The Glorious Cause

The Oxford History of the United States

C. Vann Woodward, *General Editor*

Volume II

ROBERT MIDDLEKAUFF
THE GLORIOUS CAUSE:
The American Revolution, 1763–1789

THE
GLORIOUS CAUSE

The American Revolution
1763-1789

ROBERT MIDDLEKAUFF

New York   Oxford
OXFORD UNIVERSITY PRESS

Oxford University Press

Oxford London New York Toronto
Delhi Bombay Calcutta Madras Karachi
Kuala Lumpur Singapore Hong Kong Tokyo
Nairobi Dar es Salaam Cape Town
Melbourne Auckland

and associated companies in
Beirut Berlin Ibadan Mexico City Nicosia

First published in 1982
by Oxford University Press, Inc.
200 Madison Avenue, New York, NY 10016

First issued as an Oxford University Press paperback, 1985

Library of Congress Cataloging in Publication Data
Middlekauff, Robert.
The glorious cause.
(The Oxford history of the United States; v. 2)
Bibliography: p.   Includes index.
1. United States—History—Revolution, 1775–1783.
2. United States—Confederation, 1783–1789.
I. Title. II. Series:
Oxford history of the United States; v. 2.
E173.094 vol. 2 [E208]   973s [973.3]   81–9660
ISBN 0–19–502921–6 AACR2
ISBN 0–19–503575–5 (pbk.)

Printing (last digit): 9 8 7 6 5 4 3 2 1
Printed in the United States of America

For Holly

Preface

The title that I have given this book may be understood in this day—when all is suspect—as irony. I do not intend that it should be. The Americans, the "common people," as well as soldiers and great leaders, who made the Revolution against Britain believed that their cause was glorious—and so do I. But their cause, however glorious, had its inglorious sides, and the Americans' manner of advancing it was sometimes false to the great principles they espoused. And therefore, while I have tried to convey a sense of the achievements of the Revolution, I have also pointed to its failures, and tried to understand both achievements and failures and their peculiar relationship.

This book is largely a narrative. To be sure, several chapters and sections within chapters analyze events with the intention of extracting meanings beyond those narration reveals. But in the main, I have chosen to tell the story of the Revolution in the belief that the process of reconstructing what happened may be made to provide an explanation of events and their importance. The narrative form, I believe, allows one to recover much that is central to an understanding of the Revolution and to revive at least a part of the passions and commitments of the people who struggled and fought. A narrative, moreover, can recapture some of the movement of the years of conflict, movement which saw the cause grow into something considered glorious by a people who came to recognize themselves as set apart from others by Providence.

Some readers will note that I have not given a full discussion of foreign affairs and the American West. These subjects will be treated further in the volume following this one in the Oxford History of the United States. I have concentrated on questions of governance, politics, constitutionalism, and on the war. Historians who emphasize these matters often argue that the Americans' desire to preserve rights was preeminent, and hence their Revolution was conservative. In my account the Americans may appear especially conservative because I have tied their convictions about rights and politics to their Protestant past. The appearance does not correspond to reality. The Americans did wish to preserve much from their past, but their struggle was not conservative, for it was shot through with hope for the future. This hope was in part a millennial hope, born of a conception of the world that was religious in origin. Nor was the rejection of monarchy a conservative— or safe—act. To conceive of a republic and to fight for it in a world dominated by monarchy took daring and imagination.

In the years that I have been engaged in writing this book I have incurred many debts. I owe much to C. Vann Woodward, general editor of the Oxford History of the United States. He has read my work and given me perceptive criticism and thoughtful suggestions. Sheldon Meyer, Vice President of the Oxford University Press, has been a supportive critic, and Leona Capeless, Managing Editor, has improved what I have written by superb editing.

Early in my research I had the help of Michael Hindus and Lucy Kerman; later on, Chuck Cohen, Wayne Carp, Michael Meranze, and Greg Schultz gave me aid of several sorts. I am especially grateful to Charles Royster, my former student and colleague, for a variety of suggestions about sources and for his careful reading of much of what I have written. Paula Shields has helped in several ways, and she and Kathleen Kook made the index. Kathleen Kook and Miss Shields read much of the galley and page proofs.

Several colleagues at Berkeley—William J. Bouwsma, Winthrop Jordan, James Kettner, Nicholas Riasanovsky, Irwin Scheiner, and Thomas Smith—also read all or part of this book in manuscript and suggested ways of improving it. Riasanovsky gave me especially detailed comments. James Kettner saved me from a number of mistakes and gave both the final draft and all the proofs extraordinarily close readings. I owe more than I can say to Kettner for this assistance and for his thoughtful comments on my work.

Librarians at the University of California, Berkeley, and the Henry E. Huntington Library and Art Gallery gave me much assistance. The Huntington Library provided a marvelous setting for the writing of a part of this book. I appreciate the kindness and support given me at the Huntington by its Director, James Thorpe, and by the Senior Research Associate, Martin Ridge. Ray Billington, whose recent death deprived the Library and American historiography of a wonderful figure, helped me in many ways. It was at his and Mr. Thorpe's suggestion that I gave a paper at a Huntington Research Seminar in August 1977 based on the first section of Chapter 20. The *Huntington Library Quarterly* published that paper as "Why Men Fought in the American Revolution" (Spring 1980). I am grateful to the editors for permission to use it in slightly altered form in this book. At several other places in this book, I have quoted from the rich collections found at the Huntington. The late Claude Simpson first suggested that I might enjoy working at the Library. Simpson, Thorpe, and Billington awarded me a Huntington Faculty Fellowship (March–September 1977) funded by the National Endowment for the Humanities. My debt to the Endowment is great: in 1973–74 I enjoyed a Senior Faculty Fellowship it provided. I have also received support from the Humanities Institute and the Committee on Research at the University of California. A part of the manuscript was typed at the Institute of International Studies at Berkeley. Early drafts of my manuscript were typed by two members of my family, mentioned below, and by Katherine Klein, Dorothy Shannon, and Louise Sullivan, who also did a skillful job on the final draft. Mrs. Shannon read proofs and helped in other ways with unfailing good humor. Two men, Mick Pont and Nate Norman, helped keep me going at a particularly difficult time, and though I will never be able to repay them for their help, I do want to thank them.

Besides typing and reading what I wrote, Beverly and Holly Middlekauff—my wife and daughter—occasionally asked me when I was going to finish this book. At no time did they ever imply that they thought I would not finish; and they successfully concealed what must have been appalled surprise when they saw its length. For their discretion, and for much else, I am grateful to them.

Berkeley   R. M.
September 1981

Contents

Maps

Illustrations appear between pages 302 and 303

Editor's Introduction

Some periods of historical scholarship, like some periods of history, are more crowded with developments and surprises than others. The findings, revisions, and innovations of the latest generation of historians have been singularly rich in changes and surprises. Some of them are superficial and ephemeral, but there remain numerous insights and revisions characterized by critical sophistication, subtlety, and depth that have banished many old simplicities and reshaped and deepened our understanding of the past. The parts that have proved durable have been mainly the contributions of specialists—often local historians or trained statisticians—whose works, methods, and analytical techniques are not readily available to the non-specialist. Yet they are sometimes essential to an understanding of American history by the modern citizen, who would otherwise confront the present and the future with outdated misconceptions of the past. To incorporate the new insights and revisions in a general history that is available to the unspecialized reader, neither the specialized monograph nor the generalized textbook would suffice, nor would dozens of books dividing history into narrow segments of time or subject.

The most satisfactory solution for the *Oxford History of the United States* seemed to be a series of ample volumes covering the large periods and aspects of the nation's history. The continuities and changes as well as the basic narrative and the contributions of recent scholarship can best be presented in this manner. One volume is assigned for each of the nine major periods of American history from the colonial period down to the present time, with two additional volumes, one on economic history and the other on diplomatic history. Each volume in the series is, finally, the responsibility of the individual author, free of any expectation of conformity in interpretation or point of view. Each author will strive for a readable text that will be readily accessible to the educated general public, and at the same time he will provide students at various levels an interpretative synthesis of the findings of recent scholarship as well as the essentials of narrative history in the period or subject being treated.

It comes as no surprise that all the historic developments of a period do not fit conveniently into chronological limits and that there are inevitable overlappings between volumes. One such instance is apparent in the present book. Although it deals with major events in the late 1780s, certain developments such as the settlement of the West and foreign relations in that decade are not covered in detail here. They will be treated fully in the volume dealing with the next stage of the nation's development, the early national period (1789–1815), and in the volume on diplomatic history. Overlaps do not present serious difficulties.

The volumes are to be published as they are completed. It is by fortunate chance that the first to appear is Robert Middlekauff's *The Glorious Cause*, treating the period of the American Revolution. His work skillfully and handsomely exemplifies the editorial purposes and goals outlined above and adds much to our understanding and appreciation of this vital era of national history through his masterful command of the subject.

In the earliest stages of planning the *Oxford History*, the editor had the enormously valuable collaboration of Richard Hofstadter, who originally served as co-editor. His death was a deeply felt personal loss as well as a grave loss to this series. His inestimable contributions to the present work are gratefully acknowledged. Over time some changes have been made in the authors of volumes, but the general conception and plan for the series retain the character fixed in the original collaboration.

C. Vann Woodward

The Glorious Cause

Prologue
The Sustaining Truths

"The use of travelling," Doctor Johnson wrote Mrs. Thrale, "is *to regulate imagination by reality, and instead of thinking how things may be, to see them as they are.*" Johnson spoke for the age in this desire to see things as they are and to avoid the dangerous imaginings of how they may be. His England and much of pre-Revolutionary America shared a suspicion of what he called "airy notions"—the illusions of dreams and fancies. Johnson's great American contemporary, Benjamin Franklin, as a young man put aside speculations on the nature of reality in favor of living as a reasonable creature in contact with the world that presented itself through the evidence of his senses.

Franklin was a practical man. Practical men usually do not make revolutions; dreamers do. Yet Benjamin Franklin became a revolutionary with several million others in America. His action suggests one of the ironies of the American Revolution: its sources in a culture of men devoted to the hard realities of life—practical men, down-to-earth men like Franklin himself, men who in 1776 threw off their allegiance to the empire in the name of "common sense," a phrase Thomas Paine had chosen as the title of his great tract on behalf of American independence. That brings us to another irony: what seemed to be only common sense to Thomas Paine, and to most Americans in 1776, would have struck them as uncommon madness a dozen years before. Paine's *Common Sense*, a sermon disguised as a political tract, informed Americans that their long-standing connection to England was preposterous, that

3

it violated the laws of nature and of human reason, indeed that it aroused a repugnancy in "the universal order of things." And as for the institution to which they had always given their loyalty—the monarchy—it was ridiculous, and as unnatural as the traditional tie to the mother country. Monarchy, according to Paine, had a heathenish origin; it had been instituted by the devil for the promotion of idolatry. The word according to Thomas Paine was accepted easily enough by most Americans; they were a church of the converted, and he gave them exactly what they wanted to hear. They declared their independence six months after his essay appeared, citing the laws of nature and of nature's God as justification.

The laws of nature and the universal order of things covered a good deal of ground, and the Americans of the revolutionary generation almost spent themselves in an attempt to map their limits. They had not often tried their hand at such things before. Besides, until the crisis with England began, the fundamentals seemed fairly clear, including the lines of universal order. That order began with a power mightier than the monarch—it began with God.

Almost all Americans—from the Calvinists in New England searching Scripture for the will of God to the rationalists in Virginia studying the divine mechanics in nature—agreed that all things fell within the providential design. Providence ordered the greatest and smallest events of men's lives; Providence controlled the workings of the universe from the turning of the planets to the flight of a bird. Men might disagree about the meaning of the occurrences of their lives, some of which seemed surprising, even inexplicable—early deaths, epidemics, droughts, plagues, wars, evil as well as good. Such things men might wonder at, and even describe as judgments, or afflictions, or marvels, or mysteries. Yet they did not doubt that these things had meaning.

But the God who gave order to the world was not only seen in externals. He was felt, sometimes in the cool hush of Virginia churches, sometimes in quiet Quaker meetings, sometimes in the spare meetinghouses in New England villages. Whether in the calm rationalism of Arminians, the unforgiving harshness of Calvinists, or the surging spirit of enthusiasts, the divine was felt. To some the power of God seemed overpowering, to some His grace gave relief, and to some God's "majestic meekness," in Jonathan Edwards's startling phrase, appeared to reveal the joining of His majesty and His mercy.

Perhaps at some point in their lives most men had a sense of the divine who gave meaning to the eternal order of things. Perhaps few sustained great religious passion for long, but they did retain faith in providential order. For most Americans, perhaps, providential order appeared most clearly in the progress of an increasing, flourishing people. They called themselves a thriving people and impressed European travelers with the ease and the zest with which they accepted their growth and success. They were not complacent—more than one European remarked on their "enthusiasm," a word that suggested that they might be dangerous as well as filled with religious extravagance. Many observers called them prolific, meaning that they produced goods as well as children at a surprising rate. And more than one commented on their ragged money, as indeed it was from changing hands in the bustling markets of American business.

Their increase in business and population did not amaze Americans, who had long had great expectations for themselves. To the heirs of people who had begun by thinking of themselves as settling the New World in the service of God, success—increase and growth in the things of this world—seemed only their just deserts, only their due, and a part of the eternal order of things.

In the second half of the eighteenth century that order still extended to the ordinary doings of life—and especially to work and family. Work seemed akin to the sacred. Work was a duty imposed by God and approved by Him as right and good. That everyone should have a trade or a calling was unquestioned. The trade should be worked at, the calling well followed, for as Franklin said, "there is much to be done" and though you may be "weak handed," "stick to it steadily and you will see great Effects."

To be sure, the higher purposes of these great effects were not so clear as they had once been, say, to the founders of the colonies. But the purpose of life was still the glorification of God. Teaching that proposition fell to all in authority and began with parents, especially fathers, who ruled the house and all in it. They did so as fathers seem to have done from time immemorial. They were commissioned by God and their word was law. They were responsible for much—for bread, for discipline, for seeing that others lived up to responsibilities, and for doing so themselves.

The order that began with the divine and expressed itself in the lives of a people embraced their government. In the second half of the eighteenth century no one in America regarded the Crown as the immediate instrument of God. Yet royal government had the sanction of the Lord, and men accepted the existing structure of government without question, though they often protested against its agents whom they faced every day.

The structure of government, they agreed, should reflect the structure of society. The good, the well-born, and the socially qualified should govern. That arrangement had apparently always existed and should continue. Maintaining it seemed all the more desirable to Americans because they knew that it conformed to the ancient lines of the British constitution, the most glorious frame of government yet devised by man. The Americans marveled at the long history of the protection—indeed encouragement—that the British constitution afforded to liberty. And it protected imperial liberty, the freedoms of Americans as well as Englishmen, a remarkable achievement when measured against the record of despotism in earlier empires, and the tyranny that infected most of European life.

Thus public life and private life, according to these widely shared assumptions, were a part of an inevitable and unchanging order. Yet what American colonials assumed seems to have flown in the face of the reality for which they professed such admiration. For in the New World much was different, and a fresh though not entirely new society was making its appearance. The assumptions about the fixed order also prevailed in England. That agreement between England and America is one of the facts that makes the Revolution so difficult to understand—how it began and what it became—a bloody war between peoples who had long been held together by having so much in common.

1

The Obstructed Giant

When George III acceded to the throne in 1760, his English subjects were singing with spirit once more. "Rule Britannia" burst from their mouths—words twenty years old (they originally formed a patriotic poem)—and they went like this:

> When Britain first, at heaven's command,
> Arose from out the azure main;
> This was the charter of the land,
> And guardian angels sung *this* strain
> "Rule *Britannia*, rule the waves;
> Britons never will be slaves."

The call to rule seemed natural in 1760; a few years earlier it had mocked the realities of British power and influence in Asia and America. For in these years of war with France, British arms took a terrible beating—and so did British pride.

The war had begun with a skirmish in the wilderness between French troops and American colonials led by young George Washington, whose description of the affair revealed that his interest in war lay in the opportunities it offered for honorable and gallant action. Honor and gallantry did not die in the next few years, though large numbers of English, American, and French soldiers and Indians did. The deaths of the English and Americans were especially galling, for they came in a series of battles marred by ineptitude, stupidity, and, some said, cowardice. General Edward Braddock, not stupid but surely inept and ignorant of his ignorance, lost his army and his life a few miles from what is now Pittsburgh. Colonel James Mercer, brave but incompetent, gave way at Oswego on Lake Ontario to General Montcalm, who pushed across Lake Champlain to Lake George and seized Fort William Henry. At sea things had gone no better, as Admiral Byng surrendered Minorca in the Mediterranean to French forces, whereupon the Admiralty charged him with cowardice and when found guilty in a court-martial ordered him shot. On the Continent disaster followed disaster. Frederick the Great, Britain's ally, sent armies against French and Austrian forces and absorbed defeat. The British and Hanoverian army did no better and after defeats in the summer of 1757 virtually surrendered Hanover to the French. In Asia Britain's prospects appeared dark as the French marched, Calcutta fell, and the entire subcontinent seemed ripe to be plucked by the French.

Up to this point in the war British leaders had squandered their resources; they had no clear idea of how or where to proceed against the French. They had failed to bring their power to bear, to focus it, and thereby make it bring victories. In 1757 these leaders gave up office, and the old king, George II, called William Pitt to head the new ministry.

Pitt was one of the marvels of the century, a leader who dazzled sober politicians and the crowd alike. He drew his peculiar appeal from some inner quality of temperament as well as mind, a quality which allowed, indeed drove, him to disregard both conventional wisdom and opposition and to push through to what he wanted. He was an "original" in an age suspicious of the original. He got away with being what he was, scorning the commonplace and the expected and explaining himself in a magnificent oratorical flow that inspired as much as it informed.

Pitt's powers of concentration shone from his fierce eyes, as did his belief in himself; in the crisis of war he said, "I know that I can save this country and that no one else can." He was obsessed even more by a vision of English greatness, a vision that fed on hatred of France and contempt for Spain. Pitt had despised the fumbling efforts of his predecessors to cope with the French on the Continent, and he was impatient with the incompetence of English generals in America. Hence he went to different men—Saunders and Boscawen in the Royal Navy, Jeffrey Amherst and James Wolfe in the army in America—and to fresh strategies in the war. Properly subsidized, Frederick the Great would take care of the French on the Continent. The navy's task was to prevent resupply of French forces in Canada, and it was in Canada and the West where Pitt ordered that the main effort should be made. Pitt was fascinated by the New World and captivated by the idea that imperial power should be forced to grow through trade in a vast arena under

British sway. And so he made the fateful decision to play his strongest hand in America while the French were occupied in Europe and held off on the sea.

The strategy worked brilliantly. In July 1758 a combined military and naval force under Admiral Boscawen and Generals Amherst and Wolfe took the French fortress of Louisbourg. Soon after, Fort Frontenac, at the site of what is now Kingston, Ontario, fell to Colonel John Bradstreet and his New England volunteers. George Washington felt the exquisite pleasure of serving with General John Forbes as that commander, retracing Braddock's steps, took Fort Duquesne after the French destroyed and then abandoned it. The British soon renamed Duquesne Pittsburgh to celebrate Pitt's daring leadership. Pitt got an unexpected series of victories in India from Clive, who set about demolishing French power there with a vigor to match Pitt's own. And on the Continent, Frederick danced and slashed his way through the encircling armies of France, Russia, and Austria.

The greatest triumphs came the following year—the wonderful year—1759. Admiral Sir Edward Hawke's naval squadrons smashed a French fleet at Quiberon Bay southeast of Brest and thereby prevented provisioning of Canada with food and troops. In the West Indies, the rich sugar island of Guadeloupe surrendered to a joint expedition of the British army and navy. Two thousand regulars and one thousand Iroquois did their bit at Fort Niagara, which Sir William Johnson, who replaced Brig. General John Prideaux killed in battle, captured in July. But the victory that left all of Europe gasping with admiration—and England swollen with pride—was won by Wolfe on the Plains of Abraham. Wolfe died there. So did the romantic Montcalm, and with him French power on the American continent.

Victories were won the next year, but the war continued as George III took the crown. The new king wanted peace, wanted it so much that he was willing to let Pitt leave office. Pitt, far from wanting peace, urged that the war be widened to include Spain. Pitt made the king uncomfortable: he was too flamboyant, too unpredictable, and there seemed to be a bloodthirsty quality in his daring. And so he had to go from office; he resigned in October 1761, and by the end of the following year terms of peace had been arranged.[1]

1. Accounts of Pitt are to be found in virtually all the standard studies of late eighteenth-century England. For his life, see Basil Williams, *The Life of William Pitt, Earl of Chatham* (2 vols., London, 1913). The Seven Years War in America is richly treated in Gipson, *British Empire*, vols. VI–VIII. There is a good short history in Howard

II

Most of George's subjects probably hated to see Pitt depart; he had given them glory and power and excitement. The rest of Europe felt differently. Europeans may have been awed by Pitt but they did not admire him. Indeed, they felt something rather different from admiration for England and Englishmen. The energy and the power of England had to be respected of course, but Europeans could detect little else that was attractive in those bluff, beef-eating, beer-drinking Englishmen who seemed bent on tearing the civilized world apart.

For all the power of the English, to cultivated Europe they appeared to be only a cut above barbarians. Granted they had won victories in war, their merchants pushed their ships all over the world, they dominated commerce almost everywhere; but despite all these successes, Europeans could not bring themselves to extravagant praise or unqualified admiration. The English were after all a people without a culture. No European collected the pictures of English artists or sent his sons to England for education, and the Grand Tour did not include stopovers at English salons.[2]

France, not England, was the great nation. European aristocrats admired French culture, collected French art and books, and chose French furniture for the well-appointed room. The fashionable wore French clothes and spoke French—not English, unless they happened to be English. French *philosophes* set the intellectual standard for all in Europe who admired daring and imagination. Europe found much else in France worthy of emulation: French science as revealed in the *Encyclopédie* and the Academy dazzled scholars everywhere; merchants and statesmen envied France her modern roads and canals, and especially the growing wealth and population of the nation. Presiding over this strength and culture, this magnificence, was a great monarchy, unhobbled by the limits placed on the Hanoverians in England.[3]

In the eyes of European aristocrats, English monarchy was indeed a pale imitation of the real thing. A century earlier the English had taken off one king's head and driven another to flight. In Europe's eyes they were an unstable lot, obsessed with parliamentary government, with bills of rights and liberty that cut monarchs down to the size of mayors.

H. Peckham, *The Colonial Wars, 1689–1762* (Chicago, 1964). A list of abbreviated titles used in footnotes will be found on page 666.

2. J. H. Plumb, *Men and Centuries* (Boston, 1963). I have learned much from this volume and from Plumb's *The Origins of Political Stability* (Boston, 1967).

3. Plumb, *Men and Centuries*, 4–7.

They were an unpredictable people, apparently abandoned to limited government and wild adventures overseas—at the expense of European empires.

As extravagant as these fantasies about the English were, they contained an important truth: English energies were formidable and bent on finding expression in war, trade, and domination. In the capacity to grow, to concentrate power and energy, to bring force to bear in the service of an expansionist policy, no nation in 1760 could match England—not Germany and Italy, which did not exist as modern states but only as hopelessly divided fragments, squabbling powers and principalities unable to pull themselves together; not Prussia, which had a great leader but lacked resources in iron, steel, and coal; not Austria, which also needed industry and commerce; not Spain, once a mighty power, now flatulent, her wealth spent, her energies dissipated, her state in decay; not Portugal, now little more than an English satellite; not the Netherlands, disabled in a paralyzing federal system of government; not Sweden, obviously weak; not Poland, weak, corrupt, and about to endure partition by rapacious neighbors.

And France, for all her cultivation, her taste, her philosophy, art, and style, was in 1760 also weaker than England. Progressive and advanced in many respects, France had not been able to throw off the remnants of vested interests in church and state. A privileged nobility and a self-indulgent church controlled an antiquated government. The French paid for these ancient luxuries in the war with England, when all Europe came to see that French glories could not be translated into military and political power sufficient to deal with the upstart English, surely the wild men of Europe but—just as surely—the victorious throughout the world.

There was something askew in the condescension of Europe; English culture was not barbarous. It lacked the imagination and daring that gave French culture its brilliant vitality. And yet the apparent cultivation of the French aristocracy was not responsible for the art and literature of France. French aristocrats patronized the arts of course, but so did the English; neither shaped them nor provided standards of taste and appreciation. French taste was more discriminating than English: one has only to look at the great country houses of English aristocrats to see that size, extravagance, and prodigality charmed the Walpoles and the Pelhams—representatives of the breed—as little else did. Here French sensibilities were surer—more civilized, as eighteenth-century commentators might say.

What English culture lacked was the almost uniform brilliance of the French. The houses of the English aristocracy were usually vast and cold, but Georgian architecture also had beauty and often showed dignity and restraint. French painting established the European standards; the English was confined largely to portraiture. In France, creativity seemed to thrive; in England, Reynolds with his crowd of assistants carefully depicted stolid English faces with stolid artistic conventions. Gainsborough, who worked alone and who defied prevailing style in favor of his own difference, earned the displeasure of the critics and the public. Hogarth's savage perceptions went unappreciated. Still, in painting, in architecture, and above all in prose and poetry, the English, if not always breathing beauty, avoided the backwardness that Europe saw.[4]

If English high culture was not guilty of the barbarism that fashionable Europe attributed to it, society from the meaner sort to the upper classes was. There was still a ferocity to English life that seemed hard to reconcile with the mania for progress and development. Criminals were hanged publicly; an execution often became an occasion for a celebration. Six months after George III was crowned, an immense London crowd witnessed the hanging of Lord Ferrers at Tyburn for the murder of his steward. Lord Ferrers chose to go to the gallows dressed as he had been for his wedding; all London appreciated this decision, for it was well known that His Lordship had started on the road to the noose on the day he married. The leading role in such spectacles was not usually played by aristocrats, but the occasions were appreciated nonetheless. And they were widely approved; as Dr. Johnson observed, the people of England had the right to see the penalties of their laws enacted on criminals. Criminals thrived in London and on the roads of the countryside. Among the populace they excited fear and admiration. Celebrated in popular ballads and transfixed in Hogarth's sketches—along with every other order in English society—and skillfully rendered in Fielding's *Jonathan Wild*, they evaded the hangman more often than not.

No doubt the average citizen rarely encountered a highwayman, but avoiding the filth, disease, and shabby housing was more difficult. English life had its elegance and beauty—in Georgian houses and in the countryside still bursting with flowers, greenery, and woods untouched by highways and developers. Yet there were slums in villages as well as in

4. Readers interested in English painting and prose should probably pursue their interests first by looking at the pictures of English artists and by reading the great writers of the century.

London—and ugliness in both. John Byng, a thoughtful traveler, described the dark huts of Alderminster as "mud without and wretchedness within."[5] Disease in this unsanitary age was widespread, and not only among the common sort, but among the rich and well-born, who were as ignorant and filthy as any. Understandably, perhaps, the rich sought relief in dissipation and prodigal display; the poor, in gin and rioting. The middle classes flocked after Wesley and revivalism and perhaps did not suffer badly at all.

This is a grim picture—a society torn by crime and suffering from inadequate housing, disease, filth, and riot. Social conditions, however, were improving when George III was crowned and had been improving for at least ten years. The underlying reasons were the appearance of industry and the increase in national wealth. English business had made its way all over the world—to Asia and India, to the West Indies, to the farthest reaches of the Mediterranean. The mechanisms of commerce had also improved, fiscal practices had gradually been rationalized, and banking helped in mustering resources. The importance of good transportation was recognized, and better roads, bridges, and canals were constructed. In these circumstances industry took hold; the profits from trade could provide a start, and the new commercial practices helped free resources for development. Inevitably, perhaps, the lives of ordinary people were affected to some small degree, but for the most part only a few benefited from the appearance of industrialism.[6]

III

And the few continued to run things, especially the aristocratic few, the great landowners. Land remained the key to society, to political power, and to prestige.

Understandably this society of landowners and their servants—accustomed to the slow rhythm of the seasons, annual tasks, one year looking like every other year, familiar and for the most part comfortable relations within the ranks of men—did not value imagination and change highly. Tied to the land, they trusted their situations, and though not always found easy, were apparently content in, or at worst resigned to, them. They accepted the improvements in transport and communications: bridges and roads made life easier. They did not at first resist commercial development, especially as it seemed to offer new sources of revenue—

5. Quoted in Dorothy Marshall, *English People in the Eighteenth Century* (London, 1956), 165.

6. Plumb, *Men and Centuries*, 9–14.

and perhaps relief from taxes on land. Progress in transportation and commerce and in manufacturing was appreciated by those whose lives were affected, and perhaps ignored by the mass of men in the countryside who because remote were unaffected. But other sorts of changes and reforms were resisted with an obstinacy that reveals how profoundly traditional, conventional, and conservative English society was in the eighteenth century.

Public measures at the middle of the century afford a variety of examples of the bias against change. In 1751, Parliament had received a bill for naturalizing foreign Protestants; it reached a committee before protests from the City of London and elsewhere persuaded Henry Pelham, first lord of the Treasury, to abandon it. Two years later a similar effort was made on behalf of Jews. This "Jew Bill" earned an incredible notoriety despite its limited objectives. Its central provisions provided that Jews might be naturalized by private acts from which the words "on the true faith of a Christian" had been omitted from the oaths of supremacy and allegiance, which were still required. A similar statute had been accepted in the American colonies without opposition. The English bill slipped through an apathetic Parliament only to be repealed the next year after an immense public outcry. A careful Pelham tried to explain that only wealthy Jews would be able to afford a private bill and that the capital investments by this minority would add to public revenue. These restrained and reasonable arguments made no headway against ingrained prejudice and religious conservatism.[7]

Religious conservatism was surely involved in resistance to another reform at about the same time—the adoption of the Gregorian calendar in England in 1752. Before this change the new year began on March 25 in England; and the Julian calendar used in England lagged eleven days behind the Gregorian, long since adopted in continental Europe. The disparity was awkward for anyone who had anything to do with peoples outside of England, with merchants and diplomats suffering the greatest inconvenience. The Earl of Macclesfield, president of the Royal Society, threw the prestige of science behind the bill which would

---

7. I have drawn on several works for my picture of English society. Among them: G. E. Mingay, *English Landed Society in the Eighteenth Century* (London, 1963); J. Steven Watson, *The Reign of George III, 1760–1815* (Oxford, 1960); T. S. Ashton, *An Economic History of England: The Eighteenth Century* (New York, 1955). For the "Jew Bill," see Thomas W. Perry, *Public Opinion, Propaganda, and Politics in Eighteenth-Century England: A Study of the Jew Bill of 1753* (Cambridge, Mass., 1962).

bring English practice into conformity with the eighteenth century's, and an uneasy Parliament went along. The new act remained in force, but not without Pelham and other leaders of Parliament hearing ugly cries about profanation of the saints' days, which of course were altered by the new calendar. "Give us back our eleven days"—the days between September 2 and 14 had been eliminated—expressed the popular mood and popular enlightenment perfectly.[8]

Attempts to reduce the consumption of gin ran into another kind of resistance. In 1736 Walpole had forced prohibitive duties on distillers and retailers of gin. Cheap gin had corrupted business, destroyed families, and seriously weakened lower class life. The Gin Act, well intentioned but poorly designed and impossible to enforce, hardly slowed the rate of consumption and the consequent demoralization of the poor. When Walpole left office five years later, gin flowed as easily as ever. Hogarth's *Gin Lane* (1751) provided a bleak picture of its effects on ordinary people in London. Parliament acted again soon after, with more success though with no more popular support.[9]

Beneath these curious episodes involving naturalization, calendars, and gin was a powerful conservatism that suggests that they were in no way aberrations, but rather characteristic of the deepest instincts of the culture. The excesses of the seventeenth century—antinomianism, fanaticism, and a bloody civil war—had not left a legacy of moral weariness or social fatigue, but they had created a suspicion of inspiration, extravagance, and innovation—especially, though not exclusively, in day-to-day behavior, religion, and politics. There were, of course, cranks and fanatics in England throughout the eighteenth century, and there were political radicals, but all these sorts were outsiders, butting their heads against a social order resistant to all but the familiar, the known, and the conventional.

For the English air was no longer full of ghosts and sprites, furies and fairies, witches and goblins. It did not nourish the prophets and sectarians who had sought to make the world over in the full tide of the Spirit a century earlier. The process of clearing the atmosphere had begun while it was still full of fancies, and while men still dreamed extravagant dreams of the New Jerusalem incarnate in England. The dreams had given some men the strength to cut off the head of Charles I and to establish a holy commonwealth. Inspired, others drew up marvelous plans for the new order. But in this heady atmosphere, still others

8. Dorothy Marshall, *Eighteenth Century England* (New York, 1962), 222–23.
9. *Ibid.*, 224–25.

shrank and drew back—none with more skepticism toward romances and delusions than Thomas Hobbes.

Perhaps with more hope than realism it was Hobbes who, in 1651, consigned superstition to the past and who assumed that rationality distinguished the mind of his day. In the past, now happily departed according to Hobbes, men explained invisible agencies by calling up "a god, or a Divel." Their own mental quirks and events in nature which seemed inexplicable were explained, and men had "invoked also their own wit, by the name of Muses; their own ignorance, by the name of Fortune; their own lusts, by the name of Cupid, their own rage, by the name of Furies."[10]

But such explanations had long since lost their power to persuade. Reason and light apparently governed the eighteenth century, along with the down-to-earth, the solid, the dependable, the commonsensical realities.

IV

The general understanding in the eighteenth century about the nature of government and what it should do reflected faithfully the bias of this conservative culture. There was nothing remotely resembling the present-day idea that government ought to promote the general welfare and the public interest. Of course eighteenth-century government was not hostile to these purposes, but something rather different—much more limited—was expected of it. Government existed to maintain "the king's peace," as the common law and ancient tradition had it. This notion implied more than keeping order, more than catching lawbreakers and punishing them; it involved taking action, or remaining inactive if that were necessary, to see that things went on pretty much as they always had. Maintaining the king's peace constituted the core of domestic policy; foreign policy ordinarily entailed the analogous provision for national security. In practice, the one abiding problem in foreign affairs before the American Revolution was the question of Hanover, which Britain had taken on when the first of the Georges was crowned.

All government was the king's. From the lowest official in the parish to the greatest minister, service undertaken was in the name of the monarch; it was personal, not institutional, service, though of course it was in fact institutionalized in an elaborate and clumsy structure of government. At the top the king himself took an active part. He was

10. Thomas Hobbes, *Leviathan*, ed. Michael Oakeshott (Oxford, 1957), 73–74.

the leader of the executive, those ministers who exercised the powers of the Crown. Within limits the king chose the ministers who served him—the limits being essentially the willingness of the leaders of Parliament to combine with others to do the government's work, and their ability to command the support of the membership of the two houses. No combination—nor individual—could be forced on the king, and great leaders commonly did not refuse the monarch's request that they put together a ministry to do his bidding, provided, of course, that they could work with others acceptable to the king.

The great source of leadership, and ultimately of power, in government was the House of Commons, a body of some 558 members. Eighty of these were sent from the counties, the universities sent four, and the remaining sat for the cities and boroughs. Why men wished to act in Commons reveals much about English politics. Few apparently came with great ideas about policy or even with the purpose of serving some organized social or economic interest. Rather, they came for power and status, or to serve some local purpose, or because their families expected them to.

With most members animated by purposes so limited, and with the nation agreed that no fundamental issues existed, it is not surprising that politics usually came down to the question Charles Dickens puts in the mouth of Lord Boodle in *Bleak House:* "What are you going to do with Noodle?" Bewildered by the shifting alignments of the day and sorely put to find a place for every deserving man, Lord Boodle saw the awful choices facing the Crown in forming a new ministry should the present government be overthrown, choices which "would lie between Lord Goodle and Sir Thomas Doodle—supposing it to be impossible for the Duke of Foodle to act with Goodle, which may be assumed to be the case in consequence of the breach arising out of that affair with Hoodle. Then, giving the Home Department and the Leadership of the House of Commons to Joodle, the Exchequer to Koodle, the Colonies to Loodle, and the Foreign Office to Moodle, what are you to do with Noodle? You can't offer him the Presidency of the Council: that is reserved for Poodle. You can't put him in the Woods and Forests, that is hardly good enough for Quoodle. What follows? That the country is shipwrecked, lost and gone to pieces . . . because you can't provide for Noodle!"[11]

The Lord Boodles of the political order rightfully attributed great

11. *Bleak House*, chapter 12.

importance to the distribution of offices; the system after all depended upon providing for one's friends and followers. Boodle, of course, overestimated the size of the catastrophe that would overtake the nation should Noodle go unprovided for—the country would not go to ruin, but the ministry might, and given the myopia endemic to this sort of politics, the temptation to regard the ministry as the nation is understandable.

In fact, if parliamentary government only imperfectly represented the nation, it did manage to contain, if not always to express, the interests of landed society. No matter how severe the shuffling of ministers and governments, this capacity remained intact. William Pitt, one of the rare men of ideas who played the game, entered the government in 1757 and left it in 1761; Newcastle held various offices over a forty-year period. His departure a year after Pitt's did not shake the system. The same men, or the same sorts of men, popped up, played their parts, passed off, and perhaps reappeared, but the government continued to do about the same kinds of things, as did the Parliament. What Parliament did so far as what we would call public policy was not very much. It was not the ruler, nor a source of energy and activity impressing its will upon the nation. The nation was best served when left alone and liberty would flourish if unattended to by meddlers in Parliament. The landed interests took care of themselves and thereby served the nation and the king.

V

Every British monarch in the eighteenth century accepted this system and worked willingly within it. None admired it more than George III, who in a characteristic statement declared his "enthusiasm" for "the beauty, excellence, and perfection of the British Constitution as by Law established."[12] He wrote these words in 1778 when he had been the monarch for eighteen years, thoroughly experienced in playing his part as the executive in a mixed form of government.

George III had come to the throne unprepared for this role, though unlike his grandfather, George II, he was British-born, and though he had a better-than-average formal education. Yet his incapacity on becoming king did not lie in his education but in his temperament and his lack of understanding of men—or, as the eighteenth century put it, of human nature. Although he learned much of men during his long reign,

12. Fortescue, ed., *Correspondence of George the Third*, IV, 220–21.

he was never able to understand the subtleties in their behavior.[13]

Born in 1738 at Norfolk House, St. James's Square, the first son and second child of Frederick, Prince of Wales, George III had a difficult and lonely childhood. His mother, Augusta of Saxe-Gotha, was not, as commonly thought, a stupid woman, only a rather frightened one who kept her son cut off from other children on the grounds that they were "ill-educated" and vicious. George's only real companion in his early years was his brother Edward.

Lady Louisa Stuart, a perceptive observer, remarked that the prince was "silent, modest, and easily abashed." His parents' behavior toward him undoubtedly prompted silence and modesty, for they did not conceal their preference for his brother. George observed the petting of Edward and learned to stay within himself. He was usually ignored, at least in Edward's company, and when he spoke seems occasionally to have been rebuked with the gentle rejoinder, "Do hold your tongue, George: don't talk like a fool."[14]

If there was a fool in the household, it was Frederick, George III's father, who at the age of thirty-nine still found amusement in breaking other people's windows at night. Frederick, however, had much to recommend him: he was a good husband (though a not very sensitive father), a patron of the arts, and interested to some degree at least in science and politics. His interest in politics came naturally to one who expected in the normal course of things to become king. Frederick did not handle this situation well, quarreling with his father, George II, and going into opposition. A following collected around him at Leicester House, composed of some of those excluded from power who looked forward to enjoying it when the king died and the prince took the throne. They received a nasty surprise in 1751 when Frederick died, not his father the king.

Prince George was thirteen years old in 1751, and became immediately the center of great interest. His education, control of the shaping of his mind and opinions, was recognized as a subject of importance. The king might have taken the boy from his mother, but he did not. The

13. Thoughtful assessments of George III may be found in John Brooke, *King George III* (New York, 1972); Sir Lewis Namier, *Personalities and Powers: Selected Essays* (New York, 1965); Richard Pares, *King George III and the Politicians* (Oxford, 1953); and Romney Sedgwick, ed., *Letters from George III to Lord Bute, 1756–1766* (London, 1939).

14. Quoted in Brooke, *King George III*, 41.

prince was now even more isolated; his mother feared the king's intentions and took pains to shelter her son from all but the most carefully scrutinized influences. In 1755 the key influence was John Stuart, the Earl of Bute, a Scot, the adviser—not, as some whispered, the lover—of George's mother.

Princess Augusta introduced Bute to her son, and for the next five years he served as the prince's tutor and friend. The friendship seems to have developed easily—in part, we may suppose, because George craved affection and kindness and Bute responded with both. Yet warm as their relationship was, it was not between equals. Bute held the upper hand: he was twenty-five years older, strongly opinionated, obviously intelligent, and he was in charge of the prince's education. Although Bute possessed the learning required, he was not a good teacher. To be sure, he launched the prince on an impressive series of studies and saw to it that George continued those already under way. And George at this time had sampled books and subjects far beyond those ordinarily taken up by an English gentleman.

When Bute became the prince's tutor the prince was seventeen years of age. He had at least an elementary knowledge of French, German, and Latin, less Greek, some mathematics and physical science. He had read fairly widely, though superficially, in history, and he had, in the manner of those of birth and breeding, studied military fortification. His previous tutors had not neglected to introduce their pupil to the social attainments necessary to a monarch—riding, fencing, dancing, music. And, of course, the prince had received careful religious instruction according to the creed of the Church of England.

Bute saw to it that his charge continued these studies and personally supervised a more thorough study of English and European history. In the process, the prince absorbed much knowledge of the British constitution and of statecraft and yet did not understand either. In Bute's unpracticed hands the prince's insecure, rather rigid personality grew more rigid and no more confident, though he became proud, and intolerant of others whose views did not agree with his or his tutor's. Bute himself knew much but did not understand men or human conduct. His pride reinforced the prince's; his propensity to judge others by abstract principles—he lacked the experience which wiser men rely upon—strengthened a similar tendency in the prince. Master and pupil then and later commonly mistook inflexibility for personal strength and character. Understandably, George's studies did not produce the qualities needed by a monarch: good judgment and a capacity to take fully into account the principles and interests of others without giving over one's own.

George III was twenty-two when he ascended the throne in 1760. For the next few years he clung to his prejudices and to Bute with a tenacity that reflected his and Bute's miscomprehension of the political world. He would reform their world, he thought, and make virtue his real consort. Factional politics, which were of course based on interest, not ideology, revolted him—and he would somehow change them. If this dream soon disappeared in disappointment, the king's rigidity did not, and though he learned to play the game—at times with remarkable skill—his early mistakes and his attachment to Bute bred a suspicion in Parliament that introduced a dozen years of instability to his government.

VI

Instability in Parliament occurred at a most inopportune time—the beginning of the American crisis. Quite clearly, English political arrangements worked better in periods of calm than in crisis. They reflected the views of the satisfied, of the haves more than the have-nots, and by their inertia protected the liberties of the subject, defined negatively. But how else was liberty to be defined? Fortunately, a static order stood in the way of change, which no one of consequence—that is, no one with land who had connections—wanted anyway. Had these men who ran things been able to declare explicitly the assumption on which they lived, they would have said that the world was essentially perfect, fixed, and unchanging.

And their world changed very little in the eighteenth century, at least before the American Revolution. Their assumptions were widely shared in the villages and parishes of England, as well as in London. There was a good deal of energy in English local government, but it arose in isolation and it remained uncoordinated from above. For the most part, the Crown and Parliament ignored government in the municipal boroughs and corporations, in parishes, in the Quarter Sessions of the counties, and in the Statutory Authorities for Special Purposes. Parliament, at least, recognized their existence and over the course of the century passed hundreds of statutes concerning local affairs. But the manner in which this was done reflected the regnant ideas about the proper role of government in the life of the nation.

Parliament had begun early in the seventeenth century to pass "Local Acts," which applied not to the whole kingdom as a Public General Act did, but to a designated locality. These Local Acts created the

Statutory Authorities for Special Purposes—the Commissioners of Sewers, the Incorporated Guardians of the Poor, the Turnpike Trusts, and the Improvement Commissioners (charged with lighting, watching, paving, cleaning, and improving streets). At the time of the American Revolution, there were over a thousand such bodies; eventually their number would reach eighteen hundred, with responsibilities extending over a larger area and more people than all the Municipal Corporations taken together. These statutory authorities differed from all other types of local governing agencies, parishes, counties, and boroughs, for each of them was created by a special act of Parliament to fulfill one function, prescribed by the establishing statute, in a designated place. Commissioners of Sewers built and maintained in hundreds of localities trenches and drains to carry off storm water; they also constructed drains and other works to reclaim marshes and to keep out the sea. The verdant Midlands of England were in a sense the creation of these bodies, which drained off the water and kept it out, turning marshland into lovely and productive fields and pastures.

Most of the hundreds of statutory authorities operated independently of other local agencies; the Guardians of the Poor, who handled relief of the indigent, vagrants, idlers, and others commonly despised by eighteenth-century society, were a notable exception. They were usually connected by the laws with parish and sometimes county and borough governments. But they had no ties, neither responsibilities nor claims, to any agency of the ministerial government: their accounts were not audited, they published no accounts or reports, their actions passed uninspected by anybody, and yet they possessed the power to arrest, detain, and punish the poor in their charge.

This freedom to act irresponsibly came from the form of their creation and from Parliament's indifference. The special authorities got their bearings not as the result of a considered policy of Parliament or the government, but from the initiative of interested local groups. The Local Acts which set them up did not enter the full debates of either house, but usually were discussed only in small meetings by the members of the counties and boroughs to be affected by their passage.

Thus these special authorities, like the Municipal Corporations and the Quarter Sessions, operated unchecked by the Privy Council or the Assize Judges, and virtually ignored by their parent, the Parliament. In this way the localities were governed—the poor supervised, the streets improved, the marshes drained, the roads built and maintained, and a variety of other essential services provided, or unprovided—all without a governing policy or without a central direction. The result was, in the fine phrase of the Webbs, "an anarchy of local autonomy."[15]

VII

The Webbs' phrase also describes the situation of the American colonies before the American Revolution. All but Georgia had been founded in the seventeenth century, and by the eighteenth century, though all were under the supervision of Britain, they pretty well ran their own affairs. The general outlines of their formal relationship to the Crown were known, but their objective situation—their virtual autonomy—was not. The disparity between reality and what was imagined in England is not surprising: the distance between England and America was great and communication imperfect, and no very enlightened colonial administration which might have explained each to the other existed.

The colonies had been founded under the authorization of the Crown, and governmental authority in them had always been exercised in the king's name, though rather ambiguously in the three proprietary colonies, Maryland, Pennsylvania, Delaware, and tenuously in Rhode Island and Connecticut, the two corporate colonies. What had lasted long apparently seemed best left unchanged. The administrative structure on which the Crown relied to "govern" the colonies was old and never really adequate to govern the vast holdings in the New World. In England the Privy Council and the Secretary of State for the Southern Department did the actual work of administration before 1768. The Privy Council's primary responsibilities lay elsewhere, or its interests did; and the chief concern of the Secretary of State for the Southern Department was relations with Europe. For advice the Secretary relied on the Board of Trade, an advisory body primarily concerned with trade.[16]

If this structure made for confusion because responsibility for the conduct of colonial affairs was not clearly placed, the differences among the colonial governments themselves added to it, as did the problem of communication among governments separated by the Atlantic Ocean. The one relatively steady hand in this structure was provided by the Board of Trade, which funneled information received from the colonies

15. Sidney Webb and Beatrice Webb, *English Local Government from the Revolution to the Municipal Corporations Act*, IV: *Statutory Authorities for Special Purposes* (London, 1922), 353.
16. Oliver Morton Dickerson, *American Colonial Government, 1696–1765* (Cleveland, Ohio, 1912); Andrews, *Colonial Period*, IV.

to the Secretary and relayed his instructions to governors and other officials in America. For a time early in the eighteenth century the Board lost influence as certain English officials succeeded in curbing its authority. But in 1748 the Earl of Halifax became its president and increased its influence and his own. In 1757 Halifax was made a member of the Privy Council; his appointment alleviated the confusion in colonial administration, for he remained president of the Board of Trade.

When Halifax resigned in 1761, the Board lost influence and the colonies lost an intelligent administrator. Administrative order never again really attained the level reached at midcentury. The most important effort to establish such order made between Halifax's retirement and the Revolution was the creation in 1768 of the office of the Secretary for Colonial Affairs, a department charged with supervision of the colonies. Unfortunately, this office aroused the jealousy of other ministers and fell into the hands of inept secretaries.

At another time in British history, administrative inefficiency, even stupidity and an absence of understanding, would not have mattered much. But late in the century it did. Administrative agencies did not make policy on crucial matters, but they contributed to it by supplying information and advice. And they had a responsibility to keep the colonials and the ministry in touch with one another. A well-conceived structure staffed by enlightened and well-informed personnel could prevent mistakes policymakers might make and could assist in the drafting of successful policy.

The makers of colonial policy included Parliament, though important aspects of its relations with and authority over the colonies were unclear in the eighteenth century. Parliament had of course defined the economic relations of England to the colonies in a series of statutes, most passed in the seventeenth century. Acts of navigation and trade had confined colonial trade to ships owned and sailed by British and colonial subjects, and they had regulated colonial trade in other ways largely to the benefit of British merchants. In the eighteenth century, before the revolutionary crisis began, Parliament had also attempted unsuccessfully to stop the importation of foreign-produced molasses into the colonies, and it had placed limits on the production of woolens, hats, and iron. Yet despite these statutes, the extent of Parliament's authority to legislate for the colonies had not been closely examined by anyone. When it was, it became a center of controversy.

The common presumption in England, wholly unexamined, was that all was clear in the colonial relation. The colonies were colonies, after all, and as such they were "dependencies," plants set out by superiors, the "children" of the "mother country," and "our subjects." The language used to describe the colonies and their subordination expressed certain realities. The colonial economy had long been made to respond to English requirements; the subordination in economic life was real, though not absolute. Moreover, there was a theoretical basis for the subordination: several generations of writers had analyzed mercantilism, a theory which described state power in terms of the economic relations of the imperial center to its colonial wings. Mercantilism had evolved over the years from "bullionism," which had defined power largely in terms of gold, to a sophisticated set of propositions about exchange, balance of trade, manufacturing, and raw materials. Whatever the emphasis, the versions current in England in the middle of the eighteenth century prescribed a distinctly secondary position for colonies on any scale of importance.[17]

Although political thought offered much less on the colonies, the political realities seemed as clear as the economic. The mother country sent out governors who acted in the king's name; Parliament legislated for the colonies; the Privy Council reviewed the statutes passed by their assemblies, and the Crown retained a veto. In America the law was English and so were most political institutions.

The sense of superiority and the snobbery that underlay all the theory were far more important than any of the formal statements of mercantile or political thought. For this sense permeated, or seemed to, all ranks of Englishmen conscious of American existence. And it may be that the colonials in America, in the peculiar way of colonials, accepted both the truth of the explicit propositions and the unconscious assumption that they somehow were unequal to the English across the sea. Certain it is that the most sophisticated among them yearned to be cosmopolites, followed London's fashions, and aped the English style. If this imitation did nothing else, it confirmed the prevailing feeling in Britain that the lines of colonial subordination were right and should remain unchanged.

17. Andrews, *Colonial Period*, IV, esp. chap. 10.

2

The Children of the Twice-Born

English rigidities in government and in political imagination did not cramp the eighteenth-century American colonies. The colonies owed allegiance, and paid it, to the same king as England itself, but because their experience was different from the parent country's, this connection and those to imperial agencies of government did not restrict them. Distance from England and the slowness of communications helped keep the ties, those "political bands" Thomas Jefferson was to mention in the Declaration of Independence, slack. So also did the robust political institutions found in the mainland colonies—the provincial assemblies or legislatures and the county, town, and parish governments which gave order to their lives. Before 1776, the Americans had become almost completely self-governing.

And yet the crisis that came upon the English colonies in the American Revolution was constitutional. It raised the question of how men should be governed, or as the Americans came to say, whether they as free men could govern themselves. There had been conflict between individual colonies and the home government before; in fact there had been rebellions within several colonies against constituted authority; and there may have been a long-standing though submerged resentment within the colonies against external control. All the earlier upheavals, however, differed from the Revolution. For one thing, they lacked the scale and the convulsive quality of the Revolution. But more than that, they had not engaged the moral sensibilities of ordinary people in a profound way. In contrast the conflict that tore the British empire apart between

1764 and 1783 drew upon the deepest moral passions of Americans of virtually every sort and status.[1]

Why these Americans engaged in revolution had much to do with the sort of people they were. First of all, the Americans were a divided people, cut up among thirteen colonies on the mainland. They had no common political center, and London was really too far away to serve as such. When problems of governance arose the colonists naturally looked to their provincial capitals; many perhaps never gazed beyond town, parish, or county lines. They often looked farther afield in business, but their economies scarcely drew them together. If an American raised tobacco or rice he shipped it overseas; if he raised grain or milled flour or baked bread he often dealt in local markets, although a significant proportion of these commodities also found its way to the West Indies. If he had money and wore fine clothing, furnished his house with elegant furniture, drank good wine, rode in a handsome carriage, read extensively, the chances were that he used English and European products. If he needed heavy equipment, he also looked to England. He and his fellows consumed a variety of English manufactures—cotton goods, guns, and hardware of various sorts. And if he preferred local manufactures, he usually depended upon the production of his colony. There was relatively little intercolonial trade of great value.[2]

The divided character of the colonies can be overstated, for there were forces pulling them together. In the eighteenth century their economies, for example, gradually began to merge. Merchants in the leading cities dealt with one another on increasingly frequent occasions, though of course their most important ties remained with others overseas. Farmers whose produce went to foreign markets sometimes sold it—usually grain—to traders in nearby colonies. Still, most of a colony's production went to local markets or found its way to foreign merchants.

With each colony virtually independent of every other colony, political cooperation did not flourish, and most of the time no one tried to pull the colonies together. When the attempt was made, usually to meet a problem of common concern such as Indian relations or war, it was

1. A model study of an important earlier upheaval is David S. Lovejoy, *The Glorious Revolution in America* (New York, 1972).
2. Stuart Bruchey, *The Roots of American Economic Growth, 1607–1861* (New York, 1965), 1–73; Richard Pares, *Yankees and Creoles: The Trade Between North America and the West Indies Before the American Revolution* (Cambridge, Mass., 1956); James B. Hedges, *The Browns of Providence Plantations: Colonial Years* (Cambridge, Mass., 1952).

not successful. The Albany Congress of 1754, held on the eve of the French and Indian War, as the Seven Years War was called in America, attracted delegates from six colonies. These men deliberated at length over grand plans for a union of colonies submitted by Thomas Hutchinson of Massachusetts and by no less than Benjamin Franklin of Pennsylvania and produced one of their own. Carried back to the legislatures this plan went the way of other similar proposals—into oblivion.[3]

The colonies at midcentury apparently could not attain even rudimentary unity, or at least showed no desire to attain it. Sunk in localism each clutched at its own institutions or looked across the Atlantic to Britain. All in all there seemingly could be no crisis great enough to bring them together.

II

There was, however, a standard culture throughout the colonies, not strictly American, but one heavily indebted to England. For the most part the institutions of politics and government on all levels followed English models; the "official" language, that is, the language used by the governing bodies and colonial leadership, was English; the established churches were English; prevailing social values were also English. Yet the culture was only imperfectly homogeneous. Population growth and physical expansion had weakened English dominance; the standard culture retained its English cast but the presence of large bodies of non-English populations eroded its English texture.

The largest non-English group was the blacks, slaves brought by force from Africa and the West Indies. Altogether, there were around 400,000 in the mainland colonies in 1775, approximately 17 percent of the population. To most of their white masters they seemed all cut from the same cloth, in their oppressive blackness, curly hair, and indistinguishable features. In fact, of course, they were men and women torn from cultures which had achieved their own kind of distinction several centuries earlier. The African societies had been unknown to Europe before the sixteenth century, and even after that they were slow to receive European science and technology. West African kings, however, quickly grasped the importance of firearms and also proved remarkably adept in accommodating European demands for captive labor with their own control of the long flourishing internal trade in slaves.[4]

3. See *BF Papers*, V, 337–92, 397–416, and the references cited in the footnotes.
4. *Historical Statistics of the United States: Colonial Times to 1970* (Bicentennial ed., Washington, D.C., 1975), 1168. (The figure given for 1770 is 459,822.)

Next to the Africans, the largest non-English group of immigrants was the Scotch-Irish, the Ulstermen from northern Ireland. These people were the children of another earlier migration, the thousands of Scots and English who had moved to Ulster in Ireland in the seventeenth century when Anglican kings and later the Independent Lord Protector, Oliver Cromwell, drove Irish Catholics from their lands, replacing them with good trustworthy Protestants.[5]

These beneficiaries of religious persecution soon became its victims. In the aftermath of the Glorious Revolution the English Parliament, carefully protective of Anglicans, led its Irish counterpart to bar Presbyterians from all civil and military offices under the Crown, and to remove those holding posts as judges and postmasters. More galling perhaps were the taxes the Presbyterians were forced to pay to the Church of England. These indignities might have been borne by most, but English policy soon cut down opportunities to make a living by discriminating against wool, cattle, and linen from Ireland. This blow was too much, and the poor, the desperate, and the adventurous among the Irish began to leave for the New World.

The first stop for arrivals in the early eighteenth century was New England. The Congregationalists there recognized the Scotch-Irish as part of the Protestant brotherhood and, not incidentally, as useful buffers along the frontier recently ravaged by Indians. The Scotch-Irish were a tough resourceful people—dogmatic and inflexible in their faith, and most important, given the present state of the country, ferocious in combat. They after all had endured years of persecution and bloodletting by English monarchs. Hence the Scotch-Irish were welcomed, for example, in Worcester, a frontier community in 1713 when they began to arrive. In the next few years others settled on the west bank of the Connecticut River, in southern New Hampshire, on Casco Bay in Maine, all remote and defenseless areas.

These immigrants did not come to America overburdened with money and possessions. Some had a hard time getting a start: to the west there was good land but bringing it under cultivation, building houses, buying tools and stock, required more money than they had. Not surprisingly, a number who arrived in poverty remained poor. Several New Englanders pitied them, Cotton Mather for one, but more seem to have wished that the Scotch-Irish would go elsewhere, for poor relief was expensive. In the next twenty years, some arrivals were warned to leave, others

5. James G. Leyburn, *The Scotch-Irish: A Social History* (Chapel Hill, N.C., 1962), 157–325.

were denied the right to land in Boston. In 1729, for example, a mob in Boston forcibly resisted the debarkation of Irish. The Scotch-Irish already in New England absorbed their share of abuse too. Those in Worcester attempted to build a church in 1738 only to have their Protestant neighbors tear it down. Within a few more years most of the Scotch-Irish there and elsewhere in New England gave up and looked for friendlier places to settle.

Whether they came from New England or directly from Ulster, the newcomers found hospitality in the middle colonies and after 1740 began pouring through New York City and Philadelphia to the west where they settled along the Delaware and the Susquehanna. Still others pushed to the Ohio and to what is now Pittsburgh. As these areas filled, the Scotch-Irish moved southward into western Maryland, Virginia, the Carolinas, and Georgia. Some followed a more direct route to the southern backcountry through Charleston, the one major port in the southern colonies. In all these areas, the Ulsterites turned to farming, growing grains, and raising stock, and in the process established themselves between the Indians and the East.

While the Scotch-Irish flowed in and made their way to the backcountry, another sort of immigrant arrived, lacking the toughness and, perhaps, the religious zeal of the Scotch-Irish but bringing skills of their own unrivaled anywhere in America. This group was from Germany and included large numbers of Lutherans, Reformed, Moravians, and smaller numbers of Mennonites. They had been preceded by small numbers from Germany in the seventeenth century; for example, the settlement that came to be called Germantown in Pennsylvania was made in 1683. William Penn, the founder of the colony, was largely responsible for stimulating this early migration. Penn wanted to draw the persecuted from Europe; the Germans were especially attractive in their quiet devotion to religion and farming. They were undoubtedly the best farmers in the colonies.[6]

Penn brought one group who organized themselves as the Frankfurt Company, an agency that collected men and money. A second body soon followed led by Johann Kelpius, a millenarian saint who yearned for the end of this evil world and the beginning of a better. One of his followers similarly hopeful and claiming inspiration predicted the beginning of the millennium in 1694. Though it did not come, the faith remained solid, and these Germans lost none of their zeal for God and the land.

6. Andrews, *Colonial Period*, III, 302–3.

In the eighteenth century before the Revolution, at least 100,000 Germans poured into America, settling like the Scotch-Irish in the west and drifting steadily down the Shenandoah Valley. Pennsylvania absorbed the greatest number, and by 1775 Germans made up about one-third of its population. There were also sizable companies extending as far south as Georgia by midcentury.

These peoples resembled one another more than they did anyone else, but there were differences among them—the Swiss Mennonites kept to themselves, as did the Dunkers, and the Schwenkfelders, sectarians from Silesia. Two large groups, the Lutherans and the Reformed, held conventional Christian attitudes toward war; in contrast, the Moravians and the Mennonites did not and remained quietist, passive, and uninterested in politics.

These groups contained the largest numbers of white immigrants in the eighteenth century. There were others, some of whom had come in the seventeenth century and who in various ways left their mark: the Dutch, Swedes, Finns in the middle colonies; the sprinkling of Jews in the cities; and the scattered Welsh, Irish, and French, no more than a few thousand at the most. Among the late arrivals were the Scots, of whom perhaps 25,000 came in the generation before the Revolution. The Highland Scots came last of all in the 1760s, pushed out by poverty. They settled in pockets in the middle colonies and in the Carolinas.[7]

All these peoples, Scotch-Irish, Germans, Dutch, Scots, and the rest, had one characteristic in common. They had been selected by desperate conditions at home and, surely as important, by something within themselves. Millions of their compatriots had remained in Europe, enduring religious persecution and suffering poverty, straining to get a living from thin soil and fat landlords. Those who came may or may not have been stronger than those who stayed, but whatever the case they were peoples who could not stand further oppression whether in poverty or persecution. They were those who resisted or fled; they were eccentric in this sense at least—deviants who cut themselves off from the comfortable and the successful. In class they were, in the language of the eighteenth century, "the middling and the poorer sort."

III

Besides subtly diluting the English cast of society, immigration contributed to the growth of the American population. The natural increase

7. Ian Charles Cargill Graham, *Colonists from Scotland: Emigration to North America, 1707–1783* (Ithaca, N.Y., 1956), 85–89.

of a fertile people played an even more important part throughout the eighteenth century. A comparison of population statistics will provide some notion of just how explosive population growth was. In 1700 the thirteen colonies numbered around 250,000 people, at the time of independence their population had reached 2,500,000—at least ten times what it had been. The growth was not evenly spread throughout the colonies, and it did not proceed at the same rate every year—or every decade. The most reliable estimates hold that it doubled every twenty or twenty-five years, a staggering change.[8]

Most of the growth occurred in the countryside, on farms and in villages, where more than 90 percent of all Americans lived. The cities also added people to themselves. In the thirty years before 1775, Philadelphia swelled from 13,000 to 40,000; New York from 11,000 to 25,000; Charleston from 6800 to 12,000; Newport from 6200 to 11,000. Only Boston's population remained stable in this thirty-year period at around 16,000. All of these cities were seaports, and commerce supported their existence. Each served inland areas, which sent agricultural surpluses to them and absorbed the manufactures imported from overseas or in some cases fashioned in their small shops.[9]

The increase in numbers of people in America helped produce a slow but uneven expansion in the colonies' economies. This expansion was a part of a sustained increase of population, urban and westward movements, and increases in agricultural production, shipping, and overseas trade. The southern colonies grew more rapidly than those to the north, largely as a result of the increase in the numbers of slaves in the eighteenth century.

Trade of almost all sorts expanded. In 1688 the colonies sent 28 million pounds of tobacco to Britain; in 1771, 105 million. Charleston, South Carolina, shipped eight times as much rice in 1774 as it did in 1725. Altogether the value of colonial exports to Britain in 1775 exceeded by sevenfold the value of those at the beginning of a century. Exports of bread, meat, grains, fish, plus a variety of other commodities, showed large increases in the century. Imports of goods from Britain, the West Indies, and Europe also increased—in some cases in great volume.[10]

Whether this expansion represented actual economic growth probably cannot be known with certainty—cannot, that is, if economic growth is taken to mean an increase in production or income per capita. Eco-

8. *Historical Statistics*, 1168.
9. Bridenbaugh, *Cities in Revolt*, 5, 216.
10. *Historical Statistics*, 1189–91 (tobacco exports), 1192–93 (rice).

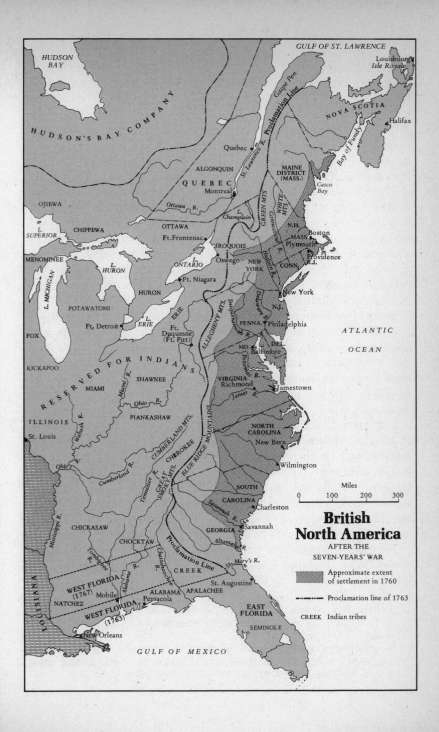

British North America

AFTER THE
SEVEN-YEARS' WAR

Approximate extent
of settlement in 1760

Proclamation line of 1763

CREEK   Indian tribes

nomic historians tell us that in the eighteenth century there was an increase in the output per unit of labor. Improvements in technology, though minor by later standards, played a part in this growth, as did foreign demands for colonial products which made a more efficient use of resources necessary. But the most important forces for expansion were the increase in land available per man—a result of the westward movement—and the increase in the number of slaves which added to labor and capital.[11]

The expansion of the population and the economy, the movement westward and, to a lesser extent, into the cities made for flux in the societies of the English colonies. The wars with the French and Spanish in the eighteenth century accentuated tendencies toward boom and recession, contributing to what has been called "variable instability."[12] Undergoing so many changes, the societies themselves are difficult to describe. Although much is known about them, less is understood about their structure and internal workings.

Besides flux they were characterized by a tendency toward the stratification of classes. At one end of society, upper classes gradually separated themselves in wealth and styles of life from everyone else. At the other end, lower classes, small in numbers but genuinely impoverished, made their appearance in the cities. The largest single group of colonials belonged to a middle group of farmers who owned and cultivated their own land.

In the countryside large landowners, a few with hundreds of thousands of acres, set themselves off; these landed magnates with their immense holdings were largely nonresident proprietors. The Penns with over forty million acres were the largest, but the Carterets in the Carolinas, the Calverts in Maryland, and Lord Fairfax in Virginia (who eventually moved there) all made claims to several million acres. A few years before the Revolution began these grandees were receiving returns from their lands rivaling the incomes of great English landed families.[13]

The cities also contained men of large fortunes. Most were merchants, though some combined commerce and law, and others branched out into manufacturing. The Browns of Providence, for example, put up

11. Bruchey, *Roots of American Economic Growth*, 22–23.
12. G. B. Warden, "Inequality and Instability in Eighteenth-Century Boston: A Reappraisal," *JIH*, 6 (1976), 593.
13. Rowland Berthoff and John M. Murrin, "Feudalism, Communalism, and the Yeoman Freeholder," in Stephen G. Kurtz and James H. Hutson, eds., *Essays on the American Revolution* (Chapel Hill, N.C., and New York, 1973), 267n, fn. 27.

an iron forge and, like several others in New England, manufactured candles from spermaceti oil, the head-matter of sperm whales. Ironmakers were more common in Pennsylvania and not all engaged in a general trade overseas. Many did, however; for them the production of pig iron was one of several money-making businesses.[14]

Commerce generated most of the great fortunes in the cities. By the middle of the eighteenth century a number of merchants in the principal cities, through their connections with the larger Atlantic world inside and outside the British empire, had made their names as well as their wealth well known—at least locally. An increasing number intermarried, and a few joined their families across colonial boundaries. Thus the Redwoods of Newport, Ervings of Boston, Allens, Shippens, and Francises of Philadelphia, DeLanceys of New York, and Izards of Charleston established familial connections in other colonies.[15]

The great landowners along the Hudson Valley in New York and the big planters in Maryland, Virginia, and South Carolina may have possessed even greater wealth. A number of these planters owned thousands of acres, cultivated a relatively small portion themselves, and leased the remainder. These landed magnates made up a rural aristocracy, and some consciously imitated English models.

Several of the great landlords owed their start to seventeenth-century charters and land patents. The charters were worthless for more than a hundred years after they were first issued even though they provided that feudal dues—rents, fees, and quit rents—should be paid their holders. The holders, however, could not collect what the charters said was owed them since the population to give these obligations reality did not exist in the seventeenth century. In the eighteenth century, when colonial population virtually exploded, the holders of the original grants— the Penns and the Calverts, for example—made the old charters pay off.

A few "feudal lords," a large number of great merchants, planters, and wealthy lawyers made their way to the top. There is some evidence that the long-run "trend" in the seventy-five years before the American Revolution entailed an increasing concentration of wealth in such groups. One historian holds that the richest 5 percent in Boston increased its share of taxable wealth between 1687 and 1774 from 30 to 49 percent. In Philadelphia a comparable group built up its holdings from 33 percent

---

14. The standard study of iron production in Pennsylvania is Arthur C. Bining, *Pennsylvania Iron Manufacture in the Eighteenth Century* (Harrisburg, Pa., 1938).

15. Bridenbaugh, *Cities in Revolt*, 346.

to 55 percent. The difficulty with these figures lies in the fact that in 1774 taxable wealth was assessed differently from 1687.[16]

Several historians have recently compiled a good many other statistics, most of which show that social stratification occurred in the eighteenth century. In Boston and Philadelphia, to cite a different sort of example, the lower half of society held 5 percent of the taxable wealth. Using another sort of measurement, a historian has established that between 1720 and 1770 in Philadelphia the percentage paying no taxes rose from 2.5 percent to 10.6 percent. He estimates that by 1772 one of four adult men in Philadelphia was poor by the standards of the day; of this poor group half either received some sort of public aid or spent part of the year in the workhouse, the almshouse, or the Pennsylvania Hospital for the Sick Poor; the other half owned so little real property that they paid no taxes.[17]

The abstractness of the statistics conceals the bleakness of the lives of these urban poor. There is little doubt that some went hungry; some lived in dreadfully cramped and unsanitary housing; some did not receive medical treatment when sick. From at least the 1750s on, these poor included new sorts of people—veterans of the midcentury wars and perhaps a larger number of victims of the instabilities produced by the wars and the increasing population growth. Not surprisingly they protested when they found the strength, rioting in the streets for bread and presumably for some public recognition of their problems.

Bread riots in the cities brought very little bread or anything else. None of these riots was large in the eighteenth century; none really threatened the control of public authority. The cities themselves, though major institutions of the colonial economy, contained relatively few people. At least 90 percent of the colonial population lived in towns and villages of no more than 8000 people. And the majority of the 90 percent lived on farms or in hamlets. The impoverished classes of the cities included a very small proportion of native-born Americans. More of the poor lived on farms and plantations than in cities. Even here they were not numerous.[18]

Although the majority of Americans who worked the soil owned their

16. Gary B. Nash, "Urban Wealth and Poverty in Pre-Revolutionary America," *JIH*, 6 (1976), 545–84.
17. *Ibid.*
18. These generalizations are drawn from social histories of the colonial period and from *Historical Statistics*.

land, landless laborers lived in all colonies. Many leased land which they cultivated with an independence approaching that of freeholders, a group they hoped to join. Three colonies—New York, Virginia, and Maryland—held the largest numbers of tenants. At first sight, a New World feudalism seemed to have existed in parts of these colonies.

On the surface no area of English America looked more feudal than the Hudson Valley in New York. Large "manors" had been carved out there, with six of the most impressive located on the east side of the river. Their holders, the landlords, may have at times fancied themselves to be Old World feudal "barons," and they did enjoy some of the privileges and exemptions of the breed. For example, some held patents which authorized them to hold courts leet and baron, exercising criminal and civil jurisdiction; several by the terms of their patents controlled hunting and fishing, the cutting of timber, and the milling of grain. A few could even appoint a clergyman for their manors. Most claimed the right of escheat, and practically all could repossess their property if tenants failed to pay the rent. Landlords could also require their tenants to work a few days a year on fences and roads.[19]

Practice often diverged from the claims to these rights. For the application of these rights proved uneven and in some cases nonexistent. Courts leet and baron rarely appeared despite the authorization of charters and patents. County courts filled their places and provided judicial services. As for most of the other rights, they remained unexercised or of minor importance when they were enforced.

Tenancy was not a desirable condition though many desired it. Tenants worked the lands of the great Hudson Valley manors and paid their rents along with a certain deference to the great men who ran things. Yet the tenants' lot was not so bad as these statements may imply, for they did not make up a European peasantry permanently tied down by their obligations to others. The Hudson Valley lords had more land than they could use, and in the eighteenth century they were under pressure from the English government—which wanted the fees that leases of land produced—to get it into production. The presence of squatters and settlers from Connecticut and Massachusetts also helped persuade the landholders to put their lands into production. As a result, landlords began to attempt to lure squatters, who paid nothing, into becoming tenants, who might be made to pay something. The landlords

19. Sung Bok Kim, *Landlord and Tenant in Colonial New York: Manorial Society, 1664–1775* (Chapel Hill, N.C., 1978), 87–128.

offered leases that required no payments of rent for the first few years, and they also lent tenants tools and livestock.[20]

These techniques worked, or at least they attracted tenants. But tenants usually aspired to become freeholders, and they signed leases only in order to get a start—not to perpetuate their own dependency. They farmed as tenants, accumulated income, and then bought their own places. By the time of the Revolution the Hudson Valley lords were getting used to a remarkable turnover among their tenants.

Tenants in Maryland, especially those of proprietary manors, led lives rather different from those of tenants in New York. For them tenancy offered little promise of moving up into the freeholder class. Rather they led stable lives, or lived for decades in the same places, usually in poverty, cultivating the same ground. They leased this land for decades, and some inherited their leases from parents who had lived and died on proprietary manors. Still others leased lands near the land leased by their fathers. Only a few owned any land, and probably fewer still owned a slave or two. Those on the eastern shore, where wheat was grown, were better off than those who cultivated tobacco. But for both sorts life went on in miserable circumstances—large families crowded into small houses, farming with primitive techniques, few livestock and barns, and indebtedness the common conditions.[21]

IV

No political system ever perfectly expresses the needs of its society. No society in the English colonies constructed political arrangements completely faithful to itself. Their governments arose from English sources such as charters, patents, and the instructions of the Crown, and their leaders counted among themselves a number who had been appointed in England by the Crown, or, in the eighteenth century, in Pennsylvania and Maryland, by proprietors.

There were other circumstances distinguishing American politics, and several more important than the English connection in giving them form and substance. Representative government prevailed in all thirteen colonies, and representation was virtually always tied to land. Since even by the middle of the eighteenth century land was still fairly easy to acquire, a majority of white adult males could exercise the vote in provin-

20. Patricia Bonomi, *A Factious People: Politics and Society in Colonial New York* (New York, 1971), 196–97.
21. Gregory A. Stiverson, *Poverty in a Land of Plenty: Tenancy in Eighteenth-Century Maryland* (Baltimore, 1977), 28–84, 137–42.

cial elections. Outright ownership—fee simple—was not always among the qualifications required of a voter. A leasehold brought the right to vote in New York, where thousands of tenants trooped to the polls on election day.[22]

Like the English government, the American divided up the spoils of office, kept the peace, and most of the time at least kept order. But they did more. Colonial assemblies had their versions of Lord Boodle, though the Boodles of America were never lords. These worthies usually held forth in the lower houses, where the real power lay by 1750. The American Boodles worried over much more than the division of political offices. The political loaves and fishes did not amount to much in the colonies, and what there was fell to some dim secretary of state in England or occasionally the royal governor, to distribute. Boodles in America chased bigger game—land which might be held for speculation or seated in plantations. They also had contracts to award, contracts for the supplies and equipment needed in the frequent wars of the century, contracts for roads, bridges, wharves, and other facilities essential to a developing economy.

These activities suggest that colonial governments had much to do compared with their English counterpart, and thirteen little Parliaments, as the assemblies liked to style themselves, offered lively arenas for their energies. With so much at stake the assemblies often found themselves the scene of considerable conflict. And indeed a factionalism sometimes described as noisy and turbulent marked most of their proceedings in the years before the Revolution. But not every colony found itself divided or disturbed by factions. Virginia, one of the greatest of all the colonies, sometimes enjoyed lively elections, but its politics were usually tranquil. A landed elite ran things, most often in the interest of a broad public and only occasionally in its own. Political life followed a course equally calm in New Hampshire in the twenty-five years before the passage of the Stamp Act in 1765 because Benning Wentworth and an elite were in charge. Wentworth and an aristocracy composed of relatives and friends dominated political life in New Hampshire between 1741 and 1767 as no other group did elsewhere. Liberal in dispensing political patronage and grants of land, Wentworth relied on a satisfied Council and judiciary to help him run the government. The lower house also learned to admire him as its members received land—once an entire township—and flattering attention. Wentworth did not just bribe his

22. Chilton Williamson, *American Suffrage from Property to Democracy, 1760–1860* (Princeton, N.J., 1960), 13, 17–28.

way into the affections of his constituents, he protected their interests, especially their interests in the trade in masts, lumber, and ships. The mast trade and lumber business so consumed labor in New Hampshire that grain sometimes had to be imported. Protecting this trade often meant that Wentworth had to violate his instructions which called on him to protect the king's right to the woods. Wentworth never seemed to mind; nor apparently did anyone else in New Hampshire, where safe and stable government prevailed.[23]

The tranquility that distinguished the politics of Virginia and New Hampshire, and one or two others, set them apart from most colonies. Next door to New Hampshire, politics in Massachusetts followed a course common to most of the colonies with factions struggling for control. In Massachusetts, as elsewhere, much of the strife twisted around the governor, who normally led a miserable life. One of those of the early part of the century, Joseph Dudley, deserved his fate; although his successors, Samuel Shute, William Burnet, and Jonathan Belcher, did not, they endured even more savage struggles with local factions. William Shirley, who served as governor between 1741 and 1757, enjoyed political peace because he had wars with France to fight. Those wars armed him with patronage and contracts to distribute, means he used to disarm his opposition.[24]

Not even war could keep Pennsylvania's factions from tearing at one another during much of the eighteenth century. As in Massachusetts, the governor customarily absorbed many blows. But the governor of Pennsylvania had his own peculiar problems—he was the representative of an absentee proprietor, one of the heirs of William Penn, who refused to allow his large holdings of land to be taxed. On the eve of the agitation of the 1760s, disenchantment with Thomas Penn, who had acceded to the proprietorship in 1746, had reached an intensity that led Benjamin Franklin and others to attempt to persuade the Crown to take over the colony's government.[25] Franklin failed, but his effort hardly contributed to a politics of calm.

23. Charles S. Sydnor, *Gentlemen Freeholders: Political Practices in Washington's Virginia* (Chapel Hill, N.C., 1952), *passim*. Jere Daniell, "Politics in New Hampshire under Governor Benning Wentworth, 1741–1767," *WMQ*, 3d Ser., 23 (1966), 76–105.

24. John A. Schutz, *William Shirley* (Chapel Hill, N.C., 1961).

25. James H. Hutson, *Pennsylvania Politics, 1746–1770: The Movement for Royal Government and Its Consequences* (Princeton, N.J., 1972). For an earlier period of Pennsylvania's politics, see Alan Tully, *William Penn's Legacy: Politics and Social Structure in Provincial Pennsylvania, 1726–1755* (Baltimore, 1977). Tully discounts conflict in Pennsylvania politics in an interesting and valuable book.

New Yorkers found other reasons for dividing into factions which contested with one another as vigorously as they did with the royal governor. Rhode Island elected its governor and scarcely even saw a royal official other than those in the Customs service. But factions appeared nonetheless and added to the colony's reputation of crankiness. Maryland and North Carolina differed from Rhode Island in many ways, and from one another, but periodically they too tied themselves and their governor in factional knots.[26]

Factions nourished themselves from offices and from the resources in the hands of the powerful. They also drew sustenance from conflict, but they did not tear the political society apart. They recognized that limits existed and that exceeding them might bring the political system to collapse. For there were rules by which the factional game was played. The rules barred the use of violence against the opposition. The colonial Boodle knew enough history to recognize the dangers of force. In the seventeenth century most of the major colonies had endured rebellion. Such upheaval dismayed men of the next century who also knew of the English Civil War. They recognized that there was much at stake— political offices, an undeveloped continent, and social order itself. The opportunities for able men to grab and then to grab more enticed many into unprincipled action and made for political struggle. But these opportunities also helped keep them in bounds, made them reluctant to go too far, and made them wary of conflict over principles from which there would be no turning back.

Factionalism thus took form in the enveloping stability of the century. The forces that made for conflict, paradoxically, contributed to political order as well. In the colonial constituencies, for example, most white men could vote. A large electorate could induce strenuous electioneering, but it gave men a sense that they had been included within the political system. Governments with considerable powers may have tempted men to strive to control them, but they also induced restraint, an accommodation to the reality of the relationships among the institutions of society. The sense of these relationships in the eighteenth century was weaker

26. Among many excellent books on New York, Stanley N. Katz, *Newcastle's New York: Anglo-American Politics, 1732–1753* (Cambridge, Mass., 1968) stands out. For Rhode Island, see Lovejoy, *Rhode Island Politics;* for Maryland, Charles Barker, *The Background of the Revolution in Maryland* (New Haven, Conn., 1940) and Donnell M. Owings, *His Lordship's Patronage: Offices of Profit in Colonial Maryland* (Baltimore, 1953); for North Carolina, Jack P. Greene, *The Quest for Power: The Lower Houses of Assembly in the Southern Royal Colonies, 1689–1776* (Chapel Hill, N.C., 1953). The best general account is Bernard Bailyn, *The Origins of American Politics* (New York, 1968).

than it had been when the colonies were founded, but it retained importance nonetheless. At its heart lay the belief that the agencies of the state were connected to all other institutions—families, churches, even schools and colleges. The precise nature of the connections appeared indistinct, yet the connections were there. Men of affairs undoubtedly took reassurance from the persistence of patrician leadership, for in virtually every colonial institution the "better sort" led the way. This leadership, drawn from the comfortable classes generation after generation, gave evidence to lesser men of the permanence of society and political institutions.

Thus colonial politics and society contained some contradictions and some surprising agreements and unities. Though dominated by property owners and entrepreneurs, the economy remained colonial—subject to regulation from abroad which aimed among other things to restrict its growth. Yet it grew nonetheless. Society on the eve of the Revolution was heavily English in composition; yet it had absorbed large numbers of migrants from the European continent. The political order, modeled in rough on the representative institutions of England, was presided over by governors who, except in Connecticut and Rhode Island, were appointed in the home country. Yet local interests managed to get their way in most matters despite instructions to the contrary that these governors carried with them. And though eagerness to govern themselves often led the American colonials to fall into factions, they observed rules that made politics tolerable.

V

Religion, especially after 1740, displayed similar contradictions. In nine colonies an established church—one that received public taxes—held forth. But the most fervent believers remained outside its doors with no intention of applying for admission. They followed the call of the Spirit and despised the formality and the rationalism—they called it sin—in the established bodies. Even these enthusiasts differed among themselves on many matters. The sacraments aroused disagreements, as did the qualifications of their clergy, the education of their children, and the order of worship.[27]

Congregationalists with a desire for purity had settled New England in the seventeenth century, and they continued to insist on their version of it for themselves, though not for others, in the eighteenth. After the turn of the century they had to contend with increasingly powerful

27. For the background of religion in early America, see Sidney E. Ahlstrom, *A Religious History of the American People* (New Haven, Conn., 1972).

groups of Anglicans, Quakers, and Baptists who fought for exemptions from paying taxes to the Congregational establishment and thereby demonstrated an aversion in common. But these groups agreed on little else. Nor did harmony prevail within the individual groups. Bitter disputes threatened unity, especially after the Great Awakening, the religious revival of the 1740s that shattered so much that was conventional in Protestantism. The Baptists, for example, divided into "separate" and "regular" branches, and struggles between "New Lights" and "Old Lights" rent the established order. Still, the Congregationalists proved their staying power, especially in Massachusetts and Connecticut, where they received public support well into the nineteenth century.[28]

The New England churches look tame compared with those of the middle colonies. There a genuine religious pluralism prevailed by the mid-eighteenth century. Pluralism helped create religious freedom eventually, but for much of the century a spirit of toleration barely breathed. Even the Quakers, who had taken the lead in founding Pennsylvania late in the seventeenth century and who had clung together under persecution in England, often disputed among themselves in America. In any case, the eighteenth century was only about twenty years old when other sects and churches in the colony could count more members. But although they were outnumbered, the Quakers continued to dominate the government until midcentury wars and the Presbyterians eased them out of power.

The Presbyterians drew their members from New England and from northern Ireland. The New English and the Scotch-Irish proved no more able to get along with one another in America than they had in England. There were sizable numbers of Presbyterians in New York, New Jersey, and Delaware, as well as in Pennsylvania; and everywhere they found more than nationality to struggle over. The qualifications of ministers, subscription to creeds, and governance all ignited fiery spirits. In 1741 the conflagration that was the Great Awakening burned them apart, as the "New Side Presbyterians" set up their own synod in New York and the "Old Side" gathered under the Synod of Philadelphia. The New Side, which favored the new measures of the revival, made itself felt from the Hudson Valley south into North Carolina; and when the schism of 1741 gave way to the reunion of 1758, the Presbyterian Church included more members than any other in the middle colonies.

Had the Old Side not proved so sluggish, the Presbyterians might have gained even more converts. The Philadelphia Synod, staggered

28. C. C. Goen, *Revivalism and Separatism in New England, 1740–1800* (New Haven, Conn., 1962).

by the schism of 1741, never really regained its balance. The most difficult problem was to reconstruct its fragmented ministry, a challenge it might have met had it established a seminary for the training of clergy. For a time after 1741 the Old Side seemed to have an opportunity of merging with the German Reformed Church in Pennsylvania. Whether this possibility was ever more than a hope is impossible to say, and had a merger occurred, the problems of the Presbyterians might have doubled. Yet it might also have encouraged efforts to convert the Scotch-Irish immigrants who were making their way to western Pennsylvania and, in many instances, moving from there down the Shenandoah Valley into Virginia and the Carolinas.[29]

The Germans in Pennsylvania could not have reached the Scotch-Irish had they tried. Cut off from much in mid-eighteenth-century life by their language and culture, the Germans remained largely isolated from those surrounding them. The German Reformed and the Lutherans faced severe problems in forming their churches. Those who emigrated to America do not seem to have had strong religious convictions, and since they came as individuals, often as bonded servants, they initially had no churches to join. German laymen had not usually offered much leadership in the Old World churches, and in America they found few ministers to pull them together. Other German churches—Mennonites, Dunkers, and Moravians were the most numerous—were better organized and held themselves together in Pennsylvania.[30]

· The colony also harbored a variety of other reformed sects of several nationalities—other Germans, Dutch, Swedes, a handful of French and Jews. None of these groups could rival the Quakers and Presbyterians in numbers or power. The one large group which could—and did— was English, and it was in the Anglican Church. The Church of England in Pennsylvania as elsewhere remained largely unaffected by the revival. Yet even in Pennsylvania there were small rumblings within a fringe, a fringe of piety that would eventually discover itself to be Methodist.

Although New York housed many of the religious groups found in Pennsylvania, a rather different religious road was followed. The Presbyterians there pushed their faith outward to New Jersey and southward,

29. This discussion of colonial Presbyterianism is based on Leonard J. Trinterud, *The Forming of an American Tradition: A Re-examination of Colonial Presbyterianism* (Philadelphia, 1949).
30. Ahlstrom, *Religious History*, 230–59; Joseph E. Illick, *Colonial Pennsylvania: A History* (New York, 1976), 243–45.

but most other churches and sects did not. If pluralism in New York did not lead to indifference, neither did it produce much piety. The Great Awakening largely left New York cold. There were small revivals in Manhattan and Staten Island, but elsewhere revival failed. Henry Muhlenberg on a visit in 1750 to a Lutheran church in New York City remarked that "it is easier to be a cowherd or a shepherd in many places in Germany than to be a preacher here. . . ."[31]

Preachers in the Dutch Reformed Church would have agreed with this assessment. And perhaps they would have preferred indifference to the bitterness that marked the struggles within their congregations. No great doctrinal principles incited the combatants, who fought instead for power. The two sides pitted America against the Netherlands—the English language against the Dutch in the affairs of the church and the authority of the local congregation against the Classis in Amsterdam. The split occurred in 1754 and was not healed until just before the Revolution. Something of the same conflict was enacted at about the same time in New Jersey.[32]

In the southern colonies the Anglican Church had most things relating to religion under its thumb, including the tax support of the public, but in the years after 1740, it learned that religious enthusiasts were not averse to challenging its dominance. The Scotch-Irish Presbyterians who moved down the Valley into the backcountry did not admire the style of the great planters and did not intend always to pay taxes for the support of a faith they did not share. The Baptists, poorer and much less aware politically, constituted silent communities of simple men and women determined to worship in their own way and to avoid the sins of excess they detected in the high-living Anglicans. Even within the established church itself an increasing number, awakened by the revival, found the old pieties and the traditional preaching unsatisfactory. Without quite knowing it, in their search for holy experience they moved toward Methodism.[33]

31. Quoted in Michael Kammen, *Colonial New York: A History* (New York, 1975), 231.
32. *Ibid.*, 235–37. I have learned much about the religion of the middle colonies from Martin E. Lodge, "The Great Awakening in the Middle Colonies" (unpub. Ph.D. dissertation, University of California, Berkeley, 1964); and Lodge, "The Crisis of the Churches in the Middle Colonies, 1720–1750," *PMHB*, 95 (1971), 195–220.
33. G. M. Brydon, *Virginia's Mother Church* (2 vols., Richmond, Va., 1947), for Anglicanism; and Rhys Isaac, "Evangelical Revolt: The Nature of the Baptists' Challenge to the Traditional Order in Virginia, 1765–1775," *WMQ*, 3d Ser., 31 (1974), 345–68, for the Baptists.

VI

Although Americans entered the revolt against Britain in several ways, their religion proved important in all of them, important even to the lukewarm and the indifferent. It did because, more than anything else in America, religion shaped culture. And different as the colonies were, they possessed a common culture—values, ideals, a way of looking at and responding to the world—which held them together in the crisis of upheaval and war. To be sure the churches in the colonies differed from one another. But beneath the surface their similarities were even more striking—a governance so dominated by laymen as to constitute a congregational democracy, a clergy much weaker than its European analogue, and a religious life marked by attenuated liturgies and an emphasis on individual experience. This last characteristic was not prominent in the Anglican Church, but worship even in Anglican establishments partook considerably of low-church practice.

Laymen assumed authority in churches of all sorts, had to assume it or else the churches might not have existed. There were no ready-made parishes in America, no rich endowments, few qualified clergymen and few opportunities for recruiting or training them. Laymen took the lead from the beginning of the colonies in creating churches and, though clergymen joined the migration across the sea and trained those who came from Europe, never gave it up. Through lay direction, and in other ways, society left its imprint on religion. Even in New England, where the Congregational churches possessed an autonomy not found in the middle and southern colonies, the surrounding society made its claims felt. Fairly early in the eighteenth century, towns began to insist on their right, if not to appoint ministers, at least to approve the choice of the churches. Cotton Mather's account of this development betrays an unease at what it implied for the faithful of the church: "Many people [inhabitants of the town but not communicants of the Church] would not allow the Church any Priviledge to go before them, in the Choice of a *Pastor*. The Clamor is, *We Must maintain him!*"[34]

Mather wrote before the Great Awakening occurred, and he described only the most obvious way that laymen reduced the authority of ministers and the faithful. How economic growth and population increases affected religious life is less clear, but they must have produced results unfavorable to established churches. For the swelling economy and the expanding population broke down institutional lines of authority, or made drawing

34. Cotton Mather, *Ratio Disciplinae Fratrum Nov-Anglorum* (Boston, 1726), 16.

them difficult. What after all could the traditional parish do about the unchurched beyond its borders, and what could it do about men on the move as well as on the make, unattached to established institutions and apparently indifferent to their standards?

If the older churches often found themselves unable to cope with growth and mobility, the newer sects—especially the Separates and the Baptists—did not. Nor did churches swept by the revival and its message that the experience of the Spirit, the New Birth, constituted true religion. For the Awakening recalled a generation to the standards of reformed Protestantism, which had prevailed at the time of the founding of America. It revived values summed up best by its greater emphasis on individual experience and its lessened concern for traditional church organization. At the same time it produced a concentration on morality and right behavior, a social ethic supple enough to insist on the rights of the community while it supported the claims of individualism. The covenanted church and Christian Union, the league of believers everywhere, were two outstanding expressions of this ethic.

The Awakening, like mobility and economic and demographic growth, fed congregational democracy. Ministers eager to further the revival of religion discovered themselves begging men to convert. Their success as ministers, they found, was measured by the number of converts they gained—thus their role as suppliants, a role that inevitably diminished their authority in the community as it made them dependent upon the actions of others.

The political ideas of Americans in 1760 did not take their origins from congregational democracy or from revivalistic religion. Most American ideas were a part of the great tradition of the eighteenth-century commonwealthmen, the radical Whig ideology that arose from a series of upheavals in seventeenth-century England—the Civil War, the exclusion crisis of 1679–81, and the Glorious Revolution of 1688. Broadly speaking, this Whig theory described two sorts of threats to political freedom: a general moral decay of the people which would invite the intrusion of evil and despotic rulers, and the encroachment of executive authority upon the legislature, the attempt that power always made to subdue the liberty protected by mixed government.

The American Revolution revealed that this radical Whig understanding of politics had embedded itself deeply in American minds. In Britain only the dissenting fringe accepted the Whig analysis. Its broad acceptance in America has been explained as one of the consequences of an imbalance in political structure which saw executive authority legally commissioned with great powers but actually weak in authority. "Swollen claims and shrunken powers," as one historian has described this institutional situation, yielded a bitter factionalism to be explained apparently only by those formulas of radical Whiggery which linked liberty to balanced government, and despotism to the over-mighty executive and to moral corruption.[35]

This interpretation is surely true in part and just as surely too simple in its concentration on the facts of institutional relationships. Radical Whig perceptions of politics attracted widespread support in America because they revived the traditional concerns of a Protestant culture that had always verged on Puritanism. That moral decay threatened free government could not come as a surprise to a people whose fathers had fled England to escape sin. The importance of virtue, frugality, industry, and calling was at the heart of their moral code. An overbearing executive and the threat of corruption through idle, useless officials, or placemen, had figured prominently in their explanations of their exile in America. For the values of the eighteenth-century commonwealthmen had earlier inspired those of the seventeenth century. They had formed an American mentality prone to conceive of politics in their terms. Thus radical Whiggery of the eighteenth century convinced Americans because it had been pervasive in their culture since the seventeenth.

The generation that made the Revolution were the children of the twice-born, the heirs of this seventeenth-century religious tradition. George Washington, Thomas Jefferson, John Adams, Benjamin Franklin, and many who followed them into revolution may not have been men moved by religious passions. But all had been marked by the moral dispositions of a passionate Protestantism. They could not escape this culture; nor did they try. They were imbued with an American moralism that colored all their perceptions of politics. After 1760 they faced a political crisis that put these perceptions to an agonizing test. Their responses—the actions of men who felt that Providence had set them apart for great purposes—gave the Revolution much of its intensity and much of its idealism.

35. Bailyn, *Origins of American Politics*, 96.

3

Beginnings: From the Top Down

The English ministers who began tightening the screws on American smugglers in 1760 and who hoped to make the Americans pay a share of imperial burdens did not know the people they were dealing with— did not know them well, that is, and had little notion of their stiff- necked quality or of their capacity for principled action. For political tacticians of considerable skill, these ministers made some surprising mistakes: making decisions in ignorance of American views was one of the worst; and refusing to compromise when these views were expressed was hardly less serious. The process of governing Americans almost seemed to rob these English ministers of their political senses as they forgot the need for accommodation and flexibility. The great distance of America from Britain surely deadened political sensitivities; governing people they never saw made the political air so thin that many a keen- nosed politician lost the scent of American interest.

The unseen people were colonials in any case. The British constitution proclaimed them subordinate—or at least the king's ministers thought it did. The language these ministers used, indeed the language of almost everyone who wrote or thought about the colonies, is revealing of rather general assumptions. The colonies were "plantations," "plants," and sometimes "children" of the English parent. All these terms implied that they were watched over, tended, managed, disciplined, and made to obey if recalcitrant. The assumption that these words conveyed is that it was right and proper for the colonies to conform to England's desires. The colonies owed something to their founders; not the least of their debt was subordination and compliance.

Framing public policy out of a sense of abstract right is a dangerous practice for any government. English ministries of the 1760s were not notably resilient, and when their American plans ran into trouble they felt outraged. Principles self-evident to them had been violated, and the colonial relationship, once so satisfactory to those in authority, seemed betrayed.

Principle hardly seemed at stake when the new king's ministry, nominally headed by one of the great figures in eighteenth-century English politics, the Duke of Newcastle, began apprising him of his responsibilities and England's problems soon after he came to the throne in October 1760. The war with France no longer raged as it had even a year before, but there was no peace. There was war fatigue: Newcastle felt it and so did his friend Bute, and so did the king. Pitt, who still dominated English public life, did not—in fact, he soon began to push for war with Spain.[1]

Newcastle, nervous, vacillating, constantly concerned about his health, could not, predictably, make up his mind. He feared and admired Pitt; he wanted to remain in office; he wanted to do his best for his king. He had held office, worked the parliamentary engines, and served two monarchs for forty years. When, in October 1761, Pitt left the government and Newcastle stayed in office, it was these inclinations to hang on, do what he had done for so long, that held him fast. Pitt departed over the king's refusal to be forced into war, even though the government had learned by October that the French and the Spanish had concluded a treaty, accomplished by their common hostility to Britain. Within three months Britain declared war on Spain, an action which led to further incredible victories.

By the spring of 1762, Newcastle, feeling shoved completely out of his king's confidence, left the government. Bute—to the king's delight—now headed the ministry.

Bute lacked Newcastle's tenacity and Pitt's brilliance. As the king's adviser before he entered the government, he had enjoyed a measure of power without responsibility. This period must have been one of the most satisfying of his life. He, a Scot, tutored a young boy who would be king some day. The advice he gave was gratefully, even worshipfully, received. And if not out of sight, he remained out of the line of fire. Now, as the king's minister, he was exposed to abuse, and he got

1. J. Steven Watson, *The Reign of George III, 1760–1815* (Oxford, 1960), 67–75. For Newcastle, see Reed Browning, *The Duke of Newcastle* (New Haven, Conn., 1975).

it. The dirty sniggers accompanying the rumors that he was the lover of George's mother were louder than ever, and all he could do was to ignore them.

Bute soon learned that though peacemakers are blessed, the world does not love them, for after the preliminary articles ending the war were concluded with France, he felt the rage of Pitt and the London mob. By February 1763 the treaty of peace in its final form was signed, and Bute fled as soon as he decently could in April.

Bute had managed to make one major decision affecting English politics and the American colonies before leaving office, or perhaps it is more accurate to say that he had headed the ministry that made the decision. His ministry decided early in 1763, apparently in February, to keep a permanent force of royal troops in America—a standing army.

King George III himself contributed in a detailed and concrete way to the decision. He took part, not out of an interest in the colonies, but because, like the Hanoverians before him, he wished to do well for the army. The army was his after all and, in 1762, as the war drew to an end the army faced uncertain days. It had grown during the Seven Years War, and it had provided employment and pay for numerous officers who gave the king and his ministries important political support. A good many colonels of regiments sat in Parliament, and they and their subordinates constituted a source of patronage for the Crown. What was to be done with these valuable officers with peace at hand and with the need to cut expenses of every sort pressing on the government? The young king worried over such questions, and therefore it is not surprising to find him writing his friend Bute in September 1762: "I have been some days drawing up a state of the troops for the Peace, and hope to send it this evening, by which the ten regiments raised at the beginning of the war remain, and yet the expense will be some hundred pounds cheaper than . . . in 1749."[2] The king continued to work for another four months on army estimates, the numbers of regiments and the money required to pay them. The American colonies entered his calculations only as they might be made to contribute to the maintenance of royal troops.[3]

Bute surely understood the king's concern and just as surely shared it, but Bute and Treasury officials had other concerns as well. Canada,

2. Romney Sedgwick, ed., *Letters from George III to Lord Bute, 1756–1766* (London, 1939), 135. For a searching discussion of the decision to keep troops in America, see John Shy, *Toward Lexington: The Role of the British Army in the Coming of the American Revolution* (Princeton, N.J., 1965), 45–83.

3. Shy, *Toward Lexington*, 68–69.

the West, and Florida all had Indian "problems" which called for solutions short of war. Pacification and security would require troops. The Board of Trade, the agency possessing the most information about the colonies, had long advocated imperial rather than local control of Indian affairs. Protection of white Americans, the Board implied on a number of occasions, could best be realized by regulating the Indian trade—and thereby preventing exploitation of the Indians by white traders, a fertile cause of conflict—and by stopping land-grabbing whites from encroaching upon Indian lands. No imperial role in Indian affairs could be conceived that did not involve the use of the British army.[4]

In the next few years further uses for a standing army in America were to occur to British officials. The army, several came to believe, might collect customs duties and control American society. These beliefs did not exist in a clear or articulated form in 1763. Common sense and imperial vision seemed to require an army in America, and so the decision to keep one there was rather easily made.

Considering the long history of English antipathy to standing armies, the decision to maintain troops in America was accepted with surprising ease in Parliament. At any rate, the matter did not become a crucial issue there, nor did it receive a full review or debate. Again, common sense probably stilled doubts: there was in America a wilderness of lightly settled territories along the borders of established—and valuable—English colonies. In Canada there was a population of Frenchmen, recent enemies of doubtful loyalty; in the West there were the Indians, long valued for their trade and long feared for their violence; in the South, in Florida, there were the Spaniards, no more trustworthy than the French. And the English-Americans themselves, though reliably loyal, were unreliable in the arts of diplomacy and quite capable of provoking conflict with all their western neighbors. How but by stationing good British troops along the rim from Canada to Florida could security and stability be guaranteed? Common sense seemed to dictate the answer, and as for the tradition that denied the Crown the services of a standing army, that tradition seemed much more compelling within the British Isles than outside them. And so Parliament, a body that always believed itself blessed by common sense and by a concern for the rights of the subject, quietly put its doubts aside and just as quietly acquiesced.[5]

4. For the West and the Board of Trade, see Arthur H. Basye, *The Lords Commissioners of Trade and Plantations, 1748–1782* (New Haven, Conn., 1925).

5. Shy, *Toward Lexington*, 72–80, emphasizes the government's deft handling of the question in Parliament.

II

When George Grenville took over from Bute in spring 1763, he was not about to reopen this question. There is no evidence that he thought anything but that royal troops ought to be stationed in America. He was in most ways a conventional English politician, though perhaps shrewder and more ambitious than most. He was well connected politically—his brother Richard, Earl Temple, had been a force in English politics for years; the two brothers, in fact, were the outstanding representatives of a thriving English political family whose power had extended from several constituencies to Parliament for a generation.

George Grenville, born in 1712, entered Parliament in 1741 to remain there until his death in 1770. Three years after his election to Commons he was asked to join a ministry and did so—perhaps evidence of his ability as well as his connections. Grenville took office again in the great Newcastle-Pitt coalition which fought the Seven Years War to its great victories. His brother was also in this government, but resigned in October 1761 with Pitt, when Pitt failed to persuade the Crown and Parliament to make war on Spain. Grenville at this point served as Secretary of State for the Northern Department and then as first lord of the Admiralty. He was very much in Bute's camp.

When Bute left office, Grenville took over at the Treasury and as the king's first minister. He was an experienced politician facing problems his experience only partially prepared him for. Within England, the first signs of a movement to reform Commons were about to appear. Neither Grenville nor anyone else could have made Commons a more representative institution in 1763; and in any case the "signs" could be read in several ways. The London mob threatened with its riots and upheavals, though it was only half-conscious of what it wanted at any given time. To Grenville and the ministry the mob simply seemed riotous and irresponsible, the scum of society out to do all the mischief it could. John Wilkes, publicist, politician, rake, was just becoming the darling of the mob, who sensed in him a power which might be bent toward reform of representative institutions which were in fact unrepresentative. To the south there was upheaval of another sort in the so-called Cider Counties—named after their chief production—where men were bitterly unhappy over the tax on cider.[6]

Wilkes, the mob, and cider seemed small-time stuff to Grenville, who had other things on his mind throughout most of his ministry. The

6. George Rudé, *Wilkes and Liberty* (Oxford, 1962), 17–36; Gipson, *British Empire*, X, 184–94.

American West continued to present difficulties, for simply deciding to keep troops there did not solve urgent problems of disposition of lands and relations with Indians. What was to be done with the lands acquired from France raised issues which had beset imperial and local officials alike for years. The facts were clear: land-hungry Americans were moving into the area in defiance of Indians and of the superintendents who sought to prevent them from forcibly taking Indian lands. Land companies competed in London and colonial capitals for grants which they hoped would give exclusive ownership and rights of sale. The Indians were restive and regarded these acquisitive whites with understandable distaste.[7]

Among the white Americans no group was more aggressive or greedy than the Virginians. On the basis of seventeenth-century charters the colony still claimed the entire region above the Ohio River. Small groups and lonely individuals from Virginia had edged into the region twenty years before the Seven Years War, and others followed, especially after the area was secured by the great victories of 1758. The most ambitious of the Virginians gathered together in 1747 and formed the Ohio Company; two years later, this group—they were planters and included young George Washington and a handful of Lees—received a royal charter conferring upon them 200,000 acres south of present-day Pittsburgh. This charter pleased them and seemed to open the door to large profits through speculation. War and a reluctance on the part of squatters to pay for something that might be taken for nothing frustrated the Ohio Company's noble desires to make money. Moreover, other Americans entered the region determined to use its resources, among them fur traders from Pennsylvania who had rather different ideas about ownership of the wilderness. The French and their Indian allies also interfered with the Virginians' designs by sending in traders and poisoning the minds of the Indians against the English. War, of course, restricted the activities of men on all sides.[8]

When the French were finally eliminated, the squatters edged back in—and beyond—the old limits. Colonel Henry Bouquet, who shared the hatred of most westerners for Indians, nevertheless tried to restrain white expansion. Bouquet acted not out of altruism but out of a sense

7. Valuable for understanding the West and British policy are John R. Alden, *John Stuart and the Southern Colonial Frontier* (Ann Arbor, Mich., 1944), and Jack M. Sosin, *Whitehall and the Wilderness: The Middle West in British Colonial Policy, 1760–1775* (Lincoln, Neb., 1961).
8. Jensen, *Founding*, 55–57.

that there would be trouble as the American whites moved into the lands Indians regarded as their own. Bouquet got the support of the Indian superintendents, William Johnson in the North and John Stuart in the South, both of whom reported to the Board of Trade on white encroachments upon Indian lands.[9]

The Board of Trade was not unmoved by such information. It had in fact acted over a year earlier in a fruitless effort to stop illegal appropriation of Indian lands. In December 1761 it had taken control of land out of the hands of colonial governors, forbidding them the right to grant lands even within the colonies should these grants interfere with Indian rights. All applications for lands were to be sent to the Board by the governors; the Board, three thousand miles away, would make the decisions about who got land and who did not.[10]

These measures were not successful in staying the settlement of the West, especially after the French had been removed. By the early spring of 1763 the Board and the Secretary of State for the Southern Department, who had formal control of colonial affairs, agreed that action, probably in the form of a royal proclamation, should be taken to reserve the newly acquired West for the Indians.[11]

The Indians, ignorant of the existence of such grand contrivances as the Board of Trade and secretaries of state, knew nothing of these benign intentions. They did know, however, that General Jeffrey Amherst, who was recalled in 1763, had stopped catering to them—had stopped trying to bribe them would put it more accurately—by the old practice of giving presents, blankets, cloth, trinkets, and tools. They knew too that, despite the army's efforts, white settlers were seeping over their lands and that white traders continued to defraud them in the primitive commerce of the West. By May 1763 the Indians had had enough and, under Chief Pontiac, the brilliant leader of the Ottawa, rose in a bloody rebellion. By July they had cut to pieces frontier settlements in Virginia, Maryland, and Pennsylvania and captured all British military posts west of Fort Pitt except Detroit. Fort Pitt itself endured desperate days and was relieved by Colonel Bouquet only after a hard fight at Bushy Run. Bouquet did not depend solely on his regulars and their muskets but seems to have resorted to trying to spread smallpox

9. *Ibid.*, 56–58.
10. *Ibid.*, 56.
11. Clarence W. Alvord, *The Mississippi Valley in British Politics* (2 vols., Cleveland, Ohio, 1917) is still the place to begin study of the West and British policy. See also note 13 (below).

among the Indians. The Indian superintendents, Johnson and Stuart, used more conventional—and more successful—techniques: bribes to detach most of the Iroquois from Pontiac and to persuade the southern tribes to remain neutral.[12]

News of this upheaval, named Pontiac's Rebellion after its great leader, strengthened official resolve in Britain to clamp down on the American westward movement. For years warnings had issued from American and knowledgeable English officials that the colonies were going to blunder into an Indian war. Now it had happened, and official action could no longer be postponed. But there was delay: not until October 7, 1763, did Grenville's ministry issue the proclamation closing the West between the Appalachian Mountains and the Mississippi River to white occupation. The proclamation also established three new colonies—Quebec, East Florida, and West Florida—carved out from the French settlements of the St. Lawrence Valley and from areas formerly claimed by Spain and ceded to Britain in the peace ending the Seven Years War.[13]

The proclamation did not end Pontiac's Rebellion; the grinding efforts of British troops and American militia did that, though fighting continued until the end of 1764. The proclamation did not end the white man's movement into the West either. British troops occasionally tried to bar emigration and succeeded only in earning the enmity of settlers, fur traders, and speculators in land. The Virginians, for example, who had settled in the Kanawha Valley almost twenty years before, and who were driven out by the rebellious Indians, insisted on going back to their farms. According to the terms of the proclamation, they could not, and British troop commanders tried to keep them out. These farmers and hundreds of other pioneers were bitterly resentful, and in late 1764 and early 1765 hundreds made their way over the mountains to the Kanawha. Other like-minded men and women, now contemptuous of British troops who had failed to protect the frontier, decided to flout the proclamation. The result was a steady migration into western Virginia, Maryland, southwestern Pennsylvania, and then northwestern Pennsylvania.[14]

As defined by Grenville's ministry, most other problems—more familiar to the ministry—can be reduced to one word: money. This is surely an over-simplification, yet the need for money played a part in every

12. Howard Peckham, *Pontiac and the Indian Uprising* (Princeton, N.J., 1947).

13. The proclamation is reprinted in *EHD*, 640–43. See also R. A. Humphreys, "Lord Shelburne and the Proclamation of 1763," *EHR*, 49 (1934), 241–64.

14. Alvord, *Mississippi Valley*, I, *passim*.

important decision made by Grenville regarding the colonies—and for that matter by the ministries that followed up to 1776.

A look at the national debt in 1763 would have sent any minister's heart down into his shoes. As of January 5, 1763, according to Exchequer accounts, the funded debt amounted to £122,603,336—an enormous sum. Moreover, it carried an annual interest of £4,409,797. A year later the debt was almost £7,000,000 larger, and by January 1766, six months after Grenville left office, it had increased another £7,000,000.[15]

Financing the interest on the debt was a problem that absorbed a good deal of attention; and retiring it, or even a part of it, seemed at times out of the question. Trade was depressed in Britain when Grenville took office, the consequences of the end of the war and the decline of heavy expenditures. Levying more taxes, or increasing existing ones, was not an attractive solution: ordinary Englishmen had grown restive under the burdens of supporting an overstuffed government and a glorious war. And well they might. Land had long been heavily taxed and no relief seemed in sight. A landowner, of course, might consider himself fortunate; by conventional social opinion he was one of the chosen of the Lord. Virtue, to say nothing of the right to vote, resided in him. So perhaps he should not mind too much when his money was spent advancing the nation's interest and glory throughout the world. But what of the poor man solaced only by beer and tobacco? Beer was heavily hit during the war and made to return over half a million pounds a year. Tobacco too was made to pay, and many other things as well: newspapers, sugar, paper, linen, advertisements. The poor did not feel the taxes on all these items, but the gentry and some of the middling sort did, and on houses, deeds, offices, brandy, and spirits, most of which paid 25 percent of their value. If a man owned a house, he not only paid a tax on it, but on every window in it; if he decided to take the air in his carriage, perhaps fleeing the tax collector, he rode with the depressing knowledge that the carriage too was taxed.[16]

Englishmen took most of the squeeze on their purses quietly, though by the end of the war they were sometimes outraged to the point of protest. In Exeter in May 1763, for example, shortly after the coming of peace, there were demonstrations against the cider tax which had just passed through Parliament despite much opposition. Apples decorated with crepe were hung over most church doors, which bore the inscription, "Excise the first fruits of Peace." The same day a procession

15. Gipson, *British Empire*, X, 200.
16. *Ibid.*, 182–84.

of several thousand people formed in the streets: "1st a man riding on an ass, and on his back this inscription; 'From Excise and the Devil, good Lord deliver us.'" A string of apples hung in crepe was placed around the ass's neck, and thirty or forty men accompanied the beast. Each man carried a white wand, with an apple also in crepe at the top. Then came a cart with an effigy of Lord Bute hanging from a gallows. Following came a cider hogshead, carried by men dressed in mourning, and thousands of people "hallooing and shouting" through the streets. The figure of Bute was eventually consigned to a bonfire where it burned to the cheers of the crowd.[17]

This demonstration was one of many in the Cider Counties; it was symptomatic of the feeling against existing taxation and evidence of what might come with tax increases. The message was not lost on Grenville, who in any case believed that troops stationed in America, ostensibly for the protection of Americans, ought to be financed by Americans. He found few who disagreed with him in Parliament and none in the ministry. The question, however, was how best to extract money from the Americans who were notorious for their ability to evade Customs duties and for their reluctance to contribute to their own defense.

George Grenville did not intend to collect money from the colonies to help retire the enormous debt the government carried, or even the interest on it. But he did think that they should help support the troops provided for their defense; he did not propose that they should bear all of the charges for troops stationed in America, however. American defense was of interest to the empire—not just to Americans—and so Britain herself would help carry the burdens of keeping troops in the wilderness. Indeed, according to estimates of what the cost would be— something over £200,000 per year for twenty battalions on the mainland and in the West Indies—Britain would pay the major share.[18]

Grenville's ministry decided to impose certain taxes on the colonies for revenue which Treasury experts reported would return only £78,000 per year. This sum, the Treasury argued, could be raised by reducing the old duty of 6d per gallon on foreign-produced molasses imported into the colonies to 3d. The Treasury and Grenville made these calculations on the assumption that this new duty could be collected. That assumption was a very large one indeed.[19]

17. *Ibid.*, 184–94.
18. Morgan and Morgan, *Stamp Act Crisis*, 22.
19. Allen S. Johnson, "The Passage of the Sugar Act," *WMQ*, 3d Ser., 16 (1959), 511.

Collecting customs duties in America had not been one of Britain's glorious successes in the eighteenth century, nor had enforcement of any of the trade regulations that the colonials decided to evade. Grenville knew the melancholy history of such efforts; the Board of Trade, Customs, and the Treasury all told it to him. There had been something approaching systematic violation of the old Molasses Act for thirty years, as colonial merchants bribed collectors to look the other way when they smuggled in molasses from the French and Dutch West Indies. The going rate in 1763 was about a penny and a half per gallon, though occasionally the smuggling merchants paid less in out-of-the-way ports. During the French and Indian War violation of the acts regulating trade seems to have become more common. War usually warps normal standards and practices, and so far as trade was concerned, normality entailed breaking the law. The Americans claimed they had good reason to act as they did: their distilleries in Massachusetts, Rhode Island, New York, and Philadelphia needed molasses for rum; their farmers who grew grain and raised cattle, and their bakers and butchers who processed these products, needed markets to sell them. The British West Indies did not, perhaps could not, produce the molasses required to keep distilleries going, the rum flowing, and the trade active, so the colonists had to turn to foreign producers. And, in fact, merchants in half a dozen colonies sent lumber, barrel staves, fish, beef, pork, bacon, horses, and a miscellany of other products into the West Indies for molasses. Distilled into rum, it was consumed locally and traded in the fisheries, sent to Africa, and to other places as well. Almost all of this produce of New England and middle colonies farms was barred from Britain, and wheat was subject to heavy duties. The law was askew here and could be enforced only at the expense of a complicated set of exchanges at the heart of the colonial economy. The law which established the prohibitive duty on foreign molasses had passed at the instigation of British West Indies planters, several of whom sat in Parliament and who made their opulence count.[20]

Defiance of the Molasses Act had begun virtually with its passage in 1733. Other sorts of violations—sending enumerated goods to Europe and importing European goods directly without stopping in Britain— had also occurred early in the eighteenth century. The war opened tempting opportunities and evasion seems to have increased—through bribery, fraud, and corruption. Britain tried to stop this trade but failed until

20. On the payments by smugglers, Morgan and Morgan, *Stamp Act Crisis*, 26.

the Royal Navy found it possible to detach a significant number of ships for the job. At one point in 1756, when smuggling seemed especially prevalent, Governor Robert Hunter Morris of Pennsylvania, an official determined to stop the trade of Philadelphia merchants with the enemy, resorted to breaking into local warehouses late at night with his bare hands in the hope of discovering contraband. Four years later, in 1760, the British navy got things under control and pretty well stopped the smuggling. In that year merchants in Philadelphia lost thirty vessels with cargoes valued at £100,000 to the navy.[21]

What worked against smuggling late in the war could not be continued in peacetime—for one reason, smugglers operated differently after the war ended—and in any case Grenville's ministry wanted trade to return revenue for the support of the troops in America. Shortly after Grenville took over from Bute, he evidently decided, on the basis of advice from Treasury officials, that molasses might be taxed for revenue. Before the act was pushed through Parliament, however, Grenville took other steps to tighten up the customs service. On the advice of the Customs Commission in July 1763, he ordered Customs collectors to report to their posts in the colonies, or to vacate their offices. This order produced an epidemic of heartburn among the collectors, most of whom resided in England enjoying fat salaries, while their deputies collected bribes in American ports. The collectors fancied life in England, not in the American provinces, and understandably a number resigned rather than assume their responsibilities some three thousand miles away.[22]

After cutting out the deadwood, Grenville turned to the main business of getting a revenue act through Parliament. This he did with surprising ease, surprising, considering that the Americans were unrepresented in Parliament, an agency which took its beginnings from the right of the people to be taxed only by their own representatives. No one reminded the members of this old right as they passed a statute imposing various duties which were intended to produce a sizable revenue. No one noted that taxes in England had always been the free gift of the people. The Revenue Act of 1764, or Sugar Act as it was popularly called, used these words, a traditional formula which set off no reaction in Parliament. The lack of opposition within Parliament can be explained in several ways—the political temper of Parliament is the most obvious and, in a sense, the most important. The leaders without office in Parliament

21. Victor L. Johnson, "Fair Traders and Smugglers in Philadelphia, 1754–1763," *PMHB*, 83 (1959), 125–49, esp. 139 and 147.
22. Morgan and Morgan, *Stamp Act Crisis*, 23.

were Newcastle and Pitt; they and others feared disagreements among
themselves. The American issue threatened to create such divisions.
Moreover, they—indeed all the opposition to Grenville—were tired and
demoralized after their losing the struggle with his ministry over general
warrants. This fight had ended in February 1764. Invigorated by his
victory, Grenville introduced the Sugar bill, which sailed past the opposition without encountering even an opposing breeze. By April 5, 1764,
it was law.[23]

Stripped down to essentials and in the nontechnical language Americans understood, the Sugar Act did more than lower the tax on foreign
molasses to three pence per gallon. That was its key provision, but the
act included others as important. It imposed other duties, several to
regulate trade as well as to return revenues; it enumerated goods which
could only be shipped to Britain, among them lumber, one of the most
valuable items in colonial trade. As productive of outrage among colonials
as any of the Act's provisions were those establishing procedures for
compliance and enforcement. Merchants and ship captains now had
to take great care in securing proper manifests and in listing cargo aboard
their ships. They were required in most cases to obtain these papers
before they loaded and unloaded their cargoes. If they did not, they
would be liable to prosecution under the statute. Prosecutions might
take place in colonial courts of record, as they always had under the
Navigation Acts, but they might also occur in vice admiralty courts at
the discretion of the officials enforcing the Customs regulations. The
rub here came in the character of the courts: colonial courts heard cases
with the help of juries, and juries composed of colonials did not regard
smuggling or other violations with unfriendly eyes. Vice admiralty courts,
on the other hand, did not use juries, and the judge who rendered
decisions and fixed penalties was a royal appointee. What made this
arrangement more unfair, in colonial minds at least, was that the supposed
offender came into a court which presumed not that he was innocent
but that he was guilty. Establishing his innocence was his problem,
and even if he succeeded, he was out the cost of the action and could
not sue to recover damages or expenses.[24]

23. Danby Pickering, ed., *The Statutes at Large* (109 vols., Cambridge, 1762–1866),
   XXVI, 33–51.
24. These matters are thoughtfully discussed in Oliver M. Dickerson, *The Navigation
   Acts and the American Revolution* (Philadelphia, 1951), 172–89. See also Thomas
   C. Barrow, *Trade and Empire: The British Customs Service in Colonial America,
   1660–1775* (Cambridge, Mass., 1967).

These Parliamentary statutes could not have been passed at a worse time as far as the colonists were concerned. An economic depression had gradually overtaken the colonies—and to some extent Britain—beginning in late 1760, as the war ground to an end. With the end of fighting in America, the orders for food and supplies for the king's military forces fell off, with predictable effects on American business. Soon all strata of society felt the change in business, especially those farmers who had become accustomed to selling their crops to commissaries. By 1763 the depression was severe. Explanations of economic distress are rarely rational, and the hard times of the 1760s soon came to be connected in American minds to the new imperial measures, among them the Sugar Act and the Currency Act, even though the first indications of depression appeared before the passage of those measures.[25]

The preoccupation with the economy had still another effect: it contributed to the disposition of Americans to couch their protests in economic rather than constitutional terms. Although more than one American pointed out that the taxation of the colonists by a body in which they were unrepresented violated a long-standing right of British subjects, most Americans who protested concentrated their attention on how the new policies cut into their purses. Even more Americans remained unconcerned of course, probably unaware of exactly what had happened in Parliament and how it affected them. Their political education was beginning, not surprisingly, in a haze of unclear issues, and was productive of indecisive and sometimes incoherent or uncoordinated responses.

Even as astute an observer as Benjamin Franklin did not grasp at first how portentous Grenville's plans for taxation were. Franklin heard the rumors that filtered into Philadelphia in 1763 about a tax on molasses with unconcern. Calm and rational in his temperament, Franklin sometimes may have been prone to attribute rationality to others who were not so rational. In November 1763, Franklin heard from his friend, Richard Jackson, M.P., and Pennsylvania's agent in England, that it was absolutely certain that "£200,000 a year will infallibly be raised by Parliament on the Plantations."[26] The trade of the colonies would be taxed, according to Jackson, and since there was no way of heading off Parliament, he would not try. But he would attempt to get the duty on molasses set at a penny and a half a gallon. The news evoked the sensible observation from Franklin—"I am not much alarm'd about

25. Bernhard Knollenberg, *Origin of the American Revolution, 1759–1766* (New York, 1960), 181–84.
26. *BF Papers*, X, 371–72; XI, 19, 181, for the quotations.

your Schemes of raising Money on us"—that he did not expect Parliament to lay heavy burdens on American business because by so doing English business would be curtailed. Franklin's easy confidence persisted for months—he did not trade in molasses, nor did he manufacture rum—though he suggested that perhaps Parliament should tax luxuries rather than necessities. But what he found reassuring was a belief that Parliament would do nothing to impair English business, and since "what you get from us in Taxes you must lose in Trade," the possibility of damaging taxes seemed remote. By early summer 1764 his confidence in the rationality of English policy had slipped, and not long afterwards Franklin was joining others in action intended to coerce Parliament into repealing the Sugar Act.

Those colonists more directly affected by the Sugar Act naturally tended to regard Parliamentary taxation with less patience. Yet the initial reactions of merchants betrayed uncertainty about Parliament's intentions and indecision about how to meet Parliamentary action. After the end of the war with France, many merchants undoubtedly expected to renew the old arrangements with Customs collectors whatever Parliament did. Bribery was cheaper than paying the duty, and better than being shut out of the trade altogether. Without bribery and corruption, the Customs collector "must starve,"[27] as Thomas Hutchinson—no friend of smugglers—pungently observed. Merchants who expected starving collectors to appear with outstretched palms as in the good old days got a nasty shock even before the Sugar Act went through Parliament. The new breed of officials sent by Grenville to the colonies disabused the merchants of any notion that things would ever be the same by passing the word that duties on trade would be collected. And the naval vessels sent to the American station to uphold the Acts of Trade and Navigation did so with a frightening zealousness.[28]

Smuggling without the connivance of Customs officials and with an unfriendly navy in coastal waters was difficult, but it could be done. Molasses imported by Providence merchants in defiance of the Sugar Act, for example, was off-loaded into scows and small boats and landed in inlets near the city. This cumbersome work had to be done at night and it was risky. Securing false papers for a ship's cargo could be done for a price, but it too carried hazards. The Browns of Providence resorted to this means in 1764 at considerable cost to their nerves as well as their purses. There always seemed to be an informer skulking about,

27. Quoted in Gipson, *British Empire*, X, 208.
28. Morgan and Morgan, *Stamp Act Crisis*, 23.

eager to tell the Customs officials that off-loading was occurring near by or that a ship's papers were false. One William Mumford of Providence—"that pussy William Mumford," in Nicholas Brown's tart description—challenged the legality of more than one ship's papers in the late spring of 1764, rousing the merchants there to try to squelch him.[29] New York City merchants showed what could be done to an informer by resourceful and powerful men. The informer was George Spencer, who was arrested for debt, paraded through the city, pelted by a mob with the filth of the streets, then jailed, to be released only on his promise to leave the city.[30]

The violence used against Spencer was condoned by the law. There were other cases in which violence was used which occurred outside— indeed, in defiance of—the law. The most extreme violence seems to have been at the expense of royal authority in Rhode Island, probably because the economy there was so fully dependent upon molasses produced in the foreign West Indies. Moreover, Rhode Island in the eighteenth century still harbored an unusual collection of extravagant personages—some called them wild men—who traced their origins back to the colony's seventeenth-century beginnings.

Whatever their origins, Rhode Islanders did not mind giving the British navy grief: the *Newport Mercury* in December 1764 reported with indignation an affair in which a lieutenant of a party boarding a colonial vessel suspected of smuggling had run his sword through one of the crew. We know from other sources that the lieutenant had at least some slight provocation—a sailor on the colonial ship had attacked him with a broadaxe, and in the fight that ensued several members of the boarding party had been thrown overboard.[31]

This fight had seen a naval officer tangle with private citizens, not an unprecedented incident in England or America. A rather more complicated struggle, and surely a more ominous one, took place in the same year between His Majesty's schooner, *St. John*, and a number of inhabitants, the sheriff, and two members of the Council, as the upper house of this legislature (an elective body in Rhode Island) was called. The details of the fray included impressment by the *St. John*, smuggling of

29. Frederick B. Wiener, "The Rhode Island Merchants and the Sugar Act," *NEQ*, 3 (1930), 471.
30. Gipson, *British Empire*, X, 209–10.
31. *Newport Mercury* (R. I.), Dec. 10, 1764. Morgan and Morgan, *Stamp Act Crisis*, cite other evidence.

molasses by the Rhode Islanders, chicken stealing by several of the ship's company, and an angry confrontation between the navy and civilians. At the climax of the struggle, the *St. John* attempted to sail out of Newport, at which time the batteries in the harbor fired upon her on the orders of the two councillors. The incident was more than ugly; it had seen civilian officials willing to order colonial guns to shoot at a ship of the Royal Navy.[32]

A more important episode involved John Robinson, the Customs collector at Newport. Robinson, one of the new appointees under Grenville's reform, arrived early in 1764, whereupon the local merchants attempted to bring him under the arrangement customarily reached with collectors: a bribe of £70,000 colonial currency a year to look the other way when illegal cargoes were landed. Robinson, an honest man, said no to this handsome offer and began enforcing the law. He soon discovered that enforcement in the local vice admiralty court was difficult because the judge and the advocate, who prosecuted cases, were both Rhode Islanders with large capacities for friendship. Among their friends were the merchants. To oblige these worthies the judge called cases on short notice when Robinson was out of town, and the advocate failed to appear. The judge thereupon dismissed the case for lack of evidence. When somehow the court convened and condemned a ship, it sold the vessel back to the owner for virtually nothing. Friends, after all, did not buy at auction the ships seized from their own kind.[33]

Robinson thought such behavior scandalous, until one April day in 1765 he discovered what scandalous meant when he seized the sloop *Polly* for failure to report all her cargo of molasses. The seizure took place in Dighton, Massachusetts. Robinson left the *Polly* there under guard while he went back to Newport to hire a crew to sail her to Newport for proper condemnation proceedings. Nobody in Dighton had been willing to serve, a fact which might have tipped off a more experienced official that the *Polly* was laden with trouble as well as molasses. While Robinson was gone, a mob took the wind out of his sails—and the sails off the *Polly*, along with her rigging, cables, anchors, and of course the cargo of molasses. For good measure, they ran her aground and bored holes in her bottom. When Robinson's unsuspecting crew arrived in Dighton to sail the *Polly* to Newport, the mob persuaded them to do something else. And when Robinson himself showed up

32. Morgan and Morgan, *Stamp Act Crisis*, 43–44.
33. *Ibid.*, 40–47, for the *Polly* and John Robinson.

to supervise, as he thought, the voyage to Newport, the local sheriff arrested him. It seemed that the *Polly*'s owner wanted £3000 damages for his damaged ship and vanished cargo.

The *Polly*'s owner lived in Taunton, Massachusetts, eight miles away, a distance Robinson walked in the sheriff's custody, followed by a jeering mob. The next two days he rested in jail because no one would put up bail for him. By the time his friends in Newport heard of his plight and got him out, he was a very bitter man.

Robinson, literal-minded, stubborn, upright man that he was, also managed to bungle, though he wished desperately to be a good official. Whatever his faults, he seems not to have been guilty of the legal harassment practiced by other Customs officials and especially by the navy. Parliament in passing the Sugar Act had not intended that the navy seize the small craft that plied the waters of every port, carrying small cargoes from one side to another. These boats—barges, dories, and the like—were not fit for the open seas, and did not stray from inland waters. Parliament had not intended that their skippers fill out papers—cockets, as the lists of cargo were called—or post bonds. The naval officers did not understand Parliament's intentions, or did not care overly about them, and began seizing these small craft on the Delaware River, in the ports of New York, Philadelphia, Charleston, Providence, Newport, indeed wherever they could. A number of naval officers saw in the Act and in their instructions to enforce it an opportunity to fill their pockets with colonial prize money; the illegal cargoes they captured were condemned and sold and the navy claimed its share. With this inducement these naval commanders did not trouble themselves with the niceties of Parliamentary intentions or with protests by colonials that they were being "legally" exploited.[34]

Merchants in the colonial ports retaliated, of course, and proved quite ingenious at making life miserable for the navy. They saw to it that no pilots were available when ships of the Royal Navy entered port, and they offered high wages to sailors the navy hoped to recruit. And when the chance appeared they incited small crowds to harass impressment parties or other groups of naval personnel isolated on shore.[35]

These encounters were relatively petty and represented small-scale organization. The merchants also attempted to organize in a larger way. Boston's merchants, who had met informally for several years before any of this, began to discuss common problems in carrying on their

34. Dickerson, *Navigation Acts*, 179–84.
35. Jensen, *Founding*, 72–74.

businesses. In April 1763, as rumors of plans for the extension of the molasses duties reached them—a full year before the passage of the Sugar Act—they gathered themselves into a Society for Encouraging Trade and Commerce and commissioned fifteen of their number to serve as a standing committee to draw up a "State of Trade," an analysis which would provide the basis of the argument that the tendency of the molasses duties was to impair the trade of the colonies, the sugar islands, and of England itself. The "State of Trade," replete with impressive statistics and commercial data, held that molasses "will not bear any duty at all," thus combining technical analysis with a prediction of commercial disaster.[36]

Boston merchants sent several of their number to meet with similar groups from Salem, Marblehead, and Plymouth, and before long all these associations submitted memorials to the General Court asking that an official protest against the duties be sent to the English ministry. And early in the next year, 250 copies of the "State of Trade," issued as *Reasons Against the Renewal of the Sugar Act*,[37] were sent to the colony's agent in England, with orders to distribute them and to protest against the proposed duties.

Merchants in other colonies also began to act in the last months of 1763. The Rhode Islanders, fully aware of the economic consequences of the proposed legislation, took action without any prompting from Boston. Governor Hopkins, a merchant himself and closely associated with Providence business, engaged in writing "An Essay on the Trade of the Northern Colonies of Great Britain in North America" for the newspapers, found the Boston document especially valuable. The merchants in Providence supplied further data on Rhode Island trade, and the governor then drafted a "Remonstrance" against the extension of the molasses duties which the legislature, sitting in special session, sent to England. Merchants in New York City met in January 1764, urged the colony's legislature to protest, and also contacted their business associates in Philadelphia, who then organized.[38]

These organizations did not speak with a single voice. Most concentrated on the inequity of the Act and its potentially disastrous effects on trade. What Parliament had failed to recognize was that the New

36. Charles M. Andrews, "The Boston Merchants and the Non-Importation Movement," CSM, *Pubs.*, 19 (Boston, 1918), 159–259.
37. Andrews, " 'State of the Trade,' 1763," *ibid.*, 379–90.
38. "An Essay on the Trade of the Northern Colonies" was printed in the *Providence Gazette* (R. I.), Jan. 14, 21, 1764.

England and middle colonies did not pay for imports from Britain simply by exporting locally produced commodities. Rather, they imported molasses from the French West Indies, turned it into rum, which was exchanged for slaves from Africa, who were commodities in a complex trade with the southern colonies and, again, the West Indies. Fish, horses, meat, grain, and bread were also carried to the French and British West Indies. These exchanges produced money as well as molasses, "credit"—usually in the form of notes or bills of exchange—which was used in the trade with Britain to pay for British manufactures: clothes, hardware, tea, furniture, beer, and necessities, as well as luxuries of all sorts.[39]

Understandably, colonial legislatures, which began sending off petitions and memorials in the autumn of 1764, also bore in on the economic consequences of the statute. By late in the following winter, nine had sent messages to England through their governors or their agents. All argued or implied that Parliament had abused its power to regulate trade. The British planters in the West Indies would surely benefit from the stoppage of exchanges with the French islands, but neither the mother country nor the colonies on the mainland would.[40]

If these legislatures, like the colonial merchants, seemed to be of one mind about the results for trade that the Sugar Act would produce, they were less sure in speaking of the rights involved. None of the nine conceded Parliament's "right" to tax for the purpose of raising a revenue in America, but only two—New York and North Carolina—forcefully denied the right. The General Assembly of New York confessed its "Surprize" that Parliament would consider such an "Innovation" and reported their "Constituents" claimed "an Exemption from the Burthen of all Taxes not granted by themselves." For such "an Exemption from the Burthen of ungranted, involuntary Taxes, must be the grand Principle of every free State. Without such a Right vested in themselves, exclusive of all others, there can be no Liberty, no Happiness, no Security; it is inseparable from the very Idea of Property, for who can call that

39. See Chapter 2 in this volume, and the references to the colonial economy, and Richard Pares, *Yankees and Creoles: The Trade Between North America and the West Indies Before the American Revolution* (Cambridge, Mass., 1956).

40. The legislatures of the following colonies acted: Massachusetts, Connecticut, Rhode Island, New York, Pennsylvania, New Jersey, Virginia, North Carolina, and South Carolina. I have included New Jersey even though the legislature probably did not meet. A committee seems to have acted for the legislature. See Knollenberg, *Origin of the American Revolution*, 214.

his own, which may be taken away at the Pleasure of another? And so evidently does this appear to be the natural Right of Mankind, that even conquered tributary States, though subject to the Payment of a fixed periodical Tribute, never were reduced to so abject and forlorn a Condition, as to yield to all the Burthens which their Conquerors might at any future Time think fit to impose. The Tribute paid, the Debt was discharged; and the Remainder they could call their own." And the New Yorkers made explicit their "disdain" of claiming "that Exemption as a *Privilege*. They found it on a Basis more honourable, solid and stable, they challenge it, and glory in it as their Right."[41]

North Carolina's legislature also resisted the Sugar Act as an encroachment upon their "right" to tax themselves. Perhaps some especially forceful—and foresighted—individual drove these protests through the legislatures of New York and North Carolina. Neither colony offered leadership later on, and these statements of rights seemed aberrant somehow. For the Americans in countinghouses and legislatures, if not exactly confused, were at the least unclear about what they were up against. They had not had to face a Parliament committed to taxing them for revenue. They had enjoyed rights without having to think about them. Unexamined rights may always be something of a luxury. The Americans were soon to think so.[42]

Of course, not many Americans had become involved in the struggles over the Sugar Act. And those who did were, for the most part, securely at the top of colonial society—merchants and representatives in colonial legislatures. Occasionally these men had found support among men less powerful than themselves. In the crisis that would occur over the Stamp Act, these leaders were to turn to such men more frequently and in the process to examine their rights more closely. Their example proved edifying to these others—artisans, shopkeepers, workers of various sorts. Quite clearly, what had begun at the top did not end there.

41. Quotations are from the documents reprinted in Morgan, ed., *Prologue*, 9–10.
42. Knollenberg, *Origin of the American Revolution*, 218.

4

The Stamp Act Crisis

While the colonists conducted operations against the duties on molasses, the most thoughtful among them worried about the possibility that still another tax would be levied on America. They owed the worry to George Grenville, who on March 9, 1764, the day he introduced the proposals for the new molasses duties, warned that to meet the national expenses "it may be proper to charge certain Stamp Duties in the said Colonies and Plantations."[1] Grenville did not say much more about what he had in mind except that he would postpone introducing the necessary legislation until the colonies had an opportunity to offer objections. But the objections should not include challenges to Parliament's right to tax the colonies; it had the right as far as Grenville was concerned, and he did not mean to be subjected to arguments to the contrary.

Grenville learned before the year was out that a disposition not to listen would not still angry American voices. At first, though, as rumors of a stamp tax reached the colonies, the Americans did not protest but instead asked for information about the duties. The reports reaching the colonies all suffered from a lack of precision, from second- and some- times third-hand observations, and from a general vagueness. Grenville had told so little that not much distortion seeped into these accounts. What seems surprising at first sight is that he was not inclined to tell more.

By the spring reports surfaced in England that Grenville had delayed in order to give the colonies time not only to furnish information but also to propose another mode of taxation. Thomas Whately, one of the Treasury secretaries, mentioned the possibility that Grenville was

1. *Commons Journals* (London, 1764), XXIX, 935.

awaiting suggestions from America for less burdensome ways of raising money. The agents of Massachusetts and Virginia wrote their respective employers that Grenville might be inclined to leave matters to the colonies—so long as the money was eventually forthcoming. But these agents' reports, like Grenville's original announcement in March, had about them an air of mystery and even unreality: no sums of money were mentioned and no plans for apportioning tax burdens among the colonies—each with its own legislature after all—were offered.[2]

To clear up the mysteries of Grenville's intentions, several agents asked him for a meeting. He obliged them on May 17, 1764, and they came away wiser, perhaps, but with very little information. When asked for a copy of the bill, Grenville replied that he could not supply one since it had not yet been drafted. When asked what would be taxed and at what rate, he replied vaguely that about the same things would be taxed as in Britain, but that he could say nothing about rates of taxation since they had not been decided. Nor did Grenville lay to rest speculation that his purpose in delaying the bill was to permit the colonies to suggest alternative modes of taxation. He neither confirmed nor denied that he would be receptive to fresh plans. Yet despite his coyness he did manage to convey knowledge of what he really wanted: approval in advance from the colonies of the general proposal. The objections he had seemed to welcome would be received—or welcomed—only after the colonies gave their assent. To be sure, he would give colonial proposals for different sorts of taxation "all due consideration," but what he seemed to have in mind was taxation by Parliament.[3]

Understandably, the agents, and soon the colonial legislatures, found all this rather bewildering. And what made matters worse, and induced a certain skepticism about Grenville's sincerity in professing to give consideration to American views, was his failure to notify the colonial governors that he had decided to ask Parliament for a stamp duty. Ordinarily when decisions were made about the colonies, the usual procedure was for the Secretary of State for the Southern Department, acting on the orders of the ministry (or officially of the Privy Council), to pass the news to the colonial governors. Information customarily was dispensed

2. Morgan and Morgan, *Stamp Act Crisis*, 55.
3. The agents' reports may be read in Morgan, ed., *Prologue*, 27–28. See also William Knox, *The Claim of the Colonies to an Exemption from Internal Taxes* (London, 1765) and Lewis Namier, "Charles Garth, Agent for South Carolina," *EHR*, 54 (1939), 632–52.

this way, though of course other means were employed as well. In this case, Grenville abandoned the normal procedures, though Thomas Whately asked several colonial officials about the nature of legal documents used in the colonies: these documents were to be subject to a tax.[4]

Whately had good reason to ask such questions, for he was charged by his chief to draw up the bill to be presented to Parliament. Whately, who had been admitted to the bar after attendance at Cambridge and study in the Middle Temple, possessed the technical qualifications to draft legislation. Moreover, he was intensely loyal to Grenville, and he believed in hard work for himself and not just for others. The ministry's ignorance of the details of colonial life was so great that considerable work proved necessary. Whately went about it with a dedication that must have gratified Grenville. Before he finished a rough draft suitable for the ministry's consideration early in December 1764, he had canvassed a variety of departments and officials, including the Board of Trade and its knowledgeable secretary John Pownall, the Customs commissioners, and the English Stamp Board. Whately also approached Americans and English officials in the colonies, though here his efforts may have been less systematic. John Temple, the surveyor general of Customs in the northern colonies, was consulted, as were lesser officials in Massachusetts, New Jersey, and New York. Whately also wrote at least one prominent private citizen in America, Jared Ingersoll in Connecticut. Ingersoll and Temple knew the colonists well and tried unsuccessfully to persuade Whately that the idea of an American stamp tax was a mistake. Ingersoll, a blunt-speaking Yankee and as far from radicalism as almost anyone in America, responded with particular directness to Whatley's questions about American attitudes. The minds of the Americans, he wrote in July 1764, "are filled with the most dreadfull apprehensions from such a Step's taking place, from whence I leave you to guess how easily a tax of that kind would be Collected; tis difficult to say how many ways could be invented to avoid the payment of a tax laid upon a Country without the Consent of the Legislature of that Country and in the opinion of most of the people Contrary to the foundation principles of their natural and Constitutional rights and Liberties." And, as other colonists had, Ingersoll added that if the colonists were asked to provide a portion of a revenue, they would do so willingly, but if even a moderate

4. [Jared Ingersoll], *Mr. Ingersoll's Letters Relating to the Stamp Act* (New Haven, Conn., 1766), 2-3, 5.

tax were laid by Parliament, he would not predict "what Consequences may, or rather may not follow?"[5]

Whately had not expected to receive warnings that a stamp tax might invite unhappy reactions in America, and he brushed them aside. Grenville could not have been disturbed by these responses, even though he had indicated that the one argument he would not listen to was a challenge of Parliament's right to tax, an argument Ingersoll and others, in letters and petitions, were making. Such arguments actually played into Grenville's hands. If there was anything intolerable to a good Parliament man, it was to be told that the Parliament lacked the right to do what it wanted to do. The colonial agents in England realized that what they were instructed to say in defense of colonial rights would only produce the result it was calculated to avoid—the passage of the stamp bill. But what could they do? English merchants trading to America were made uneasy by the conflict that was taking shape before their eyes, but they too hesitated to make the colonial constitutional case.[6]

Just before Parliament convened in February 1765, the agents, now desperate, sent four of their number to meet one final time with Grenville. They were an impressive group—Benjamin Franklin, already famous for his electrical experiments, worldly-wise and a little cynical; Jared Ingersoll, fresh from America, tough-minded and fundamentally very conservative; Richard Jackson, a member of Parliament and agent for Connecticut, Massachusetts, and Pennsylvania; and Charles Garth, another member of Parliament, agent for South Carolina, shrewd and quick-witted. Grenville received them with kindness and early in the meeting said that he regretted giving the Americans so much uneasiness, but he thought it only fair that they help pay for their own defense and that he knew no better way than by a tax levied by Parliament. The agents repeated what by now must have been familiar to everyone— that the Americans preferred to tax themselves. Richard Jackson made the reasons for this preference absolutely clear by arguing that a tax by Parliament would subvert representative government in America. Fed by a Parliamentary tax on the colonies, the royal governors there would

5. For the quotations, see Ingersoll to Whately, July 6, 1764, in The New Haven Colony Historical Society, *Papers*, 9 (1918), 299–300; and for a careful account of the preparation of the act, Morgan and Morgan, *Stamp Act Crisis*, 53–70. P. D. G. Thomas, *British Politics and the Stamp Act Crisis: The First Phase of the American Revolution, 1763–1767* (Oxford, 1975), challenges the Morgans' interpretation in certain respects. On the whole, the Morgans' conclusions remain convincing.
6. Morgan and Morgan, *Stamp Act Crisis*, 68–69.

have no reason ever to convene the local assemblies. Grenville of course denied that he had any such intention in mind, and he denied furthermore that any such thing would take place.[7]

At about this point in the meeting Grenville asked the agents if they "could agree upon the several proportions Each Colony should raise," if the colonies were permitted to raise the money through the assemblies.[8] The question has been called "fatuous," and in a sense it was.[9] The Grenville ministry itself had the responsibility of establishing such proportions, and it had had a year to do so, assuming, of course, that it had any interest in the answer. If there was any doubt that it had no such interest and no intention of allowing the colonies to tax themselves to support the troops in America, the question served to dispel it. Grenville knew that and doubtless asked the question, silly as it seemed, in order to disabuse the agents of any hope that they could deflect him from his course.

To persuade Grenville to give up the idea of a stamp tax was beyond the agents and everyone else. On February 6, 1765, he brought the resolution of 1764 before the Commons; the debates and the votes that followed demonstrated the imprudence of principled opposition. Although only William Beckford denied on the floor of Commons Parliament's right to tax, that right was clearly uppermost in the minds of most members. Anger against the colonials for presuming to challenge Parliament's absolute sovereignty was so widespread that opponents to the proposed tax phrased their arguments very carefully—but not carefully enough.[10]

Nothing that was said changed many votes. And the most eloquent defense of the American case, made in a speech by Colonel Isaac Barré, may actually have stiffened Parliament's resolve to tax. Barré's outburst came in response to a sardonic complaint by Charles Townshend: "And now will these Americans, Children planted by our Care, nourished up by our Indulgence until they are grown to a Degree of Strength and Opulence, and protected by our Arms, will they grudge to contribute

7. Jared Ingersoll wrote an account of the meeting to Governor Fitch of Connecticut, Feb. 11, 1765, *Fitch Papers* (Connecticut Historical Society, *Collections*, 18 [Hartford, Conn., 1920]), II, 324–25.

8. *Ibid.*

9. Edmund S. Morgan, "The Postponement of the Stamp Act," *WMQ*, 3d Ser., 7 (1950), 372. I have followed this article closely in reconstructing the early history of the stamp bill.

10. Bernhard Knollenberg, *Origin of the American Revolution, 1759–1766* (New York, 1960), 223.

their mite to relieve us from the heavy weight of that burden which we lie under?"[11] Barré's reply was explosive:

> They planted by your Care? No! your Oppressions planted em in America. They fled from your Tyranny to a then uncultivated and unhospitable Country—where they exposed themselves to almost all the hardships to which human Nature is liable, and among others to the Cruelties of a Savage foe, the most subtle and I take upon me to say the most formidable of any People upon the face of Gods Earth. And yet, actuated by Principles of true english Lyberty, they met all these hardships with pleasure, compared with those they suffered in their own Country, from the hands of those who should have been their Friends.
>
> They nourished up by *your* indulgence? they grew by your neglect of Em: as soon as you began to care about Em, that Care was Exercised in sending persons to rule over Em, in one Department and another, who were perhaps the Deputies of Deputies to some Member of this house—sent to Spy out their Lyberty, to misrepresent their Actions and to prey upon Em; men whose behaviour on many Occasions has caused the Blood of those Sons of Liberty to recoil within them; men promoted to the highest Seats of Justice, some, who to my knowledge were glad by going to a foreign Country to Escape being brought to the Bar of a Court of Justice in their own.
>
> They protected by *your* Arms? they have nobly taken up Arms in your Defence, have Exerted a Valour amidst their constant and Laborious industry for the defence of a Country, whose frontier, while drench'd in blood, its interior Parts have yielded all its little Savings to your Emolument. And believe me, remember I this Day told you so, that same Spirit of freedom which actuated that people at first will accompany them still.—But prudence forbids me to explain myself further. God knows I do not at this Time speak from motives of party Heat, what I deliver are the Genuine Sentiment of my heart.[12]

An American who listened to Colonel Barré thought the speech was "noble" and relished the House's initial reaction: it sat there "awhile as Amazed," unable or unwilling to speak even a word.[13] But the House soon recovered its voice and, when Barré and his friends moved to adjourn in order to avoid a vote on the proposed tax, voted 245 to 49 against. Such maneuvers were not going to stop Grenville with the Commons at his back; the stamp bill received its first reading on February 13

11. Morgan, ed., *Prologue*, 32.
12. *Ibid.*
13. *Ibid.*

and two days later the second was passed without even a division. On this day, February 15, the opposition assisted by the colonial agents did its best and failed pathetically. Charles Garth offered a petition, framed from South Carolinian protests, which carefully skirted the questions of Parliament's right to tax the colonies. Sir William Meredith, a London merchant, handed in a petition from Virginia, and Richard Jackson presented several from Connecticut and Massachusetts. The Commons refused even to receive the petitions, holding that the House of Commons simply did not hear petitions against money bills, and in any case it was not going to indulge questioners of its authority. This ruling prompted General Henry Conway to point out the paradox in the Commons' decision in 1764 to give the colonies time to prepare objections to a stamp tax and then in 1765 to refuse to receive the objections. Commons was in no mood for paradox, or logic, or anything but the passing of the bill. After the second reading no further opposition seemed possible and the bill sailed through the third, and received the king's approval on March 22.[14]

The opposition within Parliament to the Stamp Act had given its best, and it had provided some fine moments, as, for example, in Colonel Barré's answer to Charles Townshend. The opposition won the contest in rhetoric but lost it in the vote, the part of parliamentary action that counts. Those who approved of the Act had voted half in exasperation at the burden of taxation, already carried for too long, and half in the conviction that justice required the colonies to contribute to their own defense. Their votes were given rather easily, if the record of debate may be trusted; most of the objections were not considered worthy of discussion. The Commons had made up its mind quickly, and Grenville, knowing that he had the support he needed, was content to let the opposition sing its sad songs. He then pushed the measure through with an ease bordering on contempt.

II

The king's approval was the last event connected to the Stamp Act to be accomplished with ease. For the Stamp Act set off in America a crisis that had no precedents. In a sense, the rioting and mobbing that ensued during the summer and autumn of 1765 are the most interesting features of the episode; but interesting though they were, the organization of protest and the reorganization of local politics that emerged in the

14. Conway's speech is in *ibid.*, 34–35.

crisis were more important. And most important of all was the development of the colonial constitutional position, so evocative and expressive
of self-consciousness among the colonists.

News of the stamp tax arrived in the colonies in the first two weeks
of April. For the next six weeks almost nothing about the Act made
its way into the colonial press, and certainly no public body seemed
eager to take the lead in opposition. At the end of May, however, an
official body, the House of Burgesses in Virginia, took action. The Burgesses approved a set of resolves on May 31 which declared that the
constitution limited the right of taxation to the people or their representatives and that this right belonged to Virginians by virtue of the fact
that they were British subjects who lived under the British constitution.
The implication was inescapable: Parliament, a body to which they sent
no representatives, had no authority to tax them.[15]

On the face of things, this action hardly seems explosive—yet it was.
That an explosion occurred in Virginia was something of a historical
accident, or at least an event in which chance—or contingency—played
more than a normal role. Chance in this case may have been nothing
more than astute timing by several political manipulators whose spokes-
man was Patrick Henry. For Henry introduced the Virginia Resolves
at the very end of a legislative session after most of the burgesses had
already left for home. Thirty-nine members remained of 116 when Henry
got to his feet to introduce his resolves.

Patrick Henry was twenty-nine years old in 1765, a gay blade who
loved music and dancing and who in turn was loved by young ladies
for his dash and charm. He was well known for so young a man, having
made his name in a celebrated struggle over the payment of the Anglican
clergy in Virginia, a case appropriately called the Parson's Cause.[16]

The Parson's Cause began with the price of a weed—tobacco. In
the middle of the eighteenth century, tobacco dominated Virginia's economy in a way inconceivable today. Tobacco was the most important
crop raised on plantations, though some diversification had begun a

15. McIlwaine and Kennedy, eds., *Jour. Va. Burgesses*, X, 360. The resolves, along
    with many other documents essential to an understanding of the Stamp Act, have
    been reprinted in Morgan, ed., *Prologue.*
16. For the Parson's Cause, see Richard L. Morton, *Colonial Virginia* (2 vols., Chapel
    Hill, N.C., 1960), II, 751–819; Richard Beeman, *Patrick Henry: A Biography* (New
    York, 1974), 13–22; and Rhys Isaac, "Religion and Authority: Problems of the
    Anglican Establishment in Virginia in the Era of the Great Awakening and the
    Parson's Cause," *WMQ*, 3d Ser., 30 (1973), 3–36.

few years earlier; once harvested and cured, it was shipped to England for sale or for trans-shipment to the Continent. Most cultivated land in Virginia was put into tobacco production; the thousands of black slaves in the colony spent most of their waking hours with the plant; and planters seem not only to have used their days in its cultivation and sale but also to have dreamed in their nights of its expansion and increase.[17]

Notes issued on tobacco deposited in the local warehouses circulated as money, and many private contracts provided that payment of obligations was to be in tobacco rather than in money. Public acts also sometimes required that payments of debts be in tobacco—among them a statute of 1748 which required that an Anglican clergyman should be paid 17,280 pounds of tobacco a year.

In 1758, there was a drought that drastically reduced the tobacco crop, and the shortage that resulted drove up the price of tobacco to about four and one-half pence per pound, an amount about three times greater than the normal price. This inflation of price threatened the interests of debtors who of course had incurred debts when tobacco was cheaper. These debtors, for the most part tobacco planters, demanded some protection from the Virginia legislature, which responded with an act holding that debts payable in tobacco might be paid in currency for one year, at the rate of two pence per pound of tobacco—an amount well above the normal price. The statute, locally referred to as the Two Penny Act, was not aimed at the clergy, but they were clearly affected since their salaries, set by law, were ordinarily paid in tobacco.

Creditors of all kinds would have benefited had the law not been passed. But though it cut into their pocketbooks, most did not complain. Nor did many clergymen, but several did—and loudly. Not satisfied by these protests, they also sent the Reverend Mr. John Camm to England to have the law disallowed by the Privy Council. Hearings were held, arguments given, petitions received, and the Privy Council in August 1759 set aside the Act. From Virginia's point of view this was an unfortunate ruling, particularly because the councillors also declared that in the future laws which were passed in violation of the government's instruction were void from their inception. In practice, this ruling would have made governing difficult.

The clergy further soured popular feeling when a handful of their number sued to collect the full value of their salaries under the old

17. Lewis C. Gray, *History of Agriculture in the Southern United States to 1860* (2 vols., Washington, D.C., 1933) is a fine study of antebellum planting.

rate of 17,280 pounds per year. The Two Penny Act had been disallowed, and they wanted full pay; if there was drought and inflation, well, that was too bad.

In the first two cases heard by county courts in the colony, the decisions went against the clergy. The third, brought by the Reverend Mr. James Maury of Louisa County, was heard in Hanover County. The court found for Maury—the reasons are not known—and the case went to the jury which was to decide on the amount of damages to be awarded. To aid the jury in reaching an equitable decision, the county hired Patrick Henry to make the argument for the defense—in other words, for the local interest.[18]

Because Henry knew very little law at this time, he ignored legal niceties in favor of a brilliant attack: the clergy, Henry said, were enemies of the community who deserved not damages but punishment for bringing the case. The clergy, after all, had proved unwilling to obey the law. As for the British government, in disallowing the Two Penny Act, it had encroached upon colonial freedom. The climax to this address was a daring declaration that "a King, by disallowing Acts of this salutary nature, far from being the father of his people, degenerates into a Tyrant, and forfeits all rights to his subjects' obedience."[19] At this point there were cries of "Treason," but the presiding justice, Colonel John Henry, father of Patrick, unsympathetic to clergy and kings, let his son go on unreprimanded. The jury, according to the Reverend Mr. Maury, who was in anguish, sat there nodding its agreement all the while. Indeed Henry had been persuasive: the jury awarded Maury the magnificent sum of one penny.

Although this case made Henry's name in Virginia, he added to his fame by brilliant performances in hundreds of others. And Louisa County, in a demonstration of its admiration of him, chose him burgess in a special election held in the spring of 1765. Henry in fact made his first appearance in the House on May 20; ten days later, a new, untried burgess but a well-known man, he introduced the Virginia Resolves.

The main outlines of what happened that day and the next—May 30-31—are known, but several important aspects of the passing of the Virginia Resolves remain elusive. Two facts are indisputable: only thirty-nine of the 116 burgesses remained, the others having already departed for home; and these thirty-nine passed—by no means unanimously—five resolves on May 30. Henry then left the House, presumably satisfied

18. Beeman, *Patrick Henry*, 16.
19. Quoted in *ibid.*, 19.

with his first major effort. The next day, however, the fifth resolve was rescinded by what by this time was a very small rump meeting.[20]

As printed in *The Journal of the House of Burgesses*, the first four resolutions ran as follows:

> *Resolved*, That the first Adventurers and Settlers of this his Majesty's Colony and Dominion of *Virginia* brought with them, and transmitted to their Posterity, and all other his Majesty's Subjects since inhabiting in this his Majesty's said Colony, all the Liberties, Privileges, Franchises, and Immunities, that have at any Time been held, enjoyed, and possessed, by the People of Great Britain.
>
> *Resolved*, That by two royal Charters, granted by King *James* the First, the Colonists aforesaid are declared entitled to all Liberties, Privileges, and Immunities of Denizens and natural Subjects, to all Intents and Purposes, as if they had been abiding and born within the Realm of *England*.
>
> *Resolved*, That the Taxation of the People by themselves, or by Persons chosen by themselves to represent them, who can only know what Taxes the People are able to bear, or the easiest Method of raising them, and must themselves be affected by every Tax laid on the People, is the only Security against a burthensome Taxation, and the distinguishing characteristick of British Freedom, without which the ancient Constitution cannot exist.
>
> *Resolved*, That his Majesty's liege People of this his most ancient and loyal Colony have without Interruption enjoyed the inestimable Right of being governed by such Laws, respecting their internal Polity and Taxation, as are derived from their own Consent, with the Approbation of their Sovereign, or his Substitute; and that the same hath never been forfeited or yielded up, but hath been constantly recognized by the Kings and People of Great Britain.[21]

A much better attended House had approved statements of about this same tenor the year before. Hence the question of why there should have been disagreement over these resolutions is puzzling. Perhaps the answer lies in the composition of supporters of the resolutions. Patrick Henry was a young man and for the most part so were the others who backed him in the Burgesses. His opponents included several of the

20. The history of the passage of the Stamp Act Resolves has been reconstructed in Morgan and Morgan, *Stamp Act Crisis*, 88–97. The essential sources from which the Morgans drew have been reprinted in Morgan, *Prologue*, 46–48. See also Edmund S. Morgan, ed., "Edmund Pendleton on the Virginia Resolves," and Irving Brant, "Comment on the Pendleton Letter," *MdHM*, 46 (1951), 71–80.

21. McIlwaine and Kennedy, eds., *Jour. Va. Burgesses*, X, 360.

most distinguished members of the House—Peyton Randolph, John Robinson, Robert Carter Nicholas, Richard Bland, George Wythe—all older men, and all apparently resentful of the upstart from Louisa County and his youthful cohorts and their inflammatory language.[22]

That brings us to Henry's speech delivered in support of his resolutions. No copy survives, but fragments exist, as reported by an anonymous French traveler who witnessed the proceedings on May 30 and 31 from the lobby of the House. According to this French observer, Henry began in a grand style, declaring that "in former times tarquin and Julus had their Brutus, Charles had his Cromwell, and he Did not Doubt but some good american would stand up, in favour of his Country."[23] At this point John Robinson, the speaker of the House, cut Henry off by accusing him of talking treason. Henry immediately begged the pardon of Robinson and the House and stated that he was prepared to demonstrate his loyalty to George III "at the Expense of the last Drop" of his blood. Passion may have carried him too far, he said, passion and "the Interest of his Countrys Dying Liberty."

Henry backed down, but certainly not all the way. Apparently the damage was done, for the House divided. The young men there made their point in the four resolves and also succeeded in getting a fifth passed. The *Journal* of the House says nothing of it, however, and there seems to be no way of establishing its content. It may have been worded as follows—the text is from a paper Henry left behind:

> Resolved, Therefore that the General Assembly of this Colony have the *only and sole exclusive* Right and Power to lay Taxes and Impositions upon the Inhabitants of this Colony and that every Attempt to vest such Power in any Person or Persons whatsoever other than the General Assembly aforesaid has a manifest Tendency to destroy British as well as American Freedom.[24]

Several colonial newspapers printed this resolution and informed their readers that it had been passed. The *Newport Mercury* not only printed it but also a sixth and/or seventh:

22. Beeman, *Patrick Henry*, 33–35, argues persuasively that though Henry was not as well educated as most burgesses and though he had less political experience than they, he did not head a democratic insurgency in the House. None existed.
23. "Journal of a French Traveller in the Colonies, 1765," *AHR*, 26 (1921), 726–47 (quotations in this paragraph on 745–46).
24. Morgan, ed., *Prologue*, 48.

> *Resolved,* That his Majesty's liege People, the Inhabitants of this
> Colony, are not bound to yield Obedience to any Law or Ordinance
> whatever, designed to impose any Taxation whatsoever upon them,
> other than the Laws or Ordinances of the General Assembly aforesaid.[25]

The *Mercury,* however, omitted the third resolve printed in the *Journal
of the House.* The *Maryland Gazette* printed all seven, and most other
newspapers offered either six or seven.[26] The last resolve—the sixth in
the *Mercury,* which was the seventh in the *Maryland Gazette*—carried
the greatest thunder and was at least debated by the House. The French
traveler, a fascinated observer, followed the proceedings and copied down
the gist of this last resolve:

> That any Person who shall, by Speaking, or Writing, assert or main-
> tain, That any Person or Persons, other than the General Assembly
> of this Colony, with such Consent as aforesaid, have any Right or
> Authority to lay or impose any Tax whatever on the Inhabitants thereof,
> shall be deemed, AN ENEMY TO THIS HIS MAJESTY'S COLONY.[27]

Not even the remnant of the faithful who remained in Williamsburg
at the end of May had a stomach for stuff as strong as this. The first
four resolves doubtless represented the prevailing opinion of the burgesses
even though they were encumbered by the sponsorship of young men
such as Patrick Henry.

These last days of May exposed a generational split in the House,
but it did not cut deeply—and there were no other important divisions
within the body. There were, of course, differences in politics and society,
but they had not made their way into established institutions. Certainly
these potentially divisive interests had not appeared in the Burgesses.
One interest dominated the House, indeed dominated Virginia's government and politics: tobacco planters, landed, slave-owning, hard-driving
producers of a staple sold in England and on the European continent.
If the House of Burgesses was united, so was the colony as a whole
because this group ran its life. Other interests existed in the colony—
religious dissenters in the West, Baptists, Presbyterians, and Method-
ists—but these radicals of the spirit had not yet forced their way into
the government of the colony.

Every newspaper report of Virginia's action made events in Virginia

25. June 24, 1765.
26. *Maryland Gazette* (Annapolis), July 4, 1765.
27. This version appears in the *Maryland Gazette.* The French traveler's account differs
    slightly.

sound more extravagant than they were. The Burgesses had passed four resolves; Maryland printed six and Rhode Island seven; undoubtedly stories relayed in private letters, by word of mouth, the gossip of taverns, parishes, towns, and court meetings introduced further distortions. Henry's bravado was reported in these stories; his backing down was not.

III

Because official action had been taken in Virginia, the pressure built up elsewhere to respond in a similar vein. Before the end of 1765, the lower houses of eight other colonies had approved resolutions denouncing the Stamp Act and denying Parliament's right to tax the American colonies for revenue. And in October a Stamp Act Congress, composed of representatives of nine colonies, passed similar declarations of colonial rights.[28]

The statements of these bodies possess a transparent clarity and force that imply that agreement on them was complete and easily achieved. In fact, in almost every case the response was the purchase of effort and conflict, because the Stamp Act offered an opportunity for gaining political advantage in long-standing struggles. Where local divisions were deep—and felt intensely—the Stamp Act encouraged bitter conflict and usually drove divisions even deeper.

None of these legislatures passed resolutions before the fall of 1765. Most had finished their spring sessions by the time the news of the Virginia Resolves arrived, and none had been able to pull itself together sufficiently to act with a similar force. Virginia's example clearly helped them act in the fall, and so did popular action undertaken in the summer. By early 1766 politics in most of the colonies had assumed a shape rather different from that of March 1765 when the Stamp Act was passed.

Massachusetts—where violence began and where politics was transformed—offers an instructive example of a political stand-off which at first inhibited protest, and then—when it was broken—intensified conflict and violence. Indeed, long-standing political feuds contributed to at least one instance of unrestrained violence—the mobbing of Thomas Hutchinson's house—and to the general hostility to Parliament's attempt to tax the colonies. For these provincial political divisions gave the opponents of taxation the opportunity to taint their enemies with something approaching treason to America. But at first—in the spring of 1765—

28. Morgan, ed., *Prologue*, 62–63.

political division, and the peculiar cast of alignments in Massachusetts, produced only paralysis.[29]

The most important political division in Massachusetts in 1765 went back to another division between James Otis, Sr., and Thomas Hutchinson which had its origin in 1757. Division is probably too mild a word to apply to the Otis-Hutchinson conflict; their struggle took on the proportions of a feud. As is still often the case in politics, the feud was over political office—first a seat on the governor's Council which James Otis, Sr. of Barnstable wanted, and then the chief justiceship which they both wanted. Otis, Sr. hoped in 1757 that the House of Representatives would elect him to the Council, and when it did not, he blamed Thomas Hutchinson. The two men had been on opposite sides of the fence before—in a sense they were when the election to the Council was held, for Otis had been supporting the current governor, Thomas Pownall, who feared that Hutchinson coveted his place.[30]

Otis did not make much out of his disappointment until shortly after Francis Bernard replaced Thomas Pownall as governor in 1760. Colonists in Massachusetts knew Francis Bernard before they ever laid eyes on him. For Bernard was a familiar sort of figure in the colonies, a placeman who owed his appointment to his connection at "home." In this case the influential English backer was Lord Barrington, Bernard's brother-in-law and Secretary at War. Bernard had been governor of New Jersey, a place he thought beneath his ability, or at least beneath his hopes for financial reward. Bernard needed money to keep his growing family happy; all he had of his own was a rich ambition. Unfortunately, he lacked brains as well as money.[31]

Bernard arrived with instructions to enforce the Molasses Act—to stop smugglers, in other words. There is reason to suppose that he regarded these orders approvingly, for the governor received one-third of

---

29. The following are especially helpful in tracing the lines of division in Massachusetts politics: John J. Waters and John A. Schutz, "Patterns of Massachusetts Colonial Politics: The Writs of Assistance and the Rivalry between the Otis and Hutchinson Families," *WMQ*, 3d Ser., 24 (1967), 543–67; John A. Schutz, *Thomas Pownall* (Glendale, Calif., 1951) and *William Shirley* (Chapel Hill, N.C., 1961); Ellen Brennan, *Plural Office-Holding in Massachusetts, 1760–1780* (Chapel Hill, N.C., 1945); John J. Waters, *The Otis Family in Provincial and Revolutionary Massachusetts* (Chapel Hill, N.C., 1968). Bailyn, *Ordeal of Hutchinson* is especially valuable.

30. Bailyn, *Ordeal of Hutchinson*, 47–50; Waters, *Otis Family*, 104–5.

31. Insight into Bernard may best be gained from Channing and Coolidge, eds., *Barrington-Bernard Correspondence*.

the proceeds of all forfeitures of smugglers. Bernard immediately made his weight felt, light as it was, by remaining aloof from the Otis and Hutchinson factions and dealing with the Tyng interest in the House of Representatives. Tyng was a power in the House, but no governor could survive without coming to terms with either the Otis or the Hutchinson group.

Bernard had hardly been in Massachusetts a month when one of those opportunities presented itself that give politicians nightmares. The opportunity was to fill an office sought after by two powerful rivals (Otis and Hutchinson)—the office of chief justice left vacant by Samuel Sewall's death. By this time, Otis, fifty-eight years old, was speaker of the House, a formidable power there and among the inland farmers. He insisted that William Shirley, governor from 1741 to 1756, had promised to appoint him to a place on the superior court when a vacancy occurred. The vacancy was obviously there in September, but Francis Bernard quite understandably did not feel bound by Shirley's promise. To disappoint James Otis, Sr., and his tribe of family and followers was to court danger, and so Bernard, who only craved a peaceful and rewarding tenure as governor, delayed while he looked over the field.[32]

The only other seeker after the office was of course Thomas Hutchinson. Forty-nine years old in 1760, Hutchinson, like Otis, came from an old Massachusetts family. The establishment in Massachusetts had not always considered the family to be entirely honorable, for Anne Hutchinson, great-great-grandmother of Thomas, was one of its founders. Mistress Anne, a notorious antinomian, had been banished in 1638; Thomas Hutchinson had no spiritual leanings and seemed as unlikely a candidate for exile as could be found: a solid Harvard man, a prudent and successful merchant, and a pluralist second to none. A pluralist in eighteenth-century Massachusetts was not one who held several clerical livings; he was an amasser of public offices. Hutchinson in 1760 was a councillor, lieutenant governor of the colony, commander of Castle Island, and judge of probate in Suffolk County. These offices brought him around £400 sterling a year.[33]

Hutchinson's large appetite inspired his family to emulate his example (the only inspiration respected in the eighteenth-century clan). Andrew Oliver, his brother-in-law, was secretary of the Province, judge of the inferior court of common pleas in Essex County, and a councillor. Two

32. Waters, *Otis Family*, 118–19.
33. Brennan, *Plural Office-Holding*, 32.

other relatives by marriage, Peter Oliver and Benjamin Lynde, were justices of the superior court and councillors. This list could be extended without difficulty.

Governor Bernard may have thought it unkind not to feed this voracious tribe; more likely, he learned that as Chief Justice Hutchinson would be more disposed to enlist in the fight against smugglers than Otis. In any event, Bernard appointed Hutchinson in November and the fight was on—with the Otis family, their adherents, including many merchants, and a majority of the House opposed to the Bernard-Hutchinson administration.[34]

Otis had little trouble lining up enemies to the administration, for Bernard and the local vice admiralty court had been playing dirty in the rough game of suppressing smugglers. According to the law, forfeitures were to be divided into three equal parts, with the governor taking one, the officials making the seizure another, and the province the third. In practice, however, the province collected its third in a rather depleted state, for informers were paid out of it. Fairness seemed to require that such expenses be equally distributed. Fairness may not have moved Otis and his merchant supporters who, after the battle with the administration was joined, persuaded the House of Representatives to direct the province to sue for its full third. The case dragged through the year 1761 and into 1762, when the superior court, guided by Chief Justice Thomas Hutchinson, reversed a lower court ruling and decided against the province.[35]

While this case was being heard, another of greater consequence for merchant interests was decided. This involved the writs of assistance, the general search warrants used by Customs officials in the enforcement of the navigation acts. The warrants had expired at the death of George II and had to be renewed. The question before the Massachusetts courts involved the legality of writs issued by the superior court. That court could not claim chancery jurisdiction under which the court of Exchequer in England commonly issued the writs, for it after all could not hold the Customs accountable. Oxenbridge Thacher, representing the merchants with James Otis, Jr., made this point in a careful legal argument against the writs after Jeremiah Gridley, appearing for the Customs, argued that the needs of the state took priority over individual liberty. Young Otis ignored all such legal niceties in favor of constitutional argument: the writs of assistance, he maintained, violated fundamental principles of the constitution, and not even Parliament could issue such a

34. Bailyn, *Ordeal of Hutchinson*, 47–50.
35. Waters, *Otis Family*, 120–21.

writ. Thomas Hutchinson remained cool before this brilliant heat and, after consulting the authorities in England, upheld the legality of the writs.[36]

These struggles generated others: the two sides sniped at one another about the control of political office, the enforcement of Customs regulations, and a host of other matters. In 1763, Bernard, trying vainly to heal a festering wound with an inadequate poultice, offered Otis, Sr., a vacant judgeship in Barnstable County. The senior Otis took it and then proceeded to act in his usual independent way. Bernard enjoyed more success the next year, blocking the House's attempts to protest against the Sugar Act until after Parliament passed it.[37]

Understandably, the "popular" faction led by the two Otises felt overwhelmed by frustration and failure on the eve of the passage of the Stamp Act. When the legislature met in January 1765—barely a month before the Stamp Act was introduced in Parliament—it discovered that its frustration was to be renewed, not by Governor Bernard or Thomas Hutchinson, but by James Otis, Jr. For Otis was now off on one of his curious aberrations, first voting for the governor's man, Richard Jackson, as colonial agent, and then joining those voting Thomas Hutchinson additional salary as chief justice, salary Otis had opposed successfully three years earlier.

If this performance shocked the House, Otis's next actions stunned all who knew him. In the spring, Otis published two pamphlets which seemed to repudiate the constitutional position he had taken earlier in *The Rights of the British Colonies* (1764).[38] These two new tracts conceded the English case for Parliamentary sovereignty, Parliament's right to tax the colonies, and, in the strangest twist of all, argued that the colonies were represented in Parliament in law if not in fact.

The consternation these arguments produced among his friends may have surprised Otis, who never thought that he had given away his earlier defense of colonial rights. And in a sense he was correct. Both positions rested on an assumption that Parliament was a body determined to correct its own mistakes, which is exactly what Otis urged it to do the year before in *The Rights of the British Colonies*. At that time, he

---

36. L. Kinvin Wroth and Hiller B. Zobel, eds., *Legal Papers of John Adams* (3 vols., Cambridge, Mass., 1965), II, 106–47.
37. Waters, *Otis Family*, 148–49.
38. The tracts were *A Vindication of the British Colonies* (Boston, 1765) and *Brief Remarks on the Defense of the Halifax Libel on the British-American-Colonies* (Boston, 1765).

provided an elaborate case for the rights of the colonies; now in the efforts of 1765, he was redressing the balance somewhat by pointing to the sovereignty of Parliament.

To Massachusetts and to the House, Otis's assumptions mattered not at all. He seemed to be a late convert to Parliamentary orthodoxy, and his conversion to English political advocacy did not raise him to sainthood in Boston's eyes; in fact, the town almost decided it could play the game of repudiation too, and in the May election very nearly did not return him to the House. Newspapers in Boston—never gentle or subtle—suggested that the administration had bought Otis. The charge was plausible, though untrue, and Otis, a thoroughly shaken man, denied it in a piece he wrote for the *Boston Gazette* in the middle of May. The same day, Samuel Waterhouse, a Customs officer writing for another newspaper, went too far and hit Otis too hard with "light" verse called "Jemmibullero," a parody of Lillibulero. Boston's voters read:

> And Jemmy is a silly dog, and Jemmy is a tool;
> And Jemmy is a stupid curr, and Jemmy is a fool;
> And Jemmy is a madman, and Jemmy is an ass,
> And Jemmy has a leaden head, and forehead spread
>   with brass.[39]

And they decided that perhaps Otis should be given another chance. He did not lead the list of representatives, but he won re-election nonetheless.

While Otis was plunging the popular faction into disarray, news of the Stamp Act arrived in Massachusetts and with it information that Andrew Oliver, Hutchinson's brother-in-law, had been appointed stamp distributor for the colony. The House, confused and irresolute after Otis's apparent defection, could not seem to rally itself. Governor Bernard counseled submission, and the House in effect agreed. To be sure, it joined the Council in an address to Parliament protesting the Act, but by current standards this statement was not far from the description given it in July by the *Boston Gazette:* "a tame, pusillanimous, daubed, insipid thing."[40] The full extent of the House's weakness became clear when it failed to block the appointments of Oliver and Hutchinson to the Council. When the governor prorogued the House early in June, it seemed to have swallowed the bitter medicine of the Stamp Act rather meekly.

39. *Boston Evening Post,* May 13, 1765.
40. *BG,* July 8, 1765.

The medicine further soured stomachs and minds a few days later when copies of the Virginia Resolves arrived and made their way into the local newspapers. The version published by the *Boston Gazette* indicted anyone who asserted that a body other than the Massachusetts legislature had any right to tax the colony as "AN ENEMY TO THIS HIS MAJESTY'S COLONY."[41] And the *Gazette* soon published a piece denouncing the "frozen politicians" of the colony who called the Virginians' action treason, an obvious reference to James Otis, Jr., still off on his own wild tangent.

From this point on, heads, and presumably stomachs, cleared, and the frozen grew warm, heated up by the Resolves. Governor Bernard called them "an Alarm bell to the disaffected."[42] The newspapers helped too by printing essays and letters all calculated to rouse public opinion.

A small group of men, resolving to do more than publish and talk, plotted violence against Andrew Oliver, who had been selected Distributor of Stamps in Massachusetts. These men styled themselves the Loyal Nine, soon to be changed to the Sons of Liberty. They included artisans, shopkeepers, and a printer, Benjamin Edes, who with John Gill published the *Boston Gazette*. No legislative leader joined them, though Samuel Adams may have met secretly at times with several; and the only member who had any claim to social status was John Avery, a merchant, Harvard, class of 1759, who came of good stock. The Loyal Nine seem usually to have met at Chase and Speakman's distillery on Hanover Square, and there presumably they planned the riot of August 14.[43]

To do the rough work of rioting they turned to experience, the recently united North and South End mobs. These groups had entertained themselves for years, most notably in a session on Guy Fawkes Day, November 5, which the two mobs usually commemorated by brawling, a peculiar but apparently satisfying way of celebrating the frustration of an explosion. The fights between the two mobs were not gentle affairs; they used clubs, bricks, stones, and fists on one another, and in the fracas of 1764 a child who got in the way had been killed.

Understandably, neither mob kept a roster of its members, but we know that most were craftsmen, workers of lesser skills, sailors, apprentices, and boys. After the fight of 1764, some sort of rough agreement was apparently worked out between the two groups, and the leader of the South Enders, Ebenezer MacIntosh, a cobbler by trade and a man

41. *Ibid.*, July 8; Aug. 5, 12, 1765.
42. Quoted in Jensen, *Founding*, 108.
43. Morgan and Morgan, *Stamp Act Crisis*, 121–22.

of commanding presence, assumed leadership of the combined group. Persuading MacIntosh and his followers to enlist against the Stamp Act probably was not very difficult. All the Loyal Nine had to do was to induce the mob to substitute one local enemy for another—instead of the opposing mob, the enemy was Andrew Oliver and the crew of placemen who had gobbled up offices for years. Oliver was well known; he and his ilk stood to profit by the stamp tax, and current gossip had it that Oliver's brother-in-law, Thomas Hutchinson, had recommended the tax. Striking a blow for liberty meant hitting such creatures.

The identification of English and local tyranny was made evident early on the morning of August 14. The town awoke to find an effigy of Oliver hanging in a tree; beside it hung a large boot, representing the Earl of Bute, a play on his name. Bute, of course, was no longer in office in England, but he was remembered as an evil man, symbolic of, if not responsible for, the recent dangerous encroachments upon colonial liberties. The point was made clearly in the symbols in the tree, where a devil was shown crawling out of the boot.[44]

Several people living near the tree offered to take down the effigy of Oliver, but were warned not to do so. Lt. Governor Thomas Hutchinson ordered the sheriff and his officers to remove the effigy, but the sheriff soon reported that removal would cost him and his officers their lives. By this time, Governor Bernard smelled serious trouble and summoned the Council to tell them so. Several agreed but several others dismissed the hanging effigy as "trifling Business"; both groups agreed that any action would make matters worse.[45]

At the first dark of evening, Ebenezer MacIntosh and the mob took the effigy of Oliver and, parading past the Town House where the governor and Council were in worried session, gave three huzzas as if to reassure the Council that affairs were now in the right hands. The mob then marched to a new building on Andrew Oliver's dock on Kilby Street. Oliver had intended to rent rooms in the building to shopkeepers, but the mob, calling the building the "Stamp Office," tore it down in five minutes. MacIntosh then led the way to Oliver's house on nearby Oliver Street. Here in front of the house, a part of the mob beheaded the effigy, presumably for Oliver's edification, while others broke the windows in the house. Fort Hill was a few steps away, and the mob moved to it, apparently to give the town—and Oliver—a better view of the proceedings. And interesting proceedings they were: just in case

44. Governor Bernard to Lord Halifax, Aug. 15, 1765, in Morgan, ed., *Prologue*, 106–8.
45. *Ibid.*, 107.

anyone was unaware of the stamp tax, the effigy was "stamped"—with the feet of the mob—and then burned. The only thing to do then was to return to the house, which the mob did willingly enough, only to find the doors barricaded. These could be broken down and were, accompanied by calls to find Oliver and kill him. Oliver had long since departed, and his friends who had remained within the house to protect it now prudently followed after him. The mob searched several nearby houses—Oliver was hidden in one—but gave up when a neighbor told them that Oliver had fled to Castle William in the harbor. Disappointed, the mob contented itself by smashing Oliver's furniture and tearing off the wainscoting.[46]

Sometime during these events, Governor Bernard ordered the colonel of the militia "to beat an alarm," to summon his regiment which might put down the riot. The colonel replied that if a drummer could be found who was not in the mob, he would be knocked down as soon as he made a sound, and his drum would be broken. The colonel undoubtedly spoke the truth, for the mob would listen to no one in official authority. Thomas Hutchinson and the sheriff proved this to their own satisfaction about eleven P.M. when they appeared at Oliver's house to try to persuade the mob to disperse. Before they could speak, they heard, "The governor and the Sheriff my boys, to your Arms my boys," the cry followed immediately by brickbats and stones. They ran and the mob remained, not to adjourn for another hour.[47]

The following day, August 15, Oliver received another sort of delegation, a small group of gentlemen who urged him to resign his commission as stamp distributor. Oliver did not have the commission, which had not yet arrived from England, but he promised to resign as soon as it did. That night the mob again convened on Fort Hill around a bonfire, as if to remind Oliver what was expected of him. But the night's agenda was short and tame; the mob moved from Fort Hill to Hutchinson's house, pounding on his doors and shouting for him to come out. It smashed nothing, however, and Thomas Hutchinson, though a brave man, probably breathed easier.[48]

Hutchinson's turn came eleven days later. He was a natural target:

46. *Ibid.*, 107–8. See also *BG*, Aug. 19, 1765 (supplement). Morgan and Morgan, *Stamp Act Crisis*, 123–25, provide a superb account. See also Thomas Hutchinson, *The History of the Colony and Province of Massachusetts-Bay*, ed. Lawrence Shaw Mayo (3 vols., Cambridge, Mass., 1936), III, 87.

47. Morgan, ed., *Prologue*, 108.

48. Morgan and Morgan, *Stamp Act Crisis*, 125.

he was rumored to be an advocate of the Stamp Act and known by his actions to be a defender of Customs enforcement; besides, he had tried to get Oliver's effigy removed from the tree, and he had appeared at Oliver's house to attempt to convince the mob to go home. And he was proud, even stiff-necked, and brave. How tempting to introduce him to humility while defending colonial rights.[49]

On the evening of August 26, after a day of rumors that local Customs officials would be attacked, a bonfire was lighted on King Street and a great crowd gathered shouting "liberty and property," which, Bernard sardonically reported, was "the usual notice of their intention to plunder and pull down an house."[50] The mob actually had several houses in mind; to dispatch its business more efficiently it divided into two groups and each repaired to a different house. One went to the residence of Charles Paxton, the marshal of the vice admiralty court, only to discover that he rented the place. The owner of the house offered to treat them to a barrel of punch at a nearby tavern, an offer which was accepted. Now, full of liquid and patriotic spirits, the mob moved to William Story's house. Story was the deputy registrar of the vice admiralty court and evidently an unpopular man. The cry went up to kill Story, but he had escaped; the mob destroyed what it found within and carried the vice admiralty records outside where they were burned. Meanwhile, the second mob had surged to the house of Benjamin Hallowell, the comptroller of Customs. The beauty of Hallowell's house may have provided a special inducement to do a thorough job—at any rate the crowd left it a shambles, with windows and doors smashed, furniture broken, wainscoting pulled off, books and papers scattered or stolen, and the wine cellar consumed.

By now the action had become almost routine, except that the greatest prize of all lay waiting. The prize, of course, was the handsome house of Thomas Hutchinson. Most of the evening lay ahead when the mob, its two halves back together for the chief work of the night, arrived. Hutchinson and his family were eating supper, probably rather uneasily, for they had heard talk that they would have uninvited visitors. The family left just ahead of the mob, but Thomas Hutchinson decided to stay, a decision he held to until his oldest daughter returned and refused to leave unless he accompanied her. She probably thereby saved his life. As it was, he eluded his pursuers only by running through gardens and backyards to safety.

49. Bailyn provides a sensitive assessment in *Ordeal of Hutchinson*.
50. Bernard to Halifax, Aug. 31, 1765, in *EHD*, 676.

The mob took its time on his house. Virtually everything movable within was destroyed or stolen—papers, plate, furniture, clothing, and £900 sterling—and what could not be moved—walls, partitions, and roof—were severely battered. The handsome cupola was cut off, a demolition that took three hours, and much of the slate roof was pulled down. Daybreak found the mob still hard at work; a part of the roof still survived and several brick walls still stood. Dawn finally discouraged the mob, who evidently had been determined to level the house to its foundations.

Historians reflecting on this episode have concluded that things got out of hand at Hutchinson's house. Hutchinson himself opined three days later that "The encouragers of the first mob never intended matters should go this length."[51] There is other evidence along the same line, including an official statement of regret by the town meeting the following day. And Governor Bernard found much to his surprise that he would not have any difficulty in raising the militia on August 27 and for several weeks after to maintain order.

But then why should he? The opposition to the Stamp Act had expressed itself rather forcibly; no further violence seemed necessary at the end of August. The mob may have gone too far, and the town said it was sorry, but no one apologized for the riot of August 14 against Oliver, and no one repudiated opposition to taxation without consent. The riot of August 26 may have proceeded farther than the Loyal Nine intended, but they could not have felt much displeasure that it had. Hutchinson was an enemy; he was Oliver's brother-in-law; he apparently favored the Stamp Act; and he had been put in his place. In only a limited sense, then, had the action of August 26 been too extreme.

By late August two major colonies, Virginia and Massachusetts, each in its own way, had vented their anger at the Stamp Act. They in fact had started more than they knew; they had started a fire. Its spread seemed virtually inevitable.

51. Thomas Hutchinson to Richard Jackson, Aug. 30, 1765, in Morgan, ed., *Prologue*, 109; Hutchinson, *History*, ed., Mayo, III, 89–91. On August 27, the town declared its "utter detestation" of the violence. BRC, *Reports*, XVI, 152.

5

Response

Americans outside Massachusetts proved so adept in following Boston's violent example that we may suspect that they did not need it. Needed or not, Boston's action offered a model that captured attention everywhere in America. Revulsion from the Stamp Act permeated social groups of all sorts and came to focus, almost naturally it seems, on the men chosen to distribute the stamped paper—on the tax collectors and their friends. By the end of October all but two of the stamp distributors had resigned, usually in order to save their lives and property; and of the remaining two, one, William Houston of North Carolina, gave way on November 16, and the other, George Angus, appointed for Georgia, did not arrive in America until January 1766. Once in Georgia, he quickly sensed what might happen to him and promptly took the oath, passed the stamped paper to the Customs collectors, and fled the colony.[1]

By the time Angus arrived in Georgia, the pattern of coercion and violence was well established. Mobs used whatever force necessary to produce resignations, and simply by threats they prevented the landing or the distribution of the stamped paper. In several cases they scarcely had to flex their muscles to frighten distributors into sending in their resignations. James McIvers of New York, for example, submitted his resignation even before his commission and the stamps arrived. McIvers was a merchant whose business and property were located in New York City. He was no more averse than the next man to collecting the fees of office but did not want to see his house and store of goods, which

1. Morgan and Morgan, *Stamp Act Crisis,* 156–57 and *passim.*

94

he estimated to be worth £20,000 sterling, destroyed. McIvers suspected that Oliver's fate might become his own, and on August 22, a week after the first Boston riot, he resigned. In a letter to the lieutenant governor explaining his decision, McIvers put his reason succinctly: "a storm was riseing, and I should soon feel it."[2]

In nearby New Jersey, William Coxe waited a few days longer, until September 3, before the feeling of a rising storm persuaded him to surrender his office. The governor of New Jersey, William Franklin, son of Benjamin, expressed annoyance at Coxe, who, he complained, had cowardly backed out for no reason at all. No one had threatened Coxe, the governor said, nor was Coxe going to be obstructed from carrying out his duties. The governor evidently did not read the newspapers that suggested to Coxe he would be well advised to insure his house.[3]

The New Hampshire distributor, George Meserve, received less subtle hints and acted even more promptly. In England when Parliament passed the Stamp Act, Meserve got himself appointed before sailing for home. The ship he sailed aboard had not yet anchored when he was made to realize his mistake. First, the pilot who boarded the ship in Boston harbor handed him a letter from several gentlemen of Portsmouth suggesting that for his own safety he should resign before returning to the town. And then a Boston mob, convinced that the ship he was on carried stamps, refused to let anyone come ashore. Meserve stayed aboard until September 10, at which time the mob learned that the ship carried no stamps. He resigned before he touched land and sent the news to the mob, who then greeted him with praise and carried him to the Exchange Tavern for a celebration. Evidently a resignation in Boston was invalid in New Hampshire—at any rate, several days later Meserve was forced to resign publicly in Portsmouth, and in January a third time. In public, Meserve did what was expected; in private he attributed his troubles to the "damned Rebellious Spirit" which filled the crowd.[4]

That same spirit assumed more violent shapes elsewhere. As in Massachusetts, mobbing and rioting occurred in most extreme forms in colonies

2. McIvers to Cadwallader Colden, n.d., in Edmund B. O'Callaghan, ed., *Documents Relative to the Colonial History of the State of New York* (15 vols., Albany, N.Y., 1856–87), VII, 761.

3. *BF Papers*, XII, 260–61; *Pennsylvania Gazette* (Phila.), Aug. 29, 1765.

4. Jeremy Belknap, *The History of New Hampshire* (3 vols., Philadelphia, 1784–92), II, 333, for the quotation. For the episode as a whole, Morgan and Morgan, *Stamp Act Crisis*, 154.

where political divisions already existed and where one side became identified with the Stamp Act. In several cases, indeed, one faction successfully tagged another with the responsibility for the Stamp Act, accusing its political enemies of plotting with the ministry the destruction of American liberty. Thomas Hutchinson experienced the effects of this tactic and ruefully complained of its unfairness. Hutchinson, an exponent of parliamentary government, discovered that his enemies would seize his defense of the principle of parliamentary authority as evidence of his approval of all of Parliament's work. Hutchinson was a man who appreciated the fine points of court arguments; he knew it was possible to uphold parliamentary government and simultaneously condemn the Stamp Act—on grounds of expediency. The mob that gutted his house was a rather blunt instrument: it or its leaders had old scores to settle, and in any case it believed that Thomas Hutchinson had instigated the Act.

In Rhode Island there was no one quite like Thomas Hutchinson, but there were important political divisions which affected the response to the Stamp Act. Rhode Island, a colony founded in dissidence, had always harbored the strange and offbeat—some said fanatics and lunatics—but by the eve of the Revolution its politicians resembled those elsewhere in America. They operated, however, under conditions which might have aroused envy or disgust everywhere else—a seventeenth-century charter which created a virtually independent government. Almost all offices were elective, including the governor's, and to vote a man had only to own land worth £400 in currency. It has been estimated that three-fourths of all adult males could vote if they wanted to.[5]

Power in the government resided in the General Assembly, a two-house legislature that usually dominated the governor and the courts. Naturally enough, control of the General Assembly was much sought after. By the 1750s two factions had made their appearance in Rhode Island and competed for political power. Providence served as the headquarters of the Hopkins faction, so named because led by Stephen Hopkins, probably the ablest politician in the colony. Newport provided the center of the other, the Ward faction, the name derived from its leader, Samuel Ward. The two cities themselves engaged in competition for business and profit. Providence had entered a period of growth about thirty years before and by the 1750s had begun to challenge the economic supremacy of Newport, its neighbor to the south. In several respects

5. Lovejoy, *Rhode Island Politics*, 16–17. I have drawn heavily on this fine book here and later in this chapter.

Providence had a better location than Newport. It commanded a larger surrounding area, which produced foodstuffs and raw materials for export. Since the market for such commodities was increasing, the port that could supply them would grow. Newport had only the Narragansett country across the Bay. Providence could tap southern Massachusetts and Connecticut, as well as much of Rhode Island. Providence merchants in fact had begun to supply candles, rum, barrels, and rope to Newport.

Both factions called upon the same sorts of economic groups—merchants, tradesmen, professionals, and the small farmers in the towns and countryside tied to each. Thus the Ward-Hopkins struggle was in part a contest for economic power between Providence and Newport, each with satellites, struggling to control a government which could confer extensive economic advantages. For the General Assembly possessed the power to grant monopolies to manufacturers; it had public resources to spend on roads, buildings, bridges, and lighthouses, among other things; it apportioned taxes among the towns, and not surprisingly when Providence and the northern towns ran things, the tax bills in Newport and to the south had a way of going up, and when Newport and the southern towns won the legislature, Providence and to the north felt the bite. Control of the General Assembly also entailed control of political spoils. At the middle of the eighteenth century there were more than 150 justices of the peace to be appointed by the Assembly, and there were sheriffs, clerks, some militia officers, and others also in the gift of the Assembly.

These opportunities for economic and political advantage and one of the most democratic constitutions of the century gave rise to a raucous and exuberant factionalism. Elections were bitterly fought, and fraud—stuffing the ballot box, for example—was not uncommon. At times voters were bought to vote the right way and some were bribed not to vote at all. In 1758, for example, only 400 out of 600 freemen in Newport voted; "one third lie still," Ezra Stiles noted, "silenced by Connexions."[6] The Assembly itself was frequently the scene of disorder: shrill charges, deals, and undignified squabbles.

Most Rhode Islanders apparently enjoyed and valued all this political smoke, and the politicians played their parts with enthusiasm if not with aplomb. But not everyone found the spectacle of brawling politicians and a large and apparently unstable electorate to his liking. In Newport a small group, probably no larger than fifteen, despised the course of

6. *Ibid.*

government and politics in Rhode Island. The two most important members were Martin Howard, Jr., of a well-established family, a leading lawyer, an Anglican, a man of supercilious bearing and possessing an aristocratic temperament found only in provincials, and Dr. Thomas Moffat, a physician who had lived in Newport since sometime in the 1730s when he arrived to be near Bishop Berkeley. Among the others were George Rome, an agent of an English commercial house; Augustus Johnston, the attorney general; and Peter Harrison, the architect who designed the Redwood Library and the Touro Synagogue. Most of these men and their followers were Anglicans, most felt some special affinity to England, and several seemed to yearn for place and influence.[7]

This Tory Junto, as these men have been called, also shared a common revulsion from Rhode Island's coarse factionalism and from the accommodation in the political system of the "Herd," as Thomas Moffat designated the people. They proposed to change this system by securing the repeal of the charter of 1663 and by persuading Parliament to impose royal government on the colony. The contempt they felt for the charter government is manifest in Martin Howard's characterization of it as "Nothing but a Burlesque upon Order and Government."[8]

The open pursuit of royal government by the Tory Junto was signaled by a letter to the *Newport Mercury* published on April 23, 1764, and signed Z. Y. The letter attacked popular government in Rhode Island and insisted that only Parliament could end the disgraceful disorders of party and factional strife. Six weeks later, the newspaper reprinted, at the request of its readers it said, the commission Charles I issued to Archbishop Laud in the seventeenth century giving him power to revoke colonial charters. The point was obvious: the power to revoke colonial charters had a long history.[9]

In August "O. Z." made his appearance in the *Mercury*. (Why Howard and Moffat discarded Z. Y. for this designation is not known.) The letters by O. Z. appeared off and on until March 1765. O. Z. professed to offer advice on the production of sheep, hemp, and flax in the colony, a much healthier activity, he implied, than protesting against the Sugar Act and challenging generally the sovereignty of Parliament. Hemp appeared especially attractive to O. Z., for it received a bounty from the

7. Carl Bridenbaugh, *Peter Harrison: First American Architect* (Chapel Hill, N.C., 1949), 124–25.
8. Moffat to Benjamin Franklin, May 12, 1764, *BF Papers*, XI, 192, for "Herd"; Howard to Franklin, Nov. 16, 1764, *ibid.*, 459, for second quotation.
9. Lovejoy, *Rhode Island Politics*, 49–50.

English government far greater than any taxes imposed on trade.[10]
These engaging themes probably deceived no one in Rhode Island
as to O. Z.'s real purpose—to attack the charter government. In any
case O. Z. soon let his mask slip and in a discourse on politics and
government recommended the example of Pennsylvania, where the legislature had recently sought to replace proprietary with royal government.
O. Z. did not publish the fact, but the Tory Junto, emboldened by
Pennsylvania's action, in October sent Joseph Harrison with a private
petition for an end to the charter. And Martin Howard attempted in
November to persuade Benjamin Franklin, to whom he attributed "Intimacy with the *Great*" in the English government, to represent this
royalist interest.[11]

Newport was much too small to keep secret an attempt to get the
charter revoked. And the Tory Junto had let the cat out of the bag by
their public praise of Pennsylvania's pursuit of royal government. What
they were about was soon widely known and brought them unwanted
attention: in September they were stained with the charge that they
constituted a "club" of conspirators "against the Liberties of the
Colony."[12] This charge soon grew more specific and seemed more portentous as anonymous writers in the newspapers indicted the Junto as part
of the forces behind the Stamp Act. On November 4, 1764, Governor
Hopkins sent a message to the Assembly which reported that a petition
against the charter had been sent. The governor followed up his address
with a full-scale attack a few weeks later in his *Rights of the Colonies
Examined.* Martin Howard's answer, *A Letter from a Gentleman at Halifax,* met the governor head-on with sneers and barbs, but also offered
a version of the constitution in which colonial rights were severely cut
back. From this point on, the printing presses were well oiled, as pamphlets and essays poured out. Hopkins hit the *Halifax Letter* through
the columns of the *Providence Gazette;* and he received support from
James Otis, who had relatives in Newport, in *A Vindication of the British
Colonies against the Aspersions of the Halifax Gentleman in his Letter
to a Rhode Island Friend.* Neither man subdued Howard, who issued
A Defense of the Letter from a Gentleman at Halifax, but Otis's *Brief
Remarks on the Defense of the Halifax Libel* managed to reduce the
constitutional issues to simple abuse of the Tory Junto as a "little, dirty,

10. *Newport Mercury* (R.I.), Aug. 20, 1764. See also issues of Aug. 27, Sept. 3, 10,
    17, 24, Oct. 1, 29, Nov. 12, 19, 26, and Feb. 25, March 11, 18, 1765.
11. *BF Papers*, XI, 460.
12. *Providence Gazette* (R.I.), Sept. 15, 1764.

drinking, drabbing, contaminated knot of thieves, beggars and transports, or the worthy descendents of such, collected from the four winds of the earth, and made up of Turks, Jews and other Infidels, with a few renegade Christians and Catholics, and altogether formed into a club of a scarce a dozen at N-p-t. From hence proceed Halifax-letters, petitions to alter the colony forms of government, libels upon all good colonists and subjects, and every evil work that can enter into the heart of man."[13]

By spring 1765 the anger at Howard, Moffat, and their friends was clear, and the identification of their cause, the replacement of the charter by royal government, with English encroachments upon colonial liberties, had been made. The crude suggestions that these Newport gentlemen were somehow behind both the Sugar Act and the tighter enforcement of trade regulations had convinced many. To attribute plotting for the Stamp Act to them did not seem farfetched.

Still, when news of the Act arrived, no violence occurred even though Newport's libertarian sensitivities were quivering. They were soon to explode, not over the Stamp Act, but over the Royal Navy. Earlier in the year the navy had contributed its bit to the alienation of Newporters by conducting a brutal program of impressment. The navy needed sailors and it was not overly scrupulous in getting them. In May, after a series of raids which had caused trade to stagnate because ships had begun to avoid Newport where their crews might be impressed, the HMS *Maidstone* foolishly sent her boat to the dock. A mob numbering around five hundred seized and burned it.[14]

Late in June the *Newport Mercury* reprinted the Virginia Resolves, including the two most sensational ones which had not passed. On August 14, of course, Boston provided the edifying example of how a stamp distributor might be persuaded to resign. It was an important lesson, and it was studied closely in Newport.

Although rioting had a long and apparently honorable history in Newport, there was no mob-in-being such as the North and South Enders of Boston. The opposition to the Stamp Act in Newport was organized by Samuel Vernon and William Ellery, both merchants, who proved inventive and unafraid to begin action themselves. They first planned to hang effigies of Stamp Distributor Augustus Johnston, and of Thomas Moffat and Martin Howard, presumably expecting that Johnston's resignation would soon follow. Their plans leaked out, and Howard and Mof-

---

13. *Brief Remarks on the Defense of the Halifax Libel on the British-American Colonies* (Boston, 1765).
14. Lovejoy, *Rhode Island Politics*, 37–38.

fat, who learned on August 20 that their effigies would be hung on August 27, appealed to Governor Ward to stop the demonstration. Ward professed to believe that the whole business had been exaggerated, but he apparently cautioned Vernon and Ellery against going ahead. These two were not easily deterred and may have already begun a campaign they could not stop. A special issue of the *Providence Gazette* appeared four days later, relaying the Providence town meeting's condemnation of the Stamp Act and also reporting that Augustus Johnston had promised not to execute his office against the will of the people. Johnston had made no such statement, but denying it would leave him looking like an enemy of the people. For the next few days Johnston held his tongue.[15]

The day before the scheduled effigy hanging, August 26, the *Mercury* carried full accounts of the riot against Andrew Oliver of Boston; the same issue contained a plea by Martin Howard for liberty of opinion, an argument calculated to head off the activities of the next day. The argument failed, and the next morning saw the opening of four days of upheaval in Newport.

Early on Tuesday, August 27, the demonstrations began with the effigies hung on gallows hastily erected on Queen Street near the Town House, where the freeholders were to meet later in the day. Adorning the effigies were placards inscribed with language that left no one in doubt as to the meaning of this spectacle. The inscription on Johnston's simply identified him as "THE STAMP MAN." Doctor Moffat did not escape so easily, for a paper pinned to his breast described him as "THAT INFAMOUS, MISCREATED, LEERING JACOBITE DOCTOR MURFY."[16] James Otis had tagged Moffat with this name in one of his abusive pamphlets and apparently it had stuck. There was more written across Moffat's figure, but perhaps the most effective touch of all came with the boot hanging over his shoulder with the devil peeping out, an obvious imitation of Boston. Howard's effigy also bore inscriptions, including another inspired by Otis, "THAT FAWNING, INSIDIOUS, INFAMOUS MISCREANT AND PARACIDE MARTINUS SCRIBLERIUS."[17] But the most devastating touch was locally spawned: a rope tied Howard's neck to Moffat's, and a placard had them saying "We have an Hereditary Indefeasible Right to a Halter, Besides we Encourag'd the Growth of Hemp you know."[18] Vernon, Ellery, and Robert Crook, another merchant, all muffled in big coats

15. *Providence Gazette*, Aug. 24, 1765.
16. *EHD*, 674.
17. *Ibid.*
18. *Ibid.*

and hats and carrying bludgeons, guarded these images until late afternoon when a crowd fortified by "strong Drink in plenty with Cheshire
cheese," sent by the merchants, gathered and burned the effigies after
sunset.[19] The honorees—Johnston, Howard, Moffat—had long since fled
the town after receiving warnings that they might be murdered.

The next three days provided evidence that the threats had substance.
On Wednesday, the day following the effigy burning, Howard, Moffat,
and Johnston made their way back into town, but so did the news of
the great riot in Boston against Thomas Hutchinson. That night in
Newport, the mob struck Howard's house three times (at eight, eleven,
and two o'clock in the morning) and Moffat's twice. The two houses
went the way of Hutchinson's, and when the mob finished its work
they were little more than shells. Johnston's escaped—he still commanded
some popularity in Newport, and his friends interceded with the mob
by promising that Johnston would resign the next day.

The next morning, Thursday, August 29, Johnston returned and resigned in public, but the mob had not yet exhausted itself. Indeed,
one of its working leaders, an English sailor named John Webber, boasted
in the streets of his leadership and in a thinly veiled attempt at extortion
insulted his merchant-patrons. These merchants set the sheriff on Webber; in custody, Webber was delivered to HMS *Cygnet* for safekeeping.
Webber's followers thereupon threatened to tear the town apart, especially the houses and warehouses of the merchants, and the merchants
sent an abject sheriff to fetch Webber from the *Cygnet*. Back on the
streets of Newport, Webber proved unsubdued, threatening once more
to pull down houses. The merchants in something of a panic bribed
him to quiet down; and the sheriff, now thoroughly humiliated, offered
to lie down while Webber trod on his neck. The day ended with all
parties retiring uneasily to their beds.

Webber arose with the sun and once more promised to destroy his
onetime sponsors. By this time, Augustus Johnston, now a former stamp
distributor but still the attorney general, was back in town. Johnston
was a brave man and doubtless more than a little angry. Running into
the swaggering Webber on the streets and hearing his renewed threats,
Augustus Johnston solved Newport's problem by clapping him into jail.[20]

In Connecticut, as in Rhode Island, political factions seized upon
the Stamp Act as an opportunity to wound hated rivals. But whereas

19. Morgan, ed., *Prologue*, 112.
20. For Webber, see Morgan and Morgan, *Stamp Act Crisis*, 191–94.

in Rhode Island the Ward-Hopkins groups joined in battering the Tory Junto, which they perceived as a threat to the charter government, in Connecticut the two factions sought to use the crisis over the Act to destroy one another. The two factions are sometimes referred to as the New Lights and the Old Lights; the New were the supporters of the Great Awakening of the 1740s, and the Old the opponents. Religion had given these two factional groups their beginnings, but originally the New and Old Lights had no political cast at all. They gradually acquired one in the fifteen years following the climax of the revival in 1741–42, thanks to attempts to cool its enthusiasm and to several issues having nothing to do with it.[21]

The Awakening had naturally frightened some solid citizens, just as it had inspired others. It was a frightening, even shattering event, with thousands of men, women, and children convinced that the spirit possessed them, with revivalists denouncing the established ministry as unconverted, with churches splitting, and with excess in personal behavior everywhere in evidence. The solid citizens who controlled the legislature—indeed, most reputable institutions—tried to deflate what they considered to be a spirit of madness. In the legislature in 1742, they pushed through statutes prohibiting itinerants from preaching and barring the unordained from pulpits. The next year they repealed a longstanding statute providing religious toleration.[22]

Such action gave the New Lights pause and virtually forced them to begin to think politically. A major dispute at Yale College in the next decade, pitting the New Light rector against the First Church of New Haven, encouraged this disposition to think about politics and kept Old Light rage smoldering. The issue at Yale revolved around the plan of Thomas Clap, the rector or head of Yale, to appoint a professor of divinity who would then preach the true faith to faculty and students. Yale College would in this way become a church, a most desirable circumstance in Clap's view, because the Reverend Joseph Noyes of the First Congregational church in New Haven preached in such a cold and insipid style. Yale College was an important institution, and the struggle, which continued until 1756 when Clap got his way, further divided the colony.[23]

21. *Ibid.*, 221–37.
22. For the Awakening in New England, see Edwin Scott Gaustad, *The Great Awakening in New England* (New York, 1957); for details in this paragraph, Edmund S. Morgan, *The Gentle Puritan: A Life of Ezra Stiles, 1727–1795* (New Haven, Conn., 1963), 20–41.
23. Morgan, *Gentle Puritan*, 103–7.

Money and land also contributed to division. The Connecticut charter which was issued in 1662 provided that the colony's western boundary should be the Pacific Ocean. To insist in the 1750s on the validity of this limit, in part the result of seventeenth-century ignorance of American geography, was not altogether reasonable, as some in Connecticut recognized. Nevertheless, in 1754, the Susquehannah Company, an organization of land speculators with expansionist visions, was formed and immediately began planning the settlement of the upper Wyoming Valley. One of the company's problems was that the Wyoming Valley lay within Pennsylvania. Another was that the legislature took a dim view of the company and its claims.[24]

In the 1750s the legislature and the governor were Old Light. There were Old Lights in every part of the colony, but most were in the western half and concentrated especially heavily in Fairfield County. The New Lights had also spread themselves, but they too were concentrated, mostly in two eastern counties, Windham and New London. Most of the stockholders in the Susquehannah Company also lived in these eastern counties and most were New Light.[25]

Jared Ingersoll, the stamp distributor for Connecticut, was an Old Light, a graduate of Yale College, a lawyer, a onetime king's attorney for New Haven County, a man well acquainted with England and fond of it. He had opposed Thomas Clap's scheme to turn Yale College into a New Light church, and he had opposed the Susquehannah Company's claims to the Wyoming Valley and its attempt to get itself incorporated by the Crown. Not surprisingly, Jared Ingersoll enjoyed a certain reputation in the colony; indeed, the New Lights detested him.[26]

The Stamp Act was one more thing Ingersoll had opposed, but though he had predicted heavy weather for the tax in America, he accepted appointment as distributor while still in England. He may have found reassurance in the first reactions from America to his appointment, which became public knowledge late in May 1765. For the postal service soon groaned under the weight of letters to Ingersoll from office-seekers who wrote from towns all over Connecticut asking for appointments as his local representatives. Some of these letters have an obsequious flavor common to such communications: "I should Esteem myself honoured to be thought Worthy your Service; and would Recive the Favour with

24. Julian P. Boyd and Robert J. Taylor, eds., *The Susquehannah Company Papers* (11 vols., Wilkes-Barre, Pa., 1930–71).

25. Morgan and Morgan, *Stamp Act Crisis*, 228–30.

26. Gipson, *American Loyalist*.

Gratitude . . . and I hope I shall be able to Convince you—as much as the Difference of station will admit—how much I am your sincere Friend and Obedient Servent."[27]

Ingersoll discovered shortly after his return from England on July 28 that these sincere friends had rather brittle desires to assist him. Local animosities to the new tax were just beginning to be revealed publicly, inspired at least in part by the Virginia Resolves. There were other reasons of course—no one relishes the obligation to pay taxes, and the people of Connecticut, already overburdened and in default many thousands of pounds, shrank before still another demand. Hence the attacks on the Act and its local representative, Ingersoll, who became an object of vituperation.

Old enemies took advantage of Ingersoll's precarious situation to settle old feuds. Naphtali Daggett, professor of divinity at Yale and a New Light, struck him hard in the pages of the *Connecticut Gazette*. Daggett doubtless hated the Stamp Act as an encroachment upon American rights, but Ingersoll was also a welcome target because of his part in the fight in the 1750s over the professorship of divinity. Daggett described Ingersoll as a man of guile who in justifying his acceptance of the stamp distributorship asked, "But had you not rather these duties should be collected by your brethren than by foreigners?" Daggett marked Jared Ingersoll as a betrayer, and when another attacker pointed out that his initials, J. I., were also those of Judas Iscariot, his "treachery" was made to seem even more reprehensible.[28]

Ingersoll and a few hardy friends answered as best they could, but they were up against a growing passion. The first violence seems not to have been used on Ingersoll but on one of his assistants, the venerable Nathaniel Wales of Windham. Sometime after August 15, a crowd surrounded Wales's house and warned him not to travel to New Haven to receive his commission from Ingersoll. Wales broke immediately and wrote to Ingersoll that he had decided not to take the post after all. Other representatives of the stamp distributor did not escape so easily, especially if they proved stubborn about resigning. In New Providence a crowd threatened to bury the distributor alive when he insisted on remaining in office. The crowd put this stout-hearted soul inside a coffin, nailed the lid shut, and lowered him into a grave. They then began shoveling dirt on the coffin. The official listened to the awful sound of

27. New Haven Colony Historical Society, *Papers*, 9 (1918), 327.
28. *Connecticut Gazette* (Hartford), Aug. 9, 1765.

dirt striking wood and called for release and thereupon submitted his resignation.[29]

The chief object of crowd action, led by men calling themselves the Sons of Liberty, was of course the chief villain in Connecticut, Jared Ingersoll. On August 21 the Sons hanged his effigy in Norwich and the next day in New London. Windham and Lebanon followed suit on August 26, Lyme on August 29, and West Haven burned "a horrible Monster, or Male Giant, twelve Feet High, whose terrible Head was internally illuminated."[30] New Haven, where Ingersoll lived, burned no effigies, but on a September evening a crowd surrounded Ingersoll's house threatening to pull it down should he not resign. Ingersoll appeared before this crowd and explained that he could not resign until the government of Connecticut took a stand; in the meantime, he would not execute his office and would even allow the people to destroy any stamps sent to him.

Following, evidently, the example of Boston's treatment of Andrew Oliver, the crowd usually tied Ingersoll's effigy in some fashion to the devil's, or the connection of the two was described by a speaker at a large meeting. The Earl of Bute also figured prominently in these pageants, usually as a prime instigator of the Stamp Act—in New London, for example, where an orator referred to Pitt as Moses and Stamp Distributor Ingersoll as "the Beast that Lord Bute set up in this Colony to be worshipped"—a confused but effective evocation of the fear of the Antichrist.[31] The Boston Sons had set this pattern; now the Connecticut wing added its own innovations. The Sons of Liberty of several towns held mock trials with elaborate proceedings, forceful prosecutions, and farcical defenses. In Lyme, for example, the Sons charged J—d Stampman with conspiracy "to kill and destroy his own mother, Americana"; the murder weapon was to be a "Stamp, which came from an ancient and lately Bute-fied Seat in Europe."[32] The defense was that as his mother's fate was "absolutely determined, and could not possibly be avoided, he had good right himself to be the Executioner, since he should by that means save 8 per cent out of her Estate, to himself (which probably

29. Gipson, *American Loyalist*, 167–68, 168n, fn. 1.

30. *Ibid.*, 168–72; quotation on 172. See also Ingersoll's account of his resignation, which was forced from him during events of September 18 and 19, in *Connecticut Gazette*, Sept. 27, 1765, and in *Mr. Ingersoll's Letters Relating to the Stamp Act* (New Haven, Conn., 1766), 62–68.

31. Gipson, *American Loyalist*, 169.

32. *Ibid.*, 171.

would be a living worth 5 or 600 per ann.) which might as well be put into his Pocket as another's." With such a defense, guilt was a foregone conclusion. The sentence prescribed that the prisoner should be tied "to the tail of a Cart, and drawn through all the principal streets in Town, and at every corner and before every House should be publicly whipped; and should be then drawn to a Gallows erected at least 50 feet high, and be there hanged till he should be dead."

Ingersoll was tried in absentia in Lebanon. The trial contained the only subtle touch in all these affairs, an argument by the prosecution that the trial in absentia was legal because Ingersoll was "virtually represented" and thus was denied none of the sacred rights of Englishmen.[33]

II

While resistance gathered in America, sentiment for both enforcing and repealing the Act built in England. Had the Grenville ministry succeeded in remaining in office, an attempt would have been made to collect the stamp tax everywhere in the colonies, but George Grenville had been dismissed from office on July 10, three and a half months before the Act was to take effect. Grenville had been forced out for several reasons. He had become personally unacceptable to the king for his part in the attempt in Parliament to exclude the king's mother from the regency council. This council was set up to govern in event of the king's illness and was to exercise the monarch's power until he recovered or, in case of his death, until his heir reached maturity. George III had fallen sick in early 1765—he was not insane as later rumored—and the bill establishing the council was proposed because his death was feared for a time. Members of the ministry persuaded him that the House of Commons would not agree to his mother's membership in the council. When the bill reached Commons, it was amended to include his mother's name and then approved. The king was embarrassed and annoyed and blamed his chief minister, George Grenville, who in fact had declined to make any recommendations about appointments to the regency council. This affair plus a series of unhappy experiences with Grenville set the king's mind, and when the opportunity presented itself he got rid of the ministry.[34]

The new ministry stood on wobbly legs. Lord Rockingham, heading

33. See the account in the *Georgia Gazette* (Savannah), Oct. 10, 1765.
34. John Brooke, *King George III* (New York, 1972), 109–22; J. Steven Watson, *The Reign of King George III, 1760–1815* (Oxford, 1960), 109–12.

it as first lord of the Treasury, possessed a following—the so-called "Rockingham Whigs"—but it was neither very stable nor strong. Rockingham himself lacked experience, and he was virtually incapable of making himself understood in Parliamentary debate. Although his ministry was not to be one of great principles or policies, he did have some idea about what should be done in colonial affairs. Moreover, he could call on Edmund Burke, member from Bristol and his private secretary, for advice. Yet this source of strength could do little to keep the government in office or Rockingham at its head, which posed a problem, for two of Rockingham's new colleagues, Secretaries of State Conway and Grafton, wanted Pitt to replace him. And two other ministers, the Lord Chancellor, Northington, and the Secretary at War, Barrington, were King's Friends and carry-overs from the previous ministry. Altogether, it would be hard to imagine a more unpromising beginning.[35]

The problem of America fell on the Rockingham Whigs even as they took office. Trade had been depressed for months as the Americans cut back on the consumption of British goods in an attempt to get the Sugar Act repealed. And British merchants discovered just how difficult it is to collect debts in a period of economic depression. These merchants soon announced these facts to the country in a series of complaints about trade and public policy.

Parliament in adjournment was enjoying the summer silence while the merchants wept bitter tears, but in October even Parliament had to listen as alarming stories of mob violence in America arrived. As the extent of this violence became known and its effects on the stamp distributors became evident, outrage grew. Even before the Parliament resumed, the words "treason," "anarchy," and "rebellion" were spoken in describing American behavior. And when the session began in December, many members had set themselves against repeal of the Stamp Act, evidently convinced that repeal would establish a precedent so dangerous as to affect the power to govern.[36]

The king shared many of their fears, although he seems not to have felt the anger at Americans that was common in Parliament. Rather, the accounts of mobbing and rioting saddened him and filled him with gloomy forebodings. As he wrote Secretary of State Conway, "I am

35. P. Langford, *The First Rockingham Administration, 1765–1766* (Oxford, 1973).
36. Horace Walpole noted that asking Parliament to repeal the act before enforcement was really attempted did not go down parliamentary throats easily: "When do princes bend but after a defeat?" Walpole, *Memoirs of the Reign of King George the Third* (4 vols., London, 1845), II, 219.

more and more grieved at the accounts in America. Where this spirit will end is not to be said."[37]

George's address on December 17, 1765, to the reconvened Parliament betrayed little of this anxiety. The king did not write the speech of course; the Cabinet council took care of that delicate chore, and in the process took care that the king did not say too much, in particular that he did not reveal the extent of the defiance in America. Hence his address offered a general description of the American situation, stopping well short of concrete examples with a vague reference to "Matters of Importance." The House in its reply matched this vagueness, but only after it put down an amendment by George Grenville, still a member of Parliament, calling upon it to express resentment and indignation at the riots. The House might suppress its own anger, but not Grenville's, and he spoke with bitterness in these December meetings. Edmund Burke, who in private correspondence sardonically referred to Grenville as the "Grand Financier," reported a few days afterwards that Grenville had addressed the House every day "taking care to call whore first." The House listened, voted against Grenville's amendment, and on December 20 adjourned in order that special elections might be held to fill vacancies.[38]

The ministry in these December days did much more than put vague words in the king's mouth and rebuff George Grenville. Because the ministry was so weak in Parliament and because its continuation in office depended upon meeting the crisis over the Stamp Act successfully, it turned to out-of-doors support—namely, the merchants and manufacturers in cities all over England who were enduring the depression in business. These merchants themselves proved responsive to Rockingham and had met in London early in December to plan a national campaign for repeal. With the assistance of Rockingham and Burke, the London merchants formed a committee and began writing to friends, associates, and soon to similar committees in England and Scotland. Barlow Trecothick, a rich merchant who had been reared in New England, headed the London group and provided first-rate leadership. By the end of Janu-

---

37. Gipson, *British Empire*, X, 373.
38. Copeland, ed., *Correspondence of Edmund Burke*, I, 223–24. Of Grenville: "The Grand Financier behaved like a rash hot headed boy," *ibid.*, I, 225. The king's address is in William Cobbett, comp., *Parliamentary History of England from the Earliest Period to the Year 1803* (36 vols., London, 1806–20), XVI, 83–84. Grenville said that the king's address seemed as if it were written by the "Captain of the Mob." Fortescue, ed., *Correspondence of George the Third*, I, 202.

ary 1766 many individual merchants had written their representatives, and several dozen memorials and petitions from large groups had been received by Parliament.[39]

These appeals for relief were couched in terms calculated not to raise the constitutional scruples of Parliament. The colonists with all their talk about representation had already trampled on these scruples; the merchants, if not wiser at least more prudent, framed their petitions in terms of the health of the economy. The present situation, they forecast, could only worsen should action not be taken; indeed, according to the London committee, it threatened to "annihilate" the trade to North America. Everyone knew something of the commercial depression in progress; the merchants also reported bankruptcies caused by the Sugar Act and Stamp Act and on the difficulty of collecting debts in America. No exact estimate of defaults could be given, but more than one group predicted that losses might reach several million pounds sterling.[40]

Even with this powerful support from out-of-doors, Rockingham had his work cut out and he knew it. When Parliament reconvened on January 14 of the new year, he and the ministry had resolved to attempt to get the Stamp Act repealed. Earlier in the winter they had played with the idea of amendments—for example, of allowing each colony to pay the tax in its own currency rather than sterling. Events disabused the ministry that anything short of repeal would end the upheavals in America.

Facing a Parliament angry over the riots and the challenge to its sovereignty, Rockingham decided to tap the discontent of English merchants and manufacturers. If he could demonstrate that the consequence of a failure to repeal would be economic disaster, he had a good chance of ridding the statute books of the Act. His problem was how to deal with the embarrassing defiance of Parliament's authority. The colonies had denied that authority: Parliament had no right to tax Americans, they said, because Americans were unrepresented in Parliament. To be sure, Parliament was the sovereign body in the empire and it might

39. Copeland, ed., *Correspondence of Edmund Burke*, I, 231–33; Morgan, ed., *Prologue*, 130–31; G. H. Guttridge, ed., *The American Correspondence of a Bristol Merchant, 1766–1776: Letters of Richard Champion* (Berkeley and London, 1934), 9–12; Lucy S. Sutherland, "Edmund Burke and the First Rockingham Ministry," in Rosalind Mitchison, arr., *Essays in Eighteenth-Century History from the English Historical Review* (London, 1966), 45–71.

40. *EHD*, 686–91; Morgan, ed., *Prologue*, 129–31.

pass statutes affecting the colonies. Legislation was one of its rights as the center of sovereignty, but legislation did not include the right to tax, which belonged to representative bodies. Whatever the distinctions that the colonies made between legislation and taxation, the fact remained that they had challenged a right Parliament had long cherished. How to blunt that challenge, or better yet how to bury it?

How indeed when—doubtless to Rockingham's despair—these issues were raised by William Pitt, upon whom the Rockingham Whigs counted to help solve problems, not create them. Pitt entered the debate soon after it began on January 14—"entered" does not begin to describe the sensation his speech produced. He began in a voice so low as to be inaudible, and then, explaining that he had not heard the address from the Crown, asked that it be read again. As in the speech of December, the ministry had given the king only vagueness to espouse, a fact Pitt quickly grasped. He could proceed to speak his mind, an opportunity he almost immediately used to announce to the House and to George Grenville, who sat one place away from him, that "every capital measure" taken by the late ministry "has been entirely wrong!"[41] Having disposed of the Grenville ministry, Pitt defended the constitutional case made in America. "It is my opinion," he said, "that this Kingdom has no right to lay a tax upon the colonies. At the same time, I assert the authority of this kingdom over the colonies, to be sovereign and supreme, in every circumstance of government and legislation whatsoever." For in Pitt's view the Americans shared all the rights of Englishmen, were bound by England's laws, and were subject to all the protections of its constitution. And the crucial one in this case was the right to be taxed by one's representatives. Taxes after all were "no part of the governing or legislative power." Rather, "taxes are a voluntary gift and grant of the Commons alone. In legislation the three estates of the realm are alike concerned, but the concurrence of the peers and the crown to a tax, is only necessary to close with the form of a law. The gift and grant is of the Commons alone."

Pitt then asked what happened when Commons levied a tax. The answer seemed obvious to him—"we give and grant what is our own." But in taxing America what did the Commons do? "We your Majesty's Commons of Great Britain, give and grant to your Majesty, what? Our own Property? No. We give and grant to your Majesty, the property of your Majesty's commons of America. It is an absurdity in terms."

41. Cobbett, comp., *Parliamentary History*, XVI, 97. The quotations in this paragraph and the next two are from the speech, pp. 97–100.

Pitt knew that several Englishmen, among them perhaps George Grenville, had anticipated the objection to taxation without representation
by insisting that the Americans were "virtually represented" in Parliament. Pitt dismissed this notion in half a dozen sentences. Who in
England represented the Americans, he sneered—the knights of the
shire, the representative of a borough, "a borough, which perhaps, its
own representative never saw." Here was another absurdity, "the most
contemptible idea that ever entered into the head of man."

The *Parliamentary History*, wherein this speech was printed, reports
that a "considerable pause" ensued after Pitt's speech—members understandably disliked following Pitt—but Secretary Conway gathered his
courage and said that he agreed with Pitt, though in fact he disagreed
on several points unrelated to the constitutional argument.[42] The House
did not want to hear Conway, and no doubt he knew it. Everyone
waited for Grenville, who now rose to answer Pitt.

Grenville's answer was brilliant rhetorically, capturing much of the
doubt and resentment of the House. He began by censuring the ministry
for delay in reporting the rebellion in America and predicted that should
Pitt's "doctrine" be upheld the rebellion would become a revolution.
And he declared that he could not "understand the difference between
external and internal taxes."[43] Nor could he understand the difference
between legislation and taxation. Taxation, he insisted, was both part
of the sovereign power and "one branch of the legislation." Moreover,
taxation had long been exercised over many who were unrepresented—
the great manufacturing towns, for example. As for America, no member
had objected to Parliament's right to tax the colonies when the Stamp
Act was introduced.

Up to this point, Grenville had kept his anger in check; now it broke
through in a powerful denunciation of the Americans' lack of gratitude
for the military protection and economic advantage afforded them by
the empire.

> Protection and obedience are reciprocal. Great Britain protects Amer-
> ica; America is bound to yield obedience. If not, tell me when the
> Americans were emancipated? When they want the protection of this
> kingdom, they are always ready to ask for it. That protection has always
> been afforded them in the most full and ample manner. The nation
> has run itself into an immense debt to give them their protection;

42. *Ibid.*
43. Grenville's speech is in *ibid.*, 101–3.

and now they are called upon to contribute a small share towards the public expence, an expence arising from themselves, they renounce your authority, insult your officers, and break out, I might almost say, into open rebellion.[44]

Grenville said more, but these few words aroused Pitt, who got to his feet at the completion of the speech. Pitt now spoke with extraordinary eloquence and probably carried many members with him—at least temporarily. In several respects, however, he made the task of the ministry all the more difficult. For Pitt praised American resistance: "I rejoice that America has resisted. Three millions of people, so dead to all the feelings of liberty, as voluntarily to submit to be slaves, would have been fit instruments to make slaves of the rest." He also reasserted that Parliament possessed full authority to legislate for the colonies. England and her colonies were connected and "the one must necessarily govern; the greater must rule the less; but so rule it, as not to contradict the fundamental principles that are common to both."[45]

Grenville had given him an opportunity to explain what ruling entailed by asking the question "when were the colonies emancipated?" Pitt's brief reply—"I desire to know when they were made slaves?"—struck through all the rhetoric to the central issue of liberty within constitutional order. Of course the Americans could be crushed by armed force, Pitt noted, but the dangers of crushing them would be great. For "America, if she fell, would fall like a strong man. She would embrace the pillars of the state, and pull down the constitution along with her."[46]

Pitt's eloquence so thoroughly dazzled several of his listeners that they failed to understand what he was saying. One member wrote in a letter after hearing Pitt:

It seems we have all been in a mistake in regard to the Constitution, for Mr. Pitt asserts that the legislature of this country has no right whatever to lay internal taxes upon the colonys; that they are neither actually nor virtually represented, and therefore not subject to our jurisdiction in that particular; but still as the Mother Country we may tax and regulate their Commerce, prohibit or restrain their manufactures, and do everything but what we have done by the Stamp Act; that in our representative capacity we raise taxes internally and in our legislative capacity we do all the other acts of power. If you understand the difference between representative and legislative capacity it

44. For Pitt's answer, *ibid.*, 103–8.
45. *Ibid.*
46. *Ibid.*

is more than I do, but I assure you it was very fine when I heard it.[47]

If Pitt created confusion, he also gave offense to many members by his statement approving of colonial resistance. Rockingham did nothing to remove the confusion, but he acted soon to shift the House's attention from the treacherous sand of constitutional theory to the firm ground of economics. Between January 17 and 27 the petitions from merchants from all over the realm were presented and read. These petitions argued against the Stamp Act on economic grounds: they described the decay of trade, the inability of merchants to collect American debts, the hardships resulting to all classes in Britain, and several hinted that the merchants might remove themselves from the islands if repeal were not achieved.[48]

From this point on, the ministry asserted greater control in the House. First of all, on January 28, it persuaded the House to resolve itself into a committee of the whole and then to consider motions embodying a program of action in response to the crisis. This program made no concessions to Pitt's argument that Parliament had no right to tax the colonies. That right had to be stated at the outset if the ministry was to obtain repeal. Therefore, on February 3, 1766, Conway moved a resolution declaring that Parliament possessed the power to make laws binding the colonies "in all Cases whatsoever."[49] In introducing this resolution—which was the basis of the Declaratory Act—Conway explained that while the right to tax was clear, the expediency of it was not. Whether this resolution had any meaning given the ministry's intention to propose repeal of the stamp tax was immediately questioned by Hans Stanley, a highly respected member. Others clearly shared Stanley's doubt—the declaration did not seem to comport well with repeal. Attorney General Yorke answered as well as he could for the ministry that the resolution did have meaning, and the resolution passed overwhelmingly on the next day with only Pitt, who had displayed unwonted indecisiveness in this debate, and three or four others voting against it. Over the next

47. Historical Manuscripts Commission, *Report on the Manuscripts of Mrs. Stopford-Sackville* (London, 1904), I, 104.
48. Morgan, ed., *Prologue*, 130–31; Copeland, ed., *Correspondence of Edmund Burke*, I, 231–33.
49. For Conway's resolution, see Lawrence Henry Gipson, "The Great Debate in the Committee of the Whole House of Commons on the Stamp Act, 1766, as Reported by Nathanael Ryder," *PMHB*, 86 (1962), 11–14; Conway to George III, Feb. 4, 1766, Fortescue, ed., *Correspondence of George the Third*, I, 254–55.

two days resolutions passed declaring that the riots in America violated the law, that the legislative assemblies in America had countenanced them, that those persons who suffered injury or damage on account of their desires to comply with the laws should be compensated by their colonies, that such persons who had desired to comply with the laws or assisted in their enforcement would have the protection of the House of Commons, and that anyone suffering penalties because stamped paper was unavailable ought to be compensated.[50]

These last two resolutions were offered by Grenville and accepted by the ministry. Their passage must have pleased him, though he could have been under no illusions that the House was disposed to take a hard line against the colonies. Still, on February 7, he offered a resolution calling for an address to the king informing him that the Commons would back him in enforcing the Stamp Act. Although this proposal went down to defeat 274 to 134, the debate was rough, with Grenville accusing the ministry of sacrificing the sovereignty of Britain to placate the colonies. Pitt hit the resolution hard, demonstrating, according to Horace Walpole, "the absurdity of enforcing an Act which in a very few days was likely to be repealed."[51] The absurdity might produce the spilling of blood, according to Pitt, who argued that orders countermanding the instruction to enforce the Act might be delayed—should enforcement and then repeal be approved. In the interval who knew what disasters this "absurdity" might produce?

Having beaten Grenville again, and having clearly established that Commons believed in its right to tax the colonies, the ministry now proceeded to demonstrate the inexpediency of levying this particular tax. The petitions presented by the merchants in January had prepared the way for a motion for repeal. There was a bad moment when the king seemed to back away from repeal, but Rockingham went to him and demanded his support. The king gave it—grudgingly (and in the end about fifty of his "Friends" who sensed that his heart was not with the ministry voted against repeal). What remained for the ministry to do was to renew—or establish—in the minds of members the impression that economic ruin faced the nation if the statute remained on the books. This task appeared all the more difficult as the ministry came under especially bitter attack in the newspapers, attacks designed more to influence Parliament than the public. Anti-Sejanus, the cover of James

50. The debate may be followed in Gipson, "Great Debate," *PMHB*, 86 (1962), 11–25.
51. *Ibid.*, 25–31. The quotation is in Walpole, *Memoirs*, II, 285.

Scot, chaplain to the Earl of Sandwich, asked the most embarrassing question—how did the ministry ever expect to collect taxes in America if it gave way on the stamp tax?[52]

The merchants paraded before Commons by the Rockinghams did not exactly answer this question. But these sad-eyed fellows made an impression as they appeared before the committee of the whole, dripping with pathos and full of the descriptions of present horrors, to be followed by worse if repeal failed. And to reassure the House that the Americans did not object to all taxes, and were really loyal subjects, the ministry called on the redoubtable Benjamin Franklin. Members of the ministry prepared themselves and Franklin for this examination, but, since they could not control the questioning, Grenville's supporters asked slightly more than half the questions. Franklin performed brilliantly, meeting the hostility of the Grenville group with patience and tact, and cultivating the impression that the Americans were nothing but loyal subjects much put upon by a tax destructive to their interests. He also used the questions to feed the fears of Parliament that Grenville's policies had begun a movement for economic independence in America. Repeal, however, he assured the House, would start the Americans consuming English manufactures once more. To the question "What used to be the pride of Americans?" he answered: "To indulge in the fashions and manufactures of Great-Britain." And to the question that followed—"What is now their pride?"—the reply was "To wear their old cloaths over again, till they can make new ones."[53]

Franklin's most masterful comments came in answer to a question similar to the one posed by Anti-Sejanus—why should anyone expect them to pay taxes again if they succeed in escaping this one? In answer, Franklin made a distinction between internal and external taxes. The colonies, he told the House, objected only to internal taxes; they would willingly pay duties on trade to Britain in return for the protection the Royal Navy provided on the high seas. Franklin knew that some in England denied that there was any difference between the two sorts of taxes and reminded the House of it with a series of shrewd remarks to the effect that "At present they do not reason so, but in time they may possibly be convinced by these arguments."

52. P. D. G. Thomas, *British Politics and the Stamp Act Crisis: The First Phase of the American Revolution, 1763–1767* (Oxford, 1975), 194–210; Morgan, ed., *Prologue*, 131–34.
53. *EHD*, 686–91; Gipson, "Great Debate," *PMHB*, 86 (1962), 31–33. Franklin's statements are in *BF Papers*, XIII, 159.

The ministry gave the House a week to consider this testimony along with the massive evidence from the merchants, and on February 21, Conway introduced the resolution to repeal the Stamp Act. This was the point to pull together the case against the Act. Conway did the job effectively, taking care to reaffirm once more that though the ministry believed in Parliament's right to tax the colonies, enforcement would produce civil war to the disadvantage of trade and to the advantage of such vulturous nations as France and Spain. The hard core around Grenville remained unconvinced and said so. Grenville himself, trying one last desperate measure, interrupted Conway to say that repeal of the Act was premature since reports that morning had arrived which indicated that the southern colonies were complying with the Act. A listener to Grenville styled this attempt as "dilatory finesse"; in less polite language it was pure fabrication. Conway in any case was not deflected and neither was repeal, which passed 276 to 168.[54]

By early March the resolutions which had been approved in February had been embodied in a Declaratory bill and a Repeal bill. After one more attempt by Pitt to remove the phrase "in all cases whatsoever," which described Parliament's claim to bind the colonies, both passed the House on March 4 with resounding majorities.[55]

The Commons sent the bills to the House of Lords the next day. The Lords too had listened to the addresses from the throne in December and January, and the Lords contained members who, like George Grenville, wished to reply with expressions of indignation at the "rebellion" in the colonies. Debate in the Lords included ferocious denunciations of the Americans and a few defenses of the American position that Parliament lacked the right to tax the colonies.

After these preliminaries were got out of the way, the Declaratory bill was quickly approved; the Repeal bill received its last reading on March 17 and the next day the king gave his assent.

54. Quotations in this paragraph and the one preceding it are from *BF Papers*, XIII, 156; and D. S. Watson, "William Baker's Account of the Debate on the Repeal of the Stamp Act," *WMQ*, 3d Ser., 26 (1969), 261.
55. Gipson, "Great Debate," *PMHB*, 86 (1962), 39–41.

6

Selden's Penny

My penny is as much my own as the King's ten pence is his: if the
King may defend his ten pence, why not Selden his penny?

John Selden, member of Parliament during the struggles with Charles I,
a learned lawyer whose work was used by the seventeenth-century
opposition to the king, was only a minor hero to colonial pamphleteers
and intellectuals. His name graced their writings far less often than
Milton's, Sidney's, or Locke's. Yet his maxim—"My penny is as much
my own as the King's ten pence . . ."—was quoted during the crisis
over the Stamp Act and for good reason: it captured the importance
of property in this crisis.[1]

On the surface the Americans' preoccupation with their property—
more particularly their determination to resist the levy of taxes on it—
seems petty, demeaning, poor stuff with which to make a revolution
as they were soon to do with the cry "no taxation without representation."
Their concern with property, indeed their obsession with it, should not
be dismissed easily; they meant what they said, and they felt more than
they could express about the importance of property. Their understanding
of property, in fact, was profoundly embedded in their thinking not
only about the nature and purposes of political society, but also about
the character and meaning of liberty itself.

Although the intellectuals—the planters, lawyers, ministers, and others
who wrote about public policy—generally agreed that political society
had its ultimate origins in the divine will, they believed that its purposes
were the preservation and regulation of property. It had been formed
by agreement or compact among property owners for these purposes.

1. *New London Gazette* (Conn.), Nov. 1, 1765, reprinted in Bernard Bailyn, "Religion
and Revolution: Three Biographical Studies," *PAH*, 4 (1970), Appendix B, 163.

This theory had already had a long life in political speculations, though the Americans learned of it from John Locke's *Two Treatises of Government*. Locke had used the word "property" in at least two ways, one to mean material possessions, things, land; and another to refer to "lives, liberties, and estates."[2] Property in material possessions arose through the mixing of one's labor with things—cultivating or improving the land, for example. By lives, liberties, and estates as property, Locke seems to have intended that the word "property" represent one's rights—man's freedom and his equality and his power to execute the law of nature. Like man's material possessions, these rights are separate or distinguishable from himself: man can alienate them, can give them up. But a person's consent is required if his rights are to be alienated, just as it is when he surrenders material possessions. In fact, as Locke described slavery and freedom, slavery existed when consent was not required, when one's person or one's property was subjected to the arbitrary and absolute will of another.

Property in the Lockeian scheme of things conferred political character, or being, on a man. A slave has no political rights because he has no property—that is, he has not liberty in himself and he has no material possessions. Jonathan Mayhew, the Congregationalist pastor of the West Church in Boston, insisted during the crisis over the Stamp Act that the tax threatened "perpetual bondage and slavery." He defined slavery in terms indebted to the narrower definition of property by Locke: slaves—he said—are those "who are obliged to labor and toil only for the benefit of others; or what comes to the same thing, the fruit of whose labor and industry may be *lawfully* taken from them without their consent, and they justly punished if they refuse to surrender it on demand, or apply it to other purposes than those, which their masters, of their mere grace and pleasure, see fit to allow." But Mayhew invoked the broader definition of property—lives, liberties, and estates—in explaining that freedom entailed "a natural right to *our own*," a premise he offered as the "general sense" of the colonies.[3]

Mayhew might well have based these statements on political practice in the colonies, for the Americans were Lockeians by experience as well as by persuasion or general opinion. In societies where families for the most part had not been able to entrench themselves on the basis of ancestry or lineage—society was much too mobile for that—wealth

---

2. John Locke, *Two Treatises of Government*, ed. Peter Laslett (Cambridge, 1960), II, 123. See also *ibid.*, I, 42–43; II, 32–40, 101–2.

3. Jonathan Mayhew, *The Snare Broken* (Boston, 1766), 13, 4.

counted for a great deal. Land provided much of the wealth, of course, but money in commerce was not to be minimized. At any rate, one acquired status with material property—family, breeding, and education counted much less. Property also conferred political rights. In every colony ownership of real property was required of voters, and political leadership, by a common if tacit agreement, was vested in those who owned.

The history that educated groups imbibed until it became almost their own experience recounted the development of representative institutions to serve in effect as extensions of the rights of property. The Saxon myth found believers in America from New England to Virginia and was repeated by such worthies as Jonathan Mayhew and Thomas Jefferson. According to this beguiling story, the old Saxon Witan, the ancestor of the modern Parliament, took its rise as representative of the landholders of England. The Normans under William the Conqueror disbanded it, but in a century or two it made its appearance once more as the Parliament of England, the agency of property owners. In its modern form it served as the model for the colonial assemblies.[4]

When we see the political rights and obligations of the individual, and the institutions and purposes of the state, tied to property, indeed expressed in a sense by property, colonial disquiet at the stamp tax becomes understandable. This unease was transformed into a constitutional position during 1765–66, a position maintained intact until just before the Continental Congress declared independence.

At the time of upheavals over the Stamp Act, American leaders had not thought systematically or coherently about the constitutional order that presumably included the colonies. They had long acknowledged Parliamentary supremacy and colonial subordination without troubling to ask exactly what these grand phrases involved. They continued in 1765 and 1766 to profess to believe in Parliament's absolute sovereignty and in their own subordinate place. At its most extreme, this constitutional position came down to James Otis's sonorous sentence: "The power of Parliament is uncontrollable but by themselves, and we must obey." This proposition appeared in *The Rights of the British Colonies Asserted and Proved*,[5] a tract which purported to demonstrate that Parlia-

4. H. Trevor Colbourn, *The Lamp of Experience: Whig History and the Intellectual Origins of the American Revolution* (Chapel Hill, N.C., 1965), 30, 183–84, 194–98.
5. (Boston, 1764), reprinted in Bernard Bailyn, ed., *Pamphlets of the American Revolution, 1750–1776*, I: *1750–1765* (Cambridge, Mass., 1965), 418–82. The quotation is on page 448.

ment had no right to tax the colonists because they were unrepresented in it and therefore unable to give—or to withhold—their consent to levies on their property. By itself Otis's assertion that Parliament's power could be controlled only by itself stated Parliament's attitude perfectly, but not that of most colonists. And Otis himself did not intend that his statement be understood as a standard of equity, but only of power. Parliament, he argued, had the power to do what it wished but not the right, and when it erred the executive courts of England would in time recall it to the right, as they had in the seventeenth century in Bonham's case, a celebrated proceeding Otis had read of in Coke's *Reports*. Otis seems to have misinterpreted Coke and based his argument for colonial compliance on his misunderstanding. He also assumed that Parliament as a benign body would wish to correct its mistakes once they were pointed out to it by the executive courts. The entire procedure had a slightly mechanical cast, with a benevolent Parliament acting to rectify its errors when the executive courts kindly discovered them. But as naïve as the scheme appears, it solved, in Otis's mind at least, the requirements of equity within a system in which an undivided sovereignty resided in the Parliament.[6]

It was a curious line to take about the British constitution and not altogether satisfying even to Otis. Its inadequacies were obvious: uncontrollable power cannot be reconciled with a claim that men possess political and civil liberty in organized society. And, of course, all English and American theorists agreed on this claim to liberty. Otis met the difficulty as well as he could by arguing that despite Parliament's uncontrollable power there were limits it could not transgress; the colonists, after all, retained their natural rights and their rights as British subjects. Nature clearly served as the source of the first of these rights, but what was the source of subjects' rights? The answer was awkward: Parliament itself and the common law. What, aside from its own good intentions, would prevent an uncontrolled Parliament from trespassing on rules it set for the protection of the subject was a question Otis did not answer.

As convoluted and vulnerable as Otis's views were, they did help establish an important colonial contention about the British constitution. That constitution did not simply consist of what Parliament legislated, but of some fundamental law derived from nature and ultimately from God which protected the political and civil freedom of all subjects wher-

6. Bailyn's introduction and notes to Otis's tracts are valuable. See *Pamphlets*, I, 409–17, 717–24.

ever they lived. Otis never fully explained what the fundamental law consisted of, nor did anyone else in America in these years of crisis over the Stamp Act. Yet we can sense in the fragmentary references in newspaper essays, learned tracts, and "political" sermons that American theorists—Otis, Mayhew, Bland, Moore, Carter, Dulany, and others—believed that some basic constitutional order existed which limited in equity if not in actuality the powers of all political agencies, including the sovereign body in the empire, the British Parliament. These half-formulated comments were of two kinds: one explicitly insisted that there were limits beyond which even Parliament could not go, because the Americans as British subjects retained certain fundamental rights and privileges from that ancient and mysterious day when they left the state of nature for civil society; the other implicitly assumed that, because a free man was distinguished from a slave only by his independence of the arbitrary will of another, limits existed curbing the power of all men, whatever their station and authority.[7]

The relation between the fundamental law and actual institutional protections—Otis's executive courts and the common law, to cite two examples frequently adduced by Americans—did not appear clearly in these years. Presumably the common law followed the subject wherever he went, but though it included seemingly permanent protections, it was subject to revision in courts and in Parliament. The charters issued to the colonies by the Crown appeared to be made of more solid stuff, but despite a number of flat statements that they incorporated fundamental rights, including the right to be taxed only by one's representatives, there was an uneasy recognition in these assertions that the Crown had vacated them in the past and might do so again.[8]

Yet even with all these uncertainties about the nature of the constitution, a half-articulated constitutionalism made its appearance by 1766. It held that there were limits, outside of and independent of Parliament. Their essence might not be altogether clear and their sources might be a matter of dispute, but they existed nonetheless.

7. See in particular, Mayhew, *The Snare Broken;* Richard Bland, *The Colonel Dismounted* (Williamsburg, Va., 1764) and *An Inquiry into the Rights of the British Colonies* (Williamsburg, Va., 1766); Maurice Moore, *The Justice and Policy of Taxing the American Colonies* . . . (Wilmington, N.C., 1765); Jack P. Greene, ed., "Not to be Governed or Taxed," *VMHB*, 76 (1968), 259–300; Daniel Dulany, *Considerations on the Propriety of Imposing Taxes in the British Colonies* (Annapolis, Md., 1765).

8. See, for example, Bland, *Inquiry*, 14–26.

The fact remained, however, that the American colonies were a part of the empire, and an argument that Parliament, like all political bodies, was limited did not establish where its legal lines of jurisdiction began and ended. Drawing these lines proved extraordinarily difficult, and the initial attempt made by the colonial assemblies in 1764 soon after they heard of the possibility of a stamp tax, though clear on at least one essential, was not altogether satisfactory to them and simply confusing to the English government. The essential on which these legislative bodies agreed was that Parliament could not levy internal taxes in the colonies, a proposition clear on its face but full of unsuspected implications.

Not all the assemblies issued statements—petitions, resolutions, memorials, and remonstrances—in 1764 when the stamp bill was being drafted. The five which did were probably even more concerned about the recently enacted Sugar Act. Yet all showed an unease about the proposed stamp taxes and all declared their opposition. The New York Assembly decried Parliament's right to tax the colonies in three forthright petitions to the king, the Lords, and the Commons. Declaring its "Surprize" that Parliament would even consider taxing the colonies, an "Innovation" which will "reduce the Colony to absolute Ruin," the Assembly insisted that the colonies should be exempt "from the Burthen of all Taxes not granted by themselves."[9] The New Yorkers protested at the same time that they had no desire for independence, and as evidence of their loyalty and reasonableness conceded the authority of Parliament to regulate colonial commerce "so as to subserve the Interests of her own."

With the exception of Virginia's House of Burgesses and its Council, which claimed a right to be taxed only by their own consent, the other legislatures which produced resolutions in 1764 were less emphatic—and less clear. Rhode Island ducked the issue of Parliament's right to raise a revenue by taxing colonial trade while arguing that the proposed stamp taxes would violate long-established rights. Massachusetts made a similar though cautiously worded claim to an exemption from internal taxes but left the issue of external taxes unexplored. Unexplored, that is, in the official address of the House and Council; behind that prudent document lay a bitter dispute between the two bodies, a dispute the Council under the leadership of Thomas Hutchinson won. The House had originally prepared a protest against any tax to be levied on the colonists without their consent. When the Council refused its approval,

9. Morgan, ed., *Prologue*, 9, 11.

the House gave in and endorsed the weaker document in the belief that a mild protest was better than none.[10]

Only the Connecticut legislature in some of the fastest footwork displayed in any of these official statements conceded Parliament's authority to raise a revenue in America. Connecticut's statement, drafted by a committee which included Governor Thomas Fitch and Jared Ingersoll, was published as a pamphlet, *Reasons Why the British Colonies Should Not Be Charged with Internal Taxes*.[11] In it the Connecticut legislature formulated one of the early versions of distinct but connected jurisdictions which it saw operating in the empire. These jurisdictions were "internal" and "external" as they bore on the colonies. In the internal affairs of the colonies only their legislatures had authority to legislate and tax. On this ground the Connecticut legislature stood fast—Parliament had no authority to levy internal taxes. In external affairs, the legislation of trade and foreign relations, on the other hand, the jurisdiction of Parliament was undoubted. Indeed, the Connecticut legislature was so impressed by the "capacious and transcendent" character of this jurisdiction that it could not bring itself to deny Parliament's right to raise a revenue by duties on trade and even went so far as to suggest two taxable commodities, Negroes and furs, both items which rarely appeared in local ports. If Parliament ever decided to levy such taxes, the Connecticut legislature piously insisted that it should manage the job without impinging upon the rights of the colonists, rights which guaranteed that "No Law," including statutes levying taxes, "CAN BE MADE OR ABROGATED WITHOUT THE CONSENT OF THE PEOPLE BY THEIR REPRESENTATIVES."[12]

Whatever confusion these paradoxical assertions engendered was eliminated in 1765 when these five colonies and four others produced unequivocal denials of Parliament's right to levy any sort of taxes for revenue in America. The Virginia Resolves, of course, began this process of clarification; their strong rejection of Parliament's claims inspired other colonial assemblies. In a sense, the most impressive action of all came in October 1765, when the Stamp Act Congress, a gathering in New York City of delegates from the colonial assemblies of Massachusetts, Connecticut, Rhode Island, New York, New Jersey, Pennsylvania, Delaware, Maryland, and South Carolina, issued resolutions and petitions

10. For Virginia, *ibid.*, 14–17; for Rhode Island and Massachusetts, Morgan and Morgan, *Stamp Act Crisis*, 34–36.
11. (New Haven, Conn., 1764), reprinted in Bailyn, ed., *Pamphlets*, I, 385–407.
12. Bailyn, ed., *Pamphlets*, I, 394, 405, 391, for the quotations.

to the king, the Lords, and the Commons, all rejecting any claim of Parliament to tax the colonies.[13]

Neither the Stamp Act Congress nor the assemblies suggested that Parliament had no authority over the colonies. The Stamp Act Congress in fact offered as a leading premise the statement "That his Majesty's Subjects in these Colonies, owe the same Allegiance to the Crown of *Great-Britain*, that is owing from his Subjects born within the Realm, and all due Subordination to that August Body the Parliament of *Great-Britain*."[14] Maryland referred to its long history of self-government, noting in particular the rights of its citizens to give their consent to measures of taxation and "internal Polity." The implication was that in the sphere of "external" polity, Parliament might legislate for the colonies. This was elaborated upon elsewhere to mean the right to take such action, including enacting legislation on matters of common concern in the empire, the most notable being, of course, the commerce of the colonies and Great Britain.[15]

Because the colonists were primarily concerned at this time in resisting Parliament's claim to a right to tax them, they did not fully work out the implications of their ideas about separate, or internal and external, jurisdictions. The question was incredibly complicated in any case, and the legislatures did not attempt to explore it in depth. They concentrated on taxes, the immediate issue at hand, and may have skirted broader considerations for fear of diverting attention from what seemed absolutely essential.

Pamphleteers dared more, perhaps because they had less to lose, but even their productions only grazed the target rather than boring in on it. This "unofficial" colonial position was a good deal clearer when it dealt with the internal sphere than the external. It held that since the colonials as Englishmen were born free, a contention with Lockeian overtones, they were subject only to laws made with their own consent. Moreover, their rights had received royal approval through the various charters issued to the colonies. Although these charters amplified and extended these rights, they did not provide an absolute basis for them. The colonists were English, and Englishmen could be governed only by their own consent given through their own representatives.

The question of why the colonists were subject to any regulation by

13. Morgan, ed., *Prologue*, 62–69.
14. *Ibid.*, 62.
15. *Ibid.*, 53, for "internal Polity."

Parliament, or just what constituted the external sphere, interested these colonial writers much less. Every tract assumed that the colonists were subject to Parliament, an assumption which obviously followed from the argument that the colonists were English subjects. All English subjects were in some sense under Parliament. The right of Parliament to regulate trade seemed just as clear—it was a matter of "necessity," Stephen Hopkins wrote. The empire had a center, England, and it had constituent parts, the colonies. To pull it together, superintend its commerce, and make decisions relating to matters of common concern were necessary, and Parliament seemed the only agency capable of so doing.[16]

II

These abstractions of constitutionalism and political theory carry an antiseptic flavor; by themselves they seem bland and juiceless, and uncontaminated by human feeling or passion. We have to remind ourselves as we read such words as rights, sovereignty, and representation that they pertain to human affairs, and never more so than in these eighteenth-century struggles. For in the reality of the controversy over the Stamp Act these terms were anything but disembodied and detached; rather, they were set out in a framework which conveyed profound fears and anxieties.

The fear and anxiety arose from one compelling conviction: a conspiracy existed to deprive Americans of their liberties and to reduce them to slavery, and the Stamp Act was merely the "first step to rivet the chains of slavery upon us forever."[17] These notions were much too widely disseminated and accepted to be dismissed as propaganda; and virtually every sort of colonial leader—ministers, merchants, lawyers, and planters—sounded them through all the available means. There was John Adams, in the privacy of his diary branding the Stamp Act as "That enormous Engine, fabricated by the british Parliament, for battering down all the Rights and Liberties of America"; and Stephen Johnson, pastor of the Lyme (Connecticut) church, writing anonymously in the *New London Gazette* of the purpose of the Act to bring the colonists to "slavish nonresistance and passive obedience"; Andrew Eliot, informing Thomas Hollis in England of the plot against the colonies in which the Stamp Act was "calculated" to enslave the colonies; Landon Carter,

16. Stephen Hopkins, *The Rights of Colonies Examined* (Providence, R.I., 1765), in Bailyn, ed., *Pamphlets*, I, 507–22.
17. *New London Gazette*, Sept. 20, 1765, reprinted in Bailyn, "Religion and Revolution," *PAH*, 4 (1970), Appendix B, 146–49.

a great Virginia planter, assailing it in the *Virginia Gazette* as "the first resolution to enslave us." These charges were typical of hundreds of others, all marked by varying degrees of anger and outrage, but to the greater extent suspicion and fear.[18]

These charges appeared clear on the surface. What made them sinister were the murky details—the specifications of the plot—surrounding them. A natural question to ask was who conspired? The ministry drafted the statute, the Parliament passed it, and the king gave his approval. Did they conspire together? Were they in league against the American colonies? No one suggested that they were; indeed, the king was "the best in the world," and the Americans were his loyal subjects who never tired of professing their loyalty; and the Parliament furnished the model of their own representative assemblies. The ministry, however, could not draw on such affection in America.

In the attacks on the stamp masters, one minister absorbed more abuse than any other. He was, of course, George Grenville, and behind him lurked the dastardly *"Thane,"* the Earl of Bute, with his constant companion, apparently a minister-without-portfolio, the Devil. The pamphleteers relayed some of the same information to their readers, but ordinarily contented themselves with an inclusive indictment of the entire ministry, which was grasping, aspiring, and ambitious for power and dominion. Beyond these generalities few ventured, though Jonathan Mayhew included the king and Parliament among those ensnared by the plotters. The suggestion of conspiracy imputed a larger design than the enslavement of America: the plotters aimed to destroy liberty in both Britain and America. Most American writers agreed the ministry had actually advanced their malignity further in England than in America.[19]

There were local variations on these charges. Where Protestant zeal burned fiercely and where the Catholic presence in Canada seemed ominous, the conviction grew that the threat against civil liberty posed

18. Butterfield et al., eds., *Diary of John Adams*, I, 263; *New London Gazette*, Sept. 20, 1765, in Bailyn, "Religion and Revolution," *PAH*, 4 (1970), Appendix B, 146–49; "Letters from Andrew Eliot to Thomas Hollis," MHS, *Colls.*, 4th Ser., 4 (Boston, 1858), 400; Greene, ed., "Not to be Governed," *VMHB*, 76 (1968), 266–68.

19. Morgan and Morgan, *Stamp Act Crisis*, 290–91, briefly discuss American fears of conspiracy. For a full elaboration of the importance of conspiracy in American thought before the Revolutionary War, see Bernard Bailyn, *The Ideological Origins of the American Revolution* (Cambridge, Mass., 1967), 144–59, and *passim*, especially chapters 3 and 4. I have drawn heavily on Bailyn's and the Morgans' books.

by unconstitutional taxation was partly a papist conspiracy to subvert Protestantism. In New England and to some extent New York, this fear attached itself to the rumors, the gossip, the baleful stories about the Anglican hierarchy's intention of importing a bishop into America. When the Society for the Propagation of the Gospel established a mission in Boston the stories gained credence, and a pamphlet campaign broke into print and continued long after the repeal of the Stamp Act. Even after agitation against the Stamp Act subsided and amid celebrations on its repeal, the tale was spread that a Frenchified, Catholic party in England had designed it in the interests of the House of Bourbon and the Catholic Church.[20]

A single act of Parliament led by an evil ministry would not immediately fasten chains on colonial wrists, of course. As far as the American writers were concerned, the Stamp Act was simply the visible edge of the dark conspiracy. If the Act were accepted, they asked, what guarantee did the colonists have that their lands, houses, indeed the very windows in their houses, and the air breathed in America would not be taxed? A people virtually represented in Parliament would have no choice once they swallowed that pernicious doctrine which was in reality shackles for the enslaved. And there would be many hungry men in England eager to do the work of the enslavers. Colonial accounts of the conspiracy lingered over long and horrified descriptions of the officeholders, placemen, taskmasters, and pensioners who would descend upon the colonists ostensibly to serve His Majesty but in reality to eat out the colonial substance. The corruption they would bring would complete the ruin of the colonies.[21]

What accounts for the elaboration of these fears into almost paranoid delusions of covert designs and evil conspiracies against colonial liberty? Only recently have historians begun to take these charges seriously, though not as descriptive of the realities of English politics and government, but as indicative of a genuine—and pervasive—belief in America about English intentions. As rhetorically extravagant as the colonists' responses may appear, they were not contrived; they were not what we call propaganda. Rather, they were deeply felt and honest reactions.[22]

20. Carl Bridenbaugh, *Mitre and Sceptre: Transatlantic Faiths, Ideas, Personalities, and Politics, 1689–1775* (New York, 1962) discusses thoroughly American fears of the episcopacy. For a typical reference to the "Frenchified party," see Stephen Johnson, *Some Important Observations* . . . (Newport, R.I., 1766), 15.

21. Bailyn, *Ideological Origins*, 99–102.

22. The Morgans and Bailyn in works cited in these notes were among the first to take seriously American arguments as statements of principle.

That these responses were products of emotion as well as of mind should not lead us to dismiss them as irrational. Reason inspired them just as passion did. On one level, the colonists estimated quite rationally what the stamp taxes would cost economically as well as politically. Because the taxes would have to be paid in sterling, it seemed that hard money would disappear from the colonies already chronically short of coin. As for who would bear the heaviest burden, even so stalwart a conservative as Jared Ingersoll wrote the ministry that the poor would feel the taxes most heavily. Small claims before justices of the peace would be taxed, for example—cases ordinarily brought only by poor men.[23]

To be sure, the political meaning of the stamp taxes preoccupied the colonists even more. The ministry might cite all the precedents it liked, from the Post Office Act of 1711 to the recently enacted duties on molasses, but it seemed obvious to the colonists that something new, in actuality something unprecedented, had been done. At any rate, the colonists looked at the Stamp Act in a context rather different from that assumed by the ministry. The Stamp Act followed other actions and official statements which indicated that from now on life in America would be different, especially as it pertained to governance and getting and spending. The Sugar Act had let the colonists know of official displeasure at the conduct of juries in cases involving seaborne commerce. So out with trial-by-jury and in with vice admiralty courts unencumbered by juries. Concern for ancient liberties at this substitution seems understandable—and reasonable.

One can also see rationality in the disquiet expressed at the explanation given for the new policies: reduction of the English national debt and the defense of the colonies. Perhaps selfishness and a notorious propensity to starve public bodies account for the lack of sympathy for English taxpayers, but the concern over regular troops stationed in America hardly arose from merely a mean spirit. A standing army in time of peace, after all, had helped occasion the Glorious Revolution. For their part, the colonists professed not to understand why such an army was needed in America after the French had been driven out of Canada, unless to be used to force them to yield to such oppressions as unconstitutional taxes. Considering all these matters together—taxes, governance, and security—concern and even suspicion seemed eminently rational to the colonists, and one can agree that the discontent they felt on these scores seems so—on its face.

23. For a full exposition of Ingersoll's opinions, see Gipson, *American Loyalist*.

If this discontent was explicable by rational calculation and expressed itself as anger, even rage, against English public policy and in particular the Stamp Act, there must have been still another kind of discontent that vented itself in this crisis. This discontent may justly be termed nonrational, for its ultimate sources had nothing to do with public affairs. No doubt every society generates a certain amount of frustration, tension, and anxiety in its members. Some may be neurotic, some not; some may find outlet in personal relations, some is contained or directed at the self; and at least occasionally some seeks discharge in a political or a social movement. The varieties and sources of individual discontents must often seem endless and were surely diverse in the colonies. The present state of knowledge of the psychology of Americans in the second half of the eighteenth century will not reveal with certainty why this sort of discontent—or aggression—focused against public authorities in England and America. There are clues, however, in the controversies over the Stamp Act about the connections between private rage and public behavior. For one thing, the movement in opposition to English policy commanded not only the support of most leaders in society, but also their talents and resources. The leading supporters of the Stamp Act, on the other hand, besides feeling divided within themselves, had already incurred suspicion and hostility on other grounds—Thomas Hutchinson in Massachusetts, for example, and the Tory Junto in Rhode Island.[24]

In 1765 the privately engendered anger of a son against his father, a husband against his wife, a worker against his employer, still encountered the usual powerful constraints inhibiting its release, but might find a socially approved target in English public policy. The traditional prohibitions against the discharge of discontent against public authority had been suspended. The new focus undoubtedly freed a good deal of aggression which otherwise would have had to find other channels.

Whether "rational" or "nonrational," the discontent expressed in this crisis was so explosive that had the Stamp Act not been repealed five months after taking effect, it might have produced revolution in 1766. The pervasiveness and the intensity of the conviction in the colonies that a conspiracy had placed liberty on a precarious footing explains in part the American response. Yet the Americans' political sensitivities and their almost instinctive willingness to explain their crisis in terms of dark plots and sinister conspiracies require further explanation. They

24. See Bailyn, *Ordeal of Hutchinson,* and Lovejoy, *Rhode Island Politics.*

may have been brought to the edge of revolution by their conviction that they were the victims of an evil conspiracy, but what made them believe in the conspiracy, a conspiracy that had no basis in fact?

Two sorts of circumstances conditioned these responses. The first was political; the second, religious or, more accurately, moral. For at least two generations politically aware Americans had been a suspicious lot, smelling plots and conspiracies in all sorts of circles, including those surrounding governors and royal officials serving in the colonies. Of course their politics gave them reason for entertaining suspicions; their politics bred a turbulent factionalism and an atmosphere, if not always the actuality, of conspiracy. The "outs" plotted to replace the "ins" who conspired to remain where they were. In fact, colonial politics possessed so much fluidity, with interest groups forming to achieve short-term objectives, then dissolving, only to coalesce once more in different alignments in the service of another set of temporary purposes, that no group maintained its hold on the government for long.[25]

This instability persisted in spite of conditions which would in time contribute to a remarkably durable political order. By eighteenth-century standards almost all the thirteen colonies were ruled by governments that included strong popular, if not democratic, elements. With land ownership widely spread, the typical American male was an independent yeoman and a voter because the franchise was tied to the land. Representation, though not always well apportioned, was by the standards of the time responsible, especially in the lower houses of the legislatures. Since society was relatively simple, representatives tended to have interests in common with the voters; and constituencies often instructed their representatives. And institutions outside governments which in Europe still retained political authority had largely lost it in America—for example, the established churches could no longer persecute dissenters.

Yet despite these circumstances, instability proved a chronic condition and often appeared in a sinister guise. For it involved outside—royal or proprietary—authority in the person of the governor who was everywhere out of reach of popular control except in Connecticut and Rhode Island. The governors seemed to hold, and in fact legally did hold, power to deprive the colonies of their liberties. Governors, as agents of an English ministry, could legally convene and prorogue and dissolve the legislatures; they could veto legislation; they could create courts, appoint

25. Bernard Bailyn, *The Origins of American Politics* (New York, 1968) discusses the political circumstances.

and remove judges, or routinely insisted that they had these powers. The Crown had lost all these powers in England in the Revolution of 1688, but in the colonies populated by English subjects they survived in law, apparently a legacy of a persistent tyranny. In the realities of colonial politics, despite these legal or constitutional powers, the governor lacked the "influence"—the control of patronage—that gave ministerial authority its substance. This disparity between formal constitutional structure and the reality of politics contributed to the instability and the atmosphere of conspiracy, with the governor playing a part in the incessant combining and fragmentation of factions, and with his authority, shadowy and mysterious as it was, often in dispute.[26]

In this environment conventional wisdom came to hold that plots and conspiracy always ruled political action. This had not been an original discovery of the colonists. At least fifty years before the American Revolution they had in fact begun to absorb the ideas and assumptions of the radical opposition in England, the so-called eighteenth-century commonwealthmen. The name was derived from the radicals of the previous century, the Roundheads, the makers of the English Civil War and the Commonwealth. The seventeenth-century writers of this ideological bent included John Milton, James Harrington, and Algernon Sidney, among others. Their political ideas received something of a revision in the exclusion crisis of 1679–81—the attempt to bar James II from the throne—and eighteenth-century radicals continued the process, adapting the older ideology in order to make it useful in the opposition to ministerial governments.[27]

The eighteenth-century commonwealthmen have not survived as great names—John Trenchard, Thomas Gordon, and Benjamin Hoadly, bishop of Winchester, were the most important—but in the fashioning of revolutionary ideology in America they had an influence that surpassed Locke's. To be sure, they drew upon Locke and others more original than themselves. Indeed, their ideas were not original, and the heart of their political theory resembled closely the great Whig consensus of the century. They praised the mixed constitution of monarchy, aristocracy, and democracy, and they attributed English liberty to it; and like Locke they postulated a state of nature from which rights arose which the civil polity, created by mutual consent, guaranteed; they argued that a contract formed government and that sovereignty resided in the people. These ideas were

26. *Ibid.*, 66–83, and *passim*.
27. The basic study of eighteenth-century radical Whig ideology and its seventeenth-century background is Caroline Robbins, *The Eighteenth-Century Commonwealthman* . . . (Cambridge, Mass., 1959).

so widely shared in England as to be conventional, but the eighteenth-century radicals put them to unconventional uses. These radicals rarely got into Parliament—and never in numbers—but they formed an opposition to a succession of ministries and to the complacency of the age. While Whigs and English governments sang the praises of English institutions, English history, and English liberty, the radicals chanted hymns of mourning, dirges for the departing liberty of England and the rising corruption in English politics and society. Within all states, from ancient Rome to the present, they argued, there had been attempts to enslave the people. The history of politics was nothing other than the history of the struggle between power and liberty. Trenchard and Gordon called one of *Cato's Letters: Essays on Liberty* (1721) "Cautions against the Natural Encroachments of Power"; in that essay they declared that "it is natural for Power to be striveing to enlarge itself, and to be encroaching upon those that have none." *Cato's Letters* likens power to fire—"it warms, scorches, or destroys, according as it is watched, provoked, or increased. It is as dangerous as it is useful . . . it is apt to break its bounds." There was in the radical ideology a profound distrust of power, then, power as force, as coercion, as aggression. What did power coerce or encroach upon? Liberty, usually defined as the use and enjoyment of one's natural rights within the limits of law made in civil society.[28]

In the radicals' understanding of history, England had enjoyed liberty for so long because her constitution, her laws, and her institutions had successfully checked power and confined it to useful functions. But these writers did not share the general confidence that liberty would continue to flourish, for they detected relentless plots against it. Their writings from the late seventeenth century to the American Revolution are studded with laments for the vanishing liberties of England. In a typical warning, "Cato" declared that "public corruptions and abuses have grown upon us; fees in most, if not all, officers, are immensely increased; places and employments, which ought not to be sold at all, are sold for treble value; the necessities of the public have made greater impositions unavoidable, and yet the public has run very much in debt, and as those debts have been increasing, and the people growing poor, salaries have been augmented, and pensions multiplied."[29]

"Public corruptions and abuses": the phrase or similar ones appeared

28. The quotations are from *Cato's Letters*, numbers 33 and 25, by John Trenchard and Thomas Gordon. I have used the 1724 London edition, in four volumes. David Jacobson provides a fine selection in *The English Libertarian Heritage* (Indianapolis, Ind., 1965).

29. Number 98.

repeatedly in the oppositionist literature. Just as frequently the radicals bewailed the growing "luxury," officeholding by "wicked men," the degeneration of manners, the bribery of officeholders and the electorate. The climax of all this corruption, this pervasive moral decline, according to these political Jeremiahs, would be the destruction of liberty, and its replacement by a ministerial tyranny.

In England these grim predictions never persuaded the great Whig leadership or its massive following. But in America they were taken in deadly seriousness by a vast company of responsible men. When the crisis of the Stamp Act reached its peak, they seemed all the more compelling.

The other sort of circumstance leading Americans to accept charges of conspiracy as simply commonsense truth was the character of their Protestantism. The children of the awakened, the evangelical, the revivalistic could not have been astonished at the news that an evil plot against their liberties had been hatched in a corrupt and faintly "Catholic" England. The founders had come to America in the seventeenth century to escape an earlier version of what seemed by the eighteenth a persistent conspiracy. Christian history afforded many such examples.

Protestant Americans were especially sensitive to the pictures of hordes of placemen and taskmasters that the pamphleteers predicted would descend upon the colonies. The traditional Protestant virtues—purity and simplicity in life, work, thrift, and frugality—shaped their lives and conduct, after all. Hence the revulsion they felt at the accounts of the degeneracy, idleness, and profligacy which threatened to pass from England to America in the persons of placemen and their satellites.[30]

This feeling suggests that the uprising in the colonies, half-articulated and partially disguised as it was, occurred in part over values. The hatred of English corruption set off fears in many colonists that their society too might give way to effeminacy, sloth, luxury, and moral decay. Thus the victims chosen by the mobs at the time of the Stamp Act were struck not simply because they supported or were presumed to support English policy. Such men as Andrew Oliver, Jared Ingersoll, and in particular Thomas Hutchinson represented a dangerous moral order. In attacking them, and others like them, the mobs not only defended political liberty in America but also virtue and morality.

The mobs and no doubt popular leaders as well acted in the belief

---

30. On the background of these themes, Edmund S. Morgan, "The Puritan Ethic and the American Revolution," *WMQ*, 3d Ser., 24 (1967), 3–43.

that they face an unqualified evil. The Devil's specter had been summoned up in the denunciation of the stamp men. Protestant concerns and mental patterns had fostered an exaggerated clarity of morality and immorality, thereby heightening the emotional receptivity to fear of unseen, utterly evil forces. This disposition was broadly diffused in colonial society, and it seized ways of thinking and feeling because it was encouraged by a Protestantism that also supplied many moral and psychological values. It seemed to explain political conduct because it had always explained private behavior. It aligned the colonists with much that was old, comfortable, and good in their moral code, for a hatred of idle, dissolute placemen who served the designs of tyrants implied a love of honest, hard-working freemen committed to constitutional government. There is irony, of course, in fears and delusions fostering a national and responsible public order, but ultimately that occurred in the prolonged crisis that began with the passage of the Stamp Act.

7

Chance and Charles Townshend

Rumors that Parliament had repealed the Stamp Act, or soon would, seeped through the colonies soon after Grenville's dismissal in July 1765. Ships from England brought most of these reports and occasionally less happy news as well—of a reluctant Commons and a beleaguered ministry trying unsuccessfully to get the Act off the books. Certainty replaced rumor on May 2, 1766, when the *Virginia Gazette* published copies of the repealing and Declaratory acts, and in a few weeks printers spread the statutes all over their newspapers.

News of repeal set off celebrations in small towns and cities through America. The cities, of course, made more of the opportunity than the towns. New York proved itself especially rowdy, with the Sons of Liberty there consuming an incredible amount of hard drink, offering toasts to a long list of English heroes and to themselves, exploding fireworks, shooting guns, and finally marching in a body to the fort to "congratulate" the governor. That eminence received three of them, drunk as they were, as representatives of the rest. An officer in the British army who witnessed the celebration reported sourly that the night "ended in Drunkeness, throwing of Squibbs, Crackers, firing of muskets and pistols, breaking some windows and forcing off the Knockers off the Doors."[1] Far to the south, the citizens of Charleston in their joy did some of these things, but more sedately and with restraint. Boston thoroughly enjoyed itself with fireworks, music, "a magnificent Pyramid" decorated with 280 lamps, and the recitation of a surprising number of grandilo-

1. *Journals of Capt. John Montresor* (New York, 1881), 368.

quent verses. Several wealthy citizens put up the money to obtain the release of all debtors in jail, and perhaps the wealthiest, John Hancock, "treated the populace with a Pipe of Madeira Wine."[2] Hancock also gave a lavish party for his friends. Philadelphia behaved itself—it had been warned to do so by none other than Benjamin Franklin, who had written that repeal should not occasion either boasting or recriminations. The city gave a handsome dinner, presided over by the mayor and attended by the governor and other officials. There was an "illumination" by fireworks for ordinary people which, according to one of Franklin's friends, "was conducted with great Prudence."[3]

As the colonial legislatures convened throughout the remainder of the year, they too declared their pleasure over the repeal, and most sent addresses of gratitude to the king. None matched the Massachusetts House of Representatives in professions of loyalty or in fulsome sentiment. Only the Virginia House óf Burgesses, where opposition had first declared itself, failed to rise to the occasion. In refusing to send thanks to the king, the Burgesses maintained the integrity it had shown a year earlier.[4]

The Burgesses was not in session when the report of repeal reached America in May, and it did not convene until the following November. In the interval, enthusiasm for Parliament's action inevitably cooled and just as surely the meaning of the previous year penetrated more Americans' minds. As it did, thoughtful people asked what all the celebrating was about.

Not that the Americans had not felt genuine joy and relief in May. They had, and they quite rightly said so. What they felt but conveyed only rarely was a mood, a feeling of uneasiness at what had befallen them and distrust of the English across the sea, even of those merchants who had interceded in their behalf. The belief that a sinister ministry had conspired to deprive them of their liberties remained strong, though expressions of this conviction were naturally muted after the Rockingham Whigs took over. The plotters had long since identified themselves— George Grenville ostensibly led them, but behind him lurked the Earl of Bute.

If the Americans who had written and rioted against the Stamp Act hated these men, they regarded with something less than love the "friends of the colonies"—those who had pushed through repeal. These friends

2. *BG*, May 26, 1766. See also "Diary of John Rowe," 62.
3. *BF Papers*, XIII, 282.
4. Gipson, *British Empire*, XI, 9.

had also passed the Declaratory Act with its curious phrase about Parliament's right "to bind the colonies in all cases whatsoever." At first, most colonists who read this line seemed to believe that by this claim Parliament did not include taxation. Others were not so sure. More ominous was the curiously patronizing, even arrogant, attitude of the so-called friends of the colonies. The merchants, for example, who had organized support outside of Parliament seemed more than smug over their success—they acted as if the colonists were under great obligation to them, when everyone knew that they had favored repeal in order to get trade flowing again, and profits flowing too. The Americans had felt no cynicism or even surprise that British merchants defended America to protect British commerce; they understood this motive and indeed had depended upon it. The British merchants, however, persisted in talking as if they had saved the foolish Americans from themselves and not from a policy which the Americans regarded as subverting their rights and which had cut into British profits. Yet the British merchants betrayed no understanding of these facts—at least not in their warnings to Americans against repeating claims to be exempt from Parliamentary taxation. The manner of the merchant addresses to the colonies was all wrong and had been from the beginning of the crisis. It approached, as George Mason the distinguished Virginia planter said,

> the authoritative Style of a Master to a School-Boy: "We have, with infinite Difficulty and Fatigue got you excused this one Time; pray be a good boy for the future; do what your Papa and Mama bid you, and hasten to return them your most grateful Acknowledgments for condescending to let you keep what is your own; and then all your Acquaintance will love you, and praise you, and give you pretty things; . . . but if you are a naughty Boy, and turn obstinate, and don't mind what your Papa and Mama say to you, but presume to think their Commands (let them be what they will) unjust or unreasonable, or even seem to ascribe their present Indulgence to any other motive than Excess of Moderation and Tenderness, and pretend to judge for yourselves, when you are not arrived at the Years of Discretion, or capable of distinguishing between Good and Evil; then everybody will hate you, and say you are a graceless and undutiful Child; your Parents and Masters will be obliged to whip you severely, and your Friends will be ashamed to say anything in your Excuse: nay they will be blamed for your Faults."[5]

5. Robert A. Rutland, ed., *The Papers of George Mason, 1725-1792* (3 vols., Chapel Hill, N. C., 1970), I, 65–66; James Truslow Adams, ed., "London Merchants on the Stamp Act Repeal," letters of Feb. 28, March 18, June 23, 1766, MHS, *Procs.,* 55 (Boston, 1923), 215–23.

Disquieting as the supercilious tone was, what lay beneath it appeared worse—an uncomprehension of the American constitutional argument, or even a glimmer of suspicion that the Americans really believed in the principles they professed. Historians of the American Revolution sometimes argue that a lack of communication divided the British and their colonies. After all, the Atlantic Ocean lay between England and America, and getting information back and forth took months. When news arrived it was often out of date. There is some truth in this contention, but despite the slowness of ship crossings a surprising amount of knowledge was exchanged. In the case of the aftermath of the Stamp Act crisis, one might suggest that there was too much communication; surely the Americans who read the merchant letters published in the newspapers understood their meaning. And the American position had been amply laid out in Britain; yet few took it seriously or brought much sympathy to it.

The problem the British had was an inability to see that they had a problem—despite the letters, petitions, and memorials of the previous year. Years of dominance over the colonies had deadened their sensitivities. In the seventeenth century when the colonies began to trade with the Dutch, Parliament confined their trade to British ports; and when the colonies showed a fancy for European goods, Parliament soon nipped it in the bud. Did the colonies threaten the market for English manufactures? Pass a statute stopping them. They were "our colonies," "our subjects," and, as George Mason noted, "our children"; Parliament the parents, the mother and father, and they should obey.

The colonists played their parts in this relationship with proper deference, in fact with willingness, for years. They connived at their own subordination: they were provincials, and provincials in the eighteenth century may have admired the metropolis, but they did not deceive themselves that they were its equals. They also resorted to the familial metaphors in describing their subordination—England was the mother country and they were children owing deference. But there were distinct limits to these colonial attitudes, and in the crisis produced by the Stamp Act, Parliament and the Grenville ministry had blundered across those limits. The immediate aftermath revealed how few in Britain possessed the insight to see the full extent of this blundering.

II

The lingering suspicion of Britain did not quiet the bitter factionalism of American politics, and in fact in several colonies the defeat of the

Stamp Act permitted important shifts of local power. These alterations sometimes entailed the control of offices, sometimes of legislatures, and everywhere forced men to make clear their allegiances. More important, provincial politics now had an abiding issue which carried the potential of unifying the colonies: hostility to control from Britain.

Drastic changes in local alignments occurred where colonial politicians were able to exploit this issue, an event which depended largely on their ability to impute to the opposition support of ministerial policies. In Massachusetts the Otis faction had no trouble in smearing Governor Bernard and Thomas Hutchinson and their friends with the tar of the Stamp Act and for sucking up offices and patronage and disgorging them in bribes to supporters. Many of the charges were no smear, and Otis and company made the most of them. Their opportunity came in the elections held in May 1766, the first chance they had since the violence of the previous summer to rid the House and Council of, as they said, the enemies of the people. They opened their campaign in the *Boston Gazette*, their house organ, with an assortment of attacks. They charged the governor and the council with appropriating money to their friends without the consent of the House; they protested against the practice of "treating" (some delicacy made them use this word rather than "bribing")—supplying the electorate with rum and wine in return for votes—a practice, of course, only of the administration. They condemned anyone who had urged compliance with the Stamp Act or who referred to the "Sons of Liberty" without due respect—Hutchinson's crowd choked on the name and suggested a more apt designation would be "Sons of Violence."[6]

These charges were offered for the edification of Sons of Liberty all over Massachusetts. Lest anyone miss the point, the *Gazette* published model instructions for representatives to the House and urged the towns to use them. Believing that at least thirty-two representatives had demonstrated their unfitness for office, the *Gazette* published their names with the suggestion that the best instruction for them would be retirement to private life.[7]

Governor Bernard detested unseemly behavior, especially in public and particularly at his expense. Thomas Hutchinson did not admire it either, but he had friends who took up his cause in the *Boston Evening Post*. The defense, however, worked under the handicap of respect for the truth, at least the truth so far as the Stamp Act was concerned.

6. *BG*, March 31, 1766, April 14, 1766 (for the quotations).
7. *BG*, March 31, 1766.

Neither Hutchinson nor Bernard had urged its passage; Hutchinson had deplored it in private. Announcing their opposition long after the event left their critics unmoved—indeed in control of the battlefield. The *Boston Evening Post* attacked as well as defended, and its victim, James Otis, took a savage lashing in its columns. Otis's *Brief Remarks on the Halifax Libel*, which had revealed a rather different emphasis on Parliament's power from his *Rights of the Colonies*, drew particular scorn for its "inconsistencies and *Prevarications.*" And Otis himself received rough handling as a "double-faced Jacobite Whig" and as a *"slight of hand-man."*[8]

None of this saved Bernard's supporters from taking a drubbing at the polls. Nineteen of the thirty-two representatives chosen for purging were defeated. In Massachusetts the new House and the outgoing Council chose the new Council, and in the May election four incumbents—Judge Peter Oliver, Secretary Andrew Oliver (who had been slated to be the stamp distributor), Attorney General Edmund Trowbridge, and Chief Justice Thomas Hutchinson—were removed. All were notorious as plural officeholders and friends of the administration, and all, except Trowbridge, were related to one another by blood or marriage. A fifth councillor, Benjamin Lynde, a judge of the superior court, resigned before he could be dispatched. Bernard vetoed the popular supporters chosen in the place of these comfortable old standbys, and he vetoed the election of James Otis as speaker of the House. But Bernard was in a much weakened position and he knew it.[9]

In Massachusetts the governor at least survived; in Connecticut, where the office was elective, the governor, Thomas Fitch, did not. Fitch had contributed to his own defeat in spring 1766 by swearing the previous November to enforce the Stamp Act. Failure to take the oath would have cost Fitch £1000 in a fine, but he was a stubborn man who probably would have taken the oath whether or not the fine existed. He and several members of the Connecticut Council were turned out of office when the Sons of Liberty succeeded in identifying them with the Stamp Act. These men had to carry the dead weight of Jared Ingersoll around their necks. Like them, Ingersoll was an Old Light and an opponent of the ambitions of the Susquehannah Company in the Wyoming Valley, Pennsylvania. The Sons of Liberty, mostly New Light, of course, and in the case of those from New London and Windham counties eager to maintain the claims of the Susquehannah Company, hung Ingersoll

8. *Boston Evening Post,* May 5, 1766.
9. Jensen, *Founding,* 193–97.

on them and thereby linked Old Light religion to advocacy of the Stamp Act, an unfair equation and a damaging one because so widely believed.[10]

When the elections approached in 1766, the Sons of Liberty, dominated by contingents from Windham and New London counties, organized a colony-wide meeting in Hartford in late March. The first order of business was innocuous, a resolution to maintain correspondence with Sons of Liberty in other colonies. After this was accomplished the convention went into closed session, an action which caught some delegates from western counties by surprise. Windham and New London delegates soon revealed their purposes—the nomination of a slate of candidates for governor, deputy-governor, and the Council (the lower house was already safely in popular hands). After much discussion, an adjournment of a day, and more debate, the convention decided to limit its slate to governor and deputy-governor and avoid endorsements of councillors, since a wholesale overturning might "make too great an Alteration in the Body Politick at once." The Sons delivered on their promises in May when William Pitkin, who was deputy-governor, replaced Fitch as governor, and Jonathan Trumbull was chosen in Pitkin's stead.[11]

Elsewhere the aftermath of the Stamp Act in provincial politics was less clear—as in New Jersey, Maryland, and the Carolinas—or delayed—as in New York, which had no election in 1766. Rhode Island, savage in its resistance to the Stamp Act, had no important royalist faction—or willing surrogates once Thomas Moffat and Martin Howard and their cohorts departed. The Tory Junto had never shown anything more than a nuisance value at any rate and could not be discharged from offices they never held.[12]

Pennsylvania presents the strangest case of all. Neither of the two old alignments—the Quaker and Proprietary parties—had opposed the Stamp Act strenuously. The Quakers, led by Benjamin Franklin in pursuit of royal government to replace the much despised proprietor, had muted their discontent—they could not expect the Crown to revoke the charter if they led riots against ministerial policy. Hence they remained quiet—as did the Proprietary party, also hoping that their loyalty would help prevent the Crown from revoking their charter rights.[13]

10. Morgan and Morgan, *Stamp Act Crisis*, 234–35.
11. The quotation is from Gipson, *American Loyalist*, 221. See also Morgan and Morgan, *Stamp Act Crisis*, 235–37.
12. Jensen, *Founding*, 186–214, provides a fine discussion of reactions in politics.
13. For Pennsylvania politics and the Stamp Act, see James H. Hutson, *Pennsylvania Politics, 1746–1770* (Princeton, N.J., 1972), 192–215, and *passim*.

By mid-1766 something approaching a fresh political alignment had emerged from fragments of these two groups—the Presbyterian party, a group especially fearful of the importation of an Anglican bishop. The Declaratory Act had aroused those fears, for it seemed to imply that the colonies could claim no protection against episcopacy. The party was a coalition—and still incomplete in 1766—of Presbyterians, Quakers, Germans, and Scotch-Irish. The party's main contingent of recruits, the mechanics of Philadelphia and the farmers of the West, did not align with it for another two years.

III

Altogether the Stamp Act had at least temporarily united several sorts of colonial groups, even though it could not subdue the factionalism of colonial politics. By late spring 1766 the Act was an issue of the past, but the suspicions it had aroused of British purposes in America lingered, suspicions reinforced by still unresolved grievances. There were the restrictions on colonial trade, in particular the duty on molasses which, though reduced to one penny per gallon, was collected on all molasses imported into the colonies—even that from the British West Indies. There were currency restrictions in the mid-1760s that seemed to cramp the trade of New York merchants more than others. At any rate, the New Yorkers complained the loudest. There was the ministry's request to compensate the victims of the Stamp Act riots which occasioned predictable fights between governors and legislatures.[14]

In Massachusetts, Bernard in his usual tactless way told the House to vote the money as an act of justice before it was requisitioned— presumably by the Crown. The House asked who had the authority to requisition the people's money and then blandly suggested that any compensation would be an act of generosity, not of justice. Shortly after the exchange, towns outside began to ask why they should pay anything since the riots had occurred in Boston. Faced with the unappealing prospect of paying the whole bill, the Boston meeting flip-flopped and agreed that the colony should compensate the sufferers from the riots. Somehow Boston's leaders persuaded the House that the issue was not a local matter but that all towns should contribute. The House then agreed to pay and coupled payment to a pardon for those charged with riot. In December 1766 a statute providing both compensation and pardon passed and was sent to Governor Bernard. The legislature lacked

14. Jensen, *Founding,* 196–97.

the power to pardon, traditionally the prerogative of the executive, and Bernard knew it. The legislature had trapped him: Thomas Hutchinson and other victims were friends and stood to get the money. Bernard approved the statute.[15]

New York also made an issue of compensation. There the legislature agreed to pay Major James, the commander of the fort, for his losses of personal property, and it also compensated the owner of the house where James lived, which had sustained damage in the riots. But Lt.-Governor Colden remained uncompensated; as the House coldly remarked, Colden had earned his losses by his own "misconduct."[16]

Colden did not suffer alone. General Gage, commander of British forces in America, also received a rebuff from the New York legislature in 1766. The occasion was provided by the legislature's refusal to abide by the terms of the Quartering Act (enacted in 1765), which required that the colonies house the troops stationed in settled areas in barracks, taverns, or vacant buildings—not in private homes, however. The Act also ordered the colonies to supply certain provisions and firewood, candles, and cider or beer. At the time the Act was passed the army had posted most troops in the West, but soon after it removed many to the East, in part to have them available as resistance to the Stamp Act grew violent. Most were assigned to New York, many in the Hudson Valley, especially in and around Albany, where in spring 1766 the great landlords requested that they be used to put down a large-scale uprising of tenant farmers. General Gage, to his credit, disliked using the troops in this way but eventually did so. He was then all the more surprised when the legislature—which contained a large contingent of landlords—continued to turn down his requests for compliance with the Quartering Act. What followed had some of the qualities of a farce: the general and the new governor, Sir Henry Moore, quoting the Quartering Act to the legislature—the governor sent a complete copy at one point—and the legislature refusing to acknowledge either the army's need or the existence of the statute.[17]

The issue, however, was not farcical. In the legislature's eyes the Quartering Act represented still another attempt by Parliament at taxing the colonies. Principle and property were again involved, and the legislature was determined not to give over either. In early summer it did provide some support, £3200 from old funds, to equip barracks in Albany

15. *Ibid.*, 209–11.
16. *Ibid.*, 211.
17. *Ibid.*, 211–14.

and New York City, but it refused to supply the drink, salt, and vinegar required by the Quartering Act. And, in fact, the legislature refused to acknowledge that in giving this limited support it was complying with the statute. Appropriating funds which it contended had been available since 1762 allowed the legislature to maintain the fiction that no compliance was involved.[18]

These events were not known in England in summer 1766 when the king dismissed Lord Rockingham from office. Never very strong in Parliament, Rockingham's administration had begun cracking in the spring as the alliance of merchants trading to North America and the West India merchants parted company. These groups which had meant so much in securing the repeal of the Stamp Act fell out with one another over the proposal to establish a free port in the West Indies, and the West Indies planters deserted Rockingham when he backed the proposal. Weak in Parliament, the ministry was also divided within itself. The Duke of Grafton, discontented because Pitt had not been taken into the government, resigned in the spring; in early July, Lord Northington went to the king and asked for permission to resign the Great Seal. Rockingham desperately wanted Pitt's support, but every application to Pitt had been refused. The ministry might have survived a little longer had it been willing to give Bute's friends more offices; this price, however, was too high. The king did not admire Rockingham, but he feared having to accept Grenville in his stead. In May the king learned that Pitt was willing to form a government, and at the end of July when the opportunity arose, he dismissed Rockingham and summoned Pitt.[19]

Pitt was fifty-seven years old and still a great national hero despite his aberrant behavior since leaving office five years before. He had been sought after by the king three times and had always found a reason not to serve. He had rarely attended Parliament in these years, and when he did he usually professed ignorance or indifference to the concerns that interested ordinary politicians. He lacked a following, an "interest," in Commons, men tied to him for patronage and influence; indeed, he despised ordinary connections. Yet he could arouse great enthusiasm in Commons with his compelling oratory and of course had done so in the debates over the Stamp Act. Now, as he agreed to head the

18. Gipson, *British Empire*, XI, 39–66, discusses the Quartering Act and the Restraining Act (which did not go into effect).
19. P. Langford, *The First Rockingham Administration, 1765–1766* (Oxford, 1973), 236–63.

government, he accepted elevation to the peerage and became the Earl of Chatham, an advancement that took him out of the House of Commons where any government needed powerful leadership.[20]

The ministry Chatham formed contained several men whose abilities approached brilliance but whose temperaments and ambitions held them apart. Chatham himself took the Privy Seal, a place without a function. His friend and admirer, the Duke of Grafton, received the Treasury and nominally headed the government. Grafton lacked experience and maturity, and he lacked too a genuine desire to exercise power, but he regarded Pitt with an affection bordering on worship, an attitude of mind that recommended if it did not qualify him for office. The Earl of Shelburne, another warm friend of Chatham, became Secretary of State for the Southern Department. Shelburne had genuine intellectual gifts, but he was disabled by a temperament, aloof and cold, which led him to avoid the political arena, where he was needed to exercise the arts of persuasion and conciliation. Henry Conway remained in the government as Secretary of State for the Northern Department; Camden became Lord Chancellor; Egmont, who despised Chatham, headed the Admiralty, and Northington, a stout King's Friend, became president of the Council.

After Chatham, the most interesting man in the government was Charles Townshend, who became Chancellor of the Exchequer. Townshend, forty-one years of age, was the second son of Charles, Viscount Townshend, a well-connected and formidable man who tried to dominate his son and partially succeeded. Townshend's mother, née Audrey Harrison, was a bright, witty, and promiscuous woman who saw little of her son after she and his father separated. Townshend remained with his father when his parents' marriage collapsed, even though he apparently felt no great love for him. A troubled youth suffering from epilepsy and struggling with his father over money and career, Townshend emerged a troubled adult, brilliant but unpredictable in both private and public conduct.

Townshend has often been described as erratic, yet he remained absolutely faithful to one key conviction about America—the need to make royal officials there independent of popular control. At the beginning of his career, as a member of the Board of Trade, he drafted instructions

20. My account of the formation of the new government follows John Brooke, *The Chatham Administration, 1766–1768* (London, 1956), chap. 1. For Townshend, see especially Sir Lewis Namier and John Brooke, *Charles Townshend* (New York, 1964).

to the new governor of New York directing that the legislature should be instructed to make a permanent provision for the salary of the governor and other royal officials, thereby establishing the independence of the executive. As a member of Grenville's administration, Townshend favored the Stamp Act but opposed the resolution of December 1765 declaring the colonies in rebellion, and in the debate, according to Burke, he handled George Grenville "very roughly." The following spring he voted for repeal of the Act. By this time he had earned a reputation as a dazzling orator and an amusing but unreliable man.[21]

With this unlikely collection, Chatham proposed to work a great change in English politics. He would crush faction, end the instability of the previous half-dozen years, and restore peace and harmony to the government of England. By accepting a peerage, which took him out of the Commons into the Lords, Chatham had made attacking his problem all the more cumbersome, for he had removed himself from where the great battles were fought. He had also handicapped Conway, his leader in the Commons, by giving the Treasury to the Duke of Grafton. The Treasury, of course, was the source of much of the patronage that made the Commons amenable to a ministry's desires. Conway had to look to Grafton, in the Lords with Chatham, for this necessary resource.[22]

The first six months of Chatham's administration brought home to him the difficulties inherent in his design. One of his colleagues, Egmont, first lord of the Admiralty, left the government a few weeks after it took office. In November most of the remaining Old Whigs, loyal to Rockingham, left office, driven out by Chatham, who now turned to the Bedfordites for support. The price in offices asked by Bedford was too high, however, and Chatham was forced to take aboard the King's Friends. Outside the government stood an opposition, now stronger than ever but, happily for Chatham, divided and distrustful of one another. Faction, however, had not been subdued, and in December, Chatham, nursing his gout and his frustration, removed himself to Bath.[23]

Chatham's two other major purposes—bringing the East India Company under control and settling colonial problems—did not prosper either. Before taking himself to Bath, Chatham had begun to push for a Parliamentary inquiry into the affairs of the East India Company. These affairs were in an uncertain state, though rumors abounded of abuses in the management of the company's finances and its recently

21. Copeland, ed., *Correspondence of Edmund Burke*, I, 224.
22. Brooke, *Chatham Administration*, 11.
23. *Ibid.*

acquired territories. Chatham wished to deprive the company of its territorial holdings, which were especially large in Bengal; these lands, he
pointed out, had been acquired with the help of the army. Why then
should the company enjoy revenue from lands conquered by the king's
troops? Conway and Townshend opposed taking over the company's
territories, and there were many in Parliament who agreed with them.
The motives of many members were hardly pure, for many owned and
speculated in East India stock, Townshend among them. Townshend
proposed that the territories remain the company's property and that
negotiations for a share of the revenue be undertaken.[24]

As seen by the ministry, American problems came down to matters
of making government in the colonies responsible and finding the resources to pay for royal expenditures there. New York's defiance of the
Quartering Act became known during the year, and the reluctance of
Massachusetts and New York to compensate sufferers from Stamp Act
riots was also recognized. Awareness of problems in the West grew more
slowly.

Since the Proclamation of 1763 the West had proved virtually ungovernable. Royal officials, most notably the superintendents of Indian
Affairs, found themselves helpless to regulate the fur trade and consequently to prevent frauds against the Indians. And settlers defied the
ban against settlement and encroached upon lands supposedly reserved
to the Indians. Shelburne, as Secretary of State for the Southern Department whose responsibility it was to make recommendations about the
West, delayed any action for a year while he studied the issues. The
pressures on him were enormous: fur traders in Canada, Pennsylvania,
and the southern colonies wanted a free hand and hoped to prevent
the intrusion of thousands of land-hungry colonists from the East. Other
business interests, among them the Illinois Company, one of whose
promoters was Benjamin Franklin, urged that large grants of land be
made to them and that at least two colonies be carved out of the West
to assure orderly settlement and the protection of profits. There was
still another interest to contend with—those men in and out of Parliament who insisted that expenses in America be cut, or at least made
an American responsibility.[25]

Money indeed connected all the various problems of America and
the East India Company. Beyond extracting revenue from the company,

24. *Ibid.*, 73–74, and *passim.*
25. R. A. Humphreys, "Lord Shelburne and British Colonial Policy, 1766–1768," *EHR*,
    50 (1935), 257–77.

Chatham had no clear ideas on how to strengthen the finances of the government. His refusal to try to persuade Townshend and Conway to support his plan for the company killed whatever chances it had. And his withdrawal to Bath, followed by his collapse in March 1767, after a brief foray into London and the government once more, opened the way for Townshend to take the lead.[26]

Townshend's manner of taking the lead evidently caught his colleagues by surprise. In January 1767 debate began on the army estimates; for America, the army proposed costs of some £400,000. During the discussions of this sum George Grenville moved that it be halved and that the colonies bear the expense of troops stationed in America. The government beat back this proposal, but Townshend in the course of the debates pledged that the government would raise at least a part of the revenue from the colonies. Although this promise distressed Conway and others in the government, it did not attract great attention in Parliament. Grenville did not respond, nor did others, probably because all agreed that Parliament possessed the authority to tax the colonies, a view which they believed had been embodied in the Declaratory Act.

If Townshend had rather casually committed the government to raise money in America, the necessity to do so soon appeared anything but casual. For in February the Rockingham Whigs with the support of much of the opposition pushed through a reduction in the land tax from four shillings on the pound to three. This cut forced the government to look for an additional £500,000.

Chatham still withheld himself from the struggles in Parliament. A despairing Grafton wrote him of the reduction of the land tax and begged him to return to defend his position on the East India Company. The king indicated his support, were it to be called for, but still Chatham remained aloof. By mid-February it looked as though Townshend would settle the East India business in his own way, but two weeks later Chatham exerted himself to pull his administration together. He saw he must rid the government of Townshend; hence on March 4 he offered Townshend's place at the Exchequer to Lord North. North refused. Chatham sank back into himself and did not take part in the affairs of the government for the next two years.

Grafton simply lacked the drive and the experience, and perhaps the intellect, to replace Chatham. Townshend possessed these qualities in abundance though his temperament sometimes disabled him, but for

26. Brooke, *Chatham Administration*, 68–116.

the next few months he was in command. He spent a part of this period in graceless flirtation—a political matchmaking, not an affair of the heart—as the Rockingham Whigs courted him in a fruitless effort to entice him out of the government. By May, Townshend seems to have had his fill of courtship—he had more powerful suitors in the ministry, in any case—and he offered his American program. His proposals were of three sorts: the New York Assembly should be suspended until it agreed to comply with the Quartering Act; import duties should be collected in the colonies on lead, glass, paper, painter's colors, and tea; an American Board of Customs Commissioners with its headquarters in the colonies should be established. By the end of June all three proposals had been embodied in legislation and approved with virtually no opposition. George Grenville wanted to go farther and argued that Parliament should enact legislation requiring colonial officials, including governors, councillors, and representatives, to take an oath upholding the Declaratory Act. The oath included a statement that "the colonies and plantations in America are, and of right ought to be, subordinate unto, and dependent upon the imperial Crown and Parliament of Great Britain," a sentiment that commanded almost unanimous approval in Parliament but which seemed unnecessarily redundant and perhaps provocative at this point. Commons turned it down.[27]

In the debate over the Revenue Act of 1767, Townshend explained that he did expect the duties on lead, glass, tea, and the other items to return more than £40,000 a year. This admission must have startled some members (but apparently not many), for the sum expected did little to reduce the loss from the reduced tax on land; and in any case this American revenue would be placed at the disposal of the Crown to be used to pay the salaries of royal officials in the colonies, thereby removing them from local control. Townshend seemed quite proud that his proposal to raise revenue entailed only what was called in England an "external tax." In the confusion over the repeal of the Stamp Act some members had evidently been persuaded that the colonists did not object to such taxes but only to internal taxes. Of course the colonists made no such distinction and opposed all taxes for revenue, though they conceded the expediency of Parliament's regulation of trade through use of certain duties.[28]

What Townshend and Parliament had done in the Revenue Act was

---

27. The account in this paragraph and the three preceding is based on Namier and Brooke, *Charles Townshend,* and Brooke, *Chatham Administration, passim.*
28. Jensen, *Founding,* 224–27.

to revive fears and resentments in a people already convinced that a plot against their liberty and property had been hatched in 1765. Moreover, the plan to pay royal officials with the money raised simply made the statute worse. Not only were colonial pockets about to be picked, but another constitutional protection was to be removed.

The suspension of the New York Assembly was to become effective October 1, 1767. It deprived the legislature of its right to pass acts after that date and declared them "null and void" in advance if the legislature persisted. And, in a strange redundancy, the governor was ordered to veto any legislation passed in defiance of the suspension. Once the legislature complied with the Quartering Act these prohibitions would be lifted. Taken with the civil list to be financed by the Revenue Act, this statute seemed to give firmer evidence of Parliament's intentions to destroy constitutional rights in America.[29]

Along with the statute creating an American customs service, the Revenue Act and the Suspending Act expressed some long-standing attitudes toward the colonies, especially the persuasion that they were somehow subordinate to Parliament and must be brought under control. The Townshend legislation did more, however: it vented an anger and frustration bordering on the emotions parents often feel over rebellious children. Like inexperienced children, the colonies had misbehaved and must be disciplined. To be sure, reason took a part in the internal history of the Townshend program as it had in Grenville's policies. Britain bore a heavy debt and the colonies, lightly taxed, might take over a part of the burden. Yet questions might be raised about how reasonable the taxation of imports was. Reason had always urged the expansion of commerce; given colonial resentments against Parliamentary taxation, how reasonable was it to expect that the duties would not impair commerce? And how reasonable was it to expect the colonies to pay? These questions were not really broached in Parliament.

The irony in this episode is that an administration at least nominally headed by a man who opposed Parliamentary taxation of America approved Townshend's policies. Of course Chatham was sick, or incapable of action, in 1767, but Grafton and Conway, who had pushed the repeal of the Stamp Act, were well. And the ministry included Shelburne and Camden, both of whom had opposed the Declaratory Act the year before. If this ministry were incapable of settling American affairs on a basis of friendship and cooperation, it might at least have managed to avoid

29. *Ibid.*, 227–28.

the explosive mixture Charles Townshend bestowed upon it. Accident and chance seem prominent in the history of this disastrous year. The timing of Chatham's collapse could not have been worse for American affairs. Chatham's removal from the political scene in March left a tired and dispirited leadership—Grafton, Conway, and Shelburne—facing a strange, irresponsible, but finally tough and determined man who got his way. Had the Rockinghams succeeded in wooing Townshend to their side, his program probably would not have been proposed; or had his energy encountered an opposing force, he probably would not have won. But the Rockinghams failed to persuade Townshend to leave the ministry, and his colleagues in the ministry went along with his proposals. Townshend did not live to see the consequences; his death on September 4, 1767, like so much in his life, came abruptly and with shocking surprise.[30] But before his death Townshend had made his mark on policies affecting England and America. That was the final irony: this man, apparently memorable only for personal eccentricities, succeeded in leaving an impression on public affairs such as few men have ever done.

30. The "definitive" life of Townshend remains to be written, even though the study by Namier and Brooke is useful in many ways.

8

Boston Takes the Lead

Perhaps more than most crises in the past, revolutions take on the appearance of inevitable, even natural, events. They usually have small beginnings that grow into large confrontations between political bodies and a people. Riots become rebellions, and rebellions, war; at the climax, power shifts—or seems to—as a ruler or a class is deposed and the state transformed.

In some ways the appearance resembles reality: the populace experiences the growth of popular emotion, of disaffection from old authority, of new loyalties, and perhaps of actual power. But these developments are by no means inevitable. Frequently, established authority emerges not only unscathed but stronger after putting down upheavals against itself. And in the course of "successful" revolutions the way is never free of failure, of loss of popular support, for example, of weariness, declining faith, and confusion.

Certainly confusion and weariness abounded in the American colonies early in the struggle over the Townshend acts. At this time no self-conscious revolutionary movement existed in America, but rather a determination to resist unconstitutional authority, which was much stronger in urban communities and among professionals, merchants, skilled craftsmen, and the great planters in the southern colonies who produced staples for the market than it was in the countryside remote from markets and communications. Yet there were divisions within these groups, especially among the merchants, who resented their financial losses in the resistance to the Stamp Act.

Confusion, weariness, and resentment affected the initial reactions among Americans to the Townshend program. Whether the new duties constituted a violation of colonial rights was a question honestly asked; the answers did not always dispel the confusion. Long after the appearance of John Dickinson's *Letters from a Farmer in Pennsylvania* (1767–68), which insisted that the duties encroached upon the constitutional rights of the Americans just as the Stamp Act had, Richard Henry Lee, the Virginia planter, wrote that the duties were "not perhaps, literally, a violation of our rights," though he added that they were "arbitrary" and "unjust." Lee read Dickinson's essays on the Townshend program and he eventually became convinced that American rights had been violated, but he with others was slow to come to this conclusion.[1]

Others, especially merchants who knew that they would be called upon to give up the importation of English goods if the public construed the new duties the way they had the stamp tax, simulated confusion about whether rights were at stake, or attempted to avoid the constitutional issue altogether. Rather than discuss rights and liberties, they moved immediately to the issue of nonimportation as if to head off any demand that they reinstitute what had apparently worked so well the year before. They showed themselves first in Boston, whose example everyone knew would be important elsewhere in America. Early in September, news of the Townshend policies having arrived in August, the *Boston Evening Post* opened the campaign against nonimportation. Among the earliest articles, one held forthrightly that nonimportation pressed too hard on the merchants who had to bear the sacrifices virtually alone and without reimbursement. Two weeks later "a true Patriot" attacked the "Blow-coals," presumably the group around Otis, as giving way to "political enthusiasm" in their opposition to British measures; and "Libernatus" stressed that as a "remedy" nonimportation fell unequally on the merchants. Nonimportation, he concluded, is a "partial" method, "the consent partial, the execution partial." In October "A Trader" argued that besides violating the "civil liberties" of merchants, nonimportation would ruin business. According to the "Trader," only those who have "no property to lose" favored it, and he pronounced them "brawling boys" and "hectoring bullies."[2]

1   Richard Henry Lee to John Dickinson, March 1768, James Curtis Ballagh, ed., *The Letters of Richard Henry Lee* (2 vols., New York, 1911–14), I, 27. In July, he wrote Dickinson a letter of praise for giving a "just alarm" to Americans about their endangered liberties; *ibid.*, 29.

2. *Boston Evening Post*, Sept. 7, 16, 27, Oct. 12, 1767.

Naturally, little of this went unanswered. The *Boston Gazette* made the case for nonimportation, though only after a period of indecision, in late summer 1767. Eventually it created or picked up a slogan that served well in the controversy: "Save your money, and you save your country."[3] Elsewhere in the colonies—Philadelphia, for example—this slogan caught on and appeared in newspapers and tracts. But in most colonies little was published about Townshend's policies until after the appearance of John Dickinson's *Letters from a Farmer in Pennsylvania*.[4]

John Dickinson called himself a farmer in these letters, but his ties to the soil were rather remote by 1767. He was the son of a planter in Maryland, where he was born in 1732 and where his father practiced law. The family moved to Dover, Delaware, when Dickinson was still a boy; in Delaware he received a classical education and began his legal training. In 1754 he entered the Middle Temple in London for the study of law and remained there until 1756. On his return he practiced law in Philadelphia, earned a small fortune, and eventually established a handsome country estate in Delaware. Like so many lawyers, he found politics irresistible, and in 1760 he was elected to the assembly in Delaware and two years later to the assembly in Pennsylvania.[5]

Dickinson's *Letters* struck the colonies with a peculiar impact, unsurpassed, according to many historians, until Thomas Paine's *Common Sense* appeared in 1776. The letters were published first in the *Pennsylvania Chronicle* and reprinted in all but four colonial newspapers. Collected, they made their appearance as a pamphlet in several editions—three in Philadelphia, for example, two in Boston, and still others in New York and Williamsburg. Benjamin Franklin, ordinarily on the opposite side of the political fence in Pennsylvania, was sufficiently impressed to write a brief preface for the edition published in London in June 1768. And others, sensing the importance of the essays, had them reprinted in Paris and Dublin.[6]

The essays appealed to a people fatigued by the strain of extravagant

3. *Ibid.*, Nov. 2, 1767.
4. The "Farmer's Letters," as they were immediately called, appeared in twelve installments in the *Pennsylvania Chronicle and Universal Advertiser* (Phila.). The first appeared Dec. 2, 1767. I have used the edition edited by Forrest McDonald, *Empire and Nation* (Englewood Cliffs, N.J., 1962).
5. David L. Jacobson, *John Dickinson and the Revolution in Pennsylvania, 1764–1766* (Berkeley and Los Angeles, 1965) provides biographical details and a shrewd analysis. McDonald, *Empire and Nation* contains a short sketch.
6. McDonald, *Empire and Nation*, xiii.

rhetoric and violent measures. Their tone is established by Dickinson's modest recommendations of further petitioning as a method of obtaining repeal of the Townshend duties; he also proposed economy, frugality, hard work, and home manufacturing, all for the purpose of lessening the consumption of English goods. His language is mild, even meek in places—as, for example, in the suggestion, "Let us behave like dutiful children who have received unmerited blows from a beloved parent," a proposal George Mason had scorned the year before in the aftermath of the Stamp Act. Within these submissive inflections, the message was inescapable: although Parliament possessed the right to regulate commerce, it had no right whatsoever to levy duties for revenue. And however disguised as regulation, the Townshend duties were taxes to raise money on the colonies, an "experiment," Dickinson wrote, to test the colonists' disposition, and, if it were acquiesced in, "A direful foretel-ler of future calamities." Dickinson's clarity of analysis and his modest phrasing forced Americans to confront the constitutional implications of the Townshend duties—or, perhaps more accurately, made it possible for the reluctant and the confused to confront them without endorsing the popular upheavals that had marked the crisis of the Stamp Act. Still, action bent toward forcing the repeal of the Townshend duties did not follow hard on the heels of the *Pennsylvania Farmer.*[7]

The reasons lie in that gray area of public will and mood. Dickinson had informed men's minds as to the constitutional issues but left their passions unmoved—indeed, left them in the trough of exhaustion where popular emotion had fallen in summer 1766. Normal desires prevailed then—desires for business and profits as usual. Recognizing these desires, Dickinson offered an incisive critique of the constitutional issues raised by the Townshend duties and with it sweet reason and condemnation of mobbish violence. His appeals for childlike submissiveness, his quiet calls for petitioning and home manufacturing, seem to have comforted many precisely because they asked for so little. What Dickinson could not supply were lurid descriptions of plots against liberty, of sinister conspiracies of a degenerate ministry determined to enslave the liberty-loving Americans. The colonists read the *Letters*, agreed, and with few exceptions did nothing.

The exceptions—who, not surprisingly, lived in Boston—turned out to be rather important. They did not include James Otis—at least they did not until sometime after the first of January 1768. On one of his curious gyrations in the autumn, Otis evidently argued in the Boston

7. For the quotations, see Letters 3 ("Let us behave . . .") and 11 ("a direful fortel-ler . . .") from Virgil, *Aeneid*, Book 3.

meeting for the constitutionality of the Townshend duties. The town may have been impressed; in any event it turned down demands that it endorse nonimportation of British goods. It contented itself with a resolution calling for reduced consumption of certain specified British goods which, according to the town, were superfluous anyway. Curiously, the articles slated for the Townshend duties were not included, but the town did resolve to encourage the manufacture of paper and glass.[8]

A week later the Customs commissioners arrived from England. Their arrival had been expected—they were already odious figures—but its timing was a stroke of bad luck: November 5, Guy Fawkes Day, a day ordinarily of riotous behavior. Somehow they avoided all abuse, though they were greeted by a large crowd parading with effigies of "Devils, Popes, & Pretenders," all with labels on their breasts reading "Liberty & Property & no Commissioners."[9]

The presence of the commissioners, visible embodiments of a parasitic policy, might have given the faction an advantage, but still they were unable to push through a nonimportation agreement. Late in December they evidently persuaded the town to instruct its representatives in the legislature to protest against the Townshend duties, and by this time several small towns, eventually numbering around twenty-five, passed nonconsumption agreements in obvious imitation of Boston. Although the spread of the boycott must have been encouraging, all the signs indicated that the province would submit to the Townshend program.[10]

Governor Bernard confessed to an uneasy delight at the absence of opposition. In December, just before the legislature convened, Otis seemed less threatening to the governor and, as the new session stretched into January 1768, calm evidently prevailed. Bernard remained anxious—wounds, he wrote Secretary of War Barrington, sometimes "skinned-over" without healing. Bernard did not know and could not find out during these peaceful January days that the House, under Sam Adams's tutelage, was writing a series of protests to its agent Dennys De Berdt, Secretary Shelburne, and others it considered friendly, asking that the Townshend acts be repealed. The House also sent a moderate but clear appeal to the king—again without informing the governor.[11]

8. BRC, *Reports*, XVI, 227–29.

9. [Ann Hulton], *Letters of a Loyalist Lady* . . . (Cambridge, Mass., 1927), 8.

10. BRC, *Reports*, XVI, 229–30; Jensen, *Founding*, 270.

11. For Bernard's statement, Channing and Coolidge, eds., *Barrington-Bernard Correspondence*, 132. For the letters to De Berdt and Shelburne, see Harry Alonzo Cushing, ed., *The Writings of Samuel Adams* (4 vols., New York, 1904–1908), I, 134–52, 156.

At the end of January the "skinned-over" wounds burst, and the governor got a good look at the infection below. By this time James Otis had reasserted his claim to leadership of the popular faction, and now with Sam Adams he called upon the House to approve a letter to all the colonies which urged a united stand against the new program of Townshend. The response from the House, a rejection of the proposal by a majority of two to one, came as a nasty shock.[12]

Otis and Adams rarely misjudged the temper of their colleagues. They had in this case, probably because the House had proven willing to petition king and ministers a few days earlier. Petitioning, of course, was the right of subjects and of legally constituted bodies such as colonial legislatures; a letter to official bodies in the colonies calling for opposition to a statute passed by Parliament was another matter. The House, heavily composed of representatives from small towns which as yet did not feel deeply threatened by the Townshend program, hesitated to issue such a challenge.

Not quite two weeks later, on February 11, 1768, the Otis-Adams faction tried again and this time succeeded in passing the Circular Letter. A shocked and disappointed Bernard attributed their success to "private Cabals" and unscrupulous tampering with House members. Sam Adams, who had a common touch lacking in Otis, undoubtedly used all his no-nonsense charm and his influence on the membership.

Adams was born September 16, 1722, in Boston, a son of Deacon Samuel Adams and Mary Fifield Adams. His father was a small businessman, a maltster, who provided Boston a part of the malt that went into its beer. Besides his house and lot the elder Adams owned several slaves and a small amount of land. He was never wealthy but he was well-fixed.

Sam Adams's father was a justice of the peace and active in the town meeting. He seems usually to have been in opposition to the royal governor. He helped organize the Land Bank in Massachusetts in 1740, a bank that issued notes against the security of land. It was an inflationist scheme, and Parliament, urged on by the governor, ended it shortly after it began. The elder Adams suffered financially in the collapse of the Bank. Not surprisingly, his losses did not increase his fondness for royal government in the colony. Sam Adams may have shared his father's feelings during this episode.

Although the elder Adams had not attended college, he wanted his

12. Jensen, *Founding*, 270–71.

son to. He sent Sam to the South Grammar School and then across the river to Harvard College, class of 1740. Sam did not cover himself with honors at Harvard. He was once fined for "drinking prohibited Liquors," but that hardly distinguished him. Perhaps the most unusual feature of his stay at Harvard was that he was so infrequently disciplined.

For a while Sam, or his father, thought of the ministry as a possible career, but though a strict Calvinist, he felt no great calling to the pulpit. After graduation he worked in the malt shop and then was apprenticed to an important merchant. His merchant-master soon decided that young Sam had no aptitude or interest in business and sent him home. Sam's father, probably beginning to feel uneasy about his son's future, then attempted to set him up in business. He lent his son £1000, which was soon lent to a friend and lost.

The senior Adams died in 1748. Sam inherited his father's property including the malt house. His father had left large debts, the result of the disastrous collapse of the Land Bank. His creditors attempted to have the estate, which had passed to Sam, sold to satisfy the debts. At the first sale Sam appeared and threatened the sheriff, charged with the responsibility for conducting the sale and the would-be purchasers. Nobody bought. This engaging spectacle was repeated four times: the sale was called, purchasers with cash showed up, Sam Adams appeared and spoke harsh words, the purchasers put away their still-bulging purses and stole off followed by the crestfallen sheriff. Adams proved much better at defending his property than increasing it or even maintaining it, and by the late 1750s when his creditors gave up he had spent most of the estate.

In 1756, after holding several minor town offices, Adams was elected tax collector, an important post. Public finance in Boston barely survived his tenure in office. Adams was not a dishonest collector, but he was inefficient. He remained in office for almost ten years, meeting his obligations to the town by using the money collected one year to pay the town for taxes not collected the preceding year. In 1765 he gave up the game with his accounts in arrears of £8000. Adams never paid up. The town's treasurer sued him and won a judgment of £1463. The town, however, refused to press for payment and in a few years forgave him the entire debt.

Boston's sympathy for Adams may have been stimulated by the Caucus Club, a political organization composed of artisans, merchants, tradesmen, a few lawyers and doctors. The club had formed perhaps thirty years before the Revolution, apparently in order to influence the town meeting. It nominated its own slate of candidates for local office and then did everything in its power to get them elected. John Adams reported in 1763 that the club met in the garret of Tom Daws, a bricklayer who served as the adjutant in the Boston militia. Sam Adams was a quiet but effective member.

The club seems to have been absorbed into the Sons of Liberty during the struggle against the Stamp Act in 1765. Sam Adams's part in the resistance of that year and the years immediately following was real though shadowy. Now in the crisis over the Townshend acts and the Circular Letter he came into his own.

To secure passage of the Circular Letter, Adams must have pronounced "due" all the political debts owed him. More important, timing favored the faction, for late in any session the representatives from interior towns tended to go home. Now in early February, the winter session drawing to a close, several conservatives from these towns departed, evidently secure in the belief that all important business had been dispatched. The remainder of the House, prompted and perhaps prodded by Adams, Otis, and company, passed the Circular Letter addressed to the speakers of the other colonial legislatures.[13]

The Circular Letter was not a "radical" document; it did not explicitly suggest that any measures be taken other than an attempt by the colonial legislatures to "harmonize with each other." As oblique as this proposal was, it was important, for it was calculated to invigorate the kinds of cooperation which had grown at the time of the Stamp Act. The major part of the letter included a firm statement of the colonial constitutional position. Nothing new appeared here except a firm rejection of the idea that the colonies could ever be represented in Parliament. The letter also stated well a view increasingly common in America that although Parliament was the supreme legislative body in the empire, it, like all governmental and political agencies, derived its authority from the constitution, the fundamental law which not incidentally guaranteed all subjects the right to be taxed only with their own consent. The grounds for objecting to the payment of salaries of royal officials from tariff revenues were scarcely less important—the equity, security, and happiness of the subject. As for the American Board of Customs Commissioners, its power to multiply subordinates and offices threatened colonial liberty.[14]

13. For "private cabals," Channing and Coolidge, eds., *Barrington-Bernard Correspondence*, 146. Jensen, *Founding*, gives a good account of the passage of the "Circular Letter," 249–50.

14. *EHD*, 714–16.

Speaker Cushing sent the Circular Letter to the speaker of every other colonial assembly. Several assemblies were not sitting, but by late spring, New Jersey's and Connecticut's had responded favorably and Virginia's House of Burgesses dramatically. The Burgesses, which had led the colonies in 1765, had not been in session since April 1767. Governor Francis Fauquier, who had absorbed the meaning of the Virginia Resolves, now saw the Burgesses as virtually a seditious body and prudently refrained from calling it except when he believed he had no choice. Fauquier died on March 1, 1768, and in his stead old John Blair, president of the Council, served until a successor arrived. Blair summoned the legislature at the end of the month and asked it to consider several pressing problems, among which Indian affairs seemed especially crucial. The speaker, Peyton Randolph, had no intention of ignoring such matters; nor did he mean to ignore the Circular Letter, which he promptly placed before the House. The Burgesses responded in a way that far exceeded the Massachusetts request for concerted representations to Britain. Armed with petitions from Virginia counties against the suspension of the New York Assembly, as well as against Parliamentary taxation, the Burgesses approved firm protests to king, Lords, and Commons. While making the conventional concession that Parliament might regulate imperial trade, the Burgesses insisted upon its equality as a legislature. It had no desire for an independent Virginia, but neither did it intend to see Virginia's rights infringed.[15]

This sort of argument had become familiar three years before. By May 16 the Burgesses moved onto less familiar terrain and issued a circular letter of its own. This letter advocated joint measures by the colonies against any British actions which "have an immediate tendency to enslave them." This proposal, vague on its face, was surely meant to imply that the colonies should not hesitate to reproduce all those engines of opposition they had developed in 1765–66. And if there was any doubt about the Burgesses' intentions, it went a long way toward clarifying them by announcing its hopes for a "hearty union" among the colonies.[16]

Most of the remaining assemblies had adjourned by the time the

15. McIlwaine and Kennedy, eds., *Jour. Va. Burgesses*, XI, 143, 145, 149, 151, 157, 161, 165–71. The petitions from the counties—Chesterfield, Henrico, Dinwiddie, and Amelia—protest against the suspension of the New York legislature as "a fatal Tendency, and seemed so destructive of the Liberty of a free People." *Ibid.*, 145.

16. Jensen, *Founding*, 252, quoting Charles F. Hoban, ed., *Pennsylvania Archives*, 8th Ser., VII (Harrisburg, Pa., 1935), 6189–92.

Massachusetts Circular Letter reached them. At least one—Pennsylvania's—had not, but, after hearing the letter read in May, did nothing. The legislature was in the hands of the Quaker party, now in a period of decline but unaware of the fact, and it feared the consequences of ruffling Parliamentary feathers. As in 1765, the Quaker party was in pursuit of a royal charter—a vain desire, but one which deflated any notions of challenging royal authority.[17]

II

While these colonies acted and delayed, in Massachusetts and London events were taking place which would make a favorable response to the Circular Letter almost inevitable and contribute to a further estrangement of the colonies from Britain. Compared with what took place between the governor and the faction after February 11, the Circular Letter looms as an act of disinterested statesmanship. Within two weeks both sides reverted to form—the faction resorting to invective, scurrility, and eventually to terror in an assault on Bernard and the Customs commissioners, and those royal worthies turning wildly to advocacy of a colonial representation in Parliament and, when the fatuity of that scheme became obvious to their obtuse minds, begging for troops to put down their tormentors. Locating the beginnings of this savagery is impossible—in one way or another it had begun with Bernard's arrival eight years earlier—but the Otis-led House gave a clear expression of its feelings when it accused Bernard of lying about it to the ministry at home. It then asked for copies of the governor's letters to the secretary of state, knowing that he would refuse, and when he refused, demanded his removal. Otis and Adams then gave Joseph Warren, a Boston physician, a chance to prove his mettle in the *Boston Gazette*. Warren did so in an article which approached the libelous, failing to reach it only by carefully omitting the governor's name, while accusing him of surrendering totally to "wickedness" and suggesting that he was closely related to the devil. Bernard should have realized that he could not win anything for himself or royal authority by taking on the *Boston Gazette*. But he evidently did not realize and, pronouncing the article a "virulent Libel," laid it before the Council and prepared to prosecute the printers of the newspaper. The Council wanted no part in this fray and advised bringing in the House of Representatives. Bernard's political masochism

17. *Ibid.*

was aching for satisfaction by this time and he followed the Council's advice. For two days the House pretended to deliberate and then dismissed the charge as without merit. According to Bernard, not an unprejudiced observer, the House's deliberations were enlivened by Otis—"the Canker Worm of the Constitution of this Government"—who raged "like a madman" in the House and abused everyone in authority.[18]

Chief Justice Thomas Hutchinson then made an effort to come to Bernard's defense. Hutchinson probably hated these brawls with the faction even more than Bernard, and he must have recognized that he would not succeed in getting the grand jury in Boston to indict the printers of the Gazette for libel. But Hutchinson, a loyal and determined man, ordered the attorney general to draw a bill against the printers and he presented it to the grand jury, which predictably voted it down. The agents of the faction who made no effort to conceal their activities— they "were seen publicly to haunt the Grand Jury-men"—proved more persuasive than the chief justice, governor, and attorney general combined. The grand jury made no indictment. While all this maneuvering was going on the "TRUE PATRIOT" made himself heard again in the Gazette, saying that he would not attempt to explain the "strange kind of compliment" that some paid to his recent piece by applying it to Governor Bernard. As for himself, he would "sooner cut my hand from my body" than impeach the reputation of an honest man. But, on the other hand: "whoever he is whose conscience tells him he is not the monster I have portraited, may rest assured I did not aim at him; but the person who knows the black picture exhibited, to be his own, is welcome to take it to himself." Bernard, perhaps realizing that he was diminishing his authority in these exchanges, now, belatedly, lapsed into public silence.[19]

Whatever moral authority Bernard might have exercised had long since vanished. A group of local merchants did not even consider asking his advice about how they might proceed against the Townshend Revenue Act; nor did they trouble to inform him of a nonimportation agreement they made early in March. He could not have persuaded the merchants to delay action any more than he could stop the mob from celebrating the anniversary of the repeal of the Stamp Act two weeks later. That

18. BG, Feb. 22, 28 (Warren's quotation), March 7, 1768 (Bernard's exchange with the Council); Letters to the Ministry from Governor Bernard, General Gage, and Commodore Hood (Boston, 1769), 8 ("virulent libel"), 9 (Bernard on Otis).

19. For the quotations, Letters to the Ministry, 11; BG, March 7, 1768. Hutchinson's part is explained in Jensen, Founding, 254–55.

night, March 18, a lonely group—Commissioner Burch, his family, and Thomas Hutchinson—spent the evening with the governor, while the mob—a great number of people of all kinds, ages, and both sexes—swirled through Boston's streets, parading, yelling, and occasionally gathering around the houses of the Customs commissioners. Little damage was done—a group of gentlemen leaders saw to that—but Bernard and his associates felt fear nonetheless.[20]

In this atmosphere of tension and—for royal officials, at least—terror, the Customs commissioners blundered as badly as the governor. They yielded to an impulse to strike back at one who had openly expressed his contempt for them and all their works. Their victim, whom they soon found to be an elusive target, was John Hancock, one of Boston's richest merchants. Hancock had snubbed the commissioners shortly after their arrival the previous year by refusing to allow the Cadet Company, a military organization which he captained, to participate in official exercises of welcome planned by Governor Bernard. Soon afterwards, he announced that he would not permit the company to attend a public dinner scheduled by the governor for the May election if the commissioners were to be present. The town backed up Hancock, who of course carried considerable influence in its meeting, by refusing the use of Faneuil Hall for the dinner.[21]

The commissioners saw an opportunity to square accounts in April when Hancock had two tidesmen, minor Customs officials, forcibly removed from below decks of his brig Lydia. The tidesmen had boarded the Lydia soon after she tied up; Hancock did not object to their presence until they went below without authorization and without a writ of assistance. When the matter came to the attention of the commissioners they instructed the province's attorney general to file a criminal information against Hancock. The charge was interference with Customs officers in the performance of their duty. After an investigation, the attorney general declined to proceed on the grounds that the tidesmen had exceeded their authority and that Hancock had acted legally in having them removed.[22]

The attorney general's opinion failed to satisfy the commissioners, who promptly appealed to the Treasury Board in England. The case they made reveals much about the sources of the British failure to

20. *Letters to the Ministry*, 13–17; "Diary of John Rowe," 65–66; and George G. Wolkins, "The Seizure of John Hancock's Sloop *Liberty*," MHS, *Procs.*, 55 (Boston, 1923), 269–70.
21. Jensen, *Founding*, 281.
22. *Ibid.*

govern successfully in America. Almost all of what the commissioners wrote indicates that they had proceeded with the intention of making an example of Hancock for what they deemed his political offenses. The procedural and legal issues of the matter were secondary to the challenge Hancock presented to royal authority. He was—they wrote— one of the leaders of the "disaffected" in Boston; he had affronted them when they arrived and then again over the public dinner. He was an avowed opponent of Customs policy. The commissioners' argument for criminal action against him rested on the assumption that if he were not prosecuted, royal authority in America would have sustained still another blow.[23]

For it was royal authority that concerned the Customs commissioners even more than the mundane job of collecting import duties and clearing entering and departing ships. Royal authority was a fascinating phrase, which to these officials seemed redolent of a declining empire. Thinking of its condition in America conjured up visions of popular government, an upstart equalitarianism, and the mob—frightful visions all, and all crying for exorcism. In an attempt to understand the Americans who entertained such madness, one of the commissioners, Henry Hulton, had traveled throughout Massachusetts and Connecticut to observe the delusions at first hand. Hulton's sense of superiority is clear in his descriptions of what he found: in their behavior in day-to-day life, as well as in those mobs which had terrorized Boston, the Americans showed a contempt for social rank. Yet they were energetic; a people of less energy could not have made the barren land pay. Even in this admission, grudgingly given, Hulton's incomprehension and his social remoteness are plain. He felt himself dealing with a lesser breed, hence his and the entire range of the placemen's prescriptions for Americans—bring them to order, make them respect authority—have origins in felt social differences as well as in the traditional policies of colonial government.[24]

Not that the Customs commissioners were indifferent to strict enforcement of regulations governing commerce. They were determined to see these regulations observed by the service they supervised and by the merchants. When they arrived in November 1767 they had been shocked by the state of the Customs in America—at least Hulton and Burch had been, for they were new to Boston. Temple and Paxton, who were experienced, had long recovered from whatever shock they felt when

23. Customs Commissioners to Lords of Treasury, March 28, 1768, in Wolkins, "Seizure," MHS, *Procs.*, 55 (1923).
24. Wallace Brown, "An Englishman Views the American Revolution: The Letters of Henry Hulton, 1769–1776," *HLQ*, 36 (1972), 15–24.

they first joined Customs, and Robinson, who had received a rough initiation when he tried to seize the *Polly* for smuggling molasses, knew something of American attitudes. With the exception of Temple, who had little use for the others, the commissioners intended to tighten up the system. Upon looking into the conduct of business in New England, they found smuggling "to a very great height" but only six seizures for violations in the past two and one-half years. And in these six seizures only one successful prosecution had followed; the other ships had either been retaken by mobs or released by local juries in court.[25]

The commissioners recognized that a part of their difficulty lay with their subordinates, some of whom took bribes, perhaps even solicited them. Their solution was to hire more officials, a curious decision and sure to fail unless they found some way to introduce honesty into the discharge of duties. Time soon demonstrated that they had failed.

Beaten by Hancock in the *Lydia* affair, the commissioners nursed their disappointment, and then on June 10 ordered Comptroller Benjamin Hallowell and Collector Joseph Harrison to seize Hancock's sloop *Liberty*. The *Liberty* had tied up on May 9 after a voyage from Madeira; she carried a cargo of wine, some of it "the best sterling Madeira," intended for Hancock's own table. The day the *Liberty* arrived, two tidesmen boarded to make certain that no cargo was unloaded that was not declared. The ship unloaded twenty-five casks of wine the next day; Hancock paid the required duty, and the tidesmen reported that nothing else was taken off. In the month that followed, the *Liberty* took on board barrels of whale oil and tar.[26]

On June 10, the day of the seizure, one of the tidesmen, Thomas Kirk, swore that he had lied in his report on the unloading of the *Liberty* in May; that, in fact, after refusing a bribe from one of Hancock's captains, he had been forcibly confined below decks on the night the ship arrived. Locked below, he had heard sounds of unloading for about three hours, and when released he had been threatened with violence if he did not hold his tongue. The other tidesman could give no evidence on any of this because, according to Kirk, he was home sleeping off too much drink. Kirk had decided to come forward, he said, because he was no longer afraid for his life, Hancock's captain who had terrorized him having died. The captain, it should be noted, had died on May 10.[27]

25. Wolkins, "Seizure," MHS, *Procs.*, 55 (1923), 264.
26. *Ibid.*, 251, 262–63.
27. *Ibid.*, 273–76.

Whatever the truth in this story—Kirk's account seems of doubtful authenticity—it served as a pretext for the action against the *Liberty*. The charge on which she was seized did not mention wine or the circumstances of her unloading in May, but rather indicted Hancock for loading the oil and tar without a permit. By a strict interpretation of the relevant statutes, Hancock was guilty; he had not posted the bonds and other papers before the cargo was taken aboard. He had not because the practice in Boston and almost every other colonial port was to load and then to take out the required papers, when the exact size and composition of cargo were known. The commissioners, emboldened by Kirk's "evidence," obviously ordered seizure on a technicality never before honored in Boston. As in the case of the *Lydia*, they believed they had the opportunity to strike a blow for royal authority by bringing low one of the most obnoxious opponents of the Crown in America. They may have totally believed Kirk's story, though if they did they must have discounted the popular explanation of his new-found honesty and courage: as an informer he stood to collect one-third of the proceeds from the confiscated ship and cargo.[28]

Hallowell and Harrison seized the ship at sunset and immediately signaled the *Romney*, a fifty-gun man-of-war, to move her away from the wharf and out into the harbor. The *Romney* dispatched a small boat to accomplish the job. Removing the *Liberty* proved to be difficult: a mob gathered and fought the contingent from the *Romney* to keep her tied up at Hancock's wharf. No one was killed or even seriously injured in the struggle, and the men from the *Romney* getting the upper hand towed the *Liberty* out under the guns of their ship. Thwarted at the wharf, the crowd, "chiefly sturdy boys and Negroes" according to Thomas Hutchinson, turned its attention to Harrison and Hallowell, who were lucky to escape with their lives. Hallowell absorbed more blows than Harrison, who ducked into an alley after being hit hard on the body. Left on the ground, bruised and covered with blood, Hallowell was rescued by several gentlemen in the mob—so much for Hutchinson's "boys and Negroes." The usual reprisals were made on the houses of the officials, windows broken and other minor damage done, though the houses escaped the gutting that had been standard practice in 1765. Before the night ended, the mob evidently grew to several thousand, surging through the streets hunting other Customs officials, beating them

28. Oliver M. Dickerson, *The Navigation Acts and the American Revolution* (Philadelphia, 1951), 231–42.

when it found them, and not calling quits until one in the morning.[29]

The weekend was quiet—"Saturday and Sunday evenings are sacred," Hutchinson observed.[30] Beneath the surface calm on both sides, Hancock and the Sons of Liberty and the authorities were planning their next moves. The Customs commissioners had little trouble in deciding what they should do and fled with their families and subordinates to the security of the *Romney*. That recourse did not seem appropriate or necessary to Governor Bernard, who on Monday met with the Council in an unsuccessful effort to persuade the councillors to ask for troops. The councillors were cool to the idea, telling the governor that "they did not desire to be knocked on the Head." In contrast, the Sons of Liberty were hot, announcing that they proposed "to clear the Land of the Vermin, which are come to devour them."[31]

Before the week was out the Sons were, as both Bernard and Hutchinson admitted, in complete control of the town. They converted a mass meeting at Liberty Hall (as the ground under Liberty Tree was called) into a succession of legal town meetings; they listened to all sorts of wild proposals from the cranks in their midst (such as bringing all men-of-war in the harbor under the orders of the town meeting) and then quietly petitioned the governor to order the *Romney* to leave Boston; they restated the familiar case against Parliamentary taxation; and they instructed the town's representatives to the House to do all they could to prevent further impressments and to inquire into the report that the Customs commissioners or someone else had requested that royal troops be sent to Boston.[32]

The town's resolution about troops carried an ominous meaning. Bernard must have read it with a special sort of horror, for he had long wanted troops sent in but dared not ask for them without the Council's approval. The Customs commissioners were under no such restraints and had long since requested troops, explaining in justification that the "Governor and Magistracy have not the least Authority or power in this place." Bernard knew of the commissioners' desires—he had pleaded his own inability to gratify them often enough—but he would not act on his own, even though he was now admitting that his power had

29. Wolkins, "Seizure," MHS, *Procs.*, 55 (1923), 281 (Hutchinson quotation). Bernard's account, written the next day, is in *Letters to the Ministry*, 20–21. See also "Diary of John Rowe," 67.
30. Wolkins, "Seizure," MHS, *Procs.*, 55 (1923), 281.
31. *Letters to the Ministry*, 24, 22.
32. BRC, *Reports*, XVI, 259; *Letters to the Ministry*, 25.

evaporated. He does not seem to have been terribly frightened for his own safety, though a friend had told him to "get out of the way" should troops arrive; rather, he was deeply depressed by the weakness of his government in Massachusetts. And he knew that he faced still another crisis, for Hillsborough's instructions to "require" the House to rescind the Circular Letter had just arrived. Bernard must have known that the House would refuse, and he must have known that dissolving the House when it refused, as ordered by Hillsborough, the Secretary of State for the American Colonies, would not answer anything.[33]

Still, Bernard had no choice, and on June 21, in an atmosphere still acrid with the smoke of the *Liberty* riot, he transmitted Hillsborough's order to rescind. The House stalled for a few days, and Otis gave a feverish speech, once more seemingly unrelated to the issues at hand but in fact calculated to rouse American revulsion at English degeneracy, while the faction carefully measured its supporters. Bernard pressed for a reply three times and on June 30 received what he dreaded: a negative vote of ninety-two to seventeen and a message from the House describing its Circular Letter as "innocent," "virtuous," and "Laudable." The governor then did as ordered: he dissolved the legislature.[34]

Sending the House packing only made matters worse for Bernard and royal authority. The Sons of Liberty now had still another issue: the freedom of the people's representatives to gather and petition for redress of grievances was now being denied. Hillsborough's bad-tempered letter to Bernard, soon spread all over the newspapers, did not soothe troubled spirits either. Together, Hillsborough and Bernard had given the popular party opportunities it would not fail to use.

House members who had voted against rescinding the Circular Letter, now raised to sainthood as the "Glorious Ninety-two," soon had the exquisite pleasure of reading their names in the *Boston Gazette*. The rescinders, invariably described in less flattering terms, also found their names in print. Those members who had been unfortunate enough to be absent when the vote was taken got the point and began falling all over themselves in their haste to write Speaker Cushing announcing that had they been present the Glorious Ninety-two would have been an even larger group. Speaker Cushing obliged them by giving their letters to the *Gazette*, which printed them. This sort of pressure to

33. Wolkins, "Seizure," MHS, *Procs.*, 55 (1923), 270.
34. *BG*, July 4, 1768, for the quotations and the vote. See also "Diary of John Rowe," 68; and *Letters to the Ministry*, 32.

conform to the popular line was hardly subtle, but it was mild compared with the attacks in the *Gazette* on several of the rescinders.[35]

By this time Otis, Adams, and their cohorts were old hands at using the press. They very nearly outdid themselves during summer 1768. Constitutional issues were skillfully explained—especially the threat to liberty created by the dissolution of the House—and new versions of the ministerial plot against the colonies relayed. Sam Adams did much of the writing in the summer, often under the name "Determinatus." As "Determinatus" he summed up the reasons for the people's anger in these words:

> I am no friend to *"Riots*, Tumult, and unlawful Assemblies," I take upon me to say, any more than his Excellency is: But when the People are oppressed, when their Rights are infringed, when their property is invaded, when taskmasters are set over them, when unconstitutional acts are executed by a naval force before their eyes, and they are daily threatened with military troops, when their legislature is dissolved! and what government is left, is secret as a *Divan*, when placemen and their underlings swarm about them, and Pensioners begin to make an *insolent* appearance—in such circumstances the people will be discontented, and they are not to be blamed. . . .[36]

Adams did not exaggerate the popular unease; the governor also reported it to his superiors in London.

There were signs other than newspaper reports. A little more than a week after the dissolution of the House, around fifty Sons of Liberty attempted to capture John Robinson, a Customs commissioner, at his home in Roxbury. Rumor had it that Robinson had left the safety of the castle where he had fled in June. The rumor was false, and the Sons settled for breaking down Robinson's fruit trees and the fence around his house. Later in July a much larger crowd tried to extract a resignation from John Williams, the inspector general of Customs, but he refused to be intimidated.[37]

The governor was frightened, however, by these rumblings and said so in a series of despairing letters home. A "trained mob," he reported, controlled the town. He felt himself to be between "two fires," the mob, which would blame him if he requested troops, and the British authorities, who would blame him if he did not. A few days after writing he decided to ask the Council to join him in a request for troops and received the reply he expected—a unanimous "no." Deeply depressed,

35. *BG*, July 11, 18, 1768.
36. *Ibid.*, Aug. 8, 1768.
37. *Letters to the Ministry*, 38, 45–46; "Diary of John Rowe," 68.

he wailed to Barrington, "it is all over now," unaware that things would soon look darker.[38]

In the summer the Otis-Adams group may have exuded a confidence that they did not feel. There were stories circulating that troops were on the way, and troops would at least temporarily strengthen the hands of Bernard and the commissioners. To keep up popular enthusiasm for the cause, Otis and Adams kept the presses screaming and on August 15, the anniversary of the Oliver riot, put on a lavish celebration complete with cannon firing, music (including the "American Song of Liberty"), a great parade, and fourteen toasts, ending with one to the "Glorious NINETY-TWO." Then more cannon were fired, and the gentlemen present repaired to the Greyhound Tavern in nearby Roxbury for a "frugal but elegant" dinner. More toasts followed, and after the Liberty Tree in Roxbury was consecrated, the entire group returned to Boston.[39]

III

Governor Bernard hated such expressions of the "popular" will, but his nerve held until early September, when an article in the Gazette, "containing a System of Politicks, exceeding all former Exceedings," forced him into a strategic mistake. The article, actually a series of queries by "Clericus Americanus," purported to deal with the various grievances long discussed by Americans. What caught Bernard's eye was the answer to "Sidney's" question: What shall we do if troops are sent to Boston? Clericus Americanus answered with horrifying bluntness: the colonies must declare their independence. Bernard had received word on August 27 that troops had been dispatched to Boston. Dreading an "insurrection" should they arrive unannounced—and convinced by Clericus Americanus that the situation would be explosive—on September 9 he leaked the information he had of the troops' coming and thereby made more trouble for himself. For on telling what he knew, he gave the popular leaders time to prepare. An unannounced arrival surely would have gone unopposed and just as surely would have deprived the faction of its opportunity to organize a good deal of barely latent hostility. As it was, the popular leaders used the troops' coming both before and after their actual arrival to organize outlying towns. In seeking to forestall opposition, Bernard helped spread it.[40]

Boston's town meeting gave Bernard an inkling that he had miscalcu-

38. Channing and Coolidge, eds., Barrington-Bernard Correspondence, 167–70.
39. BG, Aug. 22, 1768; "Diary of John Rowe," 68–69.
40. Letters to the Ministry, 52. Bernard mentioned an article in BG, Sept. 5, 1768. See also ibid., Aug. 29, Sept. 19, 1768.

lated by sending a committee to see him to ask officially about his knowledge of the coming of troops; it also requested that he call the legislature. The governor replied immediately that his information was "of a private nature" and that he had no authority to call another assembly until he received orders from the king. Bernard has been accused of lying in both these statements, a severe accusation but not as strained as his reading of his instructions from Hillsborough.[41]

The town simply refused to be denied. If it could not have the legislature, it would call a convention of towns to consider the crisis at hand. The selectmen also dredged up an old statute—"a good and wholesome law of this Province"—providing that every soldier and householder should have a musket and ammunition and urged compliance. Their reasons: the "prevailing apprehension, in the minds of many, of an approaching war with France," a grim joke substituting France for England, but not amusing to the governor. To ensure that no one missed the point, the selectmen brought four hundred muskets into the meeting, where they lay on display.[42]

A little more than a week later, on September 22, the convention of towns met in Boston. Otis, Cushing, Samuel Adams, and John Hancock represented Boston; Cushing was chosen to preside and Adams to serve as clerk. The convention opened with seventy representatives from sixty-six towns and several districts in attendance, and before it closed on September 27 representatives from another thirty towns arrived. A contemporary observer, the Reverend Andrew Eliot of Boston, reported that the convention was divided into three "parties": one, fearing that it was illegal, wished it to disband; another willing to trust the people without any restraints; and a third wishing to sit until the troops arrived and then to take things—presumably the government—into their own hands. The actions of the convention suggest that moderates eventually controlled its deliberations, however divided its delegates.[43]

The first order of business was a skirmish with the governor, set off by a petition to that worthy. The convention denied in its opening shots that it had any claim to "authoritative or governmental Acts," but it also pointed out that its members came from all over the province, a fact, it suggested, which indicated that anxiety was widespread. To ease the people's fears, the governor should call the legislature, which

41. BRC, *Reports*, XVI, 260, 261.
42. *Ibid.*, 264.
43. "Letters from Andrew Eliot to Thomas Hollis," MHS, *Colls.*, 4th Ser., 4 (Boston, 1858), 428.

could then deliberate on how to meet the threat of a standing army and request a redress of grievances. The governor refused to receive this petition and urged the convention to break up, hinting in a brief note that the delegates might face criminal action if it did not. This brought a stiff message from Thomas Cushing asking "wherein the Criminality of our Proceedings consists." Bernard again refused to receive any communication from the convention, and it went into secret session. What came out of these meetings was a "Result of the Convention" and a petition to the king. These documents did not advance colonial constitutional theory, nor did they threaten to oppose the landing of troops with force. After reviewing the recent history of colonial affairs, the "Result" simply made plain the convention's desire for a meeting of the legislature.[44]

This demand was less important for the development of colonial resistance than the fact that the convention met at all. It was not a criminal body, nor was it illegal; yet it did mark an extension of defiance of royal authority. There seems to have been little disposition among its members to fight the British army. Otis apparently said little; Adams may have spoken more, but he did not demand the use of force; Cushing opposed armed resistance, though he did recommend that Bernard and Hutchinson be driven from the colony. But Boston was not Massachusetts, and the hatred, the tensions, and the awareness of the threat to political liberty posed by the troops were all less intense in the towns and on the farms of the interior than in Boston.[45]

The day after the convention ended, transports carrying troops from Halifax, elements of the 14th and 29th Regiments, began entering Boston harbor. More arrived the next day accompanied by warships. On October 1 they disembarked under the guns of men-of-war all in a line.[46]

The governor may have felt relief, but he confessed to pessimism about the future of royal government in the province. The Sons of Liberty seem to have shared this feeling but were happy. There was no reason to be happy—Bernard's ordeal was not yet complete, and Boston's and America's had not yet really begun.

44. *BG*, Sept. 26, 1768. The *BG* printed the "Result" on Oct. 3, 1768.
45. There is a thoughtful review of these events in Jensen, *Founding*, 294–96.
46. "Diary of John Rowe," 69.

9

The "Bastards of England"

British troops did not end Boston's disaffection; they simply gave it another focus—themselves. The immediate problem they faced was the refusal of town and provincial authorities to pay for their housing. Governor Bernard blustered and threatened in an unsuccessful attempt to extract money from the legislature; Colonel Dalrymple spoke coolly but to no purpose; and General Gage arrived from New York only to discover that he could accomplish nothing. For a short time, the "Manufactory House," a building the province sometimes used to house a spinning school and a linen-making works, seemed available but just as Dalrymple was about to quarter some of his men there, several dozen poor families took up residence—and refused to be moved. Otis, Adams, and company probably "encouraged" these families to claim the building, in any case Dalrymple recognized that evicting the poor would bring him more grief than space.[1]

While all these little conflicts were enacted, a part of the troops pitched tents on the common, some went into Faneuil Hall, still others resorted to Castle William. Before too long Gage and Bernard authorized the use of royal funds for the renting of several large warehouses which were then converted to rough barracks. The owners of these buildings encountered little if any public enmity—taking British money apparently did not compromise one's opposition to the quartering of troops.

1. *Letters to the Ministry from Governor Bernard, General Gage, and Commodore Hood* (Boston, 1769), 57–60, 67–68; "Diary of John Rowe," 69.

II

Such transactions might not have been understood elsewhere in the colonies. They were not widely known but news of the troops' arrival in Boston soon was. The coming of the soldiers topped off a summer of ferment and virtually assured that the Massachusetts appeal in the Circular Letter would receive powerful support.

Hillsborough prepared the way for colonial action; some colonists said that he left them no choice. For in April, when he sent Governor Bernard orders which eventually produced the smashing anti-rescinding vote, he also dispatched his own circular letter to the other colonial governors instructing them to inform their assemblies that no notice was to be taken of the letter from Massachusetts. Should the assemblies ignore this command, the governors were to dissolve them.[2]

Hillsborough's fatuity, the scorn heaped on him by the House of Representatives in Massachusetts, the arrival of soldiers in Boston, along with information about the *Liberty* riot and the Customs commissioners, all helped call forth official declarations endorsing the Circular Letter and protesting against the Townshend acts. But beyond these events and the circumstances surrounding them, local politics continued to affect the form, the substance, and the timing of colonial resistance.

New Jersey, Connecticut, and Virginia had required none of the provocation these events supplied and had acted in late winter or early spring. The Maryland assembly may have needed no more, but Governor Horatio Sharpe in a well-meaning and dutiful act gave it a spur it could not ignore. In late June, Sharpe sent along Hillsborough's letter with a message of his own meant to be reassuring but saying that he trusted the assembly would take no "notice" of the Circular Letter. A repetition of Hillsborough's language was about as inept a tactic as he could have used. The delegates replied that they would not be "intimidated by a few sounding Expressions, from doing what we think is Right," but refused to say what they considered right. They did not keep the "right" from Sharpe for long: the next day they approved a petition to the king protesting against the Townshend duties and appealing for redress. The leading assumption of the petition varied little from what by this time had become virtually an American doctrine: it was, the assembly declared, "a fixed, and unalterable principle in the nature of things, and a part of the very idea of property that whatever a man hath honestly

2. *EHD*, 716–17.

acquired cannot be taken from him without his consent."[3] After receiving the caustic reply, Sharpe did not have to see the petition to know what he must do—and dissolved the assembly immediately.

During the autumn and early winter three other colonies, Delaware, North Carolina, and Georgia, which had played minor parts in the Stamp Act crisis, responded. The Delaware assembly formally received only the Virginia letter, but in October in a petition to the king it aligned itself with those who challenged the constitutionality of the new taxes. North Carolina approved a similar petition and conducted itself with a skill its governor, William Tryon, confused with "moderation." Tryon had learned three years earlier that the North Carolinians could be tough in a fight, and he chose not to dissolve the assembly despite Hillsborough's order. In Georgia the Commonshouse of Assembly decided to wait until late December, but it got off an address to the king modeled on the Circular Letter before Governor James Wright could dissolve it.[4]

In these colonies local factions either did not exist or managed to submerge their conflicts in the shared discontent over Townshend's program. Several other colonies did not act so easily. The Ward and the Hopkins factions in Rhode Island took the entire spring dividing up political spoils and working out a deal for the governorship, but over the summer they decided that the assembly should petition the king against the new taxes. By the time the king rejected the petition, the assembly, now running smoothly, informed the ministry that it shared the view of anti-rescinders in Massachusetts.[5]

Factions did not ordinarily disturb the sway of the tidewater planting elite in South Carolina. These rice planters had long enjoyed having things their own way in and out of government when in 1768 two sorts of challengers appeared. One, the Regulators in the backcountry, had actually begun to make themselves known the year before. The Regulators, so-named apparently because they sought to bring regularity, social order, law, and government to the West, were planters themselves though they did not raise rice. They also included other solid middle-

---

3. For Maryland and the quotations in this paragraph, William H. Browne et al., eds., *Archives of Maryland* (65 vols., Baltimore, 1883–1952), XXXII. 243, 244–45; LXI, 406–7, 420.

4. Jensen, *Founding*, 258–59 (Delaware); William W. Abbot, *The Royal Governors of Georgia* (Chapel Hill, N.C., 1959), 148–49; William L. Saunders, ed., *Colonial Records of North Carolina* (10 vols., Raleigh, N.C., 1886–90), VII, 881 ("moderation").

5. Lovejoy, *Rhode Island Politics*, 133.

class citizens, storekeepers, a few professionals, landowners, who in 1767, in exasperation at the indifference of the government, had taken the law into their own hands. They faced formidable problems—a backcountry still reeling from the ravages of the Cherokee War (1760–61), abounding with criminal gangs that plundered their respectable neighbors, and almost totally deficient in governmental and other institutions. By March 1768, organized into ranger companies, the Regulators had killed or driven out most of the criminals and, inflated with success, taken upon themselves debt collection, the supervision of family life, and an eager but crude program of putting the unemployed to work. By autumn they had beaten back eastern attempts to curb these activities and in the October election managed to elect two or three of their number to the legislature. They took no discernible stand on the Townshend measures: they had more immediate concerns such as the extension of representative government to the West. Their demands and their use of force had distracted the legislature for almost two years, however.[6]

The legislature in South Carolina had at its doorstep still another group with a different set of demands. The mechanics of Charleston had become politically aware several years earlier at the time of the Stamp Act. Now in October 1768 with elections to be held, they nominated Christopher Gadsden, a merchant and a planter, not a craftsman, and proceeded to hold mass meetings celebrating American "liberty." They drank toasts to the "Glorious Ninety-two," "consecrated" a liberty tree, sang John Dickinson's Liberty Song, praised and toasted John Wilkes, and urged the assembly to defy Hillsborough's order. Gadsden was elected but the assembly remained in the old comfortable hands. Still the old order had been shaken, both from the West and from within Charleston, and when the assembly met in November almost half its members avoided voting on the crucial issue. Governor Montagu in his address opening the session informed the House that he expected it to treat with contempt any seditious letters it had received—a transparent reference to the Massachusetts Circular Letter. The House declared that it had received no such letters and then adopted resolutions protesting against the Townshend duties and praising the letters from Massachusetts and Virginia. Of forty-eight members only twenty-six were present when these votes were taken, all from Charleston or nearby parishes; the others, either out of opposition or fear, stayed away. When the

6. Richard Maxwell Brown, *The South Carolina Regulators* (Cambridge, Mass., 1963), 1–82.

governor learned of these resolutions he followed his instructions and dissolved the assembly. It had sat for exactly four days.[7]

In Pennsylvania the Quaker party, which had successfully postponed action when the legislature received the Circular Letter, faced a gathering opposition as news of events in Massachusetts arrived. Joseph Galloway, the speaker of the Pennsylvania assembly, under the name "Pacificus" criticized Hillsborough in the *Pennsylvania Chronicle* but also urged delay until the colony's agents in London had a chance to appeal against the taxes. Galloway's actual reason for delay was to give Franklin more time to secure royal government for the colony; an official blast at Parliament or an endorsement of the Circular Letter could not make Franklin's task easier. Most of the colony seems to have opposed royal government, and in July, despite Galloway's ploy in the newspapers, a mass meeting in Philadelphia demanded united action in support of Massachusetts. By September when the assembly met, Galloway and the Quaker party seemed beaten—their patriotism was under attack for their apparent failure to protect colonial interests from an encroaching ministry while they were seeking further royal control. The assembly, now sensitized to popular feeling, sent off protests to king, Lords, and Commons denying Parliament's right to tax the colonies and claiming for Americans all the rights of Englishmen. But the assembly, prudently, did not approve the Circular Letter. Obviously Galloway had managed to salvage some of his authority.[8]

As in Pennsylvania, New York's factions sought to use imperial tensions for their own advantage. The legislature was awaiting elections when Massachusetts sent the Circular Letter. The Livingstons survived the elections in March 1768 though their grip on the assembly was loosened by the defeat of one of their chiefs, Robert R. Livingston of Dutchess County. An important leader in New York City, John Morin Scott, also lost his seat in the assembly. The Livingstons' problem was their record: under their guidance the assembly had finally complied with the Quartering Act and had supported the use of regular British troops against an upstate tenant uprising in 1766.[9]

The DeLanceys, though surely no more "patriotic" than the Livingstons, saw an opportunity in the Circular Letter to get their opponents turned out of office. Realizing that Governor Moore would dissolve the

7. Jensen, *Founding*, 260; Edward McCrady, *The History of South Carolina Under the Royal Government, 1719–1776* (New York, 1899), 603–13.

8. Charles F. Hoban, ed., *Pennsylvania Archives*, 8th Ser., VII (Harrisburg, Pa., 1935), 6168–69, 6271–80.

9. Jensen, *Founding*, 262.

assembly should it take up the Circular Letter, an event which would of course force new elections, the DeLanceys set about to compel the assembly to act. They did not have the votes indoors, but by a skillful, if heavy-handed use of newspapers, mass meetings, and an effigy-burning featuring Governor Bernard of Massachusetts, they won over a number of representatives sufficient to compel the assembly to endorse the popular constitutional case and take up the Circular Letter. No representative wanted to be tagged an "enemy" of "the country," a label the DeLanceys attached to those who refused to meet Hillsborough head-on. As soon as Governor Moore learned of the assembly's action at the end of December, he dissolved it and soon after called a new election. This election, which the DeLanceys won handily, brought home to everyone the practical meaning of the new patriotism.[10]

III

Beneath the actions of official bodies whose petitions, addresses, remonstrances, and circular letters seem on the surface remote from the passions of ordinary men lay a popular disaffection, a feeling soon to be transformed into anger. The concern of anonymous men over the new British policies had in fact helped dispose public bodies to act; the town meeting in Boston, for example, heard others besides Otis, Adams, and company. In Virginia, where strong resolves issued from the Burgesses, "sundry Freeholders" from a variety of counties met together and produced their own petitions protesting against the suspension of the New York assembly—"a fatal tendency . . . destructive of the Liberty of a free People"— and branding the Quartering Act and the Townshend duties as "cruel and unconstitutional."[11]

These petitions and similar ones elsewhere came out of small informal meetings, organized by men with no social standing and no offices but with their own interests and the public's in mind. For the next three years more and more such men took part in politics, or in those political activities directed against British policy. Protests against Britain marked a broadening of participation, a process encouraged by the atmosphere of urgency and crisis and by the fact that official bodies on all levels proved incapable of defending American interests with the effectiveness and passion a larger public demanded. The extension of this participation, however, was slow and uneven, as, for example, in the nonimportation movement of 1768 to 1770.

Economic coercion in the form of a refusal to import British goods

10. *Ibid.*, 262–64.
11. McIlwaine and Kennedy, eds., *Jour. Va. Burgesses*, XI, 145–46.

had worked three years before, and now in 1768, official and unofficial bodies looked to it again. Predictably the first attempts to conclude a nonimportation pact were made in Boston. The Junto, as the group around Sam Adams was called, tried first in the town meeting in October 1767; the legislature not sitting, the town, which had been a bellwether to the province, seemed a logical place to begin. The merchants who had already sounded their dislike of stopping trade now packed the meeting and voted down the proposals to end trade with Britain until the repeal of the new taxes. The best the Junto could get was a voluntary nonconsumption agreement, binding only those who signed not to use a list of British imports which did not even include all the dutied articles. The town also resolved to encourage local manufactures and singled out paper and glass as especially worthy of domestic production.[12]

The town recommended nonconsumption to the province as a whole and in irresistible language. Its subscribers proposed to stimulate local "industry," to cut the rise of British "superfluities," to curtail "luxury." This is the language of the Protestant ethic, appealing to values still deeply embedded in the culture of New England, and only slightly less so in the middle and southern colonies, where it later appeared in agreements banning importation of British goods. Its force was probably greatest in small towns where Protestantism survived uncorrupted by urban fashions. In any case during the next three months towns all over New England took up Boston's example and signed their own agreements not to consume British imports.

Whether the popular leaders in Boston ever believed that nonconsumption would affect British policy is not clear. But early in 1768 they pushed merchants toward closing down imports from Britain. To be sure not all merchants needed pressure; John Rowe, for example, confided to his diary his belief that the Townshend duties were "as dangerous as the Stamp Act,"[13] and Rowe agreed with other merchants in March to limit most British imports for a year. This agreement never went into effect, for these Boston merchants decided not to observe its terms until their competitors in New York and Philadelphia concurred. By mid-April virtually every merchant in New York had signed a similar agreement, but in June, a deadline set by the New Yorkers, the merchants of Philadelphia, despite pleas from John Dickinson, refused.[14]

12. BRC, *Reports*, XVI, 222–24. For the quotations in the next paragraph, see *ibid.*, 227–29.
13. "Diary of John Rowe," 63.
14. *Ibid.*, 65–66; Charles M. Andrews, "The Boston Merchants and the Non-Importation Movement," CSM, *Pubs.*, 19 (Boston, 1918), 204–6.

Philadelphia's merchants were neither grasping nor "unpatriotic." They did not lack principles, and they did not admire the new import duties. But they were freer than their colleagues in Boston and New York, freer of popular intimidation. Mobs had made themselves known in Philadelphia three years earlier but the city had not endured the convulsions of Boston and New York. And one important faction, the Quaker party led by Franklin and Galloway, playing for time and craving a royal charter, had dampened or at least divided popular enthusiasm. Hence in this atmosphere of moderation, though not of brotherly love, the merchants of Philadelphia felt able to defend their rights to business and profits even though they despised Parliamentary usurpation.[15]

Within eighteen months of the refusal of Philadelphia in June 1768, the atmospheres had darkened everywhere in America, and nonimportation had spread to every colony but New Hampshire. As before, Boston provided the impetus. Why merchants in Boston decided to draft another agreement is not hard to fathom. They had given up their first attempt only after Philadelphia backed away. Now, on August 1, another try seemed promising, indeed imperative, for revulsion against Hillsborough's circular letter was spreading; more importantly, the town had experienced riots against the racketeering of Customs commissioners, and it was listening to rumors that British troops would soon arrive. The merchants discussed their problems several times in the summer and on August 1, 1768, agreed to stop importation of most British goods for the year beginning January 1. Sixty of sixty-two merchants at this meeting signed, and within a few days almost all others in the town had followed suit.[16]

Near the end of August, merchants in New York approved an agreement requiring the importation of British goods to stop November 1 and not to resume until the repeal of the Townshend duties. Coupled with Boston's, the New York agreement drew Philadelphia to center stage. Newspapers in New York City and Boston printed letters and articles with unflattering remarks on the public spirit of Philadelphia merchants, and private correspondence must have been no less blunt. Still, the Philadelphia merchants held back until March 1769, when they finally entered an agreement similar to New York's. Most merchants subscribed within a couple of weeks, and their example inspired their associates in nearby Newcastle County, Delaware, to form a similar association in late August. New Jersey merchants also explicitly acknowledged

15. James H. Hutson, *Pennsylvania Politics, 1746–1770* (Princeton, N.J., 1972), 219–24.
16. "Diary of John Rowe," 68; Andrews, "Boston Merchants," CSM, *Pubs.*, 19 (1918), 206–8.

the importance of action in Pennsylvania and New York but delayed formal agreements until June 1770. They may have restricted trade before that time, however. When they did finally conform publicly, they moved in response to mass meetings in New Brunswick and in Essex County.[17]

While Philadelphia was dallying, nonimportation was gaining support in much of New England with the notable exceptions of Rhode Island, always a maverick, and New Hampshire, rarely one. In many of the towns of Massachusetts and Connecticut private organizations of merchants and town meetings both declared their commitments to nonimportation. Sometimes only one group acted, but in any case the town as a whole was thereby understood to be obligated to avoid bringing in or consuming goods from Britain. These agreements imposed sanctions of a sort, as for example in Norwich, Connecticut, where the town meeting promised to "frown upon all who endeavour to frustrate these good designs, and avoid all correspondence with those merchants who shall dare to violate these obligations." By autumn of the next year, 1769, the Connecticut assembly had given its approval in the form of resolutions of support of nonimportation.[18]

The southern colonies were not far behind despite the presence, especially in Virginia and Maryland, of a sizable group of Scottish factors who represented British commercial houses. Other merchants, for the most part native-born Americans, agreed with their brothers in the northern colonies that nonimportation required too great a sacrifice from a single financial interest, namely, themselves. Still Virginia acted in May 1769, Maryland in June, South Carolina in July, Georgia in September, and North Carolina in November.[19]

George Washington had helped precipitate Virginia's decision by sending a copy of the Philadelphia pact to his neighbor George Mason and by proposing in May that the House of Burgesses take the lead. When the burgesses met, they felt compelled to denounce Parliamentary taxation once more and to repeat the case for their own claims. Governor Botetourt decided against allowing this exercise to go on under his nose and dissolved the House well before it could enter any agreement. Undis-

17. Andrews, "Boston Merchants," CSM, Pubs., 19 (1918), 210–14. There is a fine account of non-importation in Arthur Meier Schlesinger, The Colonial Merchants and the American Revolution, 1763–1776 (New York, 1957).

18. F. M. Caulkins, History of Norwich, from Its Possession by the Indians to 1873 (New London, Conn., 1874), 369.

19. Andrews, "Boston Merchants," CSM, Pubs., 19 (1918), 215–21.

couraged, the former burgesses met as private citizens in the house of Anthony Hay of Williamsburg and joined in an agreement to end most importation from Britain. These Virginians did not bind themselves quite as tightly as northern subscribers did, but they proved their seriousness by prohibiting the importation of slaves after November 1. They promised also not to slaughter lambs weaned before May 1 of any year, a prohibition intended to stimulate the production of wool for home manufactures. All these restraints were to remain in force until the Townshend acts were repealed.[20]

While Virginia's nonimportation moved from the center—the Burgesses—outward into the counties, Maryland's began in the counties and eventually produced a broad agreement across the colony. The beginnings may have been in Baltimore, where in March 1769 a group of merchants, after considerable cajoling from Philadelphia's new believers, promised not to import British goods until the repeal of the Townshend acts. Two months later a meeting in Anne Arundel County concluded a similar agreement, followed by almost every other county in Maryland and on June 20 by a general meeting in Annapolis which formed a nonimportation association for the colony. Slightly more than half of the members of this meeting had sat in the lower house of the legislature the year before. In most respects the Maryland association resembled Virginia's, although it did not prohibit the importation of slaves.[21]

The third "tobacco colony," North Carolina, followed Virginia's example even more closely than Maryland. Governor Tryon dissolved the assembly early in November whereupon sixty-four of its seventy-seven members agreed on nonimportation resolutions modeled on Virginia's, including a ban on bringing in slaves. Most of these subscribers were planters—not merchants.[22]

Charleston planters and artisans carried South Carolina into nonimportation in July after a series of public meetings. By September most of the town and many in surrounding counties and parishes had subscribed to an agreement that barred importation of British goods with the exception of clothing for slaves, blankets, tools, powder, lead, wool cards,

---

20. Schlesinger, *Colonial Merchants*, 135–37. The Virginia resolutions have been published in *TJ Papers*, I, 27–31.
21. Charles A. Barker, *The Background of the Revolution in Maryland* (New Haven, Conn., 1940), 320–23. Ronald Hoffman, *A Spirit of Dissension: Economics, Politics, and the Revolution in Maryland* (Baltimore, 1973), 85–87, notes that Maryland's agreement did not contain many serious restrictions.
22. Schlesinger, *Colonial Merchants*, 148–49.

books, and pamphlets. A revised agreement included a ban on the importation of slaves.[23]

Shortly after completing this work, the general committee of planters, mechanics, and merchants of South Carolina, a group charged with the responsibility of supervising the new agreement, urged Georgia to align itself with the other colonies. The Sons of Liberty in Savannah, calling themselves the "Amicable Society," proceeded to do as they were bade and presented an agreement based on South Carolina's to a mass meeting on September 19 in Savannah. This meeting, which included few if any merchants, approved what were becoming the standard terms of the associations for restricting trade with Britain, not excepting a ban on importing slaves.[24]

All this patriotism up and down the colonies left the Rhode Island merchants cold, but not cold to trade with markets formerly controlled from nearby Massachusetts. Providence merchants now apparently succeeded in disposing of British imports in western Massachusetts, and Newporters imported goods from Britain including cargoes which had been turned back from as far away as Charleston, South Carolina. Merchants elsewhere regarded this behavior as crass profiteering, and those in the major northern cities resolved to turn the economic screws on Rhode Island by threatening to break off trade. The New Yorkers evidently did stop their business in October; an anonymous writer to the *Newport Mercury* described trade with Rhode Island as "nearly shut up, as if the Plague was there." The effects of these tactics were soon felt, and in less than a month merchants in both Providence and Newport had entered nonimportation agreements. Neither port, however, entirely satisfied colonial traders in neighboring colonies, who charged that the Rhode Islanders had left themselves ample opportunities to do business with Britain.[25]

Paralleling the gradual extension of nonimportation agreements were decisions by individuals and informal groups not to consume British products. Housewives in virtually all the colonies promised to stop serving tea to their husbands, at least tea imported from Britain. Others renounced fine clothes, the silks and satins that presumably graced the fashionable in England and America. And luxuries of all sorts were to

23. *Ibid.*, 140–47.
24. *Ibid.*, 147–48.
25. *Newport Mercury* (R.I.), Oct. 16, 1769 (quotation). See also Schlesinger, *Colonial Merchants*, 152–54. The account in the next two paragraphs is based on Schlesinger; the quotation about Lloyd is in Bridenbaugh, *Cities in Revolt*, 282.

be put aside by both men and women: college students to give up foreign wines; mourners the use of foreign-manufactured mourning dress in favor of plain homespun.

As was the case in 1765, nonimportation also spurred home manufacturing. Spinning bees assumed a new popularity, especially in small towns; spinning schools were established in cities and villages, and small-scale manufacturers of clothing and household articles appeared in greater numbers than ever before. The newspapers gave such activities a strong play and doubtless exaggerated their successes. The journey of one Henry Lloyd through the colonies, for example, was reported in many because he and his horse were decked out in American manufactures—"His clothes, Linnen, Shoes, Stockings, Boots, Gloves, Hatt, Wigg, and even Wigg Call, were all manufactured and made-up in New England." Undoubtedly the most impressive achievement was in the weaving of cloth. The women of Middletown, Massachusetts, wove 20,522 yards of cloth in 1769, and those in Lancaster, Pennsylvania, turned out almost 35,000 yards in a comparable period.

IV

Cooperation in home manufacturing and voluntary compliance by some merchants with nonimportation could not mask the need for coercion to bring others under the agreements. In fact, coercion of varying degrees was employed in all the colonies to produce the associations and to enforce their regulations. The merchants in the large cities drew particular attention, especially those whose primary business was with British ports. These merchants sent their ships along the routes of trade that permitted returns in "dry goods" manufactured in England. Naturally they felt themselves especially hard-pressed by the prohibitions against imports from Britain, and understandably they believed that they were paying the price for colonial constitutional liberties while those colleagues who traded in "wet goods," molasses and rum from the West Indies, escaped virtually untouched. They entered the same complaints against merchants whose trade was largely outside the empire.

Most merchants, at least in the northern cities, traded in and out of the empire, and they may have had difficulty in calculating precisely where economic advantage lay. Not that most did not share the popular constitutional position; they did and they said so, but they also wanted sacrifices spread as equitably as possible. The majority in Boston and New York joined the local nonimportation associations in August 1768 without much coaxing and with a minimum of pressure. The willingness of the Bostonians is easily understood; they felt threatened by the Customs commissioners, a feeling given intensity by what was popularly considered a fraud against Hancock in the seizure of the *Liberty*. Then there was the Boston mob—thoroughly outraged by a long series of oppressions, its temper frayed by riots, impressments, and the rumors of troops on the way—obviously a body willing to punish those who refused to shut off British trade. The New Yorkers also had to face popular discontents; in addition they felt the cramps of a trade depression and of currency shortages, conditions which made them all the more susceptible to suggestions that retaliation against the British was long overdue.[26]

In contrast, the Philadelphia merchants held out as long as they did because they had to contend with neither a mob nor a depressed trade. Yet they did come up against an increasingly restless collection of artisans who made and sold leather goods, furniture, clocks, tools, silverware, all items which were also imported from England. These artisans resented the English competition and sought to rid themselves of it, at least temporarily, by forcing merchants into nonimportation. Not a rootless proletariat, not rabble or scum, the artisans valued property and liberty as highly as the merchants or any other group did. But shared values did not inspire the same ideas about tactics, especially when one kind of tactic promised profits to artisans and losses to merchants.[27]

Artisans in Charleston, South Carolina, made their weight felt more effectively earlier in 1769 than did those in Philadelphia. The Charleston group had better leadership in the person of Christopher Gadsden, who in the summer helped pull them together and brought them into league with Carolina rice planters. Together the two groups insisted that the merchants agree to nonimportation. The merchants first tried to satisfy these demands by a relatively loose agreement, but after a series of mass meetings they met the terms of the artisans and planters. Previous to the general association of July the three groups had maintained separate committees; now they combined, and a committee of thirty-nine, thirteen representatives from each, was appointed with powers of enforcement.[28]

Although unconventional, this league of merchants, mechanics, and planters in Charleston was hardly more unusual than the resort to unofficial bodies in all the colonies to enforce nonimportation. Such bodies,

26. Schlesinger, *Colonial Merchants*, 105–34, *passim*.
27. Charles S. Olton, *Artisans for Independence: Philadelphia Mechanics and the American Revolution* (Syracuse, N.Y., 1975), 29–47, *passim*.
28. Edward McCrady, *The History of South Carolina, 1670–1783* (4 vols., New York, 1897–1902), 646–54.

most commonly called committees of inspection, operated without any formal sanction of government, which of course in normal times regulated trade. Merchants probably sat on most of these committees in the North; in the southern colonies, planters took the lead, for many of the merchants were foreign-born representatives of English or Scottish commercial houses. Artisans' committees played a prominent role in New York, Philadelphia, and Charleston, but in no case did they constitute a majority.

All groups were armed by the agreements to store or ship back goods that arrived in defiance of nonimportation. Slow communications accounted for some arrivals after the signing of the agreements; consignees in many cases had sent their orders long before the restrictions were imposed. Some of course were not so innocent, and should they fail to convince the local committee that they had no intention of violating their pledge, they might receive harsh treatment. At the least the committees ordered their cargoes stored or turned away. A celebrated case of this sort occurred in Maryland in early 1770 and involved the brigantine *Good Intent* carrying prohibited goods from London. The importers, the Annapolis firm Dick and Stewart, contended that their orders had been sent long before the Maryland association was established. After the agreement was signed, Dick and Stewart advertised in the *Maryland Gazette* that the goods were coming and asked for a ruling from the committee of Anne Arundel, Prince Georges, and Baltimore counties. Despite the firm's apparent openness in providing the records and correspondence surrounding their orders, the inspection committee remained suspicious and found against them. The *Good Intent*, cargo intact, sailed back to London at the end of February.[29]

The committee which heard the case of the *Good Intent*, like others in the colonies, proceeded on the assumption that those who deliberately violated the nonimportation resolutions were "Enemies to the Liberties of America." These words are from the Maryland agreement; most agreements contained similar denunciations of violators. Merchants who did not defy nonimportation but who did not subscribe to it were usually ignored—as long as they remained quiet. Those who refused to sign and who imported found their names published in the newspapers and their businesses shunned. Ostracism did not always satisfy committees of inspection and their supporters; violators sometimes received coatings of tar and feathers; sometimes they were driven from town, a favorite

29. *The Proceedings of the Committee Appointed To Examine into the Importation of Goods by the Brigantine Good Intent* . . . (Annapolis, Md., 1770), reprinted in *MdHM*, 3 (1908), 141–57, 240–56, 342–63.

punishment in New England; sometimes their warehouses were broken into and their goods damaged; and at still other times they were hung in effigy, forced to stand under gallows, and even ducked, as if they were petty criminals or accused of witchcraft.[30]

All these tactics drew upon a variety of groups—women engaged in spinning and home production, students who agreed to give up imported wines and tea, artisans and tradesmen of all sorts interested in capturing the market as well as defending constitutional principles, merchants who wanted a voice in the taxes they paid. Many had also resisted the Stamp Act; for them the Townshend crisis probably produced a confirmation of old ideas. For the others it was more of an awakening and an opportunity to make themselves known in local politics. Because the agitation over the Townshend policies lasted longer than that over the Stamp Act and, paradoxically, because there was more disagreement over how to respond, more groups—notably artisans and women—found their voices. The result was a more varied participation in public life, and a more popular politics. None of this boded well for British power in America, which after all made use of the most traditional instruments of royal control—a foreign-born bureaucracy, Parliamentary statutes, and now a large contingent of the regular army.

One of the Townshend acts augmented the "bureaucracy." The use of this word is anachronistic, but the term then favored in America, "parasites," is not altogether fair, though it suggests how deeply the colonists detested the new officials who arrived to put the Townshend policies into effect. Among these officials none received more abuse than the American Board of Customs Commissioners, which had appointed a flock of officials in the Customs, all charged with the mission of tightening up the service and increasing his majesty's revenue.

Earlier attempts along these lines had failed. About the time the Sugar Act was passed in 1764, for example, twenty-five comptrollers were appointed to supervise the collectors of customs. New Customs districts were carved out in the hope of covering the complicated American coastline, and a vice admiralty court was established in Halifax. In a most ambitious try at reform, George Grenville gave those Customs officials who chose to reside in England while deputies did their work in America a choice between resigning or taking up their posts in person.[31]

Nothing seemed to work. Customs remained in disrepair, with collec-

30. Schlesinger, *Colonial Merchants*, 156–209.
31. Thomas C. Barrow, *Trade and Empire: The British Customs Service in Colonial America, 1660–1775* (Cambridge, Mass., 1967), 186–88.

tors shirking their responsibilities, pocketing bribes, harassing traders, and yet not adding substantial sums to the king's revenue. The regulation of fees was particularly chaotic. Legislatures supervised them in several cases; more often, merchants and collectors agreed on a schedule. His majesty's purse was rarely fattened by these arrangements though collectors sometimes managed well.

The American Board of Customs Commissioners, designed to bring order and honesty, never performed as expected, nor did the new vice admiralty courts established by order in council the year after to stiffen the law. The board contained at least one able man, John Temple, but he was soon on the outs with the others; John Robinson was upright but stubborn and unimaginative; Henry Hulton had abilities but he did not bring them to bear; Charles Paxton disliked the colonists from that unfortunate day of arrival—Guy Fawkes Day—when he suffered the "indignity" of seeing his effigy burned. Little is known of Burch. Together the commissioners led a style of life that set them apart from the people they had to deal with, and together they never seemed to be able to conceive of any solution to their difficulties that did not involve the use of troops against the Americans.[32]

By itself the structure of American commerce would have challenged the talents of any officials sent to regulate it. From Quebec to Georgia there were hundreds of sites where ships might load and unload—major harbors and ports, rivers, creeks, streams, inlets. In the 1760s and 1770s there were only forty-five to fifty Customs districts—the number fluctuated slightly—where official entry or clearance might be obtained. To be sure in several of these districts deputy collectors, tidesmen, and other officials worked far from the customshouse, but in every district trade might be conducted unobserved by any officer. The dispersion of American business and agriculture, and the character of transport and shipping facilities, simply required that trade be carried on in scattered locations. A lumber and wood transporting vessel frequently had to pick up its cargoes at several places in New England, for example; the same type of ship in Georgia and the Carolinas might make several stops before its hold was full. Planters in the Chesapeake brought tobacco to creeks and rivers all around the bay, and ships sailed fifty miles up the York, loading tobacco, naval stores, bar and pig iron, hemp, and

32. George Wolkins, ed., "Letters of Charles Paxton, 1768–1769," MHS, *Procs.*, 56 (Boston, 1923), 348 ("indignity"). The standard study of the commissioners is Oliver M. Dickerson, *The Navigation Acts and the American Revolution* (Philadelphia, 1951).

agricultural products. In 1770 the Rappahannock was navigable to Fredericksburg, about 140 miles upstream, by ships of sixty to seventy tons. And ships made their way up the other streams ringing the bay as well. John Williams, the inspector general of Customs for the Chesapeake, noted in 1770 that ships from all over western Europe and the West Indies loaded and unloaded along the Potomac, sometimes as far as sixty miles from any Customs officer. As for the port of Boston, where so much trouble originated, an official description in 1770 held that it "Begins at Lyn northerly, Proceeds Westerly and Southerly along Massachusetts Bay to Cape Cod . . . Round Cape Cod to the Harbour of Dartmouth . . . Also the Island of Nantucket, Martha's Vineyard and Elizabeth Island." And the report added that no Customs officers served this area except at the port of entry and at Plymouth and Nantucket. These or similar conditions obtained in every district on the American continent and in the West Indies.[33]

Geography, an unconcentrated commerce, and an undermanned Customs service all conspired to offer opportunities for violating trade regulations, themselves none-too-enlightened in the Americans' opinion. No one knows how much evasion and smuggling occurred; Tory historians and Customs officials probably overplayed the extent of smuggling, and Whig historians and eighteenth-century Americans probably underplayed it. The systematic evasion of the Molasses Act and its successor, the Sugar Act of 1764, apparently stopped after 1766 when the reduction of the duty to one penny per gallon and its application to the production of the British West Indies as well as the foreign West Indies was made. Still, other goods were smuggled. For example, in the Rappahannock Customs district in Virginia seven ships and two snows entered from Bordeaux and other French ports "in ballast," as John Williams wryly noted, yet almost every store along the river sold French wines. These stores were also full of teas and foreign linens which were bought from ships returning from Scotland by way of Holland. Tea rarely appeared on the manifests and obviously was undeclared and smuggled. These examples are selected almost at random. Yet no one in the eighteenth century suggested that smuggling and evasion accounted for most American trade. Everyone agreed that most commerce occurred within the law.[34]

33. Joseph R. Frese, ed., "The Royal Customs Service in the Chesapeake, 1770: The Reports of John Williams, Inspector General," *VMHB*, 81 (1973), 280–318. For the quotation, Barrow, *Trade and Empire*, 269.

34. Frese, ed., "Reports of John Williams," *VMHB*, 81 (1973), 292.

The enforcement of the law by the newly created American Board of Customs Commissioners was another matter. Like all its predecessors the board failed to do what was expected—tighten the service and bring in a substantial increase of revenue. Failure was bad for the Treasury, but what was worse was the conduct of the commissioners who further alienated the Americans, including formerly uncommitted or loyal merchants, small shippers, seamen, and other undifferentiated groups who had little in common except a belief in self-government.

Although the commissioners arrived in an atmosphere soured by recent events and although undoubtedly imbued with the administration's suspicions of Americans, their own corporate ethic finally betrayed them. At least two of them, Paxton and Hulton, clearly saw their mission as political as well as administrative, and Robinson may well have felt the same way. The entire board indeed left behind evidence that they conceived of their task as somehow to reform American politics as well as the Customs. The men they hired, or caused to be hired, deputy collectors, searchers, tidesmen, and an official coast guard with twenty vessels and crews, understandably came to their posts in an uncompromising spirit—the colonial merchants, traders, and sailors were not simply businessmen and workers, they were evaders, smugglers, adversaries all. And for the unscrupulous and the greedy among the Customs service, the Americans were plums, ripe for the plucking.[35]

If the spirit of the service was pernicious, the new laws and regulations opened the way for abuse. The Sugar Act and Townshend's Revenue Act of 1767 supplied the key provisions for what has been called "customs racketeering." Under the dispensation of these statutes, bonds were to be given before any goods destined for trade outside the colony were loaded; all decked vessels and any vessel more than two leagues from shore had to carry clearance papers and bonds; every vessel engaged in trade outside its colony was to carry cockets listing every item of cargo aboard; the shipper or master had to enter his vessel at the customshouse before breaking bulk (any landing of cargo was interpreted as breaking bulk); and in vice admiralty courts ships and goods which had been seized were considered property of the Crown unless their owner claimed them. To do so he had to establish his innocence. And he paid all costs on the ruling—usually given—that there was "probable cause" for seizure.

35. Wallace Brown, "An Englishman Views the American Revolution: The Letters of Henry Hulton, 1769–1776," *HLQ*, 36 (1972), 1–26.

V

Unwittingly the army reinforced the resolve of all sorts of Americans to resist further encroachments upon colonial rights. The army made itself known in unhappy ways in three places. Its effects were least heavily felt in South Carolina in spring 1769 when a regiment with supporting artillery put into Charleston on its way to a permanent station in St. Augustine. There were barracks already in existence in Charleston which the troops could use. Supplies were another matter, and the Commons House of the assembly refused to approve an appropriation for them despite a request from General Gage. It had not asked for the troops, the House stated, but should the Parliamentary statutes laying a revenue upon the colonies be repealed, it would honor those requisitions that "appear to us just and reasonable or necessary." This line of reasoning silenced Gage, and the South Carolinians continued to maintain an easy distance from compliance with the Townshend policies, even when confronted by the army.[36]

After a short period of defiance the New York assembly had complied with the Quartering Act of 1765, and thereby angered many citizens including the Sons of Liberty. Troops had been stationed in New York City in the spring of 1766; their presence did not arouse widespread outpourings of joy. Indeed the kindest term of address used to the soldiers' faces in August seems to have been "rascal." The New Yorkers felt some justification for this rude behavior: the troops had cut down the liberty tree on the common. To one of the soldiers the tree was simply "a pine post," but post, pole, or tree, it was a cause for a brawl between several thousand New Yorkers and the troops. No one was killed in that fray, though many were wounded. There were annual riots thereafter as the Sons of Liberty put up liberty poles and the soldiers hacked them down. But no one was killed.[37]

No one was killed, that is, until January 1770. By that time New York was snugly in the nonimportation movement; the DeLanceys and the Livingstons were striving to look more patriotic than the other, and the Sons of Liberty and the troops had just about had their fill of one another. The inevitable explosion came the night of January 16, after the Sons had publicly urged that no one give off-duty soldiers employment. During the evening several soldiers chopped down the

36. Jensen, *Founding*, 339.
37. For events in this paragraph and the next see Roger J. Champagne, *Alexander McDougall and the American Revolution in New York* (Schenectady, N.Y., 1975), 23–26.

liberty pole, sawed it into pieces, and thoughtfully left them in front of a tavern which served as the headquarters of the Sons of Liberty. The Sons did not need firewood, and the next day with 3000 supporters in attendance they put up a new pole. While they were at work, the soldiers distributed an abusive broadside, provoking a skirmish followed by a full-scale battle at Golden Hill. The fight lasted, off and on, for two days and produced many wounded and one death.

As bad as civil-military relations were in New York, they were worse in Boston. New York could blame some of its own citizens for requesting that the army send troops into the colony in spring 1766 during the tenant uprising, but no one that Boston regarded as its own had asked for troops. They had arrived nonetheless at the end of September 1768 under the cover of a line of warships which seemed to menace the town. The troops resplendent in red coats, with their bayonets glistening, were ferried by small boats and barges to the long wharf, and from there had marched to drums and shrill fifes, obviously ready for anything. The manner of their landing had offended many Bostonians; the warships swinging at anchor were in a line usually assumed when armed opposition was expected and broadsides were to be delivered in support of an assault. From headquarters in New York, General Gage had authorized this disposition, with the conviction that he was sending the troops into a treasonous camp. The words he used at this time to describe the Bostonians convey something of his own grim mood—they were "mutinous," they were "desperadoes," they were guilty of "sedition."[38]

The redcoats had landed unopposed. Whatever inclination had existed to resist them with guns had evaporated with the knowledge that the squadron from Halifax was off Boston. As the ships began to make their way into the harbor, the convention of Massachusetts towns, in John Mein's unkind phrasing, "broke up and rushed out of Town like a herd of scalded hogs." The rush from Boston made its citizens realize that for the moment at least they were very much alone with the British army.[39]

Boston was frightened but not cowed by the troops. The authorities, including the Council and the selectmen, returned a firm "no" to all requests for quarters and supplies. Barracks were available on Castle Island, they said, and if the governor and British commanders did not choose to use them, there were quarters to be rented in town. Colonel

38. John Alden, *General Gage in America* (Baton Rouge, La., 1948), 161–62.
39. Hiller B. Zobel, *The Boston Massacre* (New York, 1970), 97.

Dalrymple, temporarily in command, did not choose to scatter his soldiers about in private homes, inns, and taverns. Maintaining discipline was difficult enough in the best of conditions; in a fragmented command it was almost impossible.[40]

For the time being, as we have seen, the army had to settle for less than satisfactory billets. The 29th Regiment, which was carrying full field equipment, pitched tents on the common, and the 14th settled into Faneuil Hall, drafty, cramped, and uncomfortable. The next day Bernard threw open the town house, where the Council and the House of Representatives met, and a part of the 14th shifted its quarters.

None of these arrangements would be sufficient for the coming cold weather; the 29th in particular had to be sent into winter quarters. Governor Bernard had ordered the province's "Manufactory House," once the site of spinning schools and now rented out to private tenants, cleared for occupancy by the soldiers. The tenants, however, refused to move, and for the next three weeks Sheriff Greenleaf, urged on by Bernard and Thomas Hutchinson, tried by persuasion and then by force to move them. Finding the door bolted and the windows barred, the sheriff broke in only to find himself and his party trapped by outraged tenants. A number of grotesque scenes followed, played up and doubtless embroidered by the local newspapers which took to calling the sheriff's actions the "siege of the Manufactory House" and dubbing the sheriff "the General." At the climax of the "siege," with the children of the tenants at the windows of the manufactory crying for bread, and bakers prevented by the sheriff from supplying them, some provisions were delivered after a scuffle with clubs swinging, heads cracked, and much screeching on both sides.[41]

Before the month was out the 29th evacuated the common, and the 14th, the town house and Faneuil Hall. Both moved into warehouses and other buildings rented from private citizens. Even William Molineux, one of the reliables in the Otis-Adams cohort, leased a warehouse to the army, apparently seeing nothing incongruous in taking the army's money while opposing the army's presence. The army's money may have reduced the hostility of others, however. Having the troops in Boston added to the business of victualers, bakers, and tavern owners, to name several sorts who made a good thing out of the garrison.[42]

Yet no circumstance, no arrangement, and no planning could head

40. *Ibid.*, 100–101.
41. Oliver Morton Dickerson, comp., *Boston Under Military Rule as Revealed in a Journal of the Times* (Boston, 1936), 8–9.
42. Zobel, *Boston Massacre*, 104.

off trouble between troops and civilians. Relations were abrasive from the beginning despite a persistent admiration and sympathy felt by many civilians for the soldiers. The discipline meted out to the troops, barbarous by civilian standards, conventional by military standards, increased that sympathy for a time. Soldiers received hundreds of stripes for minor offenses and as many as a thousand lashes was not unusual. The regimental drummers ordinarily delivered this punishment, a fact white Boston found hard to accept, for most of these drummers were Negroes. Most Negroes that Boston knew were slaves. On the last day of October, a more severe punishment was displayed—execution by firing squad. The victim, Richard Ames, a private convicted of desertion, was executed for the edification of the ranks, all properly drawn up on the common while the drums beat.[43]

The ranks did not learn from this spectacle, or perhaps they did; in any case desertion continued: about forty had slipped away in the first two weeks and thereafter several left almost every night. Desertion contributed to bad feeling between the troop commanders and the civilian population. The army blamed the civilians for enticing the men away and infuriated the town by the methods it used to catch them. Informers were hired and patrols sent out, some disguised as local citizens to entrap the deserters and any unwary citizens who might have offered aid.

If clashes between patrols looking for deserters and citizens all too willing to hide them cut into the residue of sympathy the town felt for ordinary soldiers, the behavior of these soldiers completely destroyed any surviving good feeling. Not that the soldiers behaved badly by the standards of the time; they behaved as if they were in a "garrison town," the term they employed in describing Boston to angry citizens. With the connivance of their officers they broke the quiet of the Sabbath with drums, fifes, and derisive renditions of "Yankee Doodle." They also drank to excess, behavior not uncommon in soldiers in the eighteenth century. Andrew Eliot, a Boston parson and a careful man, reported that the soldiers were "in raptures" at the cheapness of liquor in the town. The women in the town aroused another sort of rapture and endured rapes, assaults, and earthy suggestions. Theft of goods was more common than theft of virtue, however, as the town discovered, with burglaries and armed robberies on the streets on the rise.[44]

What set Boston teeth on edge more than any of these crimes—or

43. Ibid.
44. "Letters from Andrew Eliot to Thomas Hollis," Jan. 29, 1769, MHS, Colls., 4th Ser., 4 (Boston, 1858), 437 ("in raptures"); Dickerson, comp., Boston Under Military Rule, 29.

the soldiers' behavior—was the military presence. Having to stomach a standing army in their midst, observe the redcoats daily, pass by troops stationed on Boston Neck who occupied a guardhouse on land illegally taken it was said from the town, and having to receive challenges by sentries on the streets, their own streets, affronted a people accustomed to personal liberty, fired their tempers, and gnawed away at their honor. The sentries' challenges symbolized much of what the town felt was wrong: coming and going as they pleased subject only to civil authority had long been their right. Now with sentries and guards posted at the barracks-warehouses, officers' houses, and public buildings, coming and going were subject to challenge. Almost instinctively civilians refused to respond, and sometimes were seized by the guard for their scruples, and if they resisted they might feel a rifle butt or a bayonet. Until fairly late in the occupation these encounters occurred with neither side willing to give way. The best that could be hoped for until the troops were pulled out was an uneasy standoff. The troops might have a legal right to challenge, "A freeman" wrote in the *Boston Gazette,* but this right implied no obligation on the part of the inhabitants "black, white, or grey" to answer. "I would never quarrel with the guards for asking me the question, nor should they ever quarrel with me with impunity, for despising their question and passing by in silence."[45]

Neither the troops nor the citizens were capable of restraining themselves for long while living side by side. The troop commanders would have settled for peace and harmony. The popular leaders would not, and by a skillful, sometimes malicious, use of the newspapers they made a bad situation worse. The *Boston Gazette* under Edes and Gill continued to publish its versions of public occurrences, and in October 1768 popular leaders invented a fresh vehicle, the "Journal of the Times," reports and articles written in Boston purporting to offer a faithful account of the state of affairs in a town occupied by the army and the American Board of Customs Commissioners. The "Journal" was sent first to the *New York Journal* where it was published and then reprinted in the *Pennsylvania Chronicle.* After that it was widely reprinted throughout the colonies, in Boston by the *Evening Post* whose readers probably had forgotten the exact details of the atrocities being played upon. In some cases the stories seem to have been pure—or, according to the authorities and the army, impure—fabrications.[46]

45. *BG,* Feb. 6, 1769.
46. Dickerson, comp., *Boston Under Military Rule.*

Although the "Journal of the Times" exploited and invented incidents of violence and oppression, the winter passed without a major crisis. Townsmen were encouraged by the departure in June and July of the 64th and 65th Regiments. The relative ease of the first winter's stay apparently persuaded the home government that two regiments could handle Boston. Hence two were sent to Halifax, and the 14th and 29th remained in the town.

By spring 1769 the early awe of the troops felt by civilians had completely worn off, replaced by a grim, sometimes contemptuous familiarity. In this atmosphere fights were more common and, more often perhaps than before, picked by the inhabitants of the town who also discovered fresh ways of protecting themselves from the soldiers and of harassing them in the process. The law offered the new means of protection and harassment as the courts began enforcing a statute which allowed a person convicted of theft to be sold into indentured servitude if he could not raise a sum three times the value of the stolen goods to be paid to the victim of the theft. This procedure does not seem to have been invoked often, but it shocked the troop commanders. The first time it was used, June 1769, Gage recommended smuggling the accused soldier aboard ship; that expedient proved unnecessary when the civilian who had purchased the soldier's indenture settled out of court for a small sum.[47]

About this time the courts began taking an increasingly severe line on soldiers haled before it. There were several fights in the summer and autumn that produced judicial action and then further ugly brawls. The first began as a straightforward fistfight between Private John Riley and a victualer from Cambridge, Jonathan Winship. Afterwards Winship swore out a complaint; Riley was arrested, fined, and when he did not pay, ordered to jail. Getting him there proved difficult as grenadiers from the 14th rescued him from the constable who was taking him off. Before that struggle ended, Lieutenant Alexander Ross of the regiment made his appearance either to stop or to encourage the rescue and riot—the evidence does not make his intentions clear—only to be arrested himself. Eventually Ross and four of his men were convicted and fined. No one seems to have been satisfied by these verdicts, and the soldiers understandably enough came to feel that the judicial system they were charged to strengthen had it in for them.[48]

A second case which began in October reinforced this impression.

47. Zobel, *Boston Massacre*, 136.
48. *Ibid.*, 137–38.

The details of the case, an attack on the guard on Boston Neck, though interesting may be passed over except for three notable details: the first, the command of Captain Molesworth, given as the guard pushed its way back into Boston, to "put your bayonet" through "any man [who] strikes you"; the second, the obvious bias of Judge Dana, who addressed several soldiers in the preliminary hearing in these terms: "Who brought you here? Who sent for you? By what authority do you mount guard, or march in the streets with arms? It is contrary to the laws of the Province, and you should be taken up for so offending. We want none of your guards. We have arms of our own, and can protect ourselves. You are but a handful. Better take care not to provoke us. If you do, you must take the consequences"; the third, the explosiveness of the crowd on Boston Neck that had attacked the soldiers and now in the courtroom responded to questions about bail for the British officer in charge with the cry "Bail him with a rope."[49]

Such episodes involving the local courts exposed the weakness of the army in Boston. The courts and most of the justices had set their faces against the army, and the civil authorities most likely to support it did not. The Council by this time was in popular hands; the town meeting had long been; and the governor felt unable to order the army into action. Lacking the support of the civil government, the army writhed under the goadings of a hostile populace.

Bernard had admitted the hopelessness of his and the army's situation by leaving for England on August 1, 1769. His departure set off a raucous celebration—the newspapers published a final series of denunciations, this time in derisive verse. The militia companies fired their cannon, bonfires were lit, and Bernard had to listen to the church bells peal for joy as the ship carrying him set sail.[50]

A month after Bernard's departure, his old tormentor, James Otis, received the thrashing Bernard had long wanted to deliver. Those remarkable signs of an erratic and uncontrolled temperament had grown stronger in the tension of the occupation of Boston. Otis had always had a propensity to abuse those he disliked; after listening to one such outburst, Peter Oliver had remarked of Otis that "If Bedlamism is a Talent he has it in Perfection."[51] Now facing the troops and the Customs commissioners who hid behind the army's bayonets, he grew frantic in his inability to strike them effectively. Helping put together the newspaper assault

49. *Ibid.*, 141–42.
50. *Ibid.*, 133–34.
51. Butterfield et al., eds., *Diary of John Adams*, I, 225.

apparently was not enough. He talked incessantly, rambling through one story after another, leaving, as John Adams who detested his chatter said, no elbow room in the conversation. One of the objects of his hatred, John Robinson, became one of his partners in conversation early in September. Otis sought out Robinson to accuse him of writing defamatory letters to the home government about Otis's character and activities. Not surprisingly Otis received no satisfaction from these talks and grew more and more indignant at Robinson.

The atmosphere in Boston in these last days of summer can only be described as poisonous. While the newspapers did their bit to foul the air, the two sides—Adams, Otis, and company, and the Customs commissioners, printer John Mein, and Tory officials and sympathizers—breathed in their own dark rumors of conspiracies and plots. When Otis felt that he could stand it no longer he published a threat in the *Gazette* of September 4 that John Robinson should know that "if he 'officially' or in any other way misrepresents me [to the British government] I have a natural right if I can get no other satisfaction to break his head." This statement, the broadest extension of the natural rights theory of the year, was undoubtedly meant to be witty and not to be taken seriously.[52]

Just how seriously it was taken became apparent the following evening in the British Coffee House, a watering spot and a refuge on King Street for Tories and British civil and military officers. Whatever else it was, the British Coffee House was not a center of admiration for James Otis. Robinson lifted a glass there evenings with his friends, many of whom were present when Otis entered looking for Robinson on the night of September 5. Robinson arrived almost immediately after, whereupon Otis demanded "a Gentleman's satisfaction," that is, that Robinson fight him with his fists since dueling was against the law. Apparently Otis thought the fight should occur in the streets, a more friendly arena than the coffee house, and was turning to leave when Robinson took him by the nose. Having one's nose tweaked was particularly humiliating to an eighteenth-century gentleman, and Otis pushed Robinson's hand away, perhaps with a blow. The fight thus began inside the coffee house. Others joined in, evidently trying to strike Otis. Before this ruckus subsided at least one friend from outside came to Otis's rescue, young John Gridley, who absorbed a good deal of punishment himself. Otis emerged from the enemy's camp with a deep gash on his head and

52. Otis also attacked the other commissioners in this issue.

several bruises. The only damage Robinson suffered seems to have been to his coat which split to the pockets.

Otis lost the fight in the coffee house, but he and his friends won the struggle that followed in the newspapers. The *Gazette* of course made the most of the opportunity, picturing Otis and Gridley putting up a "manly Defence" against the horde of revenue officers who hung out in the coffee house. "The People" were equally heroic, arriving at just the right moment, saving their champions, and sending John Robinson and friends scurrying out the back door in ignominious retreat.[53]

Robinson was an inviting target but probably not as dangerous in the radicals' eyes as his friend John Mein, the printer of the *Boston Chronicle*. One of the things that enraged Otis and his colleagues at this time was the assault Mein mounted almost single-handedly in his paper against nonimportation. His method was devastating: he published names of ostensible supporters of the nonimportation agreement who in private were violating its terms. He found the names, he reported, in the local customshouse records. On the list appeared the name of John Hancock, who denied the charge that he had brought in British linen, a proscribed item, but admitted importing Russian duck, a cotton or linen cloth, which was legal. Mein did not rest with reprinting what he found in records but, as was common practice, soon resorted to personal attack. His inventiveness stung: Thomas Cushing was "Tommy Trifle Esq.," Otis was rendered as "Muddlehead," and Hancock as "Johnny Dupe Esq., alias the Milch Cow," a play on Hancock's role as the source of money for the group. If this tag was not clear enough, Mein described Hancock as "A good natured young man with long ears—a silly conceited grin on his countenance—a fool's cap on his head—a bandage tied over his eyes—richly dressed and surrounded with a crowd of people, some of whom are stroking his ears, others tickling his nose with straws, while the rest are employed riffling his pockets."[54]

Two days afterwards John Mein discovered that he had gone too far. Late on the afternoon of October 28, he was attacked on King Street by a crowd that had been waiting for him. He escaped, first by hiding in the main guard, the barracks and headquarters of British troops, and then by dressing as a British private and making his way to Colonel Dalrymple's house. That night another crowd vented its anger by tarring

---

53. *BG*, Sept. 11, 1769, for details and quotations in this and the preceding paragraph.
54. Quoted in Zobel, *Boston Massacre*, 156; John E. Alden, "John Mein: Scourge of Patriots," CSM, *Pubs.*, 34 (Boston, 1943), 571–99.

and feathering one George Gailer, widely believed to be an informer in the pay of the customshouse. Mein knew that he would probably receive worse than tar and feathers if apprehended, and in November he sailed for England on a British warship.

These activities were understood in Boston as responses of a beleaguered people, the victims of a parasitic revenue service and an occupying army. The violence of the crowds did not relieve this feeling, and as the new year began passions and violence intensified.

VI

Nonimportation and the British army continued to arouse most of the popular emotion. In January of the new year the "Body," as the merchant leaders of nonimportation were called, discovered that two sons of Thomas Hutchinson were engaged in importing tea in defiance of the ban. The Body must have relished the opportunity of striking anyone with the name Hutchinson. At any rate they demanded that the tea-importing sons give up the goods and stop the business. The Hutchinsons refused until a crowd threatened to destroy a warehouse owned by the family. At that point Thomas Hutchinson caved in.

It was difficult not to be intimidated by a crowd, especially at a time when it had attained such skill in the gentle art of tarring and feathering. Nevertheless, a merchant occasionally proved recalcitrant, at least to the point of refusing to sign the nonimportation agreement. One, Theophilus Lillie, published his reasons in the *Boston News-Letter* early in January. It seemed "strange," Lillie wrote, "that men who are guarding against being subject to Laws [to] which they never gave their consent in person or by their representative, should at the same time make Laws, and in the most effectual manner execute them upon me and others to which Laws I am sure I never gave my consent either in person or by my representative." That statement may have caused particular unease for the truth it told. Lillie's conclusion was even more infuriating. The charges of slavery against the royal government, he said, seemed misplaced: "I had rather be a slave under one Master; for if I know who he is, I may, perhaps, be able to please him, than a slave to a hundred or more, who I don't know where to find, nor what they will expect of me."[55]

Lillie marked himself by this public challenge to Boston's unofficial governors. Although clear evidence is lacking that the Samuel Adams

55. Jan. 11, 1770.

group was responsible for fomenting action against him, the usual measures taken suggest it was they who were behind it. They waited until the morning of February 22, when a crowd composed primarily of adolescent boys carried a sign to Lillie's shop that identified him as "IMPORTER," a violator of the agreement. The crowd that gathered resembled others that had been turning out in similar instances over the preceding month. They had gone after other IMPORTERS in that period, and now they had got around to Lillie.[56]

A neighbor of Lillie, Ebenezer Richardson, soon diverted the crowd by trying to tear down the sign. Richardson had provided information to the Customs office about Boston's merchants and in the process had earned the tag, "Knight of the Post," a term often applied to informers. He now behaved bravely or recklessly; his efforts on Lillie's behalf failed and the crowd followed him home, where curses were exchanged, including this one from the crowd—"come out you damn Son of a Bitch, I'll have your Heart out your Liver out." Richardson did not come out, but after windows of his house were broken, he fired a gun loaded with swanshot at the crowd, killing an eleven-year-old boy, Christopher Seider, and wounding another. The crowd then poured in on him. Only the intervention of William Molineux, a well-known Son of Liberty, saved his life. Later in the year Richardson was convicted of murder; after a second trial the king pardoned him.[57]

Christopher Seider served the Adams group well. At Seider's funeral they did not simply mourn the death of a child and bury him; they made the occasion an act of defiance of British measures. A large crowd marched in the funeral procession—it may have numbered several thousand—including what John Adams called a "vast Number of Boys" walking before the coffin and a vast number of women and men following it. The size of this gathering revealed more than the horror felt at a boy's death; it testified to the extent of popular revulsion from the British measures.[58]

This feeling took several forms in the next two weeks and helped produce further violence. In the clamor against the Townshend acts and in the effort to secure nonimportation agreements, the town had not forgotten that it was occupied by regiments of a standing army. It

---

56. L. Kinvin Wroth and Hiller B. Zobel, eds., *Legal Papers of John Adams* (3 vols., Cambridge, Mass., 1965), II, 396–98 ("Editorial Note").

57. *Ibid.*, 419. See Sarah Richardson's testimony in *Rex* v. *Richardson* for the quotation. The editorial note provides the factual details, and see the valuable account in Zobel, *Boston Massacre*, chap. 15.

58. Butterfield et al., eds., *Diary of John Adams*, I, 349, 350n.

could not forget with the daily struggles between soldiers and civilians grinding away before its eyes.

In the week following Seider's burial the fights picked up. Although no one planned or orchestrated these battles, they were not accidental. Boston's citizens had many reasons to resent the soldiers, chief among them was the fact that the soldiers occupied the town, and in the black moods occasioned by the length of the occupation and by events such as Seider's death, townsmen may have been even more open than usual about expressing their feelings.

Perhaps the most resentful among Boston's citizens were semiskilled workers and ordinary laborers. They included a rough lot in their number, young men with considerable animal energy, the sort who looked forward to fistfights after drinking rum of an evening in a tavern. They did not take to soldiers, and they did not mind saying so, particularly since those in Boston sometimes took work and pay away from them. British soldiers in Boston took advantage of army regulations that permitted them to work at civilian jobs when they were not on duty. The worst of this eighteenth-century moonlighting was the soldiers' willingness to work at less than the going rate of pay, sometimes as much as 20 percent below what civilian laborers expected. Laborers, then, had more than the usual reasons for hating the British army.

In the days following Seider's burial, those young men adept at using their fists may have been even more eager than usual for the opportunity. On March 2 they got their chance when an off-duty soldier walked into John Gray's ropewalk looking for a job. A ropemaker asked him if he wanted work. The soldier answered that he did, and the ropemaker then invited him to "clean my shithouse." The soldier struck the rope-maker, but then absorbed a beating and retreated. He returned with friends, and a great brawl followed. The next day more fights occurred, several saw clubs and cutlasses employed, and more and more men were drawn in. March 4th was a Sunday—and relatively quiet. The next day came with rumors on both sides of further fights to come.[59]

What followed that night does not seem to have been the result of a plot or plan on either side, but rather the consequences of deep hatreds and bad luck. The hatreds brought out roving bands of civilians and soldiers, all apparently in search of one another.[60]

59. Zobel, *Boston Massacre*, chap. 16, provides an excellent narrative of events leading to the massacre.
60. My account of the Boston massacre has been reconstructed from Wroth and Zobel, eds., *Legal Papers of John Adams*, III, which contains the records of the trial that followed, and from Zobel, *Boston Massacre*, chap. 16.

A small encounter near the customshouse on King Street about 8:00 P.M. helped bring the civilians together—a good many more than had been looking for a fight. Edward Gerrish, an apprentice, began the night's activities by insulting an army officer he happened to encounter on King Street. There were no gentlemen among the officers of the 29th Regiment, Gerrish cried. Private Hugh White, the sentry standing guard near the customshouse, heard Gerrish's taunt and gave him a blow under the ear for his audacity. There seem to have been other off-duty soldiers at the corner of King Street and Royal Exchange Lane at that time, and at least one of them also struck Gerrish.[61]

Although Boston's streets had no lamps in 1770, they were sufficiently well lighted by the moon and by reflection from a heavy coat of snow and ice to allow soldiers and civilians to see one another. Off-duty soldiers now pretty well left the scene, perhaps because they were heavily outnumbered by a crowd that gathered around Private White and perhaps because they had other fights in nearby streets to attend to. Word of what had happened to Gerrish had spread—no doubt extravagantly embroidered—and within a few minutes twenty or more men and boys gathered. They lost no time in telling White that they did not like him—"you Centinel, damned rascally Scoundrel Lobster Son of a Bitch."[62] White did not take this abuse quietly, threatening to run them through if they kept after him. The threat brought fresh oaths and with them snowballs and pieces of ice. White then retreated to the door of the customshouse where he placed his back and tried to stand off the growing crowd.

Up the block at the main guard and within sight of White's station and the customshouse, Captain Thomas Preston, the officer in charge during the night, watched uneasily. Preston, an Irishman, was forty years of age and an experienced officer. No experience is ever completely adequate to prepare one to deal with an angry crowd. Preston watched and waited, apparently in hope that the crowd might disperse on its own. But, far from dispersing, the crowd grew, swelled in part by well-meaning citizens who came into the streets prepared to put out a fire. For someone, surely not well meaning, had either called out "fire" or sent messages to nearby churches that there was a fire on King Street. In any case church bells began tolling, the signal that help was needed

61. Wroth and Zobel, eds., *Legal Papers of John Adams*, III, 50; Zobel, *Boston Massacre*, 185–86.
62. Wroth and Zobel, eds., *Legal Papers of John Adams*, III, 52–53.

to put out a blaze. Some who joined the crowd at the customshouse carried bags and buckets, the first to help victims of the fire to save their belongings, the second for carrying water. Others carried clubs, swords, and even catsticks, bats used in playing tipcat, a boys' game popular in England and America.[63]

Watching these new arrivals, Captain Preston decided around nine o'clock that the time had come to rescue Private White. He then ordered out the guard, six privates and a corporal at its head, apparently with the intention of marching down to White and returning with him to the safety of the main guard. Reaching White does not seem to have been too difficult. The guard in a column of twos, with muskets—bayonets attached—pushed through the crowd. Once it arrived the crowd filled in behind it and in a sense made it prisoner with White. Bad luck now made its play—both the crowd and the guard included men who had fought at Gray's ropewalk. Surrounded, Preston made two mistakes, entirely understandable mistakes, but mistakes nonetheless. He did not immediately order the guard to march back up the street with White; instead he shifted its alignment from a column of twos to a single line, a rough semi-circle, facing out from the customshouse. And he ordered his men to load their muskets.

During the next fifteen minutes there was an ugly standoff. More men entered the street and the crowd pressed against the small ring of soldiers. Shouts of "kill them" came from the crowd along with snowballs and ice. The soldiers seem to have shouted back and held their muskets half-cocked with muzzles low but pointed in the crowd's direction. A few reckless spirits ran along the line of the soldiers lightly touching each musket with a stick and daring them to fire.

While he was marching the soldiers to White's aid, Preston had been warned to "take care of your Men for if they fire your life must be answerable." Preston had replied, "I am sensible of it."[64] Now with the crowd pressing against the line, Preston took his place near one end in front of the muzzles. As the noise increased and the crowd gave signs of some further action, a merchant, Richard Palmes, stepped forward to deliver another warning to Captain Preston.

As the two spoke a piece of ice struck Private Hugh Montgomery standing near the end of the line. The blow may have knocked him down, or more likely, the pain of it caused him to step back and then

63. Zobel, *Boston Massacre*, 186–93.
64. Wroth and Zobel, eds., *Legal Papers of John Adams*, III, 55.

slip on the icy footing. When he regained his feet he fired. There was a short pause after this first shot, and then the remaining soldiers pulled their triggers. Their uneven bursts hit eleven men; three died instantly, one a few hours later, and a fifth several days later. Six wounded survived.

For the next twenty-four hours, public order threatened to break down completely. A crowd estimated at at least a thousand swirled through the streets almost immediately after the killings. So far as a crowd is capable of expression, this one called for vengeance against Preston, the guard, and the army. The governor showed courage and judgment in facing these people. Jailing Preston and the soldiers siphoned off some anger, but the presence of the 14th and 29th Regiments kept popular emotion near rage. Hutchinson did not want to order these troops out of town; a few hours of watching and listening to the town the next day told him he would have to give the order.

After the troops left, popular leaders shifted their attention to getting early trials. Here they encountered the judges of the superior court who, recognizing that a fair trial would not be obtained in the mood of the town, delayed judicial action until the autumn. By that time although popular fevers had subsided they remained capable of surging upward again. With public peace apparently secured, the trials began.

John Adams, full of honest conviction that every Englishman deserved a fair trial, not to mention self-righteous satisfaction at taking on an unpopular case, defended Preston. The court heard many witnesses who gave a bewildering variety of testimony—and found Captain Preston innocent. The soldiers also escaped punishment, but two who were found guilty of manslaughter and pleaded benefit of clergy were branded and released.[65]

Although the remaining months of 1770 offered up no further violence in Boston, the angers and the hatreds that had come to the town since 1765 did not disappear. Similar feelings elsewhere in America took fresh life from the killings in Boston. The Massacre—it was called that almost immediately—compelled attention all over again to the question of what British power was doing in America. The legitimacy of that power had been questioned since 1765; now apparently it had given one sort of answer to questioners of its purposes.

The constitutional issues dividing Britain and her American colonies had been clear since 1765. A number of Americans had attempted to clarify them for their countrymen and for the king and Parliament.

65. *Ibid.*, 312–14.

They had succeeded in America and failed in Britain. Still, they and most of their countrymen hoped for a resolution within the old constitutional order. The crisis set up by the Townshend acts and the conversion of a major city into a garrison town had made the constitutional questions all the more urgent. The gravest implications of the British case had been clear for some time; as the House of Representatives of Massachusetts pointed out the next year—"A Power without a Check is subversive of all Freedom."[66]

Unchecked power destroyed freedom and lives in Boston. The bitterness felt by the victims understandably made calm review of the political theory underlying Anglo-American relationships hard to sustain. In the next few years, however, the Americans would continue to think about the British constitution. They inevitably also thought much about themselves. A few years before, William Pitt, a man much admired in the colonies, had reminded Parliament that the Americans were "the sons, not the bastards of England." Experience made many Americans wonder at Pitt's formulation. Recent history culminating in the Massacre was leading them to the discovery that perhaps they were the bastards of England—and the legitimate children of America.

66. *BF Papers*, XVIII, 149.

10

Drift

On the first day of January 1771 Samuel Cooper, the minister of the Brattle Square Church in Boston, wrote his friend Benjamin Franklin that "There seems now to be a Pause in Politics." Cooper offered this assessment not primarily because the agitation about the Massacre and the trials of Preston and the soldiers appeared over but because, as he explained, "The Agreement of the Merchants is broken," a reference to the decision of the Boston merchants in the preceding October to give up nonimportation.[1]

The merchants had acted after they learned that Parliament had approved a bill repealing all the Townshend duties except the one on tea. A new ministry headed by Lord North had decided on this action. North's government had taken over from Grafton's early in 1770 and soon after had decided to extricate itself from colonial disputes. North possessed a peaceful temperament, a spirit that would be harshly bruised in the next twelve years. Even when aroused, North had little taste for conflict; he wanted only to serve his king. Thus he acted to remove the causes of strife with a sense of genuine relief. He also led Parliament to modify the Currency Act which had troubled New York. That colony now would be allowed to issue bills of credit which might be used to pay public—though not private—debts. Altogether it was an enlightened measure, further evidence that a reassuring colonial policy might be in the offing.[2]

1. *BF Papers*, XVIII, 3.
2. Joseph Albert Ernst, *Money and Politics in America, 1755–1775* (Chapel Hill, N.C., 1973), 278–79.

In reality, for most of the next three years the government paid little attention to the colonies. It had expected nonimportation to collapse and certainly had not intended to signal that it approved resistance to efforts to tax the colonies. Like the ministries before it, North's had no doubts about Parliament's right to do just about anything it wanted to do in America. North was content to let colonial affairs drift, as long as they drifted quietly.

Drift would not have displeased most Americans had they been convinced that Parliament had given up its old claims to powers to drive them where it desired. Most agreed with Samuel Cooper that the new ministry had the opportunity of adopting mild measures without looking weak, and should it "Place us on the old Ground on which we stood before the Stamp Act, there is no Danger of our rising in our Demands." But everyone knew that the Declaratory Act remained on the books— and so did the tax on tea.[3]

II

Despite the lingering sense of menace that these statutes imparted, the atmosphere in 1771 was different largely because no great issue had replaced the Townshend duties. Not that, below the surface of politics, issues did not exist which twisted men's desires for calm. In North Carolina and Georgia, for example, the assemblies and the governors struggled with one another, a common circumstance but one which produced more than the expected rancor because mutual trust had almost vanished in the previous five years.[4]

In South Carolina the governor and assembly fought over an issue closely related to the conflicts of the recent crises. The dispute had begun near the end of 1769 when the assembly appropriated £1500 "for the support of the just and constitutional rights and liberties of the people of Great Britain and America." This sum was to be sent to the Supporters of the Bill of Rights, an English group organized to press the claims of John Wilkes to a seat in Parliament. Because of procedures which had grown up since the 1740s, the governor, William Bull, was unable to stop it. Bull did inform his English superiors who, shocked, soon instructed him that he was not to consent to money bills that did not designate the money for specific purposes. The English officials clearly aimed to get the governor of South Carolina on a footing

3. *BF Papers*, XVIII, 4.
4. Jack P. Greene, *The Quest for Power: The Lower Houses of Assembly in the Southern Royal Colonies, 1689–1776* (Chapel Hill, N.C., 1953), 420–35 and *passim*.

enjoyed by governors in other colonies. Bull tried to comply with these instructions but the way had become slippery for governors of South Carolina. The best he could do was to withhold his approval of actions taken by the assembly. The result was deadlock—no annual tax bill passed into law after 1769, and no legislation of any kind after February 1771.[5]

Far to the north, another sort of conflict persisted, though by the early 1770s it had lost some of its corrosiveness. It would not disappear entirely, however, until Americans declared their independence, because it concerned religious freedom—in particular the freedom of Protestant sects from Anglican domination. In reality, there probably was little possibility that the Church of England would ever control religious life in the colonies. The dispositions of most Americans, those of English stock as well as the new immigrants, tended toward either evangelicalism or an unstructured arminianism or liberalism. Bishops and hierarchies had no appeal for the faithful, and establishments of any persuasion were attracting increasing criticism.[6]

Yet bishops, who did not exist in America, furnished the center of the religious controversy. Because at a distance, bishops seemed especially malignant. Their remoteness freed the fancies of dissenters who long before the Revolution professed to dread their coming and warned against attempts by the Anglican clergy—especially the missionaries of the Society for the Propagation of the Gospel whose commission ostensibly was to spread the light to the Indians—to insinuate themselves into the centers of education and religion in America.

One of the more lurid revelations of Anglican intentions was made in New York just before the French and Indian War. The defender of liberty in this case was William Livingston, a recent graduate of Yale and a man of no very strong religious beliefs. In 1753 as King's College (later Columbia) took shape, Livingston smelled a plot by Anglicans in New York to make the college their own. Livingston did not want the college under the control of any church or sect. Anglicans outnumbered all other groups on its board, and Anglicans agitated for a royal charter. To prevent them from seizing control, Livingston resorted to the press in 1753 and began to issue *The Independent Reflector*, a monthly magazine modeled on the *Independent Whig* of John Trenchard and Thomas Gordon. Livingston chose his model well—the anticlericalism of the *Independent Whig* had a wicked bite to it, a characteristic

5. *Ibid.*, 402–16.
6. On fear of the Church of England, see Carl Bridenbaugh, *Mitre and Sceptre: Transatlantic Faiths, Ideas, Personalities, and Politics, 1689–1775* (New York, 1962).

of particular utility in the struggle with the Anglicans of New York City. In the pages of the *Independent Reflector* two tactics emerged. The first was an appeal to the most prominent dissenting groups in the colony, among them Presbyterians, Lutherans, and Dutch Reformed. The second was to plead the larger implication of what at first sight appeared to be a provincial struggle over a pathetic little colonial college. That implication was political: religious and civic freedom could not really be separated, and therefore the apparently open Anglican intention to control only the college actually concealed a larger design to master church and state.[7]

The Anglicans eventually won the fight for King's, won at least the presidency, which one of their own, Dr. Samuel Johnson, held until 1763. But Livingston won too, for the struggle in the press alerted a large dissenting constituency in New York and undoubtedly helped ready it for the conflicts leading to independence. And during the 1760s, when rumors spread that an Anglican bishop was on the way to America, dissenting ministers in New York joined colleagues to the north in organizing opposition.

The rumors found their most avid audience in New England. There—especially in Boston and Cambridge—rumors could be attached to substance. The Reverend East Apthorp, the Anglican pastor in Cambridge, was surely a substantial figure when he arrived with Governor Francis Bernard in 1760. Apthorp, who had not reached his thirtieth birthday, soon married Elizabeth Hutchinson, daughter of Judge Eliakim Hutchinson, a wealthy merchant and a warden and vestryman of King's Chapel. Marrying into the Hutchinsons did not exhaust Apthorp's bright ideas, and shortly after his arrival he began announcing them in the local newspapers. For example, he proposed that Harvard introduce Anglican services into its commencement. Apthorp made this suggestion in such innocence as to make it appear as arrogance. His proposal that the Harvard Board of Overseers add Anglicans to its number revealed either ignorance of the religious realities in New England or a sublime taste for the fantastic. In any case the response was predictable, a series of savage attacks in the newspapers on Apthorp and all his schemes.[8]

By such proposals Apthorp made himself an easy target. Jonathan Mayhew, pastor of Boston's West Congregational Church, scored repeatedly off him in the skirmishes conducted in pamphlets and newspapers in the 1760s. Of all Mayhew's touches the tag he hung on Apthorp's

7. Milton M. Klein has edited a modern edition of *The Independent Reflector*, by William Livingston (Cambridge, Mass., 1963).

8. Bridenbaugh, *Mitre and Sceptre*, 211–14.

handsome house in Cambridge, the "Bishop's Palace," was one of the most effective.[9]

The Bishop's Palace, a lordly name for a lordly behaving clergy, seemed apt. For the Anglican clergy behaved as if they lived in a land of heathen. At least this interpretation occurred to Congregationalists who were subjected to incessant efforts to convert them to the Church of England, as if they were unchurched. Thus, Mayhew's charge in 1763 that there was "a formal design to carry on a spiritual siege of our churches" simply stated the obvious as far as Congregationalists were concerned. Two years later in the midst of the upheaval over the Stamp Act, John Adams linked spiritual and secular assaults on American liberties—"there seems to be," Adams wrote in the essays later called a *Dissertation on the Feudal and Canon Law*, "a direct and formal design on foot to enslave America."[10]

During the remainder of the decade the attack on the Anglican clergy in the middle and New England colonies continued. By the early 1770s, however, though the uneasiness of the dissenters remained, the worst of the threat of the "foreign" clergy seemed to have been contained. The Anglicans had been exposed and no bishop had appeared. With no further evidence of the coming of bishops, even the most sensitive dissenter had difficulty keeping his attention on the threat.

III

As tensions over bishops uncoiled early in the 1770s, they gradually wound up again over the collection of Customs duties. Only the tax on tea remained from the Townshend duties, an irritating reminder that Parliament had not yielded its right to tax for revenue when it repealed the other duties. This irritation did not prevent colonial merchants from importing British goods or their customers from buying them. During the three years beginning with 1771, the colonies' imports from Britain reached £9 million in value, almost £4 million more than in the three years 1768–70. Boston merchants proved especially hungry for British goods and overcame their distaste for duties tea sufficiently to bring in half a million pounds of the stuff.[11]

Still, illegal trade and Customs racketeering persisted despite the re-

9. *Ibid.*, 226.
10. Mayhew is quoted in *ibid.*, 231.
11. Ian R. Christie and Benjamin W. Labaree, *Empire or Independence, 1760–1776: A British-American Dialogue on the Coming of the American Revolution* (New York, 1976), 151.

sumption of legal commerce. In many ports, smuggling merchants and unfair collectors thrived together, as, for example, on the Delaware River where an illegal trade with the Dutch continued even after the Townshend duties were repealed. A prominent New Jersey collector was beaten by sailors in the autumn of 1770 when he imprudently tried to investigate a vessel off-loading its cargo into small boats in Delaware Bay. His son, who assisted him in the customshouse, received a coat of tar and feathers shortly after. A year later a Customs schooner captured a colonial vessel accused of smuggling but then was taken itself by a crowd which seems to have included several important merchants from Philadelphia. The crowd beat up the captain and the crew of the Customs schooner before stowing them in the hold. Before the night's work was completed, the schooner's prize disappeared with the crowd.[12]

Merchants and Customs collectors formed an explosive mixture everywhere in the colonies. In Rhode Island, where they were especially practiced in the art of making explosions, they combined in the familiar way a year after the worst of the encounters along the Delaware. The usual antagonism furnished the background. Nothing seemed to dampen the enthusiasm of the two groups for getting at one another's throats. The Rhode Island merchants conducted a lively trade, most of it legal though their reputation for illegality was formidable.

The Royal Navy believed that the reputation conformed to the facts and, after losing two small vessels in Narragansett waters, assigned the *Gaspee* there in late March 1772. Her skipper, Lieutenant William Dudingston, seized several craft engaged in trade only to find himself threatened with arrest by the local sheriff. Dudingston's commanding officer, Admiral Montagu, attempting to shield him, wrote a foolish letter to the sheriff in which he threatened to hang as pirates any citizens who attempted to rescue "any vessel the King's schooner may take carrying on an illicit trade." Governor Joseph Wanton replied with a letter not calculated to reassure the navy about civilian concern for the enforcement of the Acts of Navigation. The charge that local citizens had proposed rescuing by force any trader taken by the *Gaspee* was, Wanton said, "without any foundation, and a scandalous imposition." And "as to your advice, not to send the sheriff on board any of your squadron, please to know that I will send the sheriff of this colony at any time, and to any place, within the body of it, as I think fit."[13]

12. *Ibid.*, 154–55.
13. The quotations are from the letters in *EHD*, 760–61.

A few weeks later on June 9, Lieutenant Dudingston, in eager pursuit of a craft he suspected as a smuggler, ran the *Gaspee* aground. Unable to free her, he was vulnerable to unfriendly boarders. They appeared that night, apparently including John Brown of the great Providence family, and took the *Gaspee* by force. Dudingston tried to resist and received a bullet in the groin for his trouble. The boarding party took their time in their work, first laying about them with handspikes when the *Gaspee*'s crew tried to hold them off, then reading the ship's papers, finally taking off everyone and then burning the ship. Dudingston, put ashore by these gentle souls, nursed his wounds for a couple of days, only to be arrested by the sheriff for an earlier seizure of colonial cargo. Admiral Montagu eventually rescued him by paying a stiff fine imposed by a Rhode Island court. After that Montagu decided that Lieutenant Dudingston had outlived his usefulness and sent him back to England to explain to a court-martial the loss of the *Gaspee*.[14]

As things turned out, punishing Dudingston proved to be about as much as either the Admiral or the home government could do. Montagu tried to uncover the names of the leaders of the raiders who burned the *Gaspee* and may have succeeded but could not establish their guilt. The ministry had no better luck though it appointed a commission to investigate the affair. The commission met in January 1773 and returned a report in the summer declaring civil officials in Rhode Island free of guilt. Who was guilty it could not say.[15]

The report ended the *Gaspee* affair in a legal sense, but the political results were longer lasting. The commission had been empowered to send persons it accused to England for trial along with witnesses and evidence. This arrangement violated the ancient English right of trial by a jury of one's peers. The news of what the ministry had authorized spread rapidly, and within a few weeks the colonial newspapers had pointed to its dangers. Not long afterwards, in 1773, the newspapers began to carry articles openly speculating on the timing of an American declaration of independence.[16]

In Virginia, Thomas Jefferson, Richard Henry Lee, and Patrick Henry, after learning of the ministry's version of a fair trial in the *Gaspee* affair, decided that a permanent organization was needed to maintain colonial vigilance. The House of Burgesses agreed with them and in

14. Lovejoy, *Rhode Island Politics*, 158–59, provides a good account of the attack.
15. *Ibid.*, 159–66.
16. Jensen, *Founding*, 428–31.

March appointed a standing committee to correspond with other legislatures or their committees about activities deemed dangerous to America. This intercolonial committee of correspondence served as the model for others; and in another twelve months all the colonies, except Pennsylvania where Joseph Galloway blocked action, had followed suit.[17] That these committees existed proved to be more important than anything they did. They signaled an increasing awareness in America of a common cause. They also provided an example of common action.

That example was not easy to maintain in these years of drift. Virginia of course had pointed the way early in the conflict with Britain, most notably at the time of the Stamp Act crisis. But, like other colonists, Virginians returned with relief to normal occupations when threats to their liberties were eased. The others included Yankees in Massachusetts, fierce in the defense of freedom but also eager for calm. Not even Sam Adams could do much about the popular mood once the British ministry backed off.

IV

The affair over the *Gaspee* helped to rouse some in Massachusetts, but in 1772 a local conflict yielded even more discontent. The issue was a familiar sort by the summer of 1772—who should pay the salaries of royal officials serving in the colony? The legislature saw the control of salaries as a means of controlling the officials, surely a misapprehension but one widely shared outside Massachusetts. The British government counted itself among those who believed that salaries could be an important weapon in the struggle for power, and in 1768 it sought to insulate Thomas Hutchinson from the worst of popular pressures by ordering that henceforth his salary as chief justice should be paid from Customs revenues. Two years later it decided to pay Hutchinson as governor and Andrew Oliver as lieutenant governor from the duty on tea, and in the summer of 1772 it added all the superior court justices.[18]

The lengthening list of officials now out of the reach of popular influence set Sam Adams's teeth on edge. The Boston newspapers opened their columns to Adams and his friends, who lost no time in expressing their alarm at the growth of irresponsible power in Massachusetts. Adams also turned to the town meeting and guided that body into requesting

17. *Ibid.*, 430–31.
18. Oliver M. Dickerson, "Use Made of the Revenue from the Tax on Tea," *NEQ,* 31 (1958), 232–43; Christie and Labaree, *Empire or Independence*, 154.

further information from the governor about the ministry's purposes. Not getting it, the town requested that the legislature be called into session. The governor then reminded the town that calling the legislature was his business, and he had no intention of doing so just then. At this point Sam Adams claimed that all normal remedies had been exhausted and that Massachusetts should look for some extraordinary means of protecting its liberties. Sam Adams was never at a loss for ideas of what should be done in the defense of Massachusetts, and now he proposed that Boston establish a committee of correspondence "to state the Rights of the Colonists and of this Province in particular, as Men, as Christians, and as Subjects; to communicate and publish the same to the several Towns in this Province and the World as the sense of this Town, with the Enfringements and Violations thereof that have been, or from time to time may be made—Also request of each Town a free communication of their Sentiments on this Subject."[19]

The town approved this motion unanimously, an action facilitated no doubt by distaste for Hutchinson who, in turning down its petition for a meeting of the legislature, had not been able to resist the opportunity to instruct the town in its limited rights. The committee sat down to work at once and by the end of the month produced a report adopted by the town and almost immediately printed as the *Votes and Proceedings . . . of Boston,* known to contemporaries as the "Boston Pamphlet."[20] This tract resembled the productions of committees from that day to this, for it offered widely shared assumptions. But in tone at least it departed from such efforts in its uncompromising conclusion that the violence of British encroachments upon colonial rights pointed to a plot to enslave America. To demonstrate the existence of this plot it rehearsed the familiar grievances. Taxation without representation found a central place in this list, as did Parliament's assertion in the Declaratory Act that it possessed the authority to bind the colonies "in all Cases whatsoever." The Boston Pamphlet also reminded Massachusetts citizens of the unlawful force used against them by a standing army and the hordes of gluttonous placemen who rushed in to do the government's bidding: "Our Houses, and even our Bed-chambers, are exposed to be ransacked, our Boxes, Trunks and Chests broke open, ravaged and plundered, by Wretches, whom no prudent Man would venture to employ even as

19. *EHD,* 763.
20. BRC, *Reports,* XVIII, 95–108. The first three parts have been reprinted in Merrill Jensen, ed., *Tracts of the American Revolution, 1763–1776* (Indianapolis, Ind., 1967), 235–55.

menial Servants." The governor himself took part in the conspiracy; he had become in fact "merely a ministerial Engine." Justice had been taken out of reach by the stipends accorded the judges from Customs revenues and by shifting revenue cases to vice admiralty courts which sat without juries. There was much more on this list, including a reference to the danger to religion by the bishops whose coming apparently was imminent.[21]

The starkness of the threat to liberty, as described in the Boston Pamphlet, pointed up just how precious colonial rights were. The list of these rights contained nothing new, but it was phrased with great clarity. The pamphlet asserted that the colonials were British subjects and as such retained the rights of subjects. These rights took their origin in nature and reason. They were "absolute Rights"; they could not be alienated; no power could lawfully remove them from the people's control; and the people themselves could not give them up—to government or anyone else.[22]

Boston's statement of rights and grievances seemed to invite support from the towns of the colony, although the Boston committee did not flatly ask that the outlying communities form committees of correspondence and join in the search for a redress of grievances. It did not have to ask. As 1772 ended the news of what it had done spread. The Boston Gazette did its part, and no doubt travelers from the town reported what had taken place in November. The committee itself printed six hundred copies of the pamphlet which by the spring of 1773 had made their way into even the remote corners of the colony. The response seems to indicate that Boston's concerns were those of the majority of Massachusetts towns. By April 1773, almost half of the towns and districts of the colony had taken some action, forming their own committees of correspondence, passing resolutions echoing Boston's dread of the sinister plot against their liberties, and instructing their representatives to look into the matter of the judges' salaries.[23]

Although Thomas Hutchinson, who was one of those judges as well as governor, probably never realized it, he helped evoke these declarations of disaffection. He did by making a speech in January 1773 to the General Court answering the Boston committee of correspondence and

21. *Votes and Proceedings of the Freeholders and Other Inhabitants of the Town of Boston* (Boston, [1772]), 16–17, 21.
22. *Ibid.*, 9–10.
23. Richard D. Brown, *Revolutionary Politics in Massachusetts: The Boston Committee of Correspondence and the Towns, 1772–1774* (Cambridge, Mass., 1970), 92–121.

its pamphlet. For the most part Hutchinson maintained a measured tone in this speech. He also succeeded in making his understanding of the colonial status in the empire absolutely clear. That clarity spurred on the opposition. The speech deplored the resort to committees of correspondence and the claim to absolute rights. The colonists, Hutchinson said, did not need such committees. As for their rights, they were derived from the charter granted them by the Crown. From the founding on, the premise of their government was that they were subordinate to Parliament. They enjoyed some of the rights of Englishmen, but not all: they could not send representatives to Parliament, a right of Englishmen, because they had removed themselves far from England. Their own legislature enjoyed some authority, but it was not to pass laws conflicting with those of Parliament. Thus, the charter, custom, and geography all served to limit colonial rights, a limitation recognized by everyone and only recently challenged by men making extraordinary demands. These men were in the wrong, and to make their error obvious Hutchinson stated his conclusion starkly: "I know of no line that can be drawn between the supreme authority of Parliament and the total independence of the colonies."[24]

Hutchinson had badly miscalculated. There was a powerful constitutional case against the supremacy of Parliament in the colonies; it had been stated repeatedly since 1765 and now it was restated—by Samuel Adams, the committee of correspondence, and the towns. Hutchinson had not suppressed public opposition; he had strengthened it.

Sam Adams and the Boston committee took pains to see that the newly resurrected opposition did not lose direction. In June they played the strongest hand they had held in years—they published the letters of Thomas Hutchinson, Andrew Oliver, and several others to Thomas Whately, the British subminister. Benjamin Franklin had sent the letters to Thomas Cushing six months before with the injunction that they should be kept secret. How Franklin obtained the letters is not completely clear, and Cushing did not care. He and Adams soon decided that the letters must be revealed to the public so that the treachery of Hutchinson and his friends could be exposed.[25]

The letters, written in the years 1767, 1768, and 1769, revealed the extent of their writers' disenchantment with the popular opposition to the actions and policies of the British government. Little in the letters

24. Quoted in *ibid.*, 80.
25. The letters published as *The Representation of Governor Hutchinson and Others* . . . (Boston, 1773), have been reprinted with notes in *BF Papers*, XX, 539–80.

could have surprised readers in Massachusetts; what made the letters sensational was the timing of their release and the revelation—now completely clear in concentrated expression—that the agents of the Crown in America were deeply alienated from the people. And these agents, Thomas Hutchinson and Andrew Oliver chief among them, by their own words seemed to confess that they were advocates of a conspiracy, a conspiracy so frequently adduced as to lose its capacity to shock let alone frighten. Hutchinson's suggestion to Whately that English liberties be curtailed, which he infuriatingly said he offered for "the good of the colony," appalled the readers of his words. His patronizing tone— here and elsewhere he referred to those who disagreed with him as "ignorant" or in a "frenzy"—made these statements, which he had repeated in public, seem a betrayal of Massachusetts. In sentences which became notorious as soon as they were published he wrote:

> I never think of the measures necessary for the peace and good order of the colonies without pain. There must be an abridgment of what are called English liberties. I relieve myself by considering that in a remove from the state of nature to the most perfect state of government there must be a great restraint of natural liberty. I doubt whether it is possible to project a system of government in which a colony 3,000 miles distant from the parent state shall enjoy all of the liberty of the parent state. I am certain I have never yet seen the projection. I wish the good of the colony when I wish to see some further restraint of liberty rather than the connexion with the parent state should be broken; for I am sure such a breach must prove the ruin of the colony.[26]

By the time Hutchinson's letters were published, his enemies had perfected the techniques of responding to encroachments upon liberty. Now they took things a step farther—the House of Representatives petitioned the ministry for the governor's removal, and the newspapers picked up the pace of denunciation. By late summer 1773 even Thomas Hutchinson, he of good intentions and unfortunate means, recognized that the "Pause in Politics," commented on by Samuel Cooper, had ended in Massachusetts.[27]

In May, just before the publication of the letters, Parliament took an action which assured that the pause would end everywhere in the thirteen colonies. It passed the Tea Act of 1773, a statute intended to bail out the financially troubled East India Company. The Act gave to

26. *BF Papers*, XX, 550.
27. For an excellent discussion of the entire affair, see Bailyn, *Ordeal of Hutchinson*, 223–59.

the company a monopoly of the trade in tea with the colonies and retained the three pence duty on tea. Both features of the Act aroused opposition. Together they gave notice that Parliament would do what it liked in America. A "pause" in politics meant nothing. Parliament had insisted on its supremacy once more. Direction now replaced drift in America.

11

Resolution

The reception accorded the Tea Act in 1773–74 is replete with paradox. For the previous two years the Americans had drunk tea, much of it legally imported, and they had paid the duty of three pence per pound. Smuggling was still acceptable and a good deal of tea was imported illegally from Holland, but equally acceptable was the legal but quiet importation of tea from England through Customs. And yet within a year of the passage of the Tea Act, the opposition had revived and given a celebrated tea party in Boston harbor even though the duty remained the same. And anyone who brought in tea was branded an enemy to his country though many had done so without reproach during the preceding two years. Why we may ask did this convulsive reaction occur, destroying private property, provoking a fresh defiance of Parliament, and once more pulling the American colonies together?

The answer has much to do with how the colonists understood the Tea Act. They believed that the Act left them no choice; it forced the issue; it expressed still another claim by Parliament of the right to tax them. This claim meant, as far as they were concerned, that the English plot to enslave them had been revived. If they went on paying the duty now that the government's intentions were laid bare, they would be cooperating with the enslavers.

Arriving at this understanding consumed the summer following passage of the Act. Exactly what Parliament had done, let alone intended, was not known fully in America until September when a copy of the statute was printed in the newspapers. Even then confusion abounded because interpretations of the Act published in the newspapers implied and sometimes stated that the East India Company's tea would be imported duty free. The supporters of the Tea Act, most notably the company's consignees, understandably felt no urgency in explaining its terms, and as late as November several in New York insisted that the company's tea would not have to pay the old Townshend duty.[1]

As before, the Sons of Liberty resorted to the newspapers to expose the ministry's purposes. But this time the Sons in Philadelphia and New York—not in Boston—assumed leadership. The Philadelphians set the tone of the opposition and gave it direction in ways made familiar in the crises over the Stamp Act and Townshend acts. There were differences, however, in 1773: the artisans made themselves known rather earlier than before and threats of violence were issued almost at once. To be sure the constitutional argument was made in conventional terms— Parliament had no right to tax the colonists because the colonists were not represented in it—but no one suggested that the colonies should delay other action until Parliament reconsidered its position. Rather a mass meeting held in Philadelphia on October 16 pronounced anyone importing tea sent out by the East India Company "an enemy to his country" and appointed a committee to call upon the consignees to obtain their resignations. With John Dickinson lending his opposition to the East India Company, most of the consignees—wealthy Quaker merchants—agreed in November to give up their commissions. One firm, James and Drinker, attempted to avoid resigning outright, but by December it too had given in.[2]

No doubt these merchants were affected by the threats of rough treatment made against anyone who imported tea. The committees of the people, chosen in mass meetings or self-appointed in several cases, included one styling itself "The Committee for Tarring and Feathering" which promised to practice its art on any Delaware River pilot who brought tea ships up the river to the city. When it learned the name of the captain of the *Polly*, which carried company tea, it informed him that his "diabolical service" would bring him into "hot water." As if this were not enough, the captain, one Ayres, was asked how he would like a halter around his neck and "ten gallons of liquid tar decanted on your pate—with the feathers of a dozen wild geese laid over that to enliven your appearance?" The committee's advice to Captain Ayres was "to fly to the place whence you came—fly without hesitation—

1. Benjamin Woods Labaree, *The Boston Tea Party* (New York, 1964), 88–89.
2. *EHD*, 774; Labaree, *Boston Tea Party*, 97–102.

without the formality of a protest—and above all, Captain Ayres, let us advise you to fly without the wild geese feathers." The committee tendered this advice in a broadside before Ayres reached the North American coast. When he finally reached the Delaware River in late December, the Boston Tea Party had been given, the governor, John Penn, and the Customs officials were cowed, and the consignees converted to patriotism. Ayres did the only thing left to him—hauled anchor and set sail for England, his cargo of tea undisturbed.[3]

A similar set of events was enacted in New York: the Sons of Liberty revived and mass meetings were held in the autumn under their tutelage as Isaac Sears, Alexander McDougall, and John Lamb once more assumed leadership. Although consignees followed the example of those in Philadelphia and resigned their commissions, the governor, William Tryon, insisted in December that when the tea arrived it should be unloaded and stored at the Battery. Tryon had good cards in his hand: a stout-hearted Council and, better yet, a man-of-war standing off Sandy Hook awaiting the tea. Even so, he lost, for the *Nancy*, the ship carrying the tea, was blown off course by a severe storm and put into port badly damaged in Antigua in February. By the time she was repaired and made her way to New York, the game was up. After taking on fresh provisions, the *Nancy*, cargo intact, sailed for home.[4]

The only port where tea was landed was Charleston, South Carolina. There, disagreements among artisans, merchants, and planters produced indecision which Governor William Bull took advantage of. Many Charleston merchants had been importing English tea and paying the duty; others had been smuggling Dutch tea. The legal importers insisted on a ban against the importation of all tea, whatever its origin, pointing out that only the smugglers would profit from barring the product of the East India Company. The consignees proved quite willing to give up their commissions, but no agreement was reached about what to do with the company's tea that arrived on December 2, 1773. The governor solved the problem twenty days later by seizing the tea for nonpayment of duty. The tea was stored and never sold.[5]

The opposition in Charleston acted largely in ignorance of events in Philadelphia and New York. Boston was located closer to these two cities and initially took its cue from them. But even with the example

3. *EHD*, 775.
4. Labaree, *Boston Tea Party*, 154–56.
5. *Ibid.*, 248–49; Jensen, *Founding*, 443–44.

of Philadelphia before it, Boston was slow to move against tea. The reason is clear—obsessive feuding through most of 1773 with Governor Thomas Hutchinson over his letters to England. Adams and his followers also bore down hard on royal payment of salaries to superior court judges. The Tea Act did not escape all local notice, for the *Boston Evening Post* summarized it in late August. Still, well into October, Adams single-mindedly pursued Thomas Hutchinson in the newspapers, as though anything that happened within Boston must be more important than anything that took place outside it. Adams was out of touch and so was the committee of correspondence, which in late September cited the denial of the East India Company's "sacred charter rights" as the most recent example of Parliamentary tyranny.[6]

Three weeks later Edes and Gill awakened to what was troubling New Yorkers and Philadelphians and began filling the columns of the *Gazette* with attacks on the Tea Act and the local consignees. Those worthies—Thomas and Elisha Hutchinson, sons of the governor, Richard Clarke, Edward Winslow, and Benjamin Faneuil—did not suffer in silence but hit back through the *Boston Evening Post*. Richard Clarke writing as "Z" in late October pointed at the inconsistency in protesting the tax on tea after paying it for two years and while still paying duties on sugar, molasses, and wine "from which more than three-fourths of the American revenue has and always will arise."[7]

Unsuccessful in cowing the consignees through the press, Adams resolved to do it through the crowd. On November 2 handbills were posted announcing a meeting at noon the next day at Liberty Tree, where the consignees were to appear and deliver their resignations. Convening this meeting was the North End Caucus, Sons of Liberty in another guise, a group which also took a prominent part in the Boston committee of correspondence. The consignees were not members and did not attend the meeting at Liberty Tree. The caucus thereupon decided to visit the consignees and led by William Molineux and accompanied by a mob found them at Clarke's warehouse, where a small-scale riot, damaging to the building but not to its occupants, ensued.[8]

Thereafter Adams and company stepped up the pressure, first through the town meeting which on November 5 adopted the resolutions passed in Philadelphia in October and called for the consignees to give up

6. Quoted in Jensen, *Founding*, 448.
7. *Boston Evening Post*, Oct. 25, 1773; Francis S. Drake, *Tea Leaves* (Boston, 1884), 281.
8. Labaree, *Boston Tea Party*, 108–9.

their commissions. The committee of correspondence took care of unofficial action—an attack ten days later on Clarke's house, for example—but neither body could extract resignations from the consignees. By late November both sides were frozen into their positions: the consignees holding their commissions and awaiting tea and instructions from the East India Company; Adams, the Boston committee, and those of nearby towns determined that the tea should not be unloaded.[9]

The arrival on November 28 of the *Dartmouth*, the first of the ships carrying tea, opened the last stage of the crisis. After entering at the customshouse the ship had twenty days to pay the duties on its cargo; should it not pay it was liable to seizure, which meant that its cargo would be seized and stored. Francis Rotch, a young merchant who owned the *Dartmouth*, wanted her unloaded. There was other cargo besides the tea aboard and, after having it unloaded and ridding his ship of the tea, Rotch had a cargo of whale oil to put aboard. The consignees wanted to land the tea, store it, and await the instructions of the East India Company. Should the tea be returned to England, they must stand the loss, for the law provided that no tea could be re-imported into the country. Governor Thomas Hutchinson also wanted the tea put ashore—if for no other reason than to frustrate his old enemies. Whatever happened, the law must be observed, which meant that since the ship had entered at Customs the duties must be paid. For the time being, all he or anyone else could do was to wait for the twenty days to expire, on December 16.[10]

Adams and the local committees did not wait idly. A large mass meeting was held at the Old South on November 29 and again the next day. Neither meeting was a legal town meeting; each numbered 5000 people and included many from the surrounding countryside. These gatherings put the radicals' case simply—the tea must be sent back to England. Resolutions incorporating this demand were sent to the consignees, who in the way of other "enemies of the people" had fled to Castle William in the harbor. Their spines stiffened by the governor, the consignees refused, though they knew they had no chance of unloading their tea, for Adams and friends had forced the *Dartmouth* to tie up at Griffin's Wharf and had put a guard aboard.

Temporarily thwarted, the Boston committee of correspondence appealed to New England for support, and echoes of local resolutions began coming in. The committee then met with committees from nearby

9. *Ibid.*, 112–18.
10. *Ibid.*, 118–19.

towns; by this time the deadline for payment of duties was three days hence. When the decision was made to destroy the tea if it were not cleared for return to England is not clear. On December 14 another great mass meeting instructed Rotch to request clearance for the return voyage and sent ten men to accompany him as he made the rounds at Customs. The next day the collector, Richard Harrison, son of Joseph and one of the victims of the *Liberty* riot in 1768, refused clearance, and on the day following, December 16, Governor Hutchinson declined to issue a pass for sailing by the Castle. The ship had not been cleared by Customs, the governor observed in turning Rotch down; but if Rotch wanted naval protection the governor would request it for him from Admiral Montagu. Thinking of his ship and cargo, Rotch decided he did not want protection.

By the time Rotch reported his failure to the meeting in the Old South, it was nearly six in the evening—and nearly dark. There he found a gathering that knew it could wait no longer. After satisfying itself that Rotch would not return the tea and that he might attempt to unload it should the public authorities require him to do so, the meeting heard Sam Adams announce that there was nothing more they could do to save their country. There was, of course, and Adams's words signaled what should be done. War whoops greeted his announcement as the crowd flooded out of the meetinghouse, pouring along the waterfront and backing up on Griffin's Wharf where *Dartmouth*, *Eleanor*, and *Beaver* lay, the last two recent arrivals and, like the first, with tea aboard. About fifty men "dressed in the Indian manner," faces darkened and bodies wrapped in blankets, broke off from the crowd and set to work, brewing tea in Boston harbor. The men performed their mission with dispatch, hoisting the casks of tea on deck, smashing them open, and dumping the tea over the side. The water around the ships was soon covered, and before morning some of the tea had floated as far as Dorchester Neck. The ships themselves were not damaged. A newspaper reported a week later that a padlock belonging to a captain was broken, apparently by mistake, for another was soon sent to him. In all 90,000 pounds of East India Company tea, valued at £10,000, was destroyed, a small price, these men would have said, to pay for liberty.[11]

Who did the actual work of jettisoning the tea cannot be known. The crowd may have included a fairly broad spectrum of Boston's population and probably farmers from nearby villages. For the resistance to

11. My account of the Tea Party rests on Labaree, *Boston Tea Party*, chap. 7.

the Tea Act drew on the "people" in a way nonimportation had not. Merchants had contributed much of the leadership in nonimportation even though lawyers and other professionals had forced the pace. Destruction of property left men from all these groups uneasy, but they had seen the matter through. They were called the "rabble" by Dartmouth, the Secretary of State for the American Colonies, who, far removed in England, could not imagine the mood—a fear of tyranny—that compelled otherwise sober citizens into an act of rebellion.[12]

II

An official report of the Tea Party from Thomas Hutchinson reached England on January 27, 1774. By that day the news was at least a week old, for a ship carrying the story had arrived on the 19th; and on January 25 the *Polly* with the tea intended for Philadelphia sailed into Gravesend. Soon a number of witnesses arrived to be interrogated by the government, Francis Rotch, owner of the *Dartmouth*, among them.[13]

As further information seeped in about resistance to the Tea Act, the conviction grew that something had to be done about the colonies or they would become totally independent. The common way of putting this theme was to argue that if the supremacy of Crown and Parliament were not asserted it would be lost, as though—to use the language the king's ministers favored—the father must discipline the rebellious child or abandon him forever. Such pronouncements were made in an atmosphere already darkened by recent events—the publication in Boston of Hutchinson's letters to Whately, the petition from the Massachusetts House requesting the removal of Hutchinson and Lt. Governor Andrew Oliver, and the autumn disorders throughout America.

The ferocity of feeling toward America was exposed before any proposals for action could be made. The exposure occurred in the cockpit of the Privy Council two days after official news of the Tea Party arrived. The occasion was a hearing on the petition from Massachusetts asking that Hutchinson and Oliver be removed from office. As agent for the Massachusetts legislature Benjamin Franklin was ordered to appear. At

12. In a letter to Mercy Warren, Abigail Adams referred to the tea as the "weed of slavery," a widely shared sentiment; Abigail Adams to Mercy Warren, Dec. 5, 1773, *Warren-Adams Letters* . . . (MHS, *Colls.*, 72–73 [Boston, 1917–1925]), I, 19. Samuel Adams, like Abigail a prejudiced observer, reported that most people in and out of Boston were pleased by the Tea Party, *ibid.*, 20. Adams was surely correct.

13. Jensen, *Founding*, 453–54; Labaree, *Boston Tea Party*, 173–74.

the hearing he discovered that the ministry had decided to discredit him and relieve itself of accumulated frustration over American defiance of its authority. To do its work the ministry chose Alexander Wedderburn, the solicitor general, skillful in the use of invective and without scruples in its employment. For over an hour Franklin stood in silence in a room packed with the rulers of Britain while Wedderburn reviled him. The petition was barely mentioned; Franklin's character, supposedly lost in depravity, was lashed as Wedderburn rehearsed for the committee the story of Franklin's part in obtaining Thomas Hutchinson's letters. At the end Franklin, impassive in his old-fashioned full-bottomed wig and his suit of figured Manchester velvet, left the chamber knowing that more than the petition had been lost.[14]

If self-restraint was lacking in Wedderburn and in the ministers who allowed him to go on unrebuked, so also were the good faith and respect which might have permitted the government to examine American grievances seriously. But the shock and revulsion felt at the destruction of the tea was too great for a detached review of differences over policy and, more importantly, the nature of the constitution itself. Even staunch friends of the colonies refused to defend the Tea Party. There was no way it could be justified, Rockingham insisted; and Chatham said simply that it was "criminal." After a talk with General Gage, who was in England on leave, the king recommended that force be used to bring the colonies into proper dependence. North caught the mood exactly a few weeks later when he declared that "we are not entering into a dispute between internal and external taxes, not between taxes laid for the purpose of revenues and taxes laid for the regulation of trade, not between representation and taxation, or legislation and taxation; but we are now to dispute whether we have, or have not any authority in that country."[15]

This description of American affairs admitted of no compromise. On the day of Franklin's ordeal in the cockpit, the cabinet decided that action must be taken to reduce the colonies to a state of dependence or, as some imagined, to restore the sway Parliament had once enjoyed in America. The cabinet which backed this policy had not changed much since North had taken over from Grafton. North still led as chancellor of the Exchequer and first lord of the Treasury. He was, however,

14. Carl Van Doren, *Benjamin Franklin* (New York, 1938), 468–76.
15. Labaree, *Boston Tea Party*, chap. 9, reviews English responses. North's statement is quoted in Bernard Donoughue, *British Politics and the American Revolution: The Path to War, 1773–1775* (London, 1964), 77.

no stronger within himself than before. A fine helmsman in calm waters, he lacked the grip for heavy weather. Nor did he have the anger or the intensity to force through measures to smash American self-government. But neither did he have the will to stop those who wanted hard reprisals, for North too believed in Parliamentary supremacy, a belief which in this case disarmed him. North's step-brother, Dartmouth, had become American secretary in 1772. Like North he was a moderate in colonial matters, but he too believed in the supremacy of Parliament and felt no disposition to slow its exercise. Three sterner spirits in the cabinet demanded measures which would leave no one in doubt as to where sovereignty lay. They were Suffolk, Secretary of the Northern Department, an old Grenvillite and a man of considerable ability; Gower, president of the Council, and Sandwich, first lord of the Admiralty, both Bedfordites. Of the two, Sandwich may have had more personal force; he was a conventional politician but a superbly capable minister. Rockford and Baron Apsley did not count for much in the cabinet, but both supported coercive action against the colonies.

With this alignment the decision to take action came easily. Still, a month passed before the ministerial wheels began turning. During this time Dartmouth explored the possibility of limiting the government's response to punishment of the leaders of the Tea Party. He first obtained a ruling from Attorney General Thurlow and Solicitor General Wedderburn that the Bostonians had committed treason and then awaited evidence that would justify bringing them to trial. After a month of taking depositions from witnesses and deliberating on the question, Thurlow and Wedderburn replied—to the irritation of Dartmouth and the king—that the evidence was not strong enough to warrant prosecution of the ringleaders in Boston.[16]

While the law officers were considering the case, the cabinet had decided to close the port of Boston and to move the provincial government to a less explosive site. Although the legal experts agreed that the port could be shut up by executive action, the government decided to avoid asserting the prerogative in colonial affairs and to ask Parliament to do the job. Parliament was more than willing: North announced the government's plans on March 14, and four days later presented the Boston Port bill to Commons. The bill proposed that Boston be closed to all ocean-borne trade except for certain coastal vessels which would be permitted under tight supervision to enter with food and fuel. The

16. Donoughue, *British Politics*, 37–62, for this and the preceding paragraph.

port would remain closed until the king decided to reopen it, and he was not authorized to act until the East India Company had been fully compensated by the town for the destruction of the tea.[17]

The debate on the bill was not the most distinguished ever heard in the Commons. North explained that the purposes of the bill were to punish Boston, get the East India Company's money back, and secure the port for business undisturbed by riots and mobs. No one seems to have opposed these pieties, though Dowdeswell said that the government was recommending action without hearing Boston's side. Most members apparently thought that they had heard quite enough from Boston, and even the old friends of the colonies praised the bill, Isaac Barré, for example, saying of it, "I like it, adopt, and embrace it cheerfully for its moderation."[18]

Moderate or not, the bill moved through the Commons at an immoderate speed. The House did not even bother to divide at the second reading and immediately afterwards brushed aside Rose Fuller's amendment that Boston be fined rather than shut up. On March 25 the bill received its third reading and was sent on to the Lords, where it was quickly approved. By the end of the month the king had given his assent—and Boston by law was to be closed to all commerce as of June 15.

The Boston Port Act was the first of five acts the Americans called the Intolerable Acts. Parliament passed the others in the three months following passage of the Boston Port Act. The next two—the Massachusetts Regulatory Act (commonly called the Massachusetts Government Act) and the Impartial Administration of Justice Act—occasioned greater opposition and livelier debate, but both passed with large majorities. The Massachusetts Government Act embodied proposals which had been made at various times before by officials who had long insisted that Parliament must establish its supremacy in America. And if to do so involved altering a royal charter, an act for which no precedent existed, too bad for precedents and charters. In simple terms, the Act converted the Massachusetts government into a royal affair: the House would continue as an elective body but the Council from August on would be nominated by the Crown; the governor would appoint and remove, if he wished, most civil officials; towns would no longer meet except with royal permission; and sheriffs—not freeholders—would select juries. Obviously this Act considerably reduced local control in Massachusetts; a related statute, the Impartial Administration of Justice Act, further cut

17. Labaree, *Boston Tea Party*, 183–84.
18. William Cobbett, comp., *Parliamentary History of England from the Earliest Period to the Year 1803* (36 vols., London, 1806–20), XVII, 1169.

down colonial power by providing that any royal official accused of a capital crime in the colony might be sent to England or another colony for trial.[19]

During the debate on these bills Rose Fuller proposed the repeal of the Townshend duty on tea. The motion was neither irrelevant nor out of order, but presented on the assumption that the new coercive policies in America had no chance if the duty remained. Once the tax was removed the Americans might swallow their medicine. Fuller moved repeal on April 19, and Burke immediately gave his support in a speech on American taxation. The speech is memorable for its wit and its brilliant reconstruction of the government's dismal efforts to bring order into colonial affairs without the advantage of a coherent policy. The government's way, Burke said, was "meanly to sneak out of difficulties into which they had proudly strutted." But the speech also revealed once again the limits on sympathy for the colonials' version of the constitution. To be sure, Burke urged that the duty on tea should be lifted, but on grounds of expediency not of constitutional right. The Declaratory Act had stated what Parliament might do—"bind the colonies in all cases whatsoever"—from that line not even the friends of America deviated.

The king signed the two bills on May 20. Two weeks later he gave his assent to still another quartering bill, the latest attempt to force civil authorities in America to provide housing and provisions for troops. The Quartering Act of 1765 had required the authorities to furnish barracks; the next year an amended statute allowed billeting of troops in inns, taverns, and vacant buildings. This one permitted the quartering of troops with private families. It passed the Commons without a division early in May and went through the Lords easily, though Chatham spoke against it.[20]

All four statutes were meant to be punitive and were also calculated to reduce the colonies to a proper subordination. The Quebec Act which became law late in June had neither of these purposes, but because of its timing and its provisions, it was regarded as one of the Intolerable Acts, as part of Parliament's response to the Boston Tea Party.

III

Although many colonists branded the legislation closing the port of Boston and altering the government of Massachusetts the Intolerable Acts, just as many seemed in spring 1774 quite willing to tolerate the intolera-

19. Jensen, *Founding*, 456–57; Donoughue, *British Politics*, 88–95.
20. For Burke's statement in the preceding paragraph, see *Parliamentary History*, XVII, 1222. The debates on all these measures may be read in *ibid.*, 1163–1277.

ble. Sam Adams and the Boston committee of correspondence, however, were no more able to accept such complacency than they were the punishment of Boston. The full extent of Parliament's reactions became known only gradually, but news of the most drastic measure, the shutting up of Boston, arrived on May 10 and was widely dispersed through the colonies by the end of the month.

Adams did not wait for this information to spread before acting. He and the committee proposed that the town suspend all trade with Great Britain and the British West Indies and that the rest of America do the same. The town meeting gave the proposal its support almost immediately, but at that point a different spirit showed itself.

The last try at nonimportation had ended with accusations of bad faith ringing in all the colonies. John Mein's charges that John Hancock and associates had cheated had created suspicions of Boston, and the understandable desires of merchants everywhere to make money inhibited whatever enthusiasm they might once have felt about still another stoppage of business. Even those aroused enough to break off their trade were concerned that they not act alone, that such action be taken everywhere with no chiseling. By this time, with recent experience in mind, guaranteeing such united action did not seem easy. Therefore, the tendency of merchants almost everywhere was to hang back while awaiting evidence that economic coercion against Britain would be concerted in all the colonies.

The evidence of merchants' intentions promised anything but joint action. In Boston the reluctant among them must have taken heart when General Gage arrived on May 13 with a commission as governor. Soon afterwards a group of merchants proposed to pay for the tea destroyed in December and commissioned Thomas Hutchinson, who was leaving for England at the beginning of June, to carry their offer to London. The Boston committee of correspondence could not ignore this opposition and a few days later announced that it was sponsoring a "Solemn League and Covenant" for the public's signature. This covenant pledged its signers to stop all trade with Great Britain, to refuse to purchase any English goods imported after August 31, and to break off trade with anyone refusing to sign. The next step was to mobilize the town meeting; here again the radicals proved their political mastery as the town voted against payment for the tea on June 17 and ten days later endorsed the Solemn League and Covenant. Neither action came easily—the merchants fought savagely against both, moving in the town meeting that the committee of correspondence be dissolved.

That motion failed, but the intimidation intended by the "Solemn League" failed too, as more than one hundred merchants signed and published a protest against it and its parent, the committee of correspondence.[21]

Adams and the committee won these struggles, but their victory was worthless. To be sure, several New England towns supported nonimportation, and more than one committee of correspondence responded favorably to appeals from Boston for support. Outside New England there were promises of supplies for "suffering Boston" and there were denunciations of the Intolerable Acts. Perhaps the most impressive was sounded in Virginia, where in late May the House of Burgesses declared that Boston was enduring a "hostile Invasion" and set aside June 1, the day Boston was to be shut up, as a "Day of Fasting, Humiliation, and Prayer, devoutly to implore the divine Interposition for averting the heavy Calamity, which threatens Destruction to our civil Rights, and the Evils of Civil War. . . ." A fastday must have gratified Puritan Boston, where such days had a long and honorable tradition. Reverting to such a technique was intended to arouse sensitivities to threats against liberty such as had been present during the English Civil War. Jefferson claimed the inspiration for such a technique for himself and half a dozen other burgesses, among them Patrick Henry and Richard Henry Lee. These spirits, very much aware of their boldness, "cooked up" a resolution based on the forms and language, suitably modernized for eighteenth-century readers, employed in the Puritan Revolution. Derivative, "cooked up," and bold as it was, the resolution with its call for a fastday struck a pleasing note in the ears of older burgesses who speedily approved it. The governor, Lord Dunmore, reacted as governors representing outside authority always did and dissolved the House.[22]

From other colonies came similar, though less forceful, expressions of support for Boston. These muted declarations barely concealed the struggles behind them between merchants and popular leaders. The issue dividing them concerned the action to be taken in response to the Boston Port Act. Each "side" included various shadings of opinion, but most seemed to have agreed with Boston's claim that it was representing the "common cause," that its liberties stood for all, and that if Parliament suppressed it, all would lose their liberties. Acceptance of these proposi-

21. Richard D. Brown, *Revolutionary Politics in Massachusetts: The Boston Committee of Correspondence and the Towns, 1772–1774* (Cambridge, Mass., 1970), 191–99; Jensen, *Founding,* 466–70.

22. *TJ Papers,* I, 105–6, for the resolution calling for a day of fasting.

tions did not carry all groups to an agreement on what should be done. Boston's call for stoppage of all trade with Britain aroused open opposition in virtually all merchant groups, and skepticism even among some "popular" groups—among mechanics, for example, in New York. The way nonimportation had collapsed four years earlier had disenchanted many merchants and others as well. In 1770, merchants in several cities had been unable to resist large profits while the competition tied itself up. Merchants in Boston had been accused of such tactics; and appeals from Boston thereafter were always slightly suspect. Boston's merchants distrusted those in nearby Rhode Island, and there was a mutuality of suspicion in New York and Philadelphia.[23]

In an environment heavy with mistrust, the proposal to convene a continental congress drew surprising agreement. The reasons are fairly clear. Some merchants who had felt themselves betrayed in 1770 retained confidence in action that united their kind in all the colonies. If both obligations and penalties were clear, they reasoned, economic coercion had a chance of success. Other merchants, probably a smaller number, expected to be able to forestall any concerted action in a general meeting. But even these men seem to have believed that Parliament's action presented a threat to political liberty as well as to business. The question was, as before, how to respond—not whether to respond.

While Boston's leaders plotted, and arguments over this problem went on everywhere, colonial legislatures and unofficial bodies began to cut through the debate and to act. Connecticut's lower house was one of the first; early in June it instructed its committee of correspondence to choose delegates to what became the first Continental Congress. Less than two weeks later Rhode Island's General Assembly chose its own delegates. Five colonies—Maryland, New Hampshire, New Jersey, Delaware, North Carolina—resorted to provincial assemblies, extraordinary bodies substituting for legislatures dissolved by peace-loving governors. A similar agency, the convention, chose Virginia's delegates in August; local committees made the choices in New York, and in South Carolina the Commons House of the assembly ratified the selections of the inhabitants. Georgia in 1774, badly frightened by an uprising of Creek Indians on the northern frontier, decided against sending delegates, lest it be deprived of British arms. Boston was distant, the Indians close by; danger may not have revived loyalty in Georgia but it subdued daring.[24]

These local conflicts over the tactics to be used in responding to

23. *EHD*, 789 (Boston Committee of Correspondence, Circular Letter, May 13, 1774).
24. Burnett, *Continental Congress*, 20–22.

the Intolerable Acts were of great importance and affected the actions of the Congress itself. But they should not be overplayed. The fact is that a Continental Congress met and proved capable of making decisions crucial to the future of the empire. It did in part at least because the values and interests its delegates represented overrode the disagreements that marked its origins.

When the Congress met on September 5, 1774, most Americans agreed that Parliament had no power to tax the colonies. This proposition had been announced almost ten years before, and attachment to it had swollen to near unanimity long before the crisis over the Stamp Act ended. At that time almost no one openly repudiated Parliament's claim to legislate on matters of general concern to the colonies as constituent parts of the empire. Within a few years, however, that claim also met flat opposition from an occasional essayist. Parliament of course had stimulated this rejection by passing the Townshend acts in a fit of fatuity, as though the colonists were not really serious in their objections to attempts to take their property without their consent.

The denial of Parliament's authority occurred under various guises— discussions of the powers of representative bodies, for example, or in arguments over the nature of the empire. William Hicks's *Nature and Extent of Parliamentary Power* exemplifies the first in its concentration on the act of delegation as essential to legislative power. By what means, he asked, had the colonies—unrepresented in Parliament—delegated power to it? Obviously they had not delegated power to Parliament, and its decisions regarding them were nothing more than "violence and oppression." James Wilson's *Considerations on the Authority of Parliament*, which lies in the second category, assumes that the colonies owe allegiance only to the Crown. Parliament, Wilson held, simply had no jurisdiction in an empire of states virtually independent except for their connection to the Crown.[25]

The monarch too underwent some cutting down in the political theory published on the eve of the meeting of the Congress. In the fray over the Stamp Act, the king had escaped all abuse while the Parliament and ministry absorbed it. In the careful conventions observed in these writings he appeared the unwitting prisoner of evil ministers, a creature

25. William Hicks, *The Nature and Extent of Parliamentary Power Considered* (Philadelphia, 1768), xvi; James Wilson, *Considerations on the Nature and Extent of the Legislative Authority of the British Parliament* (Philadelphia, 1774). I have used the version in Robert Green McCloskey, ed., *The Works of James Wilson* (2 vols., Cambridge, Mass., 1967), II, 721–46 (see especially, 735–45).

apparently at once wise, just, and by implication blind to his subjects' interests. This delicately ironic treatment of the monarch continued in most writings published in 1774, but with one difference. In the mood of defiance engendered by the Intolerable Acts, the colonists did not hesitate to implicate the king directly in the misrule and oppression they felt themselves to be enduring. At the same time they shrank from saying that George III was evil; rather he had made mistakes; he had, as the young Thomas Jefferson said in *A Summary View*, "no right to land a single armed man on our shores." But "his majesty has expressly made the civil subordinate to the military"—in order to enforce "arbitrary measures" which began in England with the Norman Conquest and which were extended to the colonies with their founding. The worst of these measures, according to Jefferson, was the royal claim to all lands in England and America—the introduction of feudal tenures and all the exactions which accompanied them. Whatever the justice of such arrangements in England, they had no place in America, Jefferson believed, for "America was not conquered by William the Norman, nor its lands surrendered to him or any of his successors." Rather the colonies were founded by free men exercising their natural right to depart from Britain, "the country in which chance, not choice has placed them." The colonies were settled under laws and regulations these founders deemed most likely "to promote public happiness."[26]

Jefferson's assumptions about the empire appear clearly in this argument: Parliament did not have jurisdiction over the colonies—all that it had done was usurpation. The king on the other hand did have authority in America but only of a limited kind. Kings, Jefferson observed, are the "servants, not the proprietors of the people." This sort of flourish—so typical of Jefferson—described what he and others made explicit elsewhere. The king was bound by laws; he was a party to a contract and governed according to the limits and regulations it established. The empire was composed of parts virtually independent and tied together only under rules agreed to by its members.

This view of the empire did not conceal the problem of reconciling the various interests of members; nor did it resolve the question of which agency, if any, should mediate differences of interpretations of the contract. The traditional way of meeting such issues was of course to concede power to Parliament as a superintending agency. When the first Conti-

26. *A Summary View of the Rights of British America* (Williamsburg, Va., 1774). I have used the version in *TJ Papers*, I, 121–35 (quotations in order are from 133, 134, 133, 121).

nental Congress opened, many in America surely still believed that Parliament should exercise such power. One who did, Jonathan Boucher, the distinguished Anglican clergyman in Virginia, published his convictions in *A Letter from a Virginian to Members of Congress*, an extended and powerful statement on behalf of Parliamentary supremacy and colonial subordination. Boucher's argument rested in part on a denial of the realities of the previous ten years. A "British community" existed in the world, he argued, and the colonies made up only a small part of it. A majority represented in Parliament governed the empire; the colonies owed obedience to that majority as a small part owed its being to a whole.[27]

Boucher had little chance of convincing most Americans in 1774. He not only assumed that Parliament's power was unchallengeable; he phrased this assumption in language that could only infuriate most Americans. The cause of liberty, he wrote, had always attracted "knaves" and "Qua[c]ks in Politics," "Impostors in Patriotism" who imposed upon the "credulity of the well-meaning deluded Multitude."

Deluded or not, the multitude did not care to be likened to "froward children, who refuse to eat when they are Hungry, that they vex their indulgent Mother." Thomas Bradbury Chandler adopted similar language in *The American Querist*, which appeared three days after the Congress began its meetings. One of Chandler's queries was "whether some degree of respect be not always due from inferiors to superiors and especially from children to parents?" Chandler, like Boucher, found in the Declaratory Act the appropriate description of the colonies' relations to Parliament. They were to be bound by Parliament in "all cases whatsoever."[28]

That phrase from the Declaratory Act still angered Americans. John Hancock had quoted it in March in the Old South Meetinghouse in the oration he gave commemorating the Boston Massacre. The British claim to tax the colonies without their consent was one of the "mad pretensions" of the government, pretensions so mad in fact that an army had to be sent to enforce them. Hancock spoke before plans for the Continental Congress took shape. By summer with planning well advanced and more British pretensions known, many Americans responded even more harshly. The responses in general carried few substantial surprises: Parliament had no authority in America, but, as a matter of expediency born of the complexity of the empire, it might exercise a general superintending power. It might regulate imperial trade, always

27. ([New York], 1774), 20–23, and *passim*.
28. *The American Querist: or, some Questions . . .* ([New York], 1774), 4, 6.

remembering that the colonies agreed to the principle of regulation. But it could not tax or otherwise interfere with the internal governance of the colonies.

These concessions struck minor notes in the blasts directed against the British government by writers and preachers in America. The main theme of essays and sermons of the summer concentrated on what seemed apparent—the Intolerable Acts left no doubt that the British government had set out to destroy American liberties. The British "Ministry," an anonymous New Yorker wrote, "are bent on the establishment of an uncontrollable authority in Parliament over the property of Americans."[29] William Henry Drayton of South Carolina said that matters had proceeded beyond unconstitutional taxation to the point where the question was whether Britain "has a constitutional right to exercise *Despotism* over America!" Elsewhere colonials made assessments equally bleak.[30]

The remedies available to an America willing to follow a Continental Congress might produce a redress, but no optimistic predictions of easy accomplishment were made. Parliament and the British ministry appear in dark hues in these accounts, and no brightening seemed likely. Something had to be tried, however. Some Americans urged that a total prohibition of trade, including a ban on exports to Britain, should be instituted. Others suggested that military preparations should be made, and at least one minister preached on the doctrine of a "just war."[31]

In all the outrage and the proposals for getting things changed there was a sense that the Americans faced evil and corruption which would spread to their own shores if they failed to defend themselves. The sources of this conviction lay deeply within Protestant culture, especially the belief that most conflict involved questions of good and evil, and right and wrong. Self-government, in this view, rested on virtue, on righteousness, and in the conflict the Americans confronted a government, as John Hancock pointed out, that was not "righteous." The proof of the evil appeared everywhere—in the standing army the British had sent to America, an institution which, as Josiah Quincy said, "had

29. *A Serious Address to the Inhabitants of . . . New York, Containing a Full and Minute Survey of the Boston Port Act* (New York, 1774), 9.

30. [William Henry Drayton], *A Letter from Freeman of South Carolina, to the Deputies of North America . . . at Philadelphia* (Charleston, S.C., 1774), 7–8.

31. John Lathrop, *A Sermon Preached to the Ancient and Honorable Artillery-Company in Boston . . . June 6th, 1774* (Boston, 1774), 6–15, and *passim*. This sermon is also notable for its evocation of the virtues of the Protestant Ethic, its praise of the sumptuary laws of the seventeenth century, and its citation of Trenchard and Gordon on the advantages of militia over standing armies.

introduced brutal debauchery and real cowardice" among the lower classes and "venal haughtiness and extravagant dissipation" to the "higher orders of society." Proof existed too in the Quebec Act by which, Ebenezer Baldwin insisted, "Popery is established," a forecast of what awaited the thirteen English colonies. Evil and corruption appeared too in the protection extended by the Administration of Justice Act to the "harpies and bloodsuckers" of the Customs service.[32]

All these conclusions and the ones which found corruption and sin in the Massachusetts Government Act, the Boston Port Act, indeed the entire array of British actions against America since 1764, repeated old concerns. They also employed a familiar vocabulary and referred to the deepest values of Americans. What was different in 1774 was the air of near hopelessness; the corrosive feeling that almost nothing worked, nothing would recall Britain to its senses, recall it to the service of the good and the freedom that once filled Anglo-American life. Yet much could be done—a virtuous self-denial would help keep Americans free of corruption, a rejection of placemen and troops would aid in keeping their institutions pure, and a principled defense of their right to govern themselves gave the only hope possible that their liberty might be preserved.

IV

The bitterness so obvious in the essays and pamphlets published throughout the summer did not show itself immediately in the meeting of the first Continental Congress. The delegates who rode into Philadelphia in late August and early September felt excitement and pride and even awe at what they were doing—not rage at Britain. The Massachusetts delegates, John and Sam Adams, differed from their colleagues in their feelings but they kept their anger in check. They and their colleagues Robert Treat Paine and Thomas Cushing were shrewd men who proposed to serve Massachusetts and America without any display of self.

Keeping in the background came hard to John Adams, almost as hard as holding his anger in check. He was a warm, often irascible and impulsive man, open to the world, eager for its praise and recognition but throughout his life often stung by its barbs of disapproval. Historians

32. John Hancock, *An Oration; Delivered March 5, 1774* (Boston, 1774), 6–7; Josiah Quincy, *Observations on the Act of Parliament Commonly Called the Boston Port-Bill* (Boston, 1774), 33; Ebenezer Baldwin, "An Appendix," in Samuel Sherwood, *A Sermon, Containing Scriptural Instructions to Civil Rulers, and all Free-born Subjects* (New Haven, Conn., 1774), 56.

often compare John Adams and Thomas Jefferson, a man he admired, except for one difficult period in their lives, and to whom as an old man he poured out his heart. Jefferson possessed a serene surface that the perpetually uneasy Adams never developed, even for a moment. Jefferson was elegant; Adams was rough though never coarse. He lacked Jefferson's versatility, but within its range his intelligence cut as deeply as Jefferson's did. And in two fields of knowledge, the history of religion and politics, Adams's learning surpassed Jefferson's.

John Adams did not consider life a search for salvation but he felt many of the compulsions and drives of his Puritan forebears. In particular he felt the urge to work and to accomplish something—something in public life. He craved fame and reputation. But he would not do anything just for the sake of the world's approval. His conduct was governed by the moral code of his culture, a code that was still largely Puritan. While he valued honor and wealth and learning, he believed that piety and virtue were more important.

Adams's interest in public affairs was closely connected to the Puritan values that controlled so much of his life. The first essays he wrote as a young man were attacks on taverns. His objections to taverns echoed the traditional Protestant concern that thrift be observed and time and talent not be wasted. Taverns ran people into debt, took them away from their work, and offered tempting places in which to squander time.

Opposing the Stamp Act and the British measures that followed came as naturally to Adams as did criticizing the immorality of taverns. The political issues of the 1760s and 1770s were never simply matters of law or equity or constitutionalism, they were matters of moral principle. The British presented a threat because they were corrupt as well as powerful. They had to be resisted with everything America had; if they were not, virtue, piety, and liberty would be lost. These convictions governed Adams's conduct throughout the Revolution.

Despite his obsessive concern with public questions, despite his rage at the British, despite his anxiety and his fears, John Adams was a happy man when he attended Congress. He loved and received in turn the love of Abigail Smith Adams, whom he had married in 1764. Abigail Adams had wit and warmth to match his own, and on the eve of the Revolution she had a maturity of judgment that he would not attain for years. Nine years younger than he, she was the daughter of a well-to-do clergyman in Weymouth, a village close to John Adams's Braintree.

John Adams was born in 1735 in Braintree, the son of John Adams, a farmer, and Susanna Boylston. The Boylstons were socially better than the Adamses and they had more money. Young John had a happy boyhood, was sent to grammar school and Harvard College (A.B. 1755), taught school at Worcester, studied law for two years, and was admitted to the Suffolk bar in 1758. When he rode to Philadelphia to attend the first Continental Congress he was an experienced attorney. He had held several minor offices in Braintree and one important one—he had been elected a selectman in 1766—and after moving to Boston in 1768 he had begun to play a larger part in provincial politics. Boston had made him its representative to the General Court in 1770, the year he defended Captain Preston and the soldiers in the Boston Massacre trials. He was well known in Massachusetts and, though he never felt that he received his due, highly respected by its citizens.

The delegates that John Adams and his cousin Sam met in the Congress were hardly less capable than themselves. In fact several could claim much more in the way of attainments than either Adams.

The Virginians especially impressed their colleagues. They were an elegant lot, distinguished in bearing and apparently steady in purpose. That vainest of men, John Adams, called them "the most spirited and consistent, of any"; Richard Henry Lee was a "masterly Man," Peyton Randolph, a "well looking Man," Richard Bland, "a learned bookish Man." Others shared these impressions. To Silas Deane of Connecticut, Peyton Randolph's appearance was "noble"; and George Washington, though "hard" in countenance, had "a very young look, and an easy, soldier-like air and gesture." Washington had long since taken on the proportions of legend for his exploits in the French and Indian War. Now while the Congress met, his reputation grew as the story spread that "on hearing of the Boston Port Bill, he offered to raise and arm and lead one thousand men himself at his own expense, for the defense of the country, were there need of it." Deane reported that Washington's fortune was "equal to such an undertaking." The entire group of Virginians drew praise from Caesar Rodney of Delaware, who declared that "more sensible, fine fellows you would never wish to see."[33]

In an age that relished oratory, the Virginians performed brilliantly. Deane gave way to ecstasy in describing Patrick Henry—"the completest speaker I ever heard"—and admitted that he could not convey the "music" of Henry's voice "or the highwrought yet natural elegance of his style and manner." Richard Henry Lee brought to the Congress a reputa-

---

33. Butterfield et al., eds., *Diary of John Adams*, II, 120; *LMCC*, I, 28 (Deane), 27 (Rodney).

tion for eloquence as great as Henry's—both Deane and John Adams called them the "Cicero" and the "Demosthenes of the Age."

If the Virginians stood out in more than one way, it is fair to say that virtually all the delegates who left personal accounts of the Congress confessed to admiring the ability and the character of the others. John Adams wrote his wife, Abigail, that "The magnanimity and public spirit which I see here make me blush for the sordid, venal herd which I have seen in my own Province."[34] Adams's praise of the Congress is completely understandable. Besides the Virginians it included John Dickinson and Joseph Galloway of Pennsylvania, both formidable men; James Duane and John Jay of New York whose talents must have been obvious even then; Samuel Chase of Maryland, Christopher Gadsden and Edward and John Rutledge of South Carolina, less able surely but impressive in their own ways nonetheless. Moreover these men were meeting in an extraordinary gathering where the petty concerns of the "venal herd" which brought a blush to Adams were missing. Still, they were not completely disinterested men; they may not have had the conventional spoils of office on their minds but they were very much concerned to defend local—as well as continental—interests.

Nor did they give up familiar ways of working the political engines. The two Adamses, aware that they and their colleagues from Massachusetts were objects of suspicion as well as of sympathy, took care to wear masks of modesty. Early in their stay in Philadelphia they were disconcerted by having to defend their colony's religious establishment against charges that it persecuted the Baptists, but even this embarrassment did not force them from their pose as political innocents. Behind the scenes they plotted and schemed almost as if they were home in Boston. "We have been obliged to keep ourselves out of sight, and to feel pulses, and to sound the depths," John Adams reported, and added that they had used others to "Insinuate our sentiments, designs, and desires."[35]

The full extent of those "sentiments, designs, and desires" is not known. They clearly included a conviction that all colonial trade with Britain should cease until the Intolerable Acts were repealed, and they may have extended to a hope that the Congress would call upon the

34. *LMCC*, I, 20. For Adams's comments in the previous paragraph on Lee and Henry, see Butterfield et al., eds., *Diary of John Adams*, II, 128. There are three excellent studies of the Continental Congress: Burnett, *Continental Congress;* Rakove, *Beginnings of National Politics;* and H. James Henderson, *Party Politics in the Continental Congress* (New York, 1974).

35. *LMCC*, I, 60.

colonies to arm themselves for a war should Parliament refuse to yield. This second "sentiment" had little chance of being made part of the Congress's designs. Most delegates favored a policy of economic coercion, though the exact terms proved difficult to define, but aside from an occasional hothead like Christopher Gadsden, who seems to have proposed an attack on British troops in Boston, almost none wished to see war break out. Their reluctance arose not from an overpowering desire to remain within the British empire, but from fear—fear of losing the war and thereby inviting a full-scale despotism.[36]

The probability of war does not seem to have been discussed in official sessions; rather it was a subject taken up at the dinners and parties the delegates attended every day. Much was arranged at these affairs: the meeting place of the Congress, Carpenter's Hall rather than the state house which Joseph Galloway, speaker of the Pennsylvania assembly had offered; the selection of the president of the Congress, Peyton Randolph, the choice of the Massachusetts men and of the delegates of the southern colonies. A similar deal made Charles Thomson secretary, though he was not a delegate. Whether to give each colony a vote or to apportion votes according to population was doubtless discussed out-of-doors, but the question also received a full discussion in formal session. The decision—each colony would have one vote—was essential to preserve unity among the colonies, large and small.[37]

Formal sessions began on September 5. From that day until the Congress dissolved itself on October 26, two major questions occupied it: what was the basis of American rights and how should they be defended? Both questions were given to a committee which promptly began discussions which, it discovered, could not be brought to an easy agreement.

The debate on the basis of American rights, serious and informed as it was, had on one side a curiously detached quality, almost as if nothing had taken place between Britain and the colonies in the previous ten years. That "side" was represented by James Duane, John Rutledge, and Joseph Galloway, all three refusing to consider that colonial rights should be founded upon the laws of nature. Galloway indeed seemed unwilling to accept any part of the constitutional argument the colonists had made, announcing that "I never could find the Rights of Americans, in the Distinctions between Taxation and Legislation, nor in the Distinction between Laws for Revenue and for the Regulation of Trade. I have looked for our Rights in the Laws of Nature—but could not find

36. *Ibid.*, 14–17; Butterfield et al., eds., *Diary of John Adams*, II, 139, 147.
37. Butterfield et al., eds., *Diary of John Adams*, II, 122–24.

them in a State of Nature, but always in a State of political Society."
The political society he referred to was one defined by the British constitution, the common law, the colonial charters—and not the law of nature.
Galloway evidently recoiled from basing rights on nature for fear that
such a flexible support might lead to independence. But recognizing
that the disposition of the Congress was to reject all Parliamentary authority and wishing to head off anything more extreme, he declared that
all colonial rights might be reduced to one: "An Exemption from all
Laws made by British Parliament, made since the Emigration of our
Ancestors."[38]

Galloway probably did not believe in this formulation, and no one
took it seriously. Most delegates saw no inconsistency in arguing that
colonial rights rested, as Richard Henry Lee said, "on a fourfold foundation—on Nature, on the british Constitution, on Charters, and on immemorial Usage." The "broadest Bottom, the Ground of Nature," offered
the most protection to the colonists, and Lee implied that the colonists
might require such a defense against further encroachments. Jay, William
Livingston, and Roger Sherman argued the same line to the satisfaction
of the Congress, and on the day after the debate began the committee
agreed that colonial rights were founded on the laws of nature, the
British constitution, and the colonial charters.

The responsibility for putting this general statement into a declaration
of rights was given to a subcommittee while the main committee moved
to the question of what practical measures should be taken in response
to the Intolerable Acts. This problem absorbed the remainder of September and most of October until just before the Congress dissolved itself.
What took time was deciding what power, if any, Parliament might
exercise over colonial trade.

The debate began in confusion as the issues of nonimportation, nonconsumption, and nonexportation were taken up almost at random in
late September. Through Thomas Cushing and the two Adamses, the
Massachusetts delegation let it be known that they would not be satisfied
with anything less than an immediate stoppage of trade with Britain.
Local interests thereupon began to collide, for the Virginians, formerly
so steadfast in the common cause, now revealed that they had come
to Philadelphia with instructions not to agree to curb exports before
August 10, 1775, the date presumably by which Virginia's tobacco raised
in 1774 would be harvested, cured, and sent to market. The South

38. *Ibid.*, 129–30, 128; *LMCC*, I, 27, for quotations in the following paragraph.

Carolinians also had ideas about nonexportation, most simply that it should not apply to their rice and indigo, both of which went to British markets. Virginia's opposition to a prohibition that went into effect before August 1775 strengthened the Carolinians' resolve to block nonexportation altogether.[39]

The worst of the fears and the desires of the southern colonists now exposed, the Congress turned to nonimportation, a subject about which there was considerable agreement, and decided that importation from Britain and Ireland should stop on December 1, 1774. It now seemed possible to return to the question of whether exports to Britain should be prohibited. Just as the Congress braced itself for this struggle, Joseph Galloway proposed that conflict with Britain should be resolved not by coercive measures such as nonexportation but by a constitutional revision which would establish a colonial parliament elected by the legislatures. This "grand council" and the British Parliament would undertake to legislate on matters involving the joint interests of Britain and the colonies, such as commerce, for example. Both "parliaments" would have to approve any such legislation before it became law; purely local matters would be left to the individual legislatures.[40]

Galloway's plan had a simple logic to it resting on an assumption still widely held in both Britain and America: "In every government, Patriarchal, Monarchial, Aristocratical or democratical, there must be a Supreme Legislature." Galloway presented his plan with all the considerable persuasiveness at his command, and James Duane, John Jay, and Edward Rutledge spoke for it. Rutledge in fact declared that he found "it almost a perfect Plan." Others questioned its perfection. Patrick Henry, for example, who argued that by adopting the Galloway plan "We shall liberate our Constituents from a corrupt House of Commons, but thro[w] them into the Arms of an American Legislature that may be bribed by that Nation which avows in the Face of the World, that Bribery is a Part of her System of Government." The possibility that an American parliament would fall into a system of corruption similar to the English may have concerned others besides Henry. More perhaps doubted that the plan carried promise of relief from the present crisis. Richard Henry Lee, executing a maneuver favored by distressed represen-

---

39. My account rests on John Adams's notes on the debates in Butterfield et al., eds., *Diary of John Adams*, II. I have also learned much from Rakove, *Beginnings of National Politics*, chap. 3.
40. Galloway's plan for a union appears in *JCC*, I, 43–48, and in *EHD*, 811–12. The standard study of it is Julian P. Boyd, *Anglo-American Union* (Philadelphia, 1941).

tatives for centuries, insisted that his constituents would have to be consulted before he could commit himself. For the time being the Congress tabled the plan, but by a margin of only one as the colonies divided six to five.[41]

With Galloway and his conservative supporters turned aside, the Congress appointed several committees to get its work done. And there was difficult work ahead, including the fashioning of a mechanism to carry into effect the agreement on nonimportation, nonconsumption, and nonexportation. The question of right, discussed in September until virtually all delegates were exhausted, had to be settled too. Prudence suggested to some that a petition to the king asking for a redress of grievances should be dispatched, and if the Congress was going to explain itself to the monarch, why not to the British people as well? Committees could write these messages and accordingly the delegates appointed them.

These early days of October did not see the delegates twiddling their thumbs while their committees turned to real work. Everyone felt the need to get done, a feeling reinforced from out-of-doors. The Massachusetts delegation passed on rumors from Boston about the oppression that city endured, and then on October 6, Paul Revere rode in with the Suffolk Resolves and a letter from the Boston committee of correspondence.

The Suffolk Resolves, written by Dr. Joseph Warren, Sam Adams's henchman, and adopted by Suffolk County on September 9, 1774, were rhetorically extravagant even for a day rapidly becoming accustomed to the extravagant. The preamble did not stop with a declaration that the Intolerable Acts were unconstitutional—it used such words as "murderous" to describe them. And it urged resistance: until the acts were repealed the people of Massachusetts should withhold taxes from the Crown, cease all trade with Great Britain, Ireland, and the West Indies, stop consuming "British merchandise and manufactures," and prepare themselves for war.

The letter from Boston that Revere brought asked the Continental Congress what its citizens should do—the British army was fortifying the town, and with the suspension of the legislature, advice, indeed leadership, was badly needed. The inhabitants of the town might still abandon it, or they might stay. But before they did anything they wanted the counsel of the Congress.[42]

What Boston's leaders expected to hear from the Continental Congress

41. Butterfield et al., eds., Diary of John Adams, II, 143 (quotations).
42. JCC, I, 55–56.

is not clear. What they got was compromise, safe resolutions lashing those who had accepted office under the Massachusetts Government Act and urging that if force were used to execute the Intolerable Acts "all America ought to support [Boston] in their opposition."[43] Before the Congress arrived at this phrasing, it had listened to proposals that Massachusetts be left to its own devices, Galloway's noble resolution, or that the militia attack the British before they could be reinforced, Christopher Gadsden's wild idea. Beside these two, Richard Henry Lee's motion that Congress advise the evacuation of the town appeared almost reasonable, but it too was rejected.

On October 14, three days after the problems of Boston were shelved, the Congress demonstrated that it could agree on something—a Declaration of Rights. The rights of the colonies had preoccupied the delegates almost from the first day of their meeting. They now adopted a statement which declared that colonial rights were founded on the law of nature, the British constitution, and the colonial charters. The source of this threefold version of rights was a compromise, of course, but the declaration itself was not a weak statement. Neither was it genuinely fresh: the rights it claimed had constituted the American cause for almost ten years. The declaration left no doubt that the colonies would not give up the right to tax and legislate for themselves. They were not represented in the "British Parliament" and "from their local and other circumstances, cannot" be.[44]

This part of the declaration seems to have commanded broad support in the Congress. There was less, but still a majority, for what followed— the colonies would "cheerfully consent" from the necessity of the case, and "a regard to the mutual interest of both countries" to the regulation of "our external commerce." This portion of the declaration marked the triumph of the Adamses, Richard Henry Lee, and those like them who favored a clear rejection of all the claims of the right of Parliament to govern in America. The remainder of the declaration drove the point home—the colonies acknowledged their allegiance to the Crown, freely given—but they would not accept "Acts of Parliament" which violated their rights. And lest there be any doubt, the Congress listed the "infringements and violations" perpetrated by Parliament.

While the delegates worked on the declaration, they also decided on the ways nonimportation, nonconsumption, and nonexportation could be made realities. They entered rough water almost immediately. The

43. *Ibid.*, 58.
44. *EHD*, 805–8, for the Declaration of Rights and Grievances, and *JCC*, I, 63–73.

South Carolina delegation now revealed how tightly tied its tongue was to the pursestrings of planters at home. The South Carolinians told the Congress that unless rice and indigo were exempted from the ban on exports, they would not sign the "Association," as the agreement on trade restrictions was now called. This announcement drew protests, but after the Carolinians agreed that only rice had to be protected, Congress caved in.[45]

The Association provided that the ban on imports from Britain would take effect on December 1; nonconsumption of East India Company tea would begin immediately; the prohibition of exports to Britain would, if it were still necessary, be observed after September 10, 1775. Everyone recognized that these instructions had little chance of success without force behind them. To give them force the Congress called for the election of a committee "in every county, city, and town" by those qualified to vote for representatives in the legislature. The committees would enforce the Association as committees in the preceding ten years had enforced earlier agreements. Not every town had such a committee, of course, but layers of committees would not leave much room for evasion. Under the Association, the committees were charged to operate as no government in America had ever operated. They were to inspect customshouse books, publish the names of offenders in local newspapers, and "break off all dealings" with violators, now baptized as "the enemies of American liberty."[46]

The delegates signed the Association on October 20. They spent the next few days on the petition to the king and the addresses to the people of Great Britain, America, and Quebec. Petitioning the king aroused no great enthusiasm; Washington and John Adams, for example, believed that it held no promise of bringing a redress of grievances. The Congress did not even bother to send one to Parliament, in part no doubt because a petition might be understood as an admission that Parliament had some authority in America.

On October 26, Congress dissolved itself with the understanding that if need arose a second meeting would be held on May 10, 1775. An outsider reading the letters and diaries of the delegates might have concluded that dissolution came just in time. The delegates showed fatigue; they had worked hard. But they may have been as tired of one another as they were from their labors. John Adams who had squirmed under

45. Butterfield et al., eds., *Diary of John Adams*, II, 137–40, 147–49.
46. *EHD*, 813–16 (Association); *JCC*, I, 75–80.

the wit and eloquence of his colleagues throughout the meeting gave way to his temper two days before the Congress closed up. "In Congress grumbling and quibbling as usual." And then, because some got on his nerves more than others, this entry on Edward Rutledge, "Young Ned Rutledge is a perfect Bob o'Lincoln—a Sparrow—a Peacock—excessively vain, excessively weak, and excessively variable and unsteady— jejune, inane, and puerile."[47]

Despite such feelings, the delegates departed Philadelphia full of respect for one another. They had demonstrated that they and the people they represented shared common interests and values. For a while their interests, especially their economic interests, had threatened to pull them apart, but in the end they put together the Continental Association. The Association expressed values which tied Americans together and suggested that in their desire to protect their right to self-government there was a moral concern transcending the constitutional questions in conflict. Morality made its way into the Association through the resolve to "encourage frugality, economy, and industry" and in the avowal to "discountenance and discourage every species of extravagance and dissipation, especially all horse-racing, and all kinds of gaming, cock-fighting, exhibitions of shews, plays, and other expensive diversions and entertainments. . . ."[48] In declaring their intention to honor Puritan standards, Congress did not argue that it had found another weapon against tyrannical government. But of course it had. For it intended to remind Americans that their virtue—their commitment to the public interest— underlay their political freedom. Indeed the Congress intended that Americans should remember that without virtue all kinds of freedom would perish. That the Congress cited frugality, economy, and industry and scourged extravagance and dissipation was no accident. It chose the only words Americans knew, words born of the Protestantism that had existed in the colonies since their founding. The emphasis on the ethics of Puritanism recalled Americans to an older way of life, one perhaps that they were in danger of forgetting in the urge to get and spend that filled so much of their lives in the eighteenth century. Now in the crisis with Britain they continued to consider what sort of people they were, and the Congress in its incantation to lean and spare living threw up a challenge to them.

47. Butterfield et al., eds., Diary of John Adams, II, 156.
48. EHD, 814–15.

12

War

The delegates to the first Continental Congress rode home to the applause and admiration of the continent—or a part of it. The Massachusetts delegates found their pace slowed by invitations to dine and to be entertained. For a time it seemed that every town between Philadelphia and Boston wanted to pay its respects. The Massachusetts men, having been dazzled by the food and wine and elegance in Philadelphia, managed to control their appetites on the road, begging off as politely as possible from all but necessary stops. In Palmer "alias Kingston," Massachusetts, they lodged with one Scott and his wife, both "great Patriots" according to John Adams. Scott and the local physician, Dr. Dana, were delighted by the Congress, believing that Parliament would repeal the Intolerable Acts and thereafter content itself with regulating trade. "Scotts faith is very strong that they will repeal all the Acts this very Winter," Adams noted in his *Diary*, adding skeptically that "neither the Doctors nor Scotts faith are my Faith."[1]

This expectation of Parliament's surrender may have accounted for a part of the approval of the Congress. Perhaps more Americans shared John Adams's skepticism and did not mind very much that the crisis would most likely continue. Adams learned more in Palmer about the so-called "Powder Alarm," begun by the rumor that swept through many of the colonies early in September that Gage had seized the powder stored in Charlestown—learned indeed that some had been disappointed when the rumor turned out to be false, thereby depriving them of a chance to fight the regulars.[2]

1. Butterfield et al., eds., *Diary of John Adams*, II, 160.
2. *Ibid.*, 124 (and note).

Those delegates who recorded their opinions believed that prospects for peace were bleak; and peace would continue only if Britain backed down. John Dickinson wrote Arthur Lee, then in London, that "I wish for peace ardently; but must say, delightful as it is, it will come more grateful by being unexpected." Dickinson's phrasing is interesting, implying that the circumstances the colonies found themselves in were something less than war, though hardly peaceful. Dickinson's and Adams's expectations probably represented prevailing views in the Congress. Although neither man made much of the possibility that they might be seized as rebels and shipped off to England for trial for their part in the Congress, other delegates did admit to being nagged by this fear during and after the meeting.[3]

Still, the applause gratified most of the delegates, especially since it did not stop. The newspapers printed the Continental Association, and provincial conventions and local committees sent their congratulations and hastened to reimburse the delegates for the expenses incurred in Philadelphia. But if the admiration of the colonies continued to pour forth, it soon ran up against its opposite, a tide of abuse and criticism of the Congress and all its works. Much of this criticism was in the form of anonymous essays published in newspapers and tracts. Many of the answers these pieces incited were also unsigned. Almost all of them were undistinguished, though many were composed by men already distinguished or soon to become so.

The critics of Congress included one of its members, Joseph Galloway. He had thought hard before the Congress met about the relations of the colonies to England, and nothing he heard in Philadelphia changed his mind: Parliament must hold supreme power in the empire. But the colonies had rights, and Galloway remained convinced that an Anglo-American union would provide the best means to protect them. Galloway had little more of substance to offer. He had, however, in the Congress caught a glimpse of the future: he had seen a desire for independence—the "ill-shapen, diminutive brat, INDEPENDENCY"—and his vision made him unhappy.[4]

Galloway explained himself in a pamphlet which did not conceal his disdain of popular leaders. Others shared his feelings, though not necessar-

---

3. *LMCC*, I, 83.
4. Joseph Galloway, *A Candid Examination of the Mutual Claims of Great Britain and the Colonies* (New York, 1775), reprinted in Merrill Jensen, ed., *Tracts of the American Revolution, 1763–1776* (Indianapolis, Ind., 1967), 351–99. (The quotation is from this edition, p. 374.)

ily his grand plan for a union of England and America. Among the most scornful of Congress was Daniel Leonard, a lawyer who lived in Bristol County, Massachusetts. Leonard wrote as "Massachusettensis"; and John Adams answered him as "Novanglus." The letters of these two men saw rough charges exchanged—and the desire for independence raised and denied.[5]

The pamphlet conflict between Samuel Seabury, an Anglican priest, and Alexander Hamilton, a student at King's College, New York, was even harsher. Seabury predicted war would occur if Americans followed the lead of Congress. Hamilton does not seem to have feared war. His answers to Seabury showed a rhetorical skill and a firm commitment to American rights.[6]

These exchanges—and many others—revealed that divisions over Parliamentary power persisted in America. Congress was a popular body— it had the support of the majority of the American people, one suspects— but some opposed its measures. Still more held back, restrained by old loyalties and by fear of a future outside the empire.

II

In a situation of ambiguity, the initiative belonged to those on the attack, to those with a program or a policy to carry out. The Association, of course, expressed the policy and proposed the means of carrying it out— those seemingly ever-present provincial, county, and town committees whose formal power did not exist but who now assumed the powers of government. In their most successful form—that is, their most extreme form in Massachusetts and Virginia—they simply took over and all but expelled traditional authority.

General Gage unwittingly gave these bodies their opportunity when he dissolved the Massachusetts legislature early in October before it even met. The first Provincial Congress eased into its place later in the month and Massachusetts had something approaching a revolutionary

5. *Massachusettensis* was published in the *Massachusetts Gazette* (Boston) and *Boston Post-Boy* (in issues beginning Dec. 12, 1774 and ending April 3, 1775); *Novanglus* in *BG* (beginning Jan. 23, 1775 and ending April 17, 1775).
6. [Samuel Seabury], *Free Thoughts on the Proceedings of the Continental Congress* . . . ([New York], 1774) and Hamilton's reply, *A Full Vindication of the Measures of the Congress* (New York, 1774). Seabury responded with *View of the Controversy Between Great Britain and Her Colonies* (New York, 1774); Hamilton's response, *The Farmer Refuted* . . . (New York, 1775); [Samuel Seabury], *The Congress Canvassed* . . . ([New York], 1774). Hamilton's tracts have been reprinted in Syrett and Cooke, eds., *Papers of Hamilton*, I, 45–78, 81–165.

government. But long before Gage acted and the Provincial Congress convened, a small-scale political revolution had occurred in western Massachusetts.

Western Massachusetts contained two counties, Hampshire and Berkshire, and about 15 percent of the colony's population. The Connecticut River cut through the region and gave it a means for shipping its lumber, hides, meat, and crops to the outside world. The most important towns of the area grew near the river, but most of its people got their livings farming in the Connecticut River Valley and in the narrow spaces of the Berkshires.[7]

A few great men had run the West and everyone in it for more than a generation. There was Israel Williams of Hatfield, an able, tough-minded merchant, land speculator, and politician. Colonel John Worthington did the same for Springfield, and Joseph Hawley, though different in several ways from the others—he did not speculate in land—had things to his liking in Northampton. These men, their families, and a handful of others like them—in many cases related to them, the Stoddards and the Partridges, for example—dominated the valley so thoroughly as to earn the name the River Gods.

The River Gods did not ignore politics. They, their kin, and their henchmen served as judges, selectmen, town clerks, and sheriffs, or effectively controlled all these offices and virtually all others through their mastery of business and their connections to the royal governor in Boston. Only Joseph Hawley remained aloof from Boston, and largely through his own efforts he managed to keep his hand in public affairs in Northampton despite his aberrant refusal to tie himself to the governor.

The other River Gods looked upon the agitation against imperial policies with a horror similar to Bernard's and Hutchinson's. Since the River Gods actually possessed power that the eastern Tories dreamed of, they kept western Massachusetts quiet while Boston rioted and protested. They ignored the Stamp Act, and they regarded nonimportation at the time of the Townshend acts with equal indifference. They did not take offense at Hillsborough's circular letter in 1768, but six of the representatives they sent to the House voted to rescind the Massachusetts Circular Letter. Only one westerner voted with the "Glorious Ninety-Two," those worthies who chose to defy Hillsborough, and three did not even bother to attend the session which took up this celebrated issue. The next

7. The discussion of western Massachusetts that follows is based primarily on Robert J. Taylor, *Western Massachusetts in the Revolution* (Providence, R.I., 1954), especially chaps. 1–4.

year, 1769, the West returned three of its rescinders to the House; only two others survived the purge in the remainder of the colony. Nor did the West take Sam Adams's convention seriously. One delegate appeared from all the towns of Hampshire County, and none from Berkshire.

The River Gods unknowingly ran up a debt for the obedience they compelled: the hatred of thousands of ordinary men who resented all the bowing and scraping they had to do. In 1772, when news spread that the English ministry had decided to pay superior court justices from the customs rather than leave that responsibility to the legislature, part of the debt was called due in the West, as six towns passed resolutions condemning this new policy. The courts were hated anyway; the River Gods and their crowd used them against small borrowers, and used them without mercy.

The Intolerable Acts—in particular the ones revoking the charter and removing the administration of justice even farther from popular control—were simply not to be borne; all the latent animosities broke free. In July and August mobs closed the county courts; they remained closed until 1778 in Hampshire and until 1781 in Berkshire. Town and county conventions—extralegal bodies—met and established their own courts, or in some cases turned the whole business over to the town meeting, which still had claims to legitimacy. In Pittsfield, for example, the town appointed a special committee to try cases; other towns relied on already overburdened selectmen. In the East these actions were watched closely, and in Boston grand and petit jurymen refused to take oaths, thereby bringing the superior court to a close.

These actions humiliated the River Gods, but they soon felt the anger of their people more directly. Israel Williams and Colonel John Worthington were named to the mandamus council, the new royal agency created by the Massachusetts Government Act. Neither dared accept, but before they could make their refusal known they were mobbed by angry crowds and made to resign in public. Colonel Worthington was completely intimidated and in effect switched sides, breaking his old ties with the eastern establishment. Israel Williams accepted the loss of his power but spoke of his dislike of patriot actions. In February 1775, long after he had turned down the appointment to the council, he received another visit from the crowd, which evidently expected something approaching obsequious behavior from Tories. Williams did not crack, and he spent the night in a smokehouse breathing the aroma of wood fires and cured meat. After that he was quiet.

Mandamus councillors far from the protection of the troops in Boston endured similar abuse. After Timothy Ruggles's appointment became known, he was warned by a friend in Hardwicke not to return home: "There are those here who I am satisfied thirst for your blood, and they have influence enough over others to put them upon spilling it."[8] Timothy Paine, visited by a crowd of two thousand people in Worcester, was forced to write out his resignation which contained an abject apology for accepting an appointment he had not sought, and then was compelled to read it aloud, hat in hand, in the middle of the mob. The Worcester crowd included several militia companies which then marched off to Rutland, twelve miles to the northwest, in search of another councillor who fled before they arrived. Daniel Leonard also drew a crowd which "formed themselves into a Battalion before my House."[9] This group was not easily put off and that night fired shots into the house.

These tactics worked. Virtually every councillor who failed to make his way to sanctuary in Boston resigned, and the rump in Boston exercised paper powers. Outside Boston the government resided in local bodies, towns, conventions, committees, and occasionally mobs. The conventions and committees drew most of the energies of resistance to themselves— they were unencumbered by traditional methods—and took upon themselves the organization of political and military resources.

Stopping trade with Britain was the easiest task these agencies had. By closing up Boston, the British had shut off imports. Warm spirits outside Boston now wanted the civilian population to evacuate the city in preparation for an attack on the troops. The Boston committee looked askance at this proposal, as did indeed most leaders in the countryside. Throughout the summer these men gathered together to plan actions short of war but in preparation for it. The men of Worcester County were especially active, meeting in August to reject all Parliamentary claims to authority in America, calling for larger gatherings, and attending one in Boston with delegates from Middlesex, Suffolk, and Essex counties. Early in September the Worcester Convention closed the county courts and began to reorganize the militia, first forcing the resignation of all officers and then urging towns to select new ones whose loyalty to the "common cause" was unimpeachable.[10]

---

8. Albert Mathews, ed., "Documents Relating to the Last Meetings of the Massachusetts Royal Council, 1774–1776," CSM, *Pubs.*, 32 (Boston, 1937), 476.
9. *Ibid.*, 482. Timothy Paine describes his experience in a letter to the governor (Aug. 27, 1774), *ibid.*, 476–78.
10. Jensen, *Founding*, 551–53.

All these local maneuverings led finally to the meeting of a Provincial Congress early in October. Gage had already adjourned the legislature before it had a chance to meet. The representatives and a good many other delegates then convened in Cambridge. There the newly aroused countryside showed its zeal, first by sending many more delegates than it ordinarily did to the legislature—Hampshire County, for example, sent thirty-nine rather than its usual twenty—and then by driving through measures looking towards war. Within three weeks, under western leadership, the Provincial Congress approved an appropriation of £20,000 for arms and ammunition, the money apparently to come from taxes ordinarily collected by the regular government. It also created a committee of safety and, after making certain that its membership would be controlled by westerners, authorized the committee or any five of its members to arm, supply, and order the militia into action. What was said at the Provincial Congress may have been even more warlike than any of these acts, as a number of once-passive delegates urged that Boston should be evacuated and then attacked and burned to the ground with his majesty's garrison inside.[11]

At the end of October the Provincial Congress adjourned, not to reconvene until the final week of November. When it did, it had the results of the first Continental Congress to consider. The Association seemed weak to many of these Massachusetts men, and they refused to approve it until they found a means of toughening its requirements. There was a rural animus against the city in the demand that the sales of all imported goods be banned sometime after nonimportation went into effect. The Congress eventually decided that no such goods, even though they were legally imported before December 1, 1774, should be sold after October 10, 1775. They had been tricked by the merchants before, or believed so, and they did not propose to let it happen again.[12]

Early in December the Provincial Congress dissolved itself, but not before ugly words were spoken in arguments over what to do about the troops in Boston. Sam Adams had returned from Philadelphia to take part in this second series of meetings and he rather liked what he heard from western tongues. Not surprisingly, Adams favored large-scale preparations—20,000 militia seemed an appropriate number to him and an immediate attack on the redcoats an appropriate course of action. Other easterners were not so sure—Thomas Cushing among them, who argued that in an assault on the British army, Massachusetts would

11. *Ibid.*, 557–60.
12. *Ibid.*, 560–61.

fight alone, for only the most blatant outrages by the British would bring the other colonies into a war. Adams professed to believe that the other colonies would not hesitate but would rush to the defense of Massachusetts, whereupon Cushing flared out: "that is a lie, Mr. Adams, and I know it and you know that I know it."[13]

There were no such abrasive encounters among Virginia's leaders in the autumn of 1774. Even the merchants fell all over themselves in declaring their satisfaction at the Association adopted by the first Continental Congress. Well they might, for in August just before the Continental Congress convened, the provincial convention closed down the county courts. This action was a response to the attempts by Scottish factors and merchants resident in Virginia to collect debts before the association adopted by Virginia brought business to a stop. These Scottish businessmen were pressing hard on their debtors in the local courts. Now with the Continental Association replacing the local agreement, the merchants attempted to head off reprisals against themselves.[14]

They had reason to be concerned. At the urging of the rump of the Burgesses the previous spring, meetings of freeholders in at least thirty counties had discussed stopping all trade with Britain, and though they had usually agreed that nonexportation was not expedient, most favored closing Virginia to imports from Britain. And in the two months following the close of the first Continental Congress about half of Virginia's sixty-one counties had chosen committees to enforce the Continental Association; most of the remainder followed suit early in 1775.

The committees made two simple—and correct—assumptions in the enforcement of the Association: first, that the majority of Virginians approved the means recommended by Congress, and, second, that because of this support, exposure to public disapproval was the most effective technique in dealing with violators. After their election, the committees ordinarily selected their chairmen—the elder James Madison in Orange, Edmund Pendleton in Caroline, Landon Carter in Richmond, Benjamin Harrison in Charles City: all important planters—and then proceeded to require merchants and planters to sign the Association. Anyone refusing to sign or even protesting against the requirement could expect to be branded an "enemy of the country." Alexander Leckie felt the Caro-

---

13. Quoted in *ibid.*, 562.
14. Virginia's actions are well discussed in Emory G. Evans, "Planter Indebtedness and the Coming of the Revolution in Virginia," *WMQ*, 3d Ser., 19 (1962), 511–33.

line committee's displeasure, for example, when at a public meeting at which all present were expected to sign the Association he said to a young Negro standing near by: "Piss, Jack, turn about, my boy, and sign." Three weeks later Leckie published his apology for this jocularity and for other unguarded comments—he had said "damn them all" when contributions were being raised to defray the expenses of Virginia's delegates to the Continental Congress, and he had spread the story that Walker Taliaferro, a local patriot, had violated the agreement of 1770. Leckie's new mood was servile: he found the "weight of public censure and public hatred" absolutely "insupportable." He had plenty of company. John Morris was denounced to the committee for "Certain expressions foreign from the Good of this Country" and was compelled to confess publicly that he was "Heartily Sorry." David Wardrobe, a schoolmaster in Westmoreland County, was denounced for having written a letter considered "false, scandalous, and inimical" to America. The committee warmed to its work after delivering itself of this judgment and urged the local vestry to deny Wardrobe the use of its building for his school. Parents were told not to send their children to Wardrobe for instruction, and he himself was called upon to publish his contrition in the *Virginia Gazette*. He did so in the most abject terms: "I do, most heartily and willingly, on my knees, implore the forgiveness of this country for so ungrateful a return made for the advantages I have received from it, and the bread I have earned in it, and hope, from this contrition for my offence, I shall be at least admitted to subsist amongst the people I greatly esteem, and desire that this may be printed in the *Virginia Gazette*." [15]

Although procedures for protecting freedom of speech and the press were not deeply embodied in judicial process as they were to be by the end of the Revolution, the action against Wardrobe and others was clearly repressive. Nor was Wardrobe's case the most flagrantly repressive, though his fear is obvious. The Orange County committee forced John Wingate to turn over pamphlets in his possession which were critical of the Continental Congress. Terror was employed in these cases

15. I have discovered the names of chairmen of county committees by reading reports of their meetings and their published statements in the newspapers: *VG* (Pinkney), Nov. 4, 1774, *VG* (Dixon and Hunter), Dec. 5, 17, 22, 1774, and Jan. 28, 1775. For the committees' actions (and the quotations) described in this paragraph, see *VG* (P), Nov. 4, 1774, Jan. 7, 1775; David J. Mays, *Edmund Pendleton, 1721–1803: A Biography* (2 vols., Cambridge, Mass., 1952), I, 351n, fn. 20.

and in many others, as speech was controlled, the newspapers censored, and dissent crushed.[16]

Suppressing dissent enabled the committees to enforce the ban on imports from Britain and the West Indies. The committees also sometimes resorted to direct action against violators. There were several small tea parties in Virginia rivers during the autumn, for example. Merchants usually avoided the destruction of proscribed goods, however, by storing them with committees—or more commonly, asking that the committees sell the goods. This procedure allowed the merchants to save their investment in the imports, for the committees returned the costs and sent the profits to Boston's poor. Prohibiting imports opened the door to profiteers—those merchants who had large inventories and small scruples. The committees were ready to deal with such people, sometimes by setting maximum prices—as, for example, in Caroline County—or by inspecting merchants' accounts for evidence of profiteering, a technique also used in Caroline. A few merchants held out only to find their names published in the paper and themselves designated enemies to the country. When this occurred, the offender found himself ostracized and cut off from trade and society.

By the end of the year the Association was in full effect, and the local committees were, as Governor Dunmore sadly observed, the government of Virginia. The governor did his best to prevent the House of Burgesses from supporting local measures by postponing its meeting throughout the winter of 1774–75. He could not prevent the organizing of militia and the collecting of arms, however, and both proceeded within the counties. George Washington and his friend George Mason organized the militia in Fairfax; under their guidance the county committee levied a tax of three shillings on every tithable. The money collected was spent for military supplies, and the committee which had no legal authority to tax backed up the collection by requesting that the name of anyone who refused to pay be reported to it. Though most counties did not go this far, many organized independent companies with men voluntarily putting themselves under drill and discipline. The young James Madison, soon to be elected to the Orange County committee of safety which

16. Mays, *Pendleton*, I, 351n, fn. 20. For further examples of action against merchants, see *VG* (D & H), Dec. 21, 1774, Jan. 14, 28, 1775. The Henrico County Committee resolved in December 1774, to "enter into a subscription for the encouragement of all kinds of husbandry and manufactures within this county," a common measure in Virginia and elsewhere, *VG* (D & H), Feb. 11, 1775.

his father chaired, predicted that "Such firm and provident steps will either intimidate our enemies or enable us to defy them."[17]

There were pockets of indifference and even resistance to the Association and to proposals that America should arm itself. The colony of Georgia was one such pocket, where Governor James Wright, now playing on fears of the Indians and the need for British protection, now adjourning the House and discouraging a provincial congress which met in 1775, managed to keep "patriotism" off balance. Far to the north in Pennsylvania, the Quakers damped down hotheads; and in Fairfield County, Connecticut, several towns controlled by Anglicans denounced the Association and all opposition to the Crown. Yet in both Pennsylvania and Connecticut, the Association went into effect as local committees enforced nonimportation. South Carolina also saw sundry committees spring up, and imports from Britain virtually stopped. Despite western indifference, North Carolina observed nonimportation. Maryland's committees proved almost as vigorous as Virginia's, arousing so much terror in an Annapolis merchant, Anthony Stewart, that in October he burned his ship, the *Peggy Stewart*, which had recently arrived laden with tea. In Maryland in December a provincial convention ordered the regulation of prices and the enforcement of the Association by local committees.[18]

III

Parliament and the ministry learned only gradually of the American hatred of the Intolerable Acts. Both bodies regularly suspended operations around mid-August, and the year 1774 was no exception. Dartmouth followed events of the summer more closely than anyone else and even rushed back to London from the country when he heard that weapons were being smuggled from Europe to the colonies. The news that a Continental Congress would meet did not shake him even though he regarded it as an illegal body. He wrote to a friend that if the Congress should adopt an accommodating "tone" or produce a temperate proposal, its origins and character might be overlooked. The king took a less flexible line in a letter to North, writing that "the dye is now cast, the Colonies must either submit or triumph; I do not wish to come to severer measures but we must not retreat; by coolness and an unremitted

17. *JM Papers*, I, 129.
18. Arthur Meier Schlesinger, *The Colonial Merchants and the American Revolution* (New York, 1957), 389–92, and chaps. 11, 12; William W. Abbot, *The Royal Governors of Georgia* (Chapel Hill, N.C., 1959), 164–66; Kenneth Coleman, *The American Revolution in Georgia* (Athens, Ga., 1958), 39–55.

pursuit of the measures that have been adopted I trust they will come to submit." And according to the king, after the colonies were brought to their senses, "there must always be one tax to keep up the right, and as such I approve of the Tea Duty." Lord North's attitudes too were hardening as he received reports of the likelihood of the Congress adopting nonimportation. Should the colonies decide not to trade with Britain, he remarked to Thomas Hutchinson, "Great Britain, would take care they should trade no where else."[19]

North's ministry had more on its mind in the early autumn than American affairs. At the end of September it announced that elections for a new Parliament would be held. The Parliament elected in 1768 was not due to expire until 1775, but the ministry decided to surprise the opposition and secure a majority for another seven years. America figured in this decision only incidentally, though North's government expected further trouble overseas in 1775 and did not wish to have to deal with it while holding elections. American problems played little part in the elections except in those few constituencies where Wilkesite radicals demanded repeal of the Intolerable Acts. The electorate was small; policy was not an issue; and the voters were apathetic. Earlier in the year Burke had complained that "any remarkable highway robbery on Hounslow Heath would make more conversation than all the disturbances in America." And with the elections imminent he noted that the present discontent in America and the possibility of difficulties there in the future "operate as little as the division of Poland." The ministry had expected nothing else, and by mid-November the returns indicated that it had another handsome majority in the House of Commons.[20]

The day after the ministry announced that elections would be held, the bad news began pouring in from General Gage. He had attempted to enforce the Boston Port Act vigorously and thereby added to his problems. The Act provided that goods were not to be loaded or unloaded "at any wharf in the port, at any island, creek, landing-place, bank, or other place whatsoever." Gage interpreted these phrases to mean movement of goods anywhere within the harbor and proceeded to cut off nearby islands and Charlestown across the river. Smuggling followed almost inevitably. The mobbing of mandamus councillors, the closing

19. Fortescue, ed., *Correspondence of George the Third*, III, 131; Peter Orlando Hutchinson, comp., *The Diary and Letters of His Excellency Thomas Hutchinson* (2 vols., Boston, 1884), I, 245.

20. Bernard Donoughue, *British Politics and the American Revolution: The Path to War, 1773–1775* (London, 1964) (quotations on 199).

of the courts, and the preparations for war by towns, and soon the Provincial Congress, alarmed him even more.

Not surprisingly, Gage's letters to the ministry conveyed something of his desperation and panic. He was not up against the Boston "rabble" and he said so; rather, he faced the "freeholders and farmers" of New England. To crush them he needed reinforcements, and he had already ordered regiments from New York and Canada to Boston. Nor did he hesitate to tell the ministry that he needed troops from home. None of these reinforcements would arrive soon, of course. While he waited, feeling naked and vulnerable, Gage recommended the suspension of the Intolerable Acts. These acts, after all, had aroused the Americans.[21]

Although there was fear in Gage's account, there was also realism. He could not hope to put down a rebellion with the forces under his command, and lifting the Intolerable Acts surely would have undermined the most extreme radicals in America. The king and the ministry saw things differently. They shared Gage's displeasure as the news of American resistance came in; Thomas Hutchinson noted that Dartmouth and John Pownall were "thunder-struck" on learning of the Suffolk Resolves. North told Hutchinson that matters seemed "desperate" and insisted that "Parliament would not—could not—concede. For aught he could see it must come to violence." A few days later he was saying flatly that Massachusetts was "in actual rebellion, and must be subdued." The king shared these opinions—"the new England Governments are in a State of Rebellion, blows must decide whether they are to be subject to this Country or independent"—but he was repelled by Gage's proposal to suspend the Intolerable Acts—"the most absurd," he told North, "that can be suggested."[22]

Gage indeed had very nearly undone himself in his dispatches of late summer and early fall, and by December his recall was certain. The month before, Suffolk, Secretary of State for the Northern Department, had urged that Gage be relieved of his command but the king held back as news of the Congress worsened—the ministry learned from an informer what the Congress did even though its sessions were secret— and as Gage's panic deepened. With Gage simultaneously clamoring for 20,000 troops, urging that a decisive blow be struck, and recommend-

21. Clarence E. Carter, ed., *The Correspondence of General Thomas Gage* . . . (2 vols., New Haven, Conn., 1931), I, 366–72; John Alden, *General Gage in America* (Baton Rouge, La., 1948), 212–21.

22. Hutchinson, comp., *Diary*, I, 273–93, 297; Fortescue, ed., *Correspondence of George the Third*, III, 153, 154.

ing suspension of the Intolerable Acts, the king decided he had had enough. He thereupon offered the American command to Jeffrey Amherst, a soldier with wide experience in America. Amherst, however, who detested America and hated service there, turned his king down. Soon after, as a temporary expedient the king decided to send a major general to aid Gage, a decision that eventually resulted in the dispatch of Howe, Clinton, and Burgoyne.[23]

The problem of policy—what response should be given to the rebellious actions of the Americans—remained. By late January the ministry had decided on a policy—one, as it turned out, strikingly similar to the old one which, of course, had nearly brought open rebellion. The main features of this policy looked toward repression: New England's trade was to be strictly confined to the empire and the fisheries were to be closed to New England's ships; reinforcements of ships and troops were to be sent to Gage and Admiral Graves, and as a measure of conciliation an offer was made to stop taxing the colonies (while the right to tax was to remain) if the colonies agreed to support all civil and military needs. There was ambivalence in this policy though, to be sure, its main emphasis was on coercion. Both Dartmouth and North yearned for reconciliation before force had to be used. The king was not averse to trying conciliation so long as the right to tax was not yielded; he, however, had none of the hope that his ministers still retained.[24]

In January before the ministry could present its American program to Parliament, it had to head off Chatham's last great attempt to restore peaceful relations. Ever secretive and dramatic, Chatham concealed his plans from the Rockinghams, the major opposition to the ministry, and did not try to draw them to his side. His proposal involved the withdrawal of troops from Boston and the passage of legislation which would reaffirm Parliament's sovereignty but also provide that the colonies should not be taxed without their consent. Chatham also proposed that in return for recognition the Congress should grant the Crown a perpetual revenue. The Coercive Acts would be lifted and so would a dozen other statutes the colonies had complained of in the last ten years.[25]

It was a daring and hopeless proposal. It presumed to recast imperial relations in such fundamental ways as to imply that members of Parliament were creatures utterly without pride, that they would admit errors without a blush once they were exposed, and act speedily to correct

23. Donoughue, *British Politics*, 216–18.
24. *Ibid.*, 223–24.
25. Jensen, *Founding*, 577–78.

them. It also assumed that the Americans had not really meant to reject Parliament's sovereignty and that they would back off if Parliament repealed disagreeable statutes and promised not to exercise its legitimate right to tax them.

Parliament did not spend much time in disposing of Chatham's fancy, and in the next two months it moved to approve the ministry's program. In the first week of February both houses approved an address to the king declaring the colonies in rebellion and calling for forceful measures to ensure obedience to the laws and sovereignty of England. The members spoke long and the debate dragged on, but the issue was never in doubt. Two weeks later North held out his "olive branch" to the colonies; an offer to desist from taxing any colony that made acceptable provisions for the support of civil and military government within its boundaries. After this proposal received Parliamentary approval, the ministry pushed through legislation restraining New England's trade and fisheries—extended in April to all the colonies except New York and North Carolina. Burke observed sardonically that by this legislation the government proposed "to preserve your authority by destroying your dominions."[26]

Sitting in Boston, Gage was beginning to believe that British authority could be preserved in no other way. During the autumn and winter he had received a series of surprises which persuaded him that only force could bring the Americans to heel, but he also believed he lacked a body of troops large enough to do the job. What distressed him most was the ferocity and unanimity of the opposition he faced. The treatment of the mandamus councillors was harsh yet not altogether unexpected; but the response in September 1774 to his seizure of gunpowder in Charlestown and cannon in Cambridge was almost overwhelming. Militia from as far away as Connecticut marched to Boston's aid as the rumors swirled through New England. About four thousand men gathered, and they were prepared to fight.[27]

Once this episode passed, Gage had to contemplate the growing strength of the militia in Massachusetts. Every act of the Provincial Congress was forbidding, as money was appropriated and plans set afoot to purchase arms and supplies. When the Congress adjourned it left behind a committee of safety charged with calling out the provincial

---

26. *Ibid.*, 578–81; *EHD*, 839–40 (the "Olive Branch" resolution). For the debate on the trade and fisheries of New England see William Cobbett, comp., *Parliamentary History of England from the Earliest Period to the Year 1803* (36 vols., London, 1806–20), XVIII, 380–89.

27. Jensen, *Founding*, 535–36.

militia should Gage so much as send 500 regulars outside Boston.[28]
Not everything Gage tried failed. In September he set about fortifying
Boston Neck and found men in and out of Boston to do the work—
and to sell him construction materials. To be sure, unfriendly citizens—
doubtless including artisans and craftsmen put out of work by the Boston
Port Act—sabotaged the construction whenever they could, smashing
bricks and setting straw afire, but it proceeded nonetheless. Shortly the
Neck was fortified with cannon, and Gage soon discovered that information as well as labor and supplies could be purchased. Sometime in
the winter he engaged the services of several informers—the exact number is unknown—including Dr. Benjamin Church, who was close to
the inner circle of the Provincial Congress. Church and the others may
have volunteered information, though there is evidence that some expected, and received, a reward for their services. The stories they told
and the plans they betrayed did not reassure Gage as to British prospects
in America.[29]

By late January 1775, feeling exposed and ignored and increasingly
vulnerable in Boston, Gage began to scout the roads leading inland.
On one of these patrols Captain Brown, accompanied by Ensign DeBerni-
ere and one private, set out to sample public opinion in Suffolk and
Worcester counties and to map the roads. They never reached Worcester
County. A sharp-eyed tavern keeper penetrated their disguises—the three
wore civilian clothes—and passed the word of their presence. Before
long they were warned to return to Boston and were lucky to escape
without suffering physical attack. From this experience and similar ones,
Gage learned again what it was to command a standing army in an
unfriendly country where he was spied upon, sabotaged, and unable to
move a squad without its maneuvers being reported.

Among others Paul Revere did the reporting. Revere headed an informal group of unemployed artisans who watched every move of the troops.
When the troops did anything out of the ordinary, Revere sent word
to Joseph Warren, who dispatched the news to the committee of safety
in Concord.[30]

Gage may have considered an attempt to arrest the leaders of the
Provincial Congress, or more likely he was preparing to seize munitions
stored in Concord and Worcester. Whatever his intentions at this time,

28. *Ibid.*, 563–67.
29. The history of the informers is told in Allen French, *General Gage's Informers*
    (Ann Arbor, Mich., 1932).
30. *Ibid.*, 24.

he tipped his hand by sending scouts on these roads. He also exercised larger bodies of troops on roads leading from Boston and thereby alarmed eager watchers in and out of the city. What Gage badly needed during these gloomy winter months were instructions from home telling him what to do. All he received was an order to intercept guns smuggled into the colonies from Europe, a task he would have been delighted to do had he been able.

On April 14, 1775, instructions arrived: a long letter from Dartmouth which summed up the ministry's views and which, though not altogether explicit in its directions, by its reproving tone and substance compelled action. The letter reeked of the ministry's disappointment in what Gage had reported in the autumn: Gage should not have allowed Boston to maintain a town guard and he should not have allowed the militia to train in Faneuil Hall. His request for 20,000 troops could not be met, and they probably were not necessary anyway since the violence in Massachusetts was the work of a "rude Rabble" (a characterization Gage had long since repudiated) without "plan" and without "concert" and "conduct." In any case, if, as Gage had written, "actual Revolt" existed or nearly did and the people seemed determined "to commit themselves at all Events in open Rebellion," then "Force should be repelled by Force." In urging the use of force, Dartmouth did not mean to propose that Gage attack the Massachusetts militia wherever he could find it. Rather, as he told Gage, the ministry and the king agreed that the most appropriate action would be the arrest of the leaders of the Provincial Congress. Move secretly without warning, he urged, and added— somewhat ambiguously, given this exhortation for secrecy—that an unprepared and unorganized people "cannot be very formidable." Gage had long since warned that such action would set off war, and Dartmouth now replied that "it will surely be better that the Conflict should be brought on, upon such ground, than in a riper state of Rebellion."[31]

A suggestion from the colonial secretary endorsed by the king carried great weight, of course. Knowing this, Dartmouth gave Gage discretionary authority to act in another way if local circumstances seemed to require a different course of action. But act Gage must; Dartmouth had made his responsibility to do something unavoidable.

By this time Gage wanted to act despite his concern over the size of his command. He began preparations the day after Dartmouth's letter arrived, not to seize the leaders of the Provincial Congress, most of

31. Dartmouth to Gage, Jan. 27, 1775, in Carter, ed., *Gage Correspondence*, II, 178–83.

whom were out of reach, but to capture the arms and ammunition in Concord and Worcester. In putting together the expedition to be sent into the countryside, Gage made his first mistake. He ordered the grenadiers and light infantry companies detached from their regiments. They were elite troops: the grenadiers were composed of tall men, physically strong and imposing; the light infantry were highly mobile, trained to strike swiftly and move rapidly. Hence Gage's choice seemed logical, even clever. The weakness of this force was not in its rank and file but in their hasty and inevitably imperfect amalgamation. No officer in command could know all his subordinates, nor could they know one another, or what to expect of one another in the fire of battle when communications are difficult to maintain.[32]

The officer chosen for command of this makeshift force was Colonel Francis Smith of the 10th Regiment. To lead the light infantry Gage selected Major John Pitcairn, an able officer, but a marine and obviously unfamiliar with the army's way of operating. And Pitcairn and the light infantry, some four hundred strong, would make up the advance party, a crucial unit in the line of march, followed by an equal number of grenadiers.

The shortest way to Concord from Boston was across Back Bay. The boats to carry the troops had been hauled out of the water and repaired and on April 16 were rowed to the men-of-war swinging at anchor in the Charles. There they lay ready for use.

Joseph Warren heard of these preparations almost immediately. There was of course no way to conceal the repair of the small boats and their collection in the bay. On April 16 in the morning, Warren sent Paul Revere to Lexington to warn John Hancock and Samuel Adams, who were hiding there, that something was up. Revere returned that night, stopping in Charlestown on the way to arrange signals should the British move at night: one lattern to be hung in the steeple of North Church if the troops moved inland over the Neck, and two if they came by water.[33]

The British completed their preparations on April 18, and Gage dispatched small patrols of officers that afternoon to intercept any riders carrying warnings from Boston. This seemingly prudent action was fruitless and probably foolish, for the patrols themselves were observed. The nerves of the Americans had been tense for months and now began to throb. And perhaps inevitably Gage's plans leaked, as at least one sergeant

32. Ward, I, 33–35.
33. Ibid., 33–34.

talked indiscreetly, and rumors spread that "there would be hell to pay to-morrow." Walking across Boston common early in the evening, one of Gage's officers heard a civilian tell another "The British troops have marched, but they will miss their aim," and on inquiring what that aim was received the reply "the cannon at Concord."[34]

Still, Gage tried to keep his movements secret. Around ten at night, April 18, he had the troops quietly roused from bed by sergeants shaking them rather than shouting commands. The troops formed on the common a little later, entered the boats bobbing at its foot, and were rowed to Lechmere Point in East Cambridge. Because the water was shallow there the boats could not reach dry land; so the men waded ashore, getting wet to the knees. They stopped on a nearby road and executed the classic maneuver in such situations: they stood around and waited and waited. The delay was to permit provisions to be brought over and divided up. When this was finally completed and the march begun, it was two in the morning.[35]

The troops got wet again almost immediately, for on leaving the road at Lechmere Point, they forded, on Colonel Smith's orders, Willis Creek. Smith, it seems, feared that their boots stomping across the bridge over the creek would wake the Americans. Quiet as they were, the soldiers awakened citizens as they marched through Somerville, Cambridge, and, around three in the morning, Menotomy. The alarm spread and they could hear "alarm" guns firing in the distance, giving warning of their coming.

Around 4:30 in the morning, just before sunrise, the troops approached Lexington. They were expected. Joseph Warren had sent warnings inland almost simultaneously with the collection of troops on the common. After having two lanterns hung, Paul Revere had himself rowed across the water to Charlestown, where a horse was found for his ride to Concord. William Dawes, another express rider, galloped over the Neck with the same destination in mind.

There were two well-traveled roads to Concord: one, the shorter, ran from Charlestown to Medford then to Menotomy (modern Arlington) and through Lexington. The other swung around the Neck near Roxbury to Cambridge and then to Menotomy where it joined the first. Revere attempted to take a shortcut near Medford but was almost captured by a British patrol. He escaped by hard riding and reached Lexington

34. *Ibid.*, 34.
35. Allen French, *The Day of Concord and Lexington* (Boston, 1925), 68–70, 100–102, for the beginnings of the march.

around midnight. On the way he roused the militia in Medford and Menotomy and awakened as many sleepers as he could between Menotomy and Lexington. In Lexington he got Adams and Hancock out of bed and sat down to wait for Dawes, who rode in half an hour later. Together they then rode for Concord, accompanied by Dr. Samuel Prescott, who overtook them outside Lexington, where he had spent the evening courting a young woman. Revere never reached Concord. A second party of British officers intercepted them midway. Revere was captured, dismounted, and eventually released to walk back to Lexington. Others would carry the warning to Concord.

The Lexington militia company, commanded by Captain John Parker, had mustered on Lexington Green shortly after Revere rode in. There they waited for over an hour with no very clear idea of what they were about; in fact, as Captain Parker later explained, he had assembled them in order that they might decide what to do. What he and his men decided after standing in the darkness and cold was to fall out and await developments. There were about 130 of them, and now those who lived near the Green went home and the others repaired to Buckman's Tavern to escape the chill air. Parker told them to be prepared to form quickly on the beat of the drum.

The drum sounded at half-past four, when Thaddeus Bowman galloped in with the news that the regulars were near. There was immediate confusion on the Green as Parker aligned his men—some failed to hear, or heed, the drums; others lacking ammunition rushed to the meetinghouse where it was stored. But in a few minutes Parker had two ranks of a little over seventy men drawn up about a hundred yards from the road to Concord, which ran along the base of the Green.[36]

Pitcairn's light infantry, six companies in column, soon marched into view, scarlet coats, white breeches, and bayonets glittering in the early morning sun. On sighting the militia, Pitcairn ordered his column into the conventional battle formation, a line of three ranks divided into two sections or platoons. This movement was accompanied by much shouting and huzzaing from the rear ranks as they ran forward into the extended lines. Not surprisingly, at least one militiaman, unnerved by the numbers of the regulars and by their rush and noise, urged that the Americans get off the Green. "There are so few of us," he protested, "it is folly to stand here." Parker would have none of this and replied only that "The first man who offers to run shall be shot down." Almost

36. Ward, I, 36–37; French, *Day of Concord and Lexington, passim,* for these details.

immediately afterwards he changed his mind, as Pitcairn and two or three officers rode to within a hundred feet of the militia and shouted, "Lay down your arms, you damned rebels, and disperse." This brought an order from Parker to fall out and his men turned and began to leave the Green, carrying their muskets. Dispersal did not satisfy Pitcairn, who called again for the Americans to lay down their arms: "Damn you! Why don't you lay down your arms?" This curse was echoed by another officer's "Damn them! We will have them!"[37]

The sequence of events that followed is not clear, and probably never will be. Someone fired; American eyewitnesses accuse a British officer, and English eyewitnesses deny that any regular fired first. A British officer apparently then gave the command "Fire, by God! Fire," and one of the platoons delivered a volley. Pitcairn attempted to stop the firing, but before he could make himself heard, a second volley ripped into the militia. The answering fire was weak and the regulars charged. It was all over in a minute or two—eight militiamen dead, ten wounded, one British private grazed in the leg. Among the wounded—he died— was the aged Parker, who had stood his ground, fired his weapon, and then was struck by a bullet in the second volley.[38]

After a few more minutes, Pitcairn and his officers got their men in column once more, and then the grenadiers and Colonel Smith marched up, fired a volley, shouted a cheer, and once more set off for Concord. This time they made no attempt to muffle their march; they knew that all hope of concealing their mission had vanished. Hence they set off with their fifes shrilling and their drums beating.

As they marched along the road to Concord, they heard alarm guns fired in the distance summoning local militia from miles around. Express riders pounded over the roads to towns farther away, and before the day was over militia from as far away as Worcester would set out for Lexington and Concord. Much earlier, sometime after one in the morning, Prescott, who with William Dawes had escaped capture, had delivered the warning to Concord of the approaching British. A bell was rung and three small companies of Concord militiamen gathered in the village. These companies were minutemen, prepared to be ready on a minute's notice; George Minot's alarm company, composed of old men and boys, joined the others on the town square. And during

37. Ward, I, 37; A Narrative of the Excursion and Ravages of the King's Troops . . . (Worcester, Mass., [1775]), 6–7. A Narrative contains depositions by participants.
38. A Narrative, 7–14; Ward, I, 38.

the early morning hours militiamen from nearby towns—some in companies, others unattached—began to enter Concord.[39]

Colonel Smith's column arrived around seven o'clock. To reach their main objective, Colonel James Barrett's house, where supposedly most of the munitions were hidden, they had to pass by a cluster of buildings, among them the meetinghouse, two or three taverns, and twenty or thirty houses. The road passed along a ridge about sixty feet high, then cut to the right along a second ridge at right angles to the first. From the end of this second ridge it swung to the left across the North Bridge, which spanned the Concord River, and then went near Colonel Barrett's house. Overlooking the North Bridge was Punkatasset Hill, some two hundred feet high.

The column of regulars met no opposition for several hours, though one of the Concord companies marched down the road toward them as they approached the center of town. These militiamen simply showed themselves and then marched back; they fired no shots. Nor did those on the first ridge, even though Smith sent his light infantry along it. Instead, the militia on it pulled back—they were badly outnumbered— and reinforced their comrades on the second ridge. Smith's infantry soon occupied this ridge too, while the militia withdrew ahead of them to Punkatasset Hill.

After sending three light companies over the North Bridge to Colonel Barrett's house and posting another three on the bridge itself, Smith turned the grenadiers to searching the houses, taverns, and other buildings. Not much was found—some flour, 500 pounds of musket balls, trenching tools, a few wooden spoons—but the search itself proved disastrous, for while it was going on the blacksmith shop and the courthouse were set afire, whether by accident or deliberately is not known. The smoke alarmed the militia on Punkatasset Hill, now swollen to some 400 men by companies from Acton, Bedford, Lincoln, Westford, and by unattached volunteers from the countryside. Joseph Hosmer, Barrett's adjutant, asked, "Will you let them burn the town?" The answer was "no" and a resolve "to march into the middle of the town for its defence or die in the attempt." So down from the hill they came to North Bridge, which lay about half a mile from the main buildings of the village. There they met the three light companies of regulars which, fortunately for the militia, were badly deployed one behind the other, thereby masking the fire of two. The front company could fire and

39. Ward, I, 40–41.

did. The first few shots went astray and brought a cry of surprise from an American officer—"God damn it! They're firing ball!" Then the ball bit into flesh, and two militiamen fell dead and another was wounded. The American fire, from men spread out more effectively, took a heavier toll, as three red-coated privates fell and nine officers and men were wounded.[40]

The shock of the American fire confused the regulars, who soon broke and retreated in disarray, leaving their dead and one wounded man behind. The Americans showed little more discipline. Soon they were milling about and were unable to re-form until they reached the village. In this confusion the three British companies which had been at Barrett's slipped back across the bridge and rejoined the main body. It was now about eleven in the morning. By noon Colonel Smith had his forces together once more and began the march to Boston, carrying the wounded in two chaises.

The first mile passed without opposition. At Meriam's Corner the column ran into the militia, and the battle began. The battlefield was in reality a gauntlet, about sixteen miles long and never more than three or four hundred yards wide. In places where the woods pressed close by at a stream crossing, it was less than fifty yards in width. The Americans poured fire into the column, or sniped at it from behind trees, rocks, and occasionally buildings and fences. The British replied as well as they could from the column—and sometimes quite murderously when the flankers from the light infantry trapped the militia against the road. Although the advantage of numbers and cover and knowledge of the terrain lay with the militiamen, they squandered their edge as they lost all control of their units and proceeded to fight as individualists. The British companies also soon lost their integrity under the galling fire from the roadside. They were a rabble when they reached Lexington, where they first attempted to re-form on the outskirts and then again on the Green.[41]

Fortunately for Smith's command, Brig. General Percy arrived in Lexington with a relief brigade of about a thousand troops at two-thirty in the afternoon. Smith's exhausted soldiers rested an hour, while Percy's artillery worked the militia over. An hour later the enlarged column set out once more. Opposition did not show itself in strength until the column reached Menotomy, where fresh militia from other towns

---

40. *Ibid.*, 42–44; *A Narrative*, 14–17.
41. French, *Day of Concord and Lexington*, 220–39; Ward, I, 44–46.

and the trailing militia from Concord caught up with it. The fighting now took an especially vicious turn marked by hand-to-hand encounters with bayonet against hatchet and club. The British commanders, sharing their troops' frustration, made no attempt to stop their pillaging and plundering. Civilians were attacked; houses were smashed and burned; looting was common.

At Cambridge, Percy shook off his pursuers and drove his column to Charlestown. There he reached safety shortly after the sun went down. Behind him lay stragglers, wounded, dead, and missing men; and behind him too, an increasing number of militia. In all the British had received 273 casualties; the Americans, 95.[42]

In several respects the battle was unlike any other in the Revolution. Never again would there be a "front" sixteen miles long. But different as the battle was, it forecast the central problem the British would face: how to subdue not just another army but a population in rebellion. Of course the war would often resemble many of the eighteenth century, with conventional armies facing one another using well-known tactics. But it was different at times in the enlistment of civilian populations and the discard of the usual methods of battle. It never became an entirely civilian war, a people-in-revolt against an army. There were moments when that threatened, however. And throughout the long struggle, the passions of the people and their moral strength played a far more important part than in any eighteenth-century war before the French Revolution.

42. A *Narrative*, 21, a deposition on British plundering; Ward, I, 50, for the number of casualties. Peckham, *Toll*, 3, gives slightly different figures.

13

"Half a War"

The first message telling of the combat at Lexington was written around ten in the morning at nearby Watertown and sent to other towns in Massachusetts and to Connecticut. Its prose was spare: the British had attacked the militia; six men were dead and four others wounded; more regulars were coming out of Boston. The writer, Colonel Joseph Palmer, dispatched Israel Bissel with this note after adding an appeal that Bissel be supplied with fresh horses whenever he needed them. Bissel, a postrider who customarily traveled between Boston and New York, wore out his mounts and himself for the next five days until he reached Philadelphia. While he was on the road, other riders followed, several with wildly inaccurate accounts of the fighting that had occurred between Boston and Concord—the most extravagant of which reported that the British expedition was trapped on Winter Hill by 20,000 Americans. This story held that Earl Percy, who had led the party that rescued Smith's detachment on its return, had been killed. Far from dead, Percy was at that moment enjoying the adulation of the army and its friends for his conduct on April 19.[1]

Such mistakes in the messages sent out from the battle could not obscure their essential matter which was that war had begun and that the other colonies should be notified as soon as possible. One of the

1. Peter Force, ed., *American Archives*, 4th Ser. (6 vols., Washington, D.C., 1837–46), II, 363; *Diary of Frederick Mackenzie* (2 vols., Cambridge, Mass., 1930), I, 23, describes Percy as behaving with "great spirit" and with "great coolness."

messages carries the urgent endorsements of its readers south of Philadelphia as they hastened it along the way:

> Wednesday night, Christeen Bridge, twelve o'clock, forwarded to Col. Thomas Couch, Esquire, who received it this moment, and he to forward it to Tobias Randolph, Esquire, head of Elk, in Maryland. Night and day to be forwarded.

> Dumfries, April 30, Sunday. Gentlemen: The enclosed came to hand this morning, about ten o'clock. In one hour I hired the bearer to convey it to your place.

As the message moved along, the urgency to forward it seemed to increase. "For God's sake send the man on without the least delay; and write to Mr. Marion to forward it by night and by day." "Pray don't neglect a moment in forwarding." "Pray order the express you send to ride night and day." "I request, for the good of our Country, and the welfare of our lives and liberties, and fortunes, you will not lose a moment's time." Charleston, South Carolina, received the news with an endorsement that commanded attention: "We send you momentous intelligence, this instant received."[2]

Momentous it was, and it produced an immense reaction. In New England, militia from the neighboring colonies converged on Boston; within a few days thousands had gathered on the hills around the town, effectively cutting it off from the countryside. Further south, recruitment into the militia picked up, arms and ammunition were gathered, and more news from Massachusetts was eagerly sought. Undoubtedly the war plunged many still loyal to their king into despair, or stiffened their resolution to support royal authority. But for weeks after Lexington and Concord, loyalists dared not sound their sentiments. Rebels exercised less restraint: they felt betrayed, let down by his majesty's army, and felt too that the barbarous face of the conspiracy against their liberties now stood exposed. In this mood they craved action, wanted to strike back, as if, Thomas Jefferson remarked in a letter, their "last hopes of reconciliation" had been cut off. A "phrenzy of revenge," Jefferson noted of the Virginians, "seems to have seized all ranks of people."[3]

2. Force, ed., *American Archives*, 4th Ser., II, 363–70. See also Elizabeth Merritt, "The Lexington Alarm, April 19, 1775 . . . ," *MdHM*, 41 (1946), 89–114.
3. *TJ Papers*, I, 165.

II

Prudence as much as revenge moved the Americans who seized Fort Ticonderoga on Lake Champlain early in May. The fort lay on the southwestern side of Lake Champlain, commanding the entrance to it from Lake George. The French had built Fort Carillon there in 1755, a massive fortification which Montcalm had held against James Abercromby in 1758. The next year Amherst, with an overwhelming force, took it. The English repaired the damage they had inflicted on the fort during its capture and renamed it Ticonderoga.[4]

By 1775 the walls, the bastions, and the blockhouses were in a dilapidated condition—not exactly in ruins, but badly in need of reconstruction. The garrison seemed appropriate for this pile—two officers and forty-eight men with twenty-four women and children. Although this collection lived within Ticonderoga, they were incapable of defending it.

But men in New England and New York worried about the fort, and a few who knew the place coveted the heavy guns and mortars still emplaced there from the time of the French and Indian War. The worry fed on rumors that Guy Carleton, the British commander in Quebec, would bring a party of French, Indians, and all the regulars he could muster up the St. Lawrence, the Richelieu River, down Lake Champlain and Lake George, and through the Hudson River Valley to cut the colonies in two. Among the Americans determined to block the British were Ethan Allen and Benedict Arnold.

Allen, who was born in Litchfield, Connecticut, a sometime lead miner and farmer, had moved to the New Hampshire Grants (now Vermont), an area claimed by New York and much in dispute between New Hampshire and New York. There had been violence between Allen's Green Mountain Boys and New York settlers, and Allen carried a price on his head in New York. Colonel Allen, as his frontier followers called him, was not the typical backwoodsman, though he was physically large and strong, swore like a demon, and loved the rough and tumble. He enjoyed reading and he wrote, most notably a deistical tract *Reason the Only Oracle of Man*.[5]

Benedict Arnold lacked Allen's size of body but exceeded him in power of mind and in ambition. He was thirty-four years old in 1775, athletic, graceful, and charming. Arnold came from good stock; the family had made its name and fortune in Rhode Island business and he had prospered as a merchant in New Haven, Connecticut.

4. Ward, I, 63.
5. (Bennington, Vt., 1784). There is a helpful modern biography by Charles A. Jellison, *Ethan Allen: Frontier Rebel* (Syracuse, N.Y., 1969).

Shortly after the battle of Lexington, a small group of Connecticut Valley businessmen and landowners approached Allen with a plan to seize Ticonderoga. Allen was only too willing, and in early May he took his Green Mountain Boys and a small number of irregular troops gathered by his Connecticut backers to Hand's Cove, two miles below Ticonderoga. Arnold, meanwhile, had nominated himself to capture the fort and persuaded the Massachusetts committee of safety to sponsor him. That he had no troops did not prevent him from going to Hand's Cove on May 10, where he found Allen and about two hundred followers. Arnold claimed command of this force, a claim Allen refused to honor. The two men squabbled, but their argument did not deter them from moving as many men as they could aboard the few boats available for a dawn attack.

What followed was comedy—and victory. The garrison was literally surprised in their beds; the high point of the farce occurred when Allen demanded of Lieutenant Jocelyn Feltham, standing sleepily in his bedroom with his breeches in hand, "Come out of there, you damned old rat"—some accounts say "skunk" and others "bastard"—and upon being asked by what authority he was acting answered "In the name of the Great Jehovah and the Continental Congress"—presumably equal powers in the theology of deism.[6]

Crown Point fell two days later; its garrison numbered less than a dozen. No one was seriously hurt in these actions. Over the next few days Arnold took St. Johns, a post on the Richelieu River, and then abandoned it. But Allen thought this post should be held and therefore occupied it, only to be driven off by a party of redcoats from down the river. By the end of May, Connecticut had decided to retain Forts Ticonderoga and Crown Point, but with neither Arnold nor Allen in charge. New York, in whose territory Ticonderoga lay, looked on uneasily. Within the year the importance of Ticonderoga was recognized to be its heavy artillery, not its site or its fortifications.

III

The capture of Ticonderoga occurred on May 10, the day that the second Continental Congress met in Philadelphia. Its members arrived in circumstances reminiscent of the glory which cheered the departure of the first Congress. They were accompanied by military escorts along the roads to Philadelphia, and again were praised and petted by everyone—or at least everyone seemed to admire them. John Adams pretended

6. Ward, I, 64–69. For Arnold, Willard Wallace, *Traitorous Hero: The Life and Fortunes of Benedict Arnold* (New York, 1954).

to complain of "the unnecessary Parade that was made about us," but he loved every minute of it, even when his mare bolted and his sulky was dashed to pieces on rocks in the roadway.[7]

Most members of the first Congress returned though there were several notable new faces—Benjamin Franklin and James Wilson from Pennsylvania, John Hancock from Massachusetts, and in late June, Thomas Jefferson arrived to replace Peyton Randolph, who returned home. The greatest change took place in the delegation from New York, which now added five members, among them George Clinton, Robert R. Livingston, and Philip Schuyler. Only Georgia remained unrepresented, though St. John's Parish sent Lyman Hall.

These men convened when enthusiasm for war raged through the colonies. Voluntary militia companies formed in every colony, arms were collected, and in New England, at least, men shed their blood. The delegates could not remain unaffected and had no wish to; many indeed held commissions in their colonies' militia. As if to remind the Congress of the nature of the problems the colonies faced, George Washington wore his uniform to its meetings. Washington, of course, also reminded the Congress of his own experience in war, and they soon were calling upon him for advice about military affairs. John Adams, combative spirit that he was, was not in the least martial but yearned to join the army: "Oh that I was a Soldier!—I will be.—I am reading military Books.— Every Body must and will, and shall be a soldier."[8]

If everybody did not become a soldier, or desire to, everybody in the Congress agreed that soldiers were needed and that force must be used now that fighting had occurred along the road to Concord. Agreement did not exist, however, on the purpose of the war, whether there should be reconciliation or independence. Perhaps the most prominent delegate hoping for reconciliation was John Dickinson, renowned for his *Letters from a Farmer in Pennsylvania*. Like many others, Dickinson favored reconciliation if it could be obtained along with security of constitutional rights. He does not seem to have regarded this prospect with optimism; rather, his mood was gloomy. Firm ground upon which to reconcile did not seem to exist; the British, after all, had begun the war with "the butchery of unarmed Americans." And, he asked, "what topics of reconciliation are now left for men who think as I do, to address our countrymen? To recommend reverence for the monarch,

7. Lyman H. Butterfield, ed., *Adams Family Correspondence* (2 vols. to date, Cambridge, Mass., 1963–   ), I, 195.
8. *Ibid.*, 207.

or affection for the mother country? . . . No. While we revere and love our mother country, her sword is opening our veins."[9]

The bitterness in this statement was deeply felt, but it was no stronger than Dickinson's revulsion from independence. The revulsion undoubtedly had hidden and surely nonrational sources, most notably a lingering affection for traditional ties. But it rose also from fear—fear for a new nation isolated and vulnerable. With France and Spain lurking off-stage, eager to enter to smash Britain and, apparently, to seize her possessions, the independent colonies would play in a precarious world.

These possibilities were not discussed openly in the Congress, as the group that favored a complete break from Britain did not admit that independence was their objective. But they did not disguise their skepticism about the likelihood of reconciliation. The Adamses and the Lees, the Lee-Adams Junto, spoke for this group but quietly and with care. For the old suspicion of Massachusetts still lingered, and this new alliance saw that the Congress could not move faster than its slower members if unity was to be obtained. John Adams likened the Congress to "a Coach and six—the swiftest Horses must be slackened and the slowest quickened, that all may keep an even pace."[10]

Congress rarely attained an even pace during the war, and in the first six months it moved by rushes, pell mell through an accumulating pile of business, or by fits and starts. As soon as it convened, it received depositions and letters from Massachusetts telling of the events at Lexington and Concord. These accounts were read and then Congress ordered them published. Next it received a letter from Joseph Warren, president of the Massachusetts Provincial Congress, beseeching "direction and assistance" and recommending the creation of a "powerful Army" under the aegis of the Continental Congress. This request raised the painful questions most members preferred to duck—especially whether the colonies were going to organize themselves so as to be able to fight as a union. Congress was obviously unprepared to answer this question and referred Warren's letter to the committee of the whole, a resting place which it believed could be made safe, secure, and inactive.[11]

Events soon forced Congress's hand. First, it had to reply to New York's question about an appropriate response to British troops daily expected to arrive in the colony. On May 15, Congress urged that New York remain on the "defensive" so long as the troops behaved "peaceably

9. Force, ed., *American Archives*, 4th Ser., II, 444–45.
10. Butterfield, ed., *Adams Family Corr.*, I, 216.
11. *JCC*, II, 24–25.

and quietly." But if the troops erected fortifications, invaded property, or cut the city's communications to the outside, then New York should "repel force by force."[12]

Two days later word arrived that Ethan Allen and Benedict Arnold had seized Ticonderoga, an act that no one could call defensive. Congress felt uneasy not just because the capture of Ticonderoga might outrage the British, but also because it brought into the open once more the conflicting claims of New York and New Hampshire to the New Hampshire Grants. Equally embarrassing was the inescapable fact that Connecticut troops and Green Mountain Boys had taken a fort within the borders of New York without bothering to tell New York officials about it.

Congress ignored as many of these conflicts as it decently could and recommended that the cannon and the military stores taken at Ticonderoga be removed to the south end of Lake George, where they should be inventoried "in order that they may be safely returned when the restoration of the former harmony between Great Britain and these colonies so ardently wished for by the latter shall render it prudent and consistent with the overruling law of self-preservation."[13] The clumsiness of the Congressional style cannot be explained strictly in terms of the rigidity that eventually overcomes all official bodies. In this case it reflects the prudence born of internal divisions recognized by all concerned. Arnold and Allen, who cared nothing for the problems Congress had within itself, protested against any withdrawal. Congress then changed its mind and a few days later sent a letter to "the oppressed Inhabitants of Canada" calculated to persuade them to join the struggle for a "common liberty." Since the French and Indian War, the Congress wrote, the Americans had regarded the Canadians as "fellow-subjects," but since the passage of the Quebec Act which made the Canadians "slaves," the Americans considered them "fellow-sufferers." And to demonstrate its good faith the Congress on June 1 forbade the invasion of Canada by any colonial forces. Not quite a month later, on June 27, it would reverse itself and authorize General Philip Schuyler, recently appointed head of the northern department, to invade and hold Canada.[14]

This reversal of policy was not accompanied by a declaration of independence; the Congress, of course, would not bring itself to such a step for another year. Yet while it shrank from committing itself clearly to either independence or reconciliation, it was beginning to act as if

12. *Ibid.*, 52.
13. *Ibid.*, 56.
14. *Ibid.*, 68–70, 75, 109–10.

it were the representative of a sovereign nation. The decision to favor an invasion of Canada was only one sort of dramatic evidence of its disposition. A month before, even as it decided to petition the king for a redress of grievances and a restoration of peace and harmony, the Congress urged all the colonies to arm themselves. The next day, May 27, it appointed a committee on ways and means to secure military supplies. A week later it voted to borrow £6000 for the purchase of gunpowder. And on June 14 it decided to raise the Continental army by approving a plan calling for the recruitment of rifle companies from Pennsylvania, Virginia, and Maryland, which would be added to the New England forces around Boston. Congress agreed to pay for these companies. It also appointed George Washington to head a committee charged with the responsibility for drawing up rules and regulations governing this army. An army required a chief, and the following day, June 15, Congress selected George Washington as commander of "all the continental forces, raised, or to be raised, for the defense of American liberty." In the next few days the Congress proceeded to organize the army, select Washington's major subordinates, and approve the army's finances, a currency issue of $2,000,000.[15]

IV

While the Congress set about to organize the Continental army, two other armies, Britain's in Boston and New England's around it, came together for the bloody but indecisive battle of Bunker Hill. Neither side anticipated such a clash. Early in June, Gage decided to occupy Dorchester Heights, which had been ignored by everyone even though the area commanded Boston and had obvious strategic importance. Gage may have felt compelled to show some aggressiveness in order to satisfy his newly arrived colleagues, Major Generals William Howe, John Burgoyne, and Henry Clinton. This "triumvirate of reputation," Burgoyne's modest description of himself and his colleagues, arrived on the *Cerberus* late in May, and may have urged action. Their very presence bespoke the ministry's dissatisfaction with Gage's conduct, and he knew it. Feeling the need to do something, he ordered the move on the hills around Dorchester to begin on June 18. His intentions filtered out of Boston to the Massachusetts committee of safety a few days later, which then

15. *Ibid.*, 91–92, 93–94. On all the matters discussed in this section, see Burnett, *Continental Congress*, 60–79.

instructed General Artemas Ward, commander of American forces around Boston, to act before the British did and to seize Bunker Hill on the Charlestown peninsula along with the Dorchester Heights. The move to Bunker Hill was to be accomplished immediately, with the Dorchester hills to be taken later.[16]

General Artemas Ward, a Massachusetts farmer in quieter times, had fought in the French and Indian War twenty years earlier but had not, any more than any other American colonial, ever commanded an army. His inexperience may have led to a caution that often approached timidity. Ward hated to act, preferring to prepare, to husband resources, to dig in; he seems never to have felt ready for the bold stroke or the daring operation. He now had little choice, with the committee of safety demanding that the army exert itself and his subordinates in a council of war urging him on.[17]

Two among them proved too much to withstand. Connecticut furnished the more energetic, Brigadier Israel Putnam, a bear of a man, fifty-seven years old, a solid farmer, short in stature, thickset, bursting with energy, but lacking the thoughtfulness and perspective so valuable in a commander who feels himself buffeted by forces he cannot control. Putnam—"Old Put" in the legend that surrounded him—was a force, a natural force who had survived capture by the Iroquois in the French and Indian War and shipwreck on the coast of Cuba in an attempt to capture Havana. Putnam knew the attack and the smell of powder, but strategy, tactics, the careful plan which got the most out of men and supplies were as mysterious to him as the "new divinity" of western parsons. At the head of a regiment in assault he had few equals; in a staff meeting, few inferiors. Not surprisingly, he advocated the move on Charlestown peninsula. Joining him was Colonel William Prescott, forty-nine years of age, born of a distinguished and wealthy family, and commander of a Massachusetts regiment. Prescott rarely acted rashly; he exuded a quiet air that made men listen to him and heed his counsel. His approval of the proposal must have weighed heavily with Ward.

There were others in the council of war who favored the plan—General Seth Pomeroy of Connecticut, almost seventy years old, a veteran of the siege of Louisbourg in 1745, so steady in mind and manner as to seem immune to the madness that sometimes overpowers men facing the choice between battle and passivity. Joseph Warren, fresh from

16. Ward, I, 73; Allen French, *The First Year of the American Revolution* (Boston and New York, 1934), 212–13.

17. Ward, I, 74–75 and 76–78, for the details about Putnam and Prescott.

the Provincial Congress and awaiting his commission as a major general, also went along with the recommendation, though he may have shared Ward's reluctance.

Reluctant or not, Ward placed Prescott in charge of a force of around a thousand men with orders to fortify Bunker Hill, the largest of three hills on Charlestown peninsula. The peninsula was a rough triangle of land, the base of which faced Boston, half a mile away across the Charles River. The top of the peninsula, about a mile to the northwest, was joined to the mainland by the "Neck," never more than a few hundred feet in width and sometimes under water at high tide. To the northeast the Mystic River separated the peninsula from the mainland, and on the other side lay the bay where the Charles River widened. At its broadest point the peninsula was half a mile wide. Charlestown, a small village in peacetime but now almost deserted, covered the southwestern corner. Bunker Hill rose 300 yards from the Neck, reaching a height of 110 feet; 600 yards farther down lay Breed's Hill, about 75 feet in height, with especially steep slopes on its eastern and western sides, Moulton's Hill, only 35 feet high, sat at the southeastern corner where the Charles River and the Mystic River met. The ground between Breed's and Moulton's was broken by fenced pasturelands, brick kilns, clay pits, and a small swamp.

Prescott found his thousand-odd men assembled in Cambridge early in the evening of June 16. Two Massachusetts regiments besides his own, a Massachusetts artillery company of forty-nine men and two field-pieces led by Captain Samuel Gridley, and a working party of some two hundred men from Israel Putnam's regiment commanded by Captain Samuel Knowlton made up the expedition. These men wore homespun and other sorts of civilian dress—there were no uniforms—and they carried muskets of every sort and variety. Each was supposed to carry a pack, rations for a day, and entrenching tools.

This party, led by Prescott, marched from Cambridge a little after nine that night. General Putnam met them at the Neck with wagons loaded with gabions (wicker baskets which were filled with dirt and used in fortifications) and fascines (tightly bundled brushwood and sticks, also used in setting up fortifications). Putnam seems also to have had a small number of tools and barrels, presumably to be used in constructing defenses. Shortly after the arrival at the Neck, Prescott sent a company into Charlestown with orders to watch for surprises from the British. The main body then moved down the peninsula and occupied Bunker Hill, stopping just short of Breed's. Here Prescott and his officers, joined by Putnam and Colonel Richard Gridley, chief engineer of the army, decided that, despite the orders to fortify Bunker Hill, they would dig in on Breed's. Their reasons are not entirely clear, but the fact that Breed's was closer to Boston seems to have provided their principal justification. They also decided to keep a detachment on Bunker Hill and to dig in there once the principal work was completed on Breed's.

Colonel Gridley now did his job, laying out a roughly square redoubt about 130 feet on a side, with an entrance on the side facing Bunker Hill, and apparently away from any attack the British might deliver. The side facing Charlestown had a redan, a two-sided, V-shaped earth-work, projecting outward. Midnight came by the time Gridley traced this fortification on the ground. That left about four hours before dawn for the troops to dig the fortification with its deep trenches and high earth walls. Those with picks and shovels fell to work immediately despite the heat of the night and the dust which rose from their digging. When first light broke, they had raised walls about six feet high on all sides, but they still had much to do.

First light made their task easier, but it also exposed them to the observation of ships swinging at anchor in the bay. The *Lively* saw them first and opened fire almost immediately. Soon after, Admiral Graves ordered the *Lively* to stop but after thinking the matter over started the fire up again, this time from other ships near by and from the battery on Copp's Hill. This shelling did little damage, as the ships had difficulty elevating their guns high enough to bear on the hill, and the battery on Copp's was out of effective range, but its noise unnerved many of Prescott's men who had never endured battle before. Occasionally it was more than noise: it was deadly—one ball killed a soldier working outside the redoubt and another smashed two hogsheads filled with water, the entire supply brought for the troops, who were now dependent upon the wells in Charlestown. Just before noon, with the dust choking them and fatigue setting in—"We began to be almost beat out, being tired by our labor and having no sleep the night before"— Prescott's men began to slip away.[18] They were discouraged of course, and they had begun to suspect that they had been abandoned, for they believed that fresh troops were scheduled to relieve them after their night's work. Prescott saw what was happening to his command; a lesser man might have given in to his troops' anxieties. Prescott, however,

18. Peter Brown to his mother, June 28, 1775, in Sheer and Rankin, *Rebels and Red-coats,* 60.

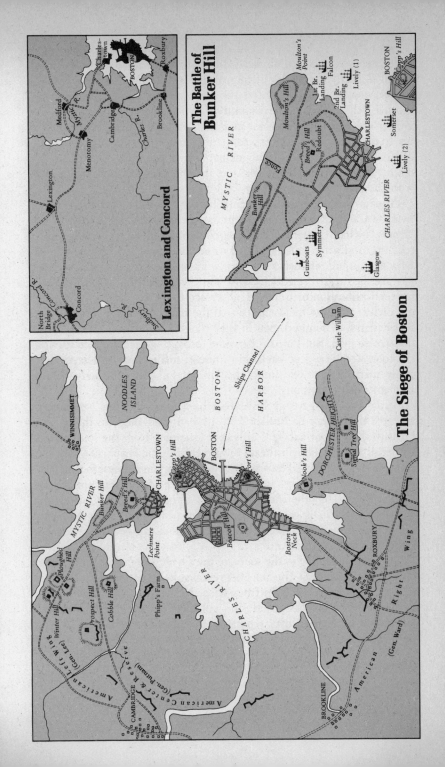

Lexington and Concord

North Bridge · Concord · Sudbury R. · Concord R. · Lexington · Menotomy · Medford · Mystic R. · Cambridge · Charles R. · Brookline · CHARLES-TOWN · BOSTON · Roxbury

The Battle of Bunker Hill

MYSTIC RIVER · Moulton's Hill · Moulton's Point · 1st Br. Landing · Falcon · 2nd Br. Landing · Lively (1) · Breed's Hill · Redoubt · FENCE · Bunker Hill · CHARLESTOWN · BOSTON · Copp's Hill · Somerset · CHARLES RIVER · Lively (2) · Gunboats · Symmetry · Glasgow

The Siege of Boston

NOODLES ISLAND · WINNISIMMET · MYSTIC RIVER · Bunker Hill · Breed's Hill · CHARLESTOWN · Copp's Hill · BOSTON · Fort's Hill · BOSTON HARBOR · Ships Channel · Castle William · Moorehead Hill · Prospect Hill · Cobble Hill · Winter Hill (Gen. Lee) · American Left Wing · Lechmere Point · Phipp's Farm · Beacon Hill · Boston Neck · Nook's Hill · DORCHESTER HEIGHTS · Signal Tree Hill · CAMBRIDGE (Gen. Putnam) · American Center Reserve · CHARLES RIVER · ROXBURY · American Right Wing (Gen. Ward) · BROOKLINE

concealed whatever doubts and fears he may have had and cajoled his troops to keep at the work of improving the redoubt. When persuasion seemed too little, he mounted the walls of the redoubt and exposed himself deliberately to the cannonade as if to show his men that the danger was in their heads, not in British cannon. There, standing over his troops, Prescott marched, sometimes shouting encouragement and orders—and sometimes harshly demanding of the men below that they ignore their thirst and hunger and the incoming rounds and get on with the job.

Putnam proved as brave, riding between Bunker and Breed's and twice to Cambridge to demand reinforcements and supplies from Ward. Others, including members of the committee of safety, made similar requests, and after prolonged delay and indecision Ward sent off two New Hampshire regiments. Zeal for work now led Putnam into a serious mistake: he urged Prescott to send him the entrenching tools necessary for the fortification of Bunker Hill. Prescott delayed as long as he could out of fear that the men who carried the tools would not return. With fewer than five hundred men in the redoubt, he realized that he could not spare a man. But Putnam persisted, promising that the men carrying the tools would be sent back, and Prescott finally gave in. Exactly how many men he sent off cannot be known, but few returned—despite Putnam's best intentions.

Before Prescott gave up his entrenching tools, and the "volunteers" to carry them back to Bunker Hill, he had used them to throw up a breastwork of about 330 feet in length extending from the southeastern corner of the redoubt northeast toward the Mystic River. Daylight had shown him how exposed he was, how vulnerable the redoubt to a flanking movement out of musket range along the side of the peninsula by the Mystic River. His other flank was nearly as open, though Charlestown and the troops in it gave some protection. The breastwork now gave some cover to his eastern flank though it remained exposed to a movement along the bank of the river.

Gage had awakened to the sound of the *Lively's* cannonade. He probably had not slept well—the anxieties revealed in his letters of the previous month would keep any man from sleep. He worried about the mouths he had to feed in besieged Boston cut off from supplies from inland farms, and he worried over reports of the spreading rebellion. In May he had written Dartmouth that Connecticut and Rhode Island were in "open rebellion," and to the south New York, Pennsylvania, and the southern colonies were arming. All this was disquieting, and nothing he saw the morning of June 17 on the Charlestown peninsula gave him confidence.[19]

Whether Gage said his prayers in the morning is not known, but he did appeal for counsel from the trinity at hand—Howe, Clinton, and Burgoyne. They gave him what often issues from military advisers and staffs—conflicting advice—with Clinton proposing a landing in the rear of the redoubt and the use of the navy to keep reinforcements from coming down the Neck. A second landing at the foot of the peninsula would allow the British to squeeze the Americans to death. Clinton's plan would have made effective use of the navy's control of the water, but it violated the convention which held that an army should not allow itself to be trapped between two enemy forces. Gage objected to Clinton's plan on this ground, and the others backed him. After further discussion they planned a landing on the southeastern corner, Moulton's Point near the hill of the same name, movement along the side washed by the Mystic River, and an assault from the rear. Although this plan showed intelligence, the decision to land at Moulton's Point did not. The tide was out and Gage had to wait until early afternoon to put Howe, who commanded the landing force, ashore. Landing at the Charlestown wharves might have been accomplished at any time and at small cost since they were lightly defended. By the time Howe's force stepped on Moulton's Point, the Americans had realized that their left flank was still vulnerable and had acted to defend it.[20]

Howe's force included ten companies of light infantry, ten of grenadiers, four regiments, and parts of a fifth—about 1500 men in all. His reserve, around 700 rank and file from two regiments and two battalions of marines, was to remain at the battery until it was needed. Brigadier General Sir Robert Pigot served as Howe's second in command.[21]

The troops embarked on twenty-eight large barges around noon and were rowed in two lines to Moulton's Point. They made an awesome picture: sitting erect and motionless on the barges, their red coats raucous in the sunlight, muskets butt down with bayonets affixed, glittering and flashing as the sun blazed down. As the barges approached the land, the men-of-war intensified their bombardment, concentrating on the Neck to isolate the troops on Bunker and Breed's, seeking also to soften

19. Clarence E. Carter, ed., *The Correspondence of General Thomas Gage* . . . (2 vols., New Haven, Conn., 1931), I, 401.
20. For British planning, see French, *First Year of the American Revolution*, 221–22; Ward, I, 82–84.
21. Ward, I, 84.

up the redoubt and finally to clear the landing area itself. The ships alone could fire eighty guns, and Gage had augmented their fire with several floating batteries and with additional guns on Copp's Hill. The smoke from all these guns drifted over the water accompanied by a nearly constant roar and flash.

Howe put his troops ashore at Moulton's Point about one o'clock. No one contested this landing, and the soldiers were quickly placed in the conventional formation for attack: three long lines. Just as they arranged themselves, Howe ordered them to fall out and rest while he brought over the remainder of his 1500 men and a part of his reserve. The breastwork which had not been there when his plan of attack was approved now gave him pause and so did the movement of a column from Bunker Hill toward Breed's—seemingly, he thought, reinforcements for the redoubt.

Had Howe known that Prescott was about to strengthen the American left flank even more, he might have struck at once. Prescott guessed correctly from Howe's choice of a landing site that the main attack would be against the American left. And the uncovered ground east of the breastwork worried him so much that he sent Captain Knowlton and about 200 men to defend it. Their defensive line was not an extension of the breastwork, but rather a rail fence 200 yards northeast of it and roughly parallel to it. Knowlton's men tore down another fence, rolled stones up against the first, and covered rails and stones with newly mown hay. This "work" appeared more formidable than it actually was. Shortly after Knowlton aligned his men behind the rail fence, the column of troops Howe had observed marched up and joined Knowlton's men. These reinforcements were the two New Hampshire regiments Ward had so reluctantly dispatched, led by Colonels John Stark and James Reed. Stark showed immediately that he had brought brains and initiative as well as troops, for not only did he place troops with Knowlton at the fence, but he also set up a breastwork of stones along the water's edge. There a beach ran along the Mystic, shielded from the fields above by a dropoff—or bluff—of around nine feet. Though narrow, this beach was wide enough to permit a column of four or five files to pass along it.[22]

So punctilious in observing the convention which forbade placing troops between two enemy forces, Howe nevertheless threw out the rules in attacking the redoubt. The old casual feeling of superiority that

22. *Ibid.*, 86–87.

puffed up imperial heads when they dealt with the "provincials" may have clouded his judgment. In any case, he ignored standard military doctrine which held that fortified positions should be attacked by columns, not by the extended lines he now chose to use in deploying his troops. An attack in columns permitted rapid movement and a concentrated assault by a mass of men. The theory was Wolfe's and had made its way into manuals of tactics. The intention was to deprive defenders within entrenchments of the advantage of picking off attackers-in-line before they could close for bayonet work. Wolfe had recommended that small parties of sharpshooters be placed between columns with orders to fire at the top of the parapet so as to divert the defenders' fire. The columns would rush the entrenchments quickly and overpower the defenders by sheer mass.[23]

On Howe's far right along the beach skirting the Mystic, he did use a column for the attack—he had no choice—placing eleven companies of light infantry in a column of fours. Above the beach, he had another twenty-six companies in two lines, the front rank composed of grenadiers. This force was to attack the rail fence; Howe joined the soldiers himself and braved American fire with them. He may have lacked skill and imagination; he did not lack courage.[24]

These thirty-seven companies composed the British right. Howe gave Pigot the left and thirty-eight companies, including three companies each of light infantry and grenadiers, the 38th, 43rd, and 47th Regiments, and the 1st Marines. These units on the left were deployed in three lines just as Howe's division was. All together the attacking British had 2200 rank and file, six field pieces, two light 12-pounders, and two howitzers.

Howe's plan called for a coordinated movement forward, with the main attack to be delivered from the British right by the light infantry on the beach and the grenadiers and supporting infantry above them against the rail fence. Pigot would move from the left, but his initial attack was apparently to be diversionary, occupying the attention and fire of the Americans in the redoubt. Once the light infantry and grenadiers broke through on the right, they would turn their attack inward away from the river. The breastwork and the redoubt lying isolated and exposed could then be taken by a flanking attack.

The plan ran into trouble because of its complexity and its need for timing and coordination. The troops moved forward together, but the

23. French, First Year of the American Revolution, 235.
24. Ward, I, 89.

fences, high grass, kilns, swamp, and clay pits which broke the ground on the British right disordered the lines almost immediately. The need to slow the march while the artillery fired, then hooked up to be rolled forward, caused more confusion and disorder. The artillery soon proved almost useless as most of its ammunition turned out to be of the wrong size. On the left Pigot also ran against fences and high grass and, in addition, fire from Americans hiding in the buildings of Charlestown, 200 yards from the redoubt. A carcass, a shell carrying hot iron or combustible material, soon landed in Charlestown and the place began to burn, driving out the defenders. Still, Pigot had trouble gaining momentum.[25]

The light infantry, led by those from the 23rd Regiment, the Royal Welch Fusiliers, met no obstructions from grass or fences, since the beach, though narrow, was smooth and flat. The Fusiliers advanced rapidly, bayonets at the ready, for they were not to fire but simply to overrun the provincials by sheer drive and mass. Stark watched them come from behind the barrier of stones and kept his men silent. When the column of scarlet got to within fifty yards of his position, he ordered his troops to fire. At that range, fire into a dense column could not miss, and the front ranks of the Fusiliers disintegrated, pitched about by the heavy musket balls. They were brave men and bravely led; their officers urged them forward despite the massed fire from Stark's soldiers. "Our Light Infantry were served up in companies," a British officer commented a few days later, and were devoured by musket fire until ninety-six died on the beach where, as another sadly noted, they "lay as thick as sheep in a fold."[26] Not even the highly disciplined Fusiliers could stand this slaughter for long, and in a minute or two they pulled back; some said they broke and ran.

Above them in the fields before the rail fence the grenadiers also fell in thick grotesque piles. They too were allowed to approach well within effective range before the Americans poured musket balls into them. The grenadiers had come forward with "laudable perseverance" in Howe's understated phrase, "but not with the greatest share of discipline, for as soon as the Order with which they set forward to the attack with bayonets was checked by a difficulty they met with in getting over some very high fences of strong railing, under a heavy fire, well kept up by the rebels, they began firing, and by crowding fell into disorder,

25. Howe to ?, June 22, 24, 1775, in Fortescue, ed., *Correspondence of George the Third*, III, 220–24.
26. Sheer and Rankin, *Rebels and Redcoats*, 62–63; Ward, I, 91.

and in this state the 2d line mixt with them." The sight of his troops entangled in fences, high grass, with one another, and chopped into a disordered crowd by the hot lead from the rail fence produced in Howe a *"Moment that I* never felt before," a moment of horror and—though he did not admit to fright—surely of fear that his command was about to be defeated and perhaps destroyed.[27]

Howe wrote later of the gallantry of his officers, who in this extremity rallied the troops for a second assault which, joined to another attempt led by Pigot on the left—"a 2d onset"—carried the redoubt and breastwork.[28] His memory may have led him to compress two attacks into one in this account, for the evidence we have suggests that a second charge was made against the rail fence and the breastwork by the grenadiers and that Pigot led his troops on the British left up against the redoubt at the same time. Both failed, encountering, as a British officer reported, "an incessant stream of fire."[29] Incessant but carefully concentrated, he might have added, because in the redoubt Prescott had hoarded his troops' fire as mindfully as the fabled miser hoarded gold. The shortage of powder and lead had concerned him from the start; his men had not been trained to fire by volleys—many had not been trained to do anything—but they could be made to conserve their ammunition until the enemy came close. Prescott saw to that.

Despite Prescott's efforts, repelling this second assault consumed most of the remaining powder and bullets. Howe's troops had followed their officers up the hill, only to go down again after approaching in some cases to within a hundred feet of the Americans. The third assault, perhaps thirty minutes later, concentrated on the breastwork and the redoubt; no attempt was made against Stark on the beach or Knowlton along the rail fence. By this time, Howe had received reinforcements— 400 fresh troops, the 2nd Battalion of Marines and the 63rd Regiment. As in the second attack, his initial advance was made by columns—he had remembered the doctrine of the textbooks—and then for the final rush by lines. This time his artillery gave him support, pushing forward so as to deliver enfilade fire along the breastwork, and the infantry led by the grenadiers ran up the hill, bayonets flashing, voices shouting "push on, push on."[30] Within the redoubt the Americans saved their

27. Fortescue, ed., *Correspondence of George the Third,* III, 222.
28. *Ibid.*
29. Sheer and Rankin, *Rebels and Redcoats,* 62. French and Ward agree that the British made three attacks.
30. French, *First Year of the American Revolution,* 247.

bullets as long as they could and then opened up. Those on the right side of the redoubt aimed well and stopped Pigot's marines, who led his assault, killing, among others, Major Pitcairn of Lexington fame. The grenadiers, however, could not be stopped. The Americans ran out of ammunition. Minutes later the grenadiers entered the redoubt, some over the parapet, others from the rear. Most of Prescott's men escaped in a disorderly withdrawal from the redoubt, but at least thirty trapped within were bayoneted by British infantry eager to settle scores.[31]

The retreat that followed did not collapse into disorder. Knowlton from the rail fence and Stark moving up from the beach gave covering fire, moving backward to Bunker Hill as they did. The men at the breastwork had already pulled back under the raking from the artillery, and Prescott's troops found a shield in Knowlton and Stark. Yet they took heavy losses as they ran back toward Bunker Hill. Joseph Warren was killed as he left the redoubt; he may have been among the last to leave.

The British pursuit developed slowly, hampered by the confusion that ruled the redoubt. The troops on Breed's had won a victory but lost their integrity as units. Getting them sorted out and into formations from which pursuit might be conducted took time. General Clinton, who had been unable to contain himself in Boston and who had come over to the peninsula in time to take part in the final assault on the left, took charge of the milling troops on Breed's and reorganized them for a move against Bunker Hill. But by the time he recovered order from disorder, the Americans were pulling back off the peninsula—some simply running without direction or leadership, but most apparently in some rough order under the command of desperate officers. By nightfall it was all over: the British held the ground all the way to Charlestown Neck. This victory, if it can be called that, cost them 226 dead and 828 wounded. American losses were 140 killed, and 271 wounded.[32]

---

31. *Ibid.*, 249–52.
32. *Ibid.*, 253. My account of Bunker Hill rests on the studies of Ward and French. Bernhard Knollenberg, "Bunker Hill Re-viewed: A Study in the Conflict of Historical Evidence," MHS, *Procs.*, 72 (Boston, 1963), 84–100, is also helpful, although Knollenberg's conclusion that fortifying Breed's Hill was done by mistake rather than calculation is surely in error. Among the participants' accounts, General Howe's letters of June 22 and 24, in Fortescue, ed., *Correspondence of George the Third*, and the diaries and letters in Sheer and Rankin, *Rebels and Redcoats*, are especially valuable.

V

George Washington arrived in Cambridge on July 2, just two weeks after the battle of Bunker Hill. He did not exude confidence in himself or in American prospects. Though the performance of the militia against Howe's regulars heartened him, he did not feel certain that the Americans could win a war with Britain or even that they could force the British to an accommodation of American liberties. In fact, he had accepted his appointment with misgivings, registering his protests with Congress: "my Abilities and Military experience may not be equal to the extensive and important Trust." Washington hated the prospect of failure and what it would do to his "reputation," a word that appeared frequently in his letters at this time. To refuse the appointment, however, would tarnish his "honor," another word he used often, and which expressed one of his basic values. By refusing to lead, he would not only dishonor himself, he would, as he explained to his wife Martha—"My Dearest"— give "pain to my friends." All these concerns—doubts about American prospects, honor and reputation, regard for friends, uncertainty about his abilities—set the ambivalence within him throbbing.[33]

For despite his apparent serenity, his massive dignity and gravity, and his obvious mastery of the problems of his life, Washington, a man now in middle age, still harbored many of the tensions and anxieties of his youth. Yet there was a difference. As a young man he had burned with desires after fame and fortune, the conventional goals of eighteenth-century youth of his class. Their attraction for him may have exceeded normal bounds, though, perhaps because he was not so securely of the gentry as many of the young men around him. Now, in 1775, though his honor still concerned him, it was no longer an obsession. He would risk his reputation for the great cause.

Washington was born in 1732 to a planting family in Virginia whose founder had emigrated to the colony in the seventeenth century. Augustine Washington, the father of George, was of the gentry but he was not a major planter. The family's social credentials were good but not distinguished. Augustine Washington did not make his mark in politics, though he did serve as sheriff and as a justice of the peace, but he never sat in the House of Burgesses. At his death in 1743 he held around 10,000 acres of Virginia land.

After Augustine Washington's death, George lived with his older brother Lawrence at Mount Vernon. His mother, Mary Ball Washington,

33. GW Writings, III, 292, 294.

did not make her sons' lives easy; she may have felt cheated by her husband's death. For whatever reasons, she brought more querulousness than comfort to her sons, with her complaints of her hard lot and of their neglect. George was not fond of her, but duty commanded that he listen to her and that he honor her. He heeded these commands and gave his mother respectful attention if not love.

As a youth, Washington was big and awkward. Everyone commented on the size of his hands, and his feet were also large and inevitably got in his way. Ease in company never came to him but he tried hard for it. Like other boys before and since, he turned to a book for help, *Youth's Behaviour or Decencie in Conversation Amongst Men*,[34] a manual of conduct which contained precepts designed to smooth the way for rough-hewn boys:

> In the Presence of Others sing not to yourself with a humming Noise, nor Drum with your fingers or feet. Shake not the head, feet or legs, rowl [roll] not the eyes, lift not one eyebrow higher than the other, wry not the mouth, and bedew no mans face with your spittle, by approaching too near him when you speak.[35]

Washington learned more than not to spit and scratch in company. Though his formal schooling was slight, he developed a good English prose style—occasionally he wrote with power and fluency—and he picked up more than an ordinary amount of mathematics. His ability in mathematics led him to surveying, and at sixteen he was a competent surveyor. This skill may have fed his passion for land, a passion he shared with most planters in Virginia. Surveying, he found, opened opportunities to speculate in land, especially in the West in 1748, where he worked as a surveyor and returned 1500 acres richer. By the time he was twenty-one, he owned several thousand acres; he had leased Mount Vernon (which would soon be his), he was a major in the militia, and he was the surveyor of his county.

At this time Washington craved fame almost as badly as he craved land. And he was soon to attain it. The opportunity came in the growing struggle between Britain and France for the American West, especially that part of it around the forks of the Ohio River. The Ohio Company, owned by speculators in land, decided in 1753 to build a fort at the forks of the Ohio, the center of a vast area claimed by the company

34. (7th impression, London, 1661).
35. Washington copied this passage which appears, in slightly different form, in *ibid.*, 1–3.

and by the French. The problem was how to get the French out. Washington, whose brother Lawrence owned stock in the Ohio Company, was sent by the governor of Virginia with a letter, demanding that the French leave the Ohio. Washington made the journey through the wilderness, received a polite rebuff, and returned to Virginia, where he wrote an account of his journey which so captivated the governor that he ordered it printed. This short narrative impressed men as far away as London, where it was reprinted. Things were looking up for Washington.

Having done one job well, Washington was given another the next year: command of an expedition which would hold the Ohio country for Virginia. This expedition ended in disaster. Washington and his men were captured by the French after a bloody fight, but Washington had performed well and emerged with his reputation unscathed. Of the battle Washington wrote to his brother, "I heard the bullets whistle, and, believe me there is something charming in the sound"—a remark which made its way into the newspapers and which added to his fame.[36]

The next five years offered few charms. Washington was given command of the Virginia militia and ordered to defend the frontier. Unfortunately, to his mind, the main arena of the war had shifted elsewhere. Leading the militia was almost impossible, for the civilians who filled its ranks were impatient of authority and unreliable in almost every way. Washington dealt with them as well as he knew how and smoldered over what he considered neglect by Virginia and his majesty's army in America. Feeling neglected and facing great problems along the frontier, he responded, immature man that he was, by complaining frequently about his burdens and of slights by regular British officers, and by seeking preferment for himself in the form of a regular commission in the British army. The Washington of these years is not an attractive figure. He lusted after glory and reward and achieved neither, and he also failed to achieve serenity or perspective, both of which he needed more than reputation.

Late in 1758 Washington resigned his commission and returned to Mount Vernon. He soon married and turned to tobacco planting. His marriage to Martha Custis, a wealthy widow, was not one of great passion,

36. Quoted in Samuel Eliot Morison, *By Land and By Sea: Essays and Addresses* (New York, 1954), 173. For my conclusions about Washington, I have drawn on his writings and from two splendid biographers, Freeman, *GW*; and James Thomas Flexner, *George Washington: The Forge of Experience, 1732–1775* (Boston, 1965) and *George Washington in the American Revolution, 1775–1783* (Boston, 1968).

but neither was it one of convenience. They seem to have been genuinely fond of one another, and their marriage was a happy one.

The fifteen years from 1759 until 1774 were quiet, but important nonetheless. When they began, Washington was a disappointed officer, an ambitious man, jealous of his honor and reputation, inclined to self-pity, sensitive to slights, selfish and self-seeking—in short, still immature. He grew in these fifteen years: his military ambition cooled, he became less concerned with himself and more concerned with others—family, friends, and neighbors. Serenity largely replaced the sensitivity to slights, and generosity, the selfishness. We can only speculate about the process by which these changes were accomplished. We do know that Washington's responsibilities increased and, perhaps more important, that they were of a new sort, unrelated to military ambition and dreams of glory. The problems of plantation management had to be faced daily; friends came for advice, money, and comfort. And there were problems of governing. Washington's public activities extended from the courtroom, where he was a justice of the peace, to the vestry, and finally to the House of Burgesses.

All these obligations he fulfilled thoroughly and, as far as is known, generously. He was not a brilliant leader in the Burgesses—not really a leader at all, although his opinion on important questions came to be valued. In these years he met the requirements of patrician leadership: concern for the community informed by balance and judgment in making decisions. Those qualities had been identified by the second Continental Congress in Philadelphia.

And now in 1775 standing with the army outside Boston, Washington's hard-won mastery of himself faced a cruel test. He was called upon to lead forces of doubtful quality, supported by colonies of still unknown resolve, against the greatest power in Europe. Those strong inner resources of mind and character which had developed so slowly in Washington sustained him in the eight years of war that followed. So also did at least two profound convictions. The first was that he was the instrument of Providence in the struggle. He characteristically put this belief more modestly than this bald statement allows: "But as it has been a kind of destiny that has thrown me upon this service, I shall hope that my undertaking it is designed to answer some good purpose."[37] The other belief approached passion—a love of what Washington called the "glorious cause," the defense of the liberties of Americans.

37. *GW Writings*, III, 294.

VI

When Washington arrived in Cambridge on July 2 to take command, the British army locked up in Boston still bled from Bunker Hill. Yet it was a dangerous enemy, well trained and on the whole well officered and equipped. In July it numbered 5000; when Howe, who replaced Gage in October, evacuated Boston the following March it had increased to 10,000.[38]

In most respects the British army was a conventional eighteenth-century European force trained to fight in the accepted style of the century. In the eighteenth century, before the French Revolution brought its immense changes, war was the preserve of the dynastic state, fought on a small scale for limited purposes. Ordinarily, two groups in society did the fighting—the aristocracy who provided the officers, and an under class, peasants, vagrants, the dregs who filled the ranks. Frederick the Great of Prussia once said that a war was not a success if most people knew that it was going on, and he, like rulers all over Europe, took pains to shield the middle classes, the solid producers and the artisans, from the bloodshed and destruction of battle.[39]

Armies composed of dregs were difficult to recruit, difficult to train, and expensive to maintain. They were also necessarily small—"necessarily" because of their expense and because of the character of the dynastic state, chronically limited in its revenues and limited too by its inability to call upon an indifferent people to support its wars. Hence wars had to be fought only for dynastic purposes—not national ones as became the rule in the nineteenth century. The eighteenth-century dynasts feared an armed people, with good reason—as the French Revolution was to show.

The composition of the army required that it be highly trained and harshly disciplined. Vagrants, ignorant peasants, and in many cases foreigners who were dragooned or hired felt neither moral commitment to their rulers nor loyalty to their nation which, in a modern sense,

---

38. Knollenberg, "Bunker Hill Re-viewed," MHS, *Procs.*, 72 (1963), 85, states that on June 17, 1775, the British had 4500 rank and file in Boston. Rank and file was a technical term for privates and corporals; it did not include sergeants, fifers, and drummers. The British lost 226 killed and 828 wounded at Bunker Hill. For the March 1776 figures, see Ward, I, 125.

39. R. R. Palmer, "Frederick the Great, Guibert, Bülow: From Dynastic to National War," in Edward Mead Earle, ed., *Makers of Modern Strategy: Military Thought from Machiavelli to Hitler* (Princeton, N.J., 1943), 49–74; Walter L. Dorn, *Competition for Empire, 1740–1763* (New York, 1940), chap. 3, esp. 80–81. Much that follows about eighteenth-century warfare is based on these two excellent studies.

did not exist. The aristocracy, however, felt such loyalties and provided the officers to drill and lead the scum who made up the rank and file. Frederick, who set the standards of organization and the direction of much military doctrine, warned against reliance on any but aristocrats; bourgeois officers he despised as deficient of any motive other than a wish to fatten their purses. But neither Frederick nor any other eighteenth-century ruler could avoid reliance on foreign-born rank and file. Press gangs swept the scum into the army and recruiters hired foreign mercenaries; and officers of noble birth subjected both to exacting and sometimes savage discipline. Still the rate of desertion proved appallingly high. A French traveler once observed that the main duty of the native half of the Prussian army was to prevent the foreign half from deserting.

With troops enlisted almost entirely from the impoverished classes, incapable of honor, difficult to train, and expensive to maintain, military commanders understandably conceived of warfare as the art of preserving the army as much as winning victories. Their preoccupation with the problems of recruitment and training led them to strive to make military practice as rational as possible. Operations ordinarily were conducted only in seasons of good weather, and winter campaigns were rare. Winter quarters were carefully selected to permit a reasonably comfortable existence and opportunities for the renewal of men and weapons. And in good weather, victories were not usually exploited for fear that defeat might follow or intolerable expense be incurred. Commanders did not seek combat with eagerness; the German officer who characterized battle as the remedy of the desperate spoke for most. The concept of total war and its corollary, total victory, remained for the future to invent.

Tactics reflected the assumptions that underlay the general rules of campaigning. Skillful tactics consisted of maneuvering troops so as to begin battle under circumstances that would prohibit heavy losses. This consideration sometimes outweighed the results of battle—with defeat and light losses tolerable, and victory with heavy losses intolerable. Skill in marching, Marshal Saxe the French military authority contended, was more important than proficiency in the manual of arms—the handling and use of weapons, including their firing at the enemy. Hence the enormous energy lavished on close-order drill, drill on the parade ground, with intricate movements precisely accomplished. These movements in formations were rigidly controlled—the intervals between men, ranks, and files exactly determined—and the troops were taught, drilled, and practiced until they could carry them out without thinking, as if they were parts in a machine animated only by the sounds of their officers' voices. Several generations of military commanders sought to create armies that were virtually machines, their soldiers mechanical pieces, moving only on order. The drill instilled more than discipline; it taught movements on the parade ground which men used on the battlefield—it was not simply for "show," as a number of American observers charged during the Revolution.

Thus the steps that the troops used in marching were calculated to hold them in precise formation. Frederick's officers insisted that their soldiers move by the "Prussian step," with the knee rigid and the entire leg swung forward. The British favored high knee-action, with the foot lifted well off the ground and stamped down hard. Troops ordinarily moved in columns, places in the column corresponding to places in the lines from which fire was delivered. The British, along with most European armies, fought with their infantry deployed in lines three deep, the front rank kneeling, the center with each soldier standing with his left foot inside the right of the man kneeling in front, and the rear rank with each soldier placed with his left foot inside the right of the man ahead in the center. "Locking," the term British regulars used to describe this alignment, reveals much about its purposes: to hold tightly a mass of men so as to permit the concentrated, and controlled, fire of their muskets. In this formation, as in most others, the troops fired on order by volley.[40]

The firing of muskets in fact involved another set of intricate procedures, each initiated and completed on command. The standard guide for British foot soldiers, Humphrey Bland's *An Abstract of Military Discipline*, called for seventeen separate commands to be given to soldiers loading their muskets.[41] Infantrymen could not fire until six more orders were relayed, seven if the command "Take Care" (which initiated the process) is counted. This elaborate set of orders seems absurd, and is customarily treated as such by modern historians, but in reality it suited the way everything was done and contributed to the rational control of the irrational process that constitutes warfare. Had troops been permit-

40. Humphrey Bland, *An Abstract of Military Discipline* . . . (Boston, 1747), especially chap. 4; [Edward Harvey], *The Manual Exercise, As Ordered by His Majesty in 1764* (Boston, 1774), 3–14, and *passim*. There were several similar guides, or manuals, published in America during the revolutionary crisis. They provide instructions on firing, marching, and maneuvering troops. See Timothy Pickering, *An Easy Plan of Discipline for a Militia* (Salem, Mass., 1775); [Lewis Nicola], *A Treatise of Military Exercise, Calculated for the Use of the Americans* (Philadelphia, 1776); Thomas Hanson, *The Prussian Evolutions in Actual Engagements* . . . (Philadelphia, 1775).

41. Chapter 1.

ted to load their weapons at their own speed, they probably would have got in one another's way, for the Brown Bess, as the British musket was affectionately called, was long, heavy, and difficult to handle and load. And the fire of troops loading it without careful supervision would undoubtedly have been difficult to control. Free-lancing was not encouraged; the heavy volleys of massed men were much more lethal.

There was another use for the foot soldier after he fired his weapon which also required unyielding discipline. Since muskets could not deliver more than three rounds per minute and had an effective range of only one hundred yards, the bayonet was usually relied upon to break up a massed, or an entrenched, enemy. And the bayonet charge returned results only when it was performed by massed men—here was still another reason for the three ranks of infantry. Marshal Saxe recommended four lines of infantry, the last line (or fourth) to be armed with pikes. British commanders relied on three, however, sometimes eschewing firing altogether in favor of the heavy shock of the bayonet charge. Howe had depended upon the bayonet at Breed's Hill with disastrous results to his troops until he delayed placing them in line until after they had come close to the redoubt. Then their charge proved effective.[42]

George Washington admired European military doctrine. He had begun reading the European authorities while serving as commander of the Virginia militia and soon confirmed their judgments for himself. That books told the truth—sometimes—did not surprise him, but his own experience with the militia did, and discouraged him as well. Under arms his fellow Virginians resembled those in civilian life—stubborn, undisciplined, and lacking in public spirit. Those citizen-soldiers he found in the lines around Cambridge were from New England, but they might have come from Virginia. "Discipline is the soul of an army," the young Washington had written in 1757, and now in 1775 he had to find a way to convert what he considered to be the rabble around Boston into an army. A week after he arrived in Cambridge, he was writing Richard Henry Lee that "The abuses in this army, I fear, are considerable and the new modelling of it, in the face of an enemy, from whom we every hour expect an attack, is exceedingly difficult and dangerous." The weakness of his army, he believed, was inherent in any nonprofessional force—its members, officers and men alike, had interests and ties which could not be reconciled with the purposes of a professional army. To a certain extent then, a militia would always remain unreliable simply

42. Saxe and Frederick the Great were cited by both British and American writers.

because of what it was, a collection of civilians on temporary duty.[43]

Washington, a Virginian with the conventional prejudices of the eighteenth-century breed, detected still another sort of weakness in the New England army. Its soldiers were for the most part from Massachusetts, a colony well known in Virginia for its leveling democracy, and democrats did not make good soldiers. Washington found "an unaccountable kind of stupidity in the lower class of these people," which "prevails but too generally among the officers of the Massachusetts *part* of the Army who are nearly all the same kidney with the Privates."[44] Unaccountable as this "stupidity" may have seemed, Washington felt quite able to account for it as the inevitable result of equality. The Massachusetts privates elected their officers, with predictable consequences for their ability to command: "there is no such thing as getting of officers of this stamp to exert themselves in carrying orders into execution—to curry favor with the men (by whom they were chosen, and on whose smiles possibly they may think they may again rely) seems to be one of the principal objects of their attention."[45]

Although Washington had a clear conception of the kind of army he wanted, he was not so wedded to traditional European ideas as to be incapable of making do with what he had. At Cambridge in 1775 and throughout the war, though he strove to create a conventional army, he proved himself capable of departing from standard doctrine. He campaigned in the winter; he used irregulars—as the militias surely were; he appealed to political principles and to the nation; and he did not attempt to confine the war to a few men of his class and to the dregs of society.

VII

Washington's first acts in Cambridge revealed the practical intelligence that served him so well. The day after his arrival he asked for a return of information on the numbers of troops in the army and the gunpowder on hand. The week that elapsed before this simple accounting could be made gave him pause and more than a hint of how badly the army was organized and administered. Nor were the answers that finally came encouraging: the army numbered 16,600 enlisted men and noncommissioned officers, of whom not quite 14,000 were present and fit for duty. Washington believed that he needed over 20,000 men for the siege; the British, he thought, had 11,500, and of course the British controlled

43. *GW Writings*, II, 114; III, 331.
44. *Ibid.*, III, 450.
45. *Ibid.*, 450–51.

the waters around Boston, and this control meant that they could concentrate their forces.[46]

The next step was to take a look at the lines. This reconnoitering took two days—not because the Americans were deeply entrenched in well-chosen positions, but because they were not. There were shallow redoubts on Winter Hill and Prospect Hill, on the north, overlooking the Charlestown peninsula; a crude abatis on the Boston Road and a trench across Roxbury's main street, presumably blocking Boston Neck; and a breastwork on Dorchester Road near the burying ground to the southeast. Dorchester Heights, which dominated Boston and the approaches from the sea, had not been occupied by either side. None of this provided reassurance to an anxious Washington, who almost immediately laid out new lines for fortifications.

If Washington were to conduct operations against the British in Boston and eventually drive them out, he had simultaneously to train an army. To train this army to besiege a city did not entail instruction in tactics— in how, for example, to wheel in columns of battalions or how to move from line of march to line of assault. Washington might have wished at times that he could afford such luxuries in training, but he could not even take the time to exercise his soldiers in siege operations. Training had to be conducted on a much simpler—indeed primitive—level. Training these men involved disciplining them, getting them to take orders and to do the simplest tasks without the shirking and slovenly behavior they were accustomed to. They slept away from their camps and entrenchments, apparently with the approval of their officers; those on guard left their posts before they were relieved; some crept out beyond the line of sentries to take long-distance shots at the British, a practice which made Washington writhe in embarrassment and shame; sentries and their officers talked with the enemy along the outpost lines. Furloughs were granted easily and in defiance of common prudence which required that units be kept at maximum strength; the camps themselves were filthy, latrines improperly placed and irregularly covered over after extensive use. Junior officers failed to inspect their men, neglecting what should have been first among their responsibilities—supervision of food and quarters.[47]

46. Freeman, GW, III, 493-94.

47. Ibid., 490-91. Washington began issuing General Orders July 3, 1775. These orders reveal much about the army and Washington's conceptions of its problems. See GW Writings, III, 305-6, 309-10, 314, 315, 316, 338-40; see also his letters of this period, ibid., 320-29, 330-31, 394-95, 450-51.

George Washington, after a miniature by Charles Willson Peale
Mount Vernon Ladies Association

Thomas Jefferson, by John Trumbull
Metropolitan Museum of Art,
bequest of Cornelia Cruger, 1923

John Adams in 1766, by Benjamin Blyth
Massachusetts Historical Society

Benjamin Franklin, by Joseph-Siffred Duplessis
Metropolitan Museum of Art

James Madison, by Charles Willson Peale
*Thomas Gilcrease Institute of American History
and Art, Tulsa, Oklahoma*

Alexander Hamilton, by John Trumbull
Museum of Fine Arts, Boston

Samuel Adams, by John Singleton Copley
Museum of Fine Arts, Boston

Abigail Adams in 1766, by Benjamin Blyth
Massachusetts Historical Society

Sir Henry Clinton, portrait engraving by H. H. Ritchie
New York Historical Society, New York City

Horatio Gates, by Charles Willson Peale
Independence National Historical Park, Philadelphia

Lord Frederick North, by Rinke, after George Dance

William L. Clements Library, University of Michigan

King George III seated on the Coronation Chair,
by Sir Joshua Reynolds
Royal Academy of Art

John Stuart, Third Earl of Bute,
by Sir Joshua Reynolds
National Portrait Gallery, London

Baron Ludwig von Closen's sketch of American army uniforms
Library of Congress

John Laurens, by Charles Willson Peale
Independence National Historical Park, Philadelphia

Baron Friedrich Wilhelm von Steuben,
by Charles Willson Peale
Independence National Historical Park, Philadelphia

Nathanael Greene by Charles Willson Peale
Independence National Historical Park, Philadelphia

Gouverneur Morris and Robert Morris, by Charles Willson Peale
Pennsylvania Academy of the Fine Arts

Charles, Earl Cornwallis, by Thomas Gainesborough
National Portrait Gallery, London

In a conventional army the commanding general did not have to concern himself with such matters, properly the concern of sergeants and lieutenants. Washington had few officers worthy of the name, and hence his general orders issued on a daily basis were filled with details about matters which should have been reserved for noncommissioned and junior officers. All betray two related concerns. The welfare of the troops: the quartermaster general is to investigate complaints that the bread is "sour and unwholesome"; company officers are to inspect the men's food and the camp kitchens; the men should have clean straw for their bedding; "the necessaries to be filled up once a week, and new ones dug; the Streets of the encampments and Lines to be swept daily, and all offal and Carrion, near the camp, to be immediately burned." The discipline of the men and the standards of performance were also much in Washington's orders. Hence he informed his soldiers immediately that with his command they were now under Congress as the Troops of the UNITED PROVINCES of North America, that since they were fighting for their liberty much was expected of them. They should refrain from "profane cursing, swearing and drunkenness"; they should know that he required "punctual attendance on divine Service, to implore the blessings of heaven upon the means used for our safety and defense." A flood of orders followed forbidding waste of powder, talking with the enemy, and slovenly standing of the guard and requiring company officers to crack down on unsoldierlike practices. Lest there be doubt about how seriously Washington took these common affairs, he convened courts-martial to drive home the point. Drumming out, cashiering of officers, fines and lashes followed with a grim regularity. The officers who allowed their troops free rein were soon departing the camps in disgrace as Washington "made a pretty good slam" among them, a phrase he used which reveals the anger he felt toward dereliction.[48]

While Washington strove to create an army from the free spirits of the militia, operations had to be conducted against the British. Digging-in commenced at once all along the line. The British were doing the same thing, and the two sides watched one another warily. By the end of August the American fortifications were virtually complete, and Washington soon after proposed an assault up the Neck from Roxbury and by boats across the bay, an idea the council of war he convened disapproved. Washington yielded to this group, believing that he was bound

48. GW Writings, III, 315, 338, 309, 451.

by congressional instruction not to act without the approval of his senior officers. It was the first instance of several in which his regard for civilian authority and the advice of others inhibited action.

By early fall one treacherous problem had been solved—the shortage of powder—but another beckoned, a shortage of troops which would commence when the enlistments of those from Connecticut and Rhode Island expired in December and January.

VIII

Even as Washington directed operations around Boston, he planned action against Canada in accordance with the wishes of Congress. Deciphering those wishes was no easy task in the early summer. For Congress did not make up its mind about an expedition until late June when it ordered Major General Philip Schuyler to take Canada if he found doing so "practicable" and not "disagreeable" to the Canadians. By far the largest number of Canadians were of French origin, and Congress may have doubted whether this group shared American principles.

While Schuyler prepared in western New York, Washington set Benedict Arnold in motion from Massachusetts. Arnold spent late August and early September collecting men and supplies and planned an expedition that would follow the rivers of Maine to Quebec. Arnold believed that in twenty days he would be demanding surrender from Sir Guy Carleton, the British general who served as governor of Canada. Arnold's optimism was equaled only by his ignorance of the geography of the Northeast—he thought that he had only 180 miles to travel; in reality he had 350 that would take him forty-five days to cover.

Soon after setting out Arnold was forced to recognize that reaching Quebec would strain his men's bodies and spirits. During the first three weeks of his march into the Maine wilderness, he seems to have believed that his men could do anything. They sailed from Newburyport to the mouth of the Kennebec, a distance of 150 miles, on September 19. The river was wide enough and deep enough to accommodate their ships which reached Gardinerstown three days later. There most of the troops either embarked in bateaux, small boats capable of carrying six or seven men and provisions, or marched along the river's edge. A few of the troops remained in the smaller sailing vessels until the narrowness of the river compelled them to join the others on land.

The expedition forced its way up the river to the Great Carrying Place, a portage of twelve miles, by October 11. Long before reaching it, the boats began to leak and, according to Arnold, a "great part" of the bread was ruined. To add to their food supply, the men fished for trout in several ponds at this portage and caught as many as "ten dozen" in an hour. Carrying the boats for twelve miles left arms and legs and backs aching—each bateau weighed 400 pounds, and arms, ammunition, and provisions had to be carried too. Spirit remained high, Arnold reported, despite pain and fatigue.

The remainder of the march was even more difficult, so difficult in fact that the expedition almost collapsed. From the Great Carrying Place, the troops entered the Dead River. Perhaps no stream in America was so badly named. The Dead River was alive with a ferocious current and snags of sunken logs and brush that slowed and sometimes stopped all progress. The men had spent so much time in the water—and under it—while going up the Kennebec that Arnold likened them to "amphibious animals." Now they were constantly wet, especially after October 19 when a heavy rain which lasted for three days sent the river over its banks. Still they dragged themselves along, often with little or nothing to eat.

Near the end of October most of the expedition had covered the thirty miles of the Dead River to the Height of Land—the watershed between the Kennebec and the Chaudière rivers. By this time many of the men were sick. They had been half-frozen for days—snow had fallen—and they were in need of food, clothing, and shoes. And they still had to cross Lake Megantic and from there sail down the Chaudière River to the St. Lawrence. On November 9, these desperately tired men made it to the St. Lawrence River. By this time they numbered 675; some 300 had turned back, others had been left sick or dead along the way.

The expedition found itself four miles from Quebec and of course across the river from it. A heavy storm stopped them from crossing until November 13; almost nothing else could have delayed Arnold, for after the misery of the march he craved battle. He did not get it until the end of December.

Quebec boasted no formidable garrison, but it could not be taken by the sick and badly equipped force Arnold commanded. The city sat on a high point of land cut out by the St. Lawrence and its tributary the St. Charles River. This point—it actually resembles a swollen thumb or several fingers pressed tightly together—looks to the northeast. On the southeastern side, Cape Diamond rises more than 300 feet above the St. Lawrence River. Along the St. Charles, to the northwest, the land slopes downward. Slightly to the northeast of Cape Diamond, Lower

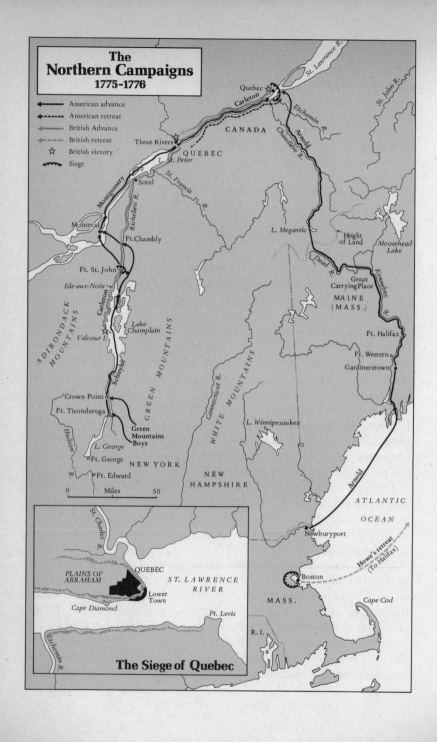

The
Northern Campaigns
1775-1776

⬅— American advance
◄----- American retreat
⬅— British Advance
◄----- British retreat
☆ British victory
〰〰 Siege

St. Lawrence R.

Quebec ☆
Carleton

Etchemin R.

St. John R.

CANADA

Three Rivers ☆

QUEBEC

Arnold

Chaudière R.

L. St. Peter

Montgomery

Richelieu R.

Sorel

St. Francis R.

L. Megantic

Height
of Land

Moosehead
Lake

Montreal

Ft. Chambly

Dead R.

Great
Carrying Place

Kennebec R.

Ft. St. John

Isle-aux-Noix

MAINE
(MASS.)

Carleton

ADIRONDACK
MOUNTAINS

Valcour I. ☆

Lake
Champlain

Schuyler

GREEN MOUNTAINS

Ft. Halifax

Ft. Western

Gardinerstown

Crown Point

Ft. Ticonderoga

Green
Mountains
Boys

Hudson R.

L. George

Ft. George

Ft. Edward

NEW YORK

NEW
HAMPSHIRE

Connecticut R.

WHITE MOUNTAINS

L. Winnipesaukee

Arnold

ATLANTIC
OCEAN

0   Miles   50

Newburyport

Howe's retreat
(To Halifax)

Boston

MASS.

Cape Cod

R.I.

St. Charles R.

QUEBEC

PLAINS OF
ABRAHAM

ST. LAWRENCE
RIVER

Lower
Town

Cape Diamond

Pt. Levis

Etchemin R.

The Siege of Quebec

Town huddled along the narrow band of land on the water's edge. At its southern side fortifications had been built, two rough palisades and a blockhouse. There was also a wall at the northern part of the Lower Town and outside it small clusters of suburbs.

The main part of the city, Upper Town, stood astride the high ground, protected by its height, the steep cliffs on three sides, and to the west by a wall thirty feet high which extended from river to river. The wall looked toward the Plains of Abraham, where Wolfe and Montcalm had fought and died. There were six strong points along the wall and three gates. Quebec's defenders concentrated their artillery at the six strong places. Within Upper Town the British assembled about 1800 troops, a strange mixture of militia, Scottish soldiers, a handful of marines, and large numbers of sailors drawn from ships in the harbor.

Arnold's force made a brave show in front of the wall for a few days and then pulled back twenty miles to Pointe aux Trembles. There early in December, Richard Montgomery, Schuyler's second-in-command in western New York, joined them. Montgomery, an attractive man in every respect, as handsome and brave as the most splendid heroes of eighteenth-century romances, had fought his way to Montreal which fell to his forces in November. He had then led his soldiers, some 300 in all, carrying provisions, heavy winter clothing, cannon, and ammunition to where Arnold's men lay suffering. Arnold greeted Montgomery with joy, and in about three weeks the two were prepared to assault Quebec.

An assault rather than a siege had to be made. Arnold's soldiers from New England would not remain in the army after the end of the year when their enlistments expired. Even had they been willing, they could not have sustained a siege for long because in the spring, when the ice melted in the St. Lawrence, transports carrying British soldiers would undoubtedly come up the river to relieve the city.

After a false start on December 27, the assault was made early in the morning of December 31 during a blizzard with the wind screaming and the temperature well below freezing. Getting the troops into place took about three hours. About two in the morning they began to move, Arnold's 600 against the northern side of Lower Town and Montgomery's 300 against the southern side. The British lay waiting—they had slept in their clothes for a week, and they had fortified Lower Town at precisely the points where the attack would be delivered.

About 5:00 A.M. the Americans struck. Arnold's troops broke through the first barrier the British had set up, but were stopped at the second. Arnold himself received a bullet in the leg and was carried, badly bleeding, out of danger. Montgomery fell dead almost immediately with a bullet in his head. Despite the gallantry of Daniel Morgan, who took charge of the van of Arnold's force, the attack on the north failed. Montgomery's disintegrated even more rapidly. Within a couple of hours both were finished with over 400 Americans captured, trapped by snow and ice and skillful British deployments, and some fifty or sixty others dead or wounded.

Arnold pulled back a mile from Quebec. Over the next few months he received small numbers of reinforcements. When spring came, still suffering from his wound, he gave up his command and slowly rode to Montreal.

The soldiers he left behind under Major General David Wooster may have hoped that they would spend the summer of 1776 inside the walls of Quebec. Bravery and spirit had carried the Americans to Quebec in 1775 on one of the great marches of the eighteenth century. Such men and those who joined them in Canada could not help but hope that they would finally capture the city. They had earned the right to hope.

IX

As American efforts in Canada unwound, to the south in Boston the end of the siege came with surprising suddenness. The American army forced its end by action which gave the British a choice of attacking to relieve the siege or evacuating Boston and thereby ending their misery. Howe chose to evacuate the town.

The beginning of the end came with extraordinarily cold weather in February. The cold made Washington hot for an attack; he had been quietly burning for action since the autumn. Now with temperatures well below freezing, ice thick enough to support the weight of troops formed between Cambridge and Boston. Washington convened a council of war and urged that it agree to send the troops across in an assault. He reported that he had 16,000 men—around 7000 militia and almost 9000 Continentals—and he had more than fifty pieces of heavy artillery recently transported from Ticonderoga and Crown Point by young Henry Knox, colonel of artillery.[49]

Henry Knox resembled nothing so much as one of his heavy mortars: he was tall, thickset—his weight at this time was nearly 280 pounds— his voice boomed; he was gay, friendly, a vastly attractive man. He

49. Freeman, *GW*, IV, 19–20; *GW Writings*, IV, 335.

also knew his craft, and he possessed the drive that allowed him to practice it in spite of great disadvantages. The first of these was probably the greatest: he had few or no guns. But in November 1775, Washington sent him to Ticonderoga to remove the captured artillery there. What followed was one of the most impressive examples of perseverance and ingenuity in the war.[50] Despite the absence of roads and wagons, Knox managed to transport to Albany forty-four guns, fourteen mortars, and a howitzer. He first moved down Lake George on flat-bottomed scows, then across the snow and ice on heavy sledges constructed for the job, and crossed the Hudson four times on the journey. From Albany, stopping only to pull a heavy gun out of the water where it had broken through the ice, he pushed over the Berkshires, the guns and artillery in a train pulled by horses and oxen. By late January, Knox was at Framingham, and early in February the artillery was being emplaced and readied for action.

Despite the artillery and the renewed forces, the council of war refused to accept Washington's plans for an attack. It recommended instead that Dorchester Heights, still ignored by both sides, be occupied in the hope that Howe would repeat the blunders of Bunker Hill. Artillery on the Heights would make Boston untenable; Howe would have to respond somehow or sit there and watch his command pounded to pieces.

Washington took the rejection of his proposal gracefully and accepted the council's suggestion that Dorchester Heights be seized. There were difficulties in this proposal: Boston harbor was frozen and so was the ground around it, including the hills on Dorchester peninsula. The immediate question was how to fortify them quickly, in one night, as Breed's Hill had been. Digging-in was not possible, at least not in one night, for the ground was too hard. But anything less would bring a British attack which probably could not be repulsed by the untested Americans unless they were entrenched. Colonel Rufus Putnam worked out the answer: fortifications of earth set upon the ground, not dug out of it. Accordingly, late in February the troops near Dorchester were put to making chandeliers, large frames from timber in which gabions, fascines, and bales of hay would be placed once the chandeliers were hauled up into place on the hills. The gabions were to be filled with earth and the hay would be covered with as much dirt as could be dug up. Putnam also recommended that an abatis from nearby orchards should ring the

50. Freeman, GW, IV, 17 and fn. 94. For Knox, see North Callahan, Henry Knox: George Washington's General (New York, 1958).

fortifications and that barrels filled with earth should be placed outside the parapets, where they would appear to give cover but would in reality stand ready to be rolled down upon troops assaulting the hills.[51]

While the soldiers near Dorchester hammered and sawed and dug up the earth to fill gabions and barrels, Washington prepared troops in Cambridge for an assault across Back Bay against Boston. "Old Put," the formidable Israel Putnam, was given command of this operation, and John Sullivan and Nathanael Greene were to lead the crossing. Though never made, this attack was intended to answer any British attempt to dislodge the Americans from Dorchester Heights. By March 1, all was ready.

To mask his intentions Washington ordered a light bombardment of Boston by American batteries on Lechmere Point, Cobble Hill, and Roxbury on the night of March 2. Only a few shots were fired and to no effect, except on American pride when "Old Sow," one of the heavy mortars, ruptured. The shelling resumed the next night, answered as on the night before by the British. On the night of March 4 the artillery on both sides opened up without restraint, and around 7:00 P.M. in darkness General Thomas took an expedition up the Dorchester Heights, a 1200-man working party to set up the breastworks and a force of 800 infantrymen to give cover. Over 300 oxcarts and wagons carried the chandeliers, gabions, fascines, and entrenching tools. The working party laid out the redoubts while the infantry took up temporary positions on Nook's Hill, which was not to be permanently held, and on the point looking out on Castle William. Early in the morning fresh workers went up the hills to relieve those already there, and by daybreak two redoubts were virtually complete.

Howe was astonished by what he saw the morning of the fifth. There were the Americans, well protected behind heavy fortifications, looking down his throat. His naval counterpart, Rear Admiral Molyneaux Shuldham, who had taken over after Graves's recall in December, gave him the next piece of nasty news: the navy could not remain in the harbor if the enemy mounted heavy guns in the hills.[52]

Several weeks earlier Howe had decided to evacuate Boston—he hated the place, he felt trapped there as Gage had. His orders from Britain permitted such discretion. But now he would have to pull out before he was ready, or drive the Americans from the Heights in order to

51. Ward, I, 126–27.
52. Ibid., 128.

give himself some time. He first decided to attack. Ships and barges began to gather; the troops were mustered; ammunition and food were issued; and plans were laid for a landing on the peninsula that night to be followed, presumably, by an assault the next morning. Before these preparations were complete, doubts, inspired by memories of Bunker Hill, ate at his resolve and caused him to cancel the attack in favor of evacuation of Boston. High winds and heavy rains the night of the fifth saved Howe's face, as ships and boats were scattered by heavy waves, a situation which made an attack impossible.[53]

While Washington, ever suspicious, watched uneasily, the British navy sent its transports to the wharves of Boston, where over the next two weeks they were stowed with arms, stores, equipment, and finally troops. Embarkation had not been carefully planned and the lading was done badly. And inevitably much was left behind, including the horses of the artillery and the dragoons. Still, despite their haste the British found time to plunder houses and stores, thereby earning more ill will for themselves. By March 17, the last of the ships were loaded and pulled away, leaving Boston to Washington's army. They did not leave the outer harbor for another ten days, however. The loading had been so sloppily done that time was required to shift cargoes in preparation for sailing on the open sea. But on March 27, 1776, they dropped down the harbor, and Boston saw the last of the British.

Almost a year of fighting was over, and if it had not been what John Adams called it at the time—"half a war"—neither had it been a full-scale effort on the American side. The attempt to take Canada refuted Adams's contention that the colonies had been satisfied by acting "upon the line of defense," fighting a defensive war in other words, but Adams's disappointment was understandable.[54] He wanted more than a siege of Boston and an expedition to the north: he wanted America to declare its independence. In March 1776 such a declaration was closer than Adams thought. He would scarcely have been satisfied had it come the day after the British sailed from Boston. John Adams never showed much patience; yet he was an astute and sometimes a wise man. In 1776 his countrymen were more patient than he—and perhaps had greater wisdom.

53. *Ibid.*, 128–29.
54. *LMCC*, I, 406.

14

Independence

While the British army was ending its long ordeal in Boston, the second Continental Congress was in the midst of deliberations that would end with the Declaration of Independence. The second Congress began its sessions on May 10, 1775, a day midway in the period marked out by the battles of Lexington and Bunker Hill. From the outset, the Congress suffered its own ordeal—a tortuous questioning of whether America could better protect its liberties inside or outside of the British empire. And while the delegates asked themselves what the purposes of American action should be, they knew they had to act.

The need to do something was urgent. The two enemies, still bleeding from their encounter on Lexington Road, faced one another around Boston. The proposal made soon after the delegates gathered thus seemed almost inevitable: the Congress should raise an army. Over the next six weeks Congress began to do just that, and in the process took the direction of the war into its own hands. Yet while it was making generals, calling out troops, and spending money that it did not have, the Congress also worriedly discussed how it should seek to defend American rights.

Few delegates in the spring of 1775 advocated independence, and of those few none advocated a declaration of independence. Rather they seem to have believed that though a try at reconciliation would fail, it must be made, if for no other reason than that most Americans preferred reconciliation.[1]

1. *LMCC*, I, 99–100.

John Adams preferred a separation from Britain though, as he said of himself, he was "as fond of reconciliation, if we could reasonably entertain Hopes of it upon a constitutional Basis, as any man." But Adams did not believe that such hopes were reasonable because the king, Parliament, the administration, and the electorate "have been now for many years gradually trained and disciplined by Corruption" in their oppressive ways. The conclusion seemed clear that "the Cancer [of official corruption] is too deeply rooted, and too far spread to be cured by anything short of cutting it out entire."[2]

To have any chance of success, political surgery required that the people support it. But the American people seem to have been divided just as the delegates were, with most probably opposing such drastic action. Adams likened the people to a "vast unwieldy machine"; they could not be forced and must be allowed to run on in their own ways in the expectation that eventually they would recognize the best means of protecting their liberties.[3]

In any case neither Adams nor anyone else suggested independence in May. Adams told the delegates that an imperial connection might be maintained through the king. Parliament, however, should play no part in governing America. John Dickinson disagreed and advocated concessions. Let us pay for the tea destroyed at Boston, he proposed, and let us concede Parliament's right to regulate our trade, and let us petition the king once more for a redress of grievances.[4]

The weeks that followed saw these differences imperfectly reconciled in the actions of Congress. The Congress authorized the raising of an army a couple of days before the battle of Bunker Hill, and almost immediately afterwards George Washington set off from Philadelphia to assume its command. John Dickinson and the moderates around him did not oppose the creation of the army; nor did they attempt to substitute one of their number for Washington, who was known to be skeptical of peaceful approaches to Britain. Early in July they persuaded Congress of the wisdom of another petition to the king, the so-called Olive Branch petition, in effect asking him to find a way out of the conflict.

John Adams despised the weakness he detected in the petition but was resigned to oscillations in congressional policy. Though Adams's spirit was rarely calm, it could find some ease in the fact that the number

2. *Ibid.*, 118.
3. *Ibid.*
4. Jack N. Rakove, "The Decision for American Independence: A Reconstruction," *PAH*, 10 (1975), 238–39.

of delegates favoring firmness was growing. One, Thomas Jefferson, arrived in Philadelphia just about the time that news came from Bunker Hill. And delegates already there were finding it increasingly difficult to advocate reconciliation as British responses became known.[5]

John Dickinson felt more divided than most: at the time he wrote the second petition to the king he was working with Jefferson on the Declaration of the Causes and Necessity for Taking Up Arms. Jefferson wrote the first version, which Dickinson, obviously feeling compelled after Bunker Hill to show that he was as fierce for liberty as anyone else, made tougher. The declaration, which indicted Parliament for having "attempted to effect their cruel and impolitic Purpose of enslaving these Colonies by Violence, and have thereby rendered it necessary for us to close with their last Appeal from Reason to Arms," was approved on July 6. Two days later Congress agreed on the second petition to the king, and at the end of the month it rejected North's so-called Conciliatory Proposal.[6]

There may have been something approaching a "whimsical cast" to these summer proceedings—so John Adams characterized them. Congress could not seem to make up its mind. It prepared for war while it begged for peace; it proclaimed its determination to protect American liberties while it petitioned for reconciliation; it expressed respect for the king while it promised death to his armies.[7]

Yet there was nothing whimsical in the tendency of action in these hot weeks. Men died at Bunker Hill, and each time an American died so did some part of moderation. Death and suffering had more than a local effect in New England. The news of the fighting spread, and soldiers from the middle and southern colonies began to march toward Boston. As they left home so also did the spirit of compromise.

Blundering British officials also helped destroy whatever support moderation possessed. Few in the ministry seem to have kept their balance once the war began. North's impulses remained peaceful, though hardly strong enough to soothe an angry king. Dartmouth might have helped North contain the ugly desires for war, but Dartmouth was not widely

---

5. On Jefferson's arrival in Congress, see Merrill D. Peterson, *Thomas Jefferson and the New Nation: A Biography* (New York, 1970), 79–81.

6. The "Declaration of the Causes and Necessity for Taking up Arms" has been reprinted in *TJ Papers*, I, 213–18. The quotation is on 213. See also Franklin's assessment in a letter to Joseph Priestley, July 7, 1775, in *LMCC*, I, 156, and John Adams's of July 11, 1775, *ibid.*, 162.

7. *LMCC*, I, 152.

trusted and left office in the autumn. His successor, Lord George Germain, was genuinely tough and fed the vulgar desire to put the Americans in their place.[8]

News of the battles at Lexington and Concord had made compromise all the more unlikely, and Bunker Hill had hardened resolves. Late in August the king expressed much of the public, and private, outrage at American behavior by proclaiming that the colonies were in "an open and avowed rebellion." Two months later in an accounting to Parliament he explained that a "desperate conspiracy" existed in America to make a rebellious war which is "manifestly carried on for the purpose of establishing an independent empire."[9]

Many in Parliament had doubtless come to the same conclusion when fighting began in America. They now followed the lead of the ministry and just before the year ended passed, on December 22, 1775, the American Prohibitory Act, which ordered all trade with the colonies stopped. This statute made American ships and their cargoes fair game for the Royal Navy; all ships trading with the colonies were to be "forfeited to his Majesty, as if the same were the ships and the effects of open enemies, and shall be so adjudged, deemed, and taken in all courts of admiralty, and in all other courts whatsoever."[10]

Had the king, his ministry, and the Parliament attempted to persuade the Americans to separate themselves from the empire they could not have chosen much more effective means than those of April onward. The British army had marched and killed on two dreadful occasions; the petition of the Congress had been considered unworthy of answer; the Americans had been described as traitors and rebels who must be subdued by force. At first sight, shutting off American commerce may not seem such a portentous act. Yet Americans considered it to be, and rightly so, for it demonstrated once more that the king's government meant what it said about crushing rebellion. Words such as "traitors," "conspiracy," and "enemies" allowed little room for negotiation, and what little there was shrank as the months slipped by. The British army continued to menace New England, and the resolve of Parliament and the ministry to destroy the American economy became clear.[11]

8. Ian R. Christie and Benjamin W. Labaree, *Empire or Independence, 1760–1766: A British-American Dialogue on the Coming of the American Revolution* (New York, 1976), 250–52.
9. *EHD*, 850–51.
10. *Ibid.*, 853.
11. The words in quotation were used by both king and Parliament.

When news of British actions began arriving in October, Americans learned that the king had proclaimed them rebels. Not long afterwards, news came of the king's refusal to receive the petition Congress had approved in July, and then came word that more troops were on the way. By February 1776, when Congress received the Prohibitory Act, the possibility of a reconciliation was remote.

Still Congress held back from declaring independence. It was waiting for unmistakable evidence that the American people favored a permanent separation. And it hesitated to act while a remnant of its membership retained hope that negotiations that might heal the terrible wounds of the last year were possible.

In several colonies, British officials proved that the king's ministry had no monopoly on blundering. During the summer the governors of North Carolina and South Carolina, after heavy-handed attempts at coercing their assemblies, simply turned tail and fled to warships off the coast. They may have consciously followed the example of Virginia's governor, Lord Dunmore, who had preceded them to the safety of a royal warship. There he sat while the Convention, the old House of Burgesses under a new name, took over the task of governing. Dunmore had dissolved the Burgesses when they rejected North's conciliatory proposal. By November, Dunmore was feeling frustration as he sat on a swaying deck and contemplated British power, which like himself was very much at sea. Early in the month he called upon the slaves in Virginia to rebel and promised them their freedom if they joined his forces and fought their masters. Whatever loyalty there was in Virginia pretty much flickered out with Dunmore's call. The possibility of a slave rebellion was never far out of white consciousness, a possibility regarded with horror. Dunmore added to white revulsion on January 1, 1776, when he ordered Norfolk shelled by ships of the British navy. The town burned in a fire which, in a sense, was seen all over Virginia.[12]

II

During these months of British mistakes, the old colonial governments searched for a new basis of authority. Massachusetts felt especially hard pressed: in the preceding year Parliament had revised its government in unacceptable ways. Now facing the war around Boston, the Provincial Congress asked the Continental Congress what it should do—abide by statutes which had helped provoke the fighting or return to the charter

12. There is an excellent account of events discussed in this paragraph in Jensen, *Founding*, 643–45.

of 1691? In June the Provincial Congress was advised that Massachusetts need not observe the requirements of the Massachusetts Government Act, one of the Intolerable Acts, but might in effect revert to its old practice, though of course it would not have a royal governor. This "solution" was realistic in that it satisfied prevailing opinion within Massachusetts and maintained a traditional basis of authority. Five months later Congress edged a little closer to telling the colonies to act as if they were independent by advising the New Hampshire Convention to call for a representation of the people. The people in convention would, if they thought it necessary, "establish such a form of government, as, in their judgment, will best produce the happiness of the people," governing as long as the "present dispute" with Britain continued. Soon after, the same recommendation was made to South Carolina in response to a request for guidance.[13]

These actions worried congressional opponents of independence, worried John Dickinson in particular. At his instigation a few days after Congress gave the lead to New Hampshire, the Pennsylvania assembly instructed its delegation not to agree to a separation from Britain or to a change in the form of Pennsylvania's government. The legislatures of Delaware and New Jersey gave similar instructions to their delegations before the end of the year, and Maryland's followed in January 1776.[14]

III

Even as these legislatures acted, a mood grew which would shake their prudence. The mood was, more precisely, a loss of faith in all things British, a mood increasingly disposed to favor independence. By January it had found able spokesmen, most notably Thomas Paine in one of the great tracts of the Revolution—*Common Sense.*[15]

Thomas Paine, the son of an English Quaker who earned his living as a corset-maker, had arrived in America only thirteen months before publication of *Common Sense.* He was thirty-nine years old, and he had failed at everything he had ever tried. He had tried, like his father, to earn a living making corsets—and failed. He had tried teaching—and failed. He had served as a tax collector, only to be dismissed from the service. He had also tried shopkeeping—and failed. He had even tried marriage—twice. His first wife died in childbirth; his second was

13. *JCC,* III, 319, 325–27.
14. These events and those discussed in the previous paragraph are discussed in Jensen, *Founding,* 641–43.
15. First published in Philadelphia and many times reprinted.

a wife in name only, for the marriage was never consummated.[16]

Paine's friend George Scott, an excise official, had introduced him in 1774 to Benjamin Franklin, who was then finishing his mission as a colonial agent. Franklin apparently saw something in Paine, some talent that had not yet found its medium, and when he learned that Paine wanted to go to America, he wrote a letter introducing him to his son-in-law Richard Bache, a Philadelphia merchant. Paine probably did not intend to go into business in America, though after his arrival on November 30, 1774, he sought out Bache. Soon he was contributing verses and essays to local newspapers.[17]

Somehow, perhaps in his various failures, Paine had learned to write. Now he put this skill to work in the service of a cause he hoped would benefit mankind. His message to Americans challenged several of their profound convictions—that their rights were rooted in the ancient constitution and that their interests were protected by the traditional connection to Britain. Paine called these convictions "illusions." None of the old political truths, it seemed, were any longer true. The British constitution, far from being one of the glories of civilization, was founded on "the base remains of two ancient tyrannies"—monarchy and aristocracy. For the most part American writers had avoided attacking the monarchy even after war began, and they professed to believe that the king was in hands of an unscrupulous ministry. Paine disdained to honor such fictions. The monarchy, he explained, was "the most prosperous invention the Devil ever set on foot for the promotion of idolatry." As for the hereditary succession of monarchs, the practice violated nature which "disapproves of it, otherwise she would not so frequently turn it into ridicule by giving mankind an Ass for a Lion." There was much more of this sort of wit in *Common Sense* along with shrewd attacks on the institutions that Americans had long believed tied them to Britain. Much of the demolition was placed in a context, or a language, sure to appeal to the mass of Americans. Thus Paine rang in the Old Testament history of monarchy, and if his readers missed the linkage to heathenism, he told them flatly that monarchy was the Popery of government.[18]

16. There are useful studies by Eric Foner, *Thomas Paine and Revolutionary America* (New York, 1976) and David Freeman Hawke, *Paine* (New York, 1974).

17. *BF Papers*, XXI, 325–26.

18. The quotations are from the W. & T. Bradford edition of *Common Sense*, reprinted by Dolphin Books. Robert Bell of Philadelphia printed the first two editions. He and Paine fell out and Paine then turned to Bradford. The Bradford edition is about one-third longer than the Bell edition. See especially 13–27.

For those presumably immune to shock and for those devoid of Protestant prejudice, Paine offered "simple facts, plain arguments, and common sense" of the American condition—that it would only deteriorate should some temporary reconciliation be achieved. To back this contention Paine cited several conventional arguments, all demonstrating the divergence of British and American interests. But perhaps his most compelling point—not much noticed since—reminded Americans that blood had recently been spilled, and with its loss American affection for the "mother country" had drained away. American passions had been engaged in the struggle, and the passion that was directed toward Britain was hatred. The conclusion to this analysis seemed obvious: "Reconciliation is now a fallacious dream."[19]

Much of what Paine wrote had already been said in the nine months following Lexington. The events of those months, giving evidence of the stubbornness and hostility of king and Parliament, made belief in reconciliation difficult to sustain. *Common Sense* helped Americans see just how far they had come in the struggle to protect their rights, made them see that they could not go back to the old relationship of 1763. If Paine was right not the king, nor the Parliament, nor the English people had any desire for the old arrangements. A part of what Paine was saying had been said by pamphleteers for a dozen years—there was a conspiracy afoot to enslave the colonies. But Paine went farther: he showed that the conspiracy inhered in the very structure of the Anglo-American arrangements. Because the conspiracy could not be separated from the monarchy or from the British constitution, the Americans, it seemed, had no choice. They must declare their independence.

A declaration of independence might be only common sense, but Paine clearly believed that it would be more—it would indeed be a break in history. He told Americans of the importance of what they were doing in only a few sentences: "We have it in our power to begin the world over again. A situation, similar to the present, hath not happened since the days of Noah until now." How seriously this phrasing was taken is impossible to say. There is no doubt though that it was calculated to appeal to the residue of Christian millennialism from the American past, and while it proposed a rupture in history it also offered a balm, the assurance that the American Revolution should take its place in Christian history.[20]

Inevitably there were answers. Inevitably the answers and the answers

19. *Ibid.*, 27, 34.
20. *Ibid.*, 59 (Appendix).

to the answers (by Paine and others as well) plumbed the depths of invective. But those who took part in the debate also reached toward the truth and caught glimpses of the American future. The critics of the contention of *Common Sense* that independence must be declared immediately offered a variety of refutations. The timing was off, some said; others argued that the idea was bad because American liberties could never attain the security long provided by the ancient constitution. Several answers sensed the importance of Paine's dream of beginning anew in America and discussed it with such scare words of eighteenth-century politics as "innovation," "Utopian," "visionary," and "anarchy." Paine responded as the "Forester," a name chosen perhaps to evoke images of a life in America free of European corruptions, with the contention that an independent America had "a blank sheet to write upon." What, he asked, did America have to fear "but her GOD"; for America, "remote from all the wrangling world, may live at ease, Bounded by the ocean and basked by the wilderness. . . ."[21]

Paine published *Common Sense* in Philadelphia, and his Forester essays first appeared in that city's newspapers. His friends also chose Philadelphia newspapers, and so did his political enemies. But since the controversy involved the "continent," *Common Sense* was reprinted in all the major American cities and the minor ones as well. Of course the debate spread, drawing in big men, John Adams, for example, and small ones as well. Within a few months over 100,000 copies of *Common Sense* had appeared, and the debates between independence and reconciliation dominated the newspapers.[22]

A part of the common sense offered by Thomas Paine was the observation that Britain's old enemies in Europe would be more likely to provide support to the colonies if they declared their independence. No European power wanted to meddle in an internal dispute which might be settled by Britain and her colonies joining forces, as they had in the past, against an external enemy. Declaring independence would reassure Europe, reassure in particular France, the nation that some in Congress looked to for money and arms.

IV

By the first months of 1776, the group in Congress which was disposed to seek foreign aid was adding to its numbers. These radicals—their

---

21. See especially *Pennsylvania Gazette* (Phila.), March 26, April 24, May 1, 1776.
22. Richard Alan Ryerson, *The Revolution is Now Begun: The Radical Committees of Philadelphia, 1765–1776* (Philadelphia, 1978), chap. 7, for the newspapers.

radicalism consisted of their belief in American independence rather than reconciliation—agreed upon a schedule of actions which they believed gave promise of a successful war for independence. The two Adamses, the Lees, and their followers thought that the formation of new state governments was the crucial first step. Although they had no clear idea about the shape of these governments, these men saw in their creation a means of tying the American people to independence. Once the colonies had given themselves new governments the next steps should be, as John Adams proposed to Patrick Henry, "for all the colonies to confederate and define the limits of the continental Constitution; then to declare the colonies a sovereign state, or a number of confederated sovereign states; and last of all, to form treaties with foreign powers." Adams was to write to Henry on June 3, when it was fairly clear that all these measures would soon follow, that perhaps, their order was not very important.[23]

In February the radicals had considered the sequence of action as critical to their plans. And their plans, though centering on the measures Adams disclosed to Henry, included a variety of moves which only solid governments could take. A memorandum drafted by John Adams listed them: an alliance should be made with France and Spain; ambassadors should be sent to both countries; coins and currencies were to be regulated; armed forces were to be raised and maintained in Canada and New York; the production of hemp, duck, saltpeter, and gunpowder was to be encouraged; taxes were to be levied; treaties with France, Spain, Holland, and Denmark were to be concluded; British ships were to be declared fair game for American privateers; independence was to be declared as was war on Britain. There were other items on the radicals' agenda, but their overriding concern remained a declaration of independence.[24]

The radicals faced determined, though shrinking, opposition in Congress after *Common Sense* signaled that the drift of public opinion was away from reconciliation. Just how the radicals should deal with such men remained a perplexing question. These moderates were no less patriotic than the radicals; nor were they any less concerned to protect American liberties which—they agreed—had been savagely trampled on in the previous year. Still they preferred to see America free within the empire rather than outside it. Several in fact seemed to doubt that

23. *LMCC*, I, 471.
24. Butterfield et al., eds., *Diary of John Adams*, II, 231.

the colonies could gain sufficient strength to survive as free states without the protection of the mother country.

Congress appointed five moderates—James Wilson, Robert Alexander of Maryland, James Duane of New York, William Hooper of North Carolina, and John Dickinson—to a committee commissioned to provide an answer to the king's charge that the colonies intended to separate themselves from Britain. The radicals probably agreed to this composition in order to force the moderates to make their position clear on independence. Wilson wrote the committee report, a much maligned statement then and since, which said that the colonists wished to remain British subjects but were determined to continue as free men. This by now time-worn formula would no longer serve, and when the committee reported, on February 13, the radicals succeeded in tabling it. The tabling of Wilson's statement does not seem to have aroused much opposition among the moderates, who were losing hope as news of British hostility continued to come in. Fresh evidence of the king's anger shook them, and then they learned that foreign mercenaries were on the way.[25]

Meanwhile, as the winter began to give way to spring, the radicals speeded up the pace of their action in Congress. In late March, Congress authorized "the inhabitants of these colonies . . . to fit out armed vessels to cruise on the enemies of these United Colonies."[26] John Adams, who earlier had lamented that the colonies were fighting only half a war, told Horatio Gates that the colonies were now engaged at least in "three Quarters of a war."[27] And early in April, after months of tortured discussion, Congress agreed to open colonial trade to all the world but Britain.

The Congress acted in part because the country seemed at last to have decided that there was nothing left to do but move toward independence. The colonial legislatures and their stand-ins, the provincial congresses, soon caught the popular mood and began removing restraints on their congressional delegations. On March 21, South Carolina gave its delegates permission to join with others in Congress to do what was necessary for the defense of America, oblique phrasing which everyone understood to mean that South Carolina was prepared to declare independence. Shortly after, Georgia's delegation received murkier in-

25. *JCC*, IV, 134–46. Richard Smith, a member from New Jersey, said the report was "very long, badly written and full against Independency," *LMCC*, I, 348; see also *ibid.*, 366.
26. *JCC*, IV, 229–33.
27. *LMCC*, I, 405–6.

structions which in effect also freed them to vote for independence. On April 12, North Carolina's Provincial Congress gave its delegates authority to "concur with the delegates of the other colonies in declaring independency, and forming foreign alliances. . . ." Rhode Island was more forthright than any colony and in the first week of May declared its own independence. It also gave its delegates in Congress a rather loose charge to combine with others in attempts to annoy the common enemy.[28]

All of these actions were uncoordinated and all stopped short of proposing that Congress pull America together. As in Congress, there was in provincial legislatures agreement that the colonies must be tied together in a league of free states before they declared themselves free of Britain. And, as in Congress, many within the states believed that a French alliance would be necessary if America was to win its war for liberty. Even Patrick Henry, always an eager advocate of the American cause, feared a declaration that preceded an American confederation.[29]

By May 15 in Virginia, others, even "old man moderation," as Edmund Pendleton was called (behind his back), had shaken off these concerns. On that day resolutions composed by Pendleton instructed Virginia's delegation to propose that Congress declare the colonies "free and independent states" and that they agree "to whatever measures" Congress thought necessary "for forming foreign alliances and a confederation of the colonies, at such time, and in the manner, as to them shall seem best: Provided that the power of forming government for, and the regulations of the internal concerns of each colony, be left to the respective colonial legislatures."[30] These resolutions reached the Virginia delegation some days later and were read in Congress on May 27.

It was a Congress now dominated by radicals strengthened by further evidence of British hostility. Rumors and reports had arrived from Europe of an English government determined to crush opposition in America by force. There seemed no other way to explain the news that the king's ministers were busy adding German mercenaries to an army bound for America. If the ministry had no intention of reconciliation by negotiation, delegates asked, how could America negotiate?

With hope of reconciliation virtually dead, the problem of how to proceed remained. The long-debated first step had been taken on May

28. Jensen, *Founding*, 677–79 (the quotation is on 679).
29. *Ibid.*, 681.
30. David J. Mays, *Edmund Pendleton, 1721–1803: A Biography* (2 vols., Cambridge, Mass., 1952), I, 106–10; *TJ Papers*, I, 291.

10, five days before Virginia acted, when Congress recommended to the colonies that they adopt governments "sufficient to the exigencies of their affairs," governments, it explained, which "best conduce to the happiness and safety of their constituents in particular, and America in general."[31] This resolution incited no opposition, but three days later John Adams proposed a preamble to it which did. The preamble approved on May 15, argued that

> Whereas his Britannic Majesty, in conjunction with the lords and commons of Great Britain, has, by a late act of Parliament, excluded the inhabitants of these United Colonies from the protection of his crown; And whereas, no answer, whatever, to the humble petitions of the colonies for redress of grievances and reconciliation with Great Britain, has been or is likely to be given; but, the whole force of that kingdom, aided by foreign mercenaries, is to be exerted for the destruction of the good people of these colonies; And whereas, it appears absolutely irreconcileable to reason and good Conscience, for the people of these colonies now to take the oaths and affirmations necessary for the support of any government under the crown of Great Britain, . . . it is [therefore] necessary that the exercise of every kind of authority under the said crown should be totally suppressed, and all the powers of government exerted under the authority of the people of the colonies, for the preservation of internal peace, virtue, and good order, as well as for the defence of their lives, liberties, and properties, against the hostile invasions and cruel depredations of their enemies. . . .[32]

The preamble seemed to discard all pretensions to a step-by-step approach to independence, and it was at odds with the body of the resolution itself which proposed important but limited action. In contrast the preamble, as the moderates protested, almost declared the colonies independent, most clearly in the remarkable sentence requiring the suppression of all governments deriving their authority from the Crown, these governments to be replaced by new ones exerting powers under the authority of the people. The moderates' assessment surely captured the mood of their radical colleagues, a mood now extending throughout the colonies.[33]

The radicals, however, distrusting the evidence of their political senses,

---

31. *JCC*, IV, 342.
32. *Ibid.*, 357–58.
33. Butterfield et al., eds., *Diary of John Adams*, II, 237–40. Adams reported that James Duane of New York protested: "Why all this Haste? Why this Urging? Why this driving?—Disputes about Independence are in all the Colonies. What is this owing to, but our Indiscretion?"

failed at this time to understand how much power had swung to them. For a few weeks they hesitated and then on June 7, Richard Henry Lee offered the motion "That these United Colonies are, and of right ought to be, free and independent States, that they are absolved from all allegiance to the British Crown, and that all political connection between them and the State of Great Britain is, and ought to be, totally dissolved."[34] The next day, Friday, and on June 10, Monday, Lee's resolution was debated by Congress. The alignments were familiar and so were the debates. Both sides spoke intelligently, though it is likely that each erred in its estimate of popular attitudes. Both agreed that the middle colonies, especially Pennsylvania and Maryland, were "not yet ripe for bidding adieu to British connection but that they were fast ripening. . . ." The moderates attributed the unripeness of the middle colonies to the people and advised Congress to delay "until the voice of the people drove us into it, for they are our power." The radicals found the people ready—"they are in favour of the measure, tho' the instructions given by some of their *representatives* are not." The people indeed only "wait for us to lead the way." There was another reason for delay according to the moderates: an alliance with foreign powers might be concluded on better terms after a favorable military campaign which they trusted the summer to bring. Back came the radical response: a declaration of independence was more likely to produce a helpful alliance.[35]

Congress listened to these exchanges and decided to postpone a final decision on Lee's motion until the first of July. While waiting, it appointed a committee to prepare a declaration of independence for possible use. This committee, John Adams, Franklin, Roger Sherman, Robert R. Livingston, and Thomas Jefferson, with Jefferson composing most of the document, finished its work on June 28.

Jefferson was thirty-three years old in 1776. He was born in Shadwell, Goochland (which became Albemarle County the year after his birth), the son of Peter Jefferson and Jane Randolph. Peter Jefferson had brought his young wife up the Rivanna River, a tributary to the James, only a short time before the birth of his son. He was an ambitious man, and before his death, fourteen years after the birth of his son, he had estab-

---

34. *JCC*, V, 425–26. See also *TJ Papers*, I, 298–99, for Lee's resolution and a valuable editorial note.

35. Jefferson's notes on proceedings in Congress between June 7 and Aug. 1, 1776, are invaluable. Julian Boyd's commentary in *TJ Papers*, I, 299–308, is perceptive and thorough. The quotations are from Jefferson's notes at *ibid.*, I, 309, 312.

lished himself as a leader in western Virginia. Though his wife brought him no property, his marriage surely helped his rise. The Randolphs were a great family, and an alliance with them set a man off from ordinary planters.

Peter Jefferson wanted his son educated and sent him to a nearby parson for instruction in Latin and Greek. Thomas Jefferson's love of the classics was born in these years. He continued his studies at William and Mary College between 1760 and 1762 and then prepared for the bar with George Wythe, a distinguished attorney in Williamsburg and a fine classicist himself. Jefferson may have met Wythe through William Small, a professor of natural philosophy at the college. Small saw something in Jefferson and made him his friend as well as his student. Jefferson could not have found better instructors and friends in Williamsburg. Both Small and Wythe were lively cultivated men; both set standards for the young Jefferson and, though he needed no encouragement to study, these mentors undoubtedly led him to make demands upon himself.

Jefferson was a serious student but not entirely a solemn young man. Wythe put him to reading *Coke Upon Littleton*, the first of four parts of Edward Coke's *Institutes of the Lawes of England*. Jefferson soon read all four parts but not without an occasional protest. To his friend John Page he confessed "I do wish the Devil had old Cooke [Coke], for I am sure I never was so tired of an old dull scoundrel in my life." He was nineteen when he wrote these words. He tired of Coke and yearned for the society of his friends—"Remember me affectionately," he told Page, "to all the young ladies of my acquaintance." A young Virginia gentleman commonly enjoyed a wide acquaintance, and Jefferson's list was long. It included one Alice Corbin from whom he planned "to win a pair of garters." His letters at this time reveal an attractive young man full of enthusiasm for his "Belinda," as he called Rebecca Burwell, and full too of his dreams of dances and young women, and of uncertainty about his future.

Whatever Jefferson dreamed, he must have believed that his future rested in the practice of law and the raising of tobacco. He began to do both with more than the usual responsibilities of a young man. His father had died when Jefferson was fourteen, and when he reached twenty-one he assumed the responsibility of looking after his mother and his younger sister Elizabeth. He was equal to the task. He managed the family's property carefully, and he began raising tobacco about the time he was admitted to the bar. The financial accounts he kept in these early years of manhood reveal a meticulous man much given to recording every detail of his expenditures. If, when traveling on legal business, he had his clothes washed and paid a shilling to the washerwoman, that fact made its way into his records. If he had his horse shod, that too was recorded.

Jefferson apparently impressed his neighbors in more important ways, and in 1769 they elected him to the House of Burgesses from Albemarle County. Three years later on January 1, 1772, he married Martha Wayles Skelton, a young widow. Although Jefferson wrote little about his wife and seems not to have spoken much about her even to his friends, the marriage was one of great love on both sides.

Up to the outbreak of war in 1775, Jefferson's life resembled that of many Virginia planters. Still, in 1776, thirty-three years of age, he was an extraordinary man. His difference did not simply lie in the range of his interests and his already formidable learning. To be sure, he seems to have been interested in everything around him and in almost everything that could be learned from books. He had studied architecture, music, classical literature, politics, law, history, and science. But what really set him apart from others was not his learning, or his interests, it was the quality of his mind. He was not a systematic thinker or a theoretician. Nor was he really interested in the formal problems of philosophy—he despised Plato. But if he had little taste for abstractions, his thought was often speculative. He asked probing questions about everything that he studied, and he sought empirical answers. He had more than a lawyer's desire for evidence; he had the bent and the appetite of a scientist. But more than most men of his time, surely more than most men of any time, he had imagination. The Revolution quickened it and almost immediately drew from him a vision of the opportunities that lay before free men in America.

By June 28 all the colonies except New York had authorized their delegates to approve independence. Pennsylvania had been especially reluctant, but popular groups there, armed by the Adams preamble of May 15, met in mobs and conventions and sent the sluggish assembly into oblivion. Thus when debate resumed in Congress on July 1, there was a large majority for independence. The vote that day found Pennsylvania's delegation joining South Carolina's in opposition, however; and Delaware's only two members present divided. New York's delegates explained that they favored independence but could not vote for it because they were bound by old instructions. The next day, July 2, with a third member on hand from Delaware, its delegation joined the majority, as did South Carolina's and Pennsylvania's. Only New York remained uncommitted to independence until the approval of its convention was laid before Congress on July 15. Before that day, on July 4, the Declaration of Independence was approved after Congress made several revisions.[36]

V

Soldiers standing in regimental formations listened to their officers read the declaration on July 9, and in the days that followed civilians heard it read or read it themselves in the newspapers. Although both soldiers and civilians responded with cheers and celebrations, there is no way of knowing what pleased them most about the declaration. It seems likely that they were moved most by the Congress declaring them independent of Britain. That they were independent had seemed obvious to many for at least a year. Now they had to prove it, with their lives if need be.

What Americans thought and felt about the declaration's "truths" which are presented as "self evident"—that all men "are endowed by their creator with inalienable rights," among them "life, liberty, and the pursuit of happiness"—is not clear. There was no immediate discussion in public of these claims; nor was there of the contention that all men were "created equal." Thomas Jefferson wrote these words and though at the time, and since, no great originality was attributed to them and to the substance of the declaration, the declaration may in fact have possessed more originality than anyone suspected.

The declaration is usually understood as a restatement of the contract theory of John Locke, holding that those governing America from Britain broke the fundamental understanding defining their relationship with the Americans. The British ruler violated the contract repeatedly and finally drove the Americans to declare their independence but only after they were denied redress. The contention of the declaration is, as Americans had argued over the previous twelve years, that they were defending their rights and that they took the final step, declaring their independence, only after all other measures failed.[37]

The document Congress approved on July 4 places most of the blame for the crisis on king and Parliament. Jefferson's original draft indicted an additional oppressor—"our British brethren," the people of Britain

36. Jensen, *Founding*, 682–701.
37. Carl Becker, *The Declaration of Independence* (1922; Vintage ed., New York, 1958), chaps. 1–3.

themselves. According to Jefferson, the British people, like their king and "their legislature,"

> have been deaf to the voice of justice and of consanguinity, and when occasions have been given them, by the regular course of their laws, of removing from their councils the disturbers of our harmony, they have by their free election re-established them in power. At this very time too they are permitting their chief magistrate to send over not only soldiers of our common blood, but Scotch and foreign mercenaries to invade and destroy us. These facts have given the last stab to agonizing affection, and manly spirit bids us to renounce for ever these unfeeling brethren. We must endeavor to forget our former love for them, and to hold them as we hold the rest of mankind, enemies in war, in peace friends. We might have been a free and a great people together; but a communication of grandeur and of freedom it seems is below their dignity. Be it so, since they will have it. The road to glory and happiness is open to us too. We will climb it in a separate state, and acquiesce in the necessity which pronounces our everlasting Adieu![38]

Congress removed most of these denunciations of the British people and kept the king as the focus of rejection. It did, however, retain a reference to the British people as "our common kindred" and in keeping Jefferson's description of them as "deaf to the voice of justice and of consanguinity" included them among the oppressors of America. In the opening of the declaration, as approved by Congress, the American people are described as dissolving the "political bands" which held them to another. Whether Congress intended to explain the decision to separate as something more than an act by which a people rejected a prince who had violated the fundamental contract, it included the British people by retaining these phrases from Jefferson's original draft.

Contrary to the long-standing judgments of historians, for many reasons the Jeffersonian draft is a much more powerful statement than the one finally approved by Congress. A rejection of one people by another once joined together by "love" is a great and moving event. It is made more affecting by the recognition that soldiers of "our common blood" had been dispatched across the ocean to kill Americans. As the Jeffersonian version puts it, the Americans declared their independence only after "the last stab to agonizing affection." There is in these lines a sense of betrayal, a sense that the Americans had been abandoned by their own kind, by their own blood, by brethren who had lost their

---

38. For the rough draft, see *TJ Papers*, I, 315–19, 423–27. (I have made several minor changes in capitalization and punctuation.)

capacity to honor justice and ties of affection, who had indeed become "unfeeling brethren."

Congress understood the American people better than Thomas Jefferson did and therefore deleted these passionate denunciations. By 1776 most Americans had long since stopped loving their British brethren if indeed they had ever felt such profound affection. Immigration had diluted the ties of "blood," and the provincialism that marked American life outside the cities, and perhaps within as well, fostered rather more restricted circles of feeling. The British connection was important, and the colonies had in the eighteenth century testified to their commitment to it in their trade, in their admiration and imitation of British constitutional arrangements, in their support of the mother country in wars with France, among other ways; but in all these cases self-interest and tradition prompted their action, not a deep feeling of affection. Thus the version of the declaration Congress adopted on July 4, 1776, substituted traditional contract theory for Jefferson's passionate evocation. The process leading to independence that the congressional declaration describes is hardly devoid of feeling, though the feeling is not of love betrayed but of anger aroused by a tyrannical oppressor, a destroyer of rights who had broken the fundamental law.

The congressional declaration is therefore a safer document and a less imaginative one than Jefferson's. For Jefferson did not simply denounce one people: he claimed that a second—the American people—were fully formed, a people capable of "grandeur and freedom." He had stated his conviction in 1774 that the American people had been free from the time of the founding of the colonies in the seventeenth century. By leaving Britain they had separated themselves from the home country and had chosen to retain only a political connection through formal allegiance to the king. The most important tie—of affection—had leagued them with the British brethren, and now it had been destroyed by the support these brethren gave the tyrant.[39]

What remained for Jefferson was the American people defending their inalienable rights. Had Congress possessed more imagination and less realism it might have accepted Jefferson's version of American history. Had it done so, the declaration would have gained greater affective and symbolic power and ended the ambiguity that surrounded the ques-

39. See *ibid.*, 429–33. Much of my interpretation of the Declaration is indebted to Garry Wills, *Inventing America: Jefferson's Declaration of Independence* (New York, 1978).

tion of just who was declaring independence—"free and independent states" or "one people" bound by ties of passion.

As a people the Americans had much in common, more indeed than they apparently recognized. They had not yet fully learned how to work together or how to concentrate their power. Congress, their central political institution, had learned much since its first meeting in 1774. But Congress and state governments did not coordinate their efforts well. In 1774, for example, Congress created the Association, the great intercolonial boycott. Special bodies, local committees for the most part, not colonial governments, enforced it. Traditional authorities had not usually responded quickly to crisis, then or earlier, during the ten years that preceded the meeting of the first Continental Congress.

But if local governing bodies had sometimes proved maladroit, or at least ineffective, behind them stood a people just beginning to recognize its unities. In the generation before the upheaval of the 1760s, these people had experienced much together, a great "awakening" that revived religious conviction, and a war with the French and Indians that stimulated their patriotism. These events were in a sense continental, if not national, experiences. The conflict that began in the 1760s had gone a long way toward making a people.

Jefferson took a long view of this national development, arguing that America had come into existence as a free people with the first settlement in the seventeenth century. His original draft of the declaration did not reconstruct this version of history; rather it described the emotional ties that fused Americans. His was a passionate statement, which might have summoned from Americans the best of themselves. For he sought to remind them that benevolence, mutual regard, love for one another, as much as concrete interests, joined them. In the war they were fighting mutual affection was important, and in the national state they would erect it would be indispensable.

VI

Many Americans owned slaves; yet Congress incorporated Jefferson's claim that "all men are created equal" into its version of the declaration. Jefferson, a slave owner, believed that in one respect, as men, blacks were the equals of whites because they possessed a "moral sense," the quality that defined men as men, that gave them their humanity. He did not believe, however, that they could ever enjoy equality in a society that mixed them with whites. A history of oppression and white prejudice made an interracial society unthinkable. Jefferson later explained this forecast in his *Notes on the State of Virginia*, in which he argued that slavery had so poisoned the affections of both blacks and whites as to make their living together—as equals—impossible.[40]

In the declaration he attempted to cast the king as the perpetuator of slavery in America as well as the instigator of racial violence. The first charge was absurd and the second true in only a limited sense— Governor Dunmore of Virginia had called upon blacks to rise against their masters and promised them freedom in return. But as Congress knew, white Americans—not the king—had instituted slavery and had maintained it. Congress removed almost all of Jefferson's denunciation, retaining only the charge, whose meaning was not altogether clear, that the king had "excited domestic insurrections amongst us." Yet Congress accepted Jefferson's claim that all men were created equal.

Congress may have intended to convey Jefferson's meaning. Perhaps, though we probably will never know, most Americans understood "created equal" to mean equal in the eyes of God. Whatever they understood, white Americans did not wish to free black slaves; nor did they attempt to extend to the small number of free blacks among them the rights at issue in the conflict with Britain.

Not many whites suggested that they should act to recognize the equality of all men. For most whites the struggle for independence assumed an importance which rendered all other concerns secondary. The Declaration of Independence approved by Congress declared the Americans free of Britain. That declaration defined American purposes and established a standard for which many had already died. And for which more would fight—and die. For most white Americans, declaring their independence from Britain was not merely enough—their brethren had given their lives—it was a glorious act.

40. Wills, *Inventing America*, 219–28.

15

The War of Posts

In early September 1776, two months after the signing of the Declaration of Independence, George Washington attempted to explain to Congress the strategy of the war he was fighting. The war, he wrote, was a "war of posts," a "defensive" war in which the American army sought to hold itself together and to avoid a "general action," a large-scale battle which might bring massive defeat. Washington's preoccupation with defeat was understandable: its taste had gradually soured his mouth throughout the summer as news of the disasters in Canada arrived. And then on August 27, sour turned bitter when Howe smashed American forces on Long Island. Nor could Washington look to the future with much hope, for his army on Manhattan seemed ready to disintegrate as its soldiers slipped away, homeward bound, and Howe prepared for still another attack.[1]

Although defeat prompted thoughts of defense, Washington had resigned himself to such strategy long before Howe pushed him from Long Island. His instincts of course were all for attack, for the offense in which courage, spirit, and honor all counted—and which returned fame and glory. These instincts of Washington's youth were now under control. Harsh experience twenty years before in the French and Indian War had taught Washington to restrain them, and so had his reading of eighteenth-century writers on war. In a sense, one set of conventions—the desire for fame—had been superseded in his mind by another—the doctrine of prudence that governed the thinking of European military

1. *GW Writings*, VI, 28.

men. The deep-lying passion sometimes broke through the crust of training—for example, in the siege of Boston, when only a decision by a
council of Washington's generals had prevented him from sending his
troops across the frozen bay in an all-out attack on the British.

In late summer 1776, other reasons for restraint bore in upon him
even before General Howe gave him to understand that New York was
not Boston. There Washington was, with still another army to be
trained—the passage of recently recruited troops in and out of his camps
never seemed to stop—while he defended a major harbor without a
navy. And there was General William Howe, whose forces had begun
arriving in June, with some 30,000 soldiers, transports, and warships
commanded by his brother, Lord Richard Howe. The Howes had more
men and ships and they had the luxury of choosing the site of battle.
Washington, for reasons which are not entirely clear, felt that it was
required of him to defend New York City whatever the odds. Congress
soon disabused him of this notion, but not before he had almost been
destroyed in a general action of the sort he dreaded.

And so after Long Island, while he uneasily awaited still another blow,
he sat down to explain the facts of war to Congress. A defensive war
seemed the only option left to his beleaguered army, but why a war of
posts—a war fought from strong fortifications? Why not a war of retreat
in which the army served as guerillas, or as partisans (to use the term
employed at the time) operating behind and around the British regulars
who were always slowed by their baggage trains and the need to protect
their magazines? Moreover, since Washington and the Congress seemed
to believe that the British would seek to reduce the American colonies
to submission by occupying them militarily, why not concentrate on
rousing the entire population against them?[2]

If a strategy of defense seemed dictated by the relative weakness of
the Americans, the sort of defense chosen—a war of posts or of strong
points—followed from Washington's understanding of his enemy and
his own troops. The British controlled the sea and coastal waters, and
in most cases the rivers as well. Even keeping them out of the East
River and the North River (as the Hudson was called) appeared almost
impossible. Control of the water made relatively rapid movement possible,
and it allowed concentration of forces. Washington had an almost instinctive sense of the importance of concentrating strength, and he recognized
that his means of bringing his force to bear at salient points would

2. Washington's letter to the President of Congress, Sept. 8, 1776, raises many of
these questions, *ibid.*, 27–32.

rarely equal his enemy's. On land too the British forces were formidable because they were regular army, professionals who knew their craft and who had the discipline and skill to practice it in adverse as well as favorable situations. As much could not be said for the Americans under arms, at least not by their general. Washington did not denounce his soldiers to the Congress even in a confidential letter. All he permitted himself was the "painful" admission "that all our Troops will not do their duty." The word in that oblique clause that aroused passion in Washington was "duty." What he meant in this unfavorable assessment of his young soldiers was that they lacked the responsibility—or loyalty— that made professional soldiers continue to fight when they knew they were about to die or to be captured. A sense of honor should bring men to such sacrifices, and Washington could never quite grasp what made some men incapable of feeling its call. "The honor of making a brave defense does not seem to be a sufficient stimulus, when the success is very doubtful, and the falling into the Enemy's hands probable," he reported sadly. Hence his reliance on "posts," which were chosen not simply for their tactical value but to persuade the American soldier to do his duty. Because "Young Troops" were not to be depended upon, he had avoided exposing them on "open ground against their Superiors both in number and Discipline." And "I have never spared the Spade and Pick Ax; I confess I have not found that readiness to defend even strong Posts, at all hazards, which is necessary to derive the greatest benefit from them."[3]

Why did his young troops repeatedly fail to stand and fight? Washington's explanation—one which made him feel both despair and pride— was that they were free men. Their freedom brought them to revolution and, paradoxically, made them incapable of fighting it well. The freedom Washington saw left its mark on character: yes, the Americans were free—a condition which made them impatient of restraint and discipline. And discipline was the heart of an army. It could be achieved only through long training, and a long period of training entailed long enlistments. As the war continued, Washington came to understand that the freedom which filled American life inhibited not only the fighting qualities of his troops but also the large-scale organization of men in a regular army and, behind the army, the political organization on all levels necessary to its support.[4]

3. *Ibid.*, 28–29, for the quotations.
4. Further aspects of the organization of the army are discussed below, especially in Chapter 20.

· Washington probably never understood the anomaly of his wishing to make a revolution with a conventional eighteenth-century army—to establish once and for all American independence with an organization which systematically broke the personal independence of its members. But he never gave up this desire. Yet he believed passionately in the American cause as its most enlightened advocates defined it: as a struggle for the rights of man. When those rights were translated into personal codes and into behavior, they did not necessarily subvert the will and discipline of an army—once a genuine army was created, an army in which orders were followed and men did their duty. But why should anyone expect the unbridled creatures who appeared in the militia to fight and to hold fast when their lives were endangered? They should fight—Washington insisted—for their honor, for fame, and glory, those aristocratic virtues which free men might value were they properly instructed and trained. Free men might fight for their honor and for a great cause. But they would not fight in their present organization— the militia, for example, with its local orientation, its incompetent and democratically chosen officers, its disdain of discipline, and its short enlistments.[5]

Washington's distrust of civilians-in-arms ran so deep as to blind him to the possibility—realized twenty years later in the French Revolution— of drawing an entire population into the war. Washington did not dread social revolution and the overturning of classes which might have occurred in a war fought by a people under arms for he did not really conceive of it as possible. The people were disabled by their lack of restraint and their inability to suffer themselves to be organized and disciplined. The best that could be done in the Revolution was to create a standing army composed of free men broken of some of the worst habits freedom engendered. They were—he believed—superior to mere mercenaries; they had a cause, and if their sense of honor could be aroused, they could be made into a reasonable facsimile of a conventional army. But until he had such an army all he could do was to substitute fortifications, the protection of breastworks, parapets, and trenches, for pride and honor so sadly deficient in the citizen-soldiers who flowed in and out of camp. Therefore he would fight a war of posts.

II

The British strategy lacked the simplicity of the American. Until Howe evacuated Boston in March 1776 the ministry had no strategy at all,

5. For representative statements by Washington about the militia, see *GW Writings*, VI, 4–5, 6, 32, 38.

no overall conception of the war. And it might be argued that the ministry never arrived at one. The ministry's difficulty in 1775 after Lexington was that it had no clear policy, and until it decided on policy no clear strategy could be maintained. Howe sat locked up in Boston for almost a year; at home the king at least knew what he wanted—colonial submission to royal and Parliamentary power. Once that was given things might resume—he thought—where they left off, before all the trouble started in 1764. North did not seem able to muster up resolution to match the king's, but as a good and loyal servant he went along. Lord George Germain, who had replaced Dartmouth as American Secretary, shared the king's ardor for first defeating the colonies and then taking them back into the empire, but like the government as a whole, he had trouble translating a desire for military victory into victory in America.[6]

Part of the ministry's problem lay with the instruments they chose to fight the war. Admiral Richard Howe, in overall command in America, possessed outstanding abilities and considerable influence. Lord Howe had headed the well-connected Howe family since 1758, when he succeeded his older brother as fourth viscount. The family had held important offices and several of its members had sat in Parliament for years. They also enjoyed friendly relations at court; Howe's mother, for example, had received a pension from George I when she married and later became a member of George III's household. Admiral Richard Lord Howe took his turn at court too. He had sailed with the brother of George III in the Seven Years War; Queen Charlotte sponsored his first child; and the king himself came to rely on his advice concerning the navy.[7]

Despite these advantages, despite the king's friendship, Howe held himself aloof in politics—he was independent—and he failed to back a policy of coercion against the colonies. In fact, he favored conciliation and had held to this line from the time troubles began until he himself was relieved of command in America. He was fond of America and Americans, and apparently had been since Massachusetts put up a monument in Westminster Abbey to the memory of his brother, George Augustus, Third Viscount Howe, killed at Ticonderoga in 1758.

6. For British strategy, see Willcox, *Portrait of a General*, 42–43, 94–97; and Willcox, "Why Did the British Lose the American Revolution?" in *Michigan Alumnus Quarterly Review* LXII (1956), 317–24. See also Piers Mackesy, *The War for America 1775–1783* (Cambridge, Mass., 1965), 32–40, and *passim*.
7. Ira D. Gruber, *The Howe Brothers and the American Revolution* (New York, 1972), 45–53, 72–80, for this and the next two paragraphs. For William Howe, *ibid.*, 56–59, and *passim*.

In February 1776 the Crown made Lord Richard Howe commander in chief in America in ignorance of his views on policy. The ministry wanted to subdue the colonies first, and in the spring it gave him unambiguous instructions to that effect. He was not to negotiate until the colonies accepted Parliament's supremacy, presumably in all cases whatsoever. Howe's instructions also provided the details of operations: he was to suppress all colonial commerce, shut up the Americans' ports, and destroy their armed ships, supplies, and fortifications.

At about the same time, Germain reached an understanding with the commander of the army in America, William Howe. Germain had believed for at least a year that New York City should be the focus of the land war. Howe agreed; and agreed too that the army in Halifax should be sent there, to be joined by Clinton's small force in the Carolinas and by a much larger number of troops from Britain. By sometime in the summer Howe would have around 30,000 soldiers in New York City. This army would push up the Hudson, to be met by a smaller force under Carleton coming south from Canada. If Washington opposed, the two would trap him and destroy him piecemeal. If he retreated, they would reduce New England, the center of the rebellion, to submission. Cutting the colonies in two was the large strategic objective; after that, submission of the colonies to the south would follow inevitably.

Whether any strategy could have accomplished the purposes of the ministry's policy is an open and unresolvable question. Had the British succeeded in smashing Washington's army, had they cut New England off and reduced it to "submission" and then subdued the other colonies, would they in fact have restored their American empire? They may well have created a persistent opposition underground which eventually might have broken into the open and brought a more savage and chaotic war. But even had peace been established, the cost in loyalty and in morale may have rendered the colonies largely useless—a collection of people with smoldering resentments whose creative energies were permanently dampened.

As formulated, the strategy of summer 1776 had a more immediate flaw: it neglected the fact that William Howe dreaded to risk his army in battle. After he landed his troops on Staten Island early in July, he let them sit there for seven weeks. He did not lack courage, but he did fear that the loss of his force might end British efforts in America. Thus Washington's fear was also Howe's, a long-standing disposition based on the scarcity of troops. Howe strained to find reasons to delay committing his men to battle: camp kettles were lacking and without

them the health of his troops might suffer; and these troops were irreplace-
able, "the stock on which the national force in America must in future
be grafted."[8] Howe was not alone in this conviction; for example, Lord
Percy, who had saved the British expedition to Concord the previous
year, wrote in the summer of 1776 that "our army is so small that we
cannot even afford a victory." The adjutant general in England sounded
a note heard throughout the army after fighting began—that British
forces might be "destroyed by damned driblets,"—and General William
Murray, another observer from afar—in Minorca—wrote after Bunker
Hill that the "Americans' plan ought to be to lose a battle every week,
till the British army was reduced to nothing: 'it may be that our troops
are not invincible, they certainly are not immortal.' " As Murray summed
up Howe's problem in a classic eighteenth-century military sentiment,
"The fate of battles at the best are precarious."[9]

III

Washington had known little of the British reluctance to join battle
when he marched his army from Boston to New York in April. His
mind was not entirely on New York or on battle, though he expected
the British to move against the middle Atlantic colonies at some time.
But for the time being he was more concerned about Canada, where
he hoped that American troops might recapture the initiative and, if
unable to seize Quebec, at least might prevent the British from cutting
New England off from the rest of the colonies. He feared that Howe
would sail into the St. Lawrence and drive out the remnants of Arnold's
tired expedition and the reinforcements sent to him on orders from
Congress. He found reassurance in the knowledge that the American
commander at the siege of Quebec, Major General John Thomas, was
an able officer. Thomas arrived at the American camp on May 1, 1776;
a month later, on June 2, smallpox killed him. In one way or another
Canada had taken a frightful toll of American leaders. Brigadier General
David Wooster, Thomas's second in command, now took over. Unfortunately, Wooster was incompetent—and did not recognize his own incapacity. June proved to be a deadly month for troops as well as generals.
As the St. Lawrence rose with the spring runoff, and green buds made
their appearance on the alder along its banks, a force of 2000 Americans
under Brig. General William Thompson attacked at Trois Rivières. The

8. Quoted in Mackesy, *War for America*, 85.
9. *Ibid.*

British threw them back easily and then cut them apart, taking prisoners with contemptuous ease. A week later Arnold pulled his pathetic little command of three hundred out of Montreal and withdrew to Ile aux Noix. There he found some 7000 American troops, at least half of whom were sick and wounded. Washington heard of these disasters by the end of the month.[10]

June also brought William Howe back to New York. The British warships and transports were sighted off Sandy Hook on the 29th, and on July 3 a heavy force put ashore on Staten Island. Two days later the British army demonstrated that it too valued the pick and shovel, as the troops on Staten Island began digging in. Over the next six weeks more ships arrived, including one on July 12 carrying Richard Howe and troops from Halifax, England, and South Carolina. By the middle of August they numbered 32,000, including 8000 Hessians.

Washington calmly observed these arrivals for himself and received rather excited reports from others. His soldiers on Manhattan dug fortifications at the island's southern tip in expectation of a landing. Brooklyn Heights on Long Island was the key to New York's defenses, and there the Americans also constructed entrenchments. The army needed troops even more than fortifications, and Washington appealed to Congress to provide them. But since he did not expect the British to delay the attack while the Americans gathered themselves, he strove to bring the soldiers he had to readiness. Washington's mastery of detail, his ability to think of the small things as well as the large, was much in evidence over the summer. Many of the soldiers needed practice with their weapons, so early in July he ordered that each man was to fire two rounds—hardly extensive exercise but all that supplies permitted. He also ordered that officers and troops should practice moving from their camps into the trenches in order to become familiar with the ground they would have to travel when the attack came. The soldiers were to fill their canteens every evening because the battle might begin early some morning before they had an opportunity to do so. Washington ordered houses stripped of lead for bullets; powder and flints remained in short supply despite efforts to increase stores.[11]

And finally there was morale to be considered. Early in the month rumors of the Declaration of Independence seeped into the army. There was no large-scale jubilation, but when official word came to headquarters

10. Ward, I, 196–201; Freeman, *GW*, IV, 121–22.
11. *GW Writings*, V, 198–99, 201, 205, 209, 230.

on July 9, Washington ordered the troops mustered and had the Declaration read aloud. In the next few weeks he himself issued orders—exhortations in everything but name—reminding his men of the great cause they were engaged in, the defense of the blessings of liberty. Not only did American rights ride on the performance of the army, but so did the natural rights of man. Near the end of August, Washington had occasion to repeat with even greater passion these calls for patriotic action. For at dawn on the 22nd, Howe began to transport a large force from Staten Island to Gravesend Bay, Long Island. Clinton and Cornwallis led the first of these troops, light infantry, grenadiers, and Colonel Carl von Donop's corps of Hessians. Four frigates covered the landing, and flatboats, bateaux, and galleys carried the soldiers to the bay. By mid-day Howe had put 15,000 men ashore, supported by forty fieldpieces; and on August 25, he sent in General Philip von Heister, a veteran of the Seven Years War, with two brigades of Hessian grenadiers.[12]

Washington at first underestimated the size of the enemy's force on Long Island. Nor was he certain of Howe's intentions, believing for two or three days following the landing that nothing more than a feint to draw off his troops from New York City was intended. Once he, Washington, committed himself to Long Island, Howe might slip in by water and take a city stripped of defenders. These concerns are understandable but may seem hard to reconcile with Washington's purposes on Long Island and his sense of how New York City should be defended. He had decided to fortify Brooklyn Heights because he recognized that it commanded the southern tip of Manhattan just as the Dorchester Heights had commanded Boston. Hence he felt compelled to divide his army even though General Howe controlled the water and might use this control to keep the Americans separated on the two islands. Washington's problem was almost unsolvable, given his lack of naval strength.[13]

To hold Brooklyn Heights, he dug in around Brooklyn Village, anchoring his right on the southwest at Gowanus Creek in salt marshes and swinging his line to the north to Wallabout Bay, where salt marshes gave protection. Out from this line about a mile stretched the Heights

12. Freeman, *GW*, IV, 132–34; Ward, I, 211–12.
13. Ward, I, 213–14. My account of the Battle of Brooklyn, including the preliminaries discussed here and in the following paragraphs, owes much to Ward's thorough treatment and perhaps even more to Freeman's account. Washington's letters in *GW Writings*, V, are helpful on certain points.

of Guan, a range of hills from 100 to 150 feet in height, covered by heavy brush and woods. The side away from Brooklyn, the south side, rose abruptly to a height of eighty feet in places and was thought to be impassable by troops in formation because of the rise and the dense woods. The woods would also prevent horse-drawn artillery from being moved up into the hills. Four passes breached the Heights of Guan—the coastal pass near Gowanus on the American right, Flatbush about a mile to the east, Bedford Pass another mile farther to the east, and Jamaica Pass almost three miles beyond.

Washington's knowledge of this terrain probably was not detailed, but he had grasped its tactical possibilities before the British landed. The decision to defend the Heights of Guan made sense presumably because Howe would have to string his army out on a line to counter the Americans, thereby reducing the importance of his overwhelming numbers. Should he be allowed to concentrate his forces against Brooklyn Heights, he would inevitably overrun the smaller American army. But if Washington's tactics were intelligent, his dispositions of his troops were not, for he failed to secure his left flank. To some extent, perhaps, General Sullivan was at fault here; the center and left—Flatbush, Bedford, and Jamaica passes—were his responsibility, and he left Jamaica, on the eastern end of the line, undefended except for a guard of five men.

The day after Howe's landing, Washington in unhappy ignorance of the state of American troops on Long Island sent over six more regiments and issued an order, amounting to a principled appeal, calling on his soldiers to "acquit yourselves like men." Though most of Washington's exhortation resorted to the "cause"—"the hour is fast approaching, on which the Honor and Success of this army, and the safety of our bleeding Country depend"—it contained equal portions of threats, invocations of recent history, and instructions on how to behave under fire: "Remember officers and soldiers, that you are Freemen, fighting for the blessings of Liberty—that Slavery will be your portion, and that of your posterity, if you do not acquit yourselves like men: Remember how your Courage and Spirit have been despised, and traduced by your cruel invaders; though they have found by dear experience at Boston, Charlestown [a reference to Bunker Hill] and other places, what a few brave men contending for their own land, and in the best of causes can do, against base hirelings and mercenaries."[14]

14. *GW Writings*, V, 479.

The "base hirelings and mercenaries" were the Hessians, of course. The general had ideas about how his soldiers should deal with them—and their British employers: "Be cool, but determined; do not fire at a distance, but wait for orders from your officers." Washington so doubted the courage of his troops that he ordered that men who attempted to "skulk" or "lay down," or who "retreated without Orders" should be instantly shot down. He was hopeful that "no such Scoundrel will be found in this army; but on the contrary, every one for himself resolving to conquer, or die, and trusting to the smiles of heaven upon so just a cause, will behave with Bravery and Resolution: Those who are distinguished for their Gallantry, and good Conduct, may depend upon being honorably noticed, and suitably rewarded: And if this Army will but emulate and imitate their brave Countrymen, in other parts of America, he has no doubt they will, by a glorious Victory, save their Country, and acquire to themselves immortal Honor."[15]

The mention of Charlestown, or Bunker Hill, and Boston was shrewd, calculated to conjure up visions of redcoats first tumbled in bloody piles and then sailing out of the harbor with defeat rusting their mouths. Washington himself could never resist an appeal for gallantry in battle nor what inevitably followed it—"immortal Honor"—and set this standard for his troops, though doubtless with few expectations.[16]

Howe probably contented himself with less fervent demands on his troops. We know that he did not ordinarily talk about the "cause"; he was not altogether sure whether he was engaged in anything nearly so grand as a cause. He sometimes praised his troops' bravery to their faces, and then urged them to look to their bayonets for the real work, a thoroughly professional recommendation. Now on Long Island he did what he often did so well—nothing. Nothing on the day after the landing, nor on the next day, the 24th, nor on the 25th.[17]

Late on August 26, he at last moved. With Clinton in the van with dragoons and light infantry, Cornwallis in reserve with grenadiers, two regiments of foot and artillery, and Percy and himself with the main body, Howe set his army moving by back roads to Jamaica Pass. Clinton reached it by three in the morning, seized the five startled Americans, and the British poured through. By daybreak the British were on the Bedford Road headed west behind the American lines on the Heights

15. *Ibid.*, 480.
16. Washington's appeals to his troops throughout the war, however, do not reflect disillusionment.
17. *Diary of Frederick Mackenzie* (2 vols., Cambridge, Mass., 1930), I, 45.

of Guan. They marched quietly and carefully, sawing rather than chopping down trees where they had to widen the road so that wagons and fieldpieces might be drawn along. Sawing would make less noise they thought, and they did not want to be discovered until the American army had been trapped.[18]

They need not have worried. About the time Clinton reached Jamaica Pass, General James Grant created a diversion at the other end of the line, the American right, by sending troops up the Gowanus Road. Small-scale skirmishing began sometime around three in the morning, and William Alexander, "Lord" Stirling, the American commander at this part of the defenses, began to prepare for a major attack. At the center of the line Heister's Hessian gunners shelled Flatbush Pass about the same time in order to hold Sullivan, who commanded the American troops there and at Bedford Pass, in place. All this worked beautifully. By nine in the morning Howe's forces had reached Bedford Village and announced themselves with heavy fire. This signal sent Heister's jaegers through Bedford Pass and over the ridge. Sullivan's outposts collapsed almost immediately, and within the hour his army had been overrun from the flank and front.

Stirling's troops on the right—principally William Smallwood's Marylanders and Colonel John Haslet's Delaware Continentals, raw and untried as they were—fought bravely. They had never fought anyone before; they could not have learned much about the terrain on Long Island, having been boated over only the day before, but they stood and slugged it out for two hours. Soon they were joined by Pennsylvanians and by Yankees from Connecticut. Stirling did not deploy them behind trees and rocks, but stood them up in the open and had them fight European fashion. By late morning they were almost surrounded. Stirling then sent most of his command across the Gowanus Creek, through the "impassable" marshes into Brooklyn. To cover the rear he held a part of Smallwood's Maryland regiment in place and stayed with these soldiers himself. Just before noon, with Cornwallis now at his rear and on his left flank, Stirling with the Marylanders, 250 strong, attacked, assaulting Cornwallis's grenadiers six times until he and his force were finally broken by overwhelming British fire. By noon on August 27 it was all over. Howe had cleared the Heights of Guan and pressed Washington's shattered command back into Brooklyn Village.

Howe did not exploit his advantage, despite the eagerness of his soldiers

18. Ward, I, 216–30, for this paragraph and the three following.

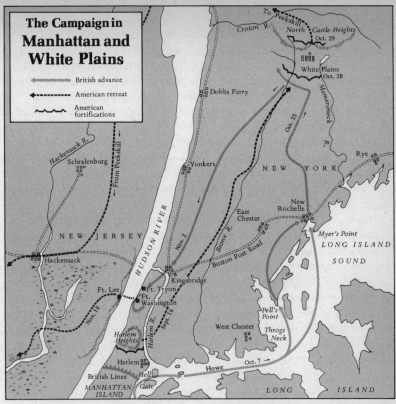

The Campaign in Manhattan and White Plains

- →→→ British advance
- ◀----- American retreat
- 〰〰 American fortifications

To Peekskill

Croton R.

North

Castle Heights
Oct. 29

White Plains
Oct. 28

Dobbs Ferry

Mamaroneck R.

Hackensack R.

Schralenburg

From Peekskill

Yonkers

NEW YORK

Rye

Oct. 25

NEW JERSEY

HUDSON RIVER

East Chester

New Rochelle

Myer's Point

LONG ISLAND

Hackensack

Nov. 2

Bronx R.

Boston Post Road

SOUND

Nov. 19

Kingsbridge

Ft. Lee

Ft. Tryon
Ft. Washington

Sept. 16

Harlem R.

West Chester

Pell's Point

Throgs Neck

Harlem Heights

British Lines

Harlem

Hell Gate

Howe   Oct. 7

MANHATTAN ISLAND

LONG   ISLAND

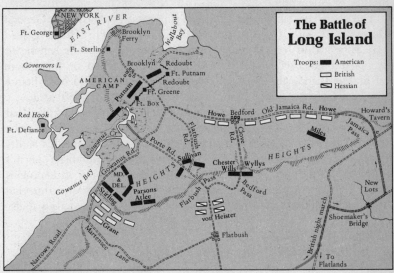

The Battle of Long Island

Troops:
- ■ American
- □ British
- ▨ Hessian

NEW YORK

EAST RIVER

Ft. George

Ft. Sterling

Brooklyn Ferry

Wallabout Bay

Governors I.

Brooklyn   Redoubt   Ft. Putnam

AMERICAN CAMP

Putnam   Redoubt

Ft. Greene

Red Hook

Ft. Box

Howe   Bedford   Old Jamaica Rd.   Howe

Howard's Tavern

Ft. Defiance

Gowanus Cr.

Gowanus Rd.

Porte Rd.

Flatbush Rd.

Clove Rd.

Miles

Jamaica Pass

Sullivan

HEIGHTS

Gowanus Bay

MD & DEL

Stirling

HEIGHTS

Chester Wills   Wyllys

Bedford Pass

New Lots

Parsons Atlee

Flatbush Pass

Grant

von Heister

Shoemaker's Bridge

Narrows Road

Martense Lane

Flatbush

British night march

To Flatlands

who had taken only light casualties and enjoyed the taste of victory. The afternoon drifted by while Washington tried to reorganize his battered army. The next day, August 28, still determined to hold Brooklyn Heights, he had three regiments transported from Manhattan to Brooklyn. That night Howe began constructing "regular approaches," as trenches and breastworks near the enemy's lines were called. It was a technique ordinarily used in siege warfare, though Howe was not facing a well-fortified enemy but a dispirited collection, badly entrenched and lacking tentage, food, and other supplies. A northeasterly came in the same day, soaking both sides and rendering the Americans vulnerable to a bayonet charge, a tactic Howe's grenadiers and light infantry were eager to use.[19]

By August 29, Washington saw, or was made to see by a council of his officers, that his position could not be held. He must evacuate Long Island while he could, for when the storm subsided Admiral Howe would be able to station his frigates in the East River, trapping the Americans once and for all. During the night and extending into the early morning of August 30, two Massachusetts regiments, adept in the use of small boats, ferried the American force across the river to New York City. In all, 9500 men were carried over, with all but a few of their cannon (several of the heaviest sank into the mud up to their hubs, Washington reported), provisions, equipment, and horses, all without the British detecting the move. It was a well-executed evacuation, for which Washington deserves the credit, just as he must take the responsibility for the disaster of August 27.[20]

The discovery that Washington had slipped away did not set General Howe ablaze with desire to close with him once more. Howe delayed here as he had in June the previous year at Boston when the Americans occupied Bunker Hill, and early in the summer when he put ashore on Staten Island, and then on August 27 when he held back before Brooklyn Heights. There is no way to explain with complete assurance this pattern of failure to exploit obvious advantage. We do know that he did not ever wish to take heavy losses to gain a victory, because he recognized that still another battle might be necessary and his ability to call on reinforcements was limited. At this time, September 1, pursuit across the East River to Manhattan would have required an enormous effort. The Americans were dug in—they had spent the summer throwing up breastworks on the southern end of the island—and the navy's ability

19. *Ibid.*, 232.
20. Freeman, *GW*, IV, 173–75.

to transport Howe depended on wind, tide, and careful organization. A landing into Washington's teeth was unnecessary anyway; putting ashore farther up the island might enable him to trap Washington in the south. And so Howe began almost immediately to get ready to clamp off escape to the north.

Washington, of course, badly wanted to discover Howe's intentions. The immediate problems of his army now demanded attention, if so disorganized and dispirited a force could be called an army. The soldiers may have been impressed by their general's ability to rescue them from disaster, but they gave no evidence of rallying themselves for the next fight. The militia proved particularly unreliable, as Washington expected, deserting almost by regiments. Their going affected the Continentals, whose discipline in September could not have been much better. There was the usual rambling about in the American camp, soldiers coming and mostly going. As usual, supplies of everything were short, and partly as a result sickness increased. A defeated army almost always has a higher rate of sickness than a victorious one.

Washington and his officers resorted to familiar techniques to pull the regiments up to some sort of standard. Exhortation always failed but it was tried, and more direct means too—courts-martial and whipping. No regular routine of training on a day-to-day basis seems to have been observed in the regiments, then or ever in 1776. But in order to stop the constant traffic that disturbed the camps and the lines, Washington ordered frequent musters to be held, and begged for returns, which would give him some idea of the number of troops he had. Low morale, lack of discipline and organization, shortages of every sort were immediate problems and persistent ones as well. Most pressing of all problems was deciding what to do. Should the American army attempt to defend New York City, or should it pull out and burn the city as Nathanael Greene urged?[21]

Congress soon gave Washington instructions on this last matter— he must not destroy the city should he decide to leave it. The Congress disabused Washington of the notion that it was requiring him to defend the city, a dangerous idea that he had harbored all summer. Freed of this "requirement," Washington began to consider evacuation of Manhattan while he could still escape. A council of his officers urged him to move to the north, at least as far as Kingsbridge, where the Harlem River emptied into the Hudson. The army began sending out its stores

21. *GW Writings*, VI, 6–7, for Washington's thinking about the defense of Manhattan.

and the sick that day, and the troops began preparations for the withdrawal, which promised to be difficult to manage, for they were stretched out on a line from the southern tip of the island sixteen miles to the north.[22]

Howe meanwhile had decided to avoid the southern end of Manhattan in favor of landing where his enemy was not so heavily concentrated and, in effect, to outflank Washington once more. On September 13 he alerted his troops, reminding them that they had smashed the Americans on Long Island and recommending, as a British officer noted in his diary, "an entire dependence upon their bayonets, with which they will ever command that success which their bravery so well deserves."[23] This appeal suited the professional character of Howe's troops—no evocation of the "sacred cause" here, nor any reference to the blessings of liberty, but simply look to your bayonets and behave bravely as British soldiers should.

To be successful the landing at Kip's Bay depended on more than bayonets. Admiral Howe put five ships up the East River about 200 yards offshore. Around eleven in the morning, they opened up with broadsides in order to—in Washington's phrase—"scour the Grounds and cover the landing of their Troops." Scour the ground they did, battering down the thin line of earthworks—hardly more than a few ditches—and causing the militia, which had not come under heavy fire before, to take to its heels. Barges carried troops from Long Island about an hour later; they landed unopposed and by late afternoon were all ashore. Long before most of these troops stepped on land, the remnants of opposition had been broken, and Washington himself, who had ridden from Harlem to Kip's Bay when he heard the ships open up, had almost been captured. As Washington approached the bay he ran into the flight of the militia, most of them from a Connecticut brigade commanded by Captain William Douglas. Appalled at what he saw, Washington lost that firm control of himself that everyone admired, and took to flogging officers and men with his riding cane. In his rage he threw his hat to the ground and was heedless of the approaching British. An aide finally grabbed the bridle of his horse and led him out of danger.[24]

The remnants of the army to the south in the city escaped too, as good luck, the determination of several leaders—or rather the guts of

22. *Ibid.*, 22, 30.
23. *Diary of Frederick Mackenzie*, I, 45.
24. The quotation is from *GW Writings*, VI, 58. For the landing at Kip's Bay, see Ward, I, 238–45, and Freeman, *GW*, IV, 189–95.

Israel Putnam—and a return of Howe's lethargy pulled them through. Israel Putnam, at his best in a disaster, helped lead and drive the militia up the west side of the island along little-traveled roads. Young Aaron Burr served as guide for several detachments. Putnam rode up and down the west side near the Hudson, hurrying, cajoling, and organizing the retreat. Most stores and the heavy artillery of Knox were abandoned as the troops fled, hoping they would not be cut off by Howe's light infantry. Howe considerately stayed on the east side, though he did send columns left and right, south and north, along the Post Road, the main highway on Manhattan. These soldiers soon entered the city, seizing stores and untended artillery. The column that moved up the Post Road paralleled the disorganized militia on the other side of the island for a time. But Howe did not push across, and by nightfall the Americans were on the high ground called Harlem Heights, their left flank on the Harlem River and their right on the Hudson.

The next day British carelessness and contempt for their enemy produced the battle of Harlem Heights, hardly more than a skirmish between several hundred light infantry and Colonel Thomas Knowlton's Connecticut regiment just forward of the American line. As Frederick Mackenzie confided to his *Diary*, the light infantry pursued the Americans without "proper precautions or support" and blundered into an unfavorable position "and were rather severely handled by them." The "victory" gave American soldiers a shred of confidence but at the cost of Knowlton's life, and Knowlton was one of the best regimental commanders in the army.[25]

IV

The next two months, until Cornwallis captured Fort Lee on the west bank of the Hudson on November 20, saw Washington's army fall back from one post to another. And in the three weeks that followed the flight from Fort Lee until December 7, 1776, when the Americans crossed the Delaware River from Trenton into Pennsylvania, the army was in full retreat, running desperately to avoid Cornwallis. For most of this period before Fort Lee fell, Washington proved indecisive and at times inept. The indecisiveness is easily understood: he did not know what Howe's plans were—would Howe strike through the highlands into southern New England? Or would he head through New Jersey toward Philadelphia? Washington's peculiar ineptness did not mar the disposition, the training, or even the leading of troops; rather it affected his dealings with his commanders, especially General Charles Lee.

On the surface at least, something approaching stagnation overtook the two armies on Harlem Heights after the battle of September 16. The Americans dug further into the ground, improved their lines, and tried to reorganize their forces. The British did some of the same though not at the frantic pace of their enemy. Below the surface, Washington was active, trying in particular to hold his forces together and—most intrusive of all his problems—recruiting in anticipation of the virtual dissolution of his army when enlistments expired in November and December. Shortly after the battle of Long Island the Congress had authorized recruitments up to 80,000 men, a well-timed and immensely heartening decision, but what the Congress gave, it—like the Lord—would take away. In this case the Congress did not so much take away as make rapid enlistment of troops impossible by requiring that state legislatures appoint committees which would then select the regimental officers who would do the actual recruiting. The state legislatures acted slowly, or rather did nothing at all for several months, and the authorized regiments went unfilled while Washington begged for soldiers.[26]

As engrossing as these problems were, Howe relieved Washington's mind of them at least temporarily on October 12, when he broke the early autumn quiet by putting 4000 men ashore on Throg's Neck. The neck, variously called Frog's Neck or Frog's Point, was sometimes a peninsula and sometimes an island, depending upon tide action and fresh-water drainage, and extended into Long Island Sound almost due east of the American lines. The Royal Navy carried the soldiers through Hell Gate in the fog; their landing was unopposed. But getting off Throg's Neck was no easy matter because American detachments guarded the exits—several fords and a small causeway over a creek.[27]

Although Howe seemed bottled up, he had outflanked the American army on Harlem Heights. Four days later Washington decided to move north to White Plains, a day-long march, and on October 18 he began pulling his forces off the Heights. Because of the shortage of horses and wagons this movement occupied four days, with the troops themselves pulling the artillery. Howe accommodatingly left the Americans unmolested, though on the day they began their move he embarked his force once more and landed farther up the Sound on Pell's Point. A small American brigade under Colonel John Glover gave the Hessian

26. Freeman, *GW*, IV, 206–10.
27. Ward, I, 254–56.

advance party a short fight, but Howe's men soon took the Point without difficulty.

The British did not make their way to White Plains for another ten days, where on October 28 they assaulted and captured Chatterton's Hill on the extreme right of the American lines. Three days later Washington pulled his army back to North Castle and a new line of entrenchments. Howe followed as far as the old lines, but during the night of November 4 he withdrew—Washington erroneously called the move a "retreat"—and ten days later Howe was in position around Fort Washington on the east side of the Hudson below Kingsbridge.[28]

During these ten days Washington speculated on Howe's intentions and prepared to pull a part of his army out of North Castle for service in New Jersey. There did not seem to be much doubt that Howe would attempt to capture Fort Washington, but that would not satisfy him. In studying Howe's behavior, Washington projected one of his own values into Howe's mind—a concern for reputation. Washington was always affected by what others thought of him. That he believed that the enemy was moved by a similar concern was clear in a rhetorical question he asked about Howe: "He must attempt something on Account of his Reputation, for what has he done yet, with his great Army?" Howe's immediate objective seemed obvious: to invest Fort Washington, but, if he succeeded, what next? Perhaps he would move to the southern colonies, and perhaps he would drive through New Jersey for Philadelphia, where the Congress held forth. For the moment, Fort Washington seemed to be the obvious objective. "Could the Americans hold it?" was a question soon translated into another: Was holding it necessary or worthwhile after British warships forced their way through the obstructions in the Hudson between Fort Washington and Fort Lee on the west bank? The American guns in these forts had fired on the warships making their way up the Hudson but with little effect beyond minor damage to rigging and sails.[29]

As soon as the British proved that the two forts could not stop their ships, Washington began to think of evacuating Fort Washington. It seemed prudent not to risk the 3000 troops there, especially since Howe's force outnumbered them three or four to one. But Washington was not on the scene, and the commander of the area, Nathanael Greene, and his subordinate, Colonel Robert Magaw, who led the garrison inside the fort, believed they could hold out. Washington expressed his doubts

28. *GW Writings*, VI, 249 ("retreat"); Ward, I, 256–66.
29. *GW Writings*. VI, 255, for Washington's question about Howe.

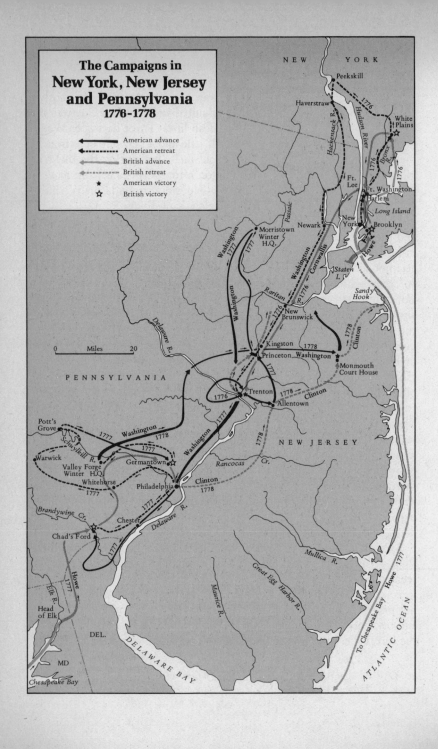

The Campaigns in
New York, New Jersey
and Pennsylvania
1776-1778

American advance
American retreat
British advance
British retreat
★ American victory
☆ British victory

NEW   YORK
Peekskill
Haverstraw
1776
Hackensack R.
Hudson River
Bronx
White Plains
1776
1776
Ft. Lee
Ft. Washington
Harlem
Long Island
Morristown Winter H.Q.
1777
Newark
New York
Brooklyn
Washington
Washington
1777
Passaic
Howe
Cornwallis
Staten I.
Sandy Hook
Delaware R.
Raritan
R. 1776
New Brunswick
1778 Clinton
Kingston
1778
Washington
Princeton
Monmouth Court House
0   Miles   20
PENNSYLVANIA
1777
Trenton
1776
1778 Clinton
Allentown
Pott's Grove
1777
Washington
1778
1777
Washington
1777
1778
NEW JERSEY
Schuylkill R.
Warwick
Valley Forge Winter H.Q.
Germantown
Rancocas Cr.
Whitehorse
Philadelphia
Clinton 1778
1777
Brandywine Cr.
Chester
Delaware R.
1777
Chad's Ford
1777
Mullica R.
Howe
1777
Head of Elk
Great Egg Harbor R.
Elk R.
DEL.
Maurice R.
DELAWARE   BAY
To Chesapeake Bay Howe 1777
ATLANTIC OCEAN
MD
Chesapeake Bay

to Greene in a letter written on November 8, 1776, but hung back from giving a direct order. He did not wish "to hazard the men and Stores at Mount Washington, but as you are on the Spot, leave it to you to give such Orders as to evacuating Mount Washington as you Judge best and so far revoking the Order given Colonel Magaw to defend it to the last."[30]

Being on the scene or "on the Spot" described a most desirable condition in Washington's mind. He was not a commander who trusted abstractions, nor did he ever wish to make decisions at a distance. He wanted to see things for himself and did so: at Cambridge, he reconnoitered the lines and inspected camps; on Long Island he did not order a withdrawal until he could supervise it himself; he raced to Kip's Bay to see the disaster with his own eyes; and he got as near the battle of Harlem Heights as he prudently could. He had the imagination to be a map general but not the inclination. He could hold a representation of troop dispositions and a battlefield in his head, but he preferred to be on the spot. One of the skills he acquired as a young man was the art of surveying, an art that required its practitioners to pace the ground. He was a planter and a land speculator, with a feel for the earth, for terrain. Though he could reason from a distance, he wanted the evidence his senses provided before bringing his judgment to bear.

Washington did not arrive on the scene until just before the British moved on Fort Washington, and when he got there he found Nathanael Greene, an attractive, confident personality and an able and articulate man who said the place could be defended. Of course Greene had not fought a major battle—he won his spurs as a tactician after this disaster—but he was obviously bright and he was self-assured, and presumably he had earned the right to predict from being on the ground.[31]

Greene had the right to make a prediction, but there was no good reason to trust him. Washington, however, did trust him—in defiance of his own instincts, whose promptings were confirmed by a visual inspection on November 14. At the decisive moment, a strong, steady personality allowed itself to be swayed by the enthusiasm of a more youthful, exuberant, and optimistic one.

On November 16, Howe destroyed Greene's illusions and confirmed Washington's fears. The British moved into position the day before

30. *Ibid.*, 258.
31. On Greene's responsibility for the loss of the fort, see Richard K. Showman et al., eds., *The Papers of Nathanael Greene* (2 vols. to date, Chapel Hill, N.C., 1976–   ), I, 352n–359, and the sources cited. See also Ward, I, 269.

around the American lines. These lines, about five miles on a side, were much too far from the fort itself, which consisted of breastworks on the Heights of Washington, 230 feet above the Hudson. Howe demanded the surrender of the fort, and Magaw refused in a grand response which soon sounded absurd: "Give me leave to assure his Excellency that activated by the most glorious cause that mankind ever fought in, I am determined to defend this post to the last extremity."[32] The next day General Percy struck Lt. Colonel Lambert Cadwalader's Pennsylvanians from the south, General Edward Mathews, Cornwallis in reserve, pressed against Colonel Baxter's militia from the east, and General Wilhelm von Knyphausen drove against Lt. Colonel Moses Rawlings's Maryland and Virginia regiments. Knyphausen's Hessians took heavy losses from the Marylanders and the Virginians, but in three hours the lines on all three sides had collapsed. Compressed into the fort, disorganized, and near panic, the Americans could not have held out long. They did not offer more resistance, and Magaw surrendered them that afternoon. British dead were numerous—almost 300—but the total American casualties were far heavier—54 killed, 100 wounded, and 2858 captured. Valuable stores, artillery, and ammunition were also taken.[33]

Four days later, on the morning of November 20, Cornwallis took 4000 regulars across the Hudson, landing at Closter, New Jersey, about six miles above Fort Lee. His objective was the American army in New Jersey, which was divided between Hackensack and Fort Lee. Washington had taken 2000 men across the Hudson at Peekskill on November 9 and 10, leaving General Heath at Peekskill with around 3200 troops guarding the approaches to southern New England; Charles Lee and 5500 men remained at North Castle. To complete the sweep of the Hudson River forts, Cornwallis marched quickly to the south and almost trapped the garrison at Fort Lee. Failing to squeeze Greene and Washington between the Hackensack and Hudson rivers, he delayed pursuit for another week.[34]

Washington and a disorganized and dispirited force of 3000 marched and straggled from Hackensack on November 21. They made it to Newark the next day and rested for the following five days. Late that week Cornwallis set his troops in motion; his advance party reached the town

32. Quoted in Theodore Thayer, *Nathanael Greene: Strategist of the American Revolution* (New York, 1960), 119.

33. Ward, I, 267–74. For casualties, Peckham, *Toll*, 26. Washington's account in *GW Writings*, VI, 243–45, is valuable.

34. Ward, I, 276–77; *GW Writings*, VI, 298.

on November 28 just as Washington's rear guard cleared out. The Americans reached New Brunswick on November 29, and a day later bade farewell to 2000 militiamen from New Jersey and Maryland whose enlistments expired. These men had stood all they cared to; they were going home. Cornwallis was in full pursuit now and moving as fast as he could over muddy roads, his pace slowed somewhat by rain and cold weather. He almost caught Washington a second time, at New Brunswick, December 1, but was stopped there by Howe's order. Washington's men had chopped down the timbers supporting the bridge over the Raritan in any case. Still, Cornwallis was criticized at the time, and ever since, for not pushing on, though his men were exhausted and he had his orders.[35]

Washington's command reached Trenton on the Delaware River on December 3; Howe, who had joined Cornwallis at New Brunswick, resumed the pursuit three days later and almost caught the Americans at Princeton on the 7th. The next day at midmorning the British moved out. When they got to Trenton, they found the river full of water and empty of boats. Washington had crossed, taking them all with him and ordering all that could be found up and down the river destroyed or floated to the west bank.[36]

Howe hovered along the Delaware for a week, his patrols looking for boats. He may have considered building a number sufficient to ferry his army across but did not pursue this possibility. On December 14 he ordered his troops into winter quarters, the weather having turned bitterly cold and no opportunity of closing with his enemy presenting itself. Most of the British regiments marched to more comfortable quarters in New York City and Howe himself went with them. Cornwallis received permission to return to England; Clinton, who by this time thoroughly despised Howe, sulked in Newport. To the Hessians went the honor and the duty of manning the outpost line along the Delaware.

During this same week Washington worried over his old, familiar problems—chief among them a shortage of troops and a lack of quality in those he did have. He had about 3000 at this time, and a little over half of them would go home at the end of the month when their enlistments ran out. Some, of course, would not wait until the end of the month. Looking at his slim force was all the more depressing when he estimated that his enemy numbered over 10,000.[37]

35. Ward, I, 280–82; Wickwires, Cornwallis, 90–93.
36. Ward, I, 283–84; Wickwires, Cornwallis, 93–94.
37. GW Writings, VI, 330–32, 345–46.

Equally depressing was the failure of General Charles Lee to join him with the 5500 troops left behind at North Castle when Washington crossed to New Jersey in early November. Washington had departed the camp with a warning to Lee that perhaps the British move into New Jersey was a feint: "They may yet pay the Army under your command a visit." But Washington also informed Lee that should the British take all or most of their army into New Jersey, Lee should then join his forces to Washington's: "I have no doubt of your following, with all possible dispatch, leaving the Militia and Invalids to cover the frontiers of Connecticut in case of need." Besides the wicked linkage of militia and invalids—the two were equivalents in Washington's mind—the interesting feature of this sentence is its indirection. Washington did not order Lee to come. At this point in the relationship of the two men, Washington, a self-conscious provincial, was too much in awe of Lee, the experienced European commander, to tell him what to do. In the next month Washington's letters continued to use the oblique: on November 21 he told Lee that the "public interest" required him to bring his army to New Jersey (that day Lee ordered Brig. General William Heath to send 2000 from Peekskill and received a cold refusal); on November 24 Washington wrote under the illusion that Lee was in motion; on the 27th he became crisp and direct: "My former Letters were so full and explicit as to the necessity of your Marching, as early as possible, that it is unnecessary to add more on that Head," but on December 10 he again reverted to the old mode, "I cannot but request and entreat you" to link up with the main army. By this time Lee had indeed crossed the Hudson but was hanging back in northern New Jersey awaiting an opportunity to strike Howe's army in the rear. He never had a chance to carry out this plan, for on December 13 he was captured by a British patrol, in White's Tavern near Veal Town.[38]

In one of his appeals to Lee to make haste, Washington revealed that he did not believe that Lee's forces added to his own would make the American army an overpowering force. He recognized that Lee's command was not large, but its numbers would strengthen his own and in any case popular "report will exaggerate them and present an Appearance of an Army." Appearance was important, the next thing to reality, important for the morale of the troops themselves and for the American people, who had to believe in their chances of winning the Revolution, or else it would collapse.[39]

38. *Ibid.*, 264–66, 299, 309, for the quotations and the substance of this paragraph.
39. *Ibid.*, 299.

Given the precariousness of the American position, the next decision Washington made may in retrospect seem surprisingly risky, more than daring surely, perhaps even foolish. He decided to venture his army in an attack on Trenton in the expectation that it would be followed by blows against Princeton and then New Brunswick, the most important magazine the British had in New Jersey. Why did he do it?[40]

The resurgence of those old passions, those instincts that could be satisfied only by attack for glory and honor, may have had something to do with his resolve to push back over the Delaware. He also wished to blunt the inevitable attack of the British against Philadelphia in the spring—"I tremble for Philadelphia," he wrote. But was the city so important as to justify the rush? It was the American capital and its loss would damage the common cause, wounding the "Heart of every virtuous American," Washington told John Hancock. That was the point then of the attack—to preserve public morale, to hold the tenuous attachments of the public. For the "great end" the British "have in view, is, to spread themselves over as much Country, as they possibly can, and thereby strike a damp into the Spirits of the people, which will effectually put a stop to the new enlistment of the Army, on which all our hopes depend, and which they will most vigorously strive to effect." All hopes depended upon the army, and the army depended upon the people, was an irrefutable proposition as far as Washington was concerned. Both army and people sometimes angered Washington: the army had melted away as it retreated across New Jersey, and as for the people, their conduct, Washington wrote his brother, was "Infamous" in the support they gave the British. The citizen-soldiers—"a destructive, expensive and disorderly mob"—so "exulted" at the success of the enemy that Washington proposed for a time to disarm them. In more reflective moments he recognized that many people of all sorts in New Jersey were simply watching to see where the balance of power lay, their sympathies were not firmly given to either side, and their "defection" was "as much owing to the want of an Army to look the Enemy in the Face, as to any other cause." Therefore he would cross the Delaware to look the enemy in the face—he had to if the army were to survive, and if it did not, the Revolution was lost.[41]

Across the river the Hessians occupying the forward line of posts felt that they looked the enemy in the face every day. They were strung

40. Freeman, *GW*, IV, 306n, fn. 15, suggests that Washington may have thought of an attack several weeks before Christmas. Ward, I, 292, agrees.
41. *GW Writings*, VI, 346, 355, 393, 397, for the quotations.

out from Trenton to Burlington under General von Donop's command. Donop stationed himself near the southern end of these posts at Mt. Holly, Colonel Rall with three regiments held Trenton, and General Leslie remained at Princeton. General James Grant in New Brunswick commanded all British forces in New Jersey and reported to Howe. Sitting in comfort in New York, Howe wrote reflectively to Germain that his forces were spread rather thin: "The chain, I own, is rather too extensive," but, he explained, he had been "induced to occupy Burlington to cover the county of Monmouth, in which there are many loyal inhabitants."[42]

Howe, like Washington, had his eye on the political dimensions of the war; if he were to hold those loyal to the king, he would have to give them protection. His proclamation offering pardons to those who made their submission to Britain had brought the wavering loyalists out into the open. Now he had to protect them. His means, however, were limited. He had troops, but thanks to Washington's policy of destroying the forage and provisions, he had shortages too. Washington of course had not had the time to scorch the earth, nor had he been disposed to do so. But he had attempted to deny the British the opportunity to live off Jersey farmers, an opportunity the farmers did not welcome. Like most occupying armies everywhere since, Howe's was in the anomalous position of simultaneously "protecting" the inhabitants and exploiting them. The inhabitants did not feel the gratitude of selfless patriots. Howe recognized these feelings and gave instructions to Donop to establish magazines but to give receipts for what he requisitioned from farmers, especially cattle and grain, which were carefully mentioned. But Howe's orders were flexible enough to permit easy abuse: "Any quantity of Salt provision or flour, exceeding what may be thought necessary for the use of a private family is to be considered as Rebel store," and could be "seized for the Crown and issued to the Troops as a saving to the public."[43]

What followed could not have greatly surprised anyone. The Hessians, who somehow failed to share Howe's political sensitivities, took what they wanted and thereby called into being an opposition never deeply dormant. Before long, Hessian commanders were complaining that the security of the chain Howe had strung them along did not exist. To get a letter to Princeton, Colonel Rall had to send a heavy patrol of fifty men. Patrols, foraging parties, and outposts were regularly mauled

42. William S. Stryker, The Battles of Trenton and Princeton (Boston, 1898), 328.
43. Ibid., 317.

by local partisans and raiders from the west bank of the Delaware. Rall did not even bother to throw up fortifications around Trenton; the enemy surrounded him—he explained—and he could not begin to cover himself adequately.[44]

Neither Rall nor his chief expected Washington to attack Christmas night. The weather was bad, with rain and snow; the Delaware, though not covered with ice, carried large pieces of it downstream. Washington planned carefully, though he had not expected the weather to conceal his movements. His attack was to have three parts: James Ewing with 700 troops would cross at Trenton Ferry and seize the bridge over the Assunpink Creek just to the south of the town. Lt. Colonel John Cadwalader farther to the south would strike over the river at Bristol and hit Donop's force at Mt. Holly, a diversion to keep the Hessians so occupied there as to prevent reinforcement of Trenton. And Trenton itself was the main objective and would be attacked by Washington, who, if all went well, planned to push to Princeton and perhaps as far as the main magazine at New Brunswick.[45]

After dark on Christmas night, the main force, some 2400 soldiers, assembled behind the low hills overlooking McKonkey's Ferry. Washington wanted to cross them all by midnight and march them south the nine miles to Trenton by five in the morning, well before daylight. The storm, the rough water, and ice prevented him from holding to this schedule. The artillery under Knox, eighteen fieldpieces in all, proved difficult to handle in the snow and sleet and was not ashore until three in the morning. Washington, who had crossed with the advance party in Durham boats, stood on the bank and watched—he knew that his presence would not go unnoticed even in the dark. By four o'clock everyone was assembled for the march into Trenton.

Two columns were formed, one on the upper or Pennington Road, the other on the lower or River Road. Washington, with Nathanael Greene, commanded the force on the Pennington, and Sullivan led on the River Road. By skill or by good luck, both groups reached Trenton within a few minutes of eight o'clock. The River Road curved into the southern end of town; the Pennington Road carried the troops to King and Queen streets, running north and south, the main thoroughfares of the town. Washington's van drove in a company on outpost duty on the north edge and within a few minutes had set up their artillery on King and Queen streets. Two young captains commanded these

44. Ibid., 329–32.
45. GW Writings, VI, 429, 434, 440–44; Freeman, GW, IV, 306–10; Ward, I, 292–93.

guns—Thomas Forrest on Queen Street and Alexander Hamilton on King.

Gunfire brought two Hessian regiments into the streets; a third remained in reserve at the southeastern edge of town. Colonel Rall, who had celebrated Christmas night with his usual exuberance, rolled out of bed and took charge on the street. An American bullet soon cut him down, and his men never really dispersed themselves to fight effectively. Much of the village was empty, the inhabitants having fled three weeks earlier, and its houses and stables were soon turned into arenas for vicious little bayonet fights. The American artillery prevented the Hessians from forming effectively, and the American infantry gradually rounded them up once the hard work had been accomplished with musket butts and bayonets. In an hour it was finished, with twenty-two Hessians dead, ninety-eight wounded, and almost a thousand prisoners. Two American officers and two privates were wounded.

At least five hundred Hessians and a handful of British dragoons escaped across the Assunpink Creek, for Ewing had not been able to cross. Nor had Cadwalader made it further south, though an advance party he sent over did, only to be withdrawn when the main body of his command found the weather and the rough water too much for them.

Washington took his tired but triumphant troops back across the Delaware to Pennsylvania that afternoon. He had learned of Cadwalader's fiasco and there seemed nothing left to do. His soldiers were much too tired to drive on to Princeton, and as far as he knew the Hessians would be coming up from the south. He was wrong on this last score. The Hessians gave up in the next few days every post they had on the river.

Feeling a little foolish perhaps, and eager to prove the mettle of himself and his men, Cadwalader crossed his command on the next day. He entered a Burlington now empty of the enemy. Two days later, Washington led his soldiers over once more, this time straight into Trenton. Once in the town, he ordered Cadwalader to march his troops up and gave the same order to General Mifflin, who had taken 1600 militia into Bordentown. As the year ended, Washington had 5000 men and forty howitzers in Trenton.[46]

A greater test than Trenton now faced the American command. Howe had sent Cornwallis galloping out of New York to Princeton in an effort

46. This account of the battle of Trenton is based on *GW Writings*, VI, 441–44; Freeman, *GW*, IV, 310–24; Ward, I, 294–305; Stryker, *Battles of Trenton and Princeton*, 361–64, 371–72.

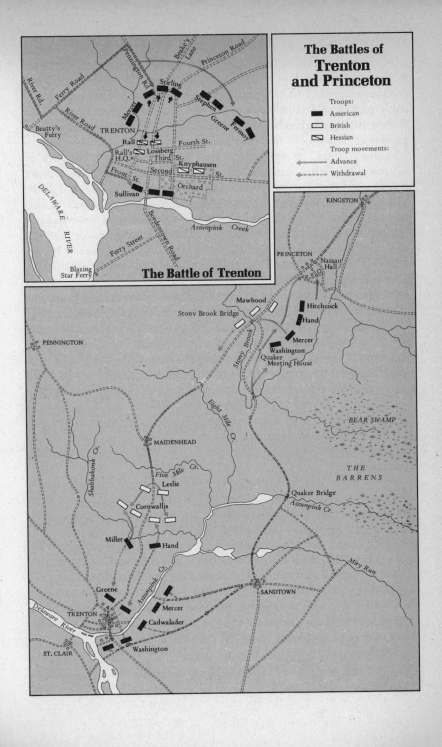

The Battles of Trenton and Princeton

Troops:
American
British
Hessian

Troop movements:
Advance
Withdrawal

The Battle of Trenton

River Rd.
Ferry Road
River Road
Pennington Rd.
Mercer
Stirling
Beake's Lane
Princeton Road
Stephen
Greene
Fernoy
Beatty's Ferry
TRENTON
Rall
Fourth St.
Rall's H.Q.
Lossberg
Third St.
Knyphausen
Second St.
Front St.
Orchard
St.
Sullivan
DELAWARE RIVER
Assunpink Creek
Bordentown Road
Ferry Street
Blazing Star Ferry

KINGSTON
PRINCETON
Nassau Hall
Mawhood
Hitchcock
Stony Brook Bridge
Hand
Mercer
Washington
Quaker Meeting House
Stony Brook
BEAR SWAMP
PENNINGTON
Eight Mile Cr.
THE BARRENS
Shabbakonk Cr.
MAIDENHEAD
Five Mile Cr.
Leslie
Cornwallis
Quaker Bridge
Assunpink Cr.
Miller
Hand
Miry Run
Greene
Assunpink Cr.
Mercer
SANDTOWN
TRENTON
Cadwalader
Delaware River
ST. CLAIR
Washington

to recover the initiative, and Cornwallis pushed down from Princeton with 5500 regulars and twenty-eight fieldpieces. Washington did not ease his way south. The Princeton Road was churned into mud, and small parties of Pennsylvania and Virginia Continentals harassed the British as they marched. Late in the afternoon of January 2 Cornwallis arrived at Trenton to find Washington drawn up along the ridge of Assunpink Creek. Several unsuccessful attempts to ford the creek by advance units left Cornwallis convinced that he should delay a major assault until the morrow. A subordinate or two protested, saying that Washington would not be there in the morning. The answer to that was a question: Where would he go? He had no boats; he was trapped.[47]

That night Washington provided a different answer by slipping away on a recently constructed road southeast of the worn highway to Princeton. The British did not discover his departure until dawn, for the Americans had left behind several hundred men who kept their campfires ablaze and who spent much of their time digging into the ground, making noise which reassured their enemies across the creek. By early morning Washington's van reached the outskirts of Princeton, where they ran into Lt. Colonel Charles Mawhood, who had been left there with two regiments. There was a desperate fight for a time with Mawhood's command roughing up troops under Hugh Mercer and John Cadwalader. Just as the American units threatened to lose their integrity as fighting organizations, Washington arrived on the scene. It was hard to resist Washington on horseback, and the Continentals pulled themselves together; the British began to fall apart. Mawhood eventually broke through to Trenton, but under severe pursuit his command virtually disintegrated.[48]

The British regiment Mawhood had left in Princeton sat there inertly and then attempted to retreat to New Brunswick. Not all made it, as a New Jersey regiment captured almost two hundred. Washington soon saw that his troops were spent and gave up his design on New Brunswick. Four days later he entered winter quarters in Morristown. Cornwallis, fearing the worst from his slippery enemy, marched his command from Trenton to New Brunswick. He was taking no chances on losing his supply depot. Hackensack and Elizabeth Town fell to American forces on January 6, 1777, the day Washington's army entered Morristown. Howe, who had dominated New Jersey two weeks before, now saw his forces confined to Amboy and New Brunswick.

47. Wickwires, Cornwallis, 95–96.
48. Freeman, GW, IV, 338–59, for this paragraph and the next.

16

The War of Maneuver

The two armies now settled in, apparently for the winter. A casual observer might have thought that it was Europe, the convention of going into winter quarters was so taken for granted. The soldiers on both sides turned to the business of making themselves comfortable or trying to find comfort in situations inherently uncomfortable. For Washington's men attaining some ease seemed almost impossible in the mean little huts they constructed for themselves. Keeping warm proved a challenge—central heating awaited the genius of a later century—but collecting firewood at least forced the men to stay active. Their opposite numbers in New York City did not swelter, but they made themselves snug in taverns, public buildings, and private homes.

Some of Washington's men at Morristown followed the ways of many who had served before them—that is, they did what was becoming the American practice, ending their military service without authorization; in other words, they deserted. Howe too lost troops to desertion, but not as many. Where, after all, could redcoats go except to the enemy?

The citizens of New York City soon came to envy the deserters. Life in the city deteriorated as winter set in, and the occupying army did nothing to improve it—for civilians at any rate. Food was scarce, as irregulars on Long Island and across the Hudson struck at foraging parties. This little war was barbarous and dirty and conducted according to none of the familiar rules. Inside the city, citizens were safe from raiding parties, but there the regulars either ignored them or pushed them around whenever they bothered to notice. Eighteenth-century garrisons and the civilians they "protected" never appreciated one another, and what the New Yorkers endured in the winter of 1776–77 had taken place many times before, most recently in Boston. The regulars in both places aimed to destroy the enemy and ended by adding to the enemy's numbers.

At the same time, Washington's troops soon lost some of their admirers in Morristown—not because they misbehaved, but because they brought smallpox with them, and because their commander insisted upon spreading out the sick among the townspeople for care and in order to "isolate" the sick. Congress had dismissed the director-general of hospitals, Dr. John Morgan, three days after Washington's forces arrived at Morristown, and hospitals which had never been adequate soon fell into deeper disrepair. Washington had no recourse other than his regimental hospitals and the town itself—thus his attempt at isolating smallpox patients and a try at inoculation, a technique which called for deliberately infecting those who had not yet contracted the disease in the hope that they would survive the less virulent form that usually resulted. Understandably, the farmers of Morristown looked with dismay at the changes in their lives that the army brought, and the cost of their principles was borne in upon them.[1]

The village itself was small—no more than fifty houses, a church, and the inevitable tavern—and by all standards a well-chosen site for winter quarters, difficult of access from the east through hills which blunted approaches. But though difficult to reach, it was close enough to New York City, about twenty-five miles away on an east-west line, to permit Washington to watch his enemy. New Brunswick and Amboy were about the same distance, so Morristown was not isolated and the army there could not be cut off, for escape to the west through passes in the hills was available. And should Howe push out from New York against Philadelphia, he could be struck on his flanks. The army at Morristown could also hit Howe if he went up the Hudson Valley.

Within two months the army had dwindled to such a size that it could not have harassed anyone. Those troops—probably around a thousand in all—who had accepted a ten-dollar bounty at Trenton in return for six weeks' service included some who did not keep the bargain once the enthusiasm of victory wore off. Others went home in early February, and by March the army numbered less than three thousand men. As usual, recruiting proved a difficult business even though Congress had

1. Ward, I, 319–20; Freeman, GW, IV, 388–89.

authorized the raising of eighty-eight battalions hard on the heels of the disaster on Long Island the previous August. In December it had added eleven battalions of infantry to the authorization besides supporting artillery, engineers, and 3000 cavalry.[2]

An army-on-paper is rather ineffective in the field. Getting the men into camp taxed the army recruiters' skill, especially since the bounties they could pay frequently were exceeded by those of the states raising militia. Washington tried persuasion on those states, explaining the effects of their practices on his army, and when that failed resorted to threats—as, for example, when he told the governor of Rhode Island that if his state did not reduce the pay it offered, it should not count on any "extraordinary attention" from the Continental army. Persuasion and the threats paid off: by early May, as the hills around Morristown turned green, the battalions Congress had authorized began to take form. Before the end of the month the army had reached almost 9000 effectives—forty-three battalions—and they could be armed, for muskets, powder, and clothing had arrived from a France still cautiously watching the struggle and surreptitiously giving aid to the Americans.[3]

Military operations also picked up in May as the British broke from their hibernation. British supplies were low and they sent out an increasing number of foraging parties. Advance units of Washington's army struck them and so did the irregulars in New Jersey. Howe disliked these savage little encounters. What he wanted was a general action which might destroy his enemy, and in mid-June he set about to lure Washington into fighting a major battle. On June 17, he moved a large force from Staten Island into New Jersey and marched them about nine miles along the road to Philadelphia. Washington was willing to have light units skirmish with the enemy but, though he feared that Howe meant to take the city, refused battle. A week later Howe again marched out, then pulled back, and when Washington followed, turned about and drove at him. Washington avoided the trap just in time, and Howe then pulled out of New Jersey completely, leaving the entire state in rebel control.[4]

2. Ward, I, 321.

3. *Ibid.*, 319–21; Freeman, *GW*, IV, 380–402.

4. James Murray, a Scottish officer, wrote bitterly of army life in New Jersey in February 1777: " . . . we have a pretty amusement known by the name of foraging or fighting for our daily bread." See Eric Robson, ed., *Letters from America, 1773 to 1780* (Manchester, Eng., 1951), 38. On the June 1777 maneuvers of Howe and Washington, Ward, I, 325–28.

II

If Howe had failed to trap Washington, he had succeeded in confusing him about British intentions. What the British were up to was a question that had been much discussed at the American headquarters in the early summer. The purpose of the forays out into the Jersey countryside in June seemed obvious enough, but what did the evacuation of New Jersey mean? In July, watchers duly reported the British going aboard ships in the New York harbor. As the fleet grew so did American uncertainty.

By this time Howe had at last decided what he was about. He was going to Philadelphia by sea. During his voyage he would change his mind about a landing place, a decision of great importance, but he would hold to his decision about his destination. He had decided on an attack on Philadelphia without consulting the ministry, although he had informed it of his plan—or plans, rather, for he had changed his mind during the spring about how best to get to Philadelphia. For most of the winter of 1776–77, he seems to have thought of a march across New Jersey to the city. However, by April he had swung his thinking to an invasion by sea, presumably out from New York to the south and up the Delaware.[5]

In England the ministry, with the approval of the king, had also decided on a strategy for the campaign of 1777. The problem for these centers of strategic thought was in making their plans somehow meet, but neither the ministry nor Howe really knew what the other intended, and the plans they made remained uncoordinated. The ministry did learn early in the winter that Howe hoped to take Philadelphia. What it did not learn until much too late was that he had switched from an expedition by land to one by sea.

During the winter the ministry, or, more exactly, the American Secretary, Lord George Germain, whose responsibility it was to develop a strategy to crush the rebellion, listened to an ambitious scheme laid out by General John Burgoyne which called for an invasion from Canada. Burgoyne had returned to England from Canada after the failure of Sir Guy Carleton's attempt in summer 1776 to drive down Lake Champlain. Burgoyne had accompanied Carleton but had escaped the blame for the failure, and back in England he pleaded the wisdom of a second similar expedition—this one under more aggressive leadership, which

5. Willcox, *Portrait of a General*, chap. 4, especially 147–52; Ira D. Gruber, *The Howe Brothers and the American Revolution* (New York, 1972).

he himself would provide. The king liked the idea, especially when Burgoyne explained that the purpose of the move was to separate New England from the rest of the colonies. By slicing down Lake Champlain and then through the Hudson Valley to Albany, the Burgoyne expedition would neatly isolate the center of the rebellion. To give his drive even more strength, he proposed that a second force under Lt. Colonel Barry St. Leger push out from Oswego down the Mohawk, a tributary of the Hudson. The two rivers joined near Albany, and so presumably would the two prongs of the invading army.[6]

Burgoyne did not insist that an expedition come up the Hudson to meet him. Clearly, he was thinking of his own role as the leading one, and only as an afterthought did he suggest that at Albany he would place himself under Howe's command. He did not propose that Howe meet him or have an army in Albany prepared to give him aid or join his force to itself. Nor did he explain what he would do in Albany or how in fact marching there would effectively isolate New England.

Germain did not ask for explanations; nor did he suggest that grand though it was, the Burgoyne plan might be difficult to execute. He did, however, sense that perhaps Burgoyne's and Howe's planning ought to be coordinated. But he did not act on this perception, which was hardly more than a vague hunch, until it was too late.

Sir Henry Clinton was in England while Burgoyne was persuading Germain and the king that a fresh try from Canada was just what the war needed. Clinton saw the dangers of independent attacks by Burgoyne and Howe, but he no more than the others in England knew at that time that Howe would take to the sea in search of Philadelphia. So, though Clinton detested Howe, he could not warn of the folly in the offing. Besides, he wanted the command of the expedition from Canada, and he knew that it was his for the asking if he could bring himself to ask, for he was Burgoyne's senior in rank. Asking for himself proved impossible to Clinton; then and later his "diffidence," his inability to exert himself to get what he really wanted, kept him silent. The command was given to Burgoyne in March; Clinton received the red ribbon of the Bath and orders to return to America as second in command to Howe. Both Clinton and Burgoyne had already sailed—Burgoyne for Canada, Clinton for New York—when Howe's final plan for the capture of Philadelphia reached England.[7]

---

6. Willcox, *Portrait of a General*, 143–47.
7. *Ibid.*, 133–41.

Howe had written Germain on April 2 that since he would not be receiving the reinforcements he had requested, he would pull his forward posts out of New Jersey, give up all idea of a march overland, and embark his forces against Philadelphia. Earlier in the year Howe had conceived of an attack by both land and sea; then he had proposed to move only by land; but now in April, with the dismal news about reinforcements, he altered his strategy once more in favor of an invasion by sea.[8]

Why he made this decision is not clear. In the dispatch he wrote on April 2 informing Germain of his intention to transport his forces by sea from New York to the Delaware, he stated that he no longer expected to end the war that year. Deprived of reinforcements, he apparently had decided against risking the army (which numbered around 21,000) in a march across the Jerseys. A move by sea, of course, would eliminate his army as a factor in the northern campaign—at least while the army was on ships, and in fact for a time afterwards—for it would be far from the Hudson Valley.[9]

Howe seemed not to care, seemed oblivious even about what was being undertaken from Canada. He may not have been obsessed with Philadelphia, as some believed then and today, but he was thinking along lines that had appeared so clear to him in the New York campaign of the previous year. The thing to do at that time was to smash Washington's army, and, failing that, to seize a major American center, cut off sea-going trade and dominate the surrounding countryside, and encourage those colonials still loyal to the king to show themselves. Capture of Philadelphia and the Delaware offered a similar opportunity: the area had important business, its farms were productive suppliers, and eastern Pennsylvania was filled with loyalists awaiting the protection of his majesty's forces to make themselves known.[10]

If strategy of this sort was not an obsession, it was a preoccupation which carried Howe's mind far from Canadian problems. The responsibility to force him to consider the war and the current campaign together lay in England, most directly with Lord George Germain, the American secretary. Germain failed to do more than make Howe vaguely aware that something was brewing in the north. Between March 3, when the decision to give command of the northern expedition to Burgoyne

8. *Ibid.*, 150–52; Gruber, *Howe Brothers*, 199–200.
9. Willcox, *Portrait of a General*, 149–50.
10. Gruber, *Howe Brothers*, 222–23.

was virtually certain, and April 19, Germain wrote Howe eight times, and neglected in each letter to tell him of Burgoyne's mission. Germain did write Carleton in Canada that Burgoyne would lead the invasion, and he sent a copy of this letter to Howe. But no explanation of strategy accompanied this letter—and no orders to Howe to coordinate his efforts with Burgoyne's. Instead, Germain contented himself with letters to Howe of approval and reassurance to the effect that the Philadelphia campaign appeared sound and that contrary to Howe's gloomy expectations would lead to the conclusion of the war.

Germain may have believed everything he wrote Howe, or if he doubted the wisdom of what Howe was about, he may have hesitated to challenge him directly. At this point in the history of the war, character and the accidents of personal relations assumed for a moment at least a decisive importance. The character that proved so important was Germain's; the relations of persons were those entangled in English politics.

Among those ministers who advocated a stiff line in dealing with the Americans, none exceeded Germain in stiffness. One of the tough men in the ministry, he was in 1777 in his sixty-second year; he had replaced Dartmouth as American Secretary in November of the year of Concord and Lexington—and Bunker Hill. North and the king found him refreshingly certain about American matters: the Americans, he argued, should give way, acknowledge Parliament's right to legislate in all cases whatsoever, and then, perhaps, grievances could be aired and complaints satisfied. These views resembled no one's as much as the king's. There is no real reason to suppose that they were not sincerely held, but it may well be that Germain hesitated to qualify them—that is, to soften them while the king maintained that the Americans must surrender—for Germain was a man always vulnerable to charges of weakness and even cowardice. His appointment to a major post in the government was a triumph of persistence and, more concretely, a strange consequence of the old feud between Leicester House, the center of the faction around the heir apparent, and the monarch, in this case George II, grandfather of George III. During the Seven Years War, Germain, then Lord George Sackville, had served on the continent with Prince Ferdinand. In the battle of Minden (1759) he had not brought the British cavalry forward fast enough to suit the prince, who brought charges against him of disobeying orders. Germain was tried before a court-martial, found guilty, and apparently relegated to disgrace and obscurity, with the stink of cowardice swirling around him. The case had attracted national attention, although only those who followed political intrigue realized that the government had pushed it so fiercely because Germain was a part of the Leicester House crowd.[11]

When the young George III assumed the throne, Germain was slowly rehabilitated through appointment to minor posts and service in Parliament. The American war was of course well under way when he joined North's ministry. He proved his worth by his unyielding attitude toward colonial claims.

But Germain never felt quite at ease in the government and may have shrunk before the unpleasant business of giving the Howes direct orders. The Howes, after all, were well connected; they were favorites of the king. Taking a firm stand on colonial issues was one thing; ordering around William Howe—telling him that he must cooperate with Burgoyne coming from Canada—was another. Germain did not issue such orders.

III

The designer of a part of British strategy for 1777, General John Burgoyne, returned to America from a London winter on May 6. The HMS *Apollo* carrying him sailed into Quebec that day, a Quebec enjoying spring sunshine and, with the general's arrival, the warmth of optimism. For Burgoyne, who always had dash, now had what he most craved: an independent command and, not incidentally, an opportunity to exercise it. He came to his army after a heady winter at home which included at least one horseback ride with the king in Hyde Park and meetings at which he convinced the king that a thrust from Canada down the Hudson would lead to the destruction of the rebellion.[12]

Sir Guy Carleton, still in command in Canada, met Burgoyne with at least surface cordiality and proceeded to give him all the cooperation he desired. The army was assembled in the next few weeks and moved to St. Johns on the Richelieu River. The army was a varied but formidable force—slightly more than 8300 men in total, composed of 3700 British regulars, 3000 Germans, mostly Brunswickers, 650 Tories and Canadians, and 400 Iroquois. Burgoyne also had a train of 138 howitzers and guns and around 600 artillerymen to service them. He could also look with confidence on his subordinates, in particular Major General William Phillips, his second in command, Brig. General Simon Fraser, who would

11. This paragraph and the two before it are based on Willcox, *Portrait of a General*, 143–46; and Gerald Saxon Brown, *The American Secretary: The Colonial Policy of Lord George Germain, 1775–1778* (Ann Arbor, Mich., 1963), 93–114.

12. Ward, I, 398–401.

lead an important striking force, and Baron Friedrich Adolph von Riede-sel, who commanded the Germans. Baron von Riedesel, accompanied by his baroness, three daughters, and their two maids, was an especially able and energetic officer, quick to sense an enemy's weakness on the battlefield and eager to take advantage of every opening. Good troops and fine senior commanders pleased Burgoyne, already pleased with him-self and with what apparently lay ahead.[13]

Had Burgoyne known of the disarray of his enemy, he would have felt even more optimism. General Philip Schuyler commanded the North-ern Department, but his hold was anything but secure and he knew it. Many of his troops were New Englanders and they despised him. Schuyler had not covered himself with glory in the earlier Canadian campaigns, and his men remembered his performance. They also disliked him for other reasons: Schuyler was a Dutch patroon, a proud man suspicious of what he took to be Yankee egalitarianism; his soldiers from New England resented his aristocratic bearing, his obvious distaste for them, and his remote manner.

The attitude of the troops from New England would not have loosened Schuyler's grip on his army had he not had a popular rival, a former officer in the British army, Horatio Gates, now a Virginian who owned a plantation and cultivated tobacco and Congressmen. Gates looked to be, and was, the polar opposite of Schuyler. Born to an English servant, Gates was a plain-looking, even homely, and comfortable man. Not a severe disciplinarian as Schuyler was, he did not conceal his admiration of the New England militia, a feeling it more than returned. Gates, moreover, was a veteran and a professional army officer who had fought with Braddock in the French and Indian War and had left the service as a major to settle in the Shenandoah Valley. His plainness and apparent lack of guile were deceptive, as George Washington, who was responsible for his appointment as brigadier general in the Continental army in 1775, came to recognize. For Gates had ambitions—in 1777, to head the northern department. Late in the winter he got his wish, after assidu-ous lobbying in Congress, only to have Congress once more place Schuyler in command. This change in command occurred in May, just as Burgoyne was beginning to gather himself for the plunge southward.[14]

Unaware of the divisions within his enemy's camp, Burgoyne set his army in motion in a mood approaching cocksureness. He had moved

13. *Ibid.*, 401–4.
14. For Gates, see Paul David Nelson, *General Horatio Gates: A Biography* (Baton Rouge, La., 1976).

his troops into position from Montreal in late May and early June. The soldiers shared their commander's certainty that victory awaited them. As an officer remarked of the prevailing conviction, the army began the campaign convinced that it was "attended with every Appearance of Success."[15] A few days into the drive, delusions of grandeur would replace this conviction: "We had conceived the Idea of our being irresistible."[16] It was a beguiling idea and reinforced by Burgoyne himself, who on June 20 issued a proclamation replete with threats and false piety, alternately calling upon the Americans to greet his warriors with loving embraces and summoning up hellfire for them if they did not. His intentions were to "hold forth Security and Depredation to the Country." He acted to restore "the Rights of the Constitution," in contrast to the "unnatural Rebellion" which sought to establish "the compleated System of Tyranny." Faced with this native-born oppression, the colonists must allow him and his army to protect them. The last thing they should do was to break up bridges and roads, and to hide their corn and cattle. But trust him, he who extended this invitation to join him "in consciousness of Christianity, my Royal Master's Clemency and the honour of Soldiership. . . . And let not people be led to disregard it by considering their distance from the immediate situation of my Camp. I have but to give stretch to the Indian forces under my direction, and they amount to thousands, to overtake the hardened enemies of Great Britain and America. I consider them the same wherever they may lurk. If not withstanding these endeavours, & sincere inclinations to effect them, the Phrenzy of hostility should remain, I trust I shall stand acquited in the Eyes of God and Men in denouncing the executing the vengeance of the State against the willful outcasts—The Messengers of Justice and of Wrath await them in the field; and devastation, famine and every concomitant horror that a reluctant but indispensable prosecution of military duty must occasion, will bar the way to their return."[17]

Burgoyne could not have adopted a more inappropriate tone or issued a message more damaging to himself and his troops. His pretensions to constitutionality, patriotism, and Christianity coupled to the barbarism of threatening to unleash the Indians aroused anger and scorn. Like so many British leaders before him, he had a talent for creating opposition.

15. S. Sydney Bradford, ed., "Lord Francis Napier's Journal of the Burgoyne Campaign," *MdHM*, 57 (1962), 324.
16. *Ibid.*, 324–25.
17. *Ibid.*, 296–97.

His countrymen at home saw his blunder as soon as they read his bombast: to Horace Walpole, he of the viper's tongue, Burgoyne was henceforth "vaporing Burgoyne," "Pomposo," and finally "Hurlothrumbo."[18] In America, Burgoyne drew disdain and bred a feeling more serious: a passion to stop him.

Burgoyne may have appeared "Pomposo" to clever men like Walpole, but to his soldiers he was a commander who combined flair with professional competence. He showed his professional side to his soldiers with the laconic injunction to rely on the bayonet, for "the bayonet in the hands of the Valiant is irresistible."[19] It was an order often tested and often proved.

The expedition of irresistibles set out on June 20 from Cumberland Head on Lake Champlain and sailed to Crown Point, eight miles north of Ticonderoga. There Burgoyne established a magazine, set up a hospital, and issued stores. A week later he was on the move again, and by the end of the month his troops were within striking distance of Fort Ticonderoga.[20]

The fort lay on both sides of the lake, but its principal works, in sad repair, were on the west side. Across the lake to the east there were defensive works on Mount Independence, a quarter of a mile away. A floating bridge connected Ticonderoga and Independence. Burgoyne, resolved to strike both sides, divided his forces: the British regulars on the west bank of the lake, the Germans under Riedesel on the east.

A little more than a mile to the west of Ticonderoga, heavily forested, Sugar Loaf Hill rose to a height of 750 feet and clearly commanded the fort. It took Burgoyne's men until July 5 to cut through the maple and pine on Sugar Loaf and emplace cannon on its summit. When the guns on the hill spoke that day, General Arthur St. Clair, commander at Fort Ticonderoga, knew he would have to abandon the fort. In the darkness of the next morning he marched his men, around two thousand effectives, across the bridge to Mount Independence. Before he made this move, he loaded his sick and as many supplies as he could get aboard into bateaux. They were to sail to Skenesboro at the head of the lake. From Independence he marched his army to Hubbardton, some twenty-four miles to the southeast.[21]

18. Quoted in Ward, I, 405.
19. James Hadden, *Hadden's Journal and Orderly Books. A Journal Kept in Canada and Upon Burgoyne's Campaign in 1776 and 1777* (Albany, N.Y., 1884), 74.
20. Ward, I, 408–9.
21. *Ibid.*, 409–12.

The British learned of this evacuation almost immediately and set out in pursuit. The pursuers, an advance party of about 850 men, were led by General Simon Fraser, an able and hardened officer. Around five o'clock the next morning, July 7, Fraser's command ran into the American rear guard, around 1000 strong, under Colonel Seth Warner. St. Clair with the main body had advanced six miles farther to Castleton. Surprised though they were, Warner's men "behaved" as the British commander of light infantry, the Earl of Balcarres, later said, "with great gallantry."[22] The battle was vicious, with neither side fully aware of where the enemy was and with the lines consequently scrambled. At the end of three hours, Warner's men were gaining the upper hand. Fraser, who had begun his pursuit the day before without waiting for Riedesel, now yearned for the sight of his German colleague—and in a stroke of good luck Riedesel, with a chasseur company and around eighty grenadiers, appeared. Their firepower and weight broke Warner's resistance, and within a few more minutes the Americans were in flight.[23]

Flight approached rout in the next week. Burgoyne, who sailed up the lake to Skenesboro, almost caught the bateaux that had carried the sick from Ticonderoga. Ashore the British took Fort Anne, but no army could keep up with St. Clair, who reached Fort Edward on the Hudson on July 12. The worst of the campaign—though not the fighting—was now over for the Americans. For the British it was really just beginning.

Burgoyne's problem in July was how to move from Skenesboro near the head of Champlain to Fort Edward on the Hudson. The best method, one which Burgoyne himself had approved while still in England, was to return to Ticonderoga, shift his boats into Lake George, and sail to the head of that lake. There he would find Fort George, a convenient base from which to follow a road already cut to the Hudson, a distance of about ten miles. Sensible though this plan was, Burgoyne discarded it; his reasons cannot be fathomed. Two years after the campaign he offered an explanation of sorts: the morale of his army concerned him, and morale would have been very much impaired by "a retrograde motion." Besides, had he pulled back, his enemy would have remained at Fort George, as their retreat could not have been cut off. The only way in that situation to dislodge the Americans would have been to

22. John Burgoyne, *A State of the Expedition from Canada* (2d ed., London, 1780), 39. A part of the value of this work lies in the testimony it reports that was given in a Parliamentary hearing.
23. *Hadden's Journal*, 91–92; Bradford, ed., "Napier's Journal," *MdHM*, 57 (1962), 300–301. Ward, I, 412–14, is excellent.

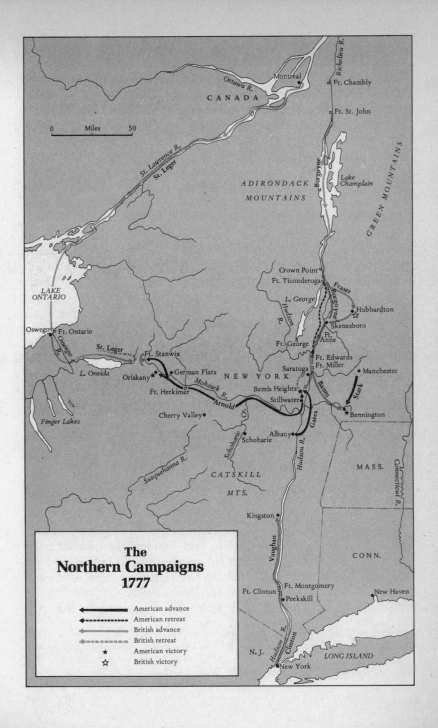

The
**Northern Campaigns
1777**

	American advance
	American retreat
	British advance
	British retreat
★	American victory
☆	British victory

"open trenches"—besiege them, in other words—an operation which would have delayed his advance even more. Then, too, marching overland from Fort Anne to Fort Edward "improved" the troops in "wood service," a justification Burgoyne apparently presented with a straight face.[24]

Whether or not the troops were "improved" in "wood service," they got their bellies full of it between Skenesboro and Fort Edward. Their way ran along Wood Creek, an aptly named stream, which twisted erratically down a valley covered with large hemlocks and even larger pines. The road crossed the stream in no fewer than forty places, many of them deep ravines spanned by long bridges. General Schuyler knew this country and saw his opportunity.[25]

Burgoyne did not strike out from Skenesboro immediately. He was short of oxen and horses to draw his wagons, and he was not traveling light. He had brought his mistress; and Baron von Riedesel had allowed his wife and three daughters to accompany him. Nor had the officers of lesser rank stripped down excess baggage: a good deal of unessential weight was being carried. Part of this weight, of course, was in servants and the inevitable camp followers.

When the army did resume its advance, it faced formidable obstacles— the trees across the road, the ruins of bridges, boulders in Wood Creek, and rough ground made rougher by the Americans. There was, however, no American opposition, Schuyler having withdrawn "deliberately," as a British officer remarked, and with his 4500 intact. By August 3 Schuyler had reached Stillwater on the Hudson, twelve miles below Saratoga. And from there he moved another twelve miles, close to the mouth of the Mohawk River. On August 4 orders went out: Gates was to replace Schuyler as commander of the Northern Department. The army, its numbers dwindling as the soldiers indulged in the American propensity to desert, rejoiced in the change. No one knew it, but the days of retreat in the face of Burgoyne's expedition were over.[26]

Just before the change in the American command, Burgoyne's advance party made its way on July 30 into Fort Edward. His men were not cheered by the ruins of the fort, though they had at last reached the Hudson. The drive from Skenesboro had consumed three weeks and exhausted them all, their animals, and their supplies.

Confronted by shortages of all sorts, except ammunition, Burgoyne

24. Burgoyne, *State of the Expedition*, 17.
25. Bradford, ed., "Napier's Journal," *MdHM*, 57 (1962), 303–4; *Hadden's Journal*, 94–95.
26. *Hadden's Journal*, 95 ("deliberately"); Ward, I, 418–21.

listened to Riedesel's proposal to send an expedition as far east as the Connecticut River to forage for cattle and horses. Riedesel recommended that a large party be sent out in the expectation that it would return with meat for the troops and mounts for his horseless Brunswick dragoons. These Germans had found the march to Fort Edward a torture. Burgoyne probably did not feel much sympathy for the Brunswickers but he needed food, and he knew that bringing it from Ticonderoga would be almost impossible.[27]

Lt. Colonel Baum was detached to lead the raid and given some 600 soldiers. Baum, who spoke no English, was instructed to enlist the support of the citizens he encountered. Burgoyne's orders contained references to Baum's expedition as "secret," and it was given a German band to, in the historian Christopher Ward's sardonic phrase, "help preserve its secrecy." This expedition departed on August 11. On the 15th near Bennington Baum's party was surrounded by a force twice its size, led by Brig. General John Stark, and virtually destroyed. Later a relief party, which had been dispatched on August 14, was also chewed up in a day by Stark's militia.[28]

News of this "disaster," as one of Burgoyne's officers called it, reached the main army on the night of August 17. Burgoyne reacted with uncharacteristic speed and had the troops instructed at 2:00 A.M. to be "in readiness to turn out at a moment's warning." Not quite two weeks later, more unhappy news arrived. Lt. Colonel Barry St. Leger had given up the siege of Fort Stanwix. Commanders who had been feeling lonely now began to sense just how isolated the expedition was.[29]

The British were not isolated, whatever else they felt about their situation. But they were at a critical juncture and Burgoyne knew it. He had about a month's supply of food and his troops were in fairly good shape. They were far from the magazine on Lake Champlain, however, and with rather short supplies and lacking winter quarters they could not remain where they were—on the east side of the Hudson far from Champlain and not close to Albany. Burgoyne might have pulled back to Ticonderoga, but he was averse to withdrawal, which everyone would have considered an admission of defeat. So he boldly and bravely decided to continue his drive to Albany.[30]

27. Ward, I, 421–22.
28. *Ibid.*, 422–23.
29. *Hadden's Journal*, 136; Bradford, ed., "Napier's Journal," *MdHM*, 57 (1962), 309–11.
30. Ward, II, 501.

Burgoyne decided at the same time that he must cross the Hudson to the west side. He might have remained on the east side and marched virtually unopposed to a point across the river from Albany. Crossing the Hudson at Albany would have been immensely difficult, however, for not only was the river wider there but the Americans would have concentrated their forces to oppose his crossing. Therefore he threw a bridge of bateaux across to Saratoga and on September 13 began sending his troops to the west bank. Two days later his army was safely over.

The American enemy had not been inactive while this movement took place. Gates had reached the army at Albany almost four weeks before, on August 19, and he had moved his forces northward. Gates's command had grown in this period to 6000 or 7000 men. The day before Burgoyne began to put his troops over to the west side, Gates undertook to fortify Bemis Heights, three miles north of Stillwater.

This stretch of the Hudson saw the river forced through a narrow defile by high bluffs 200 to 300 feet above its surface. Bemis Heights, around 200 feet above the water, was separated from nearby slopes by ravines cut by creeks which flowed into the Hudson. Much of the ground from the river to the slopes was covered by thick stands of oak, pine, and maple.

Gates's brilliant subordinate, Benedict Arnold, may have chosen Bemis Heights as the position for defense. Arnold and Colonel Thaddeus Kosciuszko, the Polish engineer, drew the lines of fortification, which extended from Bemis's Tavern near the river up the bluff to the top of the Heights. There a three-sided breastworks of earth and logs, each side about three-fourths of a mile in length, was put up. The south side, presumably the farthest from the advancing British, was left unprotected, though a ravine there afforded some protection. At the midpoint of each side of the breastworks the Americans dug a redoubt where they emplaced artillery. In most respects the Americans had built wisely, but they had left virtually unoccupied a high slope less than a mile to the west. Should the British drag artillery to this height they would command Bemis Heights.[31]

Burgoyne had crossed the Hudson about ten miles above Bemis Heights and spent the next two days crawling southward groping for his enemy. On that march with three loose columns, Riedesel on the left along the river, Brig. General James Hamilton in the center on the road (hardly more than wagon ruts), and Fraser on the right to

31. Ibid., 501–3.

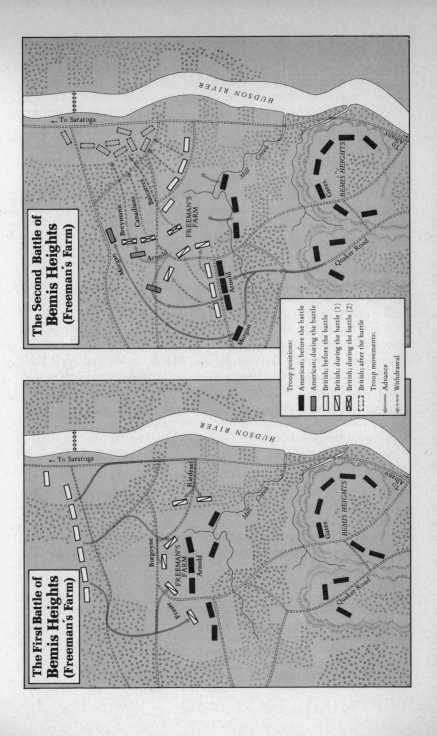

The First Battle of Bemis Heights (Freeman's Farm)

To Saratoga

HUDSON RIVER

Riedesel

Burgoyne

FREEMAN'S FARM

Arnold

Fraser

Mill Creek

BEMIS HEIGHTS

Gates

To Albany

Quaker Road

The Second Battle of Bemis Heights (Freeman's Farm)

To Saratoga

HUDSON RIVER

Breymann

Canadians

Balcarres

Morgan

Arnold

FREEMAN'S FARM

Mill Creek

Arnold

Morgan

BEMIS HEIGHTS

Gates

To Albany

Quaker Road

Troop positions:
- American; before the battle
- American; during the battle
- British; before the battle
- British; during the battle (1)
- British; during the battle (2)
- British; after the battle

Troop movements:
- Advance
- Withdrawal

the west in the woods, Burgoyne managed to cover six miles. On September 18 an American patrol roughed up a small foraging party, and Burgoyne discovered something of his enemy's dispositions. The next morning, in sunshine, he sent his three columns forward with the aim of rolling up the American left and rear. His plan called for Fraser to swing to the west, take the high ground, and then turn to the east and eventually pin the Americans on the river, where they would be chewed to pieces. The battle began at 10:00 A.M. with a cannon firing the signal to start the advance. This coordinated opening marked just about the only coordination Burgoyne's forces attained that day. The right wing under Fraser contained ten companies of light infantry and ten of grenadiers, Brunswick riflemen of company size, seven artillery pieces, a few Tories, and the battalion company of the 24th Regiment. All together they numbered around 2000 men. Hamilton led the center composed of 1100 men, four regiments, and six light fieldpieces. Generals Riedesel and Phillips, with about the same number, were on the right, with three Brunswick regiments and eight fieldpieces.[32]

When the cannon fire set these three wings in motion, the Americans were sitting behind their breastworks—Continentals on the right overlooking the river with Gates in charge, Massachusetts and New York Continentals under Brig. General Ebenezer Learned at the center, and a mixture of militia and regulars on the left under Arnold. Gates did not respond when told of the British movement toward his position. Arnold did, urging his chief to send a force out to meet the enemy so as to avoid being battered and trapped within the breastworks on the Heights. Sitting still, the Americans were vulnerable, Arnold argued; on the move in the woods, they would deprive Burgoyne of the advantage his artillery gave him. Gates remained unmoved by this argument for almost three hours, though his scouts perched high in the trees kept him informed of the flash and glitter of the advancing redcoats with their bayonets unsheathed.[33]

Around noon Gates gave way to Arnold's argument and sent Colonel Daniel Morgan and his Virginia riflemen forward on the left. Morgan, soon followed by Henry Dearborn's light infantry and then much of Arnold's force, met the British center near Freeman's Farm about a mile north of Bemis Heights. There, in a clearing about 350 yards long,

32. Ibid., 504–5; Hadden's Journal, 144–48; Bradford, ed., "Napier's Journal," MdHM, 57 (1962), 310–11.
33. Ward, II, 506–8.

the battle was fought. For most of the afternoon until early darkness the central wing of Burgoyne's army under General Hamilton's command held the northern edge of the clearing. The Americans under Arnold maintained a rough line along the southern fringe. There is no way of establishing how many times the two sides surged across the open space and into the enemy's woods. Hamilton's regulars apparently first attempted to rely on the bayonet, perhaps expecting that Morgan's men and the others would run rather than stand. But stand they did, and the long rifles cut down red-coated infantry before the heavy mass could close. Neither Arnold nor Morgan believed in static defense or in absorbing blows before delivering them. Arnold in particular loved the assault and he led his troops over the clearing into the British line. The American charge swept the British regulars back and drove artillerymen from their guns. But then the British returned under officers fully as brave as Arnold and Morgan. By late afternoon, with bodies stacked up in the clearing and the woods, British volleys began to lose their power. The troops under Hamilton had taken terrible losses, and they had probably begun the battle slightly outnumbered. The 62nd had, in particular, received extraordinarily heavy American fire, with the result that at the end of the day of its 350 men only sixty remained. British officers who had fought in Europe in the Seven Years War remarked later that they had never experienced heavier fire. Burgoyne was with them, and his bravery undoubtedly helped keep spirits up. But Fraser had not been able to enter the battle; he in fact still struggled to find his way to the high ground in the west. Nor until the center was about to collapse did Riedesel's troops force their way up the bluff from the river. Their coming prevented the disintegration of Hamilton's command, and as darkness fell it was Arnold's men, not their enemies, who fell back. The British held the field at Freeman's Farm, but they had taken casualties they could not replace. In all, 556 British regulars died or were wounded.[34]

Arnold believed that he might have completely destroyed the enemy that day had Gates acceded to his plea for reinforcements while the battle went on. Gates did not commit reinforcements, however; he, like his enemy, had not brought concentrated power to bear. Burgoyne had not because of his initial dispositions—three separate, indeed isolated, commands, groping in a maze of green woods, ravines, and steep slopes.

34. For the battle of Freeman's Farm, see *Hadden's Journal*, 164–66; Bradford, ed., "Napier's Journal," *MdHM*, 57 (1962), 315–18; Burgoyne, *State of the Expedition*, 41, 57. Ward, II, 504–12, provides a superb account.

Gates had not for reasons known only to himself. Undoubtedly what seems so clear today—that the side that successfully concentrated its forces would vanquish the other—seemed only obscure in the September sunlight. Gates may have had a clearer idea of where his enemy was than Burgoyne had, but he could not be certain that those three forces would not succeed in pinching in on Bemis Heights. A more perceptive man might have grasped the disadvantages that Burgoyne had imposed upon himself, and a bolder one surely would have poured his men into the center. If Hamilton could have been broken, Riedesel stumbling through ravines along the river's edge would have been isolated and vulnerable. As it was, both sides absorbed heavy losses, but Gates could replace his whereas Burgoyne could not.

Separated from one another by about a mile, the two armies nursed their wounded and sent out patrols which sniped at one another incessantly. Burgoyne did not yet see his situation as desperate, and two days after the battle he received a letter from Henry Clinton in New York which he read in a most unrealistic frame of mind. Clinton's letter, written on September 11, promised "a push at Montgomery in about ten days," a drive against the forts on the Hudson, Montgomery, and Fort Clinton, about forty miles above the city. Clinton considered this attack as a diversion on Burgoyne's behalf. He did not expect to reach Albany. What Burgoyne thought is not completely known, but he evidently expected much from this push, and, as he declared two years afterwards, he had no reason not to expect further cooperation from General Howe. Unfortunately for him, he had no reason to expect cooperation either.[35]

Henry Clinton proved as good as his word. Reinforced by regulars from home, he sent a large contingent of his 7000-man garrison against the forts up the Hudson River and captured them on October 4. The next day he cut through the *chevaux de frise*, boom and chain, which the Americans had placed to block passage up the Hudson. But Clinton did no more and went no farther.[36]

Burgoyne's hopes that Clinton's operations would force Gates to deplete his army in order to strengthen his rear soon collapsed. Not only did Gates hold firm on Bemis Heights, but he also received so many fresh troops, attracted by the "victory" at Freeman's Farm, that his army soon reached 11,000. Burgoyne of course received no reinforce-

35. The quotation is from Willcox, *Portrait of a General*, 177. See also Willcox, ed., *Clinton's Narrative*, 70.
36. Willcox, *Portrait of a General*, 180–81.

ments and sat in the rain watching his troops lose their spirit as his wounded suffered and died.

By early October, Burgoyne recognized how bad his situation was. He was not yet cut off from Canada, but his soldiers were in no condition to make a rapid retreat: he had many wounded and sick; his transport was short; his supplies, shorter. He decided in the midst of weakness to try to smash through his enemy. On the morning of October 7 Burgoyne sent out from Freeman's Farm a heavy force in reconnaissance to test what he thought was the American left. If weakness was found there, he intended to attack with everything he had. His generals did not enter into this plan with much conviction: Riedesel proposed withdrawal to the Batten Kill, a small stream that fed into the Hudson, and Fraser agreed; Phillips refused to give any advice. Burgoyne detested the thought of withdrawal and persisted in his plan, sending the reconnaissance in three columns supported by ten fieldpieces ranging from six pounders to light howitzers. This party crept forward for three-fourths of a mile but discovered nothing. The three columns were then realigned to form a line of about a thousand yards. There the soldiers waited.[37]

About two-thirty in the afternoon the Americans, whose knowledge of their enemy's dispositions was superior to the British, struck. Poor's brigade, New Hampshire regulars led by Enoch Poor, engaged the British left, and soon after Daniel Morgan swung wide and hit the left and found his way to the British rear. The British line began to give way, as the troops discovered Americans all around them. Burgoyne then sent his aide, Sir Francis Clarke, forward from Freeman's Farm with an order to pull the reconnoitering party back. Clarke received a bullet on the way and died before he could deliver the order.

The battle soon became Benedict Arnold's. That worthy, eager and brave, had no command, had in fact been relieved by Gates several days before and invited to take himself away. Gates despised him, and he had not even mentioned Arnold in his dispatch to Congress telling of the battle of September 19. Arnold understandably did not admire Gates; he had not taken the hint to clear out but had waited around even though he had no command. Once the bullets began to fly, Arnold decided to insert himself into the battle. He did so brilliantly, riding up and down the line and against the enemy's center and right. The troops loved Arnold and followed him in a series of wild assaults. Arnold

37. Ward, II, 525–26.

in battle was more than a little mad, but it was a derangement that led to success. The British line crumbled, then disintegrated; Arnold did not stop to savor success but hit the main entrenchments with the same wild enthusiasm. Before the end of the day, his soldiers occupied a portion of the enemy's works on the extreme right, on the northern edge of Freeman's Farm. Late in the struggle Arnold, wounded, was carried off the field, and something went out of the American attack with him. But the Americans controlled the field, and Burgoyne was left in a dreadful position.[38]

That night and the next Burgoyne withdrew his army, tired, beaten, and dispirited. The sick and wounded, numbering some three hundred, were left behind in a field hospital. On October 9, the British reached the heights of Saratoga; Gates followed but did not succeed in cutting Burgoyne off until October 12. Burgoyne had delayed too long and, unable to cross the river, had no choice but to ask for terms. Discussions were held; the two leaders met on October 16, and the next day the British regulars marched out and laid down their arms. The surrender under the terms of the "Convention," the agreement each side accepted, provided that the army was to return to England through Boston. Congress, however, disregarded this agreement, fearing that the British would send these men back against America once more. The "Convention Army" eventually was marched to Virginia, where it sat out the war. Altogether some 5800 officers and men with twenty-seven field pieces and 5000 small arms, ammunition, and various sorts of supplies were captured.[39]

IV

At the time Ticonderoga fell and Burgoyne seemed launched on a campaign of glory, a puzzled George Washington sat watching William Howe in New York City apparently preparing for action. Ships crowded the harbor but Howe delayed sending his troops aboard until July 8, and then, when he had loaded some 18,000, he kept ships and troops sitting idle for the next two weeks. The presumption in Washington's headquarters was that the ships would soon sail up the Hudson to support Burgoyne. But when on July 24 they cleared Sandy Hook and disappeared on the Atlantic, most of Washington's colleagues predicted that Philadelphia was their destination. Washington had "strong doubts"—Howe had given him unpleasant surprises before—and apparently half expected Howe to return or to turn up in some unexpected place. The ships

38. *Ibid.*, 526–31; Bradford, ed., "Napier's Journal," *MdHM*, 57 (1962), 321–22.
39. Ward, II, 533–42.

did not return, and on July 31 reports of their appearance off the Delaware Capes reached Washington. Then Howe surprised everyone by once more disappearing on the Atlantic. He had been warned against going up the Delaware, which he was told was defended by heavy fortifications. Speculation in Washington's headquarters and in Congress, which had also regarded Howe's movements suspiciously, now centered on Charleston, South Carolina. "The most general suspicion now is," John Adams wrote his beloved Abigail, "that Howe has gone to Charleston S.C. But it is a wild Supposition. It may be right however: for Howe is a wild General." Washington did not share the expectation that Howe would attack in the south and of course he was right. Early in August eager observers sighted the British convoy entering Chesapeake Bay, and on August 25, Howe began putting his troops ashore on the west side of the Elk River in Maryland. Two days later they had marched to Head of Elk where they rested until the first week in September. Rest was necessary: they had lived in crowded quarters for almost two months, and they had spent half that time at sea in weather that was hotter than most Americans living along the coast could remember.[40]

Washington put his army on the march almost immediately after learning of Howe's whereabouts. Aware of the importance of civilian morale, he marched his soldiers through Philadelphia on the way south. To the unpracticed eye, these troops appeared both formidable and yet, as John Adams said, they did not have "quite the Air of Soldiers. They dont step exactly in Time. They dont hold up their Heads, quite erect, nor turn out their Toes, so exactly as they ought. They dont all of them cock their Hats—and such as do, dont all wear them the same Way."[41] As trivial as these assessments appear, they marked one important flaw in the American army: a lack of hard discipline which assured steady performance in combat. Still, these half-soldiers fought well in the next few weeks though their leaders sometimes failed them.

Howe's soldiers were long accustomed to such discipline, but they sometimes got out of hand when they were among civilians, especially the contemptible American civilians. On the way up the Chesapeake they had encountered friendly Americans who rowed out to the ships with fruit, fowl, and milk for sale. These Marylanders from the eastern shore seemed fearless, unaware apparently that the army sometimes simply took what it wanted. The civilians in southern Pennsylvania, in con-

40. *GW Writings*, IX, 1–6, 9, 21 ("strong doubts"); L. H. Butterfield, ed., *Adams Family Correspondence* (2 vols. to date, Cambridge, Mass., 1963–   ), II, 321 (on the "wild General"). Adams reports on the weather, *ibid.*, 315.

41. Butterfield, ed., *Adams Family Corr.*, II, 328.

trast, felt fear and fled, abandoning houses and belongings, cattle, horses, sheep, and grain in the fields. Howe's soldiers dined well in early September; fresh meat appeared in the field mess twice a week, and fruit and vegetables were plentiful. The soldiers enjoyed these days, and some also found the vacant houses irresistible and plundered. Howe realized that this behavior could only erode discipline so vital in battle, and he realized too its effects on American sympathies. He responded with hangings and whippings but not before the news spread over the state and contributed to further alienation and to improved recruiting by the American army.[42]

That army strengthened by militia now moved to block the British. After the march through Philadelphia, Washington established temporary headquarters at Wilmington. He ordered several detachments forward to harass the advancing British and Germans; "hanging on" the enemy, the phrase usually employed to describe these harrying attacks, indicates something of their method. Maintaining contact kept Washington informed of the location of his foe, and the small units engaged in "hanging on" tormented enemy pickets and patrols, killing them from ambush, annoying them to the point of fury and eventually of fatigue. Howe moved on, of course, despite the irritations of his troops, and on September 10 he discovered that Washington had decided to stop and fight.[43]

Washington strung his army out on the east side of Brandywine Creek, which cut through wooded slopes. The stream itself was an obstacle and could be crossed only at fords. Greene held the center of the American position at Chad's Ford with Anthony Wayne. John Armstrong, with militia from Pennsylvania, occupied the ground to the left, and Sullivan with Stirling and Stephen covered the right. These dispositions made considerable sense: they provided strength at the center where the main road to Philadelphia ran, and they allowed concentration of forces. But they left uncovered Trimble's Ford on the west branch of the Brandywine and Jeffries Ford on the east. The right flank hung open, and behind it a hill which dominated the right and the rear sat unoccupied.[44]

The "wild general," William Howe, whose wildness had a predictable

42. Bernhard A. Uhlendorf, trans., *Revolution in America: Confidential Letters and Journals 1776–1784 of Adjutant General Major Baurmeister of the Hessian Forces* (New Brunswick, N.J., 1957), 91–96; Ward, I, 336–37.
43. *GW Writings*, IX, 140–42, 164, 198.
44. Freeman, *GW*, IV, 469–72; Ward, I, 342.

character, sent Knyphausen's Germans up against Chad's Ford to fix Washington's attention, and then from Welch's Tavern and Kennett Square he set out at 4:00 A.M. by back roads for Trimble's and Jeffries Fords. Howe had shown this design before, most recently on Long Island, and he had no reason to suppose that it would fail him now. At ten in the morning Knyphausen's guns spoke in thunderous tone as a prelude, as far as Washington could tell, to an assault across Chad's by the infantry. The American artillery replied; the main struggle seemed to be taking shape at the center. Howe and his colleague Cornwallis, meanwhile, were in the process of turning the American flank. By 2:30 in the afternoon they had their troops over the fords and behind Osborne's Hill. Washington was warned of this move against the end of his unanchored line as early as 9:00 A.M. but failed to heed the warning. When the British appeared on Osborne's Hill, no one could deny that the Americans had been outflanked once again. Sullivan acted rapidly, moving Stephen and Stirling on right angles to the creek and into a position opposite Howe and Cornwallis.

Those two seemed in no hurry. Rather, they took their time, shifting their columns into two long lines, barely deigning to notice their enemy's mad scramble to get into position. Once the British were ready, they did nothing but stand in the sunshine, their bayonets sending off flashes when they caught the light. Perhaps they hoped to unnerve the Americans; if so, they failed, but they did impress them. At four o'clock in the afternoon Howe set them in motion—a march down the hill, not fancy, but stepping out smartly to the tune of the "British Grenadier" played by an accompanying band. The troops of Sullivan, Stirling, and Stephen did not panic, but in their haste to realign themselves they had left a gap of several hundred yards in their lines. Stephen seems to have been mainly responsible for not hooking his left flank to Stirling's right; in any case, the hole there invited British penetration and the British accepted the invitation. Just as the light infantry and the grenadiers began pouring through and rolling up the American left, Nathanael Greene's brigade arrived. The brigade had been dispatched by Washington when he learned of Howe's appearance on his right. Greene's men came on a run that covered four miles in about forty-five minutes.

What had begun as a classic eighteenth-century engagement with the British regulars advancing in a dense line, bayonets at the ready, and sent off with the flourishes of the "British Grenadier" soon degenerated into a confusing and nasty fight. Smoke from cannon and muskets contributed to the confusion by obscuring the location of friend and foe. Maintaining the proper interval between units proved difficult too, as the rough terrain broke up formations. A British officer who attempted to recall his impressions of the action resorted to wit which conceded his inability to make sense out of what he had experienced:

> Describe the battle. 'Twas not like those of Covent Garden or Drury Lane. Thou hast seen Le Brun's paintings and the tapestry perhaps at Blenheim. Are these natural resemblances? Pshaw! quoth the captain, *en un mot.* There was a most infernal fire of cannon and musquetry. Most incessant shouting, "Incline to the right! Incline to the left! Halt! Charge!" etc. The balls plowing up the ground. The Trees crackling over one's head. The branches riven by the artillery. The leaves falling as in autumn by the grapeshot.[45]

The British units retained their integrity as military organizations; the same cannot be said for all the American regiments once they began their retreat. They found the ground as difficult to traverse as the British did, and when the assault brought the British infantry into close quarters they tended to give way—as individuals rather than as military units. Sergeant Major John Hawkins of Congress's Own Regiment discarded his knapsack when he was about to be "grabbed by one of the ill-looking Highlanders, a number of whom were firing and advancing very brisk towards our rear." And in his flight in the confusion and the smoke, he lost sight of his regiment and completed his retreat with troops from North Carolina.[46]

While the American right fought to hold its position, the center received an attack from across the stream by Knyphausen. The combined force of British and Germans at Chad's Ford had waited until they heard the sounds of the battle upstream. Then they plunged forward into the Brandywine and for a few minutes at least paid a frightful price. Anthony Wayne's and William Maxwell's troops "fought stubbornly," a German officer reported, sending grapeshot and musket balls over the water which was soon "much stained with blood" before the attackers captured the American guns and turned them on their enemy.[47]

By darkness the battle had ended on both "fronts." Washington's troops made their way to Chester, and Howe's pulled up short on the

45. For the battle of Brandywine, see Ward, I, 342–54; Freeman, *GW*, IV, 473–89; *GW Writings*, IX, 206–8. The British officer's comments are from *PMHB*, 29 (1905), 368.
46. Sheer and Rankin, *Rebels and Redcoats*, 272.
47. Uhlendorf, trans., *Revolution in America*, iii; Sheer and Rankin, *Rebels and Redcoats*, 270.

battlefield. The British had won a splendid victory, but like so many victories during the war it was not decisive. Washington's army had retreated in disarray but it was intact. And more important, it remained between Howe and Philadelphia.

V

Between Howe and Philadelphia was exactly where Washington wished to stay. Despite the mauling his forces had received along the Brandywine, he retained his confidence that he could stop Howe. The American troops also responded well to the defeat, though there were the usual desertions. To replace his losses Washington ordered 2500 Continentals down from Peekskill and appealed to the states for militia. Within two weeks he had received 900 Continentals and around 2200 militia from Maryland and New Jersey.[48]

Before these men arrived, the main army marched and counter-marched, always seeking to block the British from Philadelphia. Several small-scale battles marked this maneuvering; one on September 16 at Warren Tavern, between Lancaster and Philadelphia, might have developed into a general engagement had heavy rain not fallen. The rain ruined the cartridge boxes and the gunpowder carried by the American infantry. With his troops disarmed, Washington pulled back, and Howe showed no disposition to force an action. Five days later at Paoli, about two miles southeast of Warren Tavern, Major General James Grey surprised Anthony Wayne's force, which Washington had left behind to "hang on" Howe. At about one o'clock in the morning Grey led his troops into an American camp carelessly asleep. On Grey's order the British had removed the flints from their muskets—he was taking no chances that an overeager private might pull a trigger—and they used their bayonets with a cruel efficiency. Many of the sleepers never left their blankets, and when the bloody business was over 300 had been killed and wounded and still another hundred captured. Only eight of the British died. Wayne escaped, carrying with him a renewed respect for "No-Flint Grey" and the value of the bayonet.[49]

The "Paoli Massacre" shook Washington, who was maneuvering cautiously to avoid being trapped or outflanked once more. Howe took advantage of this concern on September 22 when he lured Washington's army ten miles up the Schuylkill and then crossed at Fatland Ford

48. Freeman, GW, IV, 490. Estimates of American casualties at Brandywine: 200 killed, 500 wounded, 400 captured (Peckham, Toll, 40); British losses: 90 killed, 448 wounded, and 6 missing.

49. Ward, I, 355–59; Freeman, GW, IV, 494–95.

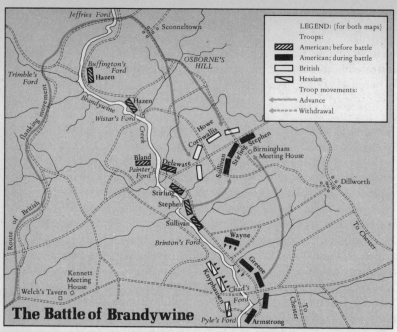

The Battle of Brandywine

Legend (for both maps):

Troops:
- American; before battle
- American; during battle
- British
- Hessian

Troop movements:
- Advance
- Withdrawal

Jeffries Ford
Sconneltown
Osborne's Hill
Trimble's Ford
Buffington's Ford — Hazen
Hazen
Wistar's Ford
Brandywine Creek
flanking movement
Howe
Cornwallis
Stirling Stephen
Birmingham Meeting House
Sullivan
Bland
Painter's Ford
Delaware
Dillworth
Stirling
Stephen
Sullivan
To Chester
Brinton's Ford
Wayne
Route of British
Greene
Kennett Meeting House
Knyphausen
To Chester
Welch's Tavern
Chad's Ford
Pyle's Ford
Armstrong

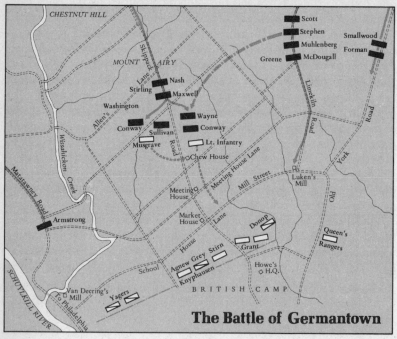

The Battle of Germantown

Chestnut Hill
Mount Airy
Skippack Lane
Scott
Stephen
Muhlenberg
McDougall
Greene
Smallwood
Forman
Limekiln Road
York Road
Nash
Stirling
Maxwell
Washington
Allen's Lane
Wissahickon Creek
Wayne
Conway
Conway
Sullivan
Musgrave
Lt. Infantry
Chew House
Meeting House Lane
Mill Street
Luken's Mill
Matsawney Road
Meeting House
Market House
Donop
Queen's Rangers
Armstrong
House Lane
Grant
School House Lane
Agnew Grey Stirn
Knyphausen
Howe's H.Q.
Van Deering's Mill
Yagers
BRITISH CAMP
Schuylkill River
to Philadelphia

from the west and slipped into Philadelphia on September 26. A year earlier the loss of the city might have hurt American morale severely. Now it did not, in part because the American army remained whole and in part because reassuring news from the north, where Burgoyne's army was gradually disintegrating, had seeped down to the middle Atlantic states.[50]

With Howe ensconced in Philadelphia, Washington made camp along Skippack Creek twenty-five miles to the west. He had no intention of sitting quietly, however. The old desire for action worked within him, drawing strength from his conviction that his troops, young and inexperienced as they generally were, would fight well given half a chance. By early October that chance had appeared. Howe had not found life in Philadelphia full of comfort and ease. He held the city but not the Delaware River, which provided an important line of access to it. The American forts on the river blocked all traffic and denied British ships the opportunity to bring in supplies and reinforcements. In his isolated circumstances Howe feared to spread all his troops throughout Philadelphia in inns and houses and had bivouacked around nine thousand at Germantown on the east side of the Schuylkill River five miles to the north. Another three thousand had been sent to protect the transport of supplies from Elktown, which of course involved a slow move over land. Four battalions remained in Philadelphia and two more had marched off to attack Billingsport twelve miles below the city on the Delaware. Howe was now spread all over the map.[51]

When Washington learned of the scattered condition of the enemy, he decided to attack the largest concentration at Germantown. His troops probably needed no persuasion to fight, but Washington felt compelled once more to review the reasons why they should. The preamble to his general order to the army conveyed something of his own eagerness and, what is probably more important, just how far his understanding of the Revolution and of his army had proceeded. He now recognized that a professional pride existed at least in several of his regiments, and he appealed to it by reminding them that far to the north their comrades had delivered a heavy blow to Burgoyne at Freeman's Farm. He coupled this reminder of the northern success to invocation of the cause of America. "This army, the main American Army, will certainly not suffer itself to be outdone by their northern Brethren; they will never endure such disgrace; but with an ambition becoming freemen,

50. Freeman, *GW*, IV, 498–99.
51. Ward, I, 360–61.

contending in the most righteous cause rival the heroic spirit which swelled their bosoms, and which, so nobly exerted has procured them deathless renown. Covet! my Countrymen, and fellow soldiers! Covet! a share of the glory due to heroic deeds! Let it never be said, that in a day of action, you turned your backs on the foe; let the enemy no longer triumph."[52]

These appeals of pride, to heroism, to honor had been made before, but their linkage to a cause which was "righteous" as well as glorious and which was shared by the "Country" marked a subtle departure, a broadening understanding. Washington ended by bringing these grand concepts into conjunction with the immediate and personal interests of his troops. The enemy, he reminded them, "brand you with ignominious epithets. Will you patiently endure that reproach? Will you suffer the wounds given to your Country to go unavenged?" These questions concerned his soldiers' families, especially since a revolution that failed would undoubtedly be regarded as treason: "Will you resign your parents, wives, children and friends to be the wretched vassals of a proud, insulting foe? And your own necks to the halter?"[53]

Perhaps only in a revolutionary war do soldiers go into battle with a conception of a "righteous cause" competing with an image of their necks in a halter. These men could have no doubts about what they were fighting for, though they may have blurred some of the fine distinctions in republican ideology. What they had to understand was that their fight was for themselves, not for an overmighty lord and master.

The first task at Germantown was to surprise the British. Washington took care to give Howe no warning by a leisurely march to the village. Rather, he broke his camp which was twenty miles to the west and, by a forced march during the afternoon and night of October 3, got into position. At 2:00 A.M. on the next day he stopped two miles away from the British pickets.[54]

Germantown, five miles northwest of Philadelphia, extended two miles on both sides of Skippack Road, which ran between Philadelphia and Reading. All of the British there were east of the Schuylkill, as indeed was most of the town. Most of their camp lay at the south end of town, though of course they had placed pickets along its northern edge. Four roads which led into Germantown seemed to make an attack on a broad front possible, and Washington decided that his army should

52. GW Writings, IX, 305–6.
53. Ibid., IX, 306.
54. Freeman, GW, IV, 505.

converge on Howe's camp in overwhelming strength. Accordingly, he drew up a plan which provided that four prongs of the American army would push into Howe simultaneously at 5:00 A.M. on October 4. Major John Armstrong and his Pennsylvania militia would advance down the Manatawny Road on the American right and behind the British left. Sullivan with his own and Wayne's reinforced brigade would deliver the main blow down the Skippack Road, which cut the town in two; Greene would lead his force, including Stephen's division and Alexander McDougall's brigade, along Limekiln Road to the northeast of Skippack; and a mile farther to the left Smallwood with Maryland and New Jersey militia would march down the old York Road and if all went well cut into the British right and into the rear of their main encampments.[55]

On the map the plan looked brilliant, and it very nearly worked on the ground. Once the American troops positioned themselves at 2:00 A.M. in the darkness of October 4, they waited quietly. Two hours later they moved forward within a few hundred yards of the outposts, and around five o'clock in early light they struck. Washington's order called for an assault by "bayonets without firing" along all four roads.[56] Sullivan's force, which Washington rode with, hit first at Mount Airy and drove over the pickets. There was firing, apparently from both sides—American fire discipline was almost never tight—and the British in confusion gave ground. A heavy fog which made seeing ahead more than fifty yards impossible created some of the confusion, especially about the size of the attacking force. Howe rode up through the fog to scout the ground for himself and immediately berated his light infantry for yielding. "Form! Form!" he called, and added that he was ashamed of his soldiers for running before only a scouting party.[57] The scouting party turned out to be Sullivan's infantry accompanied by light artillery, which soon disabused Howe of the notion that only a probe was under way. The fog also confused Sullivan's troops, who had trouble maintaining contact with one another. And within the first hour they experienced greater confusion when they ran into a strong point on Skippack Road. This point was the "Chew House," an old and large house constructed of heavy stone which Colonel Thomas Musgrave of the 40th Regiment occupied with six companies. After failing to take it, Sullivan sent his men on, but the delay had given the British time to form.

55. *Ibid.*, 502–3; Ward, I, 362–65. For Washington's general orders, Oct. 3, 1777, on dispositions of troops, see *GW Writings*, IX, 308.
56. *GW Writings*, IX, 308.
57. Ward, I, 365.

Even this delay might not have proved detrimental to the attack had Wayne, leading Sullivan's left, not been fired upon by Stephen coming in on Greene's right. Greene had attacked about forty-five minutes after the designated hour because he had to move two miles farther than Sullivan in order to reach his position of assault. This delay has often been blamed for the confusion at the center and ultimately for the loss of the battle. Of itself Greene's delay was probably not important and may indeed, had fog not covered the ground, been desirable. For when Sullivan struck, the British sent their troops forward to meet him. Greene might have been able to cut behind them had he been able to see. In the fog, however, Sullivan's left remained uncovered for an hour, and Wayne moved to secure this flank. Stephen, uncertain as to where he was to link his flank with Wayne's drove behind him and then, his vision obscured by the fog, opened fire. Wayne returned fire, and before the two groups discovered their mistakes, casualties mounted and the left-center was thrown into disorder. Whether through good luck or shrewd timing, Howe then delivered a counterattack with three regiments. A major part of this attack hit Sullivan's left and poured through almost unopposed. This drive blunted the American effort, and within minutes the impetus in the battle had swung to Howe. The Americans retreated despite Washington's efforts to reform the retreating troops. Thomas Paine, who had accompanied Washington, later called this retreat "extraordinary, nobody hurried themselves." They were much too tired to hurry and resembled nothing so much as a slow herd in motion. Greene too pulled back, for Sullivan's collapse had left him terribly exposed. One of his regiments, the 9th Virginian, which had taken around a hundred prisoners was now trapped itself and surrendered, four hundred strong. On the American right, Armstrong survived intact— he had not sent his force into battle. And on the far left Smallwood arrived much too late to exert pressure on the rear of the British, and retired almost as soon as he arrived. By late evening Washington's bedraggled army had pulled back some twenty miles to the west to Pennybacker's Mill.[58]

The failures of the day undoubtedly arose in part from a plan which was much too complicated to fulfill. The plan called for coordinated attacks by four widely separated forces. Their failures of coordination are often cited as reason for the defeat. Washington blamed the fog for a lack of coordination, but the mounted messengers and the flankers

58. Washington's account of the battle of Germantown is in *GW Writings*, IX, 308–12, 320, 327–31. See also Ward, I, 365–71; Freeman, *GW*, IV, 504–19.

each column was supposed to send out might have kept the brigades in touch with one another even through the fog. There is a possibility too that the fog enabled the attack to get off to a good beginning, as the British could not determine just who or what they faced. Moreover, American troops usually fought at their best from cover, and the fog afforded cover of sorts. What might have occurred in bright sunshine with clear visibility is anyone's guess. The British explained their recovery and victory on rather different grounds; discipline and the counterattack they made won the battle as far as they were concerned. Still, they and foreign observers conceded that the battle that had been won was almost lost. The Americans again had taken serious losses, but they had fought gallantly, as Washington remarked. And, as always, the British too had fought bravely. Perhaps Washington's army derived most from the battle: knowledge that they could carry the attack to a fine professional army and carry it well. They lost the battle, to be sure, and for reasons which we will never completely understand, given the possibilities in this engagement and given the confusions on both sides. But even in defeat they had absorbed another valuable lesson.[59]

59. Peckham, *Toll*, 42, estimates that American casualties were 152 killed, 500 wounded; 438 were captured. Total British casualties were about 550.

17

The Revolution Becomes
a European War

Howe's triumph at Germantown and his seizure of Philadelphia gave satisfaction to the British government but these events did not lift the depression that had set in when information about Burgoyne's capture arrived. The term inevitably attached to that event was "disaster." Just how disastrous the loss of Burgoyne's army was could not be known immediately, and for several months there was hope in the cabinet that its worst consequence could be avoided. What the cabinet feared was the entrance of France into the war on the side of the American colonies. French action against Britain would transform a rebellion within the empire into a worldwide conflict whose spread would necessarily result in the dispersion of British forces—and almost inevitably the establishment of American independence.

Since 1763 the French had husbanded their outrage and dreamed of revenge against the British for the defeat they suffered in the Seven Years War. Not surprisingly, the upheavals in the British colonies alerted the French government to the possibility of splintering the British empire. Choiseul, the foreign minister of Louis XV, recognizing that much of Britain's strength lay in her colonies and trade with them, watched the rising American disaffection with hope that war would occur. Choiseul, however, also had other problems to think about, for example, how he was going to rebuild French naval and military power. This problem existed because of another—a treasury depleted by the Seven Years War. The agents he sent to America in the 1760s sent back opinions that rebellion would occur, but not immediately, an assessment Choiseul accepted without question.[1]

1. Samuel Flagg Bemis, *The Diplomacy of the American Revolution* (1935; reprint ed., Bloomington, Ind., 1957), 16–17.

Of those who followed Choiseul in the French foreign office, none grasped the possibilities inherent in Anglo-American strife more clearly than Charles Gravier de Vergennes. Vergennes, who had assumed office under the young Louis XVI, shared Choiseul's hope of exploiting the problems of Britain overseas. There were limits to this hope. The yearning to reclaim the French possessions on the North American continent had died, for example. Still, Vergennes did believe that France might reclaim the fisheries off North America and that the French colonies in the West Indies might be retained. And Vergennes never lost sight of his major purpose: to reduce British power wherever possible and thereby re-establish the primacy of France in Europe. Vergennes did not mean to proceed alone against England. He intended to preserve the "family compact" with Spain as the basis of a strong position and to support the Austrian alliance as a means of forestalling England's use of Prussia against France. As for war, Vergennes believed that no war with England should be undertaken unless success seemed likely.[2]

When the strains of the 1770s in the colonies followed those of the 1760s, Vergennes reacted cautiously. The British government had shown its ability to ride out storms in colonial seas, and he did not wish to be sucked into a hurricane that would throw both Britain and America against France. There was an especially dire potential in such a situation—that premature action by France would bring the inveterate enemy, Chatham, back into power at the head of a united force. The opportunity of capturing the French West Indies might well produce such a union. By late 1775, with the outbreak of war, this possibility seemed remote and Vergennes's resolve stiffened, and he dismissed as unworthy of consideration the idea of offering neutrality in the struggle in return for an English guarantee of the French islands. Instead he sent a secret agent, Julien Achard de Bonvouloir, to America in the late summer of 1775 with instructions to observe and to offer reassurance to rebels.

Another agent with varied talents offered himself about this time. He was Caron de Beaumarchais, a dramatist (who wrote *The Marriage of Figaro*), adventurer, and a man who possibly loved intrigue more than he hated England. Dramatists require imagination, and Beaumarchais allowed his to carry him into extravagant predictions of an English collapse in the summer of the year. He was in London then avidly gobbling up gossip and rumor and believing, for the time at least, the most absurd stories of radical strength and governmental weakness. Ver-

2. *Ibid.*, 17–22, for this paragraph and the next two.

gennes may have disabused Beaumarchais of these delusions. In any case, since, dramatics aside, Beaumarchais could be useful, Vergennes proceeded to make use of him—indeed, he put Beaumarchais on the payroll of the French secret service and, after an interview in Paris, sent him back to London with instructions to listen carefully and report accurately.

In London once more, Beaumarchais met an American agent, Arthur Lee, brother of Richard Henry Lee of Virginia, a man well suited in several respects to act his new part. Although Lee was often irascible and suspicious, he was also shrewd. He had remained in London as the agent of Massachusetts after fighting began in America, and now he had a new master, the Continental Congress.

Congress had begun to look abroad for support early in 1775, in part because one of its members, Benjamin Franklin, had seen the need. But because reconciliation with Britain remained the heart's desire of many of its members even after the battles of Lexington and Concord, even in fact after Bunker Hill, Congress hesitated to deal with foreign powers. Several members had proposed opening American trade to Europe, an act equivalent to declaring independence and therefore repugnant to many in 1775. The king's declaration in August that the colonies were in a state of rebellion had added supporters to this proposal. Still Congress moved slowly and prudently.[3]

On November 29, 1775, Congress appointed a secret committee of correspondence "for the sole purpose of corresponding with our friends in Great Britain, Ireland, and other parts of the world." Franklin was named to this group along with Benjamin Harrison of Virginia, Thomas Jefferson, John Dickinson, John Jay, and, a few months later, Robert Morris. The committee wasted no time in instructing Arthur Lee to find out how European powers regarded the American rebellion. What the committee had uppermost in mind, of course, was the attitude of France. All this was done with considerable reservations—a Protestant Congress representing Protestant states retained ancient animosities toward Catholics and Catholic states. (And on the other side, European monarchs could not be expected to fancy rebellion against one of their own kind.)[4]

Throughout the winter of 1776 Beaumarchais sent strong arguments

3. Carl Van Doren, *Benjamin Franklin* (New York, 1938), 529–40. See above, Chap. 14.
4. Francis Wharton, ed., *The Revolutionary Diplomatic Correspondence of the United States* (6 vols., Washington, D.C., 1889), II, 61–64.

for intervention on behalf of the colonies against England. One of his carefully calculated warnings held that if France hesitated, the Americans would eventually have to reconcile with Britain. Vergennes sounded the same theme with more subtlety and with shrewd reminders of where French interests lay. By spring, Louis's resistance and that of most of his ministers had weakened, and secret aid to America was approved. Only Turgot, the great controller-general of finance opposed, insisting that American independence would occur in time whatever France did and that an independent America would contribute more to English commercial prosperity than the colonies had. By May 2, 1776, Louis had persuaded himself to disregard these predictions, and he authorized aid of one million livres for munitions for the colonies. Turgot resigned ten days later.[5]

The decision to provide assistance was taken in secret and covered by reassurances of friendship to Britain. And at the same time Vergennes pushed forward plans to add to French naval and military strength. The supplying of munitions, he knew, could not be done without Britain's knowledge, and war would likely result. There were, however, compelling reasons to mask the aid. Britain would protest, even if the aid were concealed, but it would not immediately feel forced to fight over it. Face-saving fiction is often more acceptable than fact in foreign relations. The fiction in this case was that a private group, Roderigue Hortalez and Company, was providing the assistance. Beaumarchais himself was the bogus company. He and a number of colleagues organized the disbursement of monies for guns, ammunition, and other military supplies. A second American agent, Silas Deane of Connecticut, who had arrived in Paris in July, served as the American representative of Congress and worked closely with Beaumarchais—too closely, according to Arthur Lee. The aid which the French government may have regarded as loans was soon confused in Deane's accounts with gifts. And both Deane and Beaumarchais while expediting the purchase of supplies, found opportunities to divert some monies into their own pockets.[6]

Aid in the form of munitions and money was one thing, but as fighting continued thoughtful Americans began to consider the possibility of drawing France and Spain, Britain's traditional enemies, into the war. They did not expect these nations to join the fight out of admiration

---

5. Bemis, *Diplomacy*, 23-28.
6. *Ibid.*, 34-37; Julian P. Boyd, "Silas Deane: Death by a Kindly Teacher of Treason?" *WMQ*, 3d Ser., 16 (1959), 165-87, 319-42.

for America and American principles. They did expect, however, that France and Spain would regard favorably any opportunity to settle old scores and more importantly to redress the balance of power which had shifted in Britain's favor a dozen years before. There were dangers in appealing for too much from these old enemies: they might come into the war and, if they won, simply insert themselves into America as the new masters of the Americans.

Benjamin Franklin had reflected on this possibility and on how European states might be used by the colonies long before fighting began. Conflict over Parliament's authority had stimulated him to examine the tactics available to colonies adrift in a world of rapacious states. A lack of power, he had concluded in 1770, did not necessarily imply weakness, for big states, at the mercy of their own desires and interests, might well act in ways protective of the small. Big states seemed more interested in damaging one another than in exploiting faraway colonies in America in any case.[7]

Franklin, John Adams, Thomas Paine, and other close observers of the European scene were, of course, correct in their belief that America might draw France and Spain into the war against Britain. But they underestimated the difficulty of the task. And until late in 1776 they underestimated what France and Spain would expect in return.

Their calculations began with the fighting. With the war under way the thought of appealing for foreign aid came naturally. In the first six months of the secret committee's existence it concentrated on securing arms and money for the army. Much more than that would have been tantamount to declaring independence, and most in Congress were to resist that act until the last moment. Thus in February of 1776, when George Wythe, a delegate from Virginia, proposed that Congress study the right to enter alliances—a right Wythe seems to have believed Congress possessed—someone responded that doing so virtually amounted to proclaiming independence. Wythe's proposal was then quietly sent off to committee, where it was discussed but not answered.[8]

Independence freed thought, although it did not entirely end the

7. For the development of Franklin's ideas, see *BF Papers*, XVI, 276–326 ("Marginalia in *Good Humour*, an Anonymous Pamphlet"), and XVII, 317–400 ("Marginalia in *An Inquiry*, an Anonymous Pamphlet"), especially 341, where Franklin writes, "The smallest States may have great Allies. And the mutual Jealousies of Great Nations contribute to their Security."

8. Butterfield et al., eds., *Diary of John Adams*, II, 229–30 (Notes of Debates in the Continental Congress); *LMCC*, I, 350–51.

confusion over just what sort of arrangements might be made with Britain's enemies. Not surprisingly, Congress received a good deal of advice on how to proceed. Much of it played on the theme of the importance of American commerce to Europe, a theme that in turn rested on the proposition that commerce should furnish the essential connection between the Old World and the New. At this time, and for a long time afterward, American statesmen held that trade should be free lest America be reduced to dependence upon a single trading nation in Europe. The long experience of such a dependence understandably was prominent in American minds. As for why European nations should welcome such arrangements, there was economic gain to consider: America bought and sold much. Eagerness to trade would exist, Thomas Paine remarked sardonically, so long as "eating is the custom in Europe."[9]

John Adams did not agree with Paine on many things, but he shared the conviction of Paine and others that for the young republic commercial policy should stand in stead of foreign policy. It was to Adams that Congress turned to draft a "model treaty" which would define the basis of America's relations with Europe—and more immediately with France in the expectation that France might enter the war. Adams pondered the matter in spring 1776 not long before independence. His notes show that he favored a most cautious policy, one that assumed that France attributed immense value to American trade and would apparently welcome a chance to cut down her chief rival in Europe. "Is assistance attainable from F[rance]?" Adams asked himself. "What connection may we safely form with her?" The answer: "1st No Political Connection. Submit to none of her Authority—receive no Governors, or officers from her. 2d No military Connection. Receive no Troops from her. 3d Only a Commercial Connection, i.e. make a Treaty, to receive her Ships into our Ports. Let her engage to receive our Ships into her Ports—furnish Us with Arms, Cannon, Salt Petre, powder, Duck, Steel." Under these conditions no "alliance," meaning a political union, would be made with France and Spain. Yet Richard Henry Lee had proposed alliances with foreign states when he made the motion for independence in June. Lee seems not to have intended a firm political connection with obligations and responsibilities, and surely not military obligations. "Alliance" had a rather elastic meaning in the eighteenth century and might be regarded as virtually synonymous with commercial treaty. In any case, Adams, and the "model treaty" that Congress adopted in September,

9. Paine's comment was made in *Common Sense*.

offered little to any foreign state that would come to America's aid. The eighth article of the model treaty recognized that any formal arrangement might bring Britain into war with France. In such case the United States promised not to aid Britain in the war, a "commitment" that reveals as clearly as any statement just how little the Congress was prepared to offer in return for French assistance.[10]

To be sure, in the next year Congress gave up this restricted conception of foreign policy. Military defeat, first on Long Island and then up the Hudson and in New Jersey, forced it to compromise these enlightened principles. The first major concession to new realities came in revised instructions at the end of 1776 to the American commissioners who were now empowered to offer France the British West Indies if France would enter the war. This change may have seemed more fundamental than it actually was. The Congress, in placing so much reliance on commerce as a force in foreign relations, did so convinced that power accompanied trade. The Congress admired political power as much as any European foreign ministry, but it did not believe that traditional arrangements were necessary to obtain it. The realities of war brought a change in perception.[11]

The commission sent to Europe seems to have shared the conviction of Congress that Europe's interest in American trade could be exploited. They knew, however, that the chance to injure Britain appealed more and that this opportunity provided the strongest card in an otherwise weak American hand.

The men Congress hoped would represent it to the French government included Thomas Jefferson and Benjamin Franklin. Jefferson refused the appointment; his wife was sick and he did not wish to leave her. Franklin accepted and so did Silas Deane, who was, of course, already

10. Butterfield et al., eds., *Diary of John Adams*, II, 236 ("Notes on Relations with France, March–April 1776"); Felix Gilbert, *To the Farewell Address: Ideas of Early American Foreign Policy* (Princeton, N.J., 1961), chap. 3, especially 44–54, and Gilbert's "The New Diplomacy of the Eighteenth Century," *World Politics*, 4 (1951), 1–38. For an important correction to Gilbert, see James H. Hutson, "Early American Diplomacy: A Reappraisal," in Lawrence S. Kaplan, ed., *The American Revolution and "A Candid World"* ([Kent, Ohio], 1977), 40–68. Hutson shows that Gilbert is mistaken in arguing that the *philosophes* influenced American thought on foreign affairs and in attributing free trade ideas to Americans. "The model Treaty [Hutson points out] proposed commercial reciprocity rather than commercial freedom."

11. Wharton, ed., *Revolutionary Diplomatic Correspondence*, II, 226–31, 240–41; Bemis, *Diplomacy*, 52–53.

in Europe. To replace Jefferson, Congress turned to Arthur Lee, who, like Deane, was in Europe on American business.

Lee had seen enough of Deane to know that he did not trust him. But Lee seems not to have trusted anyone. He had reason to suspect Deane, who was allowing French aid to fall into his own pockets. After the commission began its negotiations Deane did more than even Lee suspected—passing American secrets to Edward Bancroft, the confidential secretary of the commission who was in the pay of the British government.

Franklin, unaware of Deane's practices, arrived in France early in December 1776. The British government professed dismay that the French would receive him, the agent of rebels, and Franklin's correspondence reveals that he felt uncertain of his welcome by the French. He had reason for this uneasiness. The young king of France, Louis XVI, regarded the American Revolution with skepticism. No European monarch wished to see another rejected, action which might provide an unhealthy model. Others in France shared their king's anxiety—French merchants, who questioned whether the nation could bear the expense of another war, did not want peacetime prosperity upset. Before Franklin's arrival Turgot, while still controller-general of finance, fed French suspicions with the prediction that Anglo-American trade would flourish even after independence.

Although Franklin did not directly dispel such doubts, he almost immediately captured popular affections. He stepped off the *Reprisal*, the ship that carried him across the Atlantic, with a simple fur cap on his head which he had worn for warmth against the chill November winds. The cap, his plain spectacles, which a man conscious of fashion would not have put on in public, and, most of all, his apparent simplicity and straightforwardness attracted the admiration of Paris. The French, full of illusions about the innocence of the New World, wanted a hero, and here in this American genius they found a simple philosopher, a wise and good representative of the best of the American wilderness. Franklin enjoyed the adulation but was too sophisticated to allow his head to be turned by it. Nor did he believe that popular feeling would bring France into a treaty with America. That would take careful preparation, and so he removed himself from the eyes of the public and set up operations in Passy, a small village in the suburbs of Paris.[12]

Congress had instructed the commissioners "to press for the immediate

12. Van Doren, *Franklin*, 564-75.

and explicit declaration of France in our favor, upon a suggestion that a reunion with Great Britain may be the consequence of a delay." These initial instructions did not mention an alliance; in a few months, however, Congress authorized the commissioners to seek closer ties to France. For their part the French were determined to guide their policy by two principles—they would enter no agreement that permitted the Americans to settle for anything less than independence, and they would not act without a formal commitment from Spain.[13]

The negotiations proceeded slowly, with events in America serving to pull the two sides apart and then to push them together. In February 1777 the commissioners informed Vergennes that the United States would promise not to make a separate peace with Britain in return for the same guarantee from France. The next month they offered to join France and Spain in an alliance. Vergennes, uncertain of the war's progress, delayed, and the Spanish government would not even allow Arthur Lee to enter the country when he tried to present the American case.[14]

The commission continued over the summer to press for French recognition and a large loan. In November, at the time news of Howe's capture of Philadelphia arrived, their efforts seemed futile. On December 4, however, messages were received telling of Burgoyne's capture. Within a few days Vergennes invited the commission to renew the proposal for a Franco-American alliance. Franklin drafted it, and on December 17, 1777, Vergennes agreed that France would recognize the United States and enter into an alliance. But, before anything could be signed, Spain must be asked once more to join France and America. By the end of the month the Spanish refused, but Vergennes—his anxiety raised by knowledge that Deane and Franklin had talked with Paul Wentworth, a British agent dispatched to sound them out about reconciliation—decided to proceed alone.[15]

The two sides signed a treaty of friendship and commerce and a treaty of alliance early in February 1778. The commercial treaty included a most-favored-nation clause and opened up several ports in the West Indies and France itself to American vessels without restrictions. The treaty of alliance, which was to come into effect only if France and Britain went to war (a virtual certainty), declared that the purpose of the two nations was to maintain the liberty and independence of the

13. For the quotation, Bemis, *Diplomacy*, 47. Bemis discusses French policy in chaps. 2–4.
14. *Ibid.*, 52–53.
15. *Ibid.*, 58–61.

United States. Everyone recognized that the eighth article of this treaty was crucial: "Neither of the two Parties shall conclude either Truce or Peace with Great Britain, without the formal consent of the other first obtained; and they mutually engage not to lay down their arms, until the independence of the United States shall have been formally or tacitly assured by the Treaty or Treaties that shall terminate the War." Almost as important was France's promise not to claim any English territory on the continent of North America and its agreement that any such territory captured in the war would belong to the United States.[16]

After the signing, the treaties were sent on their way to America, arriving on May 2, just ahead of the proposals from Britain for reconciliation. The British government, however, did not mean to recognize American independence. The French treaties received the approval of Congress on May 4. By June 14, 1778, France and Britain were at war.

II

Britain now faced immense strategic problems, to say nothing of internal political and financial strains. Before Burgoyne's collapse at Saratoga, British strategy had followed an erratic course. Sandwich complained in December 1777 that the navy had not been well employed, carrying troops here and there in convoy duty and never really using its own strength effectively. His statement described clearly enough what the navy had done, and his argument made at the same time that, properly used, the navy might strangle the colonies by raiding and blockading their ports suggested one sort of strategy available to Britain. A great maritime power, as Britain was in the eighteenth century, could have chosen to fight a naval war. But when Sandwich advocated this strategy, Britain had just seen a very different sort of plan, a land campaign far from the support of the navy, bring disaster.[17]

Sandwich's advocacy of the sea notwithstanding, neither he nor anyone else had thought through Britain's problems in the war. Nor during the first two years had Britain fought with any general, or overall, conception in mind. The war had not begun on British terms, and in marching to Lexington, Gage had not chosen the circumstances for a war with America. He had acted with a much more limited purpose in mind and then surprisingly had been locked up in Boston for almost a year. From Boston, Howe had taken the army to Halifax and returned with

16. *Ibid.*, 61–65.
17. G. R. Barnes and J. H. Owen, eds., *The Private Papers of John, Earl of Sandwich, First Lord of the Admiralty 1771–1782* (4 vols., London, 1932–38), I, 328–29.

a massive force to New York, where he sought to destroy Washington's army. That design preoccupied him for the next fifteen months, although his expedition against Philadelphia in summer 1777 also looked toward bringing loyalists in southern Pennsylvania into the open. Among Howe's difficulties one stood out: an imperfect understánding that putting down a rebellion and fighting a war are not necessarily the same thing. The ministry at home shared his confusion and never really decided which of the two they were doing or how the two were related. In giving approval to Burgoyne's plan to isolate New England, the government presumably had hoped to make a military operation serve a political purpose. Had Burgoyne made his way to Albany with his army reasonably intact, he would indeed have damaged the American cause, especially if in his progress to the Hudson he had smashed Gates's army.

Burgoyne's surrender and the entrance of France into the war forced British leaders to rethink their problems, but they attained no greater coherence in planning. At first, as news of Saratoga trickled in, it seemed that all had been made clear. Sandwich evidently now felt certain enough to call into question all previous efforts and advocated in their stead a naval war, arguing that of all strategies it alone offered a means of wearying the Americans until their will to resist crumbled. During the winter of 1777–78, a naval war won over the ministry and gained the support of Amherst, probably the most admired military leader in the nation, and of the king himself. What moved these men after Saratoga was a feeling that France's coming into the war was inevitable and that Spain would follow. There was something approaching relief in their letters and conversations during the winter. They were back on familiar ground, a war with the Bourbon powers. Still, they did not welcome this war; in fact, its approach filled them with dread. But at least it was comprehensible, as the colonial rebellion was not. As Sandwich remarked in the long assessment he provided North—France and Spain are "at bottom our inveterate enemies." Amherst told the king that the colonial war was now a secondary consideration in a situation in which the primary concern had to be France. Use the navy to block up the colonial ports, Amherst urged; if anything could make the Americans see reason the navy could, by squeezing them hard.[18]

A little of this persuaded North, who felt despair at Burgoyne's failure and seemed to want nothing so much as to escape office. The king, after receiving the secret reports on the course of Franco-American nego-

18. *Ibid.*, 334, 365. The letters about a war with France may be sampled in Fortescue, ed., *Correspondence of George the Third*, IV, 5, 6, 13, 15, 30–31.

tiations, grasped the new situation as quickly as anyone. After talking with Amherst, he began speculating on strategies appropriate for the coming war. Among them was a proposal, apparently Amherst's, to withdraw altogether from the colonies and, after strengthening Canada, Florida, and Nova Scotia, to attack France and Spain in the West Indies and Louisiana. A land war against the colonies, he wrote North in February, combined with a war with France and Spain "must be feeble in all parts and consequently unsuccessful."[19]

On March 8, 1778, these assessments produced instructions to General Henry Clinton, who had replaced William Howe as commander in chief. The primary operations would now be conducted from the sea, and Clinton was ordered to cooperate with the navy in raids against the American coast from New York to Nova Scotia. Clinton was also to prepare an attack against the Carolinas and Georgia, long considered the soft spots in American resistance. Since these new efforts reduced the importance of Philadelphia, Clinton was instructed to pull his forces back to New York, although Germain, who prepared these orders, gave Clinton discretionary authority to remain if local conditions warranted keeping troops there.[20]

Five days later, when the French government announced that it had signed treaties of amity and commerce with the United States, these instructions were virtually cancelled. Though Britain and France would not be at war until June 1778, it was now certain, and the disposition to strike France first could now become policy. For a few days the king, North, and Amherst discussed the possibility of taking all British forces out of the colonies, but by March 21, when a second set of orders was drafted by Germain, nothing so drastic seemed necessary. Still, the new strategy called for a shift in direction and of resources. The planned naval blockade was not explicitly given up, but it was no longer accounted of first importance. The main effort would now be against France—"faithless and insolent" in the king's bitter phrase— and Clinton was ordered to make it. He was to send an expedition of 5000 troops against St. Lucia in the West Indies, 3000 more to reinforce the Floridas, and withdraw the remainder to New York City, which was to be held to strengthen the negotiating position of the Carlisle Commission, diplomatic agents who were about to be dispatched to America with instructions to conclude peace with the rebels without

19. Fortescue, ed., *Correspondence of George the Third*, IV, 36.
20. Willcox, *Portrait of a General*, 222–23.

agreeing to independence, a condition both ridiculous and pathetic.[21]

The ministry decided almost without thought to attack the French in the West Indies. The islands were a familiar arena, the cream of the British army was in America, and the military resources for an attack across the Channel simply did not exist. Nor did the will, and the possibility was not even considered.[22]

The West Indies were a rich prize. The economics of mercantilism seemed to suggest that the islands possessed much more value than the continental colonies. Certainly the West Indies trade returned much greater profits than trade with the mainland. The West Indies merchants clamored for protection in 1778, as always, and given the value of their business they were hard to put off. Had they been silent the result would have been the same. Striking the French in the West Indies seemed virtually preordained, and the decision was easily made.

St. Lucia was chosen for solid tactical reasons. It lay in the Windward Islands just south of Martinique, where the French had a superb harbor. Further south were British-held Grenada and Tobago and, a hundred miles to the east, Barbados, an important producer of sugar. The Windward Islands were a principal group in the Lesser Antilles. In the northern group, the Leeward Islands, the strongest British station was on Antigua. The French controlled the most important of these islands and in September 1778 would seize Dominica, a lonely English island lying between Guadeloupe and Martinique. The largest and wealthiest British island in the Caribbean, Jamaica, lay a thousand miles to the west but, because of its remoteness and the prevailing winds, could not be used in the campaigns against the French in the Lesser Antilles. St. Lucia could, however, if it were seized, for it had the anchorages from which the navy might sail against ships going in and coming out of Martinique.

Attacking the French in the West Indies pleased everyone in the ministry. What to do about the French fleet, which was stationed at Brest and Toulon, excited neither pleasure nor agreement. When the French announced the American treaties, they had twenty-one ships of the line at Brest and another twelve at Toulon. During the spring they added at least another dozen to this total. The British navy had fifty-five ships of the line, in various degrees of readiness, in March. Should the French send a significant part of their fleet to American waters the situation there, where Britain had maintained naval superiority,

21. *Ibid.*, 223–25; Gerald S. Brown, "The Anglo-French Naval Crisis, 1778: A Study of Conflict in the North Cabinet," *WMQ*, 3d Ser., 13 (1956), 1–8.

22. Piers Mackesy, *The War for America 1775–1783* (Cambridge, Mass., 1965), 181–86, for a thoughtful discussion of the West Indies in British strategy.

would be seriously changed. The British had two ways of meeting this possibility. First, they might follow their method of the previous war—a naval blockade that successfully confined the French navy to European waters. A blockade, however, offered great difficulties, especially a blockade of Brest. A close-in blockade which would see much of the fleet on station off Brest would be hard to sustain because many English ships were not in good condition, and prolonged periods at sea would not improve seaworthiness. Nor was it likely to improve the health of sailors who still fell victim to scurvy. An "open" blockade which would rely on fast frigates patrolling off Brest might be more easily maintained, but it had dangers of its own. One was that the French might divide their fleet and send a part to America. In such case, the English response would be a detachment to follow, trusting to good seamanship and luck to bring it to the place in America the French planned to attack. The Toulon fleet might be dealt with in roughly these same ways—a blockade, say at the Strait of Gibraltar, or by a detachment in case it was sent to American waters.

Soon after the French announcement, the Toulon fleet began to prepare to put to sea. The Comte d'Estaing, a landsman, was given command and rumors began to circulate in Britain about his instructions. Would he bring the Toulon line of battle up the Channel to join the main force at Brest, or would he make for America? The question and the conflicting guesses it inspired disturbed cabinet meetings for two months. Sandwich and Admiral Augustus Keppel, commander of the home fleet, or the "Great Fleet" as Keppel grandly called it, insisted that the home islands were in danger and that no division of forces for any reason should be made. They were obsessed with defense of the home islands—"our principal object must be our defence at home"—Sandwich wrote early in April. Both opposed trying to stop Estaing at the Strait, lest the attempt fail and the French slip an invasion in behind the "Great Fleet" lured away to the Mediterranean.[23]

Germain thought invasion a remote possibility and sought to prevent the loss of naval superiority in America. Stopping the Toulon fleet at the Strait seemed only prudent to him, perhaps because America had long been on his mind.

The king and North were put into a terrible dilemma by this disagreement. They agreed that the French were now their main problem, but to confine the navy so closely to home waters seemed a curious way of fighting them. Yet, if they divided the fleet between the Channel and

23. Barnes and Owen, eds., *Private Papers of Earl of Sandwich*, II, 22.

the Strait they ran the risk of exposing the nation to invasion; if they did not, their enemy would be free to overturn British preponderance in America.

Sandwich and Keppel had their way. The Toulon fleet sailed on April 13 and cleared the Strait of Gibraltar on May 16. During the month following Estaing's departure from Toulon, the king, North, and most of the cabinet, not including Sandwich, changed their minds about how best to react. By the end of the month, orders were issued to send Admiral John "Foul Weather Jack" Byron with thirteen ships of the line to reinforce Richard Howe. The cabinet at this time was betting that Estaing was bound for America. Sandwich and Keppel remained convinced that Estaing would join the Brest fleet and succeeded in so shaking the king's confidence that on May 13 he ordered Admiral Byron to stay his sailing.[24]

Indecision paralyzed the king and the navy until June 2, when the *Proserpine*, a frigate which had been stationed off the Strait, sailed in with the news that Estaing had reached the Atlantic on May 16 and set off for America. The *Proserpine* had followed Estaing for two days just to make sure that there was no trick loose on the sea. Byron was now ordered to sail, but in the face of opposing winds he did not make open seas for another week. Under way, his ships ran into a storm; scattered and badly damaged, they did not reach American waters until early August.[25]

Clinton and Admiral Howe knew nothing of these ship movements, and Sandwich did not seem eager to tell them that they would soon have visitors from France. In fact, after losing the struggle to prevent a detachment from sailing to America, he peevishly denied Germain the use of a frigate which might carry the news of Estaing's coming. As far as Sandwich was concerned Germain could use a packet. Germain dispatched the packet, and Howe learned on June 29 that before long Estaing would appear off the American coast. Clinton, who had assumed command from William Howe on May 8, received orders the next day to pull out of Philadelphia and to send troops to the West Indies and Florida.[26]

24. Brown, "Anglo-French Naval Crisis," *WMQ*, 3d Ser., 13 (1956), 9–22; Willcox, *Portrait of a General*, 214–18. Much of the indecision displayed in the government is in Fortescue, ed., *Correspondence of George the Third*, IV, 90, 98, 112–13, 119–20, 121–22, 124, 132–34, 136, 137, 145.
25. Brown, "Anglo-French Naval Crisis," *WMQ*, 3d Ser., 13 (1956), 23–25.
26. Willcox, *Portrait of a General*, 217.

A new commander who is told in effect to make preparations for the dissolution of his army does not ordinarily regard his prospects with delight. Clinton never felt satisfied with what he was given—few soldiers do—and decided that he would hang on to what he had, at least until the evacuation of Philadelphia was completed. He therefore delayed sending the 8000 troops southward.

III

George Washington had grown accustomed to seeing his soldiers disappear—often before their enlistments expired. But in 1778 he was feeling much better than he had in the winter, and not just because he had heard of the French treaties and expected help soon. Rather, the prospects of his army had improved over the winter which had been spent at Valley Forge.

Valley Forge, a name associated with suffering since the winter of 1777–78, lay eighteen miles northwest of Philadelphia, where Valley Creek entered the Schuylkill River from the south flowing from west to east. Despite the name, the "Valley" did not exist, and the "Forge," where iron once was smelted, had fallen into disuse. The ground between Valley Creek and the Schuylkill was a succession of low hills, several thickly wooded, and about two miles long and a mile and a quarter wide.[27]

Washington chose Valley Forge for winter quarters because the place was not easily accessible and because, with its high ground and streams, it could be easily defended. It was remote from settled areas, but not so distant as to prevent the army from keeping a close watch on the British in Philadelphia. Protecting Pennsylvania from "the ravages of the enemy" concerned Washington, he explained to his soldiers. At the same time he dreaded making his army a burden to those parts of the state already crowded with refugees who had fled as Howe had advanced. "To their distress humanity forbids us to add," he told his soldiers, themselves full of distress but empty of belly. Hence the choice of Valley Forge, well located strategically, easily defended, and out of the way of civilians.[28]

The army that marched into Valley Forge looked tired—and was. After fighting at Germantown in early October, it had maneuvered warily ahead of Howe's force which itself had not seemed especially eager for another battle. There were skirmishes of sorts, several bitter and

27. Freeman, *GW*, IV, 564-65; Ward, II, 544.
28. *GW Writings*, X, 168.

deadly, but the main forces of each side did not quite manage to grapple with one another. The closest they came to battle was at the American camp at Whitemarsh, twelve miles west of Philadelphia, which Washington had established early in November. Howe, who had settled back into the comforts of Philadelphia two weeks after Germantown, marched out again early in December. The two armies looked at one another for several days—Washington's troops were deployed on high ground—until Howe decided that an attack could not succeed. He then returned to Philadelphia for the winter, and a few days later, on December 21, the Americans straggled into Valley Forge.[29]

In all, Washington's army numbered 11,000 officers and men, of whom 8200 were fit for duty. They made a camp in a fine strategic site, but there was much about it that added to their misery—and they were miserable when they arrived. They lacked almost everything an army needs for survival. They had been hungry for several weeks, and their new quarters were in a part of Pennsylvania barren of provisions. They had lived for weeks in the open and required barracks or housing that would give them protection from the winter. Valley Forge had virtually no buildings; the troops would have to put up their own.

The recent campaign had worn out shoes and clothing as well as men. The hills offered no more in the way of clothing than of food. Almost everything else was in short supply as well. A few days after their arrival Washington remarked that there was no soap in the army but, he concluded, there was not much use for it since few men had more than one shirt, and some none at all. And he might have noted that, though Valley Creek and the Schuylkill bordered the camp, water for all uses had to be carried for considerable distances, in some places a mile or more.[30]

The woods afforded the materials for housing, and the soldiers fell to building huts almost immediately. Washington ordered that the camp be carefully laid out. Huts, fourteen by sixteen feet, were to be constructed of logs, roofed with "split slabs." Clay sealed the sides and was used to make fireplaces. Nails were not to be had of course, and the logs had to be notched. Each hut housed a squad of twelve men. Washington promised to share his soldiers' hardships until the first huts were completed and lived in a tent before finally moving into one of the few houses near by. By January 13 the last of the huts were completed.[31]

29. Ward, I, 379–83.
30. GW Writings, X, 195.
31. Ibid., X, 170–71, 180–81, 301.

Comfort did not abound inside the huts' walls. Many had only the ground for floors, and straw for beds was not readily available. Worst of all, the troops frequently had nothing to eat. At the time of their arrival the commissary seems to have contained only twenty-five barrels of flour—nothing else, neither meat nor fish. During the days that followed the soldiers chopped down trees and put up huts with empty stomachs. At night, according to Albigence Waldo, a surgeon of the Connecticut line, there was a general cry that echoed through the hills— "No meat! No meat!" The troops added to this "melancholy sound" their versions of the cawing of crows and the hooting of owls.[32]

Imitating bird calls suggests that the troops' sense of humor saw them through the worst of their sufferings. They had their hatreds, too, and these also may have helped sustain them. One was firecake, a thin bread made of flour and water and baked over the campfire. Another was the commissaries who were supposed to provide food for the army. Waldo reconstructed a number of conversations along the following lines: "What have you for your dinners, boys?" "Nothing but firecake and water, Sir." At night: "Gentlemen, the supper is ready. What is your supper lads?" "Firecake and water, Sir." In the morning: "What have you got for breakfast, lads?" "Firecake and water, Sir." And from Waldo, the snarl: "The Lord send that our Commissary of Purchases may live [on] fire cake and water till their glutted gutts are turned to pasteboard."[33]

During three periods even firecake was largely lacking—the last week of December, early January, and the middle weeks in February. The time in February was perhaps the worst, with Washington describing the troops as "starving" on February 6, 1778, and their condition as one of "famine" on February 16. By this time the soldiers had already endured two months of short rations; they were cold and many were sick.[34]

Washington felt their suffering and ate from a lean table himself. More important, he did his best to find food and to get it to Valley Forge. His best was carefully limited by a regard for the rights of civilians, scruples which did not put meat into the mouths of his soldiers. Members of Congress who learned of the hunger at Valley Forge urged Washington to seize the food his troops needed. Washington resisted such suggestions, recognizing that relief of his troops' hunger by such means would undercut the principles of the Revolution and the political support of the

32. "Diary of Albigence Waldo," *PMHB*, 21 (1897), 309.
33. *Ibid.*, 309–10.
34. *GW Writings*, X, 423, 469.

people. Instead he sent his commissary through New Jersey, Pennsylvania, Delaware, and the upper South in search of provisions. At times he seized supplies, or purchased them with force as well as promises of payment, but in these cases he attempted to protect the sellers' interests as much as possible. For example, at least five hundred horses died during the winter from lack of feed. Washington ordered their replacement and sent troops to nearby farms. Their orders were to leave sufficient horses for the needs of the farmers, to give receipts, and to assess the value of those taken as fairly as possible. To guarantee fair compensation impartial referees were to be used, and the farmers were allowed a voice in choosing them and to be present when the value of the horses was established.[35]

Finding supplies was not easy, and moving them to the camp was sometimes even more difficult. With army horses and wagons scarce, civilians—merchants, drayers, and others—had to be relied on, and these men, in business for themselves, frequently had better paying uses for their transport. Pork which had been purchased in New Jersey remained there to spoil for lack of wagons. In Pennsylvania, private contractors shipped flour to New England, where prices were better, while Washington's soldiers had short rations. And a number of farmers around Philadelphia preferred to sell to the British in the city, who had hard cash, than to accept Washington's promises of payment.[36]

With little to do except think of food and warmth, the soldiers at Valley Forge sometimes sought relief on their own terms. Desertions seem not to have exceeded the normal rate, which was bad enough, but the officers began to resign in such numbers as to alarm Washington. The soldiers who stayed did not have enough to do once their huts were built—one of the weaknesses of the American army was a lack of systematic routine that comes in training and drill—and some took to plundering nearby farms. The camp saw the usual coming and going, wandering soldiers who strayed here and there, and the bane of the army, those who fired their guns for the pleasure of the sound. Robbing the farmers who had little enough was more serious. Washington, who characterized it as "base, cruel, and injurious to the cause in which we are engaged," attempted to stop it by tightening discipline. Passes were required to leave camp, and soldiers found outside camp without them

35. *Ibid.*, 179, 201, 467, 474, 480–81; Nathanael Greene to George Washington, Feb. 17, 1778; Henry Lee to George Washington, Feb. 22, 1778, GW Papers, Series 4, Reel 47.

36. *GW Writings*, X, 412–13, 433–37.

were confined. Washington also ordered that frequent musters were to be taken and instructed his officers to inspect their troops' huts more often. The indiscriminate shooters were to receive twenty lashes "on the spot," and only soldiers on duty were to carry arms.[37]

The troops' misery lay at the heart of the breaches of discipline. If the conditions of their lives could be improved, most of their excesses would stop. But without supplies of food and clothing not much more than repressing criminal acts could be done. Washington's orders suggest that he did not overlook many ways of maintaining discipline. Some were vital: bury the dead horses and the offal, the troops were told. Some were less important: stop playing cards and casting dice. Inspect the troops frequently, look into their huts, the officers were instructed.[38]

Undoubtedly these orders had some effect. The gradual recovery of a sick supply system had more. When the army entered Valley Forge its supply service was almost three years old. The service had changed since its inception outside Boston in 1775, but it had not improved. A commissary department existed to provide food for the bellies that an army supposedly moves on; a second department, under a quartermaster, had as its business the responsibility of supplying most other needs including clothing. For a time before 1777–78, Joseph Trumbull, as commissary general, gave excellent service. He resigned, however, when Congress reorganized the department and among other changes, took into its own hands the appointment of the commissary general's deputies. Congressional action made the commissary general's responsibility for supervision of the deputies' work virtually impossible, and Congress itself proved unable to do the job. The deputies, who actually did most of the purchasing and issuing of provisions, found in autonomy considerable opportunities for profiteering and graft. And those who resisted temptation could not begin to meet the army's needs without proper coordination and direction.[39]

William Buchanan succeeded Trumbull as commissary general. He

37. *Ibid.*, 201, 206–7.
38. *Ibid.*, 207.
39. Supply is discussed at length below, in Chapter 20. I am much indebted here to the research of E. Wayne Carp's doctoral dissertation at the University of California, Berkeley, entitled "Supplying the Revolution: Continental Army Administration and American Political Culture, 1775–1783." Still useful are Victor L. Johnson, *The Administration of the American Commissariat During the Revolutionary War* (Philadelphia, 1941); Louis C. Hatch, *The Administration of the American Revolutionary Army* (New York, 1904); and especially Erna Risch, *Quartermaster Support of the Army: A History of the Corps, 1775–1939* (Washington, D.C., 1962).

tried, failed, and went the way of Trumbull. Later in the winter of 1778, Congress, after being made to realize that the new system was a failure, reorganized the service once more and appointed Jeremiah Wadsworth to head it. The reorganized commissary now operated under an incentive system whose control was placed with its head. The commissary general now appointed his deputies, purchasing commissaries, and their subordinates, who were paid a percentage of their cash disbursements. The more food they provided the army, the more money they made for themselves. It was not a perfect system, but it established simple lines of authority, made supervision relatively easy, and fixed responsibility.

The quartermaster department endured a similar history of congressional intervention and recovered only when Nathanael Greene took over in March 1778. A set of incentives brought vigor to its operatives, who, as in the commissary, were brought under the control of the service's head. Greene, himself, was given considerable powers of appointment. For example, he selected his own forage and wagon masters, two key posts.

At Valley Forge in February, energy proved as important as organization in rescuing the army from near-starvation. Greene, under Washington's supervision, provided both energy and organization, sending foraging parties far and wide. Anthony Wayne crossed the Delaware into New Jersey near Goshen and foraged along the river. There he found hay in abundance but the livestock and horses to feed it to were sometimes difficult to discover, for farmers hid their cattle and horses in the woods. Wayne soon learned the tricks of the hunt, and before long his troops collected large numbers of animals. Receipts were given for the stock impressed, and Wayne believed that most owners were "reconciled" to the "policy, necessity and Justice" of the seizures. Whether Wayne followed Greene's orders not to give receipts to those who concealed their livestock is not known.[40]

Henry Lee went farther afield, into Delaware and the eastern shore of Maryland where the pickings were fat. In Delaware the foragers found more cattle than horses, and almost everywhere there was more hay than grain. The islands in the Delaware River may have contained more horses than most areas—pasturage in meadows and especially marshes was good there. Greene himself scoured the islands and burned whatever hay he could not send back because of a shortage of teams and horses,

40. Anthony Wayne to Brig. General J. Ellis, Feb. 20, 1778, and Nathanael Greene to George Washington, Feb. 17, 1778, in GW Papers, Ser. 4, Reel 47.

which tactic could not have won the sympathies of farmers in New Jersey and Delaware. But Greene and Lee were both convinced that these two states were filled with loyalists anyway. Action against them, while harsh, would at least deny the British the food and forage that the Americans could not carry to Valley Forge.[41]

By March the lean, skeleton-like figures who dragged themselves around Valley Forge began to put on flesh. And the flesh was now covered by shirts and breeches. The reorganized commissary and quartermaster services could claim a part of the credit for these improvements, but so could Washington and the foraging parties.

During the winter the troops had not had enough to do. Their physical condition prevented strenuous exertion, the weather was harsh in any case, and they were left to themselves. The army had moved so often in the preceding months that no clear routine had developed. No common drill had been imposed on the regiments, and they paraded and handled their arms pretty much as their commanders decreed. Since most regimental commanders had no military training themselves, what they taught was often of limited value and sometimes worthless.

An opportunity to change all this—to give the rank-and-file military exercise and to turn them into professionals—appeared in late February in the person of an engaging Prussian who called himself Frederick William Augustus Henry Ferdinand, Baron von Steuben. He had arrived in America bearing a letter to Congress from Benjamin Franklin and Silas Deane. They recommended him highly, although not nearly as highly as he recommended himself. He had served, he said, with Frederick the Great; he had been a lieutenant general, a quartermaster general, and Frederick's aide-de-camp. The Baron was stretching things a bit, just as he stretched out his name. He had held a commission in Frederick's army fourteen years earlier but reporting that was about as close as he got to the truth about himself. He was in fact a soldier of fortune whose fortunes were rather low. Although he talked confidently about his estate in Swabia, he owned no property and had no employment. But unlike most who presented themselves to Congress, he did not ask for pay or preferment. All he wished, he said, was to place himself at General Washington's disposal. In return he expected only that his expenses would be paid. Relieved and pleased at this unusual modesty, Congress sent him off to Valley Forge.[42]

41. Henry Lee to George Washington, Feb. 22, 1778; Greene to Washington, Feb. 17, 1778, *ibid.*
42. Ward, II, 550–51; John M. Palmer, *General von Steuben* (New Haven, Conn., 1937), 3–14.

Washington liked what he saw in Steuben, and when Steuben mentioned a desire to help train the ragged troops Washington gave him his head. Steuben would for the time being serve as acting inspector general charged with the task of teaching the soldiers how to march in formations and how to handle their weapons. Despite the fact that Steuben knew what he was about, he faced a tremendous difficulty for he knew no English. Since the American army had neither written regulations nor manuals, he wrote the drill in French, and his secretary, Pierre Duponceau, a boy of seventeen, translated it into English. John Laurens and Alexander Hamilton, both on Washington's staff, polished it, rephrasing the translation when necessary in language intelligible to American troops. These instructions were then copied into the orderly books of the various regiments.

Washington then gave Steuben one hundred men who were to serve as a model company. Steuben himself took on the task of teaching this unit close-order drill. In doing so, he cast aside the usual practice in the British and American armies of having all instruction given by noncommissioned officers. The Baron began by calling a squad from the company which he marched back and forth as the company and large numbers of others looked on. He ran into trouble almost immediately. He had memorized the English and gave his commands in the language, but an imperfect memory and a heavy accent combined with a short temper led to some confusion in the ranks. Close-order drill like many simple exercises has its own strange complexities. While he sputtered curses in French and German—"God damn" exhausted his store of English profanity—Captain Benjamin Walker stepped forward and, speaking in French, offered to translate the Baron's commands into English. Steuben accepted with gratitude. From that moment on, the drill proceeded with some smoothness, although the delivery of the commands twice, first in French and then in English, was awkward.

Those officers and men who marched, and those who observed, learned. Imitation may or may not be the sincerest form of flattery, but it is an effective way of learning how to march and how to handle a musket. Those who marched under the Baron's careful eye were soon able to instruct others. The manual of arms followed and then the proper use of the bayonet. By late March all of the regiments of the army were practicing the Baron's drill.

The accounts that have survived these days indicate that this training took hold in part because the men enjoyed it and enjoyed watching Baron von Steuben. They also evidently admired him and were amused by him, especially when he indulged his temper. Soldiers of all nationalities usually have a special fondness for profanity, and many have a special proficiency in its use. Steuben was one, but even though he exploded and cursed he soon understood that an attempt to induce respect and fear in these troops would not take him very far. Republicans in arms had a special character, as he wrote an old European comrade: "In the first place, the genius of this nation is not in the least to be compared with that of the Prussians, Austrians, or French. You say to your soldier, 'Do this,' and he doeth it, but I am obliged to say, 'This is the reason why you ought to do that,' and he does it."[43]

The corollary to this conclusion is that the American soldiers knew what they were fighting for. They had a sense of the "glorious cause." And these soldiers at Valley Forge were veterans, some of Brandywine and more perhaps of Germantown. Soldiers new to the army can be disciplined, their wills shaped by vigorous exercise on the drill field. Veterans cannot be, in the usual sense. Battle has already taught them the need for both firm leadership and immediate response to orders. Close-order drill and the manual of arms aided them in doing what they must do under fire. In the tactics employed in the eighteenth century, professional armies depended on well-executed movements, and the drill on the parade field actually enabled infantry to move effectively into battle. The veterans at Valley Forge, recognizing this and recognizing too what Steuben could do for them, laughed when he exploded—he shared the pleasure he gave—but they also did as they were ordered.

In May these newly acquired skills were put to a preliminary test. Washington learned from spies in Philadelphia that the British were making preparations to leave, perhaps to return to New York City. The young officers at Valley Forge yearned for action after the dull, confining winter, none more than Marquis de Lafayette, who offered to lead a detachment which was to watch the enemy and if the opportunity arose strike his sources of supply. Washington agreed and sent Lafayette off with 2200 men. On May 20, several large British forces moving quickly from Philadelphia almost trapped Lafayette at Barren Hill, eleven miles to the west of the city. Lafayette escaped the converging forces, which might well have ground him to pieces, through skillful maneuvering and rapid marching—maneuvers and marches which could be accomplished only by troops practiced in moving efficiently in large bodies.[44]

Lafayette had learned much about fighting in his first year in America,

43. Palmer, *Steuben*, 157.
44. Ward, II, 562–67.

and he demonstrated his knowledge in this engagement at Barren Hill. Not quite twenty-one years of age, he had come to America in June 1777 over the opposition of his family and his king. Neither wished to see him risk his life in the American war. Lafayette was determined, however, to find glory and to fight British tyranny. That the tyranny was British was important, for Lafayette shared the desire of his countrymen to revenge themselves on their old enemy. Just how well he understood the principles for which the Americans struggled is not clear. Later on, after the war, when his understanding had matured, he explained his coming to America as service to the great principles of the Revolution. Whatever his convictions during the war, he remained a young nobleman of wealth, charm, and courage. These qualities impressed George Washington who had taken such a liking of Lafayette when they met in July 1777 that he had offered him a place on his staff. Lafayette, commissioned a major general by Congress, accepted eagerly. Eagerness soon developed into something approaching adoration of his chief. And Washington, who held all men at arm's length, responded with affection and warmth.

IV

General Clinton replaced Howe in May, and by the middle of June, he was prepared to evacuate Philadelphia. Almost three thousand loyalists prepared to depart with him. With the help of Lord Richard Howe, who was to retain the naval command until early autumn, Clinton loaded these people, the sick, and some supplies aboard transports in the Delaware. The remainder of his troops, about 10,000 in all, would march overland along with a supply train of 1500 wagons. His army in the eight months spent in Philadelphia had accumulated a variety of goods that helped make life tolerable and was determined to carry them to New York. Besides the soldiers' possessions and the officers' baggage, there were the laundries, bakeries, blacksmiths' shops, all vital to the life of an eighteenth-century army, and almost equally important the bat horses, private carriages, hospital supplies, and inevitably the camp followers.

Clinton set this bloated mass in motion at 3:00 A.M. on June 18. Flat-bottom boats carried them across the Delaware at Gloucester, New Jersey, in seven hours of hard work.[45] Several roads to New York were available. The most likely route, and one Clinton considered for a time,

---

45. The preparations for the removal are discussed in *ibid.*, 570–71.

ran through Haddonfield, Mount Holly, Crosswicks, Allentown, Cranbury, New Brunswick, where the Raritan River would have to be crossed, and finally to Staten Island. Clinton formed his army on the New Jersey side and began to crawl, the word is well chosen, toward New York. His supply train, principally the 1500 wagons, covered twelve miles of road. Getting them all under way must have taken several hours, and the column did not make good time. During the next six days, the army managed to move to Allentown, about thirty-five miles from Philadelphia. Clinton remained untroubled by this pace, which he knew could be improved only by the most strenuous efforts.

A report that the British had pulled out reached Washington later that same morning. He had been considering what if anything he should do if the British left Philadelphia. The day before Clinton made his move Washington called a council of his general officers and asked for advice. These officers did not agree but the preponderant opinion favored letting the British escape with little more than harassment. Charles Lee may have opposed even minor attacks, and Lee carried others with him. Washington, undecided about just how much to risk, was disposed to punish the enemy as much as possible, though he does not seem to have wanted to bring on a large-scale battle. His instincts, as always, were for action, and immediately after getting the information about the evacuation he put some of his regiments on the road. His army had grown to almost 13,500. About 1300 of them were with Brig. General William Maxwell at Mount Holly, and General Philemon Dickinson had some 800 New Jersey militia across the river. By the next day almost the entire army had left Valley Forge. By June 23, Washington had them across the Delaware at Coryell's Ferry, and the next day he camped at Hopewell, fifteen miles west of Cranbury. The army, between 10,000 and 11,000 strong, had moved fifty-seven miles in six days.[46]

The march raised the mens' spirits but it did not change the advice of Washington's commanders. Lee continued to argue against taking on the enemy. Build them a bridge of gold, he said, to speed them on their way. Most of the others agreed, impressed as amateurs usually are by professional opinion. Anthony Wayne and Nathanael Greene, young and proud, urged an attack though they did not propose that Washington seek a general engagement. Steuben gave what was perhaps the wisest counsel of all—strike Clinton when he was on the move

46. Ward, II, 570–73; *GW Writings*, XII, 82–88, 90–91; Freeman, *GW*, V, 11–15, for this paragraph and the one preceding.

and off balance. Lafayette joined Steuben and pointed out that the long British baggage train was especially vulnerable.[47]

Had Clinton attended the council of Washington's officers, he would have confessed that his long train was open to attack. Detachments under Maxwell and Dickinson had not yet ambushed his wagons, but they had made the going more difficult by breaking down bridges and the causeways over marshes. Clinton was aware of these shadows, and he soon got word that Washington had come out of Valley Forge. What worried Clinton most was the danger he would face at New Brunswick, where the Raritan would have to be crossed, where he might have to fight under dreadful circumstances. At the Raritan he feared he would have to face the combined forces of Gates—who he thought was coming down from New York—and Washington.

These odds seemed unpromising and, understandably, Clinton decided to turn at Allentown to the northeast on a route that would carry him through Monmouth Court House and Middletown to Sandy Hook and thus avoid the Raritan. This line of march could only be followed on one road and forced him to bring his troops and his wagons together. Between Gloucester and Allentown he had been able to use parallel roads and had placed most of his infantry between Washington and the baggage train. Now he had to consolidate his forces into one column—the van, some 4000 under Knyphausen, followed by the long line of wagons, and to the rear 6000 troops—the cream of the army, grenadiers and light infantry. Clinton detached about a third of these trailing soldiers and placed them under Cornwallis as a rear guard.[48]

The British hit the road early on June 25 and reached Monmouth Court House, nineteen miles from Allentown, late the next afternoon. This move in brutal heat sapped their energies. Their soldiers carried packs of at least sixty pounds, weight made especially difficult to bear by sandy roads, woolen uniforms, and cumbersome muskets. The Hessians, who wore even heavier clothing than the English, suffered the most, several dying of sunstroke along the way. With his troops worn out and the hot weather holding on, Clinton had to rest his army throughout the next day.[49]

Washington also shifted his main force on June 25. He left his baggage and his tents at Hopewell and marched seven miles to Kingston, a small village three and one-half miles north of Princeton and twenty-five miles from Monmouth Court House. The same day he sent Anthony Wayne

47. *GW Writings*, XII, 115–17.
48. Willcox, *Portrait of a General*, 232–33.
49. Ward, II, 574.

forward with 1000 regulars from New Hampshire—Poor's brigade—in order to strengthen the forces shadowing Clinton. The headquarters for this advance party was now at Englishtown about five miles west of the enemy's camp at Monmouth, but though the American van was close it was in fact divided into uncoordinated units. As if to remedy this, Washington pushed closer the night of the 25th, passing through Cranbury and pausing early the next morning within five miles of Englishtown. Like Clinton's army, the American rested on June 27.

While the troops ate, pulled their boots off, and slept, Washington brought several of his commanders to his headquarters. Among them was Charles Lee, who two days earlier had been persuaded to assume command of the advance force. Lee often appeared strange and eccentric to his colleagues and never more so than in these June days. Washington and Howe had agreed upon an exchange which freed him from British confinement in April, and in May he had returned to the American army at Valley Forge, where he was greeted with enthusiasm. While Lee was being held by the British he may have betrayed his American comrades by offering a plan of action to his captors, a plan designed, at least on its face, to end the war with a British victory. Since his return he had done little and when called upon for advice invariably couched it in language that left little doubt that he believed the American army could not stand up to the British. When, on June 25, Washington asked him to command the vanguard that trailed Clinton so closely, he at first refused and suggested that this task should properly go to Lafayette. Almost as soon as Lafayette accepted the command, now containing almost half the army, Lee changed his mind and asked that it be given to him. Washington agreed, and Lafayette generously gave way. Alexander Hamilton, who had watched these transactions with scorn, called Lee's behavior "childish." Whether or not that judgment was accurate, Lee's opposition to an attack on Clinton's army should have disqualified him from a responsible post.[50]

Nonetheless Washington gave him command and on the 27th gave orders to attack the British rear when it began to move. The exact wording of the orders is not clear but whatever Washington said, his intention to bring on a partial engagement was plain. That he gave Lee discretion to avoid battle in extraordinary circumstances did not obscure this purpose. Washington provided no detailed instructions, however, as he had not reconnoitered the ground. Nor had Lee, who on

50. Freeman, *GW*, V, 18–23; Ward, II, 574–75. Hamilton's remark in a letter to Elias Boudinot, July 5, 1778, may be read in Syrett and Cooke, eds., *Papers of Hamilton*, I, 511.

returning to the advance force made no plan and gave no orders beyond a general statement to his subordinates that they must be guided by circumstances.[51]

At five in the morning of June 28, Clinton started Knyphausen on the road to Middletown, about ten miles to the northeast. Dickinson, whose militia lay near to the British lead units, sent word immediately to Lee and Washington. Lee's units began moving from around Englishtown along the road to Monmouth Court House, and less than an hour later Clinton's rear began following the baggage train. The rear guard under Cornwallis was the last of all to move; it seems to have barely got on the road when units of Lee's cavalry discovered it. The battle that followed developed slowly as the two sides found each other and brought their troops to imperfect concentration.[52]

The terrain, largely unknown to the Americans and only slightly more familiar to the British, was in part responsible for the peculiar struggle that followed. Most of the ground was sandy pine barrens cut by small streams flowing through morasses and speckled by woods. Three fairly large ravines ran on a roughly east-west line just north of Monmouth Court House. They were West Ravine, Middle Ravine, and East Ravine. West Ravine and Middle Ravine were about a mile apart, and both were on the road. A bridge had been built over West Ravine and a causeway over Middle Ravine. East Ravine, which lay a little more than a mile east of Middle Ravine was also divided by the road.[53]

The battle of Monmouth Court House began to take on serious proportions around this last ravine, just a mile north of the court house, as Lee's forces groped along the road. How the two sides actually engaged is not clear, but within an hour of noon almost 5000 Americans in no very ordered alignment nor in any fixed position, confronted around 2000 British, mostly infantry, under Cornwallis.[54]

To this point the accounts of the battle are merely murky; after it they are confused and confusing. Artillery on both sides fired, and the American regiments evidently shifted their positions on the orders of their commanders and of Lee. What Lee was about, he kept to himself,

---

51. *GW Writings*, XII, 127–28; Ward, II, 576.
52. *GW Writings*, XII, 128–29; Ward, II, 577.
53. Ward, II, 577.
54. My account of the battle is constructed from *GW Writings*, XII, 141–44; Freeman, *GW*, V, 24–28; Ward, II, 577–85; Syrett and Cooke, eds., *Papers of Hamilton*, I, 510–14; and the testimony given at the court-martial of General Charles Lee, in *The Lee Papers* (New-York Historical Society, *Collections*, 4–7 [New York, 1872–75]), III.

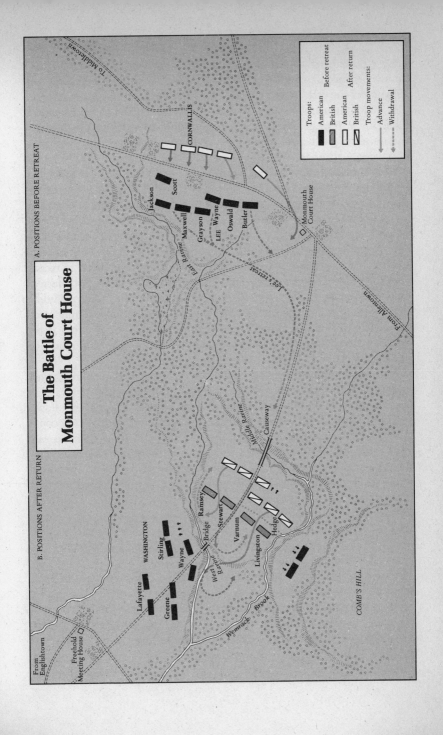

The Battle of Monmouth Court House

A. POSITIONS BEFORE RETREAT

B. POSITIONS AFTER RETURN

To Middletown

CORNWALLIS

Jackson

Scott

Maxwell

Grayson

LEE Wayne

Oswald

Butler

Monmouth Court House

Lee's retreat

From Allentown

East Ravine

Middle Ravine

Causeway

WASHINGTON

Ramsey

Stewart

Stirling

Varnum

Wayne

Bridge

Livingston

Hedge

Lafayette

Greene

West Ravine

Wemrock Brook

COMB'S HILL

From Englishtown

Freehold Meeting House

Troops:

American	Before retreat
British	
American	After return
British	

Troop movements:

American	Advance
British	Withdrawal

though he did pull a part of his force back. Whatever he intended he simply produced uncertainty in Maxwell, Colonel Charles Scott, and Wayne on the left. A withdrawal on the right left them exposed, and they pulled their troops back. Within a few minutes the entire American force was in retreat. Several regiments seem to have kept their integrity and retired in good order. Others collided and mingled, giving the impression, largely accurate, that the withdrawal was a rout.

Almost all of the American commanders—Wayne, Scott, Maxwell—reported a few days later that they had received no orders from Lee. He told neither them nor anyone else what should be done. As serious in their eyes was his failure to designate a line, or a position, from which a stand might be made. His accusers were unfair to him: Lee did not deliberately conceal his destination—he did not know it. Shortly after the retreat began he sent Duportail, the French engineer, to reconnoiter a hill to the rear where perhaps a defense could be established. Duportail followed orders, looked the hill over—it was just west of Middle Ravine—and pronounced it suitable. When Lee with his sweating army arrived at this hill, he found it less than desirable. Not far from it lay several others which would have given the British higher ground—or so Lee conjectured.

Anthony Wayne with most of the troops in the advance pulled back in complete bewilderment. Wayne had not received an order to attack nor did he receive one to retreat. But he and Scott had withdrawn their forces after repeatedly begging Lee for reinforcements so they could attack, only to discover that the American right, to the south and east of the village, had disappeared. Wayne and Scott both believed that the Americans in the advance force outnumbered the British opposing them—and they wanted to attack. Scott, a half-mile from the court house and well across East Ravine when the right evaporated, felt dreadfully exposed—and was. The British cavalry does not seem to have discovered just how vulnerable he was as most of his troops lay concealed in woods. Still, Scott's regiments were nearly cut off and escaped only by filing off to the left under cover.

Since Lee issued few orders before the retreat and drew up no plan, there is no way of telling exactly what he intended. After the battle, charged in a court-martial for failing to attack the enemy and for retreating, he defended himself by arguing that he hoped to cut the British rear guard off from the main body by attacking its flanks and rear.[55]

55. *Lee Papers*, III, 2.

As Lee reconstructed the day of the battle, retreat occurred only after Scott withdrew, leaving the American left hanging in air, while on the right the British had begun a sweep that threatened to turn his flank. About this time he received "certain intelligence" that Clinton's main body was bearing down on him from the Middletown Road. Exposed on the left, he had no choice—he concluded—but to draw back his forces, a movement performed with "order and precision." Almost no one else discerned this order and precision. Nor did any of the regimental and brigade commanders believe that the withdrawal was necessary. There had been no major battle; they had fought skirmishes and done well in them; casualties were light, though the heat, close to 100°F. by midmorning, took its toll. And yet here they were, a disorderly mass in full retreat.

Washington shared their bewilderment when, in advance of his main force, he encountered Lee's troops near West Ravine. He and his aides asked for explanations of the officers they met and soon found Lee himself. The interview that followed was short, with Washington angrily demanding to know the meaning of what he saw, and Lee managing only a "Sir! Sir!" and then a series of complaints about faulty intelligence, orders not obeyed, and finally something about not believing that the attack against Clinton was wise.[56]

There was time for no more than this short exchange, as a rider appeared with the news that the British were about fifteen minutes behind. Washington then did what he always did well—restored control when chaos surrounded him. With the assistance of others, he put together a line of troops just east of West Ravine, a line which was intended to slow, not stop, the enemy. Wayne helped and Lee himself played a part. But Washington, by his coolness and his decisiveness, more than anyone else inspired the troops and their commanders. With this defense set up, he rode back to the main body which was marching along the road from Englishtown under Greene and Stirling. Those two quickly grasped the urgency and formed along a ridge behind West Ravine, Stirling on the left and Greene on the right.[57]

When the British arrived the Americans were ready. The battle the two sides fought took most of the afternoon. The tactical skills of Clinton and Cornwallis now deserted them, or gave way to a desire to strike a decisive blow. They faced an enemy on a strong defensive position, located on high ground, a swamp in front, woods on the American

56. Freeman, *GW*, V, 28; Ward, II, 581; *Lee Papers*, II, 435–36.
57. Ward, II, 582; Freeman, *GW*, V, 29–32.

left flank and Comb's Hill on the American right, where Knox's field-pieces were emplaced. To assault such a position was risky and to turn it impossible. Yet Clinton tried to assault it—not with one overwhelming mass attack but with uncoordinated, sporadic assaults, now with infantry, now cavalry. He blundered into these tactics when the first British units to make contact rushed pell-mell into battle. Only gradually did the main British body come up, and never did it make its full weight felt. At one point in the afternoon Cornwallis, who was always tough and resourceful under fire, led his cavalry against Greene in a brave charge, only to see it cut down.[58]

By 6:00 P.M. the British had spent their energies and pulled back behind Middle Ravine. Washington then tried to mount an attack but his soldiers were as worn down as the British. Both sides then lay on their arms for the night. When morning came Washington discovered that Clinton had pulled his army from the field and was well on his way to Middletown. The Americans made no attempt to follow and the British reached Sandy Hook on July 1. Five days later the navy had transported the lot—troops, supplies, and wagons—to New York City.[59]

V

The conventions of war required General Clinton to praise his troops for their conduct at Monmouth, and when he wrote his memoirs a few years later he repeated his tributes and declared his satisfaction at the "happy conclusion" of his retirement from Philadelphia. Privately he admitted that what he called "gallantry in public was in fact indecent, ungovernable impetuosity," a reference perhaps to the pell-mell chase of Lee and the piecemeal commitment of troops into the battle at West Ravine. Clinton made little explicit comment about his own conduct, though his satisfaction with himself permeates his account. He had reason to be pleased with himself since taking command in America. He had used his head in holding his army together in the face of orders to send a large part of it off to the West Indies and Florida; he had not abandoned the loyalists who wanted to escape Philadelphia with him; and he had transported most of his troops with a heavy load of supplies safely to New York.[60]

58. Wickwires, *Cornwallis*, 111–12.
59. Ward, II, 585.
60. Willcox, ed., *Clinton's Narrative*, 98. Clinton's account of the evacuation of Phila-delphia and of Monmouth is of value.

Good luck contributed to his success, good luck in the form of winds and ocean currents that had delayed the arrival of Estaing with sixteen men-of-war. Estaing appeared off the Virginia coast a day or two after Clinton's transports put everyone ashore in New York. By July 11, he had made his way to Sandy Hook. Had he caught the British transports in open sea a few days earlier, Clinton would not have characterized the conclusion of the evacuation as "happy."[61]

George Washington also expressed satisfaction at the outcome of the battle of Monmouth Court House. His private feelings are more difficult than Clinton's to decipher, but he was obviously unhappy with Lee and, after that worthy wrote two insulting letters demanding a court-martial, decided to oblige him. The charges against Lee held that he had failed to attack in spite of orders to do so, that he had conducted "an *unnecessary*, *disorderly*, and shameful retreat," and that he had shown disrespect to the commander in chief. Lee was convicted and in August suspended from any command for a year. The prosecution of Lee distressed everyone including his critics, but Washington could not avoid seeing it through.[62]

The arrival of the French fleet lifted American spirits. Washington had long recognized the importance of controlling the sea and of coordinated land-sea attacks. He does not seem to have believed in July that Estaing's coming assured that American waters would be denied to the British, but he did see that he had the force to strike a heavy blow.

First off, the Americans and the French had to lay plans, a need that occupied both for several weeks. As soon as the location of the French ships became known, Washington dispatched his young aide, John Laurens, to Estaing. Laurens was rowed out to the French flagship and talks commenced. Estaing was polite and ready to cooperate, but he also had other preoccupations. The water carried from Toulon was almost exhausted, and he wished to replenish it. He also carried more than the usual number of sick on his ships.[63]

Though Estaing was not a sailor he did appreciate the fact that he faced a formidable man in Admiral Lord Richard Howe. The immediate problem was getting at him. Estaing's force outnumbered Howe's but Howe lay within New York harbor, apparently safe from attack behind the shallow bar that blocked easy entrance. French ships of the line late in the eighteenth century usually drew two or three feet more water

61. *Ibid.*
62. *Lee Papers*, II, 435–36; III, 2.
63. Freeman, *GW*, V, 47–51.

than British, and British warships crossed the bar only in carefully chosen places under the guidance of American pilots. Estaing could have avoided the problems of forcing his way into the harbor by pulling the heaviest guns off his ships and mounting them on Sandy Hook, then an island about four miles long that commanded the harbor. With his naval guns on Sandy Hook he might have destroyed Howe's ships which were swinging at anchor in a line awaiting their enemy. Clinton saw the danger before Estaing saw the opportunity and a week after the French appeared had placed some 1800 men on the island. Estaing prowled the waters outside the harbor until American pilots arrived and told him the dangers of trying to cross the bar.[64]

In late July with New York looking more impregnable every day, Washington and Estaing decided to hit the British where they were exposed—in Newport, Rhode Island. Newport had been a city of about 11,000 people in 1775, but it had shrunk to half that number a year after the war began. It offered a fine harbor, so fine in fact that the British had seized it in December 1776. Sir Robert Pigot and 3000 men now held it, while just to the north in Providence sat a small force of Continentals under General John Sullivan.

Estaing's departure for Newport left Clinton and Lord Howe full of uncertainty. Though they attempted to follow his movements they did not learn his destination until the end of the month. While they speculated about it, they wondered about Byron, who they knew had left England with a large fleet in the spring. They also wondered how they were going to feed their soldiers and sailors; victuallers with food and other supplies were overdue and stocks of just about everything were low. And then there was the problem presented by Clinton's orders to detach 8000 troops to the West Indies and Florida. Should he send them despite the French fleet patrolling American waters?[65]

On July 30, Estaing reduced British uncertainties when he began to enter Narragansett Bay. Four days later, August 3, he put a few French troops ashore on Conanicut, an island just to the west of Newport. About the time he had sailed from New York, Washington had begun strengthening Sullivan's force, and Sullivan himself called on New England militia. By the end of the first week of August, Sullivan had an army of around 10,000 men, most of them militia but with a core provided by General James Varnum's Rhode Islanders and John Glover's Marble-

64. Ward, II, 587–88; Willcox, *Portrait of a General*, 237–38.
65. Willcox, *Portrait of a General*, 239–40.

headers. Sullivan undoubtedly welcomed these men; he may not have felt the same pleasure at the sight of Lafayette and Greene whom Washington had sent to help him command.[66]

Cooperation between Sullivan and Estaing did not flow easily. Sullivan, the son of indentured servants from Ireland, brought an Irishman's hatred of the English to the war and much more—enthusiasm and at times an indiscreet tongue. He now used his mouth incautiously, giving orders to Estaing—he of the French nobility, tender skin, and a higher military rank than Sullivan's. It is conceivable that Estaing might have ignored Sullivan's tactlessness had it not been coupled to what Estaing evidently took to be a lack of ability. And French unease about their American colleagues was not lessened by the discovery that their own chart of Narragansett Bay was better than Sullivan's.[67]

The two sides worked out a plan for attacking Newport despite French suspicions. Sullivan was to come down from Providence, ferry to the island of Rhode Island from Tiverton, and attack Pigot on the northeast side of the island. Estaing would deliver a simultaneous attack from the west. The British saw the danger from Estaing at once and attempted to run five frigates down the middle passage, between Conanicut and Rhode Island, into Newport harbor. All five ran aground and had to be burned by their crews. In an attempt to bar the French from the harbor, Pigot ordered several transports scuttled there. These sinkings seemed to clear the way for Estaing. The attack was set for August 10. On the morning of the 9th, however, Sullivan sent his troops across to Rhode Island. He had discovered that Pigot had retired toward Newport and decided that an unopposed landing was too good to pass up. Estaing interpreted this action as further evidence of American unreliability. That afternoon Estaing received a second suprise: Howe, now reinforced by ships from Byron's fleet, appeared with twenty vessels carrying almost 100 guns more than the French had.

Estaing could have proceeded with his part of the attack. He had some 4000 troops to put ashore, and he might have debarked them before Howe entered the bay. Indeed, in confined waters the French would have been difficult to attack. Estaing, however, kept his troops aboard and took advantage of a favorable wind to sail out for battle. For the next two days the two fleets maneuvered cautiously with Estaing holding the weather advantage—the wind at his back—and Howe striving

---

66. Ward, II, 588–91.

67. *Ibid.*, 590–91. The remainder of this section is drawn from *ibid.*, 591–92; and from Willcox, *Portrait of a General*, 245–51.

to get it. Two days later a gale ended the maneuvers, blowing the two fleets out of their formations, dismasting several ships, and generally doing more damage than guns did in most engagements.

Undiscouraged, Sullivan attacked on the 14th but failed to break through. He then sat down in a half-siege to await Estaing's return. The French ships straggled in over the next few days but Estaing had seen enough, and he heard that Howe would receive even more reinforcements soon. Despite Sullivan's plea that he stay and fight for two days, Estaing set out for Boston, and repairs, on August 21. In effect, the siege of Newport was over. Sullivan's problem was now how to escape— his militia evaporated when the French took off, and Pigot was now prepared to do some attacking on his own. What Sullivan did not know was that Clinton had loaded 4000 regulars on transports and was on the way with the intention of trapping him on Rhode Island. Unfavorable winds slowed the troopships, and on the last day of August Sullivan pulled free. Clinton arrived the next day.

Events of the rest of the year gave neither side cause to rejoice. Admiral Howe, with Byron on the scene at last, went home late in September. He was a brilliant sailor and an able commander, the last naval chief in America to whom these words apply and the last Clinton met on good terms. Early in November, Clinton finally detached 5000 troops under Major General James Grant for the attack on St. Lucia in the West Indies, an attack which would capture the island in December. The Carlisle Commission departed New York about the same time, its mission unfulfilled and its spirit in tatters. Estaing also set out in November, his spirit and his pride intact and his mission unfinished. He sailed without bothering to tell Washington his destination.

VI

The meaning of these events of 1778 seemed clear to the pessimists in the ministry and in Parliament: concentration on the colonies would no longer be possible, and consequently the war in America was lost. The fact that the government somehow had to deal with was that its forces were stretched thin over the rim of the Atlantic. The government had not distinguished itself in the brilliance of its strategic thinking when faced by a colonial rebellion. What could be expected of it when it confronted war in Europe as well as in America?

One of its early decisions—to husband carefully the home fleet in the expectation of a French invasion—paid off in a limited sense in the summer of 1778. The French under Admiral Orvilliers sailed from

Brest on July 10, not with orders to invade England but simply to cruise for a month. On July 23 Orvilliers sighted the English fleet, Admiral Augustus Keppel in command, about seventy miles west of Ushant. The French maintained position with the weather gauge but did not close. The lack of firm orders to strike the enemy may have inhibited Orvilliers, and he did not fight until he was forced to by a change of the wind that enabled Keppel to drive against his rear. Orvilliers turned to face his enemy, and the two fleets sailed past one another firing as they went. Orvilliers, with twenty-seven ships against Keppel's thirty, was outgunned and, understandably, wished to avoid a prolonged engagement which would see his ships pounded to pieces by heavier metal. Outweighed, he chose to fire langrage into the British sails and rigging— a tactic that paid off. The langrage—cast-shot loaded with iron pieces of irregular shape—shattered masts and tore rigging and sails, thus reducing English maneuverability. But the British fire, directed into hulls and decks, was effective too, and French casualties were almost twice those of the British. Orvilliers found one day of battle enough and drew away. While not exactly English, the Channel would not be used for an invasion in 1778.[68]

68. Mackesy, *War for America*, 210–11.

18

The War in the South

An old delusion, born of the wishful thinking that so often follows frustration, now reappeared and made itself felt in British strategy. Before the fighting at Lexington, British ministers had persuaded themselves that their troubles in America were inspired by a conspiracy of the few, that most colonists loved Parliament and the king. Not even the fighting dislodged this conviction from many heads, including the king's own, and it no doubt was a comfort to discouraged ministers who shared the responsibility for military failure.

The Howes had believed that they would find swarms of loyalists, and the march to Trenton in 1776 only partially disabused them. Sir William Howe may even then have believed the most popular form of the myth of the loyal Americans—that those in the southern colonies were especially numerous and more warmly loyal than those in the North. Sir Henry Clinton had sailed to Charleston in June 1776 in the expectation that he would provide a center to which loyal Carolinians would flock. The Carolinians flocked—not to Clinton but to Charles Lee, who headed the city's defense. Though Clinton was joined by an expedition brought from Britain by Admiral Peter Parker, he failed both in taking Charleston and in rallying loyalists.

William Howe retained his faith that the loyalists in the southern colonies only awaited a chance to come out and put down the rebels. In the autumn of 1776 he proposed to attack South Carolina and Georgia during the following winter. But George Washington managed to take his mind off the South, and Howe also began to develop suspicions of Americans wherever he found them. His chief, Lord George Germain, removed from the disappointments of experience by 3000 miles, continued to believe that most Americans were loyal. And by summer 1777, loyalists from the Carolinas had arrived in England and had gained Germain's ear. Reassured by what he heard from them, Germain urged Howe to proceed to the South. By that time Howe had learned to beware of professions of loyalty delivered at a distance—or close up in Pennsylvania—and since he was short of troops he refused to consider undertaking another expedition.[1]

Germain now had an idea of how the war might be won—tap the loyalist support in the South and further its spread northward. From the beginning of Clinton's assumption of command, Germain had tried to push him into a new expedition. The entrance of France into the war diverted even Germain, but the order to dispatch troops from Philadelphia to Florida in March 1778 helped keep alive the possibility of a campaign in the southern colonies. By November, Clinton was prepared for a first effort. On the 27th he dispatched Lt. Colonel Archibald Campbell with the 71st Regiment, two regiments of Hessians, four Tory battalions, and a small contingent of artillery—altogether about 3500 rank-and-file on an invasion of Georgia. Two days before Christmas, Campbell arrived off Tybee Island at the mouth of the Savannah River, some fifteen miles below the town of Savannah.[2]

The American commander in Georgia, Robert Howe, rushed to the town's defense from Sunbury, a distance of thirty miles. He was badly outnumbered, however, and his force—700 Continentals, 150 militia—was soon outflanked when Campbell was guided by a slave through a swamp to a vulnerable point in the not very formidable American defenses. The battle that ensued on December 29 resembled many in the war: the Americans collapsed and fled, leaving almost 100 dead and 453 prisoners. The British lost three dead and ten wounded. In the next month, Campbell with the support of Prevost, who came up from Florida, took control of Georgia.[3]

The great prize in the South lay north of Georgia, the city of Charleston, South Carolina. Almost all of 1779 passed before Clinton made a move to take it. That year saw few great events in America, or in Britain for that matter, but it was nevertheless a momentous year in the Revolu-

1. For a perceptive study of loyalists and the making of British policy, see Paul H. Smith, *Loyalists and Redcoats: A Study in British Revolutionary Policy* (Chapel Hill, N.C., 1964).
2. Ward, II, 679–81.
3. *Ibid.*, 681.

tion. In America, with Clinton feeling himself increasingly thwarted, some new way out, some feasible way of ending the war, seemed now to lie in the South. And the year-long pause in the war, the delay in turning to the southern colonies, saw a crisis slowly build in Britain that reinforced the ministry's old fantasy that the war might be won there.

II

The crisis of 1779 within Britain had its origins in political maneuvering, as did almost every ministerial crisis of the eighteenth century. The old question of what are you going to do with Noodle was very much on Noodle's mind, and on North's. There were always several Noodles, and at this time the chief among them was possessed not merely of ordinary ambitions but also of a feeling that he had been betrayed. This Noodle was Alexander Wedderburn, the solicitor general who in 1774 had abused Benjamin Franklin in the cockpit. Wedderburn had lost none of his odious qualities, among them a greed for high office which he indulged to the point of political blackmail. He now claimed that he had been promised the chief justiceship, a post that was not vacant, but which he wanted nonetheless. Wedderburn did not much care how North delivered it, but deliver it he must.[4]

Suffolk, the Secretary of State for the Northern Department, died in March and the opportunity of replacing him inflamed the hopes of many. The composition of the ministry had been an issue ever since news arrived of the disaster at Saratoga, and now, in view of the events of 1778, in particular the evacuation of Philadelphia, the ministry's prospects had taken on a bleak look. North, Germain, and Sandwich all shared responsibility for the conduct of the war in America, and all received lashings in the newspapers. When Lord Carlisle and William Eden arrived home and their failure became known, the attackers of the ministry had further cause. Eden threw in with Wedderburn in pushing North, who soon was made to realize that appointing Hillsborough to Suffolk's vacant post would not be popular.

While this plotting was getting under way, Sir William Howe demanded a Parliamentary inquiry into his conduct in America. Howe stated to Parliament "that imputations had been thrown on himself,

4. For differing accounts of the episodes discussed in this paragraph and the next, see Herbert Butterfield, *George III, Lord North and the People, 1779–1780* (London, 1949), *passim;* J. Steven Watson, *The Reign of George III, 1760–1815* (Oxford, 1960), 225; Piers Mackesy, *The War for America 1775–1783* (Cambridge, Mass., 1965), 246–48.

and his brother, for not terminating the American war last campaign" and asked for an inquiry into "whether the fault lay in the commanders of his Majesty's fleets and armies, or in the ministries of state."[5] He then paraded witnesses before the Commons, including Lord Cornwallis and Major General Charles Grey, to substantiate his contention that fault lay with the ministry and not with himself or his brother.

Cornwallis, who said that he would confine himself to the facts and keep his opinions to himself, gave a version of the "facts" that rather subtly tarnished Howe's self-portrait as the aggressive commander in America. Grey turned out to be a much better witness, describing difficulties that would have thwarted any military chief this side of Julius Caesar. The American countryside was so rugged, Grey testified, as to make reconnoitering it almost impossible. Against an enemy determined to fight a defensive war, reconnaissance was essential, but in a country made for the defensive and inhabited by a distinctly unfriendly people, attack was difficult to prosecute.

Germain now proved his inner toughness. The implications of Grey's report were clear and easily drawn, but Germain was not about to concede that Howe required further support from home to win the war. Rather he trotted out Major General James Robertson, who proceeded to give a version of things that made Howe's failure inexplicable except in terms of his own incapacity and disinclination to fight. In Robertson's account the Americans appeared as overwhelmingly loyal to the king—in his solemn statement two-thirds of them favored the king's government— and the Declaration of Independence, far from representing popular opinion, emanated from "a few artful folks" who not surprisingly rejoiced in it by themselves. As for the countryside, it abounded in food supplies and a people eager to give information about the traitorous forces under George Washington. Moreover these people would fight for their king; they wanted nothing so much as a good chance, and capable leaders, to help them escape "Congress's tyranny."[6]

This testimony seemed damning, but the Howes struck back. Their blows were returned, and the inquiry dragged on until the end of June. And when it ended in Parliament, it was resumed in the press—to no one's satisfaction.

Meanwhile, the ministry and General Clinton, in America, agreed on a strike against Charleston, South Carolina. What could not be settled

5. John Almon, ed., *The Parliamentary Register* (17 vols., London, 1775–80), XI, 241, 242.

6. *Ibid.*, XIII, 273.

in Parliament might be played out in America. The place for a new beginning lay in the southern colonies.

III

The expedition left New York's harbor with difficulty on December 26, 1779. Loading the transports had called on all the skill of the sailors manning the small boats ferrying the troops and supplies. Temperatures had been low for several weeks, ice clogged the harbor, and winds made handling the boats a treacherous business. The 33rd Regiment, which was Cornwallis's, set out one day only to be forced back to the wharf.[7]

Clinton, always a poor sailor, who hated the sea even when it was untroubled, must have been relieved when the ships—some ninety transports and fourteen warships—departed the harbor in relatively good weather. During the night of December 28–29, whatever he was feeling was doubtless replaced by seasickness as a heavy storm heaved the ships about. Although over the next four weeks the winds occasionally abated and the seas flattened, a series of storms blew the fleet apart.

By January 6, 1780, Johann Hinrichs of the Jaeger Corps, who kept a careful diary of the voyage, was writing: "Always the same weather!" The "same" was "Storm, rain, hail, snow, and the waves breaking over the cabin, such was today's observation." During the worst of it, the ships would furl their sails and drift during the night, with the wheel lashed down and the ship buttoned up as tightly as possible. In the mornings, when they could see, each ship would discover that it was alone, or in the company of only a few others. During the day that followed the ships would attempt to collect themselves if the weather permitted. Usually the weather permitted little, as masts crashed down under the pounding, sails were ripped to shreds, and hulls sprang leaks. Captain Hinrichs watched the sinking of the *George*, a transport with the infantry aboard "throwing their belongings and themselves head over heels into the boats." The soldiers fared better than the horses, most of which were injured and had to be destroyed. Stores of all sorts were also damaged, and much was lost as ships went down.[8]

At the end of January the transports and their escorts began to drift into the mouth of the Savannah River, to Tybee Island, where the crews dried out and repaired their vessels. They were of course far south

7. Willcox, *Portrait of a General*, 301.
8. Johann Hinrichs, "Journal," in Bernhard A. Uhlendorf, ed., *The Siege of Charleston* (Ann Arbor, Mich., 1938), 121, 127.

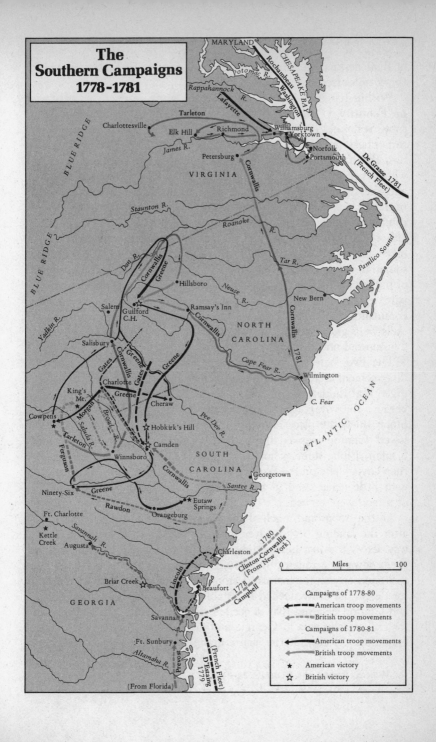

The
Southern
Campaigns
1778-1781

MARYLAND

BLUE RIDGE

Rappahannock R.
Lafayette
Tarleton
Charlottesville
Elk Hill
Richmond
Williamsburg
Yorktown
James R.
Norfolk
Petersburg
Portsmouth
Cornwallis
VIRGINIA

Rochambeau
Washington
Potomac R.
CHESAPEAKE BAY

De Grasse 1781
(French Fleet)

Staunton R.

Roanoke R.

BLUE RIDGE

Dan R.
Cornwallis
Greene
Hillsboro
Ramsay's Inn
Salem
Guilford
C.H.
Cornwallis
Salisbury
Gates
Cornwallis
Greene
Greene
Gates
Charlotte Gates
King's
Mt.
Greene
Cowpens
Morgan
Cheraw
Tarleton
Ferguson
Saluda R.
Broad R.
Hobkirk's Hill
Winnsboro
Camden
Ninety-Six
Greene
Rawdon
Orangeburg
Eutaw
Springs
Ft. Charlotte
Kettle
Creek
Augusta
Savannah R.
Briar Creek
GEORGIA
Savannah
Ft. Sunbury
Altamaha R.
(From Florida)

Tar R.

New Bern

Pamlico Sound

NORTH
CAROLINA

Neuse R.

Cape Fear R.

Cornwallis 1781

Wilmington

C. Fear

ATLANTIC OCEAN

Pee Dee R.

SOUTH
CAROLINA

Georgetown

Santee R.

Lincoln
Charleston
1780
Clinton-Cornwallis
(From New York)

1778
Campbell

Beaufort

French Fleet
D'Estaing
1779

Miles
0   100

Campaigns of 1778-80
American troop movements
British troop movements
Campaigns of 1780-81
American troop movements
British troop movements
★ American victory
☆ British victory

of their destination, which originally was the North Edisto Inlet about thirty miles from Charleston.

Within ten days Clinton declared the army ready to proceed, and on February 11 the troops began putting ashore on Simmons Island (now Seabrook) on the Edisto Inlet. This move occasioned a different sort of heavy weather between Clinton and Vice Admiral Marriot Arbuthnot, the naval commander who had followed Sir George Collier and who was Clinton's equal in rank. Clinton had liked Commodore Collier, and the two had worked well together. Marriot Arbuthnot proved to be much more difficult to work with. He was sixty-eight and did not exude energy. He was not without experience, but he had not commanded either a major station such as the North American waters nor had he taken part in a large venture with the army. He was unpredictable, sometimes determined, sometimes indecisive. He was given to bursts of both confidence and fears, and the bursts proved impossible to anticipate, let alone explain. He did not relish the responsibilities of his new command—nor should he have, for he lacked a strategic sense and the skills of a great sailor. He was, in short, just the sort of companion Clinton did not need.[9]

The two men disagreed on where the troops should go ashore, a disagreement that would be followed by others more serious. Clinton urged that the landing should be at the North Edisto Inlet, apparently because the voyage there would be a day or two shorter than to the Stono Inlet, the place Arbuthnot proposed. In the argument that followed, Clinton invoked the authority of one of Arbuthnot's skippers, Captain Elphinstone, who knew the waters around Charleston better than anyone else on the expedition. Arbuthnot gave way, but apparently with little grace. And in the exchange between the two the outlines of a feud were etched.

All the troops and much of their baggage cleared the ship three days after the landing began. Over the next ten days the army slogged its way across the marshes on Johns and James islands. Clinton then sat them down in a rough camp and, aside from establishing a beachhead at Stono Ferry on the mainland, stopped his advance. There were reasons for delay: the army needed to establish supply depots and magazines, and Clinton believed that it needed reinforcements. He promptly sent for the detachments in Georgia and ordered that troops be sent from New York. Meanwhile the quartermasters, lacking horses to draw heavy

9. Willcox, *Portrait of a General*, 284–85.

wagons over the soggy ground, proceeded slowly in building up the magazines. Clinton also had to wait on the navy to make its way into the upper harbor, where its heavy guns could be put ashore for the siege he had decided upon and where its small boats could be used to ferry troops across the Ashley River to the peninsula on which Charleston was located.[10]

Charleston, the only city of any size in the southern states, ordinarily numbered 12,000 citizens, mostly of English stock but with sizable numbers of black slaves, French Protestants, and a sprinkling of Spaniards and Germans. It lay on a peninsula cut by the Ashley River on the west and the Cooper on the east. Visitors found it beautiful and, though hot in summer, cooler than the inland areas. Wealthy rice planters aspired to houses in the city, and many built them in order to escape the worst of the summer heat. Altogether there were some eight hundred, or perhaps a thousand, houses sitting along broad streets which intersected one another at right angles. Most of the houses were of wood and rather small—at least by European standards. Along the two rivers, though, handsome and large brick houses had been built, and many owners had put in gardens behind them.[11]

Since 1776, Charleston's defenses had decayed. From the seaward side, the side that had thwarted Parker and Clinton in 1776, Fort Moultrie on Sullivan's Island on the east and Fort Johnson on the west had fallen into disrepair. They were occupied, however, and seemed to stand in the way of an enemy coming through the outer (or lower) harbor. In reality, nature offered a more formidable obstacle in the shape of a heavy sand bar. The bar could be crossed at five places, but at all these points the water was so shallow as to prevent the passage of heavy ships. Frigates and smaller vessels could make it, but not without lightening themselves. A series of terraced works of palmetto logs protected the tip of the Neck, as the peninsula was called, and along the side of each river there were redoubts, trenches, and small fortifications. The redoubt at the tip held sixteen heavy guns, and the forts along the river had from three to nine guns each. There was a small flotilla of ships in the upper harbor under Commodore Whipple when the siege began, but they were scuttled at the mouth of the Cooper when Arbuthnot crossed the bar on March 20. Their guns and crews were sent ashore

10. William T. Bulgar, ed., "Sir Henry Clinton's 'Journal of the Siege of Charleston, 1780,' " *SCHM*, 66 (1965), 147–74.

11. There is a fine contemporary description of Charleston in the "Diary of Captain Ewald," Uhlendorf, ed., *Siege*, 91.

to strengthen the defenses already in place. The ships themselves formed a barrier to entrance into the Cooper.[12]

Charleston's defenses on the north were in worse shape than those facing the harbor. Benjamin Lincoln, the commander of the city's garrison, expected invasion from the sea and consequently neglected completing the land-works that stretched across the Neck. The heart of these defenses was the citadel, or "hornwork" or "old royal work," a heavy fort made of "tapia" or "tappy," a material consisting of oystershells, lime, sand, and water. It had eighteen guns. There were redoubts on either side of it, but they were not complete; nor had their engineers located them well, had not at least in the judgment of the enemy that eventually captured them. One flaw might have been corrected had the Americans used their time more efficiently: the lonely isolation of these works. They sat apart from one another, and the main one on the left never enjoyed safe communications with the others. Communication trenches dug between the citadel and those on the right strengthened that side of the line, but the rear of even these works remained vulnerable because their defenders neglected to close them. Duportail, the French engineer who arrived late in April, urged the closing of the rear of the works, an extremely difficult process under fire.[13]

The people of Charleston did not rush into these fortifications; nor did the people from the state, and probably no more than one-third of the defenders were Carolinians. When Clinton landed, Lincoln had 800 South Carolina Continentals, 400 Virginia Continentals, around 380 of Pulaski's Legion (named after their commander, the Polish nobleman, Casimir Pulaski), 2000 militia from the Carolinas, and a small number of dragoons. In April, just before Clinton closed off the city, reinforcements, North Carolina and Virginia Continentals, arrived.[14]

Lincoln must have been grateful for the Continentals in this force. He had little else to be grateful for; he had stepped into waters over his head and he did not know how to swim. But no American commander could have stayed afloat easily in the depths of siegecraft: physical defenses in decay, or uncompleted, inadequate military forces, a civilian population eager to be defended but unwilling to expose itself, these were deep waters indeed. And of course Lincoln had no experience in defending a city under siege, nor did anyone else in his command.

12. Ward, II, 696–97.
13. "Diary of Captain Ewald," Uhlendorf, ed., Siege, 91–93, and the notes to these pages.
14. Ward, II, 697–698.

Not that Lincoln lacked ability. Before the Revolution he had got his living as a farmer in Hingham, Massachusetts, where he was born in 1733. He came up the way many able men in New England did— through hard work and service to the community as town clerk, justice of the peace, and a militia officer in a Suffolk County regiment. In the years just preceding the war he sat on Hingham's committee of correspondence and in the Provincial Congress. A lieutenant colonel of militia when the war began, Lincoln rose to major general in a short time; and Congress, following a suggestion from Washington, brought him to the same rank in the Continental line early in 1777. His service thereafter, until Congress appointed him commander of the southern department in September 1778 in place of Robert Howe, was not undistinguished but it was not brilliant. He performed well at Saratoga, where he was seriously wounded in the leg. The command in the South followed a long period of recuperation.[15]

Lincoln did not know why the enemy did not attack and may not have given the delay much thought in his haste to complete his defenses. Expecting the British to force their way across the bar and up into the harbor, he at first concentrated on the lower tip of the Neck and the mouths of the rivers. Work also proceeded up the peninsula in case the British decided to approach the city from the rear.

Clinton seems never to have considered a landing on the tip, preferring to come around to strike from the mainland. He needed the navy for this move, and on March 20, Arbuthnot succeeded in getting half a dozen frigates over the bar. A game of seagoing cat-and-mouse preceded this success, with small craft of the Royal Navy marking the shallow spots along the bar with buoys, and Whipple's boats slipping out afterwards to destroy them.

Five days later Paterson and his 1500 who had been detached to Georgia returned, and on the night of March 29, Clinton began sending his reinforced army across the Ashley at Drayton's Landing, about twelve miles above Charleston. The Ashley was only 200 yards wide at this place, and bent just below so that it shielded from American observers the small boats manned by Arbuthnot's crews.[16]

The Americans did not oppose this landing, and by April 1, Clinton's forces had moved within 1000 yards of the defenses across the Neck. The siege now began in a manner familiar in eighteenth-century warfare.

15. There is no good biography of Lincoln. Ward gives bits and pieces about him.
16. Hinrichs, "Journal," Uhlendorf, ed., *Siege*, 223–25.

Engineers opened a "parallel" across the Neck about 800 yards from the American lines. The parallel consisted of trenches and redoubts roughly paralleling the works some 800 yards away. Ten days later it was completed, and under the supervision of engineers the troops began digging saps toward the American lines. This procedure followed the usual theory and practice of sieges, which were called "regular approaches," that is, systematic and well-laid out approaches on the ground ever closer to enemy fortifications.[17]

A siege might bring the attackers close enough to permit them to make an all-out assault without exposing themselves until the last possible moment. Clinton hoped that an assault would not be necessary, hoped indeed that he could force Lincoln to surrender by cutting Charleston off from any relief. His purposes were as much political as military: to capture Charleston and its population intact and thereby help rally loyalist support to the king's cause. The destruction of the city would not contribute to this purpose, and Clinton remarked during the siege when Captain Elphinstone and "all the navy" rejoiced "at the town's being on fire": "Absurd, impolitic, and inhuman to burn a town you mean to occupy." In any case "the success of a storm [an assault] is uncertain. . . . I think we are sure of the place upon our own terms, and with it I think we conquer the southern provinces and perhaps more."[18]

No siege any more than a "storm" could be undertaken lightly. It tested the wills of the defenders watching their enemy dig his way into their guts, and it taxed the energies and resourcefulness of the attackers. The ground was generally flat north of the city; the soil sandy and marshy and full of sand fleas whose bites were "very painful" according to a German officer who experienced them. The ground had few high places to screen off American observers so most of the digging was done at night. The heat was not usually oppressive then, but the days of this April were described as "unbearable."[19]

The terrain made artillery fire especially effective—effective, that is, by the standards of the eighteenth century. The first parallel was dug out of the range of most artillery, the accuracy of which was always problematical. Generally, even heavy guns were unreliable at ranges over

17. I have constructed my history of the siege from Bulgar, ed., "Clinton's 'Journal,' " *SCHM,* 66 (1965), 147–74; Joseph Warring, ed., "Lieutenant John Wilson's Journal of the Siege of Charleston," *ibid.,* 175–82; "Diary of Captain Ewald" and Hinrichs, "Journal," Uhlendorf, ed., *Siege;* Willcox, ed., *Clinton's Narrative;* Willcox, *Portrait of a General;* and Ward.

18. The quotations are from Bulgar, ed., "Clinton's 'Journal,' " *SCHM,* 66 (1965), 160, 169.

19. "Diary of Captain Ewald," Uhlendorf, ed., *Siege,* 45.

1200 yards, and some heavy guns beyond 400 yards. Mortars might throw shells much farther—occasionally as far as two miles—but they too lacked accuracy. As the British pushed closer, however, they increased their chances of being killed not only by artillery but by small arms as well.

Push closer they did throughout April. Major Moncrieff, a skillful engineer, directed most of their operations. He began his work one night by crawling up to the abatis in order to see just what he was up against. He then organized large working parties, sometimes as many as 500 men, and put them to constructing the siege works. At several points along the parallel, redoubts were put up, consisting of heavy wooden frames ten feet high and fourteen feet long sitting on three legs. These frames, called mantelets, had been shipped from New York where they were constructed. Assembled on the scene at Charleston, sixteen were fitted together to form the skeleton of a redoubt. Then sand and earth were piled against them until their walls were at least twelve feet thick. Embrasures were cut through their parapets to permit guns and howitzers to be fired. When the last parallel was completed—the third—in late April, several of the embrasures were usually occupied by infantry with rifles and muskets. Rifle embrasures were also built with sandbags along the trenches outside the redoubts to allow infantry to fire into the embrasures of the American redoubts.[20]

Building these works and digging trenches would not have been easy in peacetime. Lifting the mantelets was difficult; each required eighteen men, and carrying them in the dark to the right place while under fire was no trifling business. The digging also presented special problems. The sand was fairly loose, but it was wet—at times the men worked in water—and drainage ditches had to be dug. The shelling was often very heavy though usually, perhaps, inaccurate. But the lack of precision added a special kind of horror. No one knew when the next round was coming or where it would land. And the Americans fired terrible stuff, canisters filled with jagged fragments of old projectiles, broken shovels, pickaxes, hatchets, flat irons, pistol barrels, broken locks, and sometimes even shards of glass. The wounds this metal inflicted could be terrible: accounts of the siege mention legs torn off, arms shattered, and men blown apart by heavy explosions. A single solid cannon ball that smashed into seven jaegers one May night tore off one man's leg, damaged another's thigh, and crashing into a tree threw splinters into five others.[21]

20. *Ibid.*, 39; Hinrichs, "Journal," *ibid.*, 231, 235.
21. Hinrichs, "Journal," *ibid.*, *passim*, and esp. 279.

The British and Germans fired more conventional rounds, but these too had the capacity to mutilate flesh and bone. As the sappers burrowed closer, artillery was dragged forward and aimed at the embrasures of the citadel and the supporting works. For this nice work, the royal artillerymen favored canisters filled with 100 bullets each. They also fired three-pound case shot and half-pound projectiles, called "bogy shot." Nor did they neglect heavy balls and explosive bombs. By late April, when the second parallel was complete and the third well under way, each side could see the damage and sometimes the casualties inflicted on the other. A shell struck an American platform behind an embrasure: "It burst as it fell, throwing two artillerymen from the embrasure into the trench and blowing up the enemy's platform."[22]

As the horror increased, men on both sides broke. The terror bred confusion as to which side was winning, and each lost deserters to the other. The worst fears came with darkness. Not that the days were tranquil or free of strain—the shells dropped on both sides, and in late April when the range shortened each kept the other under incessant rifle and musket fire. A deadly game took place: each side waited for the other to open its embrasures and then poured in musket balls and cannisters before they were closed again. The nights were worse because when the sun went down men's imaginations took over.[23]

For Lincoln's troops the darkness brought home the knowledge that the enemy's sappers were at work. When morning came the Americans looked out to an advance that seemed inexorable. The strain showed in glazed eyes and faces tight and bloated with fatigue. For the British and Germans the terrors were no less genuine. The shelling by their enemy increased as the Americans tried to slow the sappers' digging. When the Americans learned from a deserter that the relief of troops in the trenches was ordinarily done an hour before daybreak, that operation assumed a terrible danger.

Late in April as work on the third parallel was completed and the sappers burrowed toward the canal, the precariousness of their position was made especially clear to the British and German infantry. Their commander in chief had insisted from the beginning that they rely on their bayonets. Their muskets were to remain unloaded at night when no targets could be seen anyway. Reliance on the bayonet meant discipline to Clinton—discipline and pride and spirit. Clinton visited the

---

22. *Ibid.*, 257.
23. This paragraph and the next are based on the German officers' accounts already cited.

trenches often in April—he always had physical courage—and on one of his visits he discovered "GREAT NEGLECT," as he said in his journal, troops who had not fixed their bayonets.[24] The troops had not presumably because they felt easier in the dark when their muskets were loaded. Even so they panicked on the night of April 24, when 200 Americans made a sortie against one end of the third parallel. The jaegers there ran back to the second, but even so the Americans killed or wounded fifty and captured a dozen more of them. For a few dreadful minutes the Americans seemed to have cut a part of the third parallel off from the second. The following night small arms fire and yelling from the American lines produced a further panic as Germans and English abandoned the third parallel in terror. Men in flight often overpower the reason of others, and in this instance when they tumbled into the trenches of the second they set off a wild firing from those who did not actually break and run. A jaeger officer later noted that "Everywhere they saw rebels. They believed the enemy had made a sortie and fired musketry [muskets] for over half an hour, though not a single rebel had passed the ditch."[25]

Within this carnage lesser struggles were enacted. One found Clinton growling in his journal about Cornwallis and Arbuthnot, and occasionally to them about their conduct. Clinton had learned ten days before he crossed the Ashley that his resignation had not been accepted. This news may have disappointed him; it more than disappointed Cornwallis who hoped to replace Clinton—it caused him to withhold his advice from his chief. Clinton helped this sulking along by reproaching Cornwallis for having permitted someone on his staff to say with a "sneer" that if Clinton wished to resign all he had to do was to ask again. Cornwallis denied that anyone had sneered at Clinton, bitter words passed back and forth, though perhaps none so serious as Clinton's charge in his journal against Cornwallis for "UNSOLDIERLY BEHAVIOR, NEGLECTING TO GIVE ORDERS IN MY ABSENCE."[26] Although the immediate effects of this conflict defy measurement, one result is clear: Cornwallis possessed fine tactical skills and Clinton did not employ Cornwallis well.

Of more obvious importance was the near break with Arbuthnot. The background of this quarrel is to be found in events that occurred before the siege commenced. Arbuthnot rarely acted decisively, and his

24. Bulgar, ed., "Clinton's 'Journal,' " SCHM, 66 (1965), 155.
25. Hinrichs, "Journal," Uhlendorf, ed., Siege, 261; "Diary of Captain Ewald," ibid., 69–70 (the quotation is on 71). See also Bulgar, ed., "Clinton's 'Journal,' " SCHM, 66 (1965), 166.
26. Bulgar, ed., "Clinton's 'Journal,' " SCHM, 66 (1965), 149.

disagreement with Clinton left him even more reluctant than usual to exert himself. Clinton wanted him to push his ships up the Cooper River in order to trap Lincoln in the city. Arbuthnot never directly refused, but he failed to make the attempt. He offered a series of reasons—he needed more time, or he feared fireships might destroy his fleet in the confined reaches of the river—and in the process he convinced Clinton that he was an incompetent and a liar. Thus Clinton to Arbuthnot: "I find by [the] Ad[miral's] letter to Elp[hinstone] he still HARPS UPON DELAYS. He should recollect all the delays occasioned by himself. . . . I will once more enumerate them here." And: he "will LIE—NAY, I KNOW HE WILL IN A THOUSAND INSTANCES." And about two weeks later—on April 22—"In appearance we were the best of friends, but I am sure he is FALSE as HELL."[27]

During some of these worst days of bickering, Clinton's forces struck decisive blows and succeeded in cutting off the city without the navy's aid. On the night of April 14, Lt. Colonel Banastre Tarleton, commander of the Tory Legion, took Monck's Corner, a strategic point up the Cooper linking the city to the countryside to the north. And in another week, Tarleton and Lt. Colonel James Webster with two regiments dominated approaches all along the Cooper to within six miles of Charleston.[28]

With escapes closed off, Lincoln lost hope. Civilians in Charleston refused to allow him to surrender, however. Some evidently thought that Washington would march southward and save them. Lincoln tried to persuade them that defeat was inevitable, and on April 21 he offered to surrender to Clinton on the condition that he and his army would be permitted to leave on their own terms. Clinton turned him down immediately.

By the end of the first week in May the two armies were separated by only a few yards. The sappers had done their work well, digging right up to the American lines and actually draining the main ditch that cut across the Neck. Lincoln squirmed and fretted and tried to persuade Clinton both to let him surrender with full honors of war and to allow the militia to go free. Clinton would have none of this, and on the night of May 9 the two sides shelled one another heavily. This time, firing into wooden houses, the British artillery proved effective. With many houses burning, the citizens of Charleston decided they had had enough. Surrender came on May 12. The militia were paroled

27. *Ibid.*, 151, 157, 165.
28. For this paragraph and the next, Ward, II, 700–702.

and all the American officers were allowed to keep their swords until their shouts of "long live Congress" got on British nerves whereupon they were forced to give them up. Altogether 2571 Continentals were taken and 800 militia were paroled. The dead and wounded were surprisingly few on both sides—76 British killed and 189 wounded, and 89 Americans killed and 138 wounded. The American loss of weapons and supplies was heavy: 343 artillery pieces of various sizes, almost 6000 muskets, 376 barrels of powder, over 30,000 rounds of small-arms ammunition, plus large stores of rum, rice, and indigo.[29]

Three days later a dreadful accident added to the dead and wounded. The captured muskets had been thrown carelessly into a wooden building where gunpowder was also stored. A loaded musket tossed onto the pile may have gone off. An explosion followed setting six houses afire and killing some 200 people, British, Americans, Germans, soldiers and civilians alike. A German officer wrote that "a great many" suffering from terrible powder burns "writhed like worms on the ground." Pieces of bodies were scattered all about, some so "mutilated that one could not make out a human figure." Thus an agonizing siege ended in a special sort of horror.[30]

IV

Even during the worst of the siege, except perhaps for the long nights of terror, there had been some rudimentary sense of order. The lines separating the two sides were clear, and friend could identify foe. The shelling, though often ineffective, had brought fear to troops and civilians alike, but its special sort of dread had been confined to the besiegers and besieged of a city. And fear had become familiar, a part of ordinary existence, with its sources known, an enemy who lived just below ground level like one's own soldiers. Now, with Lincoln's surrender, the fear spread throughout the Carolinas, not usually so intense to be sure, but especially dreadful because it was unexpected and because it often issued from neighbors and onetime friends.

The spread took the British by surprise. Clinton did not expect that bringing order to South Carolina would be easy, but he did not think it impossible, and he had ideas on how to proceed. On June 1 he and Arbuthnot issued a proclamation offering full pardons to prisoners and other active rebels who would take an oath of allegiance. This proclama-

29. *Ibid.*, 703; "Diary of Captain Ewald," Uhlendorf, ed., *Siege*, 87. The casualties are given in Peckham, *Toll*, 70.

30. "Diary of Captain Ewald," Uhlendorf, ed., *Siege*, 89.

The Siege of Charleston

COOPER RIVER

WANDO RIVER

Ferry

Clinton →

British march from Simmons Island

ASHLEY RIVER

Canal

British lines

HOGGS ISLAND

Lamprie's Pt.

Citadel

SHUTE'S FOLLY

Haddrell's Pt.

Mt. Pleasant

Boom Redoubt

CHARLESTON

Bridge

Ft. Moultrie

SULLIVAN'S I.

Wappoo Cutoff

SWAMP

Ft. Johnson

Middle Ground

Shallows

STONO RIVER

JOHNS ISLAND

JAMES ISLAND

British fleet

Cummins Pt.

Ferry

CUMMINS ISLAND

Lighthouse

Shallows

SWAMP

Shallows

Shallows

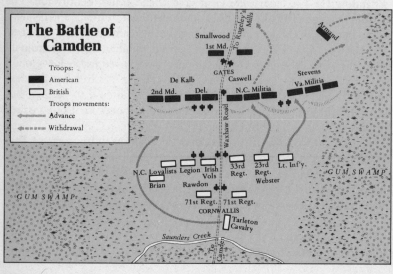

The Battle of Camden

Troops:

■ American

□ British

Troops movements:

⟵ Advance

⟵ Withdrawal

To Rugeley's Mills

Armand

Smallwood
1st Md.

GATES

De Kalb   Caswell   Stevens

2nd Md.   Del.   N.C. Militia   Va. Militia

Waxhaw Road

N.C. Loyalists   Legion   Irish Vols   33rd Regt.   23rd Regt. Webster   Lt. Inf'y.

GUM SWAMP

Brian   Rawdon

71st Regt.   71st Regt.

CORNWALLIS

GUM SWAMP

Tarleton Cavalry

Saunders Creek

To Camden

tion aroused discontent only among loyalists who expected that rebellion would be punished. And here was Clinton promising rebels who would swear allegiance that they would have the rights they had always possessed under British rule, plus exemption from Parliamentary taxation. Many rebels had already accepted parole, moved by the guarantee that in doing so their property would remain their own and perhaps by the rumors that Congress would cede the Carolinas and Georgia to Britain. Clinton did not trust all those he had captured and though he paroled several hundred, he also sent others, clearly disaffected, to islands off the coast and to prison ships in the harbor. There, in these pestilential tubs, eight hundred were to die in the next year.

Two days after the proclamation of leniency, Clinton without consulting Arbuthnot issued a second—Thomas Jones, the loyalist historian, was to observe sardonically that the British thought that they could subdue rebellion by proclamation—releasing all those on parole as of June 20, but requiring them to take an oath to support British measures. If they refused to give active support they would be treated as rebels. The effect of this requirement was to send men who might have sat out the war back into active opposition. Clinton did not remain to face it, however. He left for New York the next week with 4000 troops, most of the army's horses and wagons, and a good deal of equipment, having received word that the French might attempt to take New York in his absence. With things well under way in South Carolina he could turn the command over to Cornwallis, who had long wanted autonomy.

Just what Clinton had left Cornwallis became clear over the summer. The command in the Carolinas was independent, though of course Clinton remained at the head of the army in America. He gave Cornwallis instructions to pacify South Carolina, reclaim North Carolina, and to drive into Virginia where operations were projected with contingents drawn from the army in New York.

Cornwallis's command may have been independent but he faced formidable restraints on its exercise. The proclamations Clinton had hung around his neck could be thrown off and were, with the dispatching to jail of some of the worst rebels. But the proclamations had generated an opposition that grew over the summer, grew with every attempt to put it down. In a sense everything Cornwallis could do to destroy the king's enemies was futile. His problem in the Carolinas had been Howe's and Clinton's in the North: in order to restore the allegiance of America he had to crush the rebellion. And the process of crushing the rebellion simply fed its sources.

That process slipped out of his control almost at once in the brutal struggles that occurred over the summer between loyalists and patriots. One of the earliest of these fights took place on June 20, ten days after Cornwallis assumed command. A Tory colonel, John Moore, who had served with Cornwallis above the Cooper River, returned to his home in Ramsour's Mill in North Carolina and attempted to enlist his neighbors in the king's service. Some 1300 responded only to be defeated in a chaotic battle by a rebel force of almost equal size. Those of Moore's men who did survive disappeared, leaving him with thirty stragglers to take to Cornwallis in Camden.

Three weeks later, on July 12, rebels under Captain James McClure beat up a Tory party under Captain Christian Huck, a regular officer who ordinarily served with Tarleton's Legion. This battle was fought at Williamson's Plantation (now Brattonville), a little more than fifty miles north of Camden in the Catawba district. And on August 1, Thomas Sumter, called the "gamecock" by Tarleton, led as many as 600 men against a much smaller Tory force under Lt. Colonel George Turnbull at Rocky Mount. The loyalists held their own in this fray, but Sumter gained too from this additional example of defiance of royal authority. In the next month the loyalists absorbed heavy losses at Hanging Rock. And when they were successful, as, for example, the navy was in raiding rebel property near Georgetown, they also succeeded in calling out opposition. Near Georgetown, in the Williamsburg district, the rebel militia swarmed into organized units when the navy showed itself.

These confrontations attained a size sufficient to ensure that their history would be told. Many more, skirmishes, raids, murders, did not. Yet they were important, for they forced men into action. A raid brought Thomas Sumter back into service after he had retired to his plantation near Statesburgh. Tarleton's Legion burned Sumter's house in May. Andrew Pickens, a partisan leader of scarcely less talent, broke his parole and his oath after his plantation was plundered by Tories.

There is no way of knowing how many others took to the field for similar reasons. But throughout 1780 and well into 1781, nasty, brutish conflicts occurred in the interior of South Carolina. Many involved nothing more than small-scale raids, neighbor against neighbor. Others, better remembered, enlisted large numbers of militia on both sides and often were directed against British posts, supply trains, dispatch riders. This sort of warfare, deadly little fights, shootings, and burnings, brought out the worst in people (and the best in a few). The worst were the so-called "outliers," scavengers and jackals and renegades, their hands set against everyone while they professed to be in opposition to whichever group they plundered. Such men had appeared earlier in New York and Pennsylvania where, as in the Carolinas, they brought an indiscriminate misery.

Bringing order to this disorderly countryside was very much on Cornwallis's mind when he succeeded Clinton. By the end of June he had established posts at Ninety-Six, Camden, and Cheraw; soon after he pushed detachments into place at Rocky Mount, Hanging Rock, and Georgetown on the coast near the mouth of the Pee Dee. There were also fairly strong units at Savannah and Augusta to the south. Altogether Cornwallis could claim uneasy control of some 15,000 square miles. And he was considering a move into North Carolina and in fact was waiting only until the harvest could be completed there before beginning his march.[31]

While Cornwallis stretched his forces out in South Carolina, American regulars marched into North Carolina led by the giant Bavarian Johann DeKalb. The son of peasants, DeKalb looked as if he had spent years in grain fields doing the hardest labor, for he was a bull of a man, over six feet in height, broad in face and thick in body—though not in brain. He knew his craft, having fought in two European wars, served with Marshal Saxe, and read deeply about battles. He also knew something about America; Choiseul had sent him to report on colonial affairs during the agitation before 1776 and he had traveled widely—and observed carefully. He returned to America after the war began and though he received a commission as a major general and served at Valley Forge and Monmouth, he had never had his own command. Now he had it, from Congress, which in April had ordered him to take Delaware and Maryland Continentals to the rescue of Charleston. DeKalb never made it; in July he rested his footsore infantry at Coxe's Mill along the Deep River in North Carolina.[32]

There Horatio Gates found him on July 25 and, on the order of Congress, took command of his 1400 Continentals. Congress had appointed Gates to head the army in the South on learning of the disaster at Charleston. Washington had recommended that Nathanael Greene be appointed, but Congress, still bedazzled by Saratoga, had wanted

31. This account of the months following Charleston is based on Ward; Willcox, *Portrait of a General;* Wickwires, *Cornwallis;* and Hugh F. Rankin, *Francis Marion: The Swamp Fox* (New York, 1973).

32. Ward, II, 712–14.

its victor to recover the South for America. Given Gates's record, which is all that Congress had to go on, the choice was excellent. Most men seemed to like him instinctively, reassured by his plainness. On top of his apparent simplicity, since 1777 he carried an aura of success—he had forced surrender from a British army. The pride, and delight, that Americans felt in his triumph is clear in the word they coined to describe it—he had "burgoyned" the British.

Soldiers in the field respect victories, but they also expect renowned leaders to provide effective leadership. Doubts about Gates set in at once. The day after his arrival he ordered the "Grand Army"—his term for the worn-out Continentals—paraded, and on July 27, he set them on the road to Camden. Protest was futile and seemed churlish in the face of Gates's reassurances that "*rum* and *rations*" were only a couple of days behind him. Still, Otho Williams, his adjutant general, urged him to take a roundabout route to the west rather than a direct line which led through sand and swamp, largely barren of farms and those few long since picked clean by the militia of both sides.[33]

On August 7, Richard Caswell's North Carolina militia, some 2100 strong, joined Gates, and the next week Virginia militia under Edward Stevens came in. The militia must have wondered about the Grand Army. Gates's troops exuded fatigue, as any troops might who had existed on little more than green corn, lean beef, and peaches for several weeks. Marching from Hillsboro to Rugeley's Mills, just north of Camden, a distance of 120 miles, had taken them two weeks. They reached Rugeley's Mills short of just about everything—they had but eighteen cannon and only a small troop of cavalry, though the Carolinas generally lightly wooded and flat were made for cavalry. Gates also lacked information about his enemy, a deficiency that was to cost many lives.[34]

The enemy had increased his numbers in Camden two days before. Cornwallis, in Charleston, learned of Gates's approach on August 9. The next day he set out for Camden. There he found Rawdon, now reinforced by four companies of light troops from Ninety-Six, and small units from Hanging Rock and Rocky Mount. Rawdon had skirmished with advance parties from Gates's army and with partisans under Thomas Sumter. Gates, however, was ignorant of Cornwallis's presence and unaware that a large force, 2043 effectives, had ensconced itself in Camden.

33. Otho Williams, "A Narrative of the Campaign of 1780," in William Johnson, *Sketches of the Life and Correspondence of Nathanael Greene* (2 vols., Charleston, S. C., 1822), I. 486–87. Williams's account is in *ibid.*, I, Appendix B, 485–510.
34. Ward, II, 718–21.

There were also 800 British sick in the town, and their presence helped convince Cornwallis that he should fight rather than pull back before what he thought was a much larger army.[35]

On August 15, Gates ordered a night march which he expected would bring his army into position to trap a much smaller British force. When he issued his orders Gates thought he had 7000 men; the skeptical Williams had a tally taken and discovered that the army numbered 3052. Gates expressed surprise but ordered the army forward, commenting only that the 3000 would be sufficient. According to Williams, who wrote a perceptive account of the battle that followed, before marching the troops dined on "a hasty meal of quick baked bread and fresh beef, with a desert of molasses, mixed with mush, or dumplings." This meal, Williams reported, "operated so cathartically, as to disorder very many of the men," who "broke ranks" all night with the result that they were weaker and even more tired than usual in the morning. Whatever their condition, they marched at ten that night; by coincidence Cornwallis set his army in motion at exactly the same time. About two-thirty the next morning advance parties of each blundered into one another on the road at Saunders Creek about halfway between Camden and Rugeley's Mills. A confused fight followed with a handful of prisoners taken on both sides. From one of them, Gates learned that he faced Cornwallis and an army of 3000. Further expressions of surprise came from Gates, who now, uncharacteristically, asked his officers for advice. They obviously thought that Gates was rather late in consulting them, and all save Edward Stevens remained silent. Stevens spoke a part of what all felt: they had no choice but to fight.[36]

At first light of a very hot day, the two armies got a good look at one another and at the place where they would fight. They discovered that about 250 yards of open fields separated them, with the Americans holding slightly higher ground. On either side swamps about a mile apart bounded the field. Cornwallis had sent his troops into a long line during the night with light infantry on the far right; the 23rd Regiment stood to its left with the 33rd between it and the road. Together they composed the right wing commanded by Lt. Colonel James Webster. On the left side of the road from the swamp inward stood the North Carolina Provincials and militia, both loyalist units, the Legion infantry, and the Volunteers of Ireland, another loyalist regiment. This wing, the left, was assigned to Rawdon. Cornwallis split the 71st on either

35. *Ibid.*, 722–23; Wickwires, *Cornwallis*, 151–54.
36. The quotations are from Williams, "Narrative," in Johnson, *Greene*, I, 494.

side of the road in reserve. Tarleton's cavalry stood two abreast just to the rear of the 71st.[37]

Cornwallis had placed all his loyalist units including militia, presumably the least reliable of all, on his left. Gates did not know of these dispositions when he aligned his army and merely by chance placed his militia on the American left directly across from the British regulars. Stevens's Virginia militia stood near the swamp, and to their right, Caswell's North Carolinians. On the other side of the road, the Delaware Continentals stood close to the swamp with the 2nd Maryland Brigade between them and the road. DeKalb headed the right, Smallwood, the left. The American artillery set up near the road, and the 1st Maryland Brigade was held in reserve.

The battle began with the Virginians moving forward against the regulars on the right. Just before the order was given to them, Otho Williams was told by an artillery officer that the British seemed to be "displaying," that is, deploying, in this case from a column to a line. Williams quite properly thought that in motion the regulars were vulnerable to an attack and recommended to Gates that the Virginians be ordered forward.

Gates gave the order—his first and last of the day—and Stevens marched his men out. Cannonading on both sides had begun by this time, and the haze which hung over the field began to darken. Stevens's men reached musket range with their leader shouting to them to use their bayonets. They found the British infantry in motion, but far from displaying they were coming forward, "firing and huzzaing." Cornwallis had detected movement on the American left, probably the first steps of the Virginians, and believing that the Americans were making some change in alignment, sent Webster on the attack. The battle had begun with each side hoping to take advantage of a mistake of the other. Some of the Virginians seem to have responded to British volleys with fire but most lost their nerve and ran to the rear. The North Carolinians, panicked by the sight of the Virginians, did not squeeze their triggers but threw down their loaded muskets and ran. This opened up the left flank of DeKalb's wing. Otho Williams and the 1st Maryland Brigade in reserve attempted to come forward in these dreadful minutes, but

37. My account of the battle of Camden is based on Williams, "Narrative," in Johnson, *Greene,* esp. I, 494–97; Edward Stevens to Thomas Jefferson, Aug. 20, 1780, *TJ Papers,* III, 558–59; Stedman, *History of the American War,* II, 231–32. I have also used the brilliant study in Ward, II, 722–30; and the shrewd assessment in Wickwires, *Cornwallis,* 149–65.

their ranks were thrown into disarray by the fleeing militia pouring through them. Colonel Webster meanwhile had turned the light infantry and the 23rd to the left to strike the naked American flank. This was a brilliant move and probably destroyed whatever chances DeKalb's wing had of holding its ground.[38]

Up to the time that Webster struck, DeKalb's troops had more than held, throwing back two attacks by Rawdon's provincials and counterattacking vigorously. For thirty minutes at least Rawdon and Cornwallis were barely able to keep their left from collapsing. Neither side could see the other clearly by this time as the smoke had drifted over most of the field. Lack of visibility may have aided DeKalb in holding his soldiers to their task, for his troops could not see that their left was exposed. Gradually, however, they learned how vulnerable they were as Webster's men pressed against them. Otho Williams did his best to bring the Marylanders up to the hole vacated by the militia. Webster blocked him off, however, and by noon the American right had collapsed. DeKalb fought on for a few minutes longer until he collapsed from his wounds. Three days later he was dead.

The Americans did not withdraw from the battlefield in a manner recommended by military manuals. Rather they left in a crowd with no regiment retaining its integrity as a unit. Gates made no attempt to discipline or reorganize this herd, choosing rather to outdistance it astride a fast horse. That evening he reached Charlotte, sixty miles away, and by the 19th he was at Hillsboro another 120 miles farther on. He had gone to Hillsboro, he later explained, to secure a base and to rebuild his army. Most of his soldiers did not follow him, preferring instead to head for home.

38. The Virginians went into battle with an extended interval between each infantryman. See the account in *VG* (Dixon and Nicholson), Sept. 6, 1780. In Chapter 20 I discuss the possible psychological effect of the gaps between troops.

19

The "Fugitive War"

Camden shocked both sides. The defeat depressed patriot spirits every-where, but it did not stop the raids and ambushes on the part of the irregulars. That Camden had so little effect on the grim, inside war surprised Cornwallis and his officers. Two weeks after the battle found him promising Clinton that he would be moving into North Carolina soon. He wanted—he said—to establish a magazine for the winter at Hillsboro, stocked with rum, salt, flour, and meal from the countryside. But he hesitated to send his troops northward unless Clinton undertook to provide a "diversion" in the Chesapeake, an action that would prevent the enemy from sending southward another army, such as Gates had led. The appearance of Gates had caught Cornwallis by surprise, and in his letters to Clinton he implied that his chief should have given him warning. There was another reason to feel unease even though Camden had been a victory—the loyalists in North Carolina had not sent intelligence of Gates's coming. Nor did they show themselves imme-diately after Camden, but contented themselves with professions of friendship, very quiet professions apparently. In any case, as Cornwallis remarked to Clinton, they "do not seem inclined to rise until they see our army in motion."[1]

Cornwallis did not wait for either a diversion or a rising but began preparations for a march almost as soon as the smoke had settled at Camden. By early September he had collected the supplies he needed

1. Stevens, ed., *Clinton-Cornwallis Controversy*, I, 258–59; Charles Ross, ed., *Correspon-dence of Charles, First Marquis Cornwallis* (3 vols., London, 1859), I, 58.

and the wagons and the horses to transport them, and on the 8th the march began for Charlotte with Hillsboro the army's final destination.[2]

Two weeks later, on the morning of September 21, Colonel William Davie, a partisan who sometimes operated with Thomas Sumter, provided Cornwallis with further evidence of the dispositions of the people of the Carolinas. An advance party of the Tory Legion, under Major George Hanger, was resting on that day on Wahab's Plantation near the Catawba. Hanger resembled his chief in one respect—he was suffering from the delusion that one horseman in the legion was worth a dozen rebels. And like so many English officers who had fought in real wars, that is, European wars, he believed that his brain at the head of almost any unit would overmatch the American enemy. Hanger was completely unaware that Davie and 150 men were near by, but Davie knew exactly where Hanger was—thanks to reports from civilians in the area. Davie attacked the legion and thoroughly roughed it up—at least fifteen legionnaires were killed and forty wounded—at the cost of one partisan shot by mistake in the pursuit of the legion.

The van of Cornwallis's army reached Charlotte on September 26. Many of the soldiers had been sick in the previous two weeks, including Tarleton, who was still unable to rise from a wagon. Major George Hanger again served in his stead with almost the same results as at Wahab's. This time Hanger, heedless of the desirability of scouting the ground in and around Charlotte, led his horsemen into an ambush. Light infantry extricated the legion from the embarrassment of being shot to pieces by a small number of Davie's partisans.

The entire march had been difficult, and the losses from the raids and the sickness of the troops persuaded Cornwallis to sit in Charlotte for a time and lick his wounds. While he was there he learned little of what was going on around him and even less of what was occurring to the west, where Patrick Ferguson had been sent—in part to divert attention from the main army but more importantly to subdue the frontier.

Patrick Ferguson, a Scot who had served in the Seven Years War, possessed remarkable abilities. He had invented a breech-loading rifle, superior to anything the British army was to have for a hundred years. The army, deeply and perhaps justly fond of the musket, scorned its adoption and only two hundred were manufactured. Ferguson loved army life more than invention and yearned for a command of his own.

2. Wickwires, *Cornwallis*, 194–95.

His service did not bring him rapid promotion, and when he came to the southern campaigns he was only a major. Clinton appointed him inspector general of the loyalist militia, a post he filled with distinction until he brought disaster upon himself and British arms. The distinction and the disaster had common sources—a very good intelligence, an unyielding adherence to the conventions of a British officer, and perhaps a sense that somehow he had not demonstrated his worth to his superiors. The intelligence was obvious. The devotion to the standards and rules by which an officer was expected to comport himself had been expressed before he came to America. In the Seven Years War, for example, Ferguson once turned while retreating from an enemy charge to retrieve his pistol which had been jostled from its holster. That sort of careless bravery, the conjunction of the trivial—picking up a pistol—with the important—risking his life in an act of daring—perfectly expressed the code of an officer and a gentleman. In South Carolina, in his manner of dealing with loyalists, Ferguson showed that he had imagination as well as courage. The loyalists, who had been made to feel that they were mere appendages to the main effort, that indeed they were not quite trustworthy, discovered in Ferguson a commander who cared about them and who actually listened to their grievances and fears. The loyalists' response to Ferguson came throughout the summer of 1780 when, under his leadership, they performed well against their enemies from Ninety-Six to the North Carolina border. Ferguson and his loyalist militia did not win every engagement, but near the end of the summer they had virtually cleared northwestern South Carolina of active partisans.[3]

Their skirmish with Colonel Joseph McDowell's irregulars at Cane Creek banished that worthy to the other side of the mountains, a sanctuary to which William Campbell, Isaac Shelby, John Sevier, among others, had already retired. None of these men, nor others who led backcountrymen, were rough frontiersmen. Rather, they were men of family and property and in some cases of education. Campbell, originally from Virginia, was married to a sister of Patrick Henry. Isaac Shelby, born in Maryland, had already made a name for himself in Kentucky and was to become that state's first governor. John Sevier, a Virginian by birth, was as well known in Tennessee and would be its first governor. Joseph McDowell, though born in Virginia, was something of a local boy— he had moved to North Carolina years before and later represented the state in Congress.[4]

3. This paragraph and the three preceding are based on *ibid.*, 196–206, and on Ward, II, 739–40.
4. Wickwires, *Cornwallis*, 206–8.

These men hated Ferguson and hated being ejected from South Carolina. They seized a chance to return through a mistake Ferguson made in a moment of casual bravado, moments professional officers cherish and sometimes later regret. On September 12 Ferguson's troops had reached Gilberton, where, had their commander remained quiet, they might have stayed until they either recruited additional supporters or received reinforcements. Instead, Ferguson released a member of Shelby's family captured in a skirmish with a message to the rebels that "if they did not desist from their opposition to British arms, he would march his army over the mountains, hang their leaders, and lay their country waste with fire and sword." This threat was taken as a challenge and undoubtedly hastened the recruitment of the opposition. Within two weeks around 800 westerners had gathered at Sycamore Shoals on the Watauga and on September 26 set out for Gilberton, picking up armed recruits along the way. Ferguson did not learn of his danger for another four days and then began withdrawing toward Cornwallis in Charlotte. He could have reached Cornwallis and perhaps would have, had his information about the enemy been surer, and had his good sense overcome his pride.[5]

Pride spoke with a combative accent, good sense with a voice of prudence. On October 6, after a sixteen-mile march that began at four in the morning, Ferguson sent his men up King's Mountain, a high point in a sixteen-mile mountain ridge running across the border separating South from North Carolina. The mountain, then covered with large pines, extends for about 600 yards from the southwest to the northeast and dominates the ground around it.

Here the over-the-mountain men surrounded a willing Ferguson shortly after three in the afternoon. The battle that followed conformed to the myth of encounters between Old World tactics and New World individualism, as few battles in the Revolution did. The loyalist militia relied on volley fire and massed bayonet charges; the Americans, moving from pine tree to pine tree, picked them off with long rifles. William Campbell commanded the American individualists from the southwestern slopes. His men and Shelby's on the northwestern side absorbed much of Ferguson's early fire and received several bayonet charges, giving ground before each and then scrambling back up the ridge. In little more than an hour it was all over, with Ferguson dead, shot off a magnifi-

5. Lyman C. Draper, *King's Mountain and Its Heroes* . . . (Cincinnati, Ohio, 1881), 169, for the quotation. See also Wickwires, *Cornwallis*, 208–9. My account of the battle of King's Mountain is drawn from Wickwires, *Cornwallis*, 210–15; Lt. Anthony Allaire's diary, in Draper, *King's Mountain*, 507–10; Ward, II, 741–44.

cent white horse while leading a forlorn charge. Around his body on the mountain lay dead and wounded.

More died in the next few days from the savagery of the over-the-mountain men. Some hint of what was coming was given in the last minutes on King's Mountain when the victors, shouting "Tarleton's Quarter," shot and stabbed the wounded and those trying to surrender. A few days later nine were hanged, including three loyalist militia officers who, Lieutenant Anthony Allaire observed, "died like Romans." Their deaths were at least quick. Some of the wounded, mistreated, starved, and neglected, died slowly in agony. Several hundred escaped during the following month, further evidence of the deterioration of the control—and discipline—of the over-the-mountain men. These men who had fought so well under great pressure folded when it was removed.

Cornwallis heard of the slaughter a few days later. He did not know it, but at about the same time Lt. Colonel John Cruger at Ninety-Six felt himself in danger of being strangled by emboldened partisans. Major James in the Cheraws wrote in early October that his district was out of control. On the coast Francis Marion threatened Georgetown. And around Charlotte the loyalists, such as they were, remained discreetly silent.[6]

Cornwallis accepted the inevitable—the magazine at Hillsboro would have to wait and he would have to withdraw from North Carolina. He began to leave on October 14 and on the 29th reached Winnsboro, halfway between Camden and Ninety-Six.

The march itself was dreadful with Cornwallis and enough of his men sick so that they filled the wagons. As if the withdrawals were not bad enough, the news that came to Winnsboro in the next month worsened. Marion interrupted British communications with Charleston by a series of raids that seemed to suggest that no supply train coming inland could count on making it. Thomas Sumter contributed to the atmosphere of insecurity in similar ways, most dramatically on November 9, when he bloodied Major James Wemyss and 200 regulars at Fishdam Ford on the Broad River and then on November 22 when he fought Tarleton to a standstill at Blackstock's Plantation in the hills above the Tyger River. Sumter took a bullet in this encounter and had to be carried from the field. Though Sumter was disabled the irregular war was not, and Cornwallis's troops continued to look over their shoulders at night.[7]

6. Allaire's diary, in Draper, *King's Mountain*, 511, for the quotation in the preceding paragraph.
7. Stevens, ed., *Clinton-Cornwallis Controversy*, I, 274–79; Ward, II, 745–47.

II

When Congress heard of the debacle at Camden it recognized immediately that the remnants of the southern army required a fresh commander. By this time Congress had grown weary of trying to find someone to head up the southern department; and perhaps it felt embarrassed by its past choices—Robert Howe, whose attempt to invade east Florida in spring 1778 flopped; Benjamin Lincoln, who surrendered his army at Charleston; and Horatio Gates, who left Camden without his army. Chastened by what had happened to its chosen, Congress asked Washington to name a new man. Washington nominated Nathanael Greene, then in his third year as quartermaster general.[8]

Thirty-eight years old in 1780, Greene was a more mature and a wiser man than the amateur who in November 1776 had confidently urged the defense of Fort Washington on the Hudson River. Varied experience since then had taught him much, largely because he reflected on it to draw out its meaning and utility. He learned from Trenton, Brandywine, Germantown, Monmouth, and Newport, all battles in which he performed well. In March 1778, much against his will and with the plaintive wail, "Nobody ever heard of a quarter Master in History," he accepted appointment as quartermaster general. His acceptance bespoke as plainly as anything he was to do in the Revolution a readiness to do what had to be done and a devotion to the glorious cause.[9]

To do inglorious work for a glorious cause was the sort of proposition Greene might have absorbed from Washington. He seems to have absorbed much. Though perhaps nothing uncritically: he examined his chief's methods and tactics and was shrewd enough not to try to imitate the inimitable. Yet, over the next ten months he was to fight a war that rested on the assumption that the army must be kept intact, for in an important sense, as no one saw more clearly than Washington, the army was the Revolution. Depressed by the sluggish support from state authorities who evidently lacked an understanding of the political importance of the army, Greene soon remarked to one of them, Governor Thomas Jefferson of Virginia, that "The Army is all that the States have to depend upon for their political existence."[10]

This comment came in a letter marked by blunt talk about what would happen to the southern states if they failed to supply the army.

8. Freeman, *GW*, V, 226–27.
9. Still useful for understanding Greene is George W. Greene, *Life of Nathanael Greene* (3 vols., Boston and New York, 1867–71); for a fine recent study, see Theodore Thayer, *Nathanael Greene: Strategist of the Revolution* (New York, 1960).
10. *TJ Papers*, IV, 616.

Greene may have offended Jefferson, an extraordinarily sensitive man, and he probably angered him when he sent back to Virginia a detachment of soldiers who arrived in camp destitute of clothing and weapons. But, though Greene was a blunt man, he had a much more subtle mind than his bluntness and his penchant for quick responses and fast action seem to suggest. He understood intuitively the military problems of the southern campaign, intuitively because he had made no systematic study of the war there before he was named commander; and he decided on how he would fight before he had accumulated much first-hand knowledge.[11]

Greene's understanding of the war also rested on knowledge of tactics and of the organization of supply. He spent much of himself in pondering the usual things that any commander in war must, how to move troops, for example, and how to obtain arms, provisions, and ammunition for them. But he also thought a good deal about the men themselves; the sort of stuff they were made of, and most importantly what impelled them to fight. As most of the senior officers of the army did, Greene spoke of the glorious cause without embarrassment, believing that his soldiers were also moved by its grandeur. He may indeed have understood the soldiers' commitments better than Washington did. At the beginning of the war Washington confessed his dismay at his troops' apparent indifference to ideals and virtue, a weakness he attributed to their lower-class status and which explained to him their dismal performance in battle. Like all eighteenth-century military leaders he expected training would prepare them to fight willingly. Though Greene came from less impressive stock than Washington, he also considered himself to be set off from the common sort. Yet he brought more sympathy to the task of understanding and shaping common men. Pride or principle made a soldier, he wrote shortly after his arrival in North Carolina, and good leaders did what they could to instill both in their troops. All such attempts would fail, however, if soldiers were left in nakedness and hunger. Virtue—a sense of responsibility to the public interest—could not survive while the public gave no evidence of caring for men in its service. If Greene grasped this intuitively, he needed only a glance at the men at Charlotte, living in misery, to understand that they would never take pride in themselves as long as they were reduced to plundering nearby civilians to stay alive. As for battle, they would wilt at the first

11. This assessment of Greene is based on a reading of his correspondence of the autumn of 1780 in Nathanael Greene Papers, HL; and on his letters to Washington in GW Papers, e.g., Oct. 31, 1780, Ser. 4, Reel 72.

smell of gunpowder if they did not desert first. But clothed, fed, and properly led they might be trained to fight with spirit.

Eighteenth-century generals appeared before their soldiers in person more often than those of the twentieth. In battle they formed their lines and gave commands and set an example in person. But often they had to communicate with others in writing which meant that fluency with the pen might be more important than how they sat a horse. American generals in the Revolution dealt with an incredible number of civilians through letters, requesting recruits, money, and virtually every kind of supplies. Greene, though sometimes tactless, wrote a trenchant, muscular prose. There is much in his letters about marches and logistics, but even his most technical disquisitions do not stray far from men and their concerns. And these letters, dry as they sometimes had to be, imparted a sense that an energetic and vigorous man wrote them. This man had a talent for summing up on an aphoristic note—and for choosing images that reminded the reader that men were the reasons for being concerned with such things as logistics and battle formations. Thus in "money is the sinew of war," "good intelligence," that is, good information, is the "Soul of an Army," and "spies are the eyes of the army," Greene's reference is to some human quality.[12]

The writer of these words set out for the South almost immediately on receiving his orders from Washington on October 15. At West Point when summoned, having recently assumed command there, he stopped off in Philadelphia on his way southward. Greene knew the informal rules of commanding an American army and, though he did not much like them, he had no choice but to play the game. The "game" might better be called begging—every American army commander had to wear beggar's rags if he were to succeed. Greene began by asking Congress for money, the "sinew" his army so badly needed, and for supplies. He extracted a promise of artillery from his friend Henry Knox, but he received polite rebuffs from the city merchants he approached about a supply of clothing. He kept to this regimen after he left Philadelphia with appeals to legislatures and governors issuing from his lips and pen at every opportunity.[13]

12. For the quotations, see Greene to Samuel Huntington, Oct. 27, 1780, Greene Papers, HL; Greene to Francis Marion, Dec. 4, 1780 in Greene, *Life*, III, 81; Greene to Washington, Feb. 15, 1781, in GW Papers, Ser. 4, Reel 75.
13. Greene to Huntington, Oct. 27, 1780, Greene to Henry Knox, Oct. 29, 1780, Greene Papers, HL. See also Greene to Washington, Oct. 31, 1780, GW Papers, Ser. 4, Reel 72.

Greene did not expect and did not receive unanimously favorable responses. He took the command knowing that he would face dreadful problems, and how could it be otherwise when two American armies had disintegrated in a four-month period. He summed up his and the army's prospects in one word—"dismal."[14]

How bad things truly were surpassed even this pessimism. The troops at Hillsboro, which Greene reached on November 27, were badly clothed, armed, and fed. The word "troops" implies that the sad creatures Greene inspected were gathered in units, which they were, but only in a formal sense. In reality they were a collection of some 1400 individuals, many "naked," or virtually so with only a rag or a blanket tied around their middles—"in the Indian form," Greene remarked—devoid of shoes and just about everything else they needed. They were spiritless, understandably, many able to rouse themselves only to plunder nearby farmers and villagers. As bad as the troops were, the officers were worse. They had lost their self-respect at Camden, and they despised and blamed Gates for it. One, William Smallwood of Maryland, would not stay with the army because in the new line of command he ranked below Greene's second, General von Steuben. Smallwood may have expected to succeed Gates, and when Greene was named instead of himself he set off to plead with Congress for a redating of his commission which would place him higher on the seniority list. Greene thought Smallwood's mission to Congress an act of lunacy but could not prevent his departure and may not have really tried. Smallwood was disaffected, a source of discontent in an army amply supplied with such sources.[15]

Greene arrived at the American camp in Charlotte on December 2. There he found Gates in control of himself but of not much else. The soldiers, living in even worse conditions than he had imagined, had begun to build huts, an activity that at least showed that some initiative remained but which otherwise promised only to make their misery permanent. Greene said nothing of his dissatisfaction at this work and assumed command the next day. He brought with him a charge from Congress to convene an inquiry into Gates's conduct at Camden, but since the general officers necessary for such a review were not present he gratefully put the matter aside. Gates, who wanted to clear his name and believed that any court would exonerate him, soon after left for home dissatisfied.[16]

14. Greene to Washington, Oct. 31, 1780, GW Papers, Ser. 4, Reel 72.
15. Greene to General Steuben, Dec. 28, 1780; Greene to General Sumter, Jan. 15, 1781, Greene Papers, HL; Greene, *Life*, III, 541, 543.
16. Ward, II, 749–50.

Over the next month, Greene began to realize just what he had taken on. He did not understand the politics of North Carolina, but he did learn quickly that he faced a divided leadership. There were three "parties" in the state, he told a colleague, and none was terribly fond of the others. By "parties," Greene meant factions distinguished by no formal organization but endowed with ambitious leaders. One of them, Colonel Martin, who headed the state's Board of War, had been dismissed from the army for cowardice. The other two were the governor and a leading rival. If the prospect of dealing with Martin and "all those great and mighty men" did not lift Greene's heart, neither did it depress him. Rather than give way to despair, Greene laughed, resolving to treat all with civility and to strike a balance between "haughtiness and mean condescension." [17]

A more important division for the Revolution than these factional splits was the one between Whigs and Tories. The ferocity of the conflict between these two groups impressed Greene so much that he customarily referred to it as "savage." He was to find the same groupings in South Carolina and used identical language to describe it. In North Carolina the two sides found release in murdering and plundering one another. Greene thought that when he arrived these practices had gone so far as virtually to destroy public morals. Although he professed to believe that the Tories outnumbered the Whigs in both Carolinas, the Whigs in fact usually had the greatest number.[18]

As far as Greene was concerned the Whigs were almost as bad as the Tories—at least when they were gathered into the militia. The reason lay in the militia's appetite for everything but combat. "Like the locusts of Egypt [the militia] have eaten up every green thing," he told his friend Joseph Reed. What he particularly resented was that the Congress paid for the militia, and since Congress paid, North Carolina preferred raising militia to supporting Continental regiments. The result was that Greene, though wanting a regular—and reliable—army, had sometimes to depend upon the undependable, the militia, and even more frequently to go without fresh troops of any sort.[19]

Greene's dissatisfaction did not extend to the partisan leaders, Thomas Sumter, Francis Marion, Andrew Pickens, and William Davidson, all of whom led irregular forces drawn mostly from militia. Greene genuinely

17. Greene to General Robert Howe, Dec. 29, 1780, Greene Papers, HL.
18. Greene to Joseph Reed, Jan. 9, 1781, *ibid.*
19. *Ibid.*

admired these men though he deplored the propensity for plundering shown by, as he remarked, half their followers. In the absence of a regular army the militia was his only resource. Greene planned to use it to fight a "fugitive war," a term that he invented to describe a fighting force that would often be in flight.[20]

Putting this army together, rudimentary as it was to be, taxed all the imagination Greene possessed. To supply it, he had Steuben in Virginia working as hard as possible. Edward Carrington, a Virginia artillery officer, agreed to head up the deputy quartermaster general's office, and William R. Davie, an able North Carolinian, accepted appointment as commissary general though all his instincts were to refuse. Greene appealed to these men's devotion to the Revolution, a tactic of limited use in persuading the "haves," state officials, merchants, and planters, to give money and supplies to the "have nots," the troops of the southern department.[21]

Like any army a fugitive army could do something for itself. It could scout which rivers would be useful for transportation—and which might prove even more useful when they separated the fugitives from their pursuers. Greene sent Carrington, Kosciuszko, and several others to study the rivers. Knowing where the rivers could be forded was absolutely vital to him, for he expected to hit and then run. He could not survive a major battle, and he might have to fight one should he be so incautious as to get trapped against a river at an unfordable point. Since the rivers were deeper below the falls, prudence dictated that he fight above, where fords were not uncommon.

It was well not to rely completely on presumed knowledge of the rivers. Heavy rains sometimes deepened fords; for example, early in January 1781 the Pee Dee rose twenty-five feet in thirty hours after a heavy rain. When the rains stopped and runoff slackened, the Pee Dee might drop just as quickly. The others were the same. Boats could be almost as valuable as horses in the country, but collecting them was as difficult as collecting horses. Greene decided to build his own and to put them on wheels. Horses could pull these craft between the rivers and then float across with the army.

Before Greene had put an army together, he decided to divide it. The camp at Charlotte exuded a stench of defeat and decay, and the

20. Greene, *Life*, III, 546 ("fugitive war").
21. Greene to Carrington, Dec. 4, 29, 1780; Greene to Alexander Hamilton, Jan. 10, 1781; Greene to Board of War, Dec. 18, 1780, Greene Papers, HL.

countryside around it contained few food supplies. To rouse his command and give the men hope and training, Greene resolved to march most of his troops to Cheraw on the Pee Dee and to send Daniel Morgan with a contingent of the Maryland and Virginia militia, and Colonel Washington's horsemen, to the west side of the Catawba River. There Morgan might harass the enemy on the frontier and perhaps feed his troops better than Greene could along the Pee Dee. All textbooks of war warned against dividing an army in that it was easier for an enemy to defeat it in detail. Greene could not conduct himself according to such a sensible rule—he and his soldiers might starve to death while operating according to the textbooks. There were military advantages to splitting off Morgan anyway. Along the Catawba he threatened the British post at Ninety-Six—and smaller ones as well. If Cornwallis divided to go after Morgan, Charleston would be exposed, and if he went after Greene, the interior would be more vulnerable than usual. Morgan might also be called back to strike along Cornwallis's flanks and rear. All these possibilities figured in Greene's decision to separate Morgan from himself.[22]

Unknown to the Americans, Cornwallis was considering pushing from Winnsboro into North Carolina again. He was thoroughly fed up with South Carolina and its "perpetual risings" and its incompetent loyalist militia. To send out dispatch riders who never arrived at their destination was discouraging and to have supply trains ambushed every time they set out was equally discouraging. To crush a rebel army at Camden and see no change in the citizens was enough to make him want to give it all up. And when he learned that rebel militia had fairly successfully suppressed news of the British victory from spreading to the backcountry, confidence in his ability to bring the province back to the king's side began to evaporate.[23]

Cornwallis seems never to have comprehended why pacifying South Carolina proved so difficult. A part of his explanation reflected conventional aristocratic prejudice: the British army faced malevolent men, not simply another enemy. Moreover, the friends of the government would not behave like men even when, in the presence of the British regulars, power shifted to their side. Why wouldn't they? Cornwallis had no answer except that they were intimidated by the rebels. And

22. Greene to Daniel Morgan, Dec. 16, 1780, *ibid.*; Ward, II, 750–52.

23. Ross, ed., *Correspondence of Cornwallis*, I, 80; Stevens, ed., *Clinton-Cornwallis Controversy*, I, 265.

the rebels survived, despite their defeats at Charleston and Camden, because they were succored by their friends in North Carolina and Virginia. What he could not see was that the basis for rebellion existed in South Carolina independent of support to the north. Nor could he ever quite grasp that the British army, by its presence, nourished the rebellion it had been ordered to suppress.

Greene did not worry when he learned early in January that Tarleton, who had been about twenty-five miles west of Cornwallis at Winnsboro, had set out after Morgan. Greene had reached the new camp at Cheraw on the Pee Dee the day after Christmas. By that time Morgan was nearing a position from which he could threaten the western posts of the British.

Early in the new year Tarleton proposed to Cornwallis that they attempt to trap Morgan between them somewhere near King's Mountain. Cornwallis agreed and freed Tarleton for the chase but held up his own pursuit until he was able to learn whether the rumor that the French were at Cape Fear had any substance. It had none, and the dispositions of British troops seemed favorable to a new expedition to the north—Benedict Arnold, who had defected to the British the preceding September, had led a raiding expedition to Virginia, and Major General Alexander Leslie, who had sailed from New York in October with 2500 reinforcements, reached Camden on January 4, 1781.[24]

While Cornwallis crawled a few miles out of Winnsboro, Tarleton and Morgan played hound and hare across the South Carolina backcountry. Morgan moved on January 16 from Burr's Mills on Thicketty Creek to Hannah's Cowpens, a distance of twelve miles. He was seven miles from Cherokee Ford on the Broad River. The day before Tarleton had made it across the Pacolet at Easterwood Shoals, only six miles below where Morgan had posted his troops. Tarleton had traveled light; Morgan had pulled heavy wagons. Now with Tarleton pressing him, Morgan decided that he must fight; if he fled he was certain to be overtaken, perhaps at the fords or just over them, both places less favorable to the defense than the Cowpens.[25]

Daniel Morgan spent much of the night of January 16 with his men. He resembled his men in many ways. He was older than most, of course, but he spoke their language, a direct rough talk that has always appealed to soldiers. Moving among the campfires, Morgan may have revealed

24. Willcox, *Portrait of a General,* 349–50; Ward, II, 753.
25. Ward, II, 755.

something of his plan, certainly he revealed his confidence in his troops and himself. A more practiced tactician who knew the textbook doctrine on the deployment of troops would not have chosen Hannah's Cowpens because of what it offered the defense. According to eighteenth-century conventions, the Cowpens offered nothing—except maybe an opportunity to the attacker to envelop the defender. The Cowpens was a meadow of about 500 yards in length and almost as wide. About 300 yards from its southern edge a low hill rose, and behind it seventy or eighty yards, a second, lower, hill stood. There was little undergrowth but there were pine, oak, and hickory trees scattered over the meadow. The place was made for cavalry—and Tarleton had three times the number of cavalry available to Morgan. As the British general Charles Stedman, who inspected the field not long afterward, said, the ground was not well chosen for Morgan's purposes—his flanks were open, he was vulnerable to cavalry, and the Broad River behind his back made retreat impossible. Morgan later stated that he had chosen the Cowpens because its defects would leave his militia no choice save fighting. They all knew what had happened to Buford's men at Waxhaws when they tried to run away.[26]

Whatever his reasons for choosing Cowpens, Morgan used the terrain well. Sometime before daybreak a scout brought word that Tarleton was on the move and only about five miles away. Tarleton had roused his troops at 3:00 A.M. and set out as rapidly as possible. Morgan's men then crawled from their blankets, ate breakfast, and took their places.

The main line, composed of Maryland and Delaware regulars at the center and Virginia and Georgia militia at the ends, ran across the higher of the two hills. Altogether about 450 men made up this position. Some 150 yards to their front about 300 militia from the two Carolinas spread out for approximately 300 yards. In front of them, 150 riflemen from Georgia and North Carolina crouched behind trees forming a line of skirmishers. Morgan did not have many men in reserve, but they were well chosen, eighty cavalry of Colonel William Washington and forty-five mounted infantry from Georgia, all posted out of sight behind the second hill.

Tarleton's force included his legion, a little over 500 cavalry and infantry; a battalion each from the Royal Fusiliers (the 7th) and the Highlanders (the 71st); and smaller contingents of the 17th Light Dragoons, royal artillery, and Tory militia. In all he had about 1100 men and outnumbered Morgan slightly. This army marched into the Cowpens after daybreak and was quickly deployed in a line with dragoons on either end, the Royal Fusiliers, the legion infantry, and the light infantry in between. Two hundred cavalry and the Highlanders were held in reserve. The royal artillery—two "grasshoppers," three-pounders mounted on long legs (not wheels), hence the name—were placed with troops on the front.

This line had barely formed when Tarleton sent it forward. By this time the skirmishers in advance of the American position had already done their work, cutting down the fifteen horsemen Tarleton had ordered to advance when he first entered the Cowpens. The American militia of the second line, commanded by Andrew Pickens, awaited the British patiently, knowing exactly what their leaders expected of them. Morgan had not asked that they defend their position until death, but only that they give two effective volleys and then pull back behind the hill where they would be formed once more. They fulfilled their assignment carefully, saving their first volley until Tarleton's men came into range. They then fired, reloaded, fired again, and pulled back to the left flank of the main line. Not all made it unmolested. The British charge, though not a model of order, moved fast enough to intercept the Americans on the far right who had to cut across the entire line of battle. Before all the American militia could make it, the dragoons were among them swinging sabers and firing pistols. At just the right moment Morgan sent Washington's horsemen to the rescue. The appearance of the American cavalry surprised the dragoons and in a few minutes they retired.

The main line had continued its attack. It had taken heavy casualties from the fire of Pickens's men, but it was intact and still on the move. The British now received an unpleasant shock—the line of Continentals and Virginia militia along the hill did not retreat. Instead they delivered fire that threatened to disintegrate the assault.

Tarleton then did the only thing he could do—he called on the Highlanders in reserve. The Highlanders, with several hundred yards to cover, made for the American right. General John Eager Howard, in command of the American main line, watched them come with considerable concern. He noticed that the Highlanders extended well beyond the American right flank, and should they persist, would wrap themselves around that end of his line. Anticipating this flanking movement, Howard ordered the company on the far right to face about and wheel to the

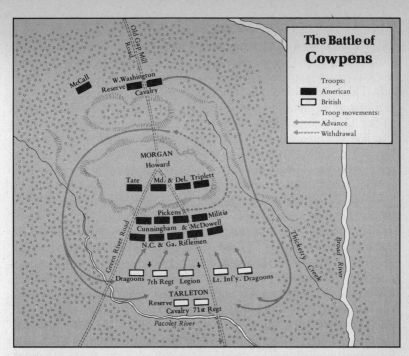

The Battle of
Cowpens

Troops:
- ■ American
- □ British

Troop movements:
- ◄— Advance
- ◄---- Withdrawal

Old Gap Mill Road

McCall

W. Washington Reserve
Cavalry

Green River Road

MORGAN
Howard

Tate   Md. & Del.   Triplett

Pickens
Cunningham & McDowell   Militia

N.C. & Ga. Riflemen

Dragoons   7th Regt   Legion   Lt. Inf'y.   Dragoons

TARLETON
Reserve
Cavalry   71st Regt

Thicketty Creek

Broad River

Pacolet River

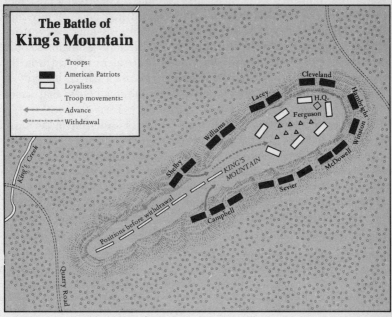

The Battle of
King's Mountain

Troops:
- ■ American Patriots
- □ Loyalists

Troop movements:
- ◄— Advance
- ◄---- Withdrawal

King's Creek

Quarry Road

Positions before withdrawal

Shelby

Williams

Lacey

Campbell

KING'S MOUNTAIN

Ferguson

H.Q.

Cleveland

Hambright

Winston

McDowell

Sevier

left, a complicated movement on the parade ground and much too demanding for militia to execute while under fire. Understandably confused, the militia company faced about and began to retire to the rear of the hill. There is nothing more contagious in battle than a move to the rear (except perhaps flight in panic), and the rest of the line also began to fall back. Surprised at what he saw, Morgan asked Howard what this line was doing and whether a retreat was in progress. Howard had the wit to see that the men were in control of themselves—and were far from panic. Upon receiving this reassurance, Morgan pulled back himself to find a place for a stand.

Tarleton's men had also seen the American right give way and convinced that a rout was in prospect broke their formation—it was already in some disorder—in order to close with the enemy that had killed so many of their comrades. This wild rush also deceived Tarleton, who, thinking to capitalize on a familiar circumstance—American panic— called up his reserve. By this time most of the Americans had reached the reverse slope of the hill and were hidden from British eyes. Whereupon Howard and Morgan ordered them to turn around and shoot into the British mob that now came over the crest of the hill about fifty yards away. The British who plunged into this fire gave way to wild fear almost immediately as their ranks crumbled. Then they were struck on their flank by Washington's cavalry which had once more ridden from concealment behind the second hill. Pickens's militia now made their second appearance of the day following behind Washington's horses and Howard's infantry. In a few minutes the Americans had won the battle, though the Highlanders, retaining at least a partial integrity as a unit, fought with particular bravery, as did the small crews that served the grasshoppers.

Courage frequently mastered the deficiencies of leadership in the Revolution, but in this case it had no chance. The Highlanders were either killed or surrendered, and the artillerymen died gallantly trying to hold their howitzers. Beaten, the British soon began to beg for quarter. Tarleton escaped with forty horsemen. He left behind 100 dead, over 800 of his men prisoners (229 with wounds), the colors of the 7th Regiment, the two grasshoppers, 800 muskets, and most of his baggage, horses, and ammunition.[27]

27. I have reconstructed the dispositions of troops and the action of the battle from the following: Daniel Morgan to Greene, Jan. 19, 1781 [copy], GW Papers, Ser. 4, Reel 74; Cornwallis to Clinton, Jan. 18, 1781, in Stevens, ed., *Clinton-Cornwallis Controversy*, I, 320–21; Lieutenant Colonel Banastre Tarleton, *History of the Cam-*

Tarleton never realized what had happened to his command at Cowpens and publicly at least did not admit that he had made serious mistakes there. He confessed that the fire from Howard's retreating line had been "unexpected" and had produced "confusion" among his soldiers. The panic that followed baffled him, however. In refighting the battle, a luxury that the vanquished relish in a perverse way as much as the victor, he ascribed a part of the defeat to the cavalry's failure to form on the right and presumably to attack there. He also—in a very confused series of comments—remarked on the "extreme extension of the files," characteristic he thought of the "loose manner of forming which had always been practiced by the king's troops in America."[28]

Loose was a well-chosen word but surely too narrowly applied by Tarleton. He had rushed into the battle, as Charles Stedman later implied, with the daring of a partisan captain heedless of the circumstances of his army and the enemy's. The attack began even before his line had formed and with his reserve, the 71st Regiment, still struggling to come forward through thick underbrush almost a mile behind. The attack appeared to Roderick Mackenzie, a young lieutenant wounded on the field, "premature, confused, and irregular." Yet at one critical moment, it might have succeeded, when the right side of the American main line began pulling back, had Tarleton been able to pour his reserve against that side. Instead, the British, irresolute and disorganized, delayed, and Howard's men re-formed themselves into an effective line.[29]

Morgan may have selected an inappropriate site, according to conventional standards, but he made it serve extraordinarily well. There was no escape for his troops in that lonely meadow. Morgan may or may not have made his decision to fight with the propensity of the militia for flight clearly in his mind. Whatever he was thinking, he devised tactics which inspired praise—and imitation—from others in the next two months.

The battle lasted until a little after 10:00 a.m. By noon Morgan had his troops with their prisoners on the road. He expected that the destruction of Tarleton's force would bring a swift reaction from Cornwallis, and he did not want to be overwhelmed while savoring his triumph.

paigns of 1780 and 1781 in the Southern Provinces of North America (London, 1787), 217–21; Roderick Mackenzie, Strictures on Lt. Col. Tarleton's History of the Campaigns of 1780 and 1781 . . . (London, 1787), 91–115; Wickwires, Cornwallis, 259–64; Ward, II, 757–62. (The Wickwires and Ward provide superb accounts.)
28. Tarleton, History, 217, 221.
29. Stedman, History of the American War, II, 360–61; Mackenzie, Strictures, 109.

The prisoners were an encumbrance, and in a few days they would be split off from his column and sent to the Virginia interior. Morgan crossed the Little Broad the next day and three days later, January 21, the Little Catawba at Ramsour's Mill. Two days after that he led his soldiers across the Catawba at Sherrill's Ford where he allowed them to rest.[30]

Cornwallis sat at Turkey Creek on the day of the battle awaiting Leslie. The news of the defeat reached him the next day, and on January 19 he set out to run Morgan to earth. He set out in the wrong direction on the wrong road. He knew whom he was looking for, but not where he had gone, a lapse in British intelligence all too common in the southern campaign It revealed a fact he found especially disagreeable: he was in the enemy's country and though he had money to buy intelligence there were few sellers. Thinking that Morgan had probably driven southward in order to take Ninety-Six, Cornwallis wasted a day marching northwestward. When he discovered his error he shifted direction and got on the road to Ramsour's Mill where earlier, had he been better informed and faster in motion, he might have intercepted Morgan.[31]

The day Cornwallis reached Ramsour's Mill, January 25, brought the news of Morgan's victory at Cowpens to Nathanael Greene at the camp on the Pee Dee. Greene realized immediately that Cornwallis would pursue Morgan and realized too that a British army stripped of its cavalry and far from its magazine might be vulnerable to attack. He resolved therefore to join his army to Morgan's. The preparations for such a movement would take several days, and Greene lusted for action. He contained himself for two days, issuing a rash of orders—Isaac Huger to bring the army from the Pee Dee to Salisbury, North Carolina, the commissaries at Salisbury and Hillsboro to prepare to evacuate stores and prisoners to Virginia, Quartermaster Carrington to collect boats on the Dan River. Then with a small escort Greene galloped off to find Morgan.[32]

Cornwallis meantime was issuing very different kinds of orders. Like most armies of the century his traveled in a column bloated with baggage and noncombatants. Officers ordinarily carried several fine uniforms, food and wine, equipment of every sort, including at times furniture and fancy dishes and glassware. They also brought along their servants and sometimes their wives and children, though more often they brought

30. Ward, II, 763–64.
31. Wickwires, Cornwallis, 268–69, 274–75.
32. Ward, II, 765–66.

women not their wives and the children of these women. To permit the rapid pursuit of Morgan, Cornwallis ordered that his army should slim down, destroy its baggage, including tents, most of its wagons, and prepare to live off the country. On January 27, he ordered the troops served an extra gill of rum. What could not be consumed on the spot, he poured into Carolina soil. The next day, as he resumed his pursuit, Cornwallis gave his men the unhappy word that supplying them with rum "for a time Will be Absolutely impossible" and recommended to them that since provisions would be none too plentiful that they learn "to bruise the Indian corn or to Rasp it after it has been soaked."[33]

The stripped-down army, sans rum but still carrying its women and children, had first to get over the Catawba, now threatening to overflow its banks after a recent heavy rain. It crossed in masterful style on February 1 at Cowan's Ford after a feint upstream at Beattie's. There were four places at which the Catawba might have been forded by the British, and Morgan had directed that North Carolina militia, under General William Davidson, cover them all. Davidson, however, had only 300 men. He was with the small force at Cowan's Ford on the morning of the crossing and lost his life attempting to stop it. Greene, who had reached Morgan the day before, waited for the militia to rally at Tarrant's Tavern near by. Intimidated by the apparent power of the British, many of these men had slipped away for home.[34]

Greene had sent Morgan ahead to the Trading Ford on the Yadkin, which was very high. Boats assembled by Kosciuszko ferried his army over on the night of February 2 with an enemy party pressing close behind. Near the ford an advance party of British cavalry under Charles O'Hara caught the American rear guard and beat it up. Even in this action the British took little satisfaction, for the American rear guard did not fight but, in the language of the Carolinians contemptuously recorded by O'Hara, "Split and Squandered—that is run away."[35] On the afternoon of the next day Cornwallis reached Salisbury. Seven miles away just across the Yadkin the Americans sat resting. The river was rising, and the British were tired and almost out of provisions. The

33. A. R. Newsome, ed., "A British Orderly Book, 1780–1781," NCHR, 9 (1932), 289.
34. Greene to Washington, Feb. 9, 1781, GW Papers, Ser. 4, Reel 75; Ward, II, 767–68; Wickwires, Cornwallis, 278–80.
35. George C. Rogers, Jr., ed., "Letters of Charles O'Hara to the Duke of Grafton," SCHM, 65 (1964), 175.

next four days they took as much ease as they could in the rain and mud and sent out foraging parties. On February 8, Cornwallis swung his army to the west to Shallow Ford, a broad spot always shallow enough for horses and men. By moving away from his enemy Cornwallis did not believe that he was giving him a chance to slip downstream and over to the Dan River, the last barrier to safety in Virginia. Rather, he thought that Morgan's army would itself have to move to the west in order to ford the Dan. As was often the case, Cornwallis's intelligence had supplied him with false information—that no boats were available farther down where the Dan was too deep to be forded.

Morgan seemed to live up to Cornwallis's expectations on February 4 by beginning a march northward. But then in a sudden turn he moved rapidly eastward to Guilford Court House, a distance of forty-seven miles covered in two days. There he met Huger and the main American army which had been diverted from Salisbury on Greene's order. At just about the same time Lee's Legion rode in. Greene once more had his army in one piece.

A few weeks earlier Greene had told Morgan that while retreat was disagreeable it was not disgraceful. He now seems to have concluded that it was so disagreeable that it must stop. Cornwallis had not drawn his admiration; Cornwallis was of a pushing disposition, inclined, like his subordinate Tarleton, to impetuous action. And impetuous action might lead to capital misfortune, Greene thought. A council consisting of Otho Williams, Huger, and a tired and sick Morgan did not agree, and when asked by Greene didn't they all think it was time to stop running and start fighting, they all said no. The council was undoubtedly right, for the troops were tired, badly clothed and equipped, and just barely outnumbered the enemy, a much better disciplined army.[36]

The decision made to continue to run, Greene proceeded to run. The run, however, was now more dangerous than ever, for no river separated Cornwallis at Salem and Greene at Guilford Court House, twenty-five miles apart. Deception is as helpful as speed in such a situation, and Greene resolved to trick Cornwallis into thinking that he would cross the Dan at the upper reaches of the river. He therefore detached Otho Williams with the best infantry and cavalry of his army, 700

36. For Greene's movements and his thinking in late January and early February 1781, see his letters to Steuben, Feb. 3, 1781; to Andrew Pickens, Feb. 3, 1781; to Thomas Sumter, Feb. 3, 1781; to Isaac Huger, Feb. 5, 1781; to Major Blair, Feb. 6, 1781; and to Governor Nash, Feb. 9, 1781; and the report on the Council of War of Feb. 9, 1781, in Greene Papers, HL.

men, to lead Cornwallis away from Irwin's Ferry where the resourceful Carrington had gathered boats to float his men across.

Williams, one of the underrated officers in the American army, performed his assignment brilliantly. Cornwallis took the bait, assuming that Williams's force was the van of the main army. The chase proved exciting and exhausting; for four days Tarleton and O'Hara nipped at the rear guard provided by Lee's Legion. The roads, half frozen at night, made muddy and rough in the day from rain and thaws, and cut up by refugees who were fleeing the British as they had over much of North Carolina, exacted a toll from shoes. Before it was over Williams's men were leaving bloody tracks on the ground. Greene's route displayed the same marks. On February 13, Greene made it to the Dan, and just behind him Otho Williams. Both crossed safely. Cornwallis's army stood on the opposite bank gazing once again at a crossing for which they had no boats.

Why did Cornwallis give up the pursuit? He might after all have repeated the whole dreary business, marching to the upper Dan where there were passable fords. A combination of circumstances seems to have prevented him from resuming the chase: he was over 200 miles from Camden where he had left supplies and men with Rawdon; he recognized that there was no clear way to force Greene to give battle; his men were tired, footsore, often hungry, and the people of the country-side had not overwhelmed them by the warmth of their welcome. Then there was the possibility—a strong one—that if he pushed Greene deep into Virginia, he pushed him into strength. Steuben was in Virginia, and he had been filling Continental battalions.

Remaining where he was on the Dan promised nothing, so Cornwallis slowly led his army to Hillsboro, where on February 20, he issued a proclamation inviting loyal Americans, with their weapons and a ten-day supply of provisions, to join him in the great task of restoring constitutional order. A copy of the proclamation made its way over the Dan immediately. Shortly after, Greene received reports that Cornwallis's appeal had drawn a very favorable response, with so many loyalists flocking to the British colors that seven independent companies had been formed in one day.

The proclamation actually produced few recruits. As Charles O'Hara, one of Cornwallis's brigadiers, observed, the chase of Greene brought "some eclat and credit to our arms." A few people in the neighborhood turned up "to stare at us" but, "their curiosity once satisfied," went home. During the long hard days of the pursuit the British had not

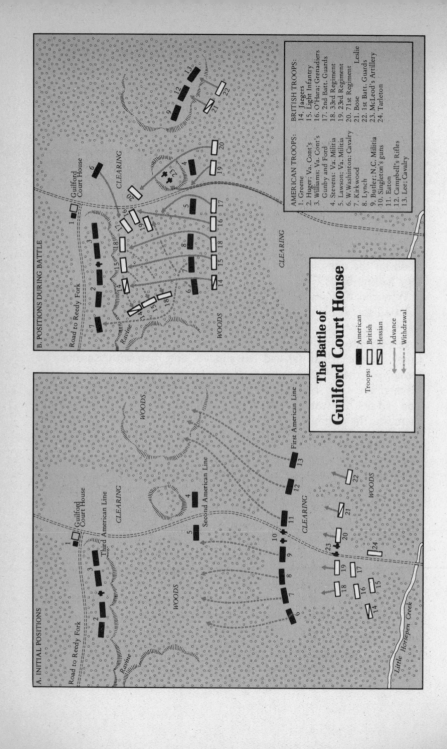

The Battle of
Guilford Court House

Troops:
American
British
Hessian

——— Advance
━ ━ ━ Withdrawal

AMERICAN TROOPS:
1. Greene
2. Huger: Va. Cont's
3. Williams: Va. Cont's
4. Gunby and Ford
5. Stevens: Va. Militia
6. Lawson: Va. Militia
7. Kirkwood
8. Lynch
9. Butler: N.C. Militia
10. Singleton's guns
11. Eaton
12. Campbell's Rifles
13. Lee: Cavalry
  W. Washinton: Cavalry

BRITISH TROOPS:
14. Jaegers
15. Light Infantry
16. O'Hara: Grenadiers
17. 2nd Batt. Guards
18. 33rd Regiment
19. 23rd Regiment
20. 71st Regiment
21. Bose   Leslie
22. 1st Batt. Guards
23. McLeod's Artillery
24. Tarleton

A. INITIAL POSITIONS

Road to Reedy Fork
Ravine
Guilford Court House
Third American Line
CLEARING
Second American Line
First American Line
WOODS
WOODS
WOODS
CLEARING
Little Horsepen Creek

B. POSITIONS DURING BATTLE

Road to Reedy Fork
Ravine
Guilford Court House
CLEARING
CLEARING
CLEARING
WOODS

had a hundred loyalists with them. Greene, however, believed the exaggerated reports and, with a vision of the Carolinas returning to the British fold dancing in his head, felt compelled to do something to dampen enthusiasm for the king. He therefore sent his army back across the Dan, first Otho Williams with the light corps, and on February 23 the main army augmented by 600 fresh Virginia militia.[37]

Cornwallis responded four days later by moving to the southern side of Alamance Creek, to a junction of roads linking Hillsboro to the east and Guilford and Salisbury to the west. Over the next two weeks each side maneuvered carefully, staying near the Alamance and tributaries of the Haw River. They fought several skirmishes but no heavy actions though Cornwallis desperately yearned for a major battle. While the American army moved, it grew as Steuben and Virginia sent 400 Continentals and 1693 militia, who were pledged to serve for only six weeks. North Carolina sent two brigades of militia, 1060 men in all. His army significantly larger than the British, Greene now felt strong enough for a battle, and on March 14, he marched to Guilford Court House. He would fight on ground of his own choosing.[38]

Guilford Court House sat on the edge of a small village clustered on a hill. Below the court house looking to the southwest a valley unfolded cut by the Great Road, a rough track from Salisbury. Although the high ground around the court house was cleared, most of the valley was wooded. The enemy coming along the road would have to enter through a defile formed by two low hills. There, at the opening of the valley, the ground on either side of the road had been cleared for the cultivation of corn. On the east side there were two fields, one abutting the road, separated from one another by woods 200 yards wide. The valley sank gradually from the defile to Little Horsepen Creek for a distance of one-fourth mile and then rose again for another fourth to the edge of a wood.[39]

The ground was Greene's; the tactics were Daniel Morgan's. Greene like Morgan at Cowpens resolved to use a defense that had depth, a defense of three lines. The first that Cornwallis's troops would hit was stretched out along the edge of the woods north of the open fields.

37. Rogers, ed., "Letters of O'Hara," *SCHM*, 65 (1964), 176, for the quotations. For Greene's movements, see his letters to Washington, Feb. 9, 15, 28, 1781, in Greene Papers, HL. (These letters are also in GW Papers, Ser. 4, Reel 75.)
38. Ward, II, 782–83. Chapters 71 and 72 in Ward provide a superb account of the chase by Cornwallis of Greene.
39. Wickwires, *Cornwallis*, 292–93; Ward, II, 785.

To reach it the British would have to go down into the valley and then climb up slopes exposed to American fire. To give that fire Greene deployed the North Carolina militia, 1000 in number, on both sides of the road. He anchored their right flank with 200 Virginia riflemen and 110 Delaware Continentals; Colonel William Washington's cavalry, probably about eighty horse, backed them. On the far left he placed about 200 Virginia riflemen and 150 of Henry Lee's Legion, about half of whom were cavalry, the others infantry. All Greene asked of this line was that it deliver two volleys before retiring. At its center on the road he set up two six-pounders, guns with a range of 600 to 800 yards.[40]

Three hundred yards behind, he set up a second line, two brigades, 600 men each of Virginia militia under Brig. Generals Edward Stevens and Robert Lawson. Historians of the battle do not agree on the relative alignments of these two, but Stevens's men seem to have been on the right (or west) side of the road. The entire line was in the woods.

The third and main line occupied the high open ground just below the court house. It was entirely to the right of the road which swung slightly northeastward as it came up the hill. Because of the configuration of the ground this line was at a slight angle to the second and between 500 and 600 yards behind it. General Huger commanded the right side composed of almost 800 Virginia Continentals, and Otho Williams, the left, of a little more than 600 Maryland Continentals.

The British began the twelve-mile march to Guilford in the darkness of early morning. They had not eaten, having run out of flour the day before. Cornwallis posted Tarleton several miles ahead, and about 10:00 A.M. Tarleton's horsemen collided with Lee's, who had been sent out to give Greene warning of the enemy's approach. Several riders were wounded on each side in this short encounter, and Tarleton took a prisoner or two. The captives were unable to tell Cornwallis anything about American dispositions, however, and when he entered the valley leading to Guilford he was ignorant of what was ahead. He had been over the ground before, of course, but seems not to have remembered much about it.[41]

The six-pounders with the first line opened up on his troops as they passed into the valley. The British artillery soon came forward to answer, and Cornwallis formed his line. On his right, under Leslie, he placed

40. Ward, II, 786–87.
41. Cornwallis to Germain, March 17, 1781, in Stevens, ed., *Clinton-Cornwallis Controversy*, I, 364. Greene explained his disposition of his troops in a letter to the Continental Congress, March 20, 1781, GW Papers, Ser. 4, Reel 75.

the regiment of Bose, the 71st, and the First Battalion of Guards in support; on the left of the road, under Webster, he assigned the 23rd and 33rd Regiments supported by grenadiers and the Second Battalion of Guards under O'Hara in support. The jaegers and the light infantry of the guards remained as a reserve in the woods to the left, and Tarleton also in reserve took the road. Altogether the army numbered about 1900 men.[42]

The North Carolinians standing behind a rail fence at the skirt of the woods watched the regulars march forward to pounding drums and squealing fifes. The British right started first, following Leslie's commands. After looking the valley over, Cornwallis had decided to begin action on the right because the trees and brush were not as dense there as on the left. The North Carolinian commander facing the British right waited while the enemy marched down the slope, crossed the creek, and moved up the hill. At 150 yards he ordered his men to fire. The Carolinians' rifles killed at that range, and the British line immediately showed great holes. An observer commented that the row of redcoats "looked like the scattering stalks in a wheat field, when the harvest man has passed over it with his cradle." A captain in the 71st gave a flat description of the sight which is even more telling of the loss of life—"one-half of the Highlanders dropped on that spot." Only superbly disciplined and proud troops would have come on without wavering. Leslie ordered the pace to be picked up, and when the line got within what he considered effective range he stopped it and gave the command to present and fire. The Highlanders, again on order, then shouted and ran toward the Carolinians with muskets, bayonets attached, thrust forward. The Carolinians seem to have panicked at the sight. Henry Lee who was on the American left with his legion later wrote that in their eagerness to escape, they dropped their rifles, threw off knapsacks, and even discarded their canteens. Lee tried to hold them in place, even threatened to shoot them if they did not remain, but the Carolinians heard only Highlander yells. They would take their chances with Lee rather than their grim enemy.[43]

The Carolinians to the right of the road may have held their places a few moments longer. Lt. Colonel Webster, the British commander opposite them, sent his troops forward after Leslie got under way. The Carolinians on the right, like those on the left, waited patiently but

42. Ward, II, 787; Wickwires, *Cornwallis*, 297–98.
43. Quotations are from Wickwires, *Cornwallis*, 298. (The Wickwires give a brilliant account of the battle.)

seem to have fired simultaneously with the Americans on their left. Webster responded immediately by commanding his men to charge, hoping to reach the line before the Americans could reload. Sergeant Roger Lamb of the Royal Welch Fusiliers said that the movement was made "in excellent order, in a smart run, with arms charged." When the British got to within forty yards of the Carolinians, they discovered that they faced men resting their rifles on the rail fence "taking aim with the nicest precision." There was a pause while each side looked the other over until Webster rode in front of the 23rd shouting, "Come on my brave Fuzileers." The line moved again, both sides fired, and finally the American "gave way." Lamb reported no panic among them.[44]

Up to this point the action can be reconstructed fairly easily. There was disagreement in the days that followed—and since—about the steadiness of the first line. In his memoirs written years later, Henry Lee blamed the Carolinians for the loss of the battle, surely an unfair charge whatever the truth about their exit from the field. Greene, who was near the court house, too far away to see the first line, also dealt them a heavy load of blame.[45]

Sergeant Lamb wrote that after the British swept over the first line and into the woods, the action took on a ragged, even unconnected, quality. Visibility in the woods was frequently obscured by the heavy undergrowth which also broke up the evenness of the line. The British complained after the battle that they had found using the bayonet almost impossible, meaning that the heavy concentration of a bayonet charge could not be maintained by men entangled in brush and deflected by trees. The Virginians on the second line understandably regarded the trees and brush differently—as cover from which to avoid the bayonet and to shoot down their attackers. In the woods the attack broke into a series of smaller assaults and charges; no unit on either side had a clear notion of what was happening on its flanks.[46]

On the extreme edges of the battlefield two separate and savage engagements were fought. Lee's and Campbell's riflemen on the American left had not joined the Carolinians in flight. Rather they had fired down the British line as it came abreast of them. So galling was this enfilade fire, that Leslie committed his support, the 1st Battalion of Guards, to clean the Americans out. The guards fought tenaciously but only suc-

44. Roger Lamb, *An Original and Authentic Journal of Occurrences During the Late American War* . . . (Dublin, 1809), 361.

45. Lee, *Memoirs*, 279; Greene to Sumter, March 16, 1781, Greene Papers, HL.

46. Lamb, *Journal*, 361–62; Stevens, ed., *Clinton-Cornwallis Controversy*, I, 364–67.

ceeded in pushing Lee and Campbell to higher ground on the American left where they fought, in virtual isolation, until the battle was decided. On the American right, Lynch's riflemen and Washington's cavalry delivered an enfilading fire. Webster shifted his line to clear them away and brought up his jaegers and the Guards, hitherto inactive, in "support." Although the Americans gave ground only slowly, give way they did, and the British left stabilized itself. These shifts outward by the two British wings left the middle relatively open. To cover this part of the field Cornwallis called up O'Hara's grenadiers and the 2nd Battalion of Guards.[47]

The Virginians along the second line soon felt the attack of the reconstituted British center. Stevens, one of the two commanders of the Virginians, had felt shame at Camden, but now his men fought with great determination. In this struggle in the woods Cornwallis himself was very nearly captured or killed. Sergeant Lamb, ever alert, spotted him remounted on a dragoon's horse—his own had been shot—seeking to lead his men forward. But so bewildering was this fight, shrouded by branches and brush, that Cornwallis was a leader with no followers. Lamb grabbed the bridle of his horse just as Cornwallis was about to blunder into a nest of Virginians and guided him back to safety, if any part of that woods of bees and bullets could be considered safe.[48]

It was Webster's men on the British left, probably of the 33rd, who smashed through first to the third American line. The 2nd Battalion of Guards soon joined them and before long so did the remaining British units, with the exception of those conducting a private battle on the far left of the American lines.[49]

The third line consisted of American regulars—two regiments of Virginians on the right and next to them the 1st and 2nd Marylanders. These men stood in the open with the Reedy Fork road to their backs, heavy woods to their right, and the Great Road on their left. On the left flank Greene stationed two six-pounders. Farther to the left across the road Washington's cavalry rested. These horsemen had been pushed there in hard fighting from the right flank of the first line. To the front of these units, the hill fell off into a ravine and small gullies. All in all, the Americans held a fine defensive position.

The battle along the third line also went through several phases with control of the field shifting back and forth. Webster's light infantry

47. Ward, II, 788–90; Wickwires, Cornwallis, 300–302.
48. Lamb, Journal, 362.
49. Stevens, ed., Clinton-Cornwallis Controversy, I, 367; Ward, II, 792.

and the 33rd made the first assault without pausing as they left the woods. They may not have realized that a new fresh line opposed them but perhaps in the eagerness of pursuit believed that their combat was almost over. The Maryland and Virginia Continentals cut them down with a volley and then drove them back in chaos with a bayonet attack. At this moment, Lee and later historians suggest, Greene might have sent his entire line forward and won the field. Greene did not want to risk everything in this battle of surges and surprises—and was satisfied simply to hold his ground.

Simply holding the line soon proved impossible. The 2nd Battalion of Guards supported by the grenadiers now hit forward and dislodged the one inexperienced regiment on the line, the 5th Maryland Regiment, which fled without firing. The Americans recovered through the action of Washington's cavalry, which plugged the hole in a fierce charge. The 1st Marylanders and small detachments of Virginians swung about and concentrated on driving back the guards. O'Hara, their commander, now steadied them, though he was wounded, and the Fusiliers and the Highlanders were soon sucked into a compressed, savage struggle—much of it hand-to-hand with the Americans gradually gaining control. Seeing that his men must lose in this tight, swirling affair where for the moment at least they were clearly outnumbered, Cornwallis took a dreadful chance. Two three-pounders had been brought to a high point along the Great Road between 200 and 300 yards from the line. Cornwallis ordered that these pieces should fire grape over the British troops immediately to their front and into the unsteady mass of guards and Americans. O'Hara, lying near by, begged him to revoke this order, but Cornwallis held fast and the grape was fired, killing men on both sides. Its effect was to separate the two, and separation worked to the advantage of the British. At close quarters they were unexcelled with the bayonet so long as they were in formation. Tumbled together incoherently, with the greater numbers on their enemy's side, they lost the advantage and were rapidly being consumed in an unbalanced conflict.[50]

Drawn apart, the two sides reformed. The British knew how to re-establish formations more effectively and soon resumed the attack. At this point Greene gave way and ordered a retreat, abandoning his artillery and his wounded. The horses that drew the guns were casualties too, and pulling these pieces out by hand could only cost more lives. The

50. This paragraph and the two preceding are based on Ward, II, 791–92; Wickwires, *Cornwallis*, 303–8; and the accounts by Cornwallis, Greene, Lamb, and Lee cited above.

British were far too disabled to pursue. That night the living gave thanks, and the wounded, as always in these eighteenth-century battles, bled and suffered and died.

III

Cornwallis sent most of his wounded from the battlefield two days later in seventeen wagons with instructions: "Each Waggon to carry as many of the wounded men as can Possibly be put into it." He and the main body followed on March 19, heading for Cross Creek, a community of Scottish highlanders who he hoped would supply him and who even might contribute recruits to his shrinking command. The Scots did neither, and Cornwallis then resumed the march, with Wilmington his destination. He had hoped to remain at Cross Creek rather than put his command on the road once more, but he needed food. American irregulars along the Cape Fear River made sending supplies up from Wilmington by water impossible, so he had no choice but to move once more. By this time he feared a trap in South Carolina—or said he did—and clearly had his fill of chasing Greene. On April 7 he made it to Wilmington with about 1400 rank-and-file fit for duty. Lt. Colonel Webster was one of many who died along the way.[51]

Two weeks after the arrival at Wilmington, Charles O'Hara noted that the "Spirit of our little Army has evaporated a good deal." Undoubtedly it had. The feeling expressed later by several who fought at Guilford—that the victory had been "honorable" and even "glorious" but of no value because of the terrible losses—was widely shared. Cornwallis did not deprecate his victory, but neither did he dwell on it.[52]

Rather, he pondered what he should do. The recent campaign had disabused him of the notion that the Carolinas housed large numbers of loyalists. It had also convinced him that he had very little chance of smashing Greene even if he managed to join his army to Rawdon's, which in April still sat in Camden. He did not know what to do, and as he wrote his closest friend, Major General Phillips, who in March had taken some troops to Virginia where he assumed command from Arnold—"I am quite tired of marching about the country in quest of adventures." He was more discreet in a letter to Clinton asking for instructions, though the letter, with its reproachful declaration that he was "totally in the dark as to the intended operations in the summer,"

---

51. Newsome, ed., "British Orderly Book," *NCHR*, 9 (1932), 388; Ward, II, 796-97.
52. Rogers, ed., "Letters of O'Hara," *SCHM*, 65 (1964), 177-78; Stedman, *History of the American War*, II, 382.

laid out a plan. The heart of this plan was an extraordinary proposal "that the Chesapeake may become the seat of war, even (if necessary) at the expense of abandoning New York." What he had in mind was of course that Clinton abandon New York and bring the northern army to Virginia. There, as he wrote to Phillips in a fit of wishful thinking, "we then have a stake to fight for, and a successful battle may give us America." These suppositions about the crucial location of the Chesapeake and the possibility of ending the Revolution with a single battle reveal once more the limitations of Cornwallis's strategic thought. Frustrated by a long, miserable, and costly campaign, he dreamed; and dreaming, he deluded himself. There was no one to stop him, and on April 25 he began the march to Virginia.[53]

Although Nathanael Greene's army had been forced from the field at Guilford Court House, its spirit remained high. Perhaps the soldiers who enjoyed the highest morale were in the militia; their enlistments were expiring and they were leaving military service, as Greene sardonically observed, to "return home to kiss their wives and sweethearts." Even they probably shared Greene's opinion that "The Enemy got the ground the other Day, But we the victory. They had the splendor, we the advantage."[54]

How to use this advantage remained a troubling question for several weeks. By April, Greene had decided that he would march into South Carolina to clear that state of the enemy. Cornwallis had taken himself far from the scene and could make his army's weight felt only by the most strenuous effort. Greene thought it unlikely that Cornwallis would follow him southward, for if he did, he gave up North Carolina. And Greene assumed, incorrectly, that Cornwallis wanted very badly to hold North Carolina. If Cornwallis followed Greene into South Carolina the advantage lay with the Americans—Cornwallis's army still suffered from the last battle, and Pickens, Marion, and Sumter would aid the main army in giving the British more grief. What Greene wished to prevent was the joining of Cornwallis's force to Rawdon's then at Camden. Late in April Cornwallis removed any possibility of concentrating troops in South Carolina. Yet in May when Greene learned conclusively that Cornwallis had left for Virginia, he felt little relief—the linking of Cornwallis and Phillips created a large enemy force.[55]

53. The quotations, in order, are from Ross, ed., *Correspondence of Cornwallis*, I, 87, 86, 87.
54. Greene to Joseph Reed, March 18, 1781, and to Steuben, April 4, 1781, Greene Papers, HL.
55. Greene to Steuben, May 14, 1781, *ibid*.

Unaware of Cornwallis's inclination to shake the Carolina dust in favor of Virginia's, Greene on April 7 started down the Cape Fear River as if he were going to Wilmington, and the next day, after this feint which was designed to confuse the British, peeled off in a march against Camden. This move was one of a series of actions which he now undertook to push the British from South Carolina. In the west, Pickens was to strike Ninety-Six, Marion and Lee were to meet below Camden to attack Fort Watson on the Santee, and Sumter, after establishing magazines with food supplies near Camden, was to add his partisans to the main army.

Lee and Marion did their part brilliantly, and Fort Watson fell on April 23. This attack seems to have marked the first use of the Maham Tower, named after its inventor, Hezekiah Maham. The tower, a high platform erected near the fort, permitted the American riflemen who stood on it to deliver a plunging fire against the enemy manning the walls. Pickens also enjoyed success though his force was far too small to reduce the fortifications at Ninety-Six. He did, however, sweep the countryside around the post and isolated its defenders. Only Greene failed to take his objective, Camden, which, he remarked immediately after his failure, "seems to have some evil genius about it [,] whatever is attempted near that place is unfortunate."[56]

The "place" may have had an evil genius, but it also had a well-constructed defense and a skillful commander, Lord Francis Rawdon, a bright and ambitious man who had served in America since 1775. Rawdon wanted at Greene as badly as Greene wanted at him, and when the Americans arrived in the vicinity was happy to oblige them. Greene set up on Hobkirk's Hill, a pine-covered ridge running east and west about a mile and a half north of Camden. Convinced that an assault on Camden would be foolhardy, he thought that he must "induce the enemy to sally." Rawdon required no persuasion, and at mid-morning on April 25 he surprised the American pickets to the southeast of the main position. Two Maryland regiments backed by North Carolina militia sat on that end of the ridge and to their right two regiments of Virginia Continentals. Otho Williams commanded the American left; Isaac Huger, the right. Rawdon came at them from the southeast with three regiments in line and three in reserve. The best he had, the 63rd, manned the far right of his attacking formation.[57]

Greene's troops scrambled into position and when the British came

56. Greene to Reed, May 4, 1781, *ibid.;* Ward, II, 799–800.
57. Greene to Steuben, April 27, 1781, Greene Papers, HL, for the quotations and an account of the battle.

on they were ready. Rawdon presented so narrow a front that Greene resolved to envelop it from both flanks. After giving Rawdon a taste of grape from his three six-pounders, he sent his two regiments from the center straight down the hill, Virginians on the right and Marylanders on the left. At the same time his regiments on either end swung down to assault the flanks. To William Washington's cavalry fell the assignment of circling behind the British to sweep up their rear.

The American attack took the British by surprise but failed nonetheless. Washington did not reach the rear until the battle had been decided, and then he wasted his time on rounding up commissaries and quartermasters and other noncombatants who had wandered out from Camden to watch the fun. Two other events proved more decisive than the cavalry's tardiness, however. The first saw Rawdon react to Greene's formation and extend his own by calling up into the line his support, an action that protected his flanks. The second involved the 1st Maryland Regiment, two companies of which broke under fire. The regimental commander, Colonel John Gunby, then ordered the remaining four companies back while he tried to rally the two that had faltered. He succeeded in reforming his regiment, but his soldiers' run to the rear had unnerved the Virginians to their left. In battle there is nothing so difficult as stopping troops who have panicked. In this case, the task became all but impossible when Colonel Ford of the 5th Maryland went down with a musket ball in him. Rawdon's infantry flowed to the hole in the American lines almost as if pulled by gravity, and though they did not succeed in destroying Greene's army they pushed it from the field.

At the end of the battle only the Virginia regiment on the right wing of the American line completely retained its integrity. The artillery was rescued just as it was about to be captured. Greene himself served as a matross for a few minutes, and Washington's cavalry, though late on the scene, fought a fierce rear-guard action. Rawdon pursued his enemy for a couple of miles, though not with much vigor, for he knew that pursuit often leads to the disorganization of the pursuers. In this affair Greene's withdrawal was ordered well enough to discourage persistent attempts to trap him. Neither side suffered heavy losses, but neither could afford to lose those who fell.

The rest of Greene's plan to clear the South Carolina interior of the enemy prospered after these days of frustration. Thomas Sumter had resisted Greene's urging that he join his force to the main army, deciding instead in favor of independent operations. But he pleased Greene by taking Orangeburg on the North Fork of the Edisto River on May 10. This post and its small garrison provided an important link between Charleston and Camden. Lee and Marion picked off another the following day, Fort Motte on the Congaree River. Motte had not given in easily, and Lee and Marion had been forced to conduct a small-scale siege, running regular approaches, until they came close enough to burn their enemy out. Meanwhile Pickens had darted south to Augusta, which held out until June 5.

Before most of these attacks had even begun, Rawdon had decided to evacuate Camden. For a few days after Hobkirk's Hill he had hoped to trap Greene and actually came up against him on Sawney's Creek. The Americans held a position too difficult to attack with the force Rawdon commanded, and a few days later he decided to leave Camden. His impression was that the backcountry had risen against him—so he wrote Cornwallis on May 24, two weeks after his column heavily laden with sick and wounded began to clear Camden. He had begun to dread a general engagement by this time, believing that a heavy loss would force him from Charleston as well as the interior. The events of the next few days did nothing to change his mind, and the slow progress southward along the Santee deepened his discouragement. There, along the river his experiences repeated Cornwallis's in North Carolina, as sullen civilians carefully kept their distance from him and his army. "I had been five Days within the Santee before a single Man of the Country came near me," he remarked to Cornwallis. Food, as well as friends, was scarce, and only revolt seemed to be in harvest.[58]

Too late Rawdon ordered Colonel John Cruger to pull his command from Ninety-Six, too late because Greene's army surrounded the post before Rawdon's message arrived. Greene, with the assistance of Lee's Legion, lay siege to the place on May 22. Its defenses were formidable and Cruger, a Tory from New York, knew how to use them. He had some 500 men against Greene's 1000 regulars. But though outnumbered, he held on and threw back a fierce attack on June 18. Two days later Greene reluctantly ended the siege, for Rawdon with 2000 men, including three regiments fresh from England marching to Cruger's rescue, now threatened to overwhelm him. There was a brief chase, but Greene's head start and the summer heat combined to discourage Rawdon after he reached the Enoree River, thirty miles to the southeast.[59]

Greene did not know it, but he had won the war in the Carolinas. For much of July and throughout August he camped in the high hills

58. Stevens, ed., Clinton-Cornwallis Controversy, I, 485.
59. Ward, II, 812-22.

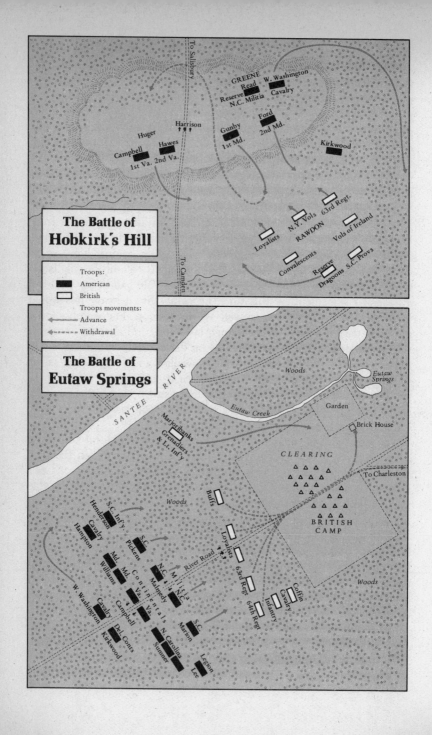

The Battle of
Hobkirk's Hill

Troops:
■ American
□ British

Troops movements:
◄——► Advance
◄----- Withdrawal

The Battle of
Eutaw Springs

of the Santee. There his regulars rested and his militia traveled in and out—mostly out. Greene occupied himself by trying to add to the size of his army and in writing letters to Congress painting in somber hues a picture of the failure of his support. Meanwhile Rawdon, his health shattered by the strenuous life he had been leading, had departed in July for England. His successor, Lt. Colonel Alexander Stewart, now held only two major posts in the southern states, Charleston and Savannah.

Greene and Stewart fought one more major engagement before the year ended, the battle of Eutaw Springs, on September 8. Eutaw Springs was thirty miles northwest of Charleston. Greene found Stewart there after maneuvering cautiously so as to conceal his desire to engage. That desire arose as his army received reinforcements and supplies and as the British lost control of the state. If Stewart could be destroyed, Charleston might be retaken and the war in the South brought to a stop.

That Greene was able to conceal the movements of his army, a force of some 2200 men, from Stewart bespeaks the loss of whatever civilian support the British had. Stewart remarked on the absence of information about his enemy, an absence so complete that he was taken almost by surprise by Greene's attack.

Greene's army included Lee's Legion, Francis Marion's partisans, militia from both the Carolinas, and Continentals from Delaware, Maryland, Virginia, and North Carolina. He also had the ever faithful Colonel William Washington and his cavalry. Stewart's force was just about equal in numbers. It consisted of companies from three regiments of regulars, eight companies of the "Irish Buffs" as the 3rd Regiment was called, and loyalist provincials commanded by John Cruger and John Coffin.[60]

Early on the morning of September 8, the Americans started toward Stewart's camp from their own at Burdell's Plantation, seven miles away. At about eight o'clock the van of Major John Armstrong's North Carolina Continentals ran into a small party of enemy soldiers who had been sent out to dig yams. Short of bread the British were substituting yams which could be found in nearby fields. Armstrong shot up the yam diggers and a small covering party of Coffin's cavalry, but the action deprived the Americans of surprise. Warned that an unknown number of enemy was approaching, Stewart placed a battalion on his far right next to the Santee in heavy blackjack, a shrub so tough and thick as to prevent cavalry from riding through it. To the south he stretched

60. *Ibid.*, 823–26.

out his regiments in a line, with most of the Tories near the center, about a hundred yards west of his camp.

Greene had formed his column as the rules of warfare enjoined, so that it might deploy into line easily with its units arrayed as he wanted them. He wanted them in two heavy lines, militia in the lead and regulars following about a hundred yards behind. He placed Lee's Legion on his right flank and partisan units under John Henderson and Wade Hampton on his left. The two sides made heavy contact about an hour after the yam diggers were driven in. Greene's lines were probably a little uneven by this time, for they had to make their way through trees and heavy brush. Nonetheless, the militia fought well until a charge by Stewart's men broke them in the center. The flanks held, however, and Greene sent the North Carolina Continentals into the gap. These men restored the American line until a second attack by the British broke them. Greene then inserted the Virginia and Maryland regulars, Richard Campbell and Otho Williams commanding, and had the satisfaction of seeing them use their bayonets as skillfully as European professionals. He later gave these regiments considerable praise in his report to Congress: "I think myself principally indebted for the victory we obtained to the free use of the Bayonet by the Virginians and Marylanders, the Infantry of the Legion and Captain Kirkwood's Light Infantry." Indeed the rush of the American regulars forced the British back, some units apparently in great disorder and confusion.[61]

In a few minutes the Americans shared this disorder and confusion. As they pursued the British they ran into the enemy's camp and paused to plunder it. What they found in ample supply seems to have been rum. The pause found them milling around entirely without discipline; and the few that maintained the attack ran into a large, heavily fortified brick house at the northeastern edge of the British camp. This house produced further confusion as the troops lost their unity in their attempts to take it. The one British battalion still in good order now asserted itself. This battalion belonged to Major John Marjoribanks. It had held together despite assaults from the cavalry of William Washington and Wade Hampton. After pretty well demolishing the American horse, Marjoribanks pulled back close to the brick house. From that position, he, aided by re-formed British regiments, drove the disorganized looters from the British camp. A battalion of Maryland regulars slowed this counterattack and prevented the withdrawal from degenerating into a rout. Still the British, despite many casualties, held the field.

61. For the quotation and an account of the battle, Greene to Congress, Sept. 11, 1781, Greene Papers, HL; Ward, II, 827–34.

IV

The British held the field, but they had lost the Carolinas and Georgia. Stewart retired to Charleston; to the south a small British force remained in Savannah. But these units were too weak to do much more than sit and wait for the end of the war. The countryside belonged to the Americans.

Shifting the war to the South had seemed especially promising to British commanders after Charleston fell in the spring of 1780. In reality they faced enormous problems even after that victory. For they had erred in their estimates of loyalist support. If they had ever had a chance of holding a population loyal to the king, they squandered it by neglecting the southern colonies after the defeats at Moore's Creek Bridge and Charleston in 1776. And until Archibald Campbell captured Savannah in January 1779, they had remained inactive.

During the years before the British turned southward again, patriot militia proved that they could maintain order in the Carolinas and Georgia. They defined this mission as one which required the suppression of loyalism. And for the most part they succeeded in putting down, or at least discouraging, loyalist attempts to organize. They continued in this work after British regulars arrived.

Cornwallis confessed to feeling disappointment at the absence of loyalist support—the Carolinians neither joined his army nor fed it willingly. Worse, they did not give him, or his successors, information about his enemy's movements. Instead Carolinians ambushed his dispatch riders, attacked his supply trains, and wiped out the Tory forces that dared to show themselves.

The South, like New England and the middle colonies, was enemy country. Southern militia may have been no more reliable in set-piece battles than most irregulars to the north, but they were brutally effective in fighting loyalist militia. They fought well in these irregular engagements for at least two reasons: they shared the faith in the glorious cause, and they had the support of most of the ordinary people of the South.

Nathanael Greene may not have recognized these realities in the dreadful days following Camden. Yet he fought his war with skill and imagination—and gradually came to understand that when he ran from the enemy he would be succored by the people of the Carolinas. The support was not lavish—the countryside's resources were lean and decimated by the war—but it was enough to enable him to make the struggle he called the "fugitive war" the means to victory in the lower South.

20

Inside the Campaigns

In the battle of Eutaw Springs, South Carolina, the last major action of the Revolutionary War before Cornwallis surrendered at Yorktown, over 500 Americans were killed and wounded. Nathanael Greene had led some 2200 men into the Springs; his casualties thus represented almost one-fourth of his army. More men would die in battles in the next two years, and others would suffer terrible wounds. The statistics, although notoriously unreliable, show that the Revolution killed a higher percentage of those who served on the American side than any war in our history, always excepting the Civil War.[1]

Why did these men—those who survived and those who died—fight? Why did they hold their ground, endure the strain of battle, with men dying about them and danger to themselves so obvious? Undoubtedly the reasons varied from battle to battle, but just as surely there was some experience common to all these battles—and fairly uniform reasons for the actions of the men who fought despite their deepest impulses, which must have been to run from the field in order to escape the danger.

Some men did run, throwing down their muskets and packs in order to speed their flight. American units broke in large actions and small, at Brooklyn, Kip's Bay, White Plains, Brandywine, Germantown, Camden, and Hobkirk's Hill, to cite the most important instances. Yet many men did not break and run even in the disasters to American arms. They held their ground until they were killed, and they fought tenaciously while pulling back.

1. Peckham, *Toll*, 90, for Eutaw Springs; pp. 132–33 for the comparison of the Revolution and the Civil War.

In most actions the Continentals, the regulars, fought more bravely than the militia. We need to know why these men fought and why the American regulars performed better than the militia. The answers surely will help us to understand the Revolution, especially if we can discover whether what made men fight reflected what they believed—and felt—about the Revolution.

Several explanations of the willingness to fight and die, if necessary, may be dismissed at once. One is that soldiers on both sides fought out of fear of their officers, fearing them more than they did battle. Frederick the Great had described this condition as ideal, but it did not exist in ideal or practice in either the American or the British army. The British soldier usually possessed a more professional spirit than the American, an attitude compounded from confidence in his skill and pride in belonging to an old established institution. British regiments carried proud names—the Royal Welch Fusiliers, the Black Watch, the King's Own—whose officers usually behaved extraordinarily bravely in battle and expected their men to follow their examples. British officers disciplined their men more harshly than American officers did and generally trained them more effectively in the movements of battle. But neither they nor American officers instilled the fear that Frederick found so desirable. Spirit, bravery, a reliance on the bayonet, were all expected of professional soldiers, but professionals acted out of pride—not out of fear of their officers.

Still, coercion and force were never absent from the life of either army. There were, however, limits on their use and their effectiveness. Fear of flogging might prevent a soldier from deserting camp, but it could not guarantee that he would remain steady under fire. Fear of ridicule may have aided in keeping some troops in place, however. Eighteenth-century infantry went into combat in fairly close lines and officers could keep an eye on many of their men. If the formation was tight enough officers might strike laggards and even order "skulkers," Washington's term for those who turned tail, shot down.[2] Just before the move to Dorchester Heights in March 1776, the word went out that any American who ran from the action would be "fired down upon the spot."[3] The troops themselves approved of this threat, according to one of the chaplains.

2. *GW Writings*, V, 480.
3. Jeanette D. Black and William G. Roelker, *A Rhode Island Chaplain in the Revolution: Letters of Ebenezer David to Nicholas Brown, 1775–1778* (Providence, R.I., 1949), 13.

Washington repeated the threat just before the Battle of Brooklyn later that year, though he seems not to have posted men behind the lines to carry it out. Daniel Morgan urged Nathanael Greene to place sharp-shooters behind the militia, and Greene may have done so at Guilford Court House. No one thought that an entire army could be held in place against its will, and these commands to shoot soldiers who retired without orders were never widely issued.[4]

A tactic that surely would have appealed to many soldiers would have been to send them into battle drunk. Undoubtedly some—on both sides—did enter combat with their senses deadened by rum. Both armies commonly issued an additional ration of rum on the eve of some extraordinary action—a long, difficult march, for example, or a battle, were two of the usual reasons. A common order on such occasions ran: "The troops should have an extraordinary allowance of rum," usually a gill, four ounces of unknown alcoholic content, which if taken down at the propitious moment might dull fears and summon courage. At Camden no supply of rum existed; Gates or his staff substituted molasses, to no good effect, according to Otho Williams. The British fought brilliantly at Guilford Court House unaided by anything stronger than their own large spirits. In most actions soldiers went into battle with very little more than themselves and their comrades to lean upon.[5]

Belief in the Holy Spirit surely sustained some in the American army, perhaps more than in the enemy's. There are a good many references to the Divine or to Providence in the letters and diaries of ordinary soldiers. Often, however, these expressions are in the form of thanks to the Lord for permitting these soldiers to survive. There is little that suggests soldiers believed that faith rendered them invulnerable to the enemy's bullets. Many did consider the glorious cause to be sacred; their war, as the ministers who sent them off to kill never tired of reminding them, was just and providential.[6]

Others clearly saw more immediate advantages in the fight: the plunder of the enemy's dead. At Monmouth Court House, where Clinton with-

4. *GW Writings*, V, 479–80; Ward, II, 786.
5. Otho Williams, "A Narrative of the Campaign of 1780," in William Johnson, *Sketches of the Life and Correspondence of Nathanael Greene* (2 vols., Charleston, S.C., 1822), I, 494; A. R. Newsome, ed., "A British Orderly Book, 1780–1781," *NCHR*, 9 (1932), 289.
6. For typical references to Providence, see Herbert T. Wade and Robert A. Lively, *This Glorious Cause: The Adventures of Two Company Officers in Washington's Army* (Princeton, N.J., 1958).

drew after dark, leaving the field strewn with British corpses, the plundering carried American soldiers into the houses of civilians who had fled to save themselves. The soldiers' actions were so blatant and so unrestrained that Washington ordered their packs searched. And at Eutaw Springs, the Americans virtually gave up victory to the opportunity of ransacking British tents. Some died in their greed, shot down by an enemy given time to regroup while his camp was torn apart by men looking for something to carry off. But even these men probably fought for something besides plunder. When it beckoned they responded, but it had not drawn them to the field; nor had it kept them there in a savage struggle.[7]

Inspired leadership helped soldiers face death, but they sometimes fought bravely even when their leaders let them down. Yet officers' courage and the example of officers throwing off wounds to remain in the fight undoubtedly helped their men stick. Charles Stedman, the British general, remarked on Captain Maitland who, at Guilford Court House, was hit, dropped behind for a few minutes to get his wound dressed, then returned to the battle.[8] Cornwallis obviously filled Sergeant Lamb with pride, struggling forward to press into the struggle after his horse was killed.[9] Washington's presence meant much at Princeton though his exposure to enemy fire may also have made his troops uneasy. His quiet exhortation as he passed among the men who were about to assault Trenton—"Soldiers, keep by your officers"—remained in the mind of a Connecticut soldier until his death fifty years later.[10] There was only one Washington, one Cornwallis, and their influence on men in battle, few of whom could have seen them, was of course slight. Junior and noncommissioned officers carried the burden of tactical direction; they had to show their troops what must be done and somehow persuade, cajole, or force them to do it. The praise ordinary soldiers lavished on sergeants and junior officers suggests that these leaders played important parts in their troops' willingness to fight. Still, important as it was, their part does not really explain why men fought.

In suggesting this conclusion about military leadership, I do not wish

7. Benjamin Fishbourne and others, Orderly Book, June 12–July 13, 1778, BR96, HL.

8. Stedman, History of the American War, II, 38.

9. Roger Lamb, An Original and Authentic Journal of Occurrences During the Late American War . . . (Dublin, 1809), 362.

10. William S. Powell, "A Connecticut Soldier Under Washington: Elisha Bostwick's Memoirs of the First Years of the Revolution," WMQ, 3d Ser., 6 (1949), 102.

to be understood as agreeing with Tolstoy's scornful verdict on generals—that despite all their plans and orders they do not affect the results of battles at all. Tolstoy did not reserve all his scorn for generals—historians are also derided in *War and Peace* for finding a rational order in battles where only chaos existed. "The activity of a commander in chief does not at all resemble the activity we imagine to ourselves when we sit at at ease in our studies examining some campaign on the map, with a certain number of troops on this and that side in a certain known locality, and begin our plans from some given moment. A commander in chief is never dealing with the beginning of any event—the position from which we always contemplate it. The commander in chief is always in the midst of a series of shifting events and so he never can at any moment consider the whole import of an event that is occurring."[11]

The full import of battle will as surely escape historians as participants. But we have to begin somewhere in trying to explain why men fought rather than ran from Revolutionary battlefields. The battlefield may indeed be the place to begin since we have dismissed leadership, fear of officers, religious belief, the power of drink, and the other possible explanations of why men fought and died.

The eighteenth-century battlefield was, compared with the twentieth, an intimate theater, especially intimate in the engagements of the Revolution which were usually small even by the standards of the day. The killing range of the musket, eighty to one hundred yards, enforced intimacy as did the reliance on the bayonet and the general ineffectiveness of artillery. Soldiers had to come to close quarters to kill; this fact reduced the mystery of battle though perhaps not its terrors. But at least the battlefield was less impersonal. In fact, in contrast to twentieth-century combat, in which the enemy usually remains unseen and the source of incoming fire unknown, in eighteenth-century battles the foe could be seen and sometimes even touched. Seeing one's enemy may have aroused a singular intensity of feeling uncommon in modern battles. The assault with the bayonet—the most desired objective of infantry tactics—seems indeed to have evoked an emotional climax. Before it occurred, tension and anxiety built up as the troops marched from their column into a line of attack. The purpose of their movements was well understood by themselves and their enemies, who must have watched with feelings of dread and fascination. When the order came sending them forward, rage, even madness, replaced the attackers' anxiety, while terror and

11. *War and Peace,* Book XI: 2.

desperation sometimes filled those receiving the charge.[12] Surely it is revealing that the Americans who ran from battle did so most often at the moment they understood that their enemy had started forward with the bayonet. This happened to several units at Brandywine and to the militia at Camden and Guilford Court House. The loneliness, the sense of isolation, reported by modern soldiers was probably missing at such moments. All was clear—especially that glittering line of advancing steel.

Whether this awful clarity was harder to bear than losing sight of the enemy is problematical. American troops ran at Germantown after grappling with the British and then finding the field of battle covered by fog. At that time groping blindly, they and their enemy struggled over ground resembling a scene of modern combat. The enemy was hidden at a critical moment, and American fears were generated by not knowing what was happening—or about to happen. They could not see the enemy, and they could not see one another, an especially important fact. For, as S. L. A. Marshall, the twentieth-century military historian, has suggested in his book *Men Against Fire*, what sustains men in the extraordinary circumstances of battle may be their relationships with their comrades.[13]

These men found that sustaining such relationships was possible in the intimacy of the American battlefield. And not just because the limited arena robbed battle of some of its mystery. More importantly, it permitted the troops to give one another moral or psychological support. The enemy could be seen, but so could one's comrades; they could be seen and communicated with.

Eighteenth-century infantry tactics called for men to move and fire from tight formations which permitted them to talk and to give one another information—and reassurance and comfort. If properly done, marching and firing found infantrymen compressed into files in which their shoulders touched. In battle, physical contact with one's comrades on either side must have helped men control their fears. Firing the musket from three compact lines, the English practice, also involved physical contact. The men of the front rank crouched on their right knees; the men of the center rank placed their left feet inside the right feet of the front; the rear rank did the same thing behind the center.

12. See Samuel B. Webb to Silas Deane, Cambridge, July 11, 1775, MHS, *Procs.*, 14 (Boston, 1876), 83.
13. (New York, 1947), especially chapter 10.

This stance was called—a revealing term—"locking." The very density of this formation sometimes aroused criticism from officers who complained that it led to inaccurate fire. The front rank, conscious of the closeness of the center, might fire too low; the rear rank tended to "throw" its shots into the air, as firing too high was called; only the center rank took careful aim according to the critics. Whatever the truth of these charges about accuracy of fire, men in these dense formations compiled a fine record of holding their ground. And it is worth noting that the inaccuracy of men in the rear rank bespoke their concern for their fellows in front of them.[14]

British and American soldiers in the Revolution often spoke of fighting with "spirit" and "behaving well" under fire. Sometimes these phrases referred to daring exploits under great danger, but more often they seem to have meant holding together, giving one another support, reforming the lines when they were broken or fell into disorder, disorder such as overtook the Americans at Greenspring, Virginia, early in July 1781 when Cornwallis lured Anthony Wayne into crossing the James with a force that was heavily outnumbered. Wayne saw his mistake and decided to make the best of it, not by a hasty retreat from the ambush but by attacking. The odds against the Americans were formidable but, as an ordinary soldier who was there saw it, the inspired conduct of the infantry saved them—"our troops behaved well, fighting with great spirit and bravery. The infantry were oft broke; but just as oft rallied and formed at a word."[15]

These troops had been spread out when the British surprised them, but they formed as quickly as possible. Here was a test of men's spirits, a test they passed in part because of their disciplined formation. At Camden, where in contrast the militia collapsed as soon as the battle began, an open alignment may have contributed to their fear. Gates placed the Virginians on the far left apparently expecting them to cover more ground than their numbers allowed. At any rate they went into the battle in a single line with at least five feet between each man, a

14. Eighteenth-century tactics are discussed with discernment by R. R. Palmer, "Frederick the Great, Guibert, Bülow: From Dynastic to National War," in Edward M. Earle, ed., *Makers of Modern Strategy: Military Thought from Machiavelli to Hitler* (Princeton, N.J., 1943), 49–74; Willcox, *Portrait of a General;* and Wickwires, *Cornwallis.* For "locking" and other aspects of firing and marching, see Humphrey Bland, *An Abstract of Military Discipline* (Boston, 1747); [Edward Harvey], *The Manual Exercise As Ordered by His Majesty in 1764* (Boston, [1774]); Timothy Pickering, *An Easy Plan of Discipline for a Militia* (Salem, Mass., 1775).
15. *The Diary of Josiah Atkins* (New York, 1975), 38.

distance which intensified a feeling of isolation in the heat and noise of the firing. And to make such feelings worse, these men were especially exposed, stretched out at one end of the line with no supporters behind them.[16]

Troops in tight lines consciously reassured one another in several ways. British troops usually talked and cheered—"huzzaing" whether standing their ground, running forward, or firing. The Americans may have done less talking and cheering, though there is evidence that they learned to imitate the enemy. Giving a cheer at the end of successful engagement was standard practice. The British cheered at Lexington and then marched off to be shot down on the road running from Concord. The Americans shouted their joy at Harlem Heights, an understandable action and one for most of 1776 they rarely had opportunity to perform.[17]

The most deplorable failures to stand and fight usually occurred among the American militia. Yet there were militia companies that performed with great success, remaining intact under the most deadly volleys. The New England companies at Bunker Hill held out under a fire that veteran British officers compared to the worst they had experienced in Europe. Lord Rawdon remarked on how unusual it was for defenders to stick to their posts even after the assaulting troops had entered the ditch around a redoubt.[18] The New Englanders did it. They also held steady at Princeton—"They were the first who regularly formed" and stood up under the balls "which whistled their thousand different notes around our heads," according to Charles Willson Peale, whose Philadelphia militia also proved its steadiness.[19]

What was different about these companies? Why did they fight when others around them ran? The answer may lie in the relationships among their men. Men in the New England companies, in the Philadelphia militia, and in the other units that held together were neighbors. They knew one another; they had something to prove to one another; they had their "honor" to protect. Their active service in the Revolution may have been short, but they had been together in one way or another for a fairly long time—for several years in most cases. Their companies,

---

16. *VG* (Dixon and Nicholson), Sept. 6, 1780, contains an account of the extended disposition on the left. Ward, II, 722–30, provides a fine study of the battle, as do the Wickwires, *Cornwallis*, 149–65.

17. Tench Tilghman to his father, Sept. 19, 1776, Henry P. Johnston, ed., *Memoir of Lieut. Col. Tench Tilghman* (Albany, N.Y., 1876), 139.

18. Francis Rawdon to the Earl of Huntington, June 20, 1775, Hastings Papers, HL.

19. Charles Willson Peale Diary, Jan. 3, 1777, HL.

after all, had been formed from towns and villages. Some, clearly, had known one another all their lives.[20]

Elsewhere, especially in the thinly settled southern colonies, companies were usually composed of men—farmers, farmers' sons, farm laborers, artisans, and new immigrants—who did not know one another. They were, to use a term much used in a later war, companies of "stragglers" without common attachments, with almost no knowledge of their fellows. For them, even bunched tightly in line, the battlefield was an empty, lonely place. Absence of personal bonds, and their own parochialism, coupled to inadequate training and imperfect discipline, often led to disintegration under fire.[21]

According to conventional wisdom the nearer the American militia were to home the better they fought, fighting for their homes and no one else's. Proximity to home, however, may have been a distraction which weakened resolve. For the irony of going into battle and perhaps to their deaths when home and safety lay close down the road could not have escaped many. Almost every senior American general commented on the propensity of the militia to desert—and if they were not deserting they seemed perpetually in transit between home and camp, usually without authorization.

Paradoxically, of all the Americans who fought, the militiamen best exemplified in themselves and in their behavior the ideals and purposes of the Revolution. They had enjoyed independence, or at least personal liberty, long before it was proclaimed in the Declaration. They instinctively felt their equality with others and in many places insisted upon demonstrating it by choosing their own officers. Their sense of their liberty permitted, even compelled, them to serve only for short enlistments, to leave camp when they liked, to scorn the orders of others—and especially those orders to fight when they preferred to flee. Their integration into their society drove them to resist military discipline; and their ethos of personal freedom stimulated hatred of the machine that served as the model for the army. They were not pieces of a machine,

20. For a fine study of a Massachusetts town and its militia, see Robert A. Gross, *The Minutemen and Their World* (New York, 1976); and for a general view of the colonial militia, John Shy, "A New Look at the Colonial Militia," *WMQ*, 3d Ser., 20 (1963), 175–85, is outstanding.

21. The conclusions in this paragraph were suggested by Edward C. Papenfuse and Gregory A. Stiverson, "General Smallwood's Recruits: The Peacetime Career of the Revolutionary War Private," *WMQ*, 3d Ser., 30 (1973), 117–32. The Nathanael Greene Papers in the Huntington Library contain materials which tend to confirm these impressions.

and they would serve it only reluctantly and skeptically. At their best, at Cowpens, for example, they fought well; at their worst, at Camden, they fought not at all. There, they were, as Greene said, "ungovernable."[22] What was lacking in the militia was a set of professional standards, requirements and rules which might regulate their conduct in battle. What was lacking was professional pride. Coming and going to camp as they liked, shooting their guns for the pleasure of the sound, the militia annoyed the Continentals, who soon learned that most could not be trusted.

The British regulars were at the opposite pole. They had been pulled out of society, carefully segregated from it, tightly disciplined and highly trained. Their values were the values of the army for the most part, no more and no less. To be sure, the officers were in certain respects very different from the men. They embodied the style and standards of gentlemen who believed in service to their king and who fought for honor and glory.

With these ideals and a mission of service to the king defining their calling, British officers held themselves as aloof as possible from the peculiar horrors of war. Not that they did not fight. They sought combat and danger, but by the conventions which shaped their understanding of battle, they insulated themselves as much as possible from the ghastly business of killing and dying. Thus the results of battle might be long lists of dead and wounded, but the results were also "honourable and glorious," as Charles Stedman described Guilford Court House, or reflected "dishonour upon British arms," as he described Cowpens. Actions and gunfire were "smart" and "brisk" and sometimes "hot," and occasionally a "difficult piece of work." They might also be described lightly—Harlem Heights was "this silly business" to Lord Rawdon. To their men, British officers spoke a clean, no nonsense language. Howe's terse "look to your bayonets" summed up a tough professional's expectations.[23]

For all the distance between British officers and men, they gave remarkable support to one another in battle. They usually deployed carefully, keeping up their spirits with drum and fife. They talked and shouted and cheered, and coming on with their bayonets at the ready "huzzaing," or coming on "firing and huzzaing" they must have sustained a sense

22. Greene to Governor Reed, March 18, 1781, Greene Papers, HL. On Feb. 3, 1781, Greene wrote Governor Nash that 20,000 militia would not provide 500 effective troops, the way they "come and go," *ibid.*

23. Stedman, *History of the American War,* II, 383, 360; Rawdon to the Earl of Huntington, Aug. 3, 1775, Sept. 23, 1776, Hastings Papers, HL.

of shared experience. Their ranks might be thinned by an American volley but on they came, exhorting one another to "push on! push on!" as at Bunker Hill and the battles that followed.[24] Although terrible losses naturally dispirited them, they almost always maintained the integrity of their regiments as fighting units, and when they were defeated, or nearly so as at Guilford Court House, they recovered their pride and fought well thereafter. And there was no hint at Yorktown that the ranks wanted to surrender, even though they had suffered dreadfully.

The Continentals, the American regulars, lacked the polish of their British counterparts, but at least from Monmouth on, they showed a steadiness under fire almost as impressive as their enemy's. And they demonstrated a brave endurance: defeated, they retired, pulled themselves together, and came back to try again. These qualities—patience and endurance—endeared them to many. For example, John Laurens, on Washington's staff in 1778, wanted desperately to command them. In what amounted to a plea for command, Laurens wrote: "I would cherish those dear, ragged Continentals, whose patience will be the admiration of future ages, and glory in bleeding with them."[25] This statement was all the more extraordinary coming from Laurens, a South Carolina aristocrat. The soldiers he admired were anything but aristocratic. As the war dragged on they came increasingly from the poor and the propertyless. Most probably entered the army as substitutes for men who had rather pay than serve, or as the recipients of bounties and the promise of land. In time, some, perhaps many, assimilated the ideals of the Revolution. As Baron von Steuben observed in training them, they differed from European troops in at least one regard: they wanted to know why they were told to do certain things. Unlike European soldiers who did what they were told, the Continentals asked why.[26]

Continental officers aped the style of their British counterparts. They aspired to gentility and, often failing to achieve it, betrayed their anxiety by an excessive concern for their honor. Not surprisingly, like their British counterparts, they also used the vocabulary of the gentleman in describing battle.

Their troops, innocent of such polish, spoke with words from their immediate experience of physical combat. They found few euphemisms for the horrors of battle. Thus Private David How, September 1776,

24. Rawdon to the Earl of Huntington, June 20, 1775, Hastings Papers, HL.
25. To his father, March 9, 1778, in William Gilmore Simms, ed., *The Army Correspondence of Colonel John Laurens in the Years 1777–1778* (New York, 1867), 136.
26. Sheer and Rankin, *Rebels and Redcoats*, 354.

in New York, noted in his diary: "Isaac Fowls had his head shot off with a cannon ball this morning." And Sergeant Thomas McCarty reported an engagement between a British foraging party and American infantry near New Brunswick in February 1777: "We attacked the body, and bullets flew like hail. We stayed about 15 minutes and then retreated with loss." After the battle inspection of the field revealed that the British had killed the American wounded—"the men that was wounded in the thigh or leg, they dashed out their brains with their muskets and run them through with their bayonets, made them like sieves. This was barbarity to the utmost." The pain of seeing his comrades mutilated by shot and shell at White Plains remained with Elisha Bostwick, a Connecticut soldier, all his life: A cannon ball "cut down Lt. Youngs platoon which was next to that of mine[;] the ball first took off the head of Smith, a Stout heavy man and dashed it open, then took Taylor across the Bowels, it then Struck Sergeant Garret of our Company on the hip [and] took off the point of the hip bone[.] Smith and Taylor were left on the spot. Sergeant Garret was carried but died the Same day now to think, oh! what a sight that was to see within a distance of six rods those men with their legs and arms and guns and packs all in a heap[.]"[27]

The Continentals occupied the psychological and moral ground somewhere between the militia and the British professionals. From 1777 on their enlistments were for three years or the duration of the war. This long service allowed them to learn more of their craft and to become seasoned. That does not mean that on the battlefield they lost their fear. Experience in combat almost never leaves one indifferent to danger, unless after prolonged and extreme fatigue one comes to consider oneself already dead. Seasoned troops have simply learned to deal with their fear more effectively than raw troops, in part because they have come to realize that everyone feels it and that they can rely on their fellows.

By winter 1779–80 the Continentals were beginning to believe that they had no one save themselves to lean on. Their soldierly qualifications so widely admired in America—their "habit of subordination,"[28] their patience under fatigue, their ability to stand sufferings and privations

27. Henry B. Dawson, ed., *Gleanings from the Harvest-field of American History*, IV: [Diary of David How] (Morrisania, N.Y., 1865), 28; Jared C. Lobdell, ed., "The Revolutionary War Journal of Sergeant Thomas McCarty," New Jersey Historical Society, *Proceedings*, 82 (Newark, N.J., 1964), 45; Powell, "Bostwick's Memoirs," *WMQ*, 3d Ser., 6 (1949), 101.

28. Laurens to his father, Jan. 14, 1779, Simms, ed., *Army Correspondence*, 108.

of every kind—may in fact have led to a bitter resignation that saw them through a good deal of fighting. At Morristown during this winter, they felt abandoned in their cold and hunger. They knew that in America food and clothing existed to keep them healthy and comfortable, and yet little of either came to the army. Understandably their dissatisfaction increased as they realized that once again the suffering had been left to them. Dissatisfaction in these months slowly turned into a feeling of martyrdom. They felt themselves to be martyrs to the "glorious cause." They would fulfill the ideals of the Revolution and see things through to independence because the civilian population would not.[29]

Thus the Continentals in the last four years of the active war, though less articulate and less independent than the militia, assimilated one part of the "cause" more fully. They had advanced further in making American purposes in the Revolution their own. They had in their sense of isolation and neglect probably come to be more nationalistic than the militia—though surely no more American.

Although these sources of the Continentals' feeling seem curious, they served to reinforce the tough professional ethic these men also came to absorb. Set apart from the militia by the length of their service, by their officers' esteem for them, and by their own contempt for part-time soldiers, the Continentals slowly developed resilience and pride. Their country might ignore them in camp, might allow their bellies to shrivel and their backs to freeze, might allow them to wear rags, but in battle they would not be ignored. And in battle they would support one another in the knowledge that their own moral and professional resources remained sure.

The meaning of these complex attitudes is not what it seems to be. At first sight the performance of militia and Continentals seems to suggest that the great principles of the Revolution made little difference on the battlefield. Or if principles did make a difference, say especially to the militia saturated with natural rights and a deep and persistent distrust of standing armies, they served not to strengthen the will to combat but to disable it. And the Continentals, recruited increasingly from the poor and dispossessed, apparently fought better as they came to resemble their professional and apolitical enemy, the British infantry.

These conclusions are in part askew. To be sure, there is truth—and paradox—in the fact that some Americans' commitments to Revolu-

---

29. S. Sidney Bradford, "Hunger Menaces the Revolution, December 1779–January 1780," *MdHM*, 61 (1966), 5–23; Worthington C. Ford, ed., *Correspondence and Journals of Samuel Blachley Webb* (3 vols., New York, 1893–94), II, 231–32.

tionary principles made them unreliable on the battlefield. Still, their devotion to their principles helped bring them there. George Washington, their commander in chief, never tired of reminding them that their cause arrayed free men against mercenaries. They were fighting for the "blessings of liberty," he told them in 1776, and should they not acquit themselves like men, slavery would replace their freedom.[30] The challenge to behave like men was not an empty one. Courage, honor, gallantry in the service of liberty, all those words calculated to bring a blush of embarrassment to jaded twentieth-century men, defined manhood for the eighteenth century. In battle those words gained an extraordinary resonance as they were embodied in the actions of brave men. Indeed it is likely that many Americans who developed a narrow professional spirit found battle broadly educative, forcing them to consider the purposes of their professional skill.

On one level those purposes had to be understood as having a remarkable importance if men were to fight—and die. For battle forced American soldiers into a situation which nothing in their usual experience had prepared them for. They were to kill other men in the expectation that even if they did they might be killed themselves. However defined, especially by a Revolution in the name of life, liberty, and the pursuit of happiness, this situation was unnatural.

On another level, one which, perhaps, made the strain of battle endurable, the situation of American soldiers, though unusual, was not really foreign to them. For what battle presented in stark form was one of the classic problems free men face: choosing between the rival claims of public responsibility and private wishes, or in eighteenth-century terms, choosing between virtue—devotion to the public trust—and personal liberty. In battle, virtue demanded that men give up their liberties and perhaps even their lives for others. Each time they fought they had, in effect, to weigh the claims of society and liberty. Should they fight or run? They knew that the choice might mean life or death. For those American soldiers who were servants, apprentices, poor men substituting for men with money to hire them, the choice might not have seemed to involve moral decision. After all, they had never enjoyed much personal liberty. But not even in that contrivance of eighteenth-century authoritarianism in which they now found themselves, the professional army, could they avoid a moral decision. Compressed into dense formations, they were reminded by their nearness to their comrades that they too had

30. GW Writings, V, 479.

an opportunity to uphold virtue. By standing firm they served their fellows and honor; by running, they served only themselves.

Thus battle tested the inner qualities of men, tried their souls, as Thomas Paine said. Many men died in the test that battle made of their spirits. Some soldiers called this trial cruel; others called it "glorious." Perhaps this difference in perception suggests how difficult it was in the Revolution to be both a soldier and an American. Nor has it ever been easy since.

II

The first contact that a new recruit had with the army could only have left him with the need for reassurance. The army was a bewildering collection of men, strange rules, and new routines. The recruit, fresh, say, from a Maryland farm where he worked for wages and his keep, had enlisted after a good deal of persuasion by local officers who had a quota to fill. He signed up for three years in return for a ten-dollar bounty and the promise of one hundred acres at the end of his service.

When the recruit made it to camp near Annapolis, he was told that the Maryland line would soon set out for Pennsylvania where the main army lay, its officers busy speculating about General Howe's intentions. Officers thought about such matters; enlisted men had other things to do. There were others to get to know. Some, the recruit learned, had entered the army for reasons very different from his own—and under very different terms. The army, in fact, consisted of several sorts of organized units: the militia, usually serving for a few months at most, owed its origins to the English Assize of Arms. More directly, long before the Revolution each colony had approved legislation requiring military service and depended upon towns and counties to supervise it. In actuality, not everyone served in local communities, but the principle of service was well established. And when Congress created the Continental Army in June 1775, the militia formed its core.

During the remainder of the war, after designating militia regiments from the New England states as Continentals, Congress relied on all the states to raise Continental units, as well as militia. Congress contracted to pay for the recruitment and service of Continentals while the states continued to meet expenses of local units. This system introduced competition for men—at the cost of corrupting soldiers and of impairing morale. Competition took the form of bidding for men, with bounties serving as bids. As the Congress and the states tried to exceed one another, bounty jumpers made their appearance, cheerfully collecting bounties for repeated enlistments. This practice disturbed honest men who, if they were unfortunate enough to enlist when bounties were low, felt somehow doubly betrayed.

When the Maryland recruit arrived, the veterans questioned him about the bounty he had received. His experience matched many others, and as the ante went up he found himself among the discontented. Washington attempted to soothe these men by urging Congress to add one hundred dollars to their pay as a one-time reward for early service. Congress delayed until 1779, when it passed the necessary legislation.[31]

Not even the payment of inflated bounties filled the Continental and militia regiments. Congress created twenty-seven Continental regiments from militia already in service at the opening of 1776; in September, after the disaster on Long Island, it authorized the raising of eighty-eight battalions, adding another sixteen in December. None of these quotas were met, and in 1779 a major reorganization was approved calling for eighty regiments. The next year this number was reduced to fifty-eight.

The recruit knew little of these plans. Most of his fellows, he discovered, had been drafted, or "levied," as conscription was sometimes called. The states appointed the conscription officers who worked through local authorities. Substitutes for those drafted were accepted, and the practice of hiring such men became common. Epping, New Hampshire, once met its entire quota by hiring substitutes from nearby towns. The result was, of course, that those on active service came increasingly to be drawn from the poor and propertyless.

Such men, including the Maryland recruit, probably did not expect much in the way of food, clothing, and pay from the army. They did not get much. Congress intended that they receive a generous ration of meat, vegetables, and bread every day. This good intention remained nothing more than an intention for most of the war, as men in the army went hungry and often nearly naked. The bloody tracks at Valley Forge made by men without shoes appeared in later campaigns as well. The hunger may have been worse at Morristown in winter 1779–80 than at Valley Forge. That winter was the coldest of the war and made Valley Forge look almost balmy by comparison. Early in the winter, Lt. Colonel Ebenezer Huntington wrote of the sufferers there—"Poor fellows, my heart bleeds for them, while I Damn my country as void

---

31. Don Higginbotham, *The War of American Independence: Military Attitudes, Policies, and Practice, 1763–1789* (Bloomington, Ind., 1971), 390–93, esp. 391.

of gratitude," a curse that must have been repeated in January, when the cold and hunger were older.[32]

III

The Maryland soldier knew no more than any other ranker of the organization behind this state of affairs, which is to say that he knew very little. He may have been aware that the official apparatus for supplying the army began with Congress. If he did not know it, he soon learned, for the army laid most of its problems at the door of Congress—and well before the war ended most of the country agreed with the army.

Shortly after it created the Continental army in June 1775, Congress established quartermaster and commissary departments charged with providing the supplies the army required. The immediate inspiration for these agencies was similar institutions of the British army. Similar yet different, for Parliament had long since turned the whole business of supply over to the Treasury, which let contracts for all the things the army in America needed. The Treasury, which devoted most of its energies to other matters, cooperated with the colonial secretary, the secretary at war, and the commissary department in America. These agencies and later the navy board worked out arrangements with London merchants and their agents which succeeded rather well in sending out food, clothing, fuel, medicines, and forage.[33]

The British worked against tremendous obstacles, perhaps the most formidable of which was the distance involved. The long voyage across the Atlantic forced the Treasury to look ahead. Even so there were mistakes and close calls with starvation very much on Henry Clinton's mind in 1779 and 1780, for example. Occasionally too, ships laden with provisions sailed to the wrong ports. After the British evacuated Philadelphia, two victualers from Cork put into the Delaware bound for the city, unaware that the hungry mouths there were American—not British.[34]

---

32. Ford, ed., *Corr. of Webb*, II, 232. See also "Letters of Ebenezer Huntington, 1774–1781," *AHR*, 5 (1899–1900), 702–29.

33. *JCC*, II, 94. For a first-class study of the British system, see Norman Baker, *Government and Contractors: The British Treasury and War Supplies, 1775–1783* (London, 1971). See also these fine studies: David Syrett, *Shipping and the American War, 1775–1783* (London, 1970), which deals with the transport of supplies across the Atlantic; and R. Arthur Bowler, *Logistics and the Failure of the British Army in America, 1775–1783* (Princeton, N.J., 1975), a study of the army's supply services in America.

34. Bowler, *Logistics*, 122–38.

Distances and communications may have provided ample problems but the British had great resources. For one thing they had been in the business of taking care of armies for a long time. They had the experience and the institutions which, although they might be severely taxed by the scope of the task, could respond. They did not have to create a system—the bureaus and agencies, the records, the means of payment, procurement, and distribution—all at once and make it work because several thousand men needed everything from beef to musket balls.

Congress had to do all these tasks while it was engaged in a good many other things, almost all for the first time. Congress had to call an army into being and supply it in a country at war which was suspicious of the army, and yet eager to make profits selling supplies to it. The men who worked within this system of supply, in and out of the army, possessed virtually no experience with it, or with any large institution. They sought, moreover, to satisfy soldiers who did not look admiringly upon large organizations and complicated procedures.

The commissary general got off to a good start. He was Joseph Trumbull of Connecticut, a merchant who had performed a similar job for his state's troops. Trumbull relied mainly on his own state for supplies as long as the army besieged Boston. There were ample stocks of food in New England the first year of the war, and Trumbull found that feeding the army, which was stationary, was not especially difficult. After this first campaign the ease disappeared and more often than not the soldiers suffered from an inadequate diet—and were sometimes near starvation.[35]

The quartermaster general, Thomas Mifflin of Pennsylvania, did not enjoy Trumbull's initial success, though the problems of his department did not make themselves felt until 1777. Mifflin, the choice of George Washington, took office in August 1775. His charge from Congress included operational responsibilities as well as supply. The quartermaster general in the British army ordinarily supervised the movement of troops. Congress decided that he would have the same duty in the American army and that he would also oversee the maintenance of roads and bridges traveled by the army, lay out and construct its camps, and furnish

35. See the articles on Joseph Trumbull and on supply of the Continental Army in Mark Mayo Boatner III, *Encyclopedia of the American Revolution* (Bicentennial ed., New York, 1976). Chapters 1–2 in Erna Risch, *Quartermaster Support of the Army: A History of the Corps, 1775–1939* (Washington, D.C., 1962), are excellent. There is scattered information in Freeman, *GW*, and Ward as well.

and maintain its wagons, teams, and boats. Mifflin resigned the quarter-master's post shortly after the British departed Boston. His successor, Stephan Moylan, served three months, until Congress persuaded Mifflin to resume the job in September.[36]

Congress regarded failures of supply in the way legislative bodies often regard failures—as evidence that the organization was flawed. In the case of supply, Congress evidently believed that the flaw was simplicity—and it began to make the system more complicated. To make institutions more complicated means that more offices and officials must be appointed and the transaction of business made cumbersome.

Over the next four years Congress experimented along these lines. In June 1777 it divided the commissary general's post into two: a commissary general of purchases and a commissary general of issue. This change made sense in that it separated two demanding and dissimilar functions. Congress assumed that the two commissaries would consult one another and that they would respond to Washington's direction. For the most part the commissaries satisfied these expectations, though at times they must have felt confused, since their ultimate master was Congress itself and Congress was not averse to speaking in several voices.[37]

It was not ambiguity that produced most of the trouble, but the firm and clear conviction of Congress that the commissaries should not profit from office. Joseph Trumbull had assumed his post when it was Connecticut's to give in 1775, and he and his deputies had come to expect that they would receive a commission of 1.5 percent of all the money they spent for supplies. This arrangement understandably induced a certain activity in the commissary department. Just as understandably, Congress thought the commissaries might prove rather expensive, and in the reorganization it put Trumbull and his men on salary. Trumbull resigned in disappointment two months later—half of his old post had been given to Charles Stewart, who was now commissary general of issue, and the old incentives had disappeared too. Stewart served until after the battle of Yorktown; William Buchanan, who had been one of Trumbull's deputies, took over as commissary general of purchases. He held on until March 1778, and in April another deputy, Jeremiah Wadsworth, accepted the job. His tenure ran until January 1, 1780, when the final holder, Ephraim Blaine, assumed the responsibility, serving until the post was abolished near the end of 1781.[38]

36. Kenneth Rossman, *Thomas Mifflin and the Politics of the American Revolution* (Chapel Hill, N.C., 1952), 49–50, 56, 107, and *passim.*
37. *JCC*, VIII, 435–36.
38. There is much on supply in Freeman, *GW*, vols. III–V, and in GW Papers.

This procession must have yearned for combat with real musket balls at times; certainly these officers—by definition a lower breed because they were staff rather than line—received fire of every other sort. After Trumbull resigned he deflected some of it by pointing to Congress, the author of the reorganization, as responsible for making his job impossible. Every head of a department ought to have control of it, he suggested in a letter to Washington. Congress had deprived him of control: "In this establishment an Imperium in Imperio is established—If I accept to Act, I must be at Continual Variance with the whole Department, and of course in Continual Hot Water, turn Accuser, or be continually applying to Congress and attending with Witnesses to Support Charges." What Trumbull meant was that the division of the department into purchasing and issuing sections had created an unworkable system— with the two commissaries bound to fall out. He was partly wrong, and he was not altogether straightforward in explaining his resignation. Congress's refusal to permit him to collect commissions gnawed at him as much as his reduced authority.[39]

Out of republican scruples, Congress had denied commissions to the commissaries. The delegates thought the salaries of the commissaries and their deputies were too high; for example, in 1775 John Adams called them "extravagant." Congress wanted not only to hold down expenses, while increasing supplies, it wished to improve control of supplies and thereby strengthen the army while protecting the public purse. Control and protection were apparently visible to Congress in records. At any rate in the reorganization of 1777 it included the requirement that henceforth elaborate records be kept. Lest the commissaries have any doubts about what was wanted the records were described in some detail—accounts, invoices (in duplicate), receipts, returns, and journals. Each deputy of purchases, for example, would keep a journal in which every purchase would be recorded, and in order that there be uniformity of accounts, each page was to be divided into ten columns in which the complete history of each purchase would be entered. If livestock were bought, "the number, colour and natural marks" would be entered, plus a good deal more. Naturally, few of these requirements appealed to the commissaries, but Congress, determined to defend the public interest, had good reasons for rationalizing a system that presented ample opportunities for corruption.[40]

Congress gave even more attention to the quartermaster general's department than it did to the commissary. The quartermaster general

39. Joseph Trumbull to Washington, July 19, 1777, GW Papers, Ser. 4, Reel 42.
40. JCC, VIII, 433–38.

may have had a more difficult set of tasks, with his operational responsibilities competing with his duties to purchase and transport supplies. Thomas Mifflin, the first quartermaster general, possessed strong abilities, but he answered too many extraordinary calls on them to allow him to serve effectively. During much of 1777, he worked closely with Congress, reorganizing the service and recruiting troops. While he was at this, the department fell apart. The usual explanation for this disintegration allocates a good deal of blame to Congress. Congress deserved some of it. In 1777 it began a practice it was to stay with throughout the war—setting rates of payment for wagons and teams, which would transport supplies, below current market values. Quartermasters found merchants and teamsters reluctant to do business with them when they could do it more profitably with others. The breakdown of supply in 1777, like most in years following, turned out to be a crisis of distribution.[41]

At times undoubtedly, Congress made matters worse by clumsy habits of supervision. Complaints brought investigations by the committees Congress worked through, and the investigations sometimes brought delay or temporary paralysis. The lines of authority always lacked clarity, though of course final responsibility for the system lay with Congress. On a practical level, however, quartermasters found it absolutely necessary to work more closely with the army command. But where money was concerned, that command had to defer to Congress, with often near-disastrous results for the army.

Congress simply did not know how to manage this business. And that inability, as common to senior army commanders as to the delegates, lay at the bottom of supply failures. Finance, supply, and management all presented uncharted ground. To solve the problems, Congress and the men of the army made an organizational revolution with all the slippages and mistakes that ordinarily attend a transformation of scale.

Congress faced one additional problem—unstable public finance. Lacking a secure revenue, it was forced into various expedients to raise money. None proved altogether satisfactory.

Although Congress blundered badly in handling supply, stinting the quartermaster general and his deputies was not among its errors. For most of the war these officials divided a commission of 1 percent of all monies they spent. Nathanael Greene, who succeeded Mifflin in

41. These impressions are derived from a reading of letters and reports to Washington in the GW Papers; see esp. T. Mifflin to Washington, March 9, 1777, Ser. 4, Reel 40; and Col. Henry Lutterloh to Washington, Dec. 25, 1777, *ibid.*, Reel 46.

March 1778, admitted a year later "that the profits is flattering to my fortune." Greene, however, lusted more for fame than money and, noting that the post was "humiliating to my military pride," declared sadly that "No body ever heard of a quarter Master in History as such or in relating any brilliant action." He was wrong in the first half of his assertion—quartermasters were not only heard of, they became notorious. Greene himself performed ably, though throughout his tenure he never ceased to sing lamentations about the graceless post he held.[42]

In an attempt to relieve the quartermaster department of some of its burdens, Congress had made two important changes late in 1776 after the evacuation of New York City. First it appointed a commissary of hides and made him responsible to one of its committees, the Board of War. The hides department took over the task of keeping the army in shoes, a challenging task, given the inflated price of leather and the fact that this army marched everywhere it went.[43]

An even more important reform saw Congress establish a separate department to supply clothing to the army. A clothier general headed this department; his name was James Mease. His performance may be estimated from the phrase soldiers coined to describe the sickness associated with inadequate clothing—they were, they grimly joked, dying of "the Meases." Mease, a Philadelphia merchant, asked Washington for the appointment with the sycophantic wish that God grant that Washington's future success "may on all occasions be equal to your merit and then I am sure it will be great as your Excellency's desires." A few months later Mease was explaining to a disgruntled Washington how it happened that one of his regiments had been dressed in red uniforms. Such an opportunity came rarely to Mease; most of the time he found his explanations had to do with the absence of uniforms of any color. Washington realized that not all of the shortages of clothing were the result of Mease's incompetence, but he could not ignore those that were, and in August 1778 he asked for Mease's removal. Congress delayed action until the following July.[44]

Mease proved to be an easy target, though he clung to his post long after his chief's patience ran out. The line officers who were so critical of him actually contributed to his problems and to the suffering of the army by their high-handed appropriation of supplies virtually wherever the opportunity arose. Supplies had to be moved from the country-

42. Greene to Washington, April 24, 1779, *ibid.*, Reel 57.
43. *JCC*, VIII, 487, 585–607.
44. Mease to Washington, Jan. 6, May 12, 1777, GW Papers, Ser. 4, Reels 39, 41.

side to the main army. On the road, open season on supply trains seems to have prevailed, as state commanders and units detached for some special service stopped the wagons and took what they needed—or wanted. The rationalization must have come naturally to them. They were defending the country, and these supplies had been provided for the use of the army. The officers were part of the army and they were in need. That some central intelligence, General Washington's headquarters, for example, might have assessed the overall needs of the army and decided on rather different priorities either did not occur to them or did not matter.

To its credit, Congress did not give up its attempt to bring order to disorderly supply arrangements. By late 1779 it had decided that much in the old procedures would have to be discarded in favor of going directly to state governments for what the army required. Early in December 1779 Congress resolved to requisition "specific supplies" from the states much as it requisitioned money. This resolve led to just about the same sort of results as the states sought to comply, sometimes succeeding, but more often failing. The plan, which went into effect in 1780, would have yielded uneven results even had the states been able to collect the supplies. Delivering beef, flour, forage, and the like to Washington's army, which was located in New York, would have been immensely difficult for the southern states. Robert Morris, the superintendent of finance, recognizing this difficulty when he inherited the problem of supply in 1781, attempted to make the best of things by ordering supplies collected at a great distance to be sold and the proceeds used to buy food and clothing located as close as possible to the army. Time and transportation costs were thereby saved.[45]

By the time Morris was to begin his tenure as superintendent, in June 1781, in those states which had tried to carry out congressional wishes more bitterness than supplies had been produced. These states had set up their own agencies of procurement, several with powers to impress what their citizens refused to sell, and set about to do their share in supplying the army. Their citizens—those in New Jersey, for example—did not lack patriotism, but they did not wish to accept paper money or certificates for what they had worked to accumulate. To accept such paper, it was pointed out, was the equivalent of giving goods away. Naturally they protested, and their government began to back off. New

<hr/>

45. E. James Ferguson, ed., *The Papers of Robert Morris, 1781–1784* (5 vols. to date, Pittsburgh, Pa., 1973–   ), I, xix–xx, 372–74.

Jersey severely reduced the authority of the state superintendent of purchases and the county contractors in June 1781 and soon gave up impressing supplies altogether. Elsewhere, where an apparatus to procure supplies had been constructed, the attempt to compel citizens to "sell" their property was discarded even earlier.[46]

The states soon stopped most of their efforts to impress, but the army did not. Under Washington's sensitive guidance, impressment was used only as a last resort. He had grown weary of civilian failures, but he also saw the dangers of impressment. Thus, though in July 1781 he characterized the subsistence of the army as "miserable," he continued to avoid as much as possible measures that would alienate civilians.[47]

When Congress placed public finance in the hands of Robert Morris, a most capable and resourceful man, it made an important attempt to revise the supply system. Morris was a wealthy Philadelphia merchant with financial connections that extended far beyond his own city. In giving him power to procure all sorts of supplies for the army, Congress did not discharge the quartermasters and commissaries of the army. It bestowed on Morris considerable power to let contracts and to use the resources of the Congress to pay them off. Since in 1781 those resources were temporarily replenished by large loans from France, Morris began with a certain advantage. He used his power well, if at times somewhat summarily, and in the last great campaign of the war, the entrapment of Cornwallis at Yorktown, his contribution was clear.[48]

In the end, however, the intangible played as great a part as organization or system in keeping the army going. The army's will to survive and to fight on short rations, its willingness to suffer, to sacrifice, made the inadequate adequate and rendered the failures of others of little importance. The army overcame the worst in itself and in others. It was indomitable.

IV

There was not much money invested in medicine in the American colonies before the Revolution, and the practice of the art had not achieved

46. *Ibid.*, II, 198n, fn. 3.
47. *Ibid.*, I, 293.
48. There are two fine books on Morris: Clarence L. Ver Steeg, *Robert Morris: Revolutionary Financier* (Philadelphia, 1954) and E. James Ferguson, *The Power of the Purse: A History of American Public Finance, 1776–1790* (Chapel Hill, N.C., 1961). Ferguson, ed., *Papers of Morris*, II, contains many letters which show Morris's contribution to the Yorktown campaign.

either distinction or prestige. The lack of investment and low public regard may have discouraged Congress from giving much attention to problems of providing for the health of soldiers. Whatever the reasons, it did not get around to establishing a hospital department until fully a month after it had created the army, late July 1775. Congressional neglect, however, did not preserve harmony in the department. Those commissioned by Congress to organize and run the service proved able to entangle themselves in controversy without external assistance—to the point of affecting adversely the care of sick and wounded soldiers.

In a sense Congress inherited its first director general and chief physician. He was Benjamin Church, and he ran the medical service of the New England army around Boston before Congress took over. Unfortunately he was also a traitor, having sold himself to General Gage several years before, apparently because he had grown fond of the fashionable and expensive life. No one in Congress knew of Church's extracurricular activities in July when he was appointed, and no one learned until September. During the summer of 1775 Congress went about ignorant of medical organization, calling for regimental surgeons to work closely with line outfits and the general hospital to do something more.[49]

Just exactly what the general hospital was to do was not altogether clear, and just exactly what the relation of the regimental surgeons was to it was no clearer. No clearer to outsiders, that is. Both the director general and the surgeons always maintained that they understood perfectly what Congress intended. They did not agree among themselves, however, on what their relation should be.

Before confusion grew into open disagreement, the army discovered Church's treason and put him under arrest. That took place in September 1775, and in October Congress named John Morgan to succeed Church. Morgan did not reach Cambridge until the end of November.[50]

Morgan did not take up his commission with many cards in his hand. Church had not done badly as director general, but he had not really

49. On Church, see Carl Van Doren, *Secret History of the American Revolution* (New York, 1941).
50. Freeman, *GW*, III, 547–53. The account that I give of the organization of the medical service of the army is based on the following studies: Howard Lewis Applegate, "The Medical Administrators of the American Revolutionary Army," *Military Affairs*, 25 (1961), 1–10; Whitfield J. Bell, *John Morgan: Continental Doctor* (Philadelphia, 1965), esp chap. 11; John Morgan, *A Vindication of His Public Character . . .* (Boston, 1777); Morris H. Saffron, *Surgeon to Washington: Dr. John Cochran, 1730–1807* (New York, 1977).

done very much. In particular he had not begun to sort out the organizational lines soon to trap Morgan in struggles that distracted him from the main business—the health of soldiers. The regimental surgeons gave him his first taste of difficulty, and after he left the service in January 1777 they gave the same treatment to his successor William Shippen, who hung on until January 1781. John Cochran, the director who performed the best and who succeeded in asserting some control over the regiments, followed Shippen and served until the end of the war.

The regimental surgeons possessed a clear notion of how they should deal with the general hospital and its director—aloofly, except when they needed something. They wished to use the hospital as a supply house that would provide them with food, instruments, medicines, and bandages. They had a point; the troops preferred the regimental hospitals to the general hospital. The regiments' facilities were always smaller, probably healthier, and nearer to comrades. And the regimental surgeon, who had usually been named by the colonel or the state assembly, was a known quantity.

The director general saw things differently. His situation may have been ambiguous, but Congress, from Morgan's time on, had authorized him or his staff to inspect regimental hospitals and to transfer patients if conditions seemed to warrant such action. Washington had strengthened Morgan's hand by giving him permission to determine the fitness of regimental surgeons and aides by examinations, which proved strenuous exercises. They so annoyed the surgeons of the regiments that when the army left Boston for New York, Morgan gave them up.

The strain between the regimental and general hospital surgeons did not really ease off until Cochran took charge. Morgan was relieved of his post by Congress at the beginning of 1777, and William Shippen, his successor, resigned early in 1781. Both men, and Samuel Stringer of the northern department, felt betrayed by Congress and the army. In fact, Shippen had connived shamelessly to get Morgan's post, and Morgan, aided by Benjamin Rush, helped to force Shippen to resign. Shippen endured court-martial during his tenure and, though he was acquitted, his reputation was shattered.

These wars within the war contributed to years of shoddy medical services. Just how badly they undermined the health care of soldiers cannot be known, though the organizational weakness persisted until the end of the war. Had the institutional arrangements been first-rate by the standards of the day, the actual medical service provided soldiers would have left something to be desired, for America did not brim with physicians or medical knowledge. Recent estimates hold that there were some 3500 medical practitioners of various sorts in America when the war began. This figure probably includes quacks as well as reputable physicians and a great number of indifferently trained men who treated the sick and worked at other occupations as well. Probably fewer than four hundred had a medical degree.

Although generalizations about such a motley group cannot be reliable, it is unlikely that any theory of disease or therapy found wide acceptance among them. The physicians among them probably believed that sickness generally represented some variation from the normal pattern of the human system, an old idea which persisted through the eighteenth century. There were diseases identified as diseases, smallpox, syphilis, and tuberculosis, for example, but both theory and practice usually dealt with body conditions, such symptoms as fevers, fluxes, and dropsies. The assumption behind this practice was that a fever indicated that the state of the system was off, not that the body was afflicted by a disease. To be sure, some physicians had come to recognize that diseases were objectively real. While treating their patients, they had observed that a medicine might be effective against one set of symptoms but not another. From this experience they inferred that they faced two different diseases.[51]

These physicians easily reconciled this inference with the ancient assumption that there was one basic cause of all disease. The most common theory held that the body's humors were somehow awry, perhaps impure or out of balance, with one or more present in excessive or insufficient amounts. The treatment followed from the diagnosis, with bleeding, purging, and sweating all calculated to reduce excessive amounts, and diets and drugs intended to build up volume. Another basic cause of sickness, it was widely thought, might be a chemical imbalance, with body fluids showing an improper blend of acidity or alkalinity. The treatments in such cases often resembled those prescribed to restore humoral balance.[52]

The ordinary soldier, of course, lived largely oblivious to theory, though

---

51. The estimate given in the preceding paragraph of the number of physicians, or medical practitioners, in America in 1775 is given by Philip Cash, *Medical Men at the Siege of Boston, April 1775–April 1776: Problems of the Massachusetts and Continental Armies* (American Philosophical Society, *Memoirs*, 98 [Philadelphia, 1973]), 1–5. For concepts of disease in the eighteenth century, see Richard H. Shryock, *Medicine and Society in America, 1600–1860* (New York, 1960), chap. 2.

52. Shryock, *Medicine and Society*, 50–51.

he, his officers, and the regimental surgeons may have shared a good deal of common lore about health and medicine. Judging from the orders that came down from on high in every American camp, one belief they did not share was that cleanliness was next to godliness. Away from home, the American soldier did not mind the filth that piled up in crowded camps—or if he minded, refused nevertheless to follow rudimentary practices which would have kept them cleaner. Soldiers throughout the war apparently disdained use of the vaults, as latrine pits were called, preferring to void whenever taken by the urge. They also scattered food scraps, carrion, and garbage throughout camps. They had to be forced to change the straw that served as bedding. And some had to be ordered to bathe. The British, professionals in this sort of thing as in all things pertaining to military life, kept clean camps and probably suffered less from disease.

Dysentery troubled the American army throughout the war. The filth the army created accounted for some of it and so did the low standards of cleanliness in cooking. Most of the time soldiers cooked for themselves, though there might be bakeries which served a brigade. Unaccustomed to the task, the soldiers did not do it well, or cleanly. Diets ran to fat meat and bread when they were available, but on the whole the army suffered more from a lack of food than an unbalanced diet.

Good officers did what they could to make camp life healthy. Washington set the standard with a flow of orders about sanitation, diet, bathing, all the concerns of a responsible commander who wanted to lead into battle men who were fit. At Valley Forge, for example, when the worst of winter had passed, he ordered renewed attention be paid to the cleanliness of troop quarters. Common opinion held that the air in each hut might be purified each day by burning of the powder from a cartridge. A small amount of tar might be substituted if gunpowder were short. Tents were to be taken down daily and the ground around them scoured. Soldiers in Washington's and Greene's armies were encouraged to bathe—moderately. Immersion in water for too long a period might weaken the body, according to the folklore that made its way into regimental orders.[53]

Good junior officers and noncommissioned officers could do much

53. George Washington, General Orders, Aug. 1–Sept. 9, 1778, BR 77, HL; Orders, American Army, Valley Forge, May 27, 1778, HM 719, I, HL. In *ibid.*, X, this instruction of Aug. 28, 1781, appears: "Moderate bathing in the Water contributes to the health, the excess of it is injurious, the Soldiers are not to stay too long in the water. . . ."

to protect the health of their charges. The memory of a Connecticut sergeant building a fire for his soldiers when they were cold and hungry stayed with one of his men for fifty years after the Revolution. No manual of leadership or of army medicine prescribed that sort of performance, but it undoubtedly contributed to the health of soldiers. Charles Willson Peale, serving as the captain of a Philadelphia militia company, found beef and potatoes for his company's breakfast two days after the battle of Princeton. His men, so fatigued they could not look for food, had gone to bed without eating. Peale shook off his exhaustion and rambled from door to door at Somerset Court House until he had collected rations for his men. A few days later, Peale found that he had a sick Ensign, one Billy Haverstock, on his hands. Peale first got some sugar for Haverstock, a remedy that did not prove effective. Next he tried "a puke of Doctor Crochwin," an emetic given to feverish patients. His final entry in his diary about the case described the use of an old standby, tartar emetic, a mixture of antimony and potassium nitrate, which he gave in a double dose. Haverstock apparently survived this treatment.[54]

Had a physician treated Haverstock, he might still have recovered. Physicians followed just about the same lore as laymen, though they may have been more inventive in their uses of medicines. What made most of them so dangerous was their fondness for bleeding patients. When they did not bleed them, they often resorted to purging and sweating, techniques not certain to cure dysentery, malaria, typhus, typhoid, pneumonia, and smallpox, the diseases which afflicted American troops in their camps.

When surgeons were available they took care of the wounded. Bleeding the wounded sometimes served as treatment and not always with fatal results. Dr. James Thacher, who was taken into the medical department of the army as a surgeon's mate, reported that one of his senior colleagues, a Dr. Eustis, once treated "a dangerous wound" of the shoulder and lungs by bleeding. While dilating the wound, Dr. Eustis "recommended repeated and liberal bloodletting, observing that in order to cure a wound through the lungs, you must bleed your patient to death." Thacher reported that the wounded man recovered; the principal reason, Thacher believed, was the treatment he received.[55]

54. Powell, "Bostwick's Memoirs," *WMQ*, 3d Ser., 6 (1949), 101; Peale Diary, Jan. 3, 10, 11, 16, 1777, HL.
55. James Thacher, *A Military Journal During the American Revolutionary War, From 1775 to 1783* (Boston, 1823), 306–7. This is a valuable account of army life as well as of medicine.

Perhaps the best guide for surgeons, *Plain, Concise, Practical Remarks on the Treatment of Wounds and Fractures* by Dr. John Jones, advocated rather different procedures.[56] Jones was a professor of surgery in King's College, New York; he had received his medical degree from the University of Rheims in 1751 and shortly after served in the French and Indian War. The first concern in the case of a wound inflicted by a musket, he wrote, should be to extract the ball and, second, to stop the hemorrhaging. Jones's manual divided wounds into categories; each sort required its own treatment. But in treating all kinds, Jones urged that care be used to clean the wound and to dress it carefully. He had a sense of the limits of surgery, noting, for example, the danger of amputation when the wounded man was reduced to a "low and weak state."

Whatever the effects of Jones's prescriptions, the treatment of wounds remained a most problematic enterprise. Soldiers who survived serious wounds doubtlessly did so through a mixture of luck and their own strong constitutions. Most surgeons tried to give their best to their patients. In the Continental army, chronically short of medicine, bandages, nurses, and food, the "best" often could not prevent death.

V

The American navy played no part in the campaigns. The war created the navy, but it could not call into being a force of great power. The financial resources for a strong navy simply did not exist; nor for that matter did the conviction that a navy equal to Britain's was needed.

The war at sea commenced before there was an American navy with the first actions occurring within a few weeks of the battles at Lexington and Concord. Perhaps the earliest—in June—involved the citizens of Machias, a small port in Maine some 300 miles northeast of Boston. These Maine patriots captured his majesty's schooner *Margaretta* commanded by a young midshipman who had threatened to fire on the town if its liberty pole was not cut down. The midshipman reconsidered this threat shortly after making it, but too late to persuade the people of Machias not to respond. In an armed attack a group captured the *Margaretta* and two sloops which had accompanied her. The midshipman died in the defense of his command.[57]

Most of the actions of sea-going patriots in the first year of the war were not against vessels of the Royal Navy. Almost all of his majesty's ships were too heavily armed and too well sailed for the Americans to

56. (New York, 1775). The quotation in this paragraph is from page 71.
57. William M. Fowler, Jr., *Rebels Under Sail: The American Navy During the Revolution* (New York, 1976), 17–20.

attack. The skippers of privateers from small Massachusetts ports preferred to engage transports and merchantmen carrying munitions and supplies to the British army in Boston. They did so to good effect—in all they brought in fifty-five prizes in the first year of the war.

George Washington commissioned many of the privateers making these captures. Washington's awareness of the importance of the sea to the land campaigns in America probably surpassed that of any of the British commanders he faced in the war. But for much of the war his strategic ideas about the use of the sea could not really affect operations, for he had no fleet. Until the French entered the war, there was no possibility that he would ever obtain one.

He could use what was available, however. There was an abundance of inlets and ports along the American coast and there was a large supply of small vessels—brigs, sloops, and schooners—as well as of shipwrights and sailors. On the eve of the Revolution, American shipyards built at least a third of the merchant ships sailing under the Union Jack. American forests yielded oak for hulls and decks and pine for masts. Sails and rope were also made in America.

The most immediate way to use the sea was to strike at British merchant ships, not only to disrupt the supply of the army under siege in Boston but also to add to the meager supply of American weapons and munitions. The first ship Washington sent into Continental service, the *Hannah*, a seventy-eight-ton schooner, failed in both missions. Nicholson Broughton, a Marblehead shipper, took command of the *Hannah* when she entered the service in August 1775. Broughton soon displayed a propensity for capturing ships owned by Americans and calling them the enemy's. This inclination led him to make a voyage to Nova Scotia with Captain John Selman, a man of similar tendencies. These two seadogs plundered Charlottetown, a small village, and kidnapped several leading citizens whom they proudly brought to Washington's headquarters in Cambridge. Washington, embarrassed by this behavior, released the prisoners and quietly let his sea captains' commissions expire at the end of December.[58]

Broughton and Selman were not alone in seizing the main chance. Many American skippers used any pretext to take the ships of friendly

58. *Ibid.*, 21–27. I have relied heavily on Fowler's fine book and on a series of books by William Bell Clark, among them *Ben Franklin's Privateers: A Naval Epic of the American Revolution* (Baton Rouge, La., 1956); *George Washington's Navy* (Baton Rouge, La., 1960); and *Naval Documents of the Revolution* (5 vols. to date, Washington, D.C., 1964–).

merchants. They also captured British ships which were privately employed and not engaged in supplying the army in Boston.

More captains acted in the Continental interest. One, John Manley of the *Lee*, made a capture in late November which delighted Washington and the Americans besieging Boston. Manley ran down the *Nancy*, an ordnance brig of 250 tons, bound for Boston with 2000 muskets fitted with bayonets, scabbards, ramrods, thirty-one tons of musket shot, plus bags of flints, cartridge boxes, artillery stores, a thirteen-inch brass mortar and 300 shells. Not long afterwards, Washington appointed Manley a commodore and gave him command of schooners charged with the responsibility of patrolling Massachusetts waters.

Disposing of prizes and cargoes before independence provided Washington and the privateersmen with a delicate problem. Since throughout 1775 and in early 1776 the possibility existed that the dispute with Britain might be settled short of independence, the question of how to sell the captures had to be faced. They could not be sold in the old vice admiralty courts. Could Americans in fact sell what they had seized without formal admiralty proceedings? Not that they expected the British to be understanding and sympathetic if the old rules were observed. They were going to take British property and hold prisoners for a time whether the two sides eventually reconciled or not. But who had jurisdiction over the captures? Was there a Continental responsibility or should they rely on provincial admiralty courts? Eventually the Massachusetts Provincial Congress came to their aid and established admiralty courts where systematic procedures for disposal of ships and cargoes were worked out.

Massachusetts acted in part because the Continental Congress, groping toward a naval policy just as it groped toward independence, had failed to respond swiftly. During the year that followed the opening of the war, Congress first seemed to suggest that the naval war should be the business of the states. And several states approved plans for fitting out armed vessels which were to attack British transports. By autumn 1775 a small-scale building program existed in several states; and Washington had six armed craft nosing about the waters off Boston. Congress itself in November ordered that four ships should be put into its service and began to frame a policy for the disposal of captures. At the end of the year it directed that thirteen frigates should be built for an American navy.

As far as Congress was concerned its vessels and those of the states should strike only those British vessels which had attacked American commerce or which were supplying the British army. Congress was not inclined to pass its own prohibitory act until it received news of Parliament's. As it began the move toward declaring independence in 1776, it also moved toward a full-scale naval war.

Congress always appeared to believe that in a committee it possessed the most useful instrument for making war. Thus in November 1775 when it first ordered that merchant ships should be fitted out as armed cruisers, it assigned the task to a naval committee. As Congress's ambitions and its building program expanded so also did its administrative committees. The naval committee sank in administrative waters early the next year, only to be replaced by a marine committee. Much of the actual work of establishing a fleet was done between 1777 and 1781 by a Navy Board of the Eastern Department. This board of three, from Massachusetts, Connecticut, and Rhode Island, did the rough work of getting ships and men together. Located in Boston, the board tried to stay out of Congress's way while carrying out its orders. To a remarkable degree it succeeded in both operations. But Congress was not satisfied with regional efforts and certainly not with regional control; late in 1779 it created the Board of Admiralty to give overall direction to the navy.

Modelled on the British Admiralty Board, the American creation included non-congressional members as well as delegates from Congress. Throughout its short life two men, Francis Lewis, a merchant and former member of Congress from New York, and William Ellery, a delegate from Rhode Island, did most of its work. These two tried to add to the number of frigates which Congress had authorized and to persuade Congress to support the navy. Congress, however, had lost interest in the navy and found uses for public money elsewhere.

The navy shrank steadily. In the summer of 1780 Congress transferred control of what remained, a handful of frigates, to General Washington, intending that their actual control would be vested in Admiral Ternay, the French officer who had brought General Rochambeau and his army across the Atlantic to Newport earlier in the year. The next year the administration of these American vessels was removed completely from the admiralty board and vested with the superintendent of finance, Robert Morris. With this transfer any possibility that the navy might gain a powerful fleet vanished. Morris had more important problems to contend with, and he like most others saw little need for a navy in 1781.

This organizational history of the early navy explains the failure of American naval power in the Revolution. Aside from the achievements of the "cruising war," Captain Alfred Thayer Mahan's term for strikes of privateers, the American efforts on the ocean were paltry. The privateering, however, did make a difference by making the problem of supplying their army more difficult for the British and by capturing arms and stores which Washington's army put to good use.

A part of the Continental navy—the regular navy—also raided commerce, and one commander did more—struck fear into the British in the home islands that their coastal towns and cities would be destroyed. The commander was John Paul Jones, a Scot with remarkable courage and daring.[59]

Jones was born John Paul at Arbigland in Kirkbean, a parish of the Lordship of Galloway—he added Jones after he came to America. Born in 1747, he left his birthplace when he was thirteen years old. In 1761 he was apprenticed to a merchant-shipowner of Whitehaven, an English port across the Solway. There he began his great career on the sea— as a ship's boy on the *Friendship*, which over the next three years made her way back and forth between England and Virginia, usually with a stop in the West Indies, where rum and sugar were taken aboard, carried to Virginia, where tobacco and occasionally lumber and pig iron were picked up for the return to Whitehaven.

John Paul's merchant-master went broke in 1764 and released his apprentice from service. Paul spent most of the next three years on slave ships. The slave trade was a brutal business, and Paul apparently left it with relief, obtaining his discharge in Kingston, Jamaica, and sailing for home in 1768 on a Scottish ship. On this voyage both master and mate died. No one on board, except John Paul, could navigate. He took over and brought her safely home.

Pleased by this demonstration of seamanship and command, the owners put Paul aboard another ship as master. He was only twenty-one years old, but he had none of the softness of youth. Outward bound in 1769, he had the ship's carpenter, Mungo Maxwell, whipped with the cat-o'-nine-tails. Maxwell left the ship after she arrived at Tobago and lodged a complaint against Paul. When the case was dismissed, the disappointed Maxwell, apparently in good health, sailed for home; but he took sick and died. When Paul returned home the sheriff arrested him on Maxwell's father's charge of murder. Paul did not completely clear himself until he returned to Tobago and was able to obtain a statement from the judge that the lash had not contributed to Mungo Maxwell's death.

An incident in 1773 proved even more serious. Paul, in command

59. My account of John Paul Jones is drawn from Samuel Eliot Morison, *John Paul Jones: A Sailor's Biography* (Boston, 1959) and Fowler, *Rebels Under Sail*, 145–70.

of a merchant ship, arrived at Tobago only to be faced with a mutiny. He ran the ringleader through with his sword and then fled the ship and the island and headed for the North American mainland. By summer 1775 he was in Philadelphia, a city in rebellion but a place he found to be a good deal more hospitable than Tobago.

Joseph Hewes, a delegate to the Continental Congress from North Carolina, eased John Paul Jones's way in Philadelphia. Jones, the name he added to conceal his identity, had met Hewes while on the run from Tobago. A sailor in search of a billet, preferably a command in the Continental navy, could choose no better friend than Joseph Hewes, chairman of the Marine Committee, which selected the officers for the Continental navy.

Jones wanted a command. He wanted to fight in the cause of the united colonies. He began to espouse the principles of liberty in these months—and he never really stopped. Early in December 1775 he received a commission as first lieutenant in the Continental navy assigned to the *Alfred*.

The *Alfred* saw considerable action in the next few months, and Jones performed well. In May 1776 he was given the sloop *Providence* to command, with a temporary rank of captain. He drove the *Providence* hard, took many prizes, fought the ship well when opportunity showed itself, and gradually began to impress Congress with his ability.

Congress proved its regard in June 1777, giving Jones command of the sloop of war *Ranger* and ordering him to France where he was expected to pick up another ship and to raid enemy commerce around the British Isles. Jones sailed later in the summer and anchored at Paimbœuf, the deep-water port of Nantes. It soon became clear that John Paul Jones did not fancy himself to be just another raider of British merchantmen. He aimed for bigger targets: he would raid British ports and tie up the Royal Navy. By April of the next year, with the *Ranger* refitted and now at Brest, he was ready. Sailing into the Irish Sea, he decided to strike Whitehaven, familiar ground to him and surrounded by familiar waters. Early on April 23 he entered the port and found it crowded with ships. He put ashore a small landing party and set afire a collier. The blaze failed to spread, and the town was soon aroused and excited. There was no way to deal effectively with the crowds that gathered and apparently little chance of doing more physical damage even though there was no armed opposition present.

Jones next took the *Ranger* across Solway Firth to St. Mary's Isle—it was now mid-morning—with the intention of abducting the Earl of Selkirk. As things turned out, he was not at home, and the landing party carried off nothing more valuable than the family silver. But the next day the *Ranger* did capture something of importance—the sloop of war *Drake*, a well-armed vessel encountered off Belfast Lough. The *Drake* fought effectively for two hours—her captain died with a bullet in his brain, and her executive officer was seriously wounded—but the *Ranger* fought more effectively.

By May 8, Jones had the *Ranger* safely back at Brest. Her voyage, though it did no great damage either to British ports or commerce, had been a sensational success. The psychological damage—the blow she struck to British pride and spirit—was extensive, though there is no evidence that her raid produced a change in the deployment of royal warships. British newspapers gave the raid a great play with shouts of outrage—at Paul Jones—and grunts of scorn—at the navy's inability to run him down.

The shouts soon after in Paris were in a lighter tone. The *Ranger*'s voyage had made Jones the lion of French society, the delight of the French government, and the ecstasy of French ladies. Jones got a larger ship, the *Duras*, to command, which he renamed the *Bonhomme Richard* in honor of Benjamin Franklin.

John Paul Jones could be patient, and he could be crafty, but he preferred to exercise other qualities. He was always an ambitious man. John Adams, who saw something of him at this time, said that he was "the most ambitious and intriguing officer in the American navy. Jones has Art, and Secrecy, and aspires very high." Adams expected the unexpected from him. "Excentricities and Irregularities are to be expected from him—they are in his Character, they are visible in his Eyes. His Voice is soft and still and small, his Eye has keenness, and Wildness and Softness in it." Adams saw, and heard, Jones in polite society—never aboard a ship in battle, which accounts for his impression that Jones spoke in a "soft and still and small" voice. But he was right about the eyes. They were sharp and could blaze with wildness, as the bust by Houdon and the portrait by Charles Willson Peale suggest. The eyes stared out from a strong face with a firm, prominent nose and a well-proportioned jaw. The eyes were important to a commander of rough and sometimes rebellious men, for Jones was not large, probably no taller than five feet, five inches, but he was lean and hard. The look of ferocity that he could throw out cowed weaker men.[60]

This tough and resourceful commander sailed with seven vessels on August 14, 1779, from Groix Roadstead, intending to create as much

60. Butterfield et al., eds., *Diary of John Adams*, II, 370–71.

havoc as possible in the British Isles. His ship, the *Bonhomme Richard*, was the largest ship—probably around 900 tons—he had commanded. She was getting old, and with all of her sails piled on, was still slow, but after he armed her she could throw out heavy fire in battle. She mounted 6 eighteen-pounders, 28 twelve-pounders (16 of them new models), and 6 nine-pounders. Of the remaining ships of his command, two were frigates, one was a corvette, one a cutter, and two were privateers. These last two took off on their own shortly after the squadron hit the open sea. Jones was not surprised; he had guessed that they would resist his orders in favor of free-lancing. Nor could he really depend on all the others for instant obedience to his orders. Their skippers were French and, perhaps, were a little jealous of their American commander. One, Pierre Landais, captain of the frigate *Alliance*, hated Jones. Landais has been described as being half-mad; on this voyage he was destined to behave as a full-fledged lunatic or as a traitor.

The squadron made its way at a leisurely pace to the southwest Irish coast and then turned north. On August 24, Landais came aboard the *Richard* and told Jones he intended to operate just as he pleased. Within the next few days the cutter *Cerf* disappeared. Jones had sent her off to find several small boats he had dispatched to reconnoiter the coast. The *Cerf* got lost and eventually made her way back to France.

Not everything went sour: the squadron captured prizes as it proceeded up the coast, and on September 3, just north of the Orkney Islands turned to the south. Off the Firth of Forth, on the east coast of Scotland, Jones decided to put a landing party ashore at Leith, Edinburgh's seaport. His purpose was to threaten Leith with fire and collect a large ransom. The city fathers were terrified by the appearance of his ships, but a gale, which forced Jones's ships out of the firth, saved them from having to buy him off. If nothing more had occurred, the cruise would have been reckoned a success. It had yielded prizes, it had produced fear in the home islands, and it had forced the British Admiralty to send ships of the Royal Navy in fruitless pursuit of John Paul Jones.

What happened next made everything else seem unimportant. On September 23, off Flamborough Head on the Yorkshire coast, the *Bonhomme Richard* fought one of the great battles in American naval history. At mid-afternoon of that day, the squadron sighted a large convoy escorted by the frigate *Serapis* (rated at 44 guns but carrying 50) and sloop of war *Countess of Scarborough* (20 guns). The *Serapis*, a new copper-bottomed frigate was commanded by Captain Richard Pearson, RN, a brave and competent officer.

Jones soon realized that he would have to defeat these escorts before he could attack the merchantmen. The wind was light, and it was sunset before he closed to firing range. The *Alliance* ignored Jones's signal to "form line of battle," as did the corvette *Vengeance*, a small lightly armed vessel. Frigate *Pallas* threatened to follow their example, sailing away rather than toward the enemy, but then put about and engaged the *Countess of Scarborough*. The *Richard* faced the *Serapis*, a more heavily armed ship, alone.

The battle opened with both ships on the same course, the *Serapis* off the *Richard*'s starboard bow. Early in the fight two of the *Richard*'s old eighteen-pounders burst with terrible effect on the crew serving them and on the entire heavy battery. This event convinced Jones that in order to win the battle, he would have to grapple with the *Serapis* and board her. The *Bonhomme Richard* was outgunned even before her eighteen-pounders exploded and, since it was unsafe to use the four that remained, could not win by trading salvoes with her enemy. Had she been nimbler, Jones, a resourceful seaman, might have used her quickness to escape a heavy battering while punching the *Serapis* with the 28 twelve-pounders. But the *Richard* was anything but quick, and a heavy slugging match could only send her to the bottom. Captain Pearson, in contrast, attempted to maneuver in such a way as to bring his superior firepower to bear while keeping the *Richard* away.

Just after the eighteen-pounders burst, Jones tried to board *Serapis* on her starboard quarter. By skillful ship-handling he brought the *Richard* close, but the boarders were driven off by the English sailors. Pearson then tried to bring *Serapis* across the bow of the *Richard*, only to have Jones put his vessel's bowsprit into the stern of the *Serapis*. It was apparently at this moment that Pearson called to Jones asking if he wanted to surrender, and received Jones's magnificent reply, "I have not yet begun to fight."

More intricate sailing followed by both ships with topsails backed and filled, vessels falling back, darting ahead (in the case of the *Serapis*), or lumbering in either direction (in the case of the *Richard*). At a crucial juncture, the *Serapis* ran her bowsprit into the *Richard*'s rigging and a fluke of her starboard anchor caught on the *Richard*'s starboard quarter. The two vessels were now locked together, starboard to starboard, with their guns pounding away. Below decks the advantage belonged to the *Serapis;* her batteries did terrible damage to the *Richard*. But on the open deck and in the top sails the *Richard* clearly had the upper hand. Jones's French marines used their muskets to deadly effect, and the American sailors hanging above them poured fire and grenades down onto the *Serapis*. Before long only her dead remained above deck, and her crew serving the batteries below gradually gave way to the bullets and grenades that came from overhead, as the Americans worked their way onto the English topsails.

Several times, both ships caught fire and the shooting fell off as their crews attempted to put them out. *Serapis* took a frightful blow when William Hamilton, one of the bravest of the *Richard*'s sailors, dropped a grenade through one of her hatches into loose powder cartridges. The explosion that followed killed at least twenty men and wounded many others. This blast may have shattered Captain Pearson's resolve; if it did not, the prospect of losing his mainmast shook him to the point of yielding. Jones had directed the fire of his nine-pounders against the mainmast—and had helped serve one of the guns himself.

It was now 10:30 P.M. The *Richard* was filling with water; her crew had suffered heavy losses; but her captain would not strike his flag, though several of his men begged him to give up. On the *Serapis* the condition of the crew was no better though the ship was in no danger of sinking. Pearson's courage, however, trickled away with the blood of his men, and he himself tore down his ensign.

John Paul Jones had carried the fight to his enemy and had won through courage, spirit, and luck. Grappling with the *Serapis* had, in fact, been accidental though of course he had badly wanted to close with her. On the other hand, luck had also served the *Serapis*, for Captain Pierre Landais of the *Alliance* had decided to enter the fight early in the evening—against his own commander. The result was the delivery of three broadsides at close range into the *Bonhomme Richard*. Somehow Jones shook off these blows and everything that the *Serapis* could hit him with.

The casualties were dreadful on both sides—150 killed and wounded out of a crew of 322 in the *Richard*, and about 100 killed and 68 wounded out of 325 on the *Serapis*. Two days after the battle Jones abandoned the *Richard*. She was a gallant old vessel, but she could not be saved. Jones transferred his flag to the *Serapis*, and joined by the *Pallas*, which had taken the *Countess of Scarborough*, sailed for friendly waters.

Nothing in Jones's career ever equaled his magnificent performance of September 23. He left Europe in December of the following year, leaving behind an admiring France and coming home to countrymen who acclaimed him. They needed heroes, and they found a great one in John Paul Jones.

21

Outside the Campaigns

What happened on the water affected what happened on the land, and both affected the lives of civilians as well as those of soldiers and sailors. The "inside" of campaigns in other words had consequences for the "outside," the civilian society which sustained the war. This distinction between the inside and the outside of the campaigns is to some extent deceptive, of course, and even false. Civilians, for example, participated directly in the campaigns, providing supplies and sometimes carrying the baggage of the armies. They also served as guides and scouts; black slaves and white freemen dug entrenchments; camp followers did laundry and nursed the sick and wounded. These examples of civilian participation can be multiplied.

Since the fighting occurred in America, the Americans suffered the physical destruction that usually accompanies war. In the opening battle of the war, in April 1775, a part of Concord burned. Two months later the battle of Bunker Hill saw almost all of Charlestown, Massachusetts, destroyed by a fire set off by British shelling. In the next seven years, towns and villages in every part of America absorbed severe losses of buildings of all sorts. South Carolina and Georgia were ravaged late in the war; there as elsewhere crops and livestock were lost to the armies of both sides along with fences, pulled down by soldiers for firewood, and farm buildings of all kinds—especially in the West. To the east, Charleston, South Carolina, received a heavy battering before Clinton captured it in May 1780.[1]

Near the end of the war, as Washington and Rochambeau squeezed Cornwallis into Yorktown, Clinton set Benedict Arnold in motion against

1. The physical destruction brought by the war needs further study. There is useful information on this subject in Broadus Mitchell, *The Price of Independence: A Realistic View of the American Revolution* (New York, 1974).

the Connecticut coast, supposedly to divert the American army from its mission in Virginia. The citizens in these towns must have known what was coming, for General William Tryon had struck their coast in 1777 and again in 1779. In an early raid Danbury, though an inland town, lost nineteen houses and twenty shops to Tryon's torches. Two years later over two hundred buildings in Fairfield, about half of them houses, were burned. Tryon tried to burn Norwalk three days after Fairfield went up in smoke, and although he met some opposition he succeeded in destroying much of the town. The towns hardest hit in September 1781, when Benedict Arnold assumed Tryon's role, were New London and Groton at the mouth of the Thames. Near Groton at Fort Griswold, Connecticut militia cut down almost two hundred of Arnold's infantry before surrendering; the British forces retaliated by killing most of the garrison after they laid down their arms. This slaughter—the word is appropriate—was followed by abuse of the wounded. Groton itself also paid with the loss of buildings, but the cost was light compared with New London's where most structures—houses, stores, warehouses, barns, a church, the courthouse, and wharves and ships which had not been able to escape—were reduced to smoldering rubble.[2]

Destruction brought one kind of pain. Less dramatic but no less deeply felt was the loneliness those at home endured. Women bore most: besides being alone with the anxiety of not knowing whether those they loved had survived battles, they had to worry about holding the family together. Life for them dragged on, with days often heavy with loneliness or darkened by dullness and unease. These feelings are clear in the letters Sarah Hodgkins wrote her husband Joseph while he was with the army.[3]

The Hodgkinses lived in Ipswich, Massachusetts. He was thirty-two years of age in 1775; she, twenty-five. When the war began, they had two children (he had five children by his first wife), a girl, born in 1773, and a boy, born in March 1775. Joseph Hodgkins's militia company joined the forces besieging Boston immediately after Lexington. Thus began his and Sarah's ordeal, lasting until he left the army in June 1779.

Sarah Hodgkins did not conceal her loneliness and anxiety from her husband. On Thanksgiving in 1775, she confessed that the day seemed

2. Ward, II, 492–95, 626–28; Mitchell, *Price*, 275–88.
3. For Sarah and Joseph Hodgkins, see Herbert T. Wade and Robert A. Lively, *This Glorious Cause: The Adventures of Two Company Officers in Washington's Army* (Princeton, N.J., 1958). The Appendix, 167–245, contains the Hodgkins letters.

"lonesome and dull," and a few weeks later she came as close to self-pity as she ever did—"I look for you almost every day but I dont alow myself to depend on any thing for I find there is nothing to be depended upon but trouble and disappointments." She repeated "I want to see you" many times in the next three years and repeated too that she feared that her husband would not survive the war.[4]

Reading these confessions did not destroy the morale of Joseph Hodgkins, in fact they may have given him comfort even as they distressed him, for they were expressions of his wife's love. Sarah also declared her love openly though usually her letters were matter-of-fact in tone. Matter-of-fact but moving was this postscript: "give regards to Capt Wade [Hodgkins's commanding officer] and tell him I have wanted his bed fellow prety much these cold nights. . . ." Joseph Hodgkins replied: "I gave your Regards to Capt Wade But he Did not wish that you had his Bed fellow But I wish you had with all my heart."[5]

News from home was always welcome. Sarah Hodgkins filled her letters with tidbits about the children, of relatives, and of Ipswich. When she was especially lonely, she was not above reminding Joseph that she was alone with their children—"I have got a Sweet Babe almost six months old but have got no father for it." She also did not hide her opposition to Joseph's re-enlistment in 1776. He was to serve almost another three years despite her protests.[6]

Sarah Hodgkins's love for her husband helped sustain her in these years. The love found its place in her faith that Providence would see them through to happiness, if not in this world, at least in the next. Her heart, she told Joseph, "akes for you" when she thought of the difficulties and fatigues he endured. Her faith in God and in God's plan helped her keep her balance; as she said, "all I can do for you is to commit you to God . . . for God is as able to preserve us as ever and he will do it if we trust in him aright."[7]

Sarah Hodgkins endured the separation from her husband, and in June 1779 he returned home. Her feelings at the separation found echoes in his. But as he told her, he fought in a glorious cause, a cause which gained intensity through the pain and suffering borne in its service.

4. Wade and Lively, *Glorious Cause*, 185, 187. (I have altered the spelling of two words in the second quotation and supplied punctuation.)
5. *Ibid.*, 191, 192.
6. *Ibid.*, 239–40, 224.
7. *Ibid.*, 220.

II

Sarah Hodgkins did not have to face redcoated soldiers at her door. She did not lose cattle and crops to marauders; no soldier put a torch to her house or cut down fruit trees in the yard or tore apart the fences and the sheds of the farm for firewood. Of course, she lived in fear for Joseph's life, but at least she did not have to worry that the enemy would take her own.

The enemy remained far enough away after Howe evacuated Boston in 1776 to permit most civilians in Massachusetts to lead fairly quiet lives. Quiet, and to some extent safety, disappeared wherever the armies marched or camped. Common rumor throughout the war had it that the Hessians, as all troops from German provinces were called, were to be feared the most. Howe's pursuit of Washington across New Jersey in late 1776 aroused a deep hatred of German troops among civilians. These soldiers probably did not behave worse than their English allies, but because they were "foreign" and spoke a strange language they excited a deep revulsion.

Eighteenth-century armies did not ordinarily deal gently with the civilians they encountered, and Howe's English and German soldiers behaved in conventional ways. They entered private houses unbidden and took what they wanted—food, clothing, and anything else they could lay their hands on. Keeping warm was difficult in winter, and, not surprisingly, troops pulled down fences and buildings for fuel.

Such actions were repeated throughout the war and not just by the enemy. Washington's soldiers endured terrible hunger and cold at Valley Forge in 1778, and during the winter of 1779–80, strung out around Morristown, New Jersey, they suffered even more. In these times and in others, the temptation to plunder nearby civilians proved irresistible to some. There were many occasions when no excuse seemed necessary, around Monmouth Court House, for example, at the end of June 1778. In the aftermath of the battle the American soldiers entered houses which civilians had fled when the two armies came together. The Americans carried off whatever they could find, only to be pulled up short by an angry Washington who ordered that they be searched.

Washington had to give such orders more than once during the war. His British opposites, Howe and Clinton and their staffs, took similar actions. Both armies indeed punished marauders, in or out of uniform, severely. James Thacher, a medical officer who kept a thorough journal, reported that soldiers near Albany in 1778 who had robbed and murdered inhabitants were hanged. Thacher called these creatures "villains," and his hatred of them seems to have been widely shared in both armies.[8] Still, soldiers robbed and killed civilians throughout the war.

Civilians learned to fear not only the army of each side but also those who traveled with them or who lived in their shadows. The camp followers of both armies, for the most part mature women—wives and a number who were not wives—committed a variety of offenses against civilians. These women normally provided useful services for officers and men. They washed clothing, cooked, nursed the sick and wounded, and gave other sorts of comfort. They did not always confine their attentions to soldiers, however. When the opportunity to steal presented itself, some took advantage of it. Several with Nathanael Greene's army in April 1781 may have joined soldiers in burning houses near Camp Gum Swamp, South Carolina. Greene threatened to execute any that were caught. Women "belonging" to regiments in Washington's army in July 1778, when it was near Newark, New Jersey, may have taken two cloaks, handkerchiefs, shirts, pillow cases, and a large "Diaper Blankett" from civilian houses. Regimental officers searched them for these items after the civilians complained of their losses.[9]

Civilians feared another group—the outlaws who lurked on the fringes of the armies. Near New York City for much of the war, around Philadelphia from September 1777 until July 1778, and throughout the Carolinas and Georgia from 1780 on, such bands roamed—often disguised as partisans serving one army or the other—plundering and killing. In reality they were jackals, possessing neither decency nor principles and seeking only their own advantage. The real partisans despised them. Francis Marion, the Swamp Fox of South Carolina, found that bandits trailed his irregulars and passed themselves off as soldiers under his command. In this guise they plundered luckless Carolinians. Marion gave his men permission to put these outlaws to death without a trial or court-martial.[10]

The Americans living in or near towns and cities occupied by the armies experienced the worst that the war could bring. Boston was the first of the cities to be occupied, but its trial ended early in the war. If the city had not ever really grown accustomed to having the army in its midst, it managed at least to hold together until fighting began

8. James Thacher, *A Military Journal During the American Revolution, From 1775 to 1783* (Boston, 1823), 156–57.
9. Nathanael Greene, General Orders, April 1–July 25, 1781, April 27, 1781, U.S. Army (Continental), Southern Department, HL; Orders, American Army, July 7, 1778, HM 719, II, *ibid.*
10. Francis Marion Orderly Book, Feb. 15–Dec. 15, 1782, HL.

at Lexington. In the month that followed this first great battle, about half its civilian population left. With their departure and with the city under siege, life in Boston assumed a bleak cast. And in June after the heavy casualties the British army suffered at Bunker Hill, almost everyone must have felt depressed and anxious.

Surely almost no one lived really well, soldiers and civilians alike, until the navy carried the troops away in March 1776. Food became scarce almost immediately. Fruits, vegetables, and fresh meat disappeared as the besieging Americans cut off access to the farms and stores of the interior. Salted meat, dried beans and peas, and a few other items continued to come in from Britain. But supply from across the sea was irregular and could not provide much variety. For civilians, as John Andrews, a merchant who remained within the city to protect his property explained, it was "pork and beans one day, and beans and pork another, and fish when we can catch it." Andrews did not starve but he lived in dread that despite his austerity he could not protect what he had. The soldiers, he said, "think they have a license to plunder every one's house and store who leaves the town, of which they have given convincing proofs already."[11]

The British soldiers, for their own reasons, must have shared some of Andrews's gloom. They had fought in two bloody battles, to no good purpose as far as they could see. And here they were confined to a virtually deserted city by an army of rebels. The winter made things worse for these troops and for the civilians as well. As the river and the bay began to freeze over, the chance of an attack increased. By itself the cold would have been bad enough.

Not surprisingly in the winter of 1775–76 the British army did not show a nice regard for civilians' rights or for civilians' property. Officers took over a number of private houses for themselves—General Henry Clinton lived in John Hancock's, and Burgoyne lived in James Bowdoin's. Other lower-ranking officers spread themselves out in lesser houses. Their soldiers also seem to have lived in houses.[12]

Public buildings were also put to the army's purposes. Dragoons used the Old South Meeting House as a riding school, tearing out the pews to make it serviceable. West Church and Hollis Street Church became barracks; the Federal Street Meeting House was made into a barn for

11. John Andrews to William Barrell, June 1, 1775, Winthrop Sargent, ed., "Letters of John Andrews, 1772–1776," MHS, *Procs.*, 8 (Boston, 1866), 408.

12. Justin Winsor, ed., *Memorial History of Boston, 1630–1880* (4 vols., Boston, 1880–81), III, 155. See *ibid.*, 156–59 for next paragraph.

the storage of hay, and the Old North was pulled down for firewood. At least one hundred privately owned houses went the way of Old North—into the fires of shivering soldiers. Besides the damaged and demolished houses and churches, Bostonians found out-buildings missing, fences destroyed, trees cut down, gardens trampled, and a general filth when they reclaimed their city in March.

The year after the British evacuated Boston they captured Philadelphia, which they held for almost nine months. In several respects the occupation of Philadelphia resembled that of Boston. The civilians who remained after the city fell had to contend with soldiers who sometimes plundered and abused and even killed them. They also had to house officers and men whether they wanted to or not.

On the whole, however, civilian life was much better than it had been in occupied Boston. No army surrounded Philadelphia, and travel to and from nearby farms and villages—and to New York—continued. To be sure, the Delaware River could not be used until late November 1777, when Howe finally succeeded in capturing the American forts which dominated its waters. But Washington's army, weak and miserable at Valley Forge, offered no threat at least until the spring of 1778. There were partisan bands, however, which attempted to stop farmers from carrying their produce into the city, and there were outlaws who robbed anyone on the road weaker than themselves.

Partisans, the occasional patrols sent from Valley Forge, even the outlaws were nothing more than a nuisance to the British army. It lived much better than it had in Boston under siege.

The civilians, however, were never completely free from harassment by soldiers. At its best a soldier's life was rarely comfortable, and soldiers in close quarters with civilians often took, or tried to take, goods civilians preferred not to give up. In the first few days of the occupation, before officers could dampen free spirits, soldiers stole from houses, tore down fences for their campfires, and took hay, vegetables, and other goods without giving receipts. Such actions never completely stopped in the next nine months, but unauthorized seizures may have fallen off. As winter came on the troops seemed to act on orders from their officers and protests from civilians.[13]

The poor suffered the most during the occupation. They may not have been robbed so frequently as those with more of the world's goods, but they felt the bite of inflated prices most keenly. Food and fuel

13. "Diary of Robert Morton," *PMHB*, 1 (1877), 8–10.

were almost always available in Philadelphia, but the prices one paid for them increased rapidly while the British were present.[14]

Inhabitants at every social level felt anxiety and fear during the occupation. Even those loyal to the king's cause had reason to fear, for soldiers looking for plunder did not care where they got it. Robert Morton, a young Tory, at first welcomed the arrival of the British and scoffed at the speed with which Congress fled the city in September. Within a day or two of the beginning of the occupation he began to record its "dreadful consequences"—the looting of houses, the seizure of his mother's hay with no pretense of payment or even a receipt, and the "ravages and wanton destruction of the soldiery."[15]

Young Morton greeted the occupation well disposed toward the British. Elizabeth Drinker, the wife of a Quaker merchant, does not seem to have cared much for either side. And like almost all Quakers, she disapproved of the violence of the war.

Several weeks before Philadelphia's capture, the Pennsylvania council seized Henry Drinker, husband of Elizabeth, on suspicion of disloyalty to the American cause. Henry Drinker and other Quakers under suspicion were sent to outlying towns and confined. Elizabeth naturally worried about her husband. The occupation added to the strain she felt.

The Drinkers had money and did not go hungry or cold. Nor did they have to give up their house, although after prolonged negotiations they had to take in a British officer, a Major Crammond, who came with three servants (one boarded at the Drinkers'), three horses, three cows, two sheep, plus assorted turkeys and chickens. All this baggage may have surprised Elizabeth Drinker, who never quite adjusted to having the major in the house. His presence, however, may have brought a benefit she did not fully recognize. Before Major Crammond took up residence the family feared that soldiers might break into the house. One did in late November, an intoxicated trooper who had taken up with their young servant Ann. Elizabeth Drinker was badly frightened by this occurrence and was made even more fearful by stories of troops who plundered Philadelphia houses. In December, after seeing men loitering in the neighborhood after dark, she confided to her journal that "I often feel afraid to go to Bed." Major Crammond may have been something of a bother—he kept late hours and entertained his friends in

14. For a detailed study of inflation during the war, see Anne Bezanson et al., *Prices and Inflation During the American Revolution, Pennsylvania, 1770–1790* (Philadelphia, 1951).
15. "Diary of Morton," *PMHB*, 1 (1877), 8, 10, 23.

the Drinkers' parlor—but his presence must have discouraged soldiers who might otherwise have entered the house.[16]

Elizabeth Drinker occasionally appealed to Joseph Galloway for assistance. Galloway was a loyalist, once a powerful Pennsylvania politician, and a man of ability. From December 4, 1777, until the army pulled out of the city, he served as "Superintendent General of the Police in the City and its Environs and Superintendent of Imports and Exports to and from Philadelphia." The grand title simply meant that he was responsible for the regulation of trade in and out of Philadelphia. The only coercive power he had was whatever the army chose to lend him.[17]

The regulation of trade during the occupation was no light matter. Business flourished during these nine months. The army ordered that regular entry of ships and cargoes should be made, and goods which were likely to be smuggled to rebels outside the city—rum, spirits, molasses, and salt—were carefully stored and sold only by permit.

Loyalist merchants made money during this period and so apparently did the British officials and naval officers who engaged in smuggling. Galloway did his best to see that the law was observed, once going so far as to break into a warehouse owned by Tench Coxe, another Tory merchant, in search of contraband arms.

Coxe had returned to Philadelphia with the army in September 1777. He found it half deserted, but exiles like himself who had fled the year before soon made their way back. Trade revived with New York and the West Indies once the American forts on the Delaware were cleared in late November. Even before the opening of the river, Coxe advertised in a local paper that he had cotton goods, satins, silk knee garters, pearl necklaces, and Keyser's pills for sale. Keyser's pills must have been highly valued, for they supposedly cured venereal disease, rheumatism, asthma, dropsy, and apoplexy.[18]

For those with money, merchants like Coxe, royal officials, and some army officers, there was a social season with balls held weekly, and occasional plays, concerts, and parties. The high point of these celebrations occurred on May 18, 1778, when General Howe's officers, directed by Captain John André, gave their commander, who was soon to give way to Henry Clinton, the Mischianza, a grand party with a mock tournament

16. Henry D. Biddle, ed., *Extracts from the Journal of Elizabeth Drinker, 1759–1807* (Philadelphia, 1889), 63–79, 72 ("I often feel afraid . . .").

17. John M. Coleman, "Joseph Galloway and the British Occupation of Philadelphia," *Pennsylvania History*, 30 (1963), 272–30.

18. Jacob E. Cooke, "Tench Coxe: Tory Merchant," *PMHB*, 96 (1952), 52.

featuring knights of the Blended Roses and the Burning Mountain, a ball, a banquet, and decorated barges on the river which hailed their commander with gun salutes. André enlisted the local gentry, and beautiful Tory girls were much in evidence. Altogether it was a memorable occasion for the general, though not everyone approved. Elizabeth Drinker sniffed that the day was to be remembered for its "scenes of Folly and Vanity."[19]

There were similar scenes in occupied New York City throughout the war, though none so lavish or extravagant as the Mischianza. New York fell to the British in September 1776 and remained in their hands until late November 1783, almost three months after the signing of the definitive treaties of peace on September 3, 1783. The city provided the headquarters for successive British army commanders in America— William Howe, Henry Clinton, and Sir Guy Carleton, who took over from Clinton in May 1783 when the war was all but over.

As the army's headquarters and as a great port, New York City naturally received a good deal of attention from the ministry at home and the military forces in America. Troops and supplies moved into it, and sometimes out of it, throughout the war. Operations were planned there, warships were refitted and in some cases repaired at its docks, and loyalists in the northern states gradually filtered into its protection. Until near the end of the war the army entertained no idea of giving it up.

But though the city provided the center for much British activity, it did not really flourish during the war. To be sure, trade resumed shortly after the occupation began. One estimate held that there were at least five hundred ships crowded into its harbor by October 1776. Several newspapers began to appear about this time, and their columns carried advertisements of a variety of goods for sale. And as business revived and the British army settled in, many inhabitants who had fled returned, their numbers swelled by loyalists seeking a haven from patriot persecution. By 1781 New York City may have housed as many as 25,000 civilians. The number of British soldiers fluctuated from around 31,000 when the city was captured to as few as 3300 early in 1777 when Howe still pursued Washington. Through much of the war there were at least 10,000 troops in the city, most in camp on Staten Island and northern Manhattan.[20]

19. Biddle, ed., *Journal of Drinker*, 103. For Major André's account of the Mischianza, see Henry Steele Commager and Richard B. Morris, eds., *The Spirit of 'Seventy Six* (Bicentennial ed., New York, 1975), 657–60.

20. This account of the occupation of New York City is based on Oscar Barck, *New York City During the War for Independence* (New York, 1931).

As in Philadelphia, many army officers and wealthy loyalists seem to have led active social lives. The theater revived, concerts were given, along with the usual round of dinners, balls, and parties. Army and navy officers in need of diversion furnished most of the actors in the plays. John André, now a major in the Guards and on Clinton's staff, took leading parts until his capture by the Americans at the time of Benedict Arnold's treason. In 1783, a few months before the war's official end, a professional troupe arrived and began giving performances. All these productions stopped at the end of the year with the close of the war and the evacuation of the city by the army and several thousand loyalists.

The amusements of the army and the loyalists have the flavor of quiet desperation. The city may not often have felt the constrictions of occupied Boston, but its inhabitants knew that an enemy lay not far away. Clinton, who certainly worried much, feared an attack several times in his years of command. And when victualing ships failed to arrive when expected, he had reason to fear that the city might starve.

For many inhabitants life was hard and depressing. Physical conditions became difficult just as the occupation began in September 1776. On the night of September 20, a fire began which burned 500 houses, about one-fourth of the city's dwellings. Trinity Church, the Lutheran church, warehouses, and stores were also destroyed. This destruction produced no immediate housing shortage, for most residents had left just as the city fell. Perhaps five thousand inhabitants remained. But as many returned in the next few months, and as loyalists from the middle Atlantic states poured in, a genuine housing shortage developed. The presence of British troops made it worse. A second great fire in August 1778, which destroyed sixty-four houses, deepened the shortage.

No strong effort was made during the occupation to rebuild the houses. The poor and the floaters who followed the army took over much of the burned area—it lay on both sides of Broadway—and put up makeshift shelters. Many of these structures were little more than tents made from sailcloth stretched over and around the fragments of walls and chimneys that remained after the fire. Locally this tent city was called "Canvas Town."

Harsh winters, especially the winter of 1779–80, caused the worst suffering. Before the war the Hudson Valley and nearby New Jersey supplied most of the city's food and fuel. Closer by, the farms on upper Manhattan furnished some vegetables and meats; Long Island sent hay, grain, meat, and wood for fires. These nearby areas remained fairly steady suppliers during the war, but they could not meet the city's needs as its population expanded. Heavy snowfalls in 1779–80 made transporting food and wood almost impossible for weeks at a time. Early in the winter the ice clogged the rivers and cut off Long Island for part of the time. By the middle of January, the Sound froze solid and sleds could be used to carry provisions to the city. But though the freezing helped in one way, it hindered transport in another, for ships were blocked out.

To govern the city, the army relied principally on itself. Howe reinstalled Governor Tryon shortly after capturing the city, but General James Robertson, named commandant of the city in September, really ran it. Robertson relied on army officers to do much of the ordinary work of the occupation, but he also looked to a group of civilians which he chose, called the City Vestry, to provide relief to the poor. Such a body existed before the war. It had collected poor rates and tried to dispense aid to paupers. Robertson's group could not collect rates, but it did have the rents from abandoned rebel houses which were leased to loyalists, and it received fines collected from offenders against various regulations made by the commandant. Altogether the vestry dispensed about £45,000 during the occupation. But neither the vestry nor any other public authority could relieve the occupied city of all its misery.

In a sense no one in America escaped the war, even those in areas remote from it. To be sure much went on as usual—farmers put in their crops in the spring and harvested them in the fall. Craftsmen made goods, and retailers sold them. Congregations gathered in churches, and children went to school. In these events the rhythms of conventional existence are clear.

Yet the war could not be forgotten. The ten years of agitation before it began had taught most Americans that they had a stake in its issues. There is considerable evidence that wherever they were, they followed the course of the fighting as best they could.

For most, perhaps, the times somehow seemed askew. Months after British troops evacuated Philadelphia, Elizabeth Drinker detected disorder in social arrangements. A new maid, hired in late 1778, entertained a visitor all day in the Drinkers' house and then invited her to spend the night—"without asking leave." Mrs. Drinker found something ominous in this behavior—"times are much changed," she said, "and Maids have become Mistresses."[21]

Soldiers and their families, the Hodgkinses of the Revolution, experi-

21. Biddle, ed., *Journal of Drinker*, 113.

enced a pain denied to the Elizabeth Drinkers. Their sense of danger was much more oppressive. It was indeed of a different sort. The question "would Joseph survive?" tormented Sarah Hodgkins until he was finally mustered out. Nothing in ordinary daily life could suppress Sarah Hodgkins's concern.

III

The length of the war and its demands on men made such experiences common in America. In the eight years between Lexington and peace some 200,000 men carried arms in the Continental army and state militias. And though some areas avoided the destruction fighting inevitably brought, none escaped the war altogether, for the British spread their armies and their efforts from one end of the new nation to the other. Men from every part of America died in opposing them.

If the lives of most Americans were touched by the war, the structure of society remained essentially what it had been before the Revolution. Social classes did not change in important ways, though the upper stratum in the cities lost significant numbers of merchants who, as loyalists, went into exile. Most merchants, of course, supported resistance and eventually war.

The major institutions survived the war as well. War disrupted families, it destroyed schools and churches, and it damaged communities, but the ways such institutions organized themselves remained intact. Not that changes were not made—the Church of England, for example, no longer received support from taxes. Disestablishing it proved difficult, especially in Virginia, where James Madison and Thomas Jefferson persuaded the legislature to act. But the character of the religion of the church did not alter drastically.[22]

Yet, though the structure of society remained about what it had always been, society in an important sense was deeply affected by the experience of revolution and war. The eight-year struggle to separate themselves from Britain could not help but transform the American people even as they held on to much in their past.

For one thing the means by which they governed themselves—the institutions of the state—were changed in important ways. To be sure government continued to be representative, but, in structure and in the disposition of its powers, it departed from colonial practice. The

22. *TJ Papers*, II, 545–53; Dumas Malone, *Jefferson and His Time* (6 vols., Boston, 1948–1981), I, 275–80.

governor, formerly the agent of the Crown or a proprietor, now existed as the agent of the legislature, where real power resided. Within the legislature, the lower house dominated. For the most part white males with real property elected the lower house just as they had always done. Pennsylvania and Georgia reduced requirements to something approaching manhood suffrage; in Massachusetts the constitution of 1780 increased the amount of property for the vote to £60. But regardless of whether suffrage requirements remained the same or became stiffer, power now shifted closer to popular desires. The state constitutions did not establish "democracy," and yet the "people" had more power than ever before.[23]

A change in the tone, or texture, of society reflected and perhaps helped produce the shift in power. If society was not exactly "democratic" or even completely "American," it was more egalitarian than before and had an awareness of itself as the society of a new nation. The Revolution after all had been made in the name of the American people. The Declaration of Independence had declared that they were separating themselves from another people. Their representatives had created a Congress that sat for the continent, and the Congress had called into being a Continental army. The great events which had led Americans to call their cause "glorious" had also led them to love their country and its independence. Thousands of men and women who shared this passion but who had never acted "politically" did so in the twenty years after 1763. Thousands who had never fought in war now did, and thousands of others worked in its service and paid taxes to keep it going.

The usual way of demonstrating the changes that these years of conflict and sacrifice wrought is to cite the evidences of an American nationalism. What has been called high culture—literature and painting most notably—gives evidence of the appearance of American nationalism in the Revolution, just as the great public documents and, perhaps more importantly, the actions of Americans do.[24]

But the experience that created national feeling is what set the society of the revolutionary generation off from all those generations which preceded—and followed—it. Those who defended American rights before 1775, those who led the way into revolution and war, those who

23. On the suffrage, see Chilton Williamson, *American Suffrage: From Property to Democracy, 1760–1860* (Princeton, N.J., 1960), 92–137.
24. On high culture and the Revolution, see Kenneth Silverman, *A Cultural History of the American Revolution* (New York, 1976).

fought, those who contributed possessions and service, and those who merely urged others on were marked by their actions. They were a part of the glorious cause, a cause which from 1776 on assumed the shape of an experiment in republican government. The precise nature of that experiment did not become immediately clear, though the five years following peace in 1783 would do much to define its meaning. In the meantime the Americans engaged in the struggle sensed that what they were doing distinguished them from other men.

The strongest expression of this sense occurred of course on the battle-field, where a feeling of identity and a commitment to virtue were most clear. That the army sometimes failed in the service of the cause does not mean that the revolutionary generation's experience was false. No society ever holds perfectly to the courses it sets for itself; and no good and honorable experience can ever be completely free of evil and dishonor.

The Continental army's sometimes erratic performance reflected the society's. The American army in fact was entangled with American soci-ety in ways unprecedented in the eighteenth century before the French Revolution. Society and the army shared problems in a common confu-sion, confusion born of the youthful, half-formed character of each. Procurement of supplies, protection of property, identification of friends (Whigs) and enemies (loyalists), and especially the recruitment of troops preoccupied both civilians and soldiers in a manner uncommon in well-established nations where institutional purposes were well understood and procedures were matters of routine. To an extraordinary extent for the eighteenth century, the army was an extension of society.

Battle gave soldiers an experience that no challenge of civilian life equaled. And yet the test of battle was endurable, as we have seen, in part because the Continental army shared so much with the people who sustained it. In the long struggle of the war, what made the cause "glorious," besides its great principles, was the fact that so many believed in it. As it took hold of Americans' imagination, the glorious cause became, in the popular phrase, the "common cause."

IV

The cause was not common to all in America. About 500,000 Americans remained loyal to Britain between 1775 and 1783, and perhaps as many as 80,000 of them left their homes to take refuge in England, Canada, Nova Scotia, and the West Indies. Altogether the "loyalists," as they called themselves ("Tories" they were to those who made the Revolution), comprised about 16 percent of the total population or a little more than 19 percent of all white Americans.[25]

Loyalty to the Crown was the normal condition of American colonials before 1775; perhaps we should not be surprised that almost one-fifth of the whites in the colonies chose not to—or could not—give up the customary allegiance to England. Somehow they resisted the call to revolution in the name of their rights. Not that many believed that those rights were not threatened in the decade before the war began. Many shared the growing revulsion against the British government's heavy-handed measures of the 1760s and early 1770s. But their loyalty ran deeper and cut them off from the politics of their time. Those who showed what their feelings were often received harsh treatment; and among those who feared for their lives or who could not stand to see the old ties broken were some who actively opposed the Revolution— in most cases by taking themselves out of their country or by joining regiments which served the British army.

In no colony did loyalists outnumber revolutionaries. The largest numbers were found in the middle colonies: many tenant farmers of New York supported the king, for example, as did many of the Dutch in the colony and in New Jersey. The Germans in Pennsylvania tried to stay out of the Revolution, just as many Quakers did, and when they failed, clung to the familiar connection rather than embrace the new. Highland Scots in the Carolinas, a fair number of Anglican clergy and their parishioners in Connecticut and New York, a few Presbyterians in the southern colonies, and a large number of the Iroquois Indians stayed loyal to the king.[26]

This rough list suggests an explanation of the weakness, indeed the failures, of the loyalists. They were disparate groups, divided among themselves, and separated from genuine power. Thus the loyal Anglicans in New England found themselves surrounded by the dominant Congregationalists. The Germans and Dutch of the middle colonies who did not always agree among themselves faced the more powerful English

25. The most careful study of loyalist numbers is Paul H. Smith, "The American Loyalists: Notes on Their Organization and Numerical Strength," *WMQ,* 3d Ser., 25 (1968), 258–77.
26. For information about the identity and location of loyalists, I have drawn on William H. Nelson, *The American Tory* (1961; paperback ed., Boston, 1964); Robert M. Calhoon, *The Loyalists in Revolutionary America, 1760–1781* (New York, 1973); Wallace Brown, *The King's Friends: The Composition and Motives of the American Loyalist Claimants* (Providence, R.I., 1966).

and Scotch-Irish. The Scots were never numerous anywhere in the colonies, and as for the tenants in the Hudson Valley, they too were a minority. All these groups were minorities—"conscious minorities" as William Nelson the historian calls them—and disabled by the traits that set them apart.

Their weakness made them dependent upon the royal government which, for its own reasons, never made effective use of them. The weakness and vulnerability these minorities felt undoubtedly contributed to their disposition to remain loyal. They recognized how they differed from the majority in America and looked across the Atlantic for support. Among the Dutch in New York and New Jersey who had not assimilated the English language and culture were to be found more loyalists than among those who had. In the Hackensack Valley the division between the two sorts of Dutch was especially clear. One group clung to the old language and customs and to the old religion; the other learned English and in the Great Awakening was swept up by revivalism. When the Revolution came, the English-speaking Dutch, imbued with evangelical values, supported it. The conservative Dutch held aloof, preferring to give their loyalty to the English king, to avoid the unknown, and to stay within the small circle of a familiar and apparently safe world.[27]

Safety resided in quiet and inaction. Those loyalists who revealed their sympathies by incautious speech and those who acted in defense of their principles found life to be dangerous. For in every colony public authority sought to suppress them. The British army offered protection, of course, but the British army had a way of moving on. When it did so—from Boston in 1776, Philadelphia in 1778, and most of the Carolinas in 1781—the loyalists who had come forward in its support either left with it or faced the consequences of staying behind.

Committees of safety and inspection which had come into being with the "Association" in 1774 sought out some of the domestic enemy. The committees listened carefully for seditious speech; they watched for tax evaders, and they took note of those who refused to serve in the militia. Once regular governments got hold of things again in 1775 and 1776, local courts and in some cases special bodies created by the legislatures assumed the responsibility of putting down the disaffected. In New York the Provincial Congress, the body succeeding the royal legislature, established a "Committee and Commission for Detecting and Defeating Conspiracies." New Jersey also turned to extraordinary

27. Adrian C. Leiby, *The Revolutionary War in the Hackensack Valley: The Jersey Dutch and the Neutral Ground* (New Brunswick, N.J., 1962), 19–41, and *passim.*

agencies. Pennsylvania satisfied itself by use of regular courts, but it armed them, as most states did, with a treason act. The one passed in Pennsylvania listed seven offenses which constituted high treason when committed by a resident against the state or the United States. These offenses, which included accepting a commission from the enemy, levying war, enlisting or persuading someone else to enlist in the enemy's army, furnishing arms or supplies to the enemy, carrying on a traitorous correspondence with the enemy, entering a treasonable combination, and providing intelligence to the enemy, might be punished by a penalty of death and forfeiture of property.[28]

Lesser offenses in Pennsylvania, misprision of treason, might bring lesser penalties—imprisonment, instead of death, and forfeiture of half one's estate. Misprision of treason introduced a vagueness into the business of discouraging opposition to the Revolution, a vagueness most useful to those with a sharp understanding of patriotism and an appetite for harassing the unpatriotic. The Pennsylvania statute made speaking or writing in opposition to the public a misprision. Attempting to convey intelligence to the enemy, attempting to incite resistance to the government or to encourage a return to British rule, discouraging enlistments, stirring up tumults or disposing the people to favor the enemy, and opposing revolutionary actions or measures were all misprisions.[29]

The year after this statute was passed the Pennsylvania legislature conferred upon itself authority to issue proclamations of attainder, and during the war it approved almost 500 acts of attainder. It also permitted the use of other means of prosecuting offenses considered subversive besides the charges of treason or misprision of treason. Charges of piracy, burglary, robbery, misdemeanor, counterfeiting, and larceny could be used.

Although loyalists found all these measures employed against themselves in Pennsylvania, and similar ones in the other states, they did not usually receive savage treatment. But they were convicted for treason and lesser offenses, and they were sometimes executed. They also saw their property confiscated.

Killing the loyalists was a proposal occasionally made in the newspapers and probably much more often in private. The killing, however, could not usually be done without patriot losses—most deaths occurred in

28. Calhoon, *Loyalists*, 397–414; Henry J. Young, "Treason and Its Punishment in Revolutionary Pennsylvania," *PMHB*, 90 (1966), 294.
29. Young, "Treason," *PMHB*, 90 (1966), 294, and 306 for attainder discussed in the following paragraph.

the bloody encounters around New York City throughout the war, or near Philadelphia in the fall and winter of 1777–78, or in the Carolinas in 1780–81. Executions occurred infrequently and almost never without judicial process.

Taking the loyalists' property from them was less dangerous but sometimes almost as difficult as taking their lives. For the law had to be observed; and then there were the friends and families of loyalists— and sometimes their creditors—all of whom had interests in seeing that the proceedings against estates followed an equitable course. The law itself recognized differences among loyalists whose property might be seized: there were those who had apparently plotted with the king's ministers to enslave America, most obviously those royal officials who had fled for their lives about the time that fighting began—the Governor Hutchinsons of the colonies. The Massachusetts General Court waited until April 1779 before it approved a statute which permitted the confiscation of Hutchinson's property, and of others like him, "Certain Notorious Conspirators" in the words of the act. A second statute dealt with less notorious loyalists who had fled—"absentees" according to the act, and sometimes referred to as "refugees," or "open avowed enemies," and "absconders." This act required that in the actual confiscations due process must be observed. The legislature passed a resolve later in the spring of 1779 permitting sales of confiscated estates. Widows and wives left behind by their absconding husbands were entitled to one-third of the estate after creditors were paid. The acts paid particular attention to the rights of creditors.[30]

Many of the loyalists in Massachusetts whose estates were seized and sold had lived in Suffolk County, which included Boston. Studies of these sales do not indicate that an alteration in the county's social structure followed. They do show, however, that men who had not owned land in Suffolk now purchased it.[31]

The changes in New York proved to be more important, though there, as elsewhere, the old social structure survived the Revolution. Still, leveling—a word that raised the hackles of landlords—occurred. Before the war tenants had rebelled in Dutchess County and elsewhere. The issues, the rents and fees extracted by landlords, had nothing directly to do with those dividing America from Britain, but the great riots in 1765 over the Stamp Act seemed to inspire tenants. The next year

30. Richard D. Brown, "The Confiscation and Disposition of Loyalists' Estates in Suffolk County, Massachusetts," *WMQ*, 3d Ser., 21 (1964), 534–50.

31. *Ibid.*, 549.

saw mobs in action in the Hudson Valley, and a good deal of blood was shed before they were put down. When the war began in 1775, tenants usually took the side opposed to their landlords'. Thus when it became known that Frederick Philipse, lord of Philipsburgh Manor in Westchester, was a Tory, his tenants happily went to the revolutionaries. The manor contained about 50,000 acres which were confiscated after Philipse chose exile. The law guaranteed preemptive rights to tenants of Tories convicted or attainted of treason, that is the law provided that the tenants had the first right of purchase at fair market value. The state sold Philipsburgh Manor under the Confiscation Act of 1784 in a series of transactions which created 287 new owners where formerly there had been only one—Frederick Philipse. The average holding of the new owners was 174 acres.[32]

Whig tenants also gained the lands of Tory landlords in Dutchess County, where the estates of Roger Morris and Beverly Robinson were confiscated in 1779. At least 401 tenants purchased 455 blocks of land in the sales that followed. Holding on to the land was another matter, and after the war many of these tenant-purchasers found making the payments difficult or impossible. A number gave up the attempt, and tenancy survived.[33]

The Livingstons in Albany County fared much better than many of their neighbors. The Livingstons favored American independence, but not personal liberty for their tenants. Not surprisingly, their tenants took the side of the Crown, especially in 1777 when they learned that Burgoyne was on his way south from Canada. Before these tenants succeeded in arming themselves, militia from adjoining Dutchess and from New England broke them apart. No real war followed, but militia and tenants skirmished and six tenants died. The militia arrested hundreds of others. Tenancy withstood these shocks on the Livingston Manor in New York and most of the other estates where it had flourished, and it continued until the mid-nineteenth century.[34]

As loyalists, the tenants in New York departed from the usual pattern: they "chose" loyalty rather than "remained" loyal. Their decision constituted a rejection of the prevailing Whig ideology. But they may have

32. Beatrice G. Reubens, "Pre-emptive Rights in the Disposition of a Confiscated Estate: Philipsburgh Manor, New York, " *WMQ*, 3d Ser., 22 (1965), 435–56.
33. Staughton Lynd, "Who Should Rule at Home? Dutchess County, New York, in the American Revolution" *WMQ*, 3d Ser., 18 (1961), 330–59.
34. Staughton Lynd, *Class Conflict, Slavery, and the United States Constitution* (New York, 1967), 63–77.

had an ideology of their own, based on the feeling that they were exploited by their landlords. Thus they, like patriots all over America, acted in the name of individual liberty.

That commitment did not set them apart from most loyalists. For the loyalists shared the revolutionaries' belief in the rights of the individual, though they parted company with the revolutionaries over the meaning of those rights. When the agitation over British measures began in the 1760s this difference was not clear, and many who later became loyalists decried Parliamentary actions, opposing, for example, the right of Parliament to tax the colonies. Some, most notably Thomas Hutchinson, even argued that Parliament could not properly tax the Americans because they were not represented. Ultimately, loyalists like Hutchinson were unable to follow their own reasoning to the conclusion most of the revolutionaries found unavoidable—Parliament had become the enemy of the subject's liberty. They could not accept the proposition that the ultimate source of liberty and order was the consent of the individual, that government dedicated to the preservation of freedom took its origins from the agreement of the people. The loyalists, so far as they explained themselves, insisted on the importance of tradition and long-established institutions, such as Parliament, in the creation and protection of liberty. And therefore, for most loyalists the crisis in America came to a head when independence was proposed. Independence found the loyalists unprepared to cast off all that they had known. They did not believe that a new basis of political authority had been fashioned in America. The old was sufficient, and they clung to it—and suffered as a result.

Understandably the sufferings of the loyalists left the revolutionaries unmoved. But the sufferings were real. The loss of property, physical injury, and the deaths of friends and members of families were hard to bear. For those who left America, there was still another sort of pain, the loneliness of exile in strange lands, and probably for many the realization that came belatedly that they were more American than British. The diaries and letters that testify to this realization are moving documents. "I earnestly wish to spend the remainder of my Days in America," Sir William Pepperell of Massachusetts wrote in 1778, "I love the Country, I love the People." Pepperell's feeling of longing and sadness took voice in many loyalist houses abroad in the years of the war—and in the years following it.[35]

35. Quoted in Mary Beth Norton, *The British-Americans: The Loyalist Exiles in England, 1774–1789* (Boston, 1972), 124.

V

Unlike loyalists, black slaves admired the principles of the Revolution, yet they were largely excluded from armed service in the patriot cause. As early as 1766, slaves, probably inspired by the agitation over the Stamp Act, paraded through the streets of Charleston, South Carolina, shouting "Liberty." The city immediately picked up its muskets while the authorities had the countryside scouted for signs of an insurrection. Liberty remained the white man's right.[36]

The ten years that followed undoubtedly taught slaves as well as their masters something more about liberty. Slaves probably had always been willing to act for freedom provided they had any chance of getting it. The coming of war in 1775 gave them the chance. Lord Dunmore's promise of freedom in return for their service brought forward several hundred slaves in Virginia within a week of his proclamation in November 1775. Those who reached him had to travel to the coast and find a boat, for he was on board a British warship in Chesapeake Bay. Slaveholders tightened their control over their slaves as soon as the proclamation was issued. Still, 300 slaves escaped to Dunmore within a week of the proclamation.[37]

Dunmore suffered military defeat in December at Great Bridge, across the Elizabeth River, ten miles below Norfolk. Thereafter slaves had an increasingly difficult time in joining him. In all, some eight hundred made it. Dunmore formed them into a regiment, but they did no fighting. They died, however, in large numbers in the king's service, victims of smallpox carried by the crews on British warships. When Dunmore sailed for England in August of the next year, only about 300 black soldiers accompanied him.

More slaves served in the American army. Virtually every Continental regiment contained a few. They enlisted, or were enlisted by their masters for conventional reasons—bounties, land, and the opportunity to earn their freedom. Some were freed before they entered the army; more perhaps were promised their freedom in return for their military service. For the most part they did not serve in separate units though there was a small Rhode Island regiment, officered by whites, composed entirely of blacks.[38]

---

36. Pauline Maier, "The Charleston Mob and the Evolution of Popular Politics in Revolutionary South Carolina, 1765–1784," *PAH*, 4 (1970), 176.
37. This paragraph and the one following are based on Benjamin Quarles, *The Negro in the American Revolution* (Chapel Hill, N.C., 1961), 19–32.
38. *Ibid.*, 80.

Military service might have provided a means by which large numbers of slaves gained their freedom. But within a year of the war's beginning whites, almost everywhere but especially where there were large numbers of slaves, opposed the enlistment of blacks. Compensating their owners would have entailed an expense a hard-pressed Congress could not meet; nor for that matter, could, or would, the state legislatures. The prospect of large numbers of armed blacks was also not smiled upon. Slavery rested on fear and coercion, and the enslavers could never entirely escape the fear that those they held against their wills would turn on them.

Why, after declaring that all men were created equal and making a revolution in the name of liberty, did Americans not free their slaves? The answer to this question lies somewhere in the tangled history of racial attitudes and American perceptions of economic necessity in the eighteenth century. White Americans had been imbued with prejudices against blacks even before slavery took hold in the seventeenth century. Fears of black animality, revulsion against their physical appearance, fantasies about their sexual proclivities had bitten deeply into white minds. These feelings help explain why blacks were enslaved.[39]

More than prejudice contributed to the development of slavery, of course. Blacks in America lacked power; their condition must have incited a disposition to exploit them. And slavery itself, as an institution of labor, gradually assumed an enormous importance in the economy, especially in the plantation colonies. Long before the Revolution, slavery had become an institution that seemed not only appropriate, when whites considered the debased character of blacks, but inescapable when they tried to imagine an economy of free labor.

The irony of white Americans claiming liberty while they held slaves did not escape the revolutionary generation. Too many men on both sides of the Atlantic remarked on it. The Society of Friends in America led the criticism, but there were others in all the new states who called for emancipation of the slaves in the name of natural rights and of Christian principles.

Not surprisingly, political leaders in the northern states reacted more positively to such appeals. In one way or another all the northern states acted to provide for the gradual emancipation of slaves. Most did so

39. Winthrop D. Jordan, *White Over Black: American Attitudes Toward the Negro, 1550–1812* (Chapel Hill, N.C., 1968), 3–98. For a brilliant argument about the importance of English attitudes toward the laboring poor in the development of racial slavery, see Edmund S. Morgan, *American Slavery, American Freedom: The Ordeal of Colonial Virginia* (New York, 1975).

by passing laws ordering that children born into slavery must be freed several years after their birth. Pennsylvania's legislature approved such a law while the war was going on; Rhode Island and Connecticut waited until the year the war ended. In Massachusetts, courts anticipated the legislature and abolished slavery. Elsewhere in the North the process took longer but by the opening of the new century it was almost complete.[40]

The southern states did not follow this example. There slavery was too deeply embedded. But these states did join those to the north in closing the slave trade. The Congress in the 1780s and the Philadelphia Convention of 1787 would also do more—the Congress would bar slavery from the Old Northwest, and the Convention would draft a constitution which permitted a national prohibition of imports of slaves after 1807.[41]

Even considered together these actions against slavery may not seem impressive. They did not destroy slavery; it would flourish until the Civil War. In taking these steps Americans still fell short of honoring their own great standards, especially Jefferson's claim that all men are created equal. But they had done much. They had made slavery a peculiar institution—peculiar in its confinement to the southern states. Had the North tried to force the South to follow its lead, the new republic would have broken apart. The people of the North were no better than those of the South, and we should consider carefully before assigning to them wisdom or a power of seeing into the future. They failed to act against slavery in the South as much out of a sense of their own weakness as out of wisdom. Whatever the reasons, white people in the North and South decided that for the time being at least the union that protected republican government was more important than a full-scale dedication to equality.[42]

40. Jordan, *White Over Black*, 345–46.
41. John Richard Alden, *The South in the Revolution, 1763–1789* (Baton Rouge, La., 1957), 346–48.
42. The most persuasive statement I know about matters discussed in this paragraph is William W. Freehling, "The Founding Fathers and Slavery," *AHR*, 77 (1972), 81–93.

22

Yorktown and Paris

On May 15, 1781, five days before Cornwallis and his army reached Petersburg, Virginia, Major General William Phillips, commander of forces in the Chesapeake, died of a tidewater fever. Cornwallis had looked forward to seeing him again, an old comrade who with Clinton and himself had cut his combat teeth in Germany in the Seven Years War. British officers who fought in Germany felt set apart from those who had not, felt superior, in fact, to all others. When they were much younger, Phillips, Clinton, and Cornwallis had dreamed of command together—"How we should agree, how act, how triumph, how love one another." Clinton and Cornwallis had long since fallen out, and Phillips and Clinton were no longer close. But Cornwallis remained fond of Phillips, whose death dampened the pleasure he felt at arriving in Virginia.[1]

Phillips, a fat and comfortable man, might have steadied Cornwallis. And at this moment Cornwallis needed some ballast. He was tired from a long and depressing campaign, and he was looking for excuses for his abandonment of the Carolinas. He was also looking for direction. He had made it to Virginia with a thousand men who had seen too much combat, but once there even he did not quite know what he should do.

Benedict Arnold greeted him, but Cornwallis could not have taken much satisfaction in Arnold's presence. The 5000 troops, present and fit for duty now in his command, offered much more reassurance. A

1. Quoted in Willcox, *Portrait of a General*, 386.

week later reinforcements arrived which he divided between his own force and the post at Portsmouth. He also pondered the orders under which Phillips had operated and which of course were now his: he was to establish a post on the Chesapeake. Clinton had also instructed Phillips to cooperate with Cornwallis but not to undertake a major campaign of his own.[2]

Clinton himself continued to display his customary restlessness and disinclination to act. He had no knowledge of Cornwallis's move to the north until late in May. He had spent much of the winter fretting over Arbuthnot and considering strikes against the French at Newport or a possible raid against Philadelphia in order to relieve Phillips in the Chesapeake. Nothing came of his ruminations, nothing could as long as Arbuthnot held command of the navy. The two chiefs had long since passed the point where they could plan, let alone carry out, joint operations. In March, Arbuthnot exerted himself to pursue the Chevalier Destouches, who had succeeded Ternay as French naval commandant at Newport. Destouches had taken a French squadron to the Chesapeake with an attack against Arnold in mind. Arbuthnot intercepted him on March 16 and though the British tactics were hardly flawless in the engagement that followed, they discouraged the French. Arnold's force was saved, and Arbuthnot was responsible for their safety.[3]

Near the end of May, Clinton learned of Cornwallis's march to Virginia. The news did not please him but he did not react decisively. What should he now do? Washington did not appear to offer an immediate threat to New York and seemed unlikely to be able to strengthen his army. American public finances and, Clinton supposed, American morale had nearly collapsed. The French at Newport were more of a threat, for they had ships as well as troops. The navy had them pretty well confined, however, in a tough and dreary blockade, and the navy would have to deal with Admiral François Joseph Paul de Grasse who, with twenty ships of the line, had sailed from Brest on March 22. Clinton had been warned of his coming by the ministry but could do little about it except pass on the news to George Rodney, naval commander in the West Indies. Grasse's force gave the French naval superiority in North America, a circumstance of immense importance but one which the ministry ignored until it was too late. No attempt was made to stop him in European waters and no reinforcement of ships was sent

2. Wickwires, Cornwallis, 326–27.
3. Willcox, Portrait of a General, 373–76.

to America until June, and that reinforcement was hardly worth the name, consisting as it did of three ships of the line. As for Cornwallis, in June Clinton sent instructions that he was to develop a base in the Chesapeake capable of sheltering warships. Clinton also wrote warningly that soon orders would be sent for the return of troops in Cornwallis's army—to join in projected operations along the Delaware. These instructions went out from New York on June 11 and 15 and reached Cornwallis on the 26th. Before they did, he had disrupted life in Virginia by first driving Lafayette from Richmond and then turning loose Lt. Colonel John Simcoe and the Queens Rangers for a strike against Baron von Steuben at Point of Fork, the juncture of the Rivanna and Fluvanna rivers. Steuben had to run before this raid—his men would not fight— and Simcoe captured arms and ammunition. Cornwallis next sent Tarleton after the Virginia legislature at Charlottesville which he reached on June 4. On this swift cut Tarleton nearly captured Governor Thomas Jefferson at Monticello. Jefferson escaped by a mere ten minutes.[4]

The day after Cornwallis reached Williamsburg he read the letters Clinton had written two weeks before. They informed him that he was not to conduct a major campaign, though he might harass the enemy, and he was to construct a naval station. Clinton by this time was attempting to ready himself for several possibilities, a Franco-American attack on New York, or a push into Pennsylvania to upset the enemy. Hence he urged Cornwallis to send troops to New York, six regiments of infantry, plus cavalry and artillery.[5]

These orders disgusted Cornwallis and perhaps confused him. At any rate, he immediately looked for a site for a naval base, first reconnoitering Yorktown. Deciding against establishing himself there, he began a march to Portsmouth, from which the troops would be sent to New York. Before he left Williamsburg he dispatched a letter to Clinton in which he virtually declared his unwillingness to remain in Virginia—under the conditions his chief had laid down—and requested permission to retire to Charleston, South Carolina. Until he heard from Clinton, however, he would remain in Virginia and scout out a naval station.[6]

The move from Williamsburg began leisurely on July 4. Lafayette followed and on July 6 sent Anthony Wayne to hit what he thought

---

4. Many of Clinton's letters to Cornwallis are in Stevens, ed., *Clinton-Cornwallis Controversy*, II.
5. Willcox, *Portrait of a General*, 392–404.
6. Stevens, ed., *Clinton-Cornwallis Controversy*, II, 57–58.

was the British rear guard near Jamestown. Cornwallis in force lay in ambush at Greenspring. Wayne led his men forward and the British sprang the trap. Lafayette helped extricate Wayne, but when it was over there were 145 dead Americans on the field. Cornwallis then led his army across the James.[7]

Before Cornwallis arrived at Portsmouth fresh letters from Clinton found him—and kept finding him—with instructions to get the troops scheduled for New York ready for a Pennsylvania expedition instead. Then as he loaded troops for Philadelphia, he was ordered to hold the Williamsburg Neck and to keep back troops for New York. Then he seemed to be instructed to fortify Old Point Comfort or Yorktown but to send any troops to New York that he no longer needed.[8]

By the end of July, Cornwallis had decided to abandon Portsmouth, keep his entire force, and fortify Yorktown. And on August 2, he began putting his troops ashore there. Clinton did not object when he learned of this disposition.

While Clinton and Cornwallis thrashed about in confusion and indecision, Washington tried to sort out his problems and to assess his possibilities. His army still dressed itself in rags and suffered from shortages of every description. The rate of desertion may have slowed but was still high. His allies, the French, sat in Newport awaiting reinforcements and eyeing the English ships that blockaded them. The naval commander, the Comte de Barras, new on the scene in May, was an unknown quantity, but Rochambeau, the lieutenant general who led the French army, had made a favorable impression since his arrival in July 1780.[9]

Rochambeau was seven years older than Washington. He had served with distinction in France's European wars, but he did not know America and he spoke no English. He had good military ability, however, and his personal qualities, honesty and tact, made him an ideal choice for command. And his acceptance of his subordination to Washington added to his value.

In May 1781, Rochambeau and Washington decided on operations around New York City, if possible in such force as to compel Clinton to recall troops from Virginia. Rochambeau would bring the French fleet to Boston where it might more easily be protected. When Washington learned in June that Admiral Grasse had sailed from Brest for the West Indies and would be coming to the American mainland during

7. Ward, II, 876–77.
8. Wickwires, *Cornwallis*, 347–53.
9. Freeman, *GW*, V, 284–96.

the summer, he did not give up his plans for an attack on New York City. He did not know the size of Grasse's force, nor did he know where Grasse intended to use it.[10]

Early in July the Franco-American operations around New York began but enjoyed no great success. There was little fighting around the city in these days largely because the allies had trouble getting into positions from which to attack. While they maneuvered, the commanders speculated about Grasse's intentions. Would he come to New York or Virginia, and would he give them naval superiority? On August 14, Washington received a letter from Barras with the answers—Grasse had left the West Indies for the Chesapeake with twenty-nine ships and over three thousand troops.

Although Grasse's naval strength was formidable it did not guarantee to the French supremacy in American waters. But it might lead to full control, and Washington decided almost immediately to act as if it would. He therefore informed Rochambeau that the two armies must move to the Chesapeake as rapidly as possible. Five days later, on August 19, he had the Continentals in motion with the French coming along soon afterwards. To conceal these movements from Clinton was impossible, but Washington could throw sand into his eyes—and proceeded to by faking preparations for an attack on New York from New Jersey. He had the roads and bridges in New Jersey near the city repaired and a large oven for baking bread constructed. Then near the end of August he started three columns marching toward the city as if positioning themselves for an attack. Clinton watched apprehensively and did not guess the destination of the allied force until September 2, when the American army passed through Philadelphia. The French, following a route recommended by Washington, marched through in the next two days.[11]

By the middle of September the two armies had transported themselves some 450 miles along with baggage and supplies. The move showed Washington's organizational talents at their best. He and a few officers planned it, selecting the routes and collecting the horses and wagons so vital in the transport of stores. Washington seems to have saturated himself in the details as well as the larger outlines of the move. Horses and oxen must be collected at strategic points, magazines with flour, beef, and rum must be set up. Wagons for tents must carry tents; if

10. *Ibid.*, 287–88.
11. *Ibid.*, 309–21, for this paragraph and the one preceding.

officers, as was their wont, piled their baggage on them, throw it off. Repair roads and bridges well in advance and find boats and small ships to transport the troops down the Chesapeake. The mastery of detail so familiar to those who knew Washington appeared in all these concerns—and in the orders that swarmed out of his pen. After sixteen paragraphs of detailed instructions to Benjamin Lincoln who was in charge of sailing down the Chesapeake, Washington added this postscript: "The Tow ropes or Painters of the Boats ought to be strong and of sufficient length otherwise we shall be much plagued with them in the Bay and more than probably lose many of them."[12]

While engaged with logistics, Washington pondered strategy and tactfully urged Grasse to use his force as vigorously as possible. Grasse's ships reached the Virginia Capes on August 26 and by the 31st were at anchor inside the Bay. At just about that time, Thomas Graves, who had succeeded Arbuthnot, sailed from New York with nineteen ships of the line. His destination was the Chesapeake, where he hoped he would find the French fleet. On September 5 he found it and fought a battle that was a standoff. While the two fleets maneuvered in the open seas, Barras who had left Newport a week earlier, slipped into the Bay behind them. The standoff left Cornwallis securely in the net, a fact Graves virtually admitted by returning to New York on September 13.[13]

Grasse suffered from shaky nerves for much of the next month. Washington carefully tutored him in the opportunities now available to their side, but Grasse feared entrapment in the Bay. Washington convinced him to prolong his stay until the end of October and then persuaded him that by taking up a station in the open seas he would unnecessarily expose the Franco-American army. Grasse gave way on both matters but steadfastly refused to send ships up the York to cut Cornwallis off after the combined army had moved into position against him.[14]

That move began at 4:00 A.M. on September 28, when French and American forces marched from Williamsburg. Together the two forces numbered around 16,000 troops, including 3000 Virginia militia. They swung out in a long column, most on foot because horses were in short supply and needed elsewhere to help drag up heavy guns and ammunition. Light artillery was spaced up and down the column rather than concen-

---

12. The quotation is from a letter of Sept. 7, 1781, in *GW Writings*, XXIII, 101. For other instructions, see *ibid.*, 38, 51–63, 78, 98–101, 102–3.
13. To Grasse, Sept. 17, 1781, *ibid.*, 123–25; Willcox, *Portrait of a General*, 414–24.
14. *GW Writings*, XXIII, 136–39, 160–65, 169; Freeman, *GW*, V, 322–44.

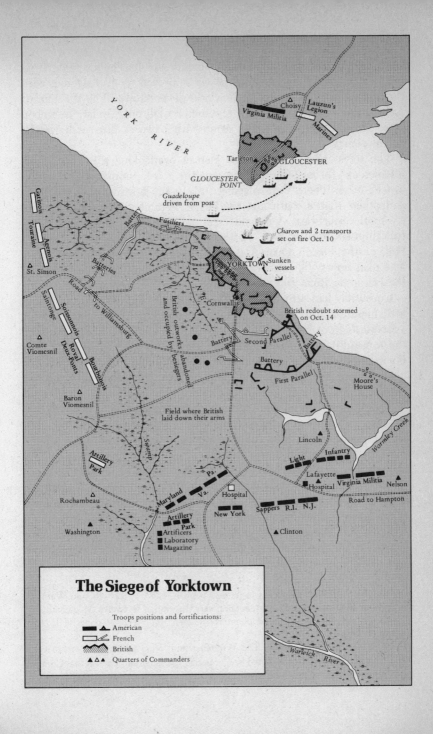

The Siege of Yorktown

trated in the rear, as was the usual practice, for fear of resistance from the British. As the sun rose in the sky it proved more dangerous than the enemy, who remained in his works at Yorktown. The sun burned down and caused more than a few men to fall out. By late afternoon most of the allied army was in camp within two or three miles of the enemy's lines.

The town itself sat on a low plateau overlooking the York River. Ravines cut through the plateau and the town, running down to the water's edge. There were marshes just to the northwest of the town and others to the south and southwest. Wormley Creek and a pond lay to the southeast. A second creek ran through the western marsh and emptied into the York. Farther to the south and west lay Pigeon's Hill, or the Pigeon Quarter, a slight rise covered by tall pine trees. The road from Williamsburg entered the town from the northwest and the Hampton Road from the south.[15]

Cornwallis had set up two lines of defense. The outer consisted of little more than three redoubts in the Pigeon Quarter, the farthest about 1200 yards from Yorktown, and the Star, or Fusiliers', Redoubt about the same distance to the northwest along the edge of the river. An inner line wandering 300 or 400 yards at the most from Yorktown had been begun, but its trenches, redoubts, and batteries were not yet complete.[16]

The allies awoke on the morning of September 30 to discover that Cornwallis had abandoned the redoubts in the Pigeon Quarter. The British continued to hold the Star Redoubt but their defenses for the most part now rested along the inner line. Over the next few days they sank several large boats close in along the shore, a measure taken to discourage an assault by water against their rear. They also gradually slaughtered their horses since they lacked forage for them. Aside from these actions, some small-scale patrolling, and the improvement of trenches and redoubts, they remained largely inactive for the next two weeks. As late as October 12, Washington called Cornwallis's conduct "passive beyond conception." A belief that Clinton would extricate him

15. For the town and approaches to it, see Freeman, *GW*, V, 345–50, and Ward, II, 887–88. There is an excellent contemporary description in Evelyn M. Acomb, ed., *The Revolutionary Journal of Baron von Closen, 1780–1783* (Chapel Hill, N.C., 1958), 139–41.

16. Wickwires, *Cornwallis*, 366. The Wickwires and Ward point to the existence of many small redoubts constructed by Cornwallis; the important point is that Cornwallis's defenses were not completed.

may explain this passivity during the first two weeks of the siege; in the last week, as this belief collapsed, passivity yielded to paralysis and despair.[17]

The mood on the other side approached enthusiasm. The French, of course, looked forward to settling old scores with their ancient enemy and had many left over from the recent war to take up. But it was the Americans who most relished the opportunities of the siege. They had endured much and absorbed so many blows in the previous six years, and now they might return one which would probably end the war and secure their independence.

This possibility led to an occasional insanity. A militiaman stood on a parapet of one of the first works constructed by the Americans "and d—d his soul if he would dodge for the buggers," the "buggers" being the British firing cannon in his direction. Captain James Duncan who watched this madness without trying to stop it later reported that the man "had escaped longer than could have been expected, and, growing fool-hardy, brandished his spade at every ball that was fired, till, unfortunately, a ball came and put an end to his capers." A few days later Captain Duncan and a detachment of light infantry just escaped service as the target. They had been sent forward in the trenches to relieve another unit. In the best tradition of the military's disdain of fear, relief was accomplished with drums beating and colors flying. If the enemy heard the drums or, more likely, noticed the colors and decided to fire at the men who were obviously under them, so be it. An eighteenth-century gentleman should always place his honor above his life.[18]

Or so the convention had it. Captain Duncan had his doubts, which grew into revulsion at the order next given by his commander, Colonel Alexander Hamilton. As Duncan told it, they arrived at the forward trench and planted their colors. "Our next maneuver was rather extraordinary. We were ordered to mount the bank, front the enemy, and there by word of command go through all the ceremony of soldiery, ordering and grounding our arms; and although the enemy had been firing a little before, they did not now give us a single shot." The British may have been filled with astonishment at this display, as Duncan later remarked. More likely, the British officers who watched admired the performance, perhaps some wished that they had ordered it themselves. Their

17. For Washington's comment, see *GW Writings*, XXIII, 210.
18. "Diary of Captain James Duncan . . . in the Yorktown Campaign, 1781," in William H. Egle, ed., *Pennsylvania Archives*, 2d Ser., 15 (Harrisburg, Pa., 1890), 748.

men, however, doubtless would have echoed Duncan's judgment of Hamilton—"One of the first officers in the American army" who in this instance "wantonly exposed the lives of his men." The French, though not so given to these wild flourishes, also relieved their infantry and working parties to the beating of drums, did at least until Rochambeau ordered the practice, which he characterized as "vain glory," to cease. A very solid and psychologically secure commander, Rochambeau noted that the drums attracted British fire. Honor evidently could survive silence and was most enjoyed by the living.[19]

Whatever else the confidence of the allies spawned, it generated a powerful zeal for work. And work the troops did in the opening days of October. The artillery had to be dragged up and emplaced and pressure had to be exerted on the British. Drawing the artillery from the James, where it had been landed, to Yorktown took time and the labor of many horses and men. While these men and animals sweated at their tasks, others began digging in, improving the redoubts captured in the Pigeon Quarter and throwing up works on both ends of the town. Once these were begun sappers started zig-zagging trenches forward toward the enemy. A few nights later in the darkness of October 6, the first parallel was opened, a trench 600 yards distant from the British and parallel to their works. This trench, some 4000 feet long initially, ran from the river on the southeast side of town to a large ravine. It was virtually completed a day later. During the next two days the French and Americans anchored it with redoubts, dug communications trenches and depots for stores and ammunition, and emplaced batteries slightly ahead of the parallel.[20]

The British did not ignore this threat. Their cannonade picked up the next few days and at times so impressed an acute American observer, St. George Tucker, that he characterized it "smart." Smart it may have been, but it was not heavy enough to stop the allied armies from emplacing their own artillery. By the afternoon of October 9 they had a sufficient number of guns and mortars in position to reply. From that time on they made life miserable for everyone in Yorktown—British and German

19. *Ibid.*, 749; for Rochambeau's order, see Acomb, ed., *Journal of von Closen*, 146.
20. Acomb, ed., *Journal of von Closen*, 143–46; Samuel C. Cobb, ed., "Diary of General David Cobb," MHS, *Procs.*, 19 (Boston, 1882), 68–69; Ebenezer Denny, *Military Journal* (Philadelphia, 1859), 41; Henry P. Johnston, ed., *Memoir of Lieut. Col. Tench Tilghman* (Albany, N.Y., 1876), 104; *GW Writings*, XXIII, 210; Edward M. Riley, ed., "St. George Tucker's Journal of the Siege of Yorktown, 1781," *WMQ*, 3d Ser., 5 (1948), 384.

soldiers, the few civilians who had not fled, and the black slaves who had volunteered or been forced to remain.

Within a few days the allied artillery established its superiority. There soon was more of it and it proved surprisingly accurate. This fire would be described today as direct fire; the cannoneers could see their targets and did not have to depend upon forward observers to "call" it in.

The French gunners, more practiced than the Americans, claimed to be able to put six consecutive rounds in the embrasures of enemy batteries. The Americans lacked this fine touch but they too fired with an accuracy that distressed the enemy. The day after the allies opened bombardment all save two of the English embrasures had closed, not necessarily destroyed, but shut up during daylight to prevent their destruction. At night they opened and returned as much fire as possible.

Not only the British works suffered under the allied pounding. From October 9 on there was little sleep for those in town. Civilians ran to "hastily contrived shelters" along the river bank, soldiers burrowed into the ground in trenches and redoubts; Cornwallis himself lived in a kind of grotto, a rough underground cave. Still the dead and wounded piled up, and a German soldier remarked on the bodies in town "whose heads, arms, and legs had been shot off." Food supplies did not run out, but the army, which had eaten "putrid meat and wormy biscuits" at least since early September, did not fare well. Sickness brought on by bad food and water incapacitated hundreds of soldiers.[21]

Two days after the allies began shelling, October 11, they dug a second parallel, this one about 300 yards from the main enemy line. The same procedure was used with sappers clawing out trenches under the watchful care of infantry. In another day the trench was almost finished. This time the British exacted a price from the infantry the allies sent forward. At two or three hundred yards the light artillery found the range. Cornwallis, who had carefully hoarded powder and shells, removed restrictions on firing. Over the next week, however, the allied artillery gradually assumed control as more forward batteries were opened and the British works brought under even heavier fire.

On the night of October 14 the allies completed the second parallel by simultaneous assaults on two British redoubts, No. 9 and No. 10. These attacks were a compound of terror and romance. Made in darkness

21. "[Steven] Popp's Journal, 1777–1783," *PMHB*, 26 (1902), 41 ("hastily contrived shelters"); "The Doehla Journal," trans. R. J. Tilden, *WMQ*, 2d Ser., 22 (1942), 251, 245, for the two other quotations. For the artillery exchanges described in the three preceding paragraphs, see the accounts cited above, fn. 20.

by troops carrying unloaded muskets, they succeeded only because of surprise—and bravery. The French who took No. 9, the larger of the two redoubts, incurred heavier casualties than the Americans. The abatis they had to force their way through may have been thicker than the one the Americans encountered or they may have been less well prepared for it. Whatever the reason, the abatis held them up and British muskets cut them down. Finally, the artificers cleared the way and the French infantry rushed through into the ditch and up the parapet. Once inside the redoubt they found the going easier as some of the British retired. To their right the Americans under Alexander Hamilton broke down the abatis as soon as they found it and swarmed over the redoubt's defenders before they could organize a defense. By morning the redoubts had been connected to the second set of trenches, and the allies had a position suitable for a final storm.[22]

A final desperate assault did not prove necessary. Not much fight remained in the British, and they exhausted what there was over the next three days. Around midnight on October 15 a small raiding party of British broke into the second parallel and spiked six pieces in two batteries, one French and one American. These raiders acted for the sake of British pride, and soon after encountering resistance they retired to their main lines. The next night, in a desperate effort to escape, Cornwallis began ferrying troops across the river to Gloucester. His intention was to mass sufficient force to break out and then to lead his army to New York. He had put about a thousand men across the river when a squall blew up and made further transport impossible. By the time the wind and rain fell off, further effort was useless. The troops were crossed back to Yorktown, and Cornwallis began to prepare himself to surrender. That day his lines took a frightful battering.[23]

On October 17, Cornwallis sent an officer to Washington with a proposal for surrender. Terms were discussed that day and the next. A little before noon on October 19, Washington signed, and at two in the afternoon, the British army marched out to surrender.[24]

---

22. For the French assault on No. 9, see "Journal of Jean-Baptiste-Antoine de Verger," in Howard C. Rice, Jr. and Anne S. K. Brown, eds., *The American Campaigns of Rochambeau's Army, 1780, 1781, 1782, 1783* (2 vols., Princeton, N.J., 1972), I, 142; for the American attack on No. 10, see Hamilton to Lafayette, Oct. 15, 1781, in Syrett and Cooke, eds., *Papers of Hamilton*, II, 679–81.

23. Wickwires, *Cornwallis*, 382–84; "Doehla Journal," tr. Tilden, *WMQ*, 2d Ser., 22 (1942), 253.

24. Wickwires, *Cornwallis*, 384–85; Freeman, *GW*, V, 378–91.

II

The surrender at Yorktown did not end the war. Britain still had an army in New York City, Charleston, South Carolina, parts of Georgia, Canada, Halifax, and the West Indies. But the yearning for peace seemed almost irresistible as the new year opened. North was more dispirited than ever, and there were no optimists in the ministry. The king hated talk of peace without an American surrender, but Parliament felt only disenchantment with the war.[25]

By late March 1782, North could hold out no longer and on the 20th resigned, his way hastened by an address by Commons that all those who would prosecute an offensive war in order to reduce the colonies to obedience were enemies of their country. A week later Lord Rockingham was back in office, heading a government the king could hardly bring himself to acknowledge. Nor did the king like Rockingham—indeed he could barely tolerate being in the same room with him—and insisted that Shelburne serve as an intermediary when the first minister had to be consulted. It was Rockingham's fate to rouse his monarch's disgust even as he saved him from disaster.

Shelburne began as Secretary for the Southern Department which now reassumed responsibility for the colonies, while Charles James Fox, his enemy, took over the Northern Department which had general responsibility for European affairs. These appointments raised awkward problems, for these two foes would both be involved in diplomacy. They did not like one another, and they did not agree on policy. Yet they would have to deal with closely related matters.

Whatever its internal condition, the new ministry had little choice. It had to make peace. An American peace commission already existed; the year before, on June 15, Congress had named it in the expectation that Austria and Russia might provide mediation. Franklin was named to this commission, as was John Adams, Henry Laurens, Thomas Jefferson, and John Jay. Laurens, who had sat in the Tower of London since 1780, when he had been captured by a British warship, was released on bail in 1782 but took little part in the negotiations. Jefferson, burdened with problems at this time, told Congress that he could not serve. Franklin, Adams, and Jay would make peace for the United States.[26]

25. John Brooke, *King George III* (New York, 1972), 219–20.
26. For peace negotiations, see the accounts by Samuel Flagg Bemis, *The Diplomacy of the American Revolution* (1935; reprint ed., Bloomington, Ind., 1957); and Richard B. Morris, *The Peacemakers: The Great Powers and American Independence* (New York, 1965).

The American commissioners began with their hands manacled. Congress instructed them to consult with the French and to take the advice they were given. It drafted these instructions at a time when the outcome of the war seemed doubtful to some, and when LaLuzerne, the French minister to the United States, had succeeded in bribing General John Sullivan, now a delegate from New Hampshire. The French bought a member of Congress because they could not corrupt John Adams, who had been named one of the American peace commissioners in 1779. Vergennes feared Adams's integrity and his devotion to the national interest of the United States. In June 1781 Congress named others to the peace commission, a measure diluting Adams's authority, and if that were not enough, Congress charged the commissioners to seek French advice and to follow it.

Only innocents in Congress could have believed in voting for such instructions that they were serving their own country. Astute men, including the commissioners, recognized that though Franco-American purposes were in general similar, in several important particulars they were different. Fishing rights in the Newfoundland Banks and the right to dry their catch ashore were of vital interest to Americans, especially those in New England. Boundaries also concerned them: to the north they did not wish to have the Canadians pushing south into the Ohio, and to the west they insisted that the Mississippi River should serve as their border. Spain at this time claimed considerable territory east of the river. None of these matters seemed of such interest to the French as to persuade them to change their plans for either peace or war. Vergennes in fact, early in 1781 would have agreed to peace that guaranteed Britain and America the territory each held in America. Britain of course held New York City and much of the Carolinas and Georgia.

Spanish interests also differed considerably from America's. Although Spain in 1779 had entered the war against Britain, in 1782 it had not yet recognized the United States. Spain's abiding interest was Gibraltar. Spanish diplomats had met secretly with the British in 1780 about the war and had not troubled to notify their French allies of the fact.

The British themselves, though looking for a settlement with America and an end to the war with their enemies on the Continent, wanted to retain their old colonial possessions. Shelburne, to whom it fell to supervise negotiations after he came to head the ministry on Rockingham's death in July, sought to separate France and the United States. If he could play one against the other, favorable terms might be obtained in the European settlement.

To represent Britain in the informal talks that began in April, Shelburne sent Richard Oswald to Paris. Oswald was a Scot, a merchant, and a much more astute man than his political masters in the ministry believed. Years before when he was young he had lived for a time in Virginia, and he still owned land in America. He had money—made in the Seven Years War and in the slave trade—and no political ambitions. His manner of presenting himself seemed to suggest that he was too old and philosophical for politics. He was known to Laurens, who had acted as his Charleston agent in the slave trade. Altogether, Oswald was the sort to get along with Franklin; both were comfortable men with few illusions and with their passions under control.[27]

The two first saw one another in April, and Franklin took Oswald to Vergennes soon after. They did not accomplish much before the summer. Oswald lacked a formal commission when they began, and Franklin lacked colleagues, with Jay sitting unhappily in Madrid awaiting some sign of recognition from Spain and Adams maneuvering at The Hague for a loan for his country. Laurens, whom Oswald had bailed out of the Tower and brought to the Continent, sank into inertia produced perhaps by sickness and grief over the death of his son, Colonel John Laurens, killed in action in August 1782.[28]

The talks almost froze at one point: Oswald's instructions did not include recognition of United States independence as a preliminary to negotiations; the Americans insisted that Britain must recognize independence before a treaty of peace was agreed upon. Franklin also pressed for accession of Canada to the United States. By late summer all parties began to move slowly toward agreement. The battle of the Saints in April made the French a bit more reasonable; their commander in the West Indies, Grasse, was captured and his fleet damaged, though not destroyed, by Admiral Rodney. The British soon sensed after a secret meeting in England with Rayneval, Vergennes's secretary, that the French were not much interested in defending American claims to the fisheries or to Canada. But the British feared the outcome of a Spanish expedition against Gibraltar. The Americans, principally Franklin and Jay, who reached Paris on June 23, feared what was going on in secret between their ally—the French—and their enemy—the British.

In September, Jay and Franklin agreed to proceed with negotiations if Oswald's commission was altered to permit him to treat with them as the representatives of the United States. The formula adopted was

27. Bemis, *Diplomacy*, 194–95.
28. *Ibid.*, 203; Morris, *Peacemakers*, 376–77.

ambiguous—Congress took it as recognition of American independence; the Shelburne ministry did not and, had negotiations broken off, would doubtless have denied that Britain had recognized the United States.

What happened in the next three months may have taken place on diplomatic quicksand, but the results were solid enough and preliminary articles of peace were signed on November 30 by the Americans and the British commissioners. A few hours before the signing, Franklin sent Vergennes word that agreement had been reached. He did not admit of course that, in negotiating, the American delegation had violated its instructions from Congress to consult the French and to follow their advice. The Americans had not, however, violated the treaty obligations to France, for the agreement with Britain was not to go into effect until France and Britain concluded peace.

The first article of the treaty stated that "His Britannic Majesty acknowledges the said United States . . . to be free Sovereign and independent States. . . ." After this supremely important article, boundaries were taken care of: in the north, a line close to the present-day line; in the south, the thirty-first parallel; in the west, the Mississippi River. The old American fishing rights off Newfoundland and the St. Lawrence were guaranteed along with "the Liberty" to dry and cure fish in the unsettled bays, harbors, and creeks of Nova Scotia, the Magdalen Islands, and Labrador. Creditors "on either side" were to meet "no lawful Impediment" in collecting debts "of the full value in Sterling Money" "heretofore contracted"; and Congress was to recommend earnestly to the state legislatures to return confiscated property of British subjects. This article, which has to be read in full to be appreciated, dealt with the tricky issue of loyalist property. The article slid over the question of how much a recommendation by Congress would be worth. If loyalists believed that Congress could force the states to act on their behalf, they were soon to change their minds.[29]

The treaty also provided that there would be no further confiscations of property or prosecutions of persons for actions taken in the war; that the British would withdraw their forces "with all convenient speed"; that the Mississippi River would be open to navigation by citizens of both Britain and the United States, and that any conquests of territory made before the articles of peace arrived in America would be returned.

Agreement between the Americans and the British stimulated the French, who wanted to end the drain on their treasury the war created,

29. The text of the "Preliminary and Conditional Articles of Peace" is reprinted in Bemis, *Diplomacy*, 259–64.

and on January 20, 1783, they and their ancient enemy signed preliminary articles of peace. Spain and Britain agreed on peace at the same time, and orders went out to suspend all military operations. The way to agreement had been eased by events—the great Spanish attack on Gibraltar had failed in September and, of course, the Americans had settled. Spain did not receive Gibraltar, but Britain did cede Minorca, which had fallen in the war to the Spanish, and east and west Florida.

All parties signed the definitive articles of peace on September 3, 1783. In America, General Carleton who had replaced Henry Clinton performed the melancholy tasks of packing up the army and evacuating America. By the end of 1783, the United States was free of British troops except for the detachments still occupying posts in the Northwest.

III

The celebrations in America greeting the news of peace often included a long series of toasts. Americans lifted their glasses to the "United States," "Congress," the "American Army," "General Washington," the "memory of the heroes who died in war," the "Peace Commissioners," "Louis XVI," "Rochambeau," and others on a list that must have drained bottles and barrels by the score. The toasts expressed joy and indicated to some extent how Americans explained their victory. Understandably, no one drank to King George III, Lord George Germain, Henry Clinton, Earl Cornwallis, William Howe, or to the British army and navy. Had these Americans been more interested in explaining their victory than celebrating it they might have mentioned the British. For the Americans had not simply won the war, the British had also lost it.[30]

The British faced problems in the war unlike any they had ever faced, and as rich as their past was, it furnished only limited guidance. The war was not just another struggle in the wilderness of the New World. The army and navy knew America; they had fought there before, and had fought well. The war was in part a civil war against a people in thirteen colonies who gained determination as they fought and sacrificed. The military problems of dealing with this people were baffling; not only were they at a great distance and scattered from Maine to Florida, they were full of surprises. Few in Britain had imagined that the Americans could pull themselves together and create a central government

---

30. For two newspaper reports on the celebration of the peace, see the *Gazette of the State of Georgia* (Savannah), May 1, 1783; and *Connecticut Gazette* (Hartford), May 9, 1783.

and an army—and then fight year after year. Fewer still sensed their "political enthusiasm," as Burke had styled their near-fanaticism for self-government.

The successful conduct of a war required that the objectives of the war be stated. Because the British did not fully understand the struggle they were engaged in, they failed to think through their purposes—most importantly their political purposes. Did they mean to crush their colonies militarily by destroying the institutions the Americans created to carry on the conflict? Or, did they mean to achieve a reconciliation by a blend of firmness and conciliation, limiting the effectiveness of the American army and thus allowing the loyalists to assert political control? With no clear objective laid out, strategy and military operations followed an erratic course even before the entrance of the French. The belligerence of the French transformed the problems the British faced but produced no greater clarity.

Failures in political comprehension were responsible in part for failures in command, strategy, and operations. Command remained a difficult problem for the ministry throughout the war. Britain did not send brilliant generals to America; as a tactician, especially in the heat of battle, Cornwallis may have been the best. The commanders in chief, William Howe and Henry Clinton, lacked strategic vision and daring. Their government probably could not have supplied them with these qualities but it could have given them firm direction and, had it possessed energy itself, might have infused them with drive and zeal. The government at home failed, however, to direct and to stimulate its generals.

Nor did it use the navy well. Before 1778, the sea belonged to Britain. France's decision to fight changed all that, but the ministry never really tried to assert its control of the sea. Instead, on the insistence of Sandwich, it kept much of its strength at home while the French, who showed no great imagination themselves, operated pretty much as they wanted to in the West Indies until Rodney defeated Grasse in 1782. And by then there was no saving the colonies from independence.

British command in America suffered from still other disabilities. Every commander in chief knew that reinforcements would be difficult to come by, knowledge which bred caution in leaders already convinced that battle must be risked only as a last resort. Naval commanders were more prepared to seek out the enemy. But Keppel proved unwilling to try to blockade the French in their European bases, and in America Arbuthnot was simply sluggish. There was another problem: the scarcity, age, and decrepitude of many British ships.

The military and naval commanders themselves were an uneven lot. General Thomas Gage had ability, but he was relieved early in the war, in part because he had frightened the ministry with his predictions of what lay in store for British power in America unless great efforts were made immediately to put down the rebellion.

William Howe was in many respects a solid officer, brave in battle and popular with most of his subordinates. But Howe seems not to have ever grasped the nature of the problems he faced, or if he did he may have been disabled by his sympathy for America. He lacked energy, and he sometimes failed to plan intelligently. He should have struck at Washington's demoralized army immediately after the battle of Brooklyn but chose to begin regular approaches instead. Washington took advantage of his opportunity and recovering quickly, boated his troops across the river to Manhattan. Howe's failure to anticipate Washington's daring strike across the Delaware on Christmas night 1776 is understandable. It was a devastating failure, for his complacency communicated itself to Rall and the officers in command in New Jersey. They, of course, were unprepared for Washington's attack. Howe's move to Philadelphia by sea in July 1777 may have been his worst blunder. A resourceful commander would have attempted to drive up the Hudson to meet Burgoyne, who himself was engaged in a badly conceived operation. To be sure, Howe's orders from Germain permitted great discretion in devising his operations. Whatever his reasons and his orders, his plan for 1777 ignored all but the narrowest strategic considerations.

Henry Clinton may have had greater ability than Howe, but his temperament, compounded of fear and suspicion of others, usually restrained whatever disposition he may have had to act. Clinton's judgment also played a part in holding him in place. He overestimated his difficulties and then did not really try to overcome them. He allowed his one great victory—the capture of Charleston in 1780—to be squandered. Cornwallis of course must bear his share of this failure, but Clinton after all gave Cornwallis command and then returned to New York. His departure ended his last burst of activity in the war and freed Cornwallis to run his own operations.

The two had regarded one another uneasily from the moment Clinton assumed command in America. Until May 1780, Cornwallis was quite prepared to give his chief loyal service, a willingness that Clinton could never quite bring himself to believe. As time passed he saw Cornwallis more and more as his rival, the natural choice of Germain and the ministry to replace him. Cornwallis's ambitions seem to have grown with his chief's suspicions. In the campaign at Charleston the two men found ways of avoiding one another, and afterwards, with Clinton in New York, neither could make the other understand what he was doing.

Clinton had even less success in dealing with Arbuthnot, the naval commander. Clinton despised Arbuthnot, and Arbuthnot did not care much for Clinton. Both men had weaknesses; unfortunately for British arms in America the weakness in one fed the weakness in the other.

Cordial personal relations among British commanders would not have won the war for them. But they might have permitted these officers to deal more effectively with problems which seemed intractable without the cooperation of the two branches of the armed forces. The possibility of coordinated efforts might also have released energies and perhaps even stimulated inventive thinking. As matters turned out, the British fought their war in conventional grooves and in an atmosphere soured by jealousy and crabbed spirits.

The morale of commanders had not been good even when the war began. Most did not like what they had to do—suppress the military forces of a people for whom they felt affection. Not that they approved of rebellion; many felt horror and rage at it. Still, the fact remained that they had to kill Americans, who, though not exactly Englishmen, were certainly not the usual sort of enemy. For officers who felt this way, perhaps the Howes among them, the whole affair from 1775 on was a dreadful business.

Unlike the British, the Americans decided on their objective in the war—the winning of independence—and shaped their actions accordingly. Just as the British irresolution affected their planning and conduct of operations, so also did the American certainty shape theirs. American strategy after Lexington emerged slowly; yet its aim seemed almost inevitable. It was to maintain the army, to seek foreign aid and recognition, both in the belief that armed opposition that refused to be subdued would eventually persuade the British government to yield. This strategy could not have been sustained had the larger purpose of the Revolution not been already stated and widely accepted. For this purpose constantly ran up against their localism, their provincial suspicions, and their unbridled individualism.

The defeats that the army absorbed and the years of sacrifice took their toll of American morale nonetheless. Civilians showed their weariness in various ways—by profiteering, refusing to honor requisitions of food and money, and avoiding military and governmental service. The army seemed about to disintegrate on several occasions. But the virtually

constant desertions and the mutinies of several regiments in 1780 and
1781 did not arise from political unease or from a divergent conception
of the cause. Rather, breakdowns in discipline occurred from concrete
grievances—lack of pay, hunger, near nakedness, and uncertainty over
the length of enlistments.[31]

The type of war the Americans fought, with its overriding political
objective and its defensive strategy, called for a particular sort of commander. In a war of defense, patience was necessary, and so was prudence
in using the army. But caution and the ability to wait were not enough.
Both civilians and soldiers needed the action which sustains hope, hope
that the war would end with America free. A general with imagination
as well as judgment would see that daring might sometimes be necessary.
George Washington was such a commander. In the course of the war
he demonstrated that he had other qualities as well.

Washington's judgment improved each year, as he assimilated the
experience of the war. His confidence in himself also grew as he learned.
When the war began he was full of concern that he would fail because
his abilities were not of the first order. This belief persisted even though
he also felt that he had been called by Providence to lead the American
army in the Revolution. By the end of 1776 with a year and a half of
the war under his belt, and with the success at Trenton and Princeton,
he was a much more confident commander. He was not arrogant, and
he continued to consult his general officers before he made important
decisions, but he no longer took advice against his better judgment, as
he had, for example, in the autumn of 1776 on the Hudson.

Washington came to his post with a feeling for the technical side
of his command. He seems always to have known about logistics, and
he seems also to have understood immediately the complexity of actually
moving an army from one place to another. In fact, whatever the impression his papers convey, his skills at these tasks probably improved just
as his staff's did. He was superb in taking the army out of danger at

---

31. The Massachusetts line mutinied on Jan. 1, 1780; in all, about 100 soldiers began
to march from camp at West Point, heading home. They were quickly brought
back, and a few were punished. In January 1781 Pennsylvania regulars at Morristown,
New Jersey, mutinied; New Jersey Continentals at Pompton, New Jersey, rose a
few days later. The Pennsylvania mutiny was especially serious and probably involved
1000 troops. Both mutinies were rapidly put down. For full accounts, see Carl
Van Doren, *Mutiny in January: The Story of a Crisis in the Continental Army
. . .* (New York, 1943). There is a short, revealing report on the Pennsylvania
mutiny in the *Pennsylvania Gazette* (Phila.), Jan. 24, 1781.

Brooklyn in 1776; his move to Trenton further demonstrated efficiency as well as his daring. And the march to Yorktown with its disguised beginnings and its transport of large numbers of men, artillery, and supplies was simply a superb achievement.

Washington also displayed wisdom in choosing men to assist him. Unfortunately the choice of subordinates did not always fall to him. Congress selected the senior officers and sometimes chose unwisely. Washington was able to make his wishes known, however, especially after the first year or two of the war. Nathanael Greene, for example, replaced Gates in the South on Washington's suggestion to Congress. Washington's "family," as the eighteenth-century army staff was known, included several brilliant young officers; and virtually every member of this group possessed fine abilities.

Successful commanders usually have a sense of strategy. Washington recognized the problems of fighting a powerful enemy with a weak and poorly trained army. He did not like the defensive war he had to fight, but he pursued it with great skill. His tactical abilities, those involved in particular in planning for a battle, were less sure. His most common mistake was to make plans beyond the capacities of his army. This tendency cost him dearly at Germantown. At Kip's Bay and at Brandywine he was out-maneuvered. His major tactical skill came from an ability to think clearly under fire. He did not flinch when disaster seemed about to overtake his army, as for example, at Monmouth Court House. Nor did he hesitate to seize his opportunities, again one thinks of Trenton and in a different sense—because larger—of Yorktown later.

As important as these talents were, Washington's temperament and his character were even more important. His fidelity to the Revolution impressed everyone who knew him, and somehow conveyed itself to the American people. Washington did not seek popularity and did not become popular in an ordinary sense. Yet he inspired others, not perhaps so much through his actions, dramatic and stunning as they sometimes were, but through his determination, his refusal to give up, and his devotion to the cause of republican liberty.

That cause inspired the deepest American resistance. The unspoken question in America during the Revolution was "What holds us together as a people?" Before 1760 some sense of commonality with Britain existed, created perhaps from language, blood, kin, trade, liberty, and constitutionalism. Over the years before the Revolution an American experience had loosened the ties. Should Britain do anything that suggested that interests were not mutual, that values were not shared, that commonality had been compromised or did not exist, then resistance to acts impairing liberty was inevitable.

English ministries and Parliament brought on a confrontation. In the war that followed, Americans recognized the ties among themselves. The most important was what they came to call the glorious cause— the defense of republican freedom. This cause and the way it was understood—as a providential struggle of good against evil—expressed the values of American culture and armed Americans for war. The language of this culture, imbued with traditional religious meanings, made the conflict much simpler and much more clear-cut than it actually was. But perhaps simplicity of understanding was an advantage to a people who fought against enormous odds in a conflict that had few precedents in history.

There is no need to take a romantic view of these people. They often faltered, and they sometimes could not match the resoluteness of Washington, but finally they sustained him as he led them. They might have broken had their army surrendered, but they could not have been held down by an eighteenth-century army. Not only were they too many and spread over a large country, in the crisis that began in 1764 they had come to know themselves. And in the war they learned that though they might be defeated, they could not be subdued.

23

The Constitutional Movement

Caesar rode into Annapolis on December 19, 1783. At least some hoped—and others feared—that he was Caesar. He turned out to be George Washington, and as much as he may have admired Caesar he admired the republic more. He had come to Annapolis, where Congress sat, to surrender the commission he had accepted eight years before.

Washington might simply have written a letter of resignation and enclosed his commission. The occasion offered too much of the dramatic and the symbolic to be passed by with such a flat performance, however, and Washington recognized the dramatic and symbolic importance of his resignation as commander in chief. The republic after all was barely on its way; its health was not yet robust; and it was surrounded by atmospheres heavy with monarchy and militarism. Hence he must seize the opportunity to reaffirm the uniqueness of a nation in which a congress, a representative body, held a weightier authority than the military.

Earlier in the year, in March, at Newburgh, New York, a small number of officers, spurred on by a handful of representatives in Congress, had seemed about ready to attempt a coup. These officers, like most in the army, felt outraged that their pay was months in arrears and that Congress opposed pensions for them. In and out of Congress a small, shadowy group resolved to tap this discontent in order to force through an accretion to the powers of Congress. Just how far each group was prepared to go is not clear—and probably was not clear at the time to either one. The officers seem not to have realized that they were being used, and the group in Philadelphia, where Congress then met, may not have known how dangerous the game was. Those in Philadelphia counted Robert Morris and Alexander Hamilton in their number; those at Newburgh had the sympathy, but probably not the support, of Horatio Gates.[1]

The army officers wanted money more than power. Washington knew of their need and had long urged that Congress come to their aid. He knew nothing of the beginnings of the plot in Philadelphia to use the army to threaten military action unless the states granted Congress the authority to tax. When he learned of what was going on, he waited until just the right moment and then confronted the officers in such a way as to bring home to them the enormity of what they seemed prepared to do. That moment occurred in a meeting at Newburgh at which Washington appeared before the officers and made clear his opposition to any military action against civilian authority. In a speech which suggested that the Revolution itself was at stake, Washington urged the officers "to rely on the plighted faith of your Country, and place a full confidence in the purity of the intentions of Congress. . . . And let me conjure you, in the name of our common Country, as you value your own sacred honor, as you respect the rights of humanity, and as you regard the Military and National character of America, to express your utmost horror and detestation of the Man who wishes, under any specious pretences, to overturn the liberties of our Country, and who wickedly attempts to open the flood Gates of Civil discord, and deluge our rising Empire in blood."[2]

This appeal and the example of their commander's own selflessness restrained the hotheads in the army at Newburgh. Shortly afterwards news of peace arrived. With the end of the war the worst of the threat against civil government disappeared, but Washington and others, especially those in Congress, remained uneasy. That anxiety no doubt contributed to the scene played at Annapolis in December.[3]

And a telling scene it was. After careful preparations ensuring that all knew their parts, General Washington appeared before Congress and galleries crowded with Annapolis gentry at noon, Tuesday, December

1. Much surrounding the events at Newburgh is shrouded in mystery. One of the best studies of the "conspiracy" is Richard H. Kohn, "The Inside History of the Newburgh Conspiracy: America and the Coup d'Etat," *WMQ*, 3d Ser., 27 (1970), 187–220, though Kohn probably exaggerates Horatio Gates's part in the affair. On Gates, see Paul David Nelson, "Horatio Gates at Newburgh, 1783: A Misunderstood Role," *ibid.*, 29 (1972), 143–51, with Richard H. Kohn's reply, *ibid.*, 151–58.

2. *GW Writings*, XXVI, 226–27.

3. Freeman, *GW*, V, 428–37; *TJ Papers*, VI, 402–14.

23. The secretary announced him and then seated him opposite the president. After the crowd quieted, President Mifflin addressed Washington in the following words, "Congress sir are prepared to receive your communications." Washington rose, bowed to Congress, who uncovered but did not bow. He then read his speech in a manner that, according to contemporary observers, brought tears to many eyes. Washington himself felt deep emotion—his hand holding the speech trembled throughout, and when he spoke of his aides, those dear members of his military "family," he gripped the paper with both hands. His deepest feeling, however, was reserved for an even finer moment—when, commending "the Interests of our dearest Country to the protection of Almighty God, and those who have the superintendence of them, to his holy keeping," he faltered and was almost unable to continue. He managed the final sentence with greater strength: "Having now finished the work assigned me, I retire from the great theatre of Action; and bidding an Affectionate farewell to this August body under whose orders I have so long acted, I here offer my Commission, and take my leave of all the employments of public life."[4]

Mifflin's reply on behalf of Congress was composed by a delegate with a skillful pen and full awareness of the symbolic significance of this occasion. That delegate, Thomas Jefferson, put the following sentence in Mifflin's mouth, which underscored the importance of all that had taken place between the General and the Congress over the preceding eight years—"You have," Mifflin told Washington, "conducted the great military contest with wisdom and fortitude invariably regarding the rights of the civil power through all disasters and changes."[5]

II

That the civil power survived the Revolution as well as it did must in part be credited to Washington. But Congress itself could also claim much credit. It was a jealous body reflecting the suspicions most Americans had long felt of the military. Some of these feelings must have helped shape Congressional attitudes toward demobilization of the army, attitudes that to veterans seemed little more than mean-spirited niggardliness.

The problem for the army and the Congress was not unusual. The army had not been paid, and many of its men faced civilian life with

4. *GW Writings*, XXVII, 284.
5. *TJ Papers*, VI, 413. There is a fine account of Washington's meeting with Congress in Freeman, *GW*, V, 472–77.

no resources. Officers felt especially badly treated. Three years earlier the Congress had promised half-pay for life to officers who served for the duration. Since then, Congress had slowly retreated from what was widely regarded as both a foolish extravagance and an importation of a European practice inappropriate to a republic. Late in the month of the Newburgh conspiracy, Congress, still frightened, approved commutation of half-pay for life to full pay for five years. And over the next three months most of the army, unpaid as yet, was either furloughed or discharged. A bad moment in the life of the young republic had passed.[6]

Equally dangerous times lay just ahead. The national debt and the lack of a revenue promised the worst. The size of the debt remained a mystery. One sort of public obligation could be calculated fairly accurately, even though it had been incurred during the war in various currencies, virtually all of which had depreciated. This debt, called "liquidated," consisted of army pay and the principal of and interest on, loan office certificates and foreign loans. The size of the second sort, "unliquidated" debt, owed for money, goods, or services supplied by citizens or the states could not be accurately determined. The evidence for this debt was not always clear—besides vouchers, claims based on lost or destroyed vouchers and even more shaky testimony were made.[7]

What the national government needed to meet its annual expenses was not known either. Early in 1783, the best estimates had it that meeting the calls of soldiers' pay, interest on loans, and day-to-day operating expenses amounted to around three million dollars. Raising this sum through requisitions once news of peace arrived was impossible. The nationalists, Robert Morris, Alexander Hamilton, and James Madison among them, argued that another attempt to secure a 5 percent impost on imports was worth a try. (The first had been made in 1781—and failed.) But with peace, suspicions of central authority rose again, and the measure Congress passed in April carried severe restrictions on the use of the revenue—provided of course that the states approved it. The impost of 1783 was to be in effect for twenty-five years; the revenues could be applied only toward the payment of the debt; and the states would appoint the collectors.

For the next two years the Congress lived in the expectation that the states would approve the impost. Nine did approve fairly soon after

6. Burnett, *Continental Congress*, 568.
7. *JM Papers*, VI, xvi-xvii.

its passage, and by 1786 only New York and Pennsylvania had not. In that year New York approved but with such paralyzing conditions that the Congress declined its terms. Pennsylvania had also imposed rigid terms and in effect was relieved of compliance by New York's action. By 1787 there clearly was no hope that the impost would win approval by all the states.[8]

The failure of the impost disappointed the nationalists in the Congress. The failure of the Congress to achieve American sovereignty in the West disappointed almost all its members—and most Americans. By far the greatest expanse of this territory conceded to the United States by the treaty of peace lay more or less under American control. The British army, however, continued to hold strategically located posts along the Lakes from which the fur trade could be managed. Though unstated, the British claim to trade and land seemed clear.

South of the Ohio River, the territory east of the Mississippi also threatened to be lifted from American control. Here Spain, which had not recognized the cession of this land to the United States in the treaty of peace, supplied the threat. The year following peace saw the Spanish close the lower Mississippi to American navigation. The Spanish expected, or at least hoped, that the settlers in what later became Kentucky and Tennessee would give up their American citizenship in favor of a Spanish connection which would allow them to do business through New Orleans. Secession from the United States was a possibility—these settlers felt neglected by Congress and the East.[9]

When news of the disaffection in the Southwest filtered back to Congress, it ordered John Jay, who had succeeded Robert Livingston as secretary of foreign affairs, to negotiate a treaty with Don Diego de Gardoqui of Spain, who had been sent to convince Congress to ratify the closing of the Mississippi. Jay's instructions were composed by a committee headed by James Monroe of Virginia. Monroe felt no sympathy for the Spanish case, and he was determined to placate the Southwest. The instructions he and his committee gave Jay took the commonsense line that the treaty of peace with Britain justly represented American interest. Hence Jay was "to stipulate the right of the United States to their territorial bounds, and the free navigation of the Mississippi, from the source to the ocean, as established in their Treaties with Great

8. E. James Ferguson, *The Power of the Purse: A History of American Public Finance, 1776–1790* (Chapel Hill, N.C., 1961), 239–40.

9. Samuel Flagg Bemis, *Pinckney's Treaty: America's Advantage from Europe's Distress, 1783–1800* (rev. ed., New Haven, Conn., 1960), 44.

Britain." Gardoqui came with firm instructions to stipulate Spain's claim to the territory east of the Mississippi and to the exclusive right to navigation of the river. The two diplomats had not discussed the conflicting claims very long when Jay decided that there was little chance of altering the Spanish position. Gardoqui insisted that the United States concede the validity of the Spanish claims—in return Spain would agree to a commercial treaty.

Although the Spanish really offered very little in the commercial treaty, Jay proved willing to talk about it before turning to the details of navigation of the Mississippi. And before the negotiations were old, he had virtually agreed to a commercial treaty on Gardoqui's terms. Jay, like many easterners, feared western growth, which he thought would come at the expense of the old established regions of the seaboard. He also argued in his explanations to Congress that, in event of a showdown with Spain, France would most likely oppose the United States.

Watching Jay in action, Monroe soon came to suspect that he was not following instructions. Jay confirmed these suspicions when he asked for a new commission which would permit him to agree to a treaty giving up the American rights of navigation to the Mississippi for at least twenty-five years. Monroe fought off this request in Congress but not without antagonizing colleagues from New England and New York who sought to protect eastern interests. Rufus King of Massachusetts may have felt especially bitter over Monroe's opposition. For Monroe accused him of favoring the treaty—and favoring the exclusion of the West from the Mississippi—because of his marriage to "a woman of fortune in New York so that if he secures a market for fish and turns the commerce of the western country down this river [the Mohawk and Hudson] he obtains his object." Whatever the sources of King's convictions, he was eager to aid the fisheries, for as he wrote Elbridge Gerry in August 1786, "our fish, and every article we sell in Spain, is sold upon the footing of the most favored nation in that country— this is favor, and not right. Should we embarrass ourselves in the attempts of imprudent men to navigate the Mississippi below the northern boundary of Florida, we can expect no favors from the Spanish government. England is our Rival in the Fisheries, France does not wish us prosperity in this branch of commerce. If we embroil ourselves with Spain, what have we to expect on this subject?"[10]

Both King and Monroe represented sectional interests and the division

10. For the quotations in this paragraph, and the instructions to Jay, see *JM Papers*, IX, 71n, fn. 5; 70; 73n, fn. 13.

held steady in the debates in Congress over Jay's instructions. The five southern states, though facing seven in the North (Delaware had no delegation in the Congress at this time), had one advantage: the Articles of Confederation required that treaties must have the approval of nine states. Thus though the northern states might vote to revoke Jay's original instructions—and did, thereby permitting him to agree to closing the Mississippi—they had no way of securing the ratification of an agreement with Spain. Before King and others came to the realization that the southern states would block a treaty which sacrificed the West to the commercial interests of the East, they had bred deep suspicions in Monroe and others from the southern states. Monroe smelled plots everywhere and soon was convinced that one was afoot which would carry the northern opposition into a separate confederacy.[11]

The mistrust of the two groups festered long after Jay dropped the negotiations with Gardoqui. Jay had been shocked by the vehemence of the southern delegates. When the question of voting and approval of treaties was raised in Congress, he saw that the game was up. There would be no treaty which recognized Spain's action in shutting Americans off from the Mississippi. And there was anger and suspicion that would make further cooperation in Congress increasingly difficult.

Congress did enjoy one major success after the conclusion of peace. It arranged for the settlement and government of the West. The arrangements entailed the reconciliation of a number of diverse—and competing—interests. That these interests could be satisfied owed much to Congress's skill in manipulating what they all had in common—a powerful acquisitive impulse—and to the fact that Congress began its work of disposing of the West before the atmosphere was fouled by Jay-Gardoqui.

The national domain had come into being on March 1, 1784, when Congress accepted Virginia's cession of the territory northwest of the Ohio claimed by the state under its seventeenth-century charters. Virginia had first ceded its claim to the Northwest in 1781, but this cession did not arouse gratitude throughout the United States because it required that all purchases from the Indians and all royal grants within the territory should be "declared absolutely void and of no Effect." At least three land companies located in other states had already made such claims,

---

11. For the vote on Jay's instructions and much else in the negotiations, I have drawn on Bemis, *Pinckney's Treaty*, esp. chap. 3.

and Virginia aimed to deny satisfaction of their large appetites. These companies—the Illinois-Wabash, Vandalia, and the Indiana—responded by urging Congress to reject the cession.[12]

There were others who wanted a share of the Old Northwest. Soldiers—later veterans—suggested strongly that lands be set aside for them as a reward for their service. One group from other states urged that a colony be created, with soldiers serving as colonists. For a time, George Washington, who wanted to see his troops reimbursed for their sacrifices, supported this proposal.

Immediately after accepting Virginia's cession, Congress acted to provide government in the territory. The development of congressional plans involved a complicated story whose leading character was Thomas Jefferson. The essential fact of this story was that Jefferson proposed an ordinance providing that new states, like the old republic in form, would be established out of the West. After a period of territorial government they would enter the Union with a status equal to the original thirteen. Jefferson called the terms of the ordinance "fundamental constitutions between the thirteen original states, and those now newly described," words which made their way into the statute Congress finally approved.[13]

Jefferson also served on the committee of Congress which was charged with the responsibility of devising a means of disposing of the new lands. He had hoped that western lands might be given to settlers—not sold to them—and thereby provide new recruits to the class of sturdy freeholders he admired so deeply. Jefferson left for Europe on a diplomatic mission before the committee finished its work, but even had he not, it is unlikely that he could have persuaded Congress to fulfill his noble hope. The national debt stood in the way of giving anything away. In an early report the committee declared that returns from land sales "shall be applied to the sinking such part of the principal of the national debt as Congress shall from time to time direct, and to no other purpose whatsoever."[14]

In May 1785 Congress adopted the ordinance which it hoped would regulate the sale of western lands. The Ordinance of 1785 provided

12. *TJ Papers*, VI, 571.

13. This discussion of policy toward western lands is based on the documents and editorial notes in *TJ Papers*, VI, 571–617; and Merrill Jensen, "The Creation of the National Domain, 1781–1784," *Mississippi Valley Historical Review*, 26 (1939), 323–42.

14. *TJ Papers*, VII, 145.

that the land was to be divided into townships six miles square. Each township would consist of thirty-six lots, or sections, one mile square. After the territory was surveyed it would be sold at public auction in lots for not less than one dollar an acre in specie or the various certificates issued by the United States. The Ordinance set aside lands for bounties which had been promised to soldiers during the war, and it reserved lot sixteen in each township for public schools. The United States was to receive four sections in each township and one-third of any gold, silver, and copper which were discovered.[15]

Although surveys began almost at once, the Ordinance did not work as it was intended to. It ran afoul almost immediately of speculators, who urged its suspension. Leading the speculators was a new Ohio Company founded in Boston, and leading the Company was the Reverend Manasseh Cutler, formerly a chaplain in the army. Cutler had the foresight to recommend that the president of the Congress, Arthur St. Clair, be made head of the Company. That touch and much skillful lobbying persuaded Congress to allow the Ohio Company to purchase a large tract carved from still unsurveyed lands. Terms of payment were especially encouraging to the Company and included the use of certificates of the United States at their face value, certificates selling in the market for ten cents on the dollar.[16]

The Ohio Company operated on a large scale. Squatters were less ambitious, but in the aggregate just as destructive of plans of orderly settlement. These men and women brought with them a craving for land and a hatred of the Indians to whom it belonged. Small-scale warfare occurred when the two peoples met, and sometimes soldiers fought both groups.

In this rough way the Old Northwest began to fill up. The Ordinance of 1784, which had provided self-government in the territorial stage, was one of the casualties. Dismayed by the barbarism in the West and convinced by the speculators that land titles were endangered by the incessant upheavals, Congress repealed the ordinance, replacing it with a new one in 1787, the so-called Northwest Ordinance. This ordinance lifted control from the hands of settlers and placed it with Congress. Officials slated to be elected locally were now to be appointed. Full self-government would not be obtained until a territory became a state.[17]

15. Merrill Jensen, *The New Nation: A History of the United States During the Confederation, 1781–1789* (New York, 1950), 354–55.

16. *Ibid.*, 355–56.

17. *Ibid.*, 358–59.

III

The high distinction Congress attained in formulating the land policies went unrecognized at the time. Rather, by 1786 a feeling of crisis pervaded Congress and much of the nation. At the center of this feeling lay a disenchantment with public finance and commercial policy which in turn bred doubts about the adequacy of republican institutions of government. Most doubts, of course, hung around Congress itself, though strong nationalists also entertained fears of the adequacy of local institutions—in particular, state legislatures and the public policies created by them. In this mood, some Americans came to fear that the American Revolution and its natural child, the republic, might soon be destroyed.

The concern about public finance extended to the economy, and for much of the period before 1789, complaints echoed in the newspapers, Congress, and in private about the decline of trade. As is so often the case, popular perceptions did not recognize the realities. And what were the economic realities? They cannot be charted precisely—given the scarcity of quantifiable data—but they indicate that, despite the damages of war and the exclusion of American ships from the British West Indies, recovery was rapid, though uneven. The middle Atlantic states may have enjoyed the quickest resurgence of business. These states—Pennsylvania, Delaware, New Jersey, and New York—had long produced agricultural products for the market, especially the West Indies. They now began processing their farm commodities for local markets, for example, cereals into beer, porter, and whiskey to slake republican thirsts. They also began to manufacture goods for themselves and the South.[18]

To the north, New England made slower going of recovery. The cod, whale oil, and the ships which Yankees had carried or sailed for English markets, especially in the West Indies, were also adversely affected by the war. And, of course, gaining entrance into British West Indies ports could not be done. By 1786 the cod fishers had brought their sales to about 80 percent of prewar quantities. They did so by pushing their ships into the French West Indies and into Spanish and Portuguese harbors.[19]

In the southern states recovery proceeded with difficulty. The rice country lost the old British bounty when America declared independence. Indigo production fell after the war—and Carolina planters generally

18. Gordon C. Bjork, "The Weaning of the American Economy: Independence, Market Changes, and Economic Development," *Journal of Economic History*, 24 (1964), 541–60.

19. *Ibid.*, *passim*, esp. 545.

struggled. Tobacco in the Chesapeake now could be shipped directly to the European continent—and was. Less Virginia tobacco was shipped to Europe in the 1780s than in the years just before the war, but full recovery was not far off. And the effort to grow wheat, corn, and flaxseed that began a generation or more before the Revolution continued.[20]

On the whole, overseas trade regained life with remarkable ease. To be sure, the exclusion from the British West Indies inhibited commerce, but elsewhere American ships found themselves welcome. Though the British excluded the Americans from the West Indies, they dealt with them on the same basis in home ports as they did those from the colonies. American shippers paid the same duties and received the same drawbacks as colonials, for example.

In this climate, prices obtained for American commodities remained high in the 1780s with tobacco and wheat doing especially well. Those American states exporting these products profited, of course, but New England and South Carolina which had to import grains found paying for it at world levels to be difficult.

Prices fell in most of the country, responding to the unfavorable balance of trade and to European levels. Public debt remained high as both Congress and the states struggled to deal with it. The debt and the flow of specie outside the country to meet the trade deficit helped to depress trade and to slow recovery.[21]

To an objective observer, economic recovery in the 1780s might have seemed promising, even impressive. At the time, however, the economic condition of the nation looked bleak, with prices depressed, public and private indebtedness heavy, and trade regulation chaotic. Americans understandably judged their prospects by short-term conditions, the circumstances that could be felt at the moment. Long-term comparisons were not available to them—and had they been, probably would not have lessened the uneasiness they felt.

Whether all Americans felt unease about the economy in the 1780s cannot be known. Nor is there any way to determine just how widespread the mood was that something had gone wrong with the Revolution. That there was anxiety about public policy is clear, and the expression of this mood did not confine itself to Congress or state legislatures. Newspapers throughout the United States published letters and essays

20. *Ibid., passim.*
21. *Ibid.,* 559; James F. Shepherd and Gary M. Walton, "Economic Change After the American Revolution: Pre- and Post-War Comparisons of Maritime Shipping and Trade," *Explorations in Economic History,* 13 (1976), 397–422.

virtually every week about grim conditions and the dangers they brought to virtue and republicanism. Ministers took up these themes on the Sabbath, and public-spirited citizen-writers produced pamphlets and poems on the American condition. And private correspondence suggests that the condition of the republic preoccupied many men who did not resort to the public prints to declare their opinions about it.[22]

This anxiety, which was perhaps fairly widespread, focused on Congress. Indeed dissatisfaction with Congress and its works—or lack of works—shaped a movement for constitutional reform in the 1780s.

The decline of Congress, a development which saw it gradually lose authority and public confidence, actually began well before the end of the war. As soon as the war started Congress found itself searching for ways to raise an army and keep it in being. Within a year the problem took on a form familiar to virtually all governments engaged in war—how money was to be raised. Congress of course resorted to currency finance, a technique much practiced in the long period before the Revolution. Before the Revolution, governments had printed money as they needed it and used it to meet their expenses. They had not proceeded without plan, however, or heedless of the obvious consequences of unrestrained printing presses. Rather they had retained their people's support by assigning taxes for the redemption of the currency at the time it was issued. This relationship of paper money and taxes specified for its redemption gave everyone confidence in the money, and it was ordinarily made legal tender not only for the payment of taxes but also for private debts. If the people of a colony lost confidence that their government would, or could, collect the taxes, the currency depreciated.[23]

The people of America lost confidence in Congress's ability to collect taxes fairly early in the Revolution. Congress issued six million dollars in paper money in 1775, a total which rose to $25 million by the end of the next year. Altogether, Congress put out around $200 million during the Revolution. Since it lacked the power to tax, it had to depend upon the states to retire the money. The states did collect the currency as payment for taxes, but they did not take it out of circulation. They needed it too badly for that, and consequently as fast as they collected it they spent it themselves. To make matters worse, they issued their own currency.[24]

22. Rakove, *Beginnings of National Politics*, 354–55, points out, however, that Congress was rarely discussed in the newspapers.

23. Ferguson, *Power of the Purse*, 3–24.

24. *Ibid.*, 29–31.

Not surprisingly, depreciation began fairly early in 1776—in part because so much money had been emitted. Intangibles—most importantly the public's faith that the war could be won—also affected the value of money. When, in November, Howe seemed about ready to push Washington out of Pennsylvania as well as New Jersey, the public found it difficult to believe that any American government would be able to redeem the debt. Nor did Congress encourage belief in itself when in 1778 it declared some $41 million it had emitted counterfeit—and offered holders the opportunity to exchange notes of this issue by purchasing loan certificates. This stratagem was really a means of compelling people to lend money to their government. People who held the "counterfeit" notes evaded this requirement, however, at considerable cost to their regard for Congress.[25]

Congress struck the worst blow against itself in late 1779 when it attempted to act responsibly. In September of that year it decided that when the total currency in circulation reached $200 million, it would stop all further emissions. At the time of this decision about $160 million had been issued; with the need for money almost desperate, the cutoff of emissions was only a few weeks in the future.[26]

The exhaustion of Congress evoked the demands on the states that followed—for specific supplies late in 1779 and larger requisitions of commodities early in the next year. Soon after, Congress added to state burdens the pay of Continental soldiers, with each state expected to pay its troops in regular service. The problem of the money supply remained, and Congress turned to a brutal resort to solve it. In March 1780 it virtually repudiated all its currency in circulation by revaluing it at one-fortieth of its face value. It tied repudiation to an emission of new currency and placed on the states the actual work of collecting the old and issuing the new. Public finance—and considerable power—had thus shifted to the states.[27]

As harsh as some of these measures appeared, they had a chance of working, and they might have forestalled much of further inflation and the decline in public morale. They did not work as they were intended to work, however. Not all these measures were compatible with one another, and in fact the way Congress and the states obtained the supplies to feed and otherwise sustain the army ruined the plan to retire the $200 million in old currency. From 1779 on both the state officials

25. *Ibid.*, 31–45.
26. *Ibid.*, 46–47.
27. *Ibid.*, 48–56.

and Continental commissaries impressed food and clothing for the army. When they took supplies they gave certificates promising payment. Since the certificates bore no interest their holders looked for ways of ridding themselves of them in the states where they were received in payment of taxes. Meanwhile the old currency remained in circulation and was only slowly withdrawn. By June 1781 a little more than $30 million had been collected by the states.[28]

Congress lost power to the states in still another fashion: through servicing its debts. When Rhode Island's rejection of the impost in 1781 destroyed hope that national obligations might be met through a uniform duty on imports, Congress resolved to try again. It did two years later with a more complicated proposal that it collect the impost and certain other duties as well. Several states approved at once but the necessary unanimity eluded Congress once more. While it waited, Congress urged the states to come forward with requisitions. Some did, though rarely with all that was requested and never with the amount in specie that Congress rashly thought it might collect.

Requisitions failed, and between October 1782 and September 1785 Congress made no new requests but waited—usually vainly—for the states to honor old ones. After 1785 it stopped paying interest on its debt to France, and in 1787 it proved unable to make all the payments on the principal. American creditors could not be paid by Congress either; nor could they be put off. They clamored for the interest owed them, and sometimes for the principal. They did not content themselves with appeals to Congress but pleaded their case to the state legislatures. As early as 1782 the states had responded with payments of interest and principal. Pennsylvania set the pattern in that year by issuing certificates of interest which were receivable for taxes. Others soon followed. And all took action to reduce their own debts. Virginia, for example, applied over $3 million collected between 1782 and 1785 toward its debt.[29]

If any possibility existed that Congress might reclaim control of public finance, it lay with the impost. By 1786 nine states had approved; several with severe conditions. Unwilling to sit on its hands while the states played with the impost and assumed real power in America, Congress tried a fresh expedient. In 1784 it had authorized the issue of indents, as certificates of interest were called, which states might use to pay

28. *Ibid.*, 65–66.
29. *Ibid.*, 220–45, esp. 234–38.

congressional requisitions. It sent loan officers into the states with instructions to provide local officials with indents. These officials were to pay interest on the debt with the indents, observing a careful schedule of payments of interest. The first expenditure was to meet past interest due through 1782. Under this plan Congress authorized the states to accept the indents for taxes and to return them with a certain percentage of specie in response to requests for requisitions.[30]

This thoughtful scheme collapsed almost immediately. The loan officers simply ignored their instructions and issued the indents not according to the congressional schedule but as they chose. The states proved as independent as the federal officials and followed their own policies of payment. They threw the schedule aside—the clamorous creditors were their citizens after all—and usually used the indents in advance for the next year's interest. They refused to receive indents, or pay them out, to any but their own citizens, and they declined to return specie as requisitions. This refusal was easy to understand and defend—hard money was scarce and states were reluctant to give up what they had when there was no assurance that Congress would return it to their citizens.[31]

Congress acknowledged its failures in public finance in 1787 when it set aside all requirements in favor of permitting the states to pay on the debt in any way they chose. Now in full control, the states chose increasingly to resort to the old colonial practice of currency finance. And when the year opened at least seven of the states were issuing paper money.

A number of men had watched uneasily the shift of control from Congress to the states. They have been called the "nationalists," a designation intended by historians to suggest that the men to whom it is applied were not only strongly committed to the increase of the central authority of the government but also that they constituted a virtual party. This party, according to several historians, looked to the replacement of the Articles of Confederation by a constitution which shifted sovereignty from the thirteen states to a national government. The leader of the group when it began to take shape in 1780, it is said, was Robert Morris, the rich Philadelphia merchant who had left Congress two years before after giving it distinguished service for three years. Morris and a small number of friends and business associates did favor a powerful national government, but they never formed anything more than a loose faction. Leadership of this group seemed almost naturally to fall to Morris, a man of great wealth and business and administrative skill. In 1781,

30. *Ibid.*, 223–29, and *passim.*
31. *Ibid.*, 226.

he added to these informal qualifications by getting himself appointed Superintendent of Finance.[32]

The post carried all the authority Congress could vest it with. The superintendent could do almost anything Congress itself might have done in managing public finances, including firing anyone in the public service who handled public money. Morris had insisted on having this sort of muscle; he was not a modest man and his demands for power caused some in Congress to hesitate before approving his appointment. When Morris had sat in Congress he had shown that he had talents besides an appetite for power. He had taken the lead in the Secret Committee of Trade, demonstrating rather impressive gifts for managing its business. He had also shown, like virtually every other merchant who undertook the public's business, that he would not shrink from using his post to turn a profit. Merchants understood the difference between private and public interests as well as anyone and knew that standards of conduct did not condone the use of office for personal gain. Yet they commonly mixed their own business with the public's, and Morris sometimes used the government's money when his own was scarce. He was not a thief nor was he dishonest; yet he sometimes misused his post in Congress. He may have felt justified by the fact that he followed common practice and that in fact holders of public office believed that they had something approaching "private rights" in their offices. In many cases standards of conduct were not high. While Morris did not raise them, neither did he confine his efforts primarily to his own interests, for he wanted to serve his country. He probably never realized that his own conduct contributed to the demoralization of a public increasingly suspicious of those who ran public finance.[33]

It was public finance that Morris expected would provide the means of constitutional reform. The Articles had denied Congress the right to tax. The states of the Confederation recognized that this power implied sovereignty, and they intended that it remain with themselves. But with the finances of Congress a shambles by 1780, many men, most delegates to Congress, accepted the argument that Congress needed the power to tax to ensure a steady revenue. Without a revenue the various sorts of notes, expressing the obligation of Congress to its creditors, would continue to depreciate. And the problem of supplying the army and keeping the Revolution going until Britain acknowledged American independence would increase in severity.

32. Merrill Jensen's *New Nation* provides the first full statement of this view.
33. Ferguson, *Power of the Purse*, 70–81, 172–74.

Thus for Morris and his friends, public finance should be made to incorporate what they took to be the central purposes of the Revolution— the protection of property and the preservation of a political order run by men like themselves. The conduct of the war had taught them much, taught them that sovereignty divided into thirteen pieces made for disorder and an ineffective nation. The disparity between the exertions of the army and the petty squabbling of the states eager to look out after their own, and little more, offended Morris. The propensity of the states to turn to the old methods of public finance frightened him. The old ways were out of step with the new, and the new—large-scale business, international finance, banking, and speculation—could flourish only if political centralization succeeded.

From 1781 until just before Morris resigned in November 1784, he worked carefully and sometimes ruthlessly for a major accretion to congressional power. The impost provided the center of all his efforts. To push it toward approval by all the states as the Articles required, he, Hamilton, and others tried to manipulate the army officers at Newburgh into a body capable of coercing Congress and the states. He failed in this measure, but he succeeded in persuading Congress to assume some of the debt which might have been parceled out to the states. His intention was to ensure that at least a part of the debts from the war remained a national obligation so that a case could be made for assigning the taxing power to Congress. Much of what Morris did succeeded as financial policy but failed as political technique. He instituted a system of bids and contracts in order to supply the army; he rationalized much of federal finance; and he established a corps of officials responsible to Congress—and himself. The end of the war robbed much of this system of its political meaning. Defeat at Yorktown would have served Morris's purposes far better than victory.[34]

With peace his disappointments piled up: the states refused his demands for specie; they corrupted his officials; and they took over the business of servicing the debt. Worst of all, though at one time or other the impost seemed on the verge of approval, in the end it failed of passage. By late 1783 Morris had played his best hand, and though he lingered in the superintendent's office until November 1, 1784, he was beaten. And his methods of attaining a strong national government had proved barren.[35]

34. *Ibid.*, 116–68.
35. *Ibid.*, 171–79.

The movement for constitutional revision did not die with Morris's resignation. Hope persisted in Congress for two years that the impost would gain the unanimous approval of the states. There were other ways of strengthening the central government in any case. Talk surfaced in these years of the possibility of holding a convention from the states which might add to congressional powers. Perhaps a favored means was to give Congress the authority to regulate commerce, especially commerce among the states. Not all delegates favored this means, and not all of course favored vesting Congress with the power to regulate trade. Jefferson and Madison both believed that Congress might legitimately claim authority to regulate commerce with foreign states under its power to make treaties. They never convinced Congress of this interpretation, and had they done so the struggles among the states amounting to a kind of war of retaliation would have continued.[36]

From the vantage of Congress, republican prospects may have looked bleaker than they actually were. Frustration and impotence often breed gloom, and Congress by 1785 was very nearly impotent, and it felt frustrated.

The vitality in America expressed itself locally, in the states, as it almost always had in the previous twenty years. In March 1785 commissioners from Maryland and Virginia met at Mount Vernon and settled long-standing differences over navigation of the Potomac River. The agreement reached at this meeting provided a model of enlightened self-interest working out a series of compromises. Thus Virginia conceded certain rights in the Chesapeake to Maryland in return for others in the Potomac.[37]

The success of this meeting convinced James Madison that a larger gathering of states in convention might seize the spirit of cooperation— where mutual interests were apparent—and place the regulation of commerce with Congress. Madison evidently also believed that the moment was right to couple such a proposal to one giving Congress the authority to tax. In any case in the following November he boldly moved in the House of Delegates, the lower house of Virginia's legislature, that Virginia's delegation to Congress "be instructed to propose in Congress a recommendation to the States in Union, to authorize that Assembly to regulate their trade, and to collect a revenue therefrom. . . ." Madison

36. Irving Brant, *James Madison: The Nationalist, 1780–1787* (Indianapolis, Ind., 1948), 376–78. The standard biography of Madison is Brant, *James Madison* (6 vols., Indianapolis, Ind., 1941–61). I have cited this work by the full title of each volume.
37. Brant, *Madison: The Nationalist,* 375–76.

may have misjudged the disposition of his colleagues for change, or he may have offered this resolution with a sense that if he were going to be forced to settle for less, say a simple power to regulate trade but not to collect a revenue from it, asking for more was tactically advisable. He got very little in fact, though in January 1786 the House agreed on a motion that merely called for a convention of states "to consider how far a uniform system in their commercial regulations may be necessary to their common interest and their permanent harmony. . . ."[38]

The invitation to a meeting went out to the states soon after, and on September 11, 1786, delegates from five states—New York, New Jersey, Pennsylvania, Delaware, and Virginia—met at Annapolis, Maryland. Maryland's legislature, theoretically the host, refused to appoint a delegation out of fear apparently that the gathering would undermine an already weak Congress. Massachusetts, New Hampshire, Rhode Island, and North Carolina sent delegates who failed to arrive in time. Several states appointed men of great distinction: Alexander Hamilton represented New York, John Dickinson appeared for Delaware, and James Madison came with Edmund Randolph from Virginia. Only the New Jersey delegation carried a commission authorizing them to consider "other important matters" besides the regulation of commerce. New Jersey had broad constitutional revision in mind, and so in fact did Madison and Hamilton. But all saw that the Convention, with only five states present, could do little. That little proved to be a suggestion to all the states that they appoint commissioners to meet in May 1787 "to take into consideration the situation of the United States, to devise such further provisions as shall appear to them necessary to render the constitution of the Federal Government adequate to the exigencies of the Union. . . ."[39]

This message reached the states almost simultaneously with news of a very different sort: there had been an armed rebellion in central and western Massachusetts. The rebellion, which has been called Shays's Rebellion after Daniel Shays, one of its leaders, was made by farmers, most of them solid, respectable men, many of them veterans who had been driven to desperation by the state's rigid financial policy. Since the early 1780s the legislature, a body under the thumb of eastern merchants and their cohorts, had funded the Massachusetts debt at close to face value, collected heavy direct taxes while abolishing legal tender currency, and resisted almost all efforts at reforming either the credit

38. *TJ Papers*, IX, 206.
39. Syrett and Cooke, eds., *Papers of Hamilton*, III, 689.

system or the tax structure. At the climax of this series of policies early in 1786, the legislature increased taxes for the payment of interest on the debt (most of which was owned in eastern Massachusetts) and resolved also to fulfill Congress's requisition. These measures had agitated the western sector for six years, and the last brought an upheaval by the debt-ridden farmers who resorted to violence to prevent the seizure of their property for the payment of debts and taxes they could not meet.[40]

Massachusetts put the rebellion down in a few months, but it had helped alter the public mood. That mood was not altogether grim, but it disposed men to favor some constitutional revision. Just how much and of what sort remained open when on February 21, 1787, Congress added its uncertain voice to the call for change by approving a resolution in favor of a convention. The convention would meet in Philadelphia in May 1787.

40. On public policy in Massachusetts in the 1780s, see Van Beck Hall, *Politics Without Parties: Massachusetts, 1780–1791* (Pittsburgh, Pa., 1972); for Shays's Rebellion, Robert J. Taylor, *Western Massachusetts in the Revolution* (Providence, R.I., 1954), 128–67.

24

The Children of the Twice-Born in the 1780s

An elite began the struggle against Britain in the 1760s, and the people followed. An elite began the movement for constitutional reform. Would the people follow again? Were the people of the 1780s different from those of the prewar and war years? Madison, Washington, and Hamilton, and the others who favored constitutional revision, did not know how to answer these questions. Nor did anyone else. One of the anomalies of the years between the making of peace and the Constitutional Convention was the uncertainty felt by such leaders about the character of the American people.

Much had changed between 1765 and 1787. Although in 1765 the Americans were not one people, they knew they had much in common. By 1787 they recognized what it was. They were a people who valued liberty and representative government. And well before 1787 they had formed a union among themselves. To be sure the central institution of that union lacked strength, but at least the union had survived. Moreover the people had a history, a short but glorious history of struggle and triumph in war. This history set apart the people of the 1780s from those of twenty years earlier. In a sense, of course, it had called them into being as a people.

The Americans in the 1780s still believed that they had been selected by Providence to do great deeds. They had been chosen, and their victory in the war and the achievement of independence demonstrated the worth of their calling. Undoubtedly some held this conviction more deeply than others did. It seems always to have existed in New England, especially among Congregationalists. It was a powerful feeling in Virginia even among planters who listened to bland sermons in the established church. Elsewhere it flourished among evangelicals and enthusiasts, among many Presbyterians and Baptists, for example. But undoubtedly there were those who did not sense the workings of Providence in America. Yet in the 1780s many of the indifferent felt the stirrings of national pride.

Nationalism, however, did not completely embody all the old values of Americans. In fact the Americans' concern for liberty retained an existence apart from their awareness of themselves as a people. It was much older and it was tied to local institutions—to the states as much as to the union.

In the 1760s and 1770s the Americans found that they could agree more easily on principles than they could on how to organize for resistance and war.[1] But in 1774 they created the Continental Congress and sent delegates to it and to its successor. This body provided the center from which the war could be directed, even though its powers remained undefined until the Articles of Confederation were ratified by the states in March 1781.

Although the states created the Congress, the Congress also created itself by taking the responsibility for leading the states. It established an army; it sent envoys abroad and entered into an alliance with the French; it issued currency and it borrowed money; it requisitioned money from the states. It did all these things and many more without any clear authority except necessity and the tacit approval of the states.

There was much that Congress could not do, however, including collecting taxes and regulating commerce. Nor apparently could it act directly on individuals and institutions within the states. There were delegates to the Congress who claimed coercive powers for it, powers they said which might be used on the citizens of a state. Congress itself made tentative efforts to flex its muscles in the states. In 1776, for example, it advised the states to try to recruit men for the army by holding out the lure of bounties to be paid in grants of land. Maryland refused, and Congress responded by insisting that no state could escape congressional instructions simply by refusing to obey them. This statement brought another protest from Maryland, and Congress backed down. About the same time, Congress considered taking upon itself the responsibility of stamping out loyalist activity in Delaware even though the state had not requested such action. Congress made other

1. Rakove, *Beginnings of National Politics*, 3–62.

motions toward taking charge in the first two years of the war although none produced a shift in power that would have made it dominant over the states. Congressional relations with the states thus remained a gray area early in the war.[2]

Gray began to give way to light when the states produced constitutions for themselves. These constitutions typically set up a frame of government and defined the powers the state governments were to exercise. They also staked out protections for citizens in bills of rights. Such actions left Congress on unstable and shrinking ground. It had to manage the war and pull together all efforts without the authority that a genuine government enjoyed. Its powers, not exactly clear at any time, threatened to become even murkier as the states acted.

Even before the action of the states, Congress had felt the need to clarify and thereby secure its authority. Two of its members, Benjamin Franklin and Silas Deane, each acting without a commission from Congress, wrote drafts of constitutions in 1775. The next year, as Congress debated about independence, a committee charged to provide a plan of confederation produced a draft which after revision became the Articles of Confederation.

The Congress did not adopt this committee's effort until November 1777. And what it approved differed in important ways from the committee's production of 1776. The committee in turn had revised a draft written by John Dickinson.

To solve the problems of confederation, Dickinson recommended granting major powers to Congress—and cutting down those of the states. Under his plan, Congress could enter the life of the states in various ways, including the regulation of state coercive powers. For their part, the states should not be permitted to interfere with congressional action. Dickinson apparently persuaded the committee, for it proposed to place most power in the hands of Congress.

Between July 12, 1776, when the committee reported and November 17, 1777, when Congress finally approved the Articles of Confederation, the delegates virtually rejected the committee's report and made drastic changes which firmly tied Congress's hands—and freed those of the states. Not all the changes concerned the relations of the states to Congress. One crucial one which did—the decision not to give Congress control of western lands—delayed ratification of the Articles until March 1781. Maryland wanted Congress to control these lands and refused

2. *Ibid.*, 164–65.

to ratify the Articles. Maryland's intransigence arose not from a desire to strengthen Congress but from an intention to weaken those states with claims on the interior of the United States. When in 1781 Virginia ceded her claims to the West, Maryland ratified and the Articles went into effect.

Article II of the new constitution disabused Congress of its pretensions to supremacy by providing that "Each state retains its sovereignty, freedom, and independence, and every power, jurisdiction, and right, which is not by this Confederation expressly delegated to the United States, in Congress assembled." Under the Articles, Congress continued to control foreign relations, and it alone could make war. But the states, as the constituting power of the Union, clearly retained the upper hand.

II

By 1783 the public spirit and the structure of government of the Union virtually dictated that Americans would look to the states—not to Congress—for direction. By this time, indeed, the states, stimulated by the great purposes of the Revolution, had already done much.

None had contributed more to the Revolution than Virginia. The credit for the state's remarkable performance must be given to an elite, the gentry, an uncommon group which led Virginia into the Revolution and continued to lead afterwards. The gentry drew the support of small Virginia planters early in the century and held it through merit—not coercion.

The gentry never included more than 5 percent of Virginia's white population in the eighteenth century and within this number, according to historian Jack Greene, lay a core of about forty major families which provided the important leaders of Virginia. If the gentry and its leaders were small in number, they were not exclusive. To be sure the gentry did not welcome just anyone to its ranks—wealth and talent were the requirements for entrance—but it remained relatively open in the eighteenth century. The gentry in England and in several colonies, most notably New York, was closed compared with Virginia's.[3]

Virginia's finest were not idle men. They worked hard at raising tobacco and, as the century went along, wheat and other grains. This hard work did not involve using their hands. A large number of slaves

3. Jack P. Greene, "Society, Ideology, and Politics: An Analysis of the Political Culture of Mid-Eighteenth-Century Virginia," in Richard M. Jellison, ed., *Society, Freedom, and Conscience: The Coming of the Revolution in Virginia, Massachusetts, and New York* (New York, 1976), 14–76.

did the planting and cultivating and harvesting crops—and carrying them to ships for transport to the European market. Not manual labor, but organizing and managing the labor of others was the task of the gentry.

The gentry also governed. They dominated government at every level, from county courts to the House of Burgesses and the Council. They did not have to force themselves on the lower orders. The franchise remained broad throughout the century, and the electorate chose able men. Lesser planters deferred to wealth and ability and apparently agreed that men with these qualifications should run things. The gentry agreed, of course, but they did not abuse the deference extended to themselves by the lower orders. They provided remarkably responsible government— not out of unalloyed nobility but out of a sense that their interests were essentially the same as those they governed. To a large extent they seem to have been right in this judgment. Everyone grew tobacco for the market, and everyone faced the same problems.

In a peculiar sense the existence of large numbers of black slaves may have helped induce the powerful to protect the liberties of poor whites. As Edmund S. Morgan, the historian, has told us, there was an affinity between slavery and freedom in Virginia. The horrors of the enslaved made the free sensitive to the blessings of liberty. The horrors did not persuade them, however, to free the slaves. Slaves were too valuable as a source of labor. And they were brutish—"vicious, idle, and dissolute" if left to their own devices, just as the English poor were. Therefore they must be kept in slavery—to provide labor and to prevent their committing outrages against whites and themselves. Long before the Revolution, Virginians had established the racist policies which perpetuated slavery. If these policies did not encourage coercive practices against slaves, they at least permitted them and gave them the approval of the law.[4]

Thus slavery encouraged white men to think of their liberties. It taught them that property was supremely important: property as ownership of the self, of land, and of others made one free. And among whites of all orders slavery established a kind of equality, an equality of free men who in large part lived from the labors of the enslaved.

In the crisis of the decade before independence, Virginia planters proved to others just how much they valued their liberties. During the year of independence they framed a constitution for the state. As the

4. Edmund S. Morgan, *American Slavery, American Freedom: The Ordeal of Colonial Virginia* (New York, 1975), 295–387.

first drafted in the new states, it exerted great influence elsewhere in America.

The fifth Virginia Convention drafted the constitution of 1776. The Convention was actually the old House of Burgesses under a new name, for it was elected by freeholders from the old constituencies. Four Conventions had preceded it as the government of Virginia. The first had met in August 1774 following the dissolution of the Burgesses the previous May by Governor Dunmore. The governor, a tough character with a nose for sedition, had acted in response to passage of a resolution in the House calling on all Virginians to express discontent at the Boston Port Bill by observing a day of fasting and prayer. In two years' time, of course, passing resolutions in favor of prayer no longer seemed enough. On June 12, 1776, the delegates issued a "Declaration of Rights," and on June 29 approved a new constitution for the commonwealth.

George Mason had a major part in the composition of both. Mason seems to have had no more use for oratory than did his old friend and neighbor George Washington. But he could write with a skill that Washington never attained. In the Convention he apparently did not speak much, but he made himself heard in the "Declaration of Rights."

The first article of the "Declaration" set its tone: "That all men are by nature equally free and independent, and have certain inherent rights, of which, when they enter into a state of society, they cannot by any compact deprive or divest their posterity; namely, the enjoyment of life and liberty, with the means of acquiring and possessing property, and pursuing and obtaining happiness and safety." In the fifteen articles that followed, the Convention established that sovereignty resided in the people, that government was the people's servant, and when it failed the majority had a right "to reform, alter or abolish it." The Convention also declared that there should be rotation in office, periodical elections, due process in criminal prosecutions; and that there should not be excessive bail, general warrants, and standing armies in time of peace. The "Declaration" stated Virginia's commitment to trial by jury, to a free press, and "to the free exercise of religion."[5]

With the approval of the "Declaration of Rights," the Convention proclaimed Virginia's faith in principles which it believed should define free government. The government established by the constitution which was approved a little more than two weeks later did not fully conform

5. S. E. Morison, ed., *Sources and Documents Illustrating the American Revolution* (2d ed., Oxford, 1929), 149–51, for the Declaration of Rights.

to these principles. The "Declaration" had located power in the people, but the people were not given the opportunity to ratify, or reject, the constitution of 1776. To be sure, there was little likelihood that they would have rejected the constitution, for except in the structure of government it proposed, it was not a "radical" document. And the shape of the government it devised is understandable. In the form the Convention gave the new government it expressed the disenchantment of the Revolution with executive power.

Ostensibly the structure expressed the American faith in balanced government, for the constitution required that "the legislative, executive, and judiciary departments, shall be separate and distinct, so that neither exercise the Powers properly belonging to the other." But in fact the constitution apportioned power in a way that assured the supremacy of the legislature, the General Assembly of Virginia. The Assembly, composed of a House of Delegates and a Senate, chose the governor annually by ballot of both houses. The governor could do little without the concurrence of a Council of State, eight men also chosen by the Assembly. Even when he acted with the Council he possessed limited force: he could not veto legislation nor could he nominate judges or other important officers of the government. The constitution also denied him authority to dissolve the Assembly or even to prorogue or adjourn it.[6]

Within the Assembly, the House of Delegates, the successor to the Burgesses, ran things. Each county elected two members while the Senate consisted of twenty-four men chosen every four years from electoral districts. Only the delegates could initiate legislation; the Senate might propose revisions except in money bills, which it had either to approve or reject as the House presented them.

The old colonial franchise was left untouched. Those with land would choose the rulers of Virginia. And, as Thomas Jefferson pointed out, most of those rulers—the delegates and the senators—would be chosen from the tidewater. The western part of the state which had always been under-represented would remain so.

III

Some men feel a persistent unease about the human condition. Thomas Jefferson was not of this sort, but in 1776 he feared that Virginia might allow the opportunities opened by the Revolution to escape. He had

6. *TJ Papers*, I, 377–83, for the constitution; the quotation is from 379.

returned to Philadelphia as a delegate to the Congress in May 1776, just as the Virginia Convention was about to frame a constitution. He was soon to write the Declaration of Independence, great work he recognized, and yet his mind remained fixed on Virginia. What he yearned to do was to have a voice in the production of a constitution for Virginia. Establishing a government, he said at this time, "is the whole object of the present controversy."[7]

Jefferson of course remained in Philadelphia to compose the "Declaration." But he wrote to members of the Virginia Convention and drafted several versions of a constitution for Virginia. His letters and his rough drafts tell us much about his ideas and help chart constitutional thought in the state.

Jefferson's constitutions resembled the one enacted in Virginia in several respects. The general frame of government was similar, but it was better balanced. The Senate, the executive, and the courts were all stronger. The Senate indeed in his first two drafts of a constitution was to be elected by the House and serve for life. The need for balance led Jefferson to this arrangement. As he explained to his friend Edmund Pendleton, he wanted "to get the wisest men chosen, and to make them perfectly independent when chosen." The people would be clearly represented in the lower house. Jefferson had a much broader conception of who composed "the people" than most men of his day—he would extend the vote "to all who had a permanent intention of living in the country"—but he did not think that good government was served by allowing them to choose both houses of the legislature. One house should be reserved to the wise. But how to discover them?[8]

Leaving the choice to the lower house appealed to him, because as he said, "a choice by the people themselves is not generally distinguished for its wisdom." Their first "secretion" is "usually crude and heterogeneous. But give to those so chosen by the people a second choice themselves, and they generally will chuse wise men."[9]

Pendleton did not agree, preferring instead to reserve the upper house for men of "great property" who would sit for life. The disadvantage

7. *Ibid.*, 292. Merrill D. Peterson, *Thomas Jefferson and the New Nation* (New York, 1970), 97–100, provides an excellent account of Jefferson's hopes for a Virginia constitution.

8. For Jefferson's draft constitutions and his comments to Pendleton, see *TJ Papers*, I, 337–64, 503, 504. Pendleton's ideas may be followed in his letters to Jefferson in *ibid.*, 296–97, 484–85, 488–91.

9. *Ibid.*, I, 503.

in giving their selection to the lower house lay in the dependence thereby created. So chosen, they would be "the mere creatures of that body and of course wholly unfit to correct their Errors or Allay casual heats which will at times arise in all large bodies." Jefferson did not disagree with all of this, but he did not share Pendleton's confidence in wealthy men—"my observations," he observed, "do not enable me to say I think integrity the characteristic of wealth."

What he was convinced of was that the Virginia constitution had placed all the powers of government in the legislature. Five years after independence, he wrote that the concentration of those powers "in the same hands is precisely the definition of despotic government." It did not matter that many hands in the legislature would exercise these powers, for "173 despots would surely be as oppressive as one."[10]

That the Constitution included no provision for popular ratification constituted further evidence of its defectiveness in Jefferson's eyes. The Convention itself was an ordinary legislature and hardly competent to lay out fundamental law. Yet when it completed its work, the work was considered a constitution.

Jefferson aimed not simply to reorder a government but also to change the society supporting it. Thus in the constitutions he drafted he recommended that fifty acres of land be allocated to all males who owned none, that the trade in slaves be prohibited, that the death penalty be abolished except in cases of murder, and that "all persons shall have full and free liberty of religious opinion: nor shall any be compelled to frequent or maintain any religious institution." None of these ideas made their way into the Virginia constitution.

Frustrated by the Convention's caution, Jefferson turned to the new government itself. Although the Convention had wanted him to remain in Congress, in September 1776 he resigned and the next month, after the freeholders of Albemarle County elected him, took his place in the House of Delegates.

There in October 1776 Jefferson introduced two important bills: one, quickly passed, abolished entails. The rule of entail confined property to a particular lineage which could not be altered by the owner except by the permission of the legislature in a special act. A related practice, primogeniture, required that property of an owner who died without a will must pass to the eldest son. Jefferson regarded both of these institutions as aspects of a feudal inheritance that had no place in a republican

10. *Notes on the State of Virginia*, ed. William Peden (Chapel Hill, N.C., 1955), 120.

society. Each provided a basis for aristocratic privilege and threatened liberty.[11]

Although Jefferson in October did not make an attempt to rid Virginia of primogeniture, the second bill he offered would open the way for an attack on it—and virtually every other vestige of feudal and monarchical practice still haunting Virginia. This bill, which passed into law as rapidly as his proposal to discard entails, required the House of Delegates to appoint a committee to revise and codify the laws of Virginia. Whether the House conceived of this revision as somehow "revolutionary," that is, as an attempt to change fundamentally the statutory basis of Virginia law, is not clear. The committee the House appointed held different opinions about what it should do, but it resolved them and set to work.

The committee of five able men soon shook down to three, Edmund Pendleton, Speaker of the House and a distinguished lawyer, George Wythe, not as well known but a fine scholar and lawyer, and Thomas Jefferson, unusually brilliant and just coming into the fullness of his powers. Over the course of a long friendship Pendleton and Jefferson agreed on much and disagreed on much. At first they disagreed about what the committee of revisers should do. The usually "conservative" Pendleton, ordinarily disposed in favor of ancient things as Jefferson observed, proposed that they abandon the existing system of laws and devise an entirely new one. Jefferson wanted only to bring the laws of Virginia into conformity with the needs of the present, and apparently without great strain persuaded the committee of his wisdom. What Pendleton wanted to do seemed almost impossible, given the research, drafting, and persuasion required to pass even one statute.[12]

In June 1779 the committee finished its work, 126 bills covering a variety of subjects from the institutions by which the war might be directed to such matters as education, crimes and punishments, the church, plus many others. A few were enacted almost immediately, for example, "A Bill Establishing a Board of War," but most of those which eventually passed did so after the war when James Madison pushed them through the Assembly while Jefferson was in France. The Assembly never acted on the revised code as a whole but took up the bills piecemeal. Thirty-five passed in the session of October 1785, and twenty-three more in the autumn session of 1786.[13]

---

11. *TJ Papers*, I, 560–64, for the bills on entail and the revision of the laws.
12. Boyd's account of the revisal of the laws is in *ibid.*, II, 305–24.
13. For a catalogue of the bills and the texts of the bills, see *ibid.*, 329–657.

The bill on slavery was not the one Jefferson hoped to see through the Assembly, a bill which would have provided for gradual emancipation. The committee of revisers thought the prospects of such a bill were so bleak as to make its introduction useless. But they did prepare an amendment by which slaves born after the passage of the act would be freed on reaching adulthood. After training in a calling at the public expense, slaves were to be sent out of the commonwealth to be colonized at a distance remote from white society. Jefferson recommended colonization because he believed that blacks and whites could not live together peacefully. Their complex and terrible history made racial harmony unthinkable: "Deep rooted prejudices entertained by the whites; ten thousand recollections, by the blacks, of the injuries they have sustained; new provocations; the real distinctions which nature has made; and many other circumstances, will divide us into parties, and produce convulsions which will probably never end but in the extermination of the one or the other race."[14]

This amendment was never introduced. Neither Jefferson nor Madison, nor the others who shared their conviction that slavery somehow must be ended, detected a spirit favorable to it in Virginia. What was approved re-enacted the prohibition against the slave trade, which had passed in 1778, and continued the customary restrictions on slaves. They could not leave their masters' plantations without permission, for example; nor could they testify in court cases involving whites. Their gatherings and their speech were also closely regulated.[15]

The revisers offered a bolder measure in the "Bill for Proportioning Crimes and Punishments in Cases Heretofore Capital." Jefferson drafted this bill, a work of scholarship as well as of law, its substance on crimes and punishments supported by citations from the modern authority, Beccaria, the classics, Anglo-Saxon laws, and the common law. The bill reduced the number of offenses calling for capital punishment to two, murder and treason, and it limited severely the number of offenses to be punished by mutilation or maiming. But it retained the principle of retaliation for certain crimes—"Whosoever on purpose and of malice forethought shall maim another, or shall disfigure him, by cutting out or disabling the tongue, slitting or cutting off a nose, lip or ear, branding, or otherwise, shall be maimed or disfigured in like sort. . . ." For men convicted of rape, polygamy, and sodomy, Jefferson prescribed castration;

14. *Notes on the State of Virginia*, ed. Peden, 138.
15. *TJ Papers*, II, 470–73.

for a woman, "cutting thro' the cartilage of her nose a hole of one half inch diameter at the least."[16]

After the bill failed to pass in 1785, Madison removed retaliation for mayhem before resubmitting it in October 1786, although the opposition may not have objected to this punishment. The opposition did, however, object to confining capital punishment to the crimes of murder and treason. The bill failed by a single vote. Madison reported its loss to Jefferson with a bitter comment—"The rage against Horse stealers had a great influence on the fate of the bill. Our old bloody code is by this event fully restored. . . ."[17]

"A Bill for the More General Diffusion of Knowledge" was equally dear to Jefferson. In it he proposed the establishment of several levels of schools at public expense in order to provide at least three years of education for all children—girls as well as boys. These three years, in "hundred" schools, were to teach reading, writing, and arithmetic and the histories of Greece, Rome, England, and America. The state would also establish grammar schools, twenty in all, where Latin, Greek, English, geography, "and the higher part of numerical arithmetick" would be taught. Most of the students in these schools would attend at their parents' expense, but a small number of able children of the poor would be entered with all costs to be borne by the public. And the most promising senior from among the poor children would be sent, again at public expense, to William and Mary College for three years.[18]

Although "all hands," according to Madison, conceded the necessity of some systematic provision for public education, the bill did not survive the scrutiny of the Assembly in 1786. The objections voiced by the delegates came down to financial cost and to doubt that the administration of this hierarchy of schools could be made to work. Some delegates apparently pointed to sparse settlements in several parts of the state, and westerners complained that the districts were laid out unequally. Madison dismissed this last protest as specious and seemed skeptical about the seriousness of the other criticisms.[19]

There may have been another reason for the bill's failure. It may have seemed to promise more social equality than most Virginia planters wanted. The bill did not propose to level society; with its assumption that the best should govern, it had elitist implications, as Julian Boyd,

16. *Ibid.*, 492–507 (498, 497 for quotations).
17. *Ibid.*, XI, 152.
18. *Ibid.*, II, 526–35 (531 for quotation).
19. *Ibid.*, XI, 152.

the editor of Jefferson's *Papers*, has pointed out. But while it proposed that men of "genius and virtue" should be educated so that they might be enabled "to guard the sacred deposit of rights and liberties of their fellow citizens," it provided that they should be "called to that charge without regard to wealth, birth or other accidental condition or circumstance." Jefferson believed that men of ability might be found in any rank in society. They must be trained to their mission—at the public expense if necessary. If they were not, the unworthy—"the weak or wicked"—might dominate government.[20]

That only the talented should have power was elitism; that the talented might be discovered anywhere was not. Jefferson's assumptions suggested that he believed that elitism and egalitarianism might be reconciled, and the means lay in education that drew on public as well as private resources.

Most of the gentry probably did not consider such a reconciliation desirable. The gentry had long been willing to look deep within itself for fresh recruits for government. All it required of candidates was that they be gentlemen and that they have talent. Now Jefferson asked the gentry to settle for talent alone on the assumption that it resided in the poor as well as in the rich. That supposition went down hard in men accustomed to assuming that quality was to be found only in their own kind.

Yet these same men gave Jefferson his greatest triumph in Virginia by approving a Bill for Establishing Religious Freedom. Their action did not come easily or quickly. When independence was declared everyone in Virginia, whatever his religion, paid taxes in support of the established church, the Episcopal Church, as the Church of England was soon called. Dissenters, especially Presbyterians and Baptists, now demanded that they at least be freed of this requirement. Although reluctant, the legislature granted relief for a year and extended it annually until 1779 when it was made permanent. At the same time the legislature suspended the requirement that members of the established church pay parish rates, but it did not abolish these rates. The church thus remained established, and the old statutes and the common law which permitted the state to punish heretical opinions continued in effect.[21]

War made conciliating the dissenters desirable, of course, and the defenders of the establishment therefore held their passions in check until peace was concluded. Restraint never came easily to Patrick Henry,

20. *Ibid.*, II, 527.
21. Peterson, *Jefferson*, 133–34.

one of those defenders, and in 1784 he gratefully took up the fight for the church again. He saw his opportunity in a question raised in the act of 1776 of "Whether a general assessment should not be established by law, on every one, to the support of the pastor of his choice, or whether all should be left to voluntary contributions." Henry revived the question apparently with the argument that the corruption of society inevitably followed the disestablishment of the church. For a time the dissenting clergy found this line, and the prospects of full treasuries, irresistible. Such distinguished Virginians as Edmund Pendleton and Richard Henry Lee also backed Henry.[22]

Laymen in and out of the establishment did not share the ardor of their clerical leaders. Episcopal laymen had long governed their church, and they recognized that a general assessment could only strengthen the clergy, still faintly tainted with loyalism. Lay Baptists and Presbyterians were suspicious, not of their own ministers but of anything that would enable the old establishment to rise again. And these dissenters seem to have been moved by the argument that held that to protect religious freedom the state must be denied any part in religious life. Madison's "Memorial and Remonstrance against Religious Assessments" offered as a petition at this time drew considerable support—in all 1552 signatures were collected. In it Madison cited the article in the "Declaration of Rights" which holds that religion "can be directed only by reason and conviction, not by force or violence" and which denies the legislature jurisdiction in matters of religion and opinion. As for rulers who interfere with churches and opinion about religion—they are "tyrants," and the people who submit are "slaves." It soon became evident that Virginia would not submit to a general assessment for churches, and in 1785 the bill quietly went to its grave without even the dignity of having been voted on.[23]

The next year, in January, the Assembly passed Jefferson's "Bill for Establishing Religious Freedom." This act disestablished the church and made clear the legislature's intention that the establishment should never be restored. The rights the Assembly was protecting, it explained, "are of the natural rights of mankind," and "any act [that] shall be hereafter passed to repeal the present or to narrow its operation, such act will be an infringement of natural right." Before the Assembly approved Jefferson's bill it stripped out some of his most forceful phrases declaring his faith that religion must be founded on reason and the free operations of the mind. But it included his statement "that all men shall be free to profess, and by argument to maintain, their opinion in matters of religion, and that the same shall in no wise diminish, enlarge, or affect their civil capacities."[24]

The making of the constitution in 1776 and Jefferson's attempts at reform suggest much about the Revolution in Virginia. Jefferson's efforts followed a decade of protest at Parliament's designs on colonial rights. Virtually all of those rights bore on governance, especially on the right of the individual to give his consent through his representative to measures affecting his life and on the freedom of traditional institutions of self-government. The Americans in the ten years before 1776 signified their devotion to principles of self-government, and in 1776 they announced them clearly in the Declaration of Independence. Jefferson and such thoughtful Virginians as James Madison believed that Virginia had an opportunity to extend the limits of freedom announced in the Declaration so as to affect the arrangements of ordinary life—the way land was held, the punishment of crimes, the legal status of blacks, the education of the young, the maintenance of religion, and the freedom of expression. Jefferson indeed thought that the Assembly should act immediately to encourage liberty while American passions were still engaged in the great struggle of the Revolution. For, he observed in 1781, "It can never be too often repeated, that the time for fixing every essential right on a legal basis is while our rulers are honest, and ourselves united. From the conclusion of this war we shall be going down hill. They will be forgotten, therefore, and their rights disregarded. They will forget themselves, but in the sole faculty of making money, and will never think of uniting to effect a due respect for their rights. The shackles, therefore, which shall not be knocked off at the conclusion of this war, will remain on us long, will be made heavier and heavier, till our rights shall revive or expire in a convulsion."[25]

From several perspectives Jefferson failed. The constitution of 1776 did not provide for a more effective expression of the consent of the governed. Slavery remained almost what it had always been; the punishment of criminals continued to be an exercise in savagery; and the state could not bring itself to educate the children of the poor.

24. *TJ Papers*, II, 546.
25. *Notes on the State of Virginia*, ed. Peden, 161.

Where Jefferson and his friends succeeded—and the Declaration of Rights, the destruction of entail and primogeniture, the Bill for Establishing Religious Freedom were remarkable achievements—they did so by making explicit the connection of their reforms to the great principles of the Revolution. Success came, for example, in disestablishing the church through the demonstration that religious and political liberty could not be separated.

Even linking the reforms to the Revolution did not inevitably carry the day. The gentry of Virginia, however seriously devoted to the principles of republicanism, did not usually agree that their radical extension would serve Virginia or the Revolution. The gentry saw themselves as the heart of the Revolution, their interests were vital to it, their leadership and power held society together. They were used to the deference of the lower orders, and they could not understand why they should be expected to undermine it. Nor could they see why racial slavery should be ended. It had served everyone well just as most of the institutions of society and government had.

IV

Men who have more than their lives to lose make one sort of revolution, and those who have only their lives to lose make another. The Virginians, like almost all the Americans, were of the first sort. Had they had nothing to lose, they might not have stopped with the disestablishment of the church, they might have destroyed it. They might not have freed access to the land; they might have abolished private property or they might have destroyed small owners. They might have encouraged the slave trade and made slavery even more barbarous. They might have toughened an already tough criminal code. They might not have simply rejected the British constitution, they might have converted constitutionalism into authoritarianism. Nowhere in America were there many men who felt they had nothing to lose; and nowhere did such men seize power.

New men, some called them "outsiders," had made their way into the unofficial committees that had helped organize resistance to Britain before independence. In Pennsylvania, the outsiders or radicals exercised more power than anywhere else in America, especially in 1776 when they captured the informal government of the state and replaced the elected Assembly. These men located themselves firmly within the movement against Britain, and they advocated independence before other patriots could bring themselves to the break. Thomas Paine served as the mentor of many of the radicals. Their deepest ties, however, were to farmers, especially in the West, and to skilled craftsmen, men of small property and ambitious to make their desires public policy.

The most important desire of radical leaders and their followers was to extend the power of ordinary people—democratic aspirations provided the cement for the radical movement. The leaders included at least two men of considerable wealth, George Bryan, a merchant, and the Quaker, Christopher Marshall, a retired druggist. Timothy Matlack was one of the most popular among workers and artisans. Not an ignorant man—he read papers before the American Philosophical Society—he had the common touch, brewing beer for a living and racing horses and fighting cocks for sport. The enlisted men of his militia regiment elected him a colonel in 1775. James Cannon, a teacher in the College of Philadelphia, assumed an important place among the radicals almost as soon as they began to form. He had emigrated from Edinburgh in 1765, and he came with an ability to write, a skill he demonstrated in the convention that drafted the constitution of 1776. There was at least one itinerant agitator among the radicals, Thomas Young, the son of Irish immigrants. Young popped up in several places during the Revolution, always as an advocate of liberty. The radicals could also claim a fine mathematician as one of their own, David Rittenhouse, a skilled watchmaker who won fame for his orrery, a mechanical representation of the relative positions and movements of bodies in the solar system. Charles Willson Peale, a captain of Philadelphia militia, was a radical. Peale, a silversmith and watchmaker for a time, painted the portraits of many of the great revolutionaries. After shoving the Assembly to the side in 1776, these men and others like them got a convention called and wrote the most democratic constitution of the era.[26]

The Pennsylvania constitution of 1776 abandoned any pretense of mixed government. The radicals believed that the people's interest was one, and any attempt to construct a government on any other assumption would deny the principles of republicanism. Thomas Paine had taught them that the structure of American society departed from Europe's. Those state constitutions which sought to balance the traditional orders of society simply ignored the important differences between Europe and America. Paine was right about society in America—there was no heredi-

26. For information about the men mentioned in this paragraph I have drawn on: Eric Foner, *Tom Paine and Revolutionary America* (New York, 1976); David Freeman Hawke, *Paine* (New York, 1974); Richard Alan Ryerson, *The Revolution Is Now Begun: The Radical Committees of Philadelphia, 1765–1776* (Philadelphia, 1978); Brooke Hindle, *David Rittenhouse* (Princeton, N.J., 1964).

tary nobility that required its own house in the legislature and of course there was no monarch.

In other states the problem of the upper house, what it was and who it represented, baffled constitution-makers. Only Massachusetts, in the constitution of 1780, made its Senate the representative of property. Virginia did not although Edmund Pendleton had hoped that it might. Jefferson, of course, envisioned the Senate as a source of greater wisdom than was available in the House. It should not be representative of a social interest, he thought, but a repository of good judgment.

Most states came, haltingly, to an understanding of a Senate similar to Jefferson's. The Senate would act as a brake on the lower house whenever the lower house behaved rashly. The Senate would balance the legislature. Something like this argument came to be accepted as the justification for bicameralism. The two houses would, in a phrase that soon became current, check and balance one another. The trouble with a single-house legislature lay precisely in its lack of balance. Whatever the protections written into a constitution against its arbitrary use of power, there was in reality only one way to check it if it wished to ignore the constitution. And that way was to establish a second body of comparable powers to block it when it threatened to overturn the constitution or act in opposition to the public interest.[27]

Nothing in such arguments persuaded the radicals in Pennsylvania of the wisdom of mixed government, and the convention, which they controlled, established a unicameral legislature. The radicals took pains to ensure that the General Assembly, as the legislature was called, would remain close to the people and never remove itself from their control. First of all the Assembly was to be elected by male taxpayers. Its members could not serve for more than four years in any seven; they must stand for election annually; they must take an oath to protect the people's interests; and their proceedings must be open to the public. The constitution also established a procedure which was designed to give the people as much knowledge as possible about proposed legislation. All bills were to be printed "for the consideration of the people, before they are read in general assembly for the last time for debate and amendment." The

27. I have learned much about American ideas about the "Senate" and mixed government from Gordon S. Wood, *The Creation of the American Republic, 1776–1787* (Chapel Hill, N.C., 1969), 206–22 and *passim*. Jackson Turner Main, *The Upper House in Revolutionary America, 1763–1788* (Madison, Wis., 1967) contains valuable information on the changes in the composition of the upper houses in the state legislatures of the 1780s.

General Assembly could not enact bills into law until after the session following their printing.[28]

Beside the General Assembly, the other branches of the government were weak. A president and supreme executive council made up the executive but lacked a veto on legislation, indeed lacked almost any power. The courts too were carefully limited. To guarantee further the rights of citizens, the convention inserted a bill of rights into the constitution. This part of the document was drawn almost completely from the Virginia "Declaration of Rights." Still the radicals were not satisfied. To protect the people and the constitution they devised an agency called the council of censors, modeled on the Spartan Ephori and Roman Censors, which was expected to review the government's performance every seven years. The council of censors, an elected body, might call a new convention if it thought amendments were needed.

In Pennsylvania the democratic impulse achieved a level of power unequaled elsewhere. But the expression of that power in the constitution of 1776 did not go unchallenged. Although the economy and the Bank of North America were issues in the politics of the 1780s, the constitution provided the center of division. Two factions which attained a remarkable level of organization grew up around the constitution—its opponents, the Republicans, and its defenders, the Constitutionalists. The split between the two did not have a class basis, though each felt considerable social antagonism toward the other. The Republicans contained more businessmen, merchants trading overseas and with other colonies, than the Constitutionalists, but a variety of groups made their way into both camps. The Quakers solidly opposed the constitution, for its requirements of an oath barred them from the General Assembly, and a law imposing a similar requirement on voters passed soon after the constitution took effect disenfranchised them. The allegiances of other religious groups were less clear.

V

Division over a constitution did not shape politics in the remaining states in the 1780s. For the most part, these constitutions attempted to provide balanced government and at the same time to restrict executive power. More often than not the balance tilted strongly to the legislature. These constitutions all incorporated bicameralism and gave the people a strong voice in one house—and usually in both. The franchise remained

28. Morison, ed., *Sources and Documents*, 167, for the quotation, and for the text of the Pennsylvania constitution.

tied to real property almost everywhere with most men apparently qualifying for the vote. The landless, who could not qualify, were apparently willing to defer to their landowning betters.

By 1787 the constitutional structure of most states seemed secure. Pennsylvania's democratic order was an exception, an exception that drew the attention of the men who wanted to strengthen the Union. Whatever good the experience of the states had to teach was not to be discovered in Pennsylvania, where democracy engendered strife and division. Yet a new constitution for the Confederation surely would have to found itself on the people.

The Revolution had been fought in the name of the natural rights of mankind. How much democracy did those rights require? Pennsylvania could not answer satisfactorily, and neither could Virginia.

Nor could the Articles of Confederation. They were a constitution in the most tenuous sense—they provided fundamental law, but they did not establish a government. Under the Articles, there was no executive and there was no judiciary. By itself Congress could not do much. It could not tax; it could not regulate trade except with the Indians. It could do few of the things ordinary governments did. State and local agencies governed the American people. And the American people did not choose Congress—state legislatures did.

By the end of the war, the inadequacy of the Articles was clear. Yet, through most of the 1780s, they could not be revised. They could not because the Americans were unable to find a way to reconcile local attachments with centralized government. One of the great strengths of the Americans—their provincialism—had weakened them in the war, and it paralyzed their effort to govern themselves after peace was concluded. There was also the lesson of the struggle with Britain—that unconfined power invariably sought to destroy liberty. Action to centralize power might solve some of the problems of governance, and it might also lead to the end of American freedom.

What, then, could be done in 1787? Much had been learned since 1781. The Articles of Confederation would not do. The state constitutions, even though they embodied much political wisdom, would not do—at least not by themselves. Something had to be done. If it were not, a confederacy of small sovereign republics, a radical institution in a world of monarchies, might collapse or be conquered.

The Constitutional Convention would have to find the answers. It needed delegates with imagination and daring. As spring came in 1787, Americans, understandably, thought about the men they had sent to Philadelphia and about what they might do there.

25

The Constitutional Convention

The delegates to the Constitutional Convention straggled into Philadelphia throughout most of May 1787. The state legislatures had not appointed delegates with undue speed, and those chosen found travel over rough roads slow and uncomfortable. May 14, the day set for the opening, came and went with only a few delegates present. Delay in getting the meeting started distressed those in the city who were committed to major reform because it suggested to them that others might not share their purposes.

The first on the scene, James Madison, the most eager for a change to a powerful central government, did not sit and suffer. He had prepared himself carefully for this meeting, and he did not mean to let the opportunity for change slip away. Madison was thirty-six years old, short of stature, with a receding hairline and a lean body. Historians sometimes describe him as an introverted little man, a classic intellectual in whom the juices of passion had dried up. His friends knew him better and their accounts confirm what his correspondence shows: he was lively and sometimes ribald, a man of passion and deep conviction. His attachments, firmly to Virginia, did not prevent him from loving the Union. Yet that love was not free of hate and fear: he hated paper money and feared the wild schemes of debtors, and most of all he feared majoritarian tyranny and its sometime offspring, anarchy. But Madison loved political liberty even more, and though he did not love the people— he had come to know them in his years of public service—he believed that political liberty could survive in a republic only if the people were faithfully represented. Ignored or frustrated, they would continue what they were doing when the Convention was called—invade the rights of property. Madison had thought more about government than anyone in the Convention; he was ready for what lay ahead in the summer; and he was determined to the point of fanaticism.[1]

Ten days after Madison's arrival George Washington rode in, to be greeted by the ringing of bells and the shouts of admiring countrymen. Persuading Washington to come had been a near thing—or seemed so—for he clung to private life after eight years of exhausting service to his country. Washington's desire to remain at Mount Vernon was undoubtedly genuine, but he also wished to aid the cause of national government. The problem for him and his friends lay in his immense reputation which he, and they, protected from all possible dangers. In the end, regard for his reputation brought him to Philadelphia after he first refused appointment to the Virginia delegation. What concerned him, he wrote Henry Knox in an appeal for advice, was "whether my non-attendance in this Convention will not be considered as deriliction to republicanism, nay more, whether other motives may not (however injuriously) be ascribed to me for not exerting myself on this occasion in support of it." Knox, Madison, and Edmund Randolph all urged him to attend, although Madison had second thoughts after Washington decided to follow their counsel. Washington had more prestige than any American, and a constitution formed with his blessing would doubtless attract the approval of many of his countrymen.[2]

Washington brought neither a clearly formulated plan of government with him nor a well-articulated political philosophy. He had no taste for theory, but he had profound convictions about the need to strengthen the Union, convictions based on far-ranging knowledge of Americans and their institutions. He also had years of experience of working with Congress. And whatever the reasons, though his service in the Revolution must have been most important, he was an unshakable republican.

By May 17 the entire Virginia delegation had arrived. It included George Wythe, in whose office the young Jefferson studied law, a learned and wise man who was called home by his wife's illness almost immediately, John Blair, a judge, John McClurg, a doctor, and two formidable planters. They were Edmund Randolph, the governor of the state, a member of a distinguished family and a man of good ability and unpredictable judgment; the other was George Mason, Washington's neighbor

1. Irving Brant, *James Madison* (6 vols., Indianapolis, Ind., 1941–61).
2. Washington to Knox, March 8, 1787, in *GW Writings*, XXIX, 171. See also *ibid.*, 193–95, 208–10.

on the Potomac, a bright sometimes cranky man whose opinions were even harder to anticipate than Randolph's despite the fact that he had written the Virginia "Declaration of Rights" and much of the state's constitution of 1776, both documents saturated with the principles of republican liberty.[3]

These men met as a delegation before the Convention commenced its work. Madison instigated their meetings in order to work out an agreement on his plan for a new government. Three among the Virginians, he knew, would be especially important in the Convention. One was George Washington, who shared Madison's desires for a national union of great power; the others were George Mason and Edmund Randolph, who were unhappy with the present government but still not certain to approve the changes he had in mind.

While the Virginians talked among themselves, other delegates drifted into Philadelphia until, on May 25, seven states were represented and the Convention opened. In a few more days the delegations were virtually complete and representatives from all the states with the exception of New Hampshire and Rhode Island were on the scene. Altogether fifty-five men served, although several left Philadelphia before the meeting ended in September.

Who were these men and what were their backgrounds? At least thirty-four had legal training and twenty-one practiced law. There were some eighteen planters and farmers; nineteen slave owners; seven merchants and another eight, all lawyers, closely associated with commerce. Many of these men had held state offices, served in Congress, and were veterans of the Revolutionary war. This short profile suggests a gathering of solid citizens, property owners, political and social leaders, and indeed it was. There were no women at the Convention, no free blacks, and no poor men. But there were few rigid conservatives, if conservatism implies a disposition to resist change. The delegates were also still young men, mostly in their thirties and forties, with few exceptions.[4]

One of the exceptions was Benjamin Franklin, eighty-one years of age and in bad health. He along with seven others represented Pennsylvania. At first glance, Robert Morris appeared the most formidable of the lot because of his extraordinary abilities. But Morris sat silent in

3. The delegations are listed in Charles C. Tansill, ed., *Documents Illustrative of the Formation of the Union of American States* (Washington, D.C., 1927), 85–86. William Pierce's sketches of delegates in *ibid.*, 96–108, are useful.

4. Forrest McDonald, *We The People: The Economic Origins of the Constitution* (Chicago, 1958), chaps. 2–3, contains much on the delegates.

the deliberations of the Convention, and there is no evidence that he threw his weight around in the inns and taverns that served as backrooms. Washington stayed with Morris and his wife during the meeting, and the two must have discussed what went on from day to day. But Morris did not contribute much to the work that produced the Constitution.[5]

Morris's colleague James Wilson did. Only Madison, with whom Wilson collaborated, proved more important in the Convention. Wilson was a legal scholar of great learning. He was born in Fifeshire, Scotland, in 1742, the son of a small farmer. His family had intended that he go into the ministry and sent him to St. Andrews University for preparation. Wilson had other plans and came to America in 1765. After service as a tutor in the College of Philadelphia, he read law under John Dickinson and began practice in Reading two years later. His splendid pamphlet, *Considerations on the Nature and Extent of the Legislative Authority of the Parliament*, published in 1774, marked him as a thinker of imaginative power who would give good service to the American side in the struggle with Britain. Wilson served in Congress, where he signed the Declaration of Independence; some thought he signed rather reluctantly. But he was not a reluctant patriot and not a reluctant supporter of the rights of the ordinary people, despite his taste for good living and his apparent need for a high income.[6]

In the Convention, Wilson expounded a democratic nationalism. His convictions arose in part from his optimistic temperament, but perhaps more from a genuine and deep belief in the premises of the Scottish Enlightenment. This version of enlightened thought, sometimes called the commonsense philosophy, held that commonsense provided a dependable means to knowledge. Man's intuition was reliable—David Hume to the contrary notwithstanding—and since it was not confined to elites of blood or wealth but fairly distributed among the people whose nature was good and benevolent, they must be trusted with power. Morality indeed required that they take part in the government of themselves.

Wilson was not a selfless enthusiast—he valued order and the things of this world. He remained a close friend of John Dickinson, who had refused to sign the Declaration, and of Robert Morris, who had hired his legal services. But Wilson came to the Convention as no one's lackey and with well-conceived political ideas.

5. This assessment of Morris is based on my reading of the Convention proceedings.
6. Charles Page Smith, *James Wilson* (Chapel Hill, N.C., 1956) is the most reliable biography.

There were others in the Pennsylvania delegation with considerable reputations, Thomas Mifflin who never opened his mouth in the Convention and Gouverneur Morris who never closed his. Morris, by far the more important of the two, had assisted the superintendent of finance three years before. In the Convention he was usually found on the side of Madison and Wilson.[7]

Nearby New York sent Alexander Hamilton, John Lansing, Jr., and Robert Yates. The last two left the meeting in the middle of July and refused to return. Hamilton might have played an important part but did not, although he made a brilliant speech in favor of constitutional monarchy.

John Dickinson represented Delaware, and William Paterson, an unknown quantity soon to make himself well known, led the delegation from New Jersey. Elbridge Gerry, Rufus King, and Nathaniel Gorham, able men all, were present for Massachusetts. The most impressive delegates from the southern states were Virginians, but South Carolina's John Rutledge, Charles Cotesworth Pinckney, Charles Pinckney, and Pierce Butler were all men of ability. Maryland's delegation contained one man with an overdeveloped capacity for boring others, Luther Martin, a verbose dogmatist.

Until mid-July when the so-called "great compromise" was agreed upon, the delegates usually fell into two groups, representing two sorts of state interests. These alignments took place almost naturally and without effort and certainly without design. The divisions seemed inevitable because they rose from fairly long-standing political and economic circumstances, at least one of which was sanctified by the Revolution itself: state equality in Congress, which had existed since that body first took shape. In fact the practice of according each state one vote whatever its population had been followed in all revolutionary gatherings. The small states—Delaware, New Jersey, Connecticut, Maryland, and even New York—were understandably reluctant to give up this customary arrangement. Custom served their interest. The large states, three of which—Virginia, Pennsylvania, Massachusetts—had almost half the American people, naturally wished to see representatives apportioned by population. These commitments—one to old practice, the other to changing it—furnished the most divisive issue at the Convention.[8]

7. For Morris, see Max M. Mintz, *Gouverneur Morris and the American Revolution* (Norman, Okla., 1970).

8. For other sorts of divisions, see McDonald, *We The People*. I have found Irving Brant, *James Madison: Father of the Constitution, 1787–1800* (Indianapolis, Ind., 1950), 55–70, especially helpful.

Political interests did not live apart from other sorts, and almost inevitably various economic interests found a common political alignment possible. Roughly speaking, businessmen in Pennsylvania and Massachusetts including overseas traders and manufacturers shared the desire of Virginian and Carolinian planters that representation be according to population. These states, especially Virginia and Pennsylvania, had a good deal of undeveloped land to develop, land which once put into use would add to their political strength in a Congress representative of population. A similar concern moved South Carolina and Georgia, both with unsettled backcountry which they hoped to fill up. These southern states had another sort of concern—slavery, an institution they expected to have to defend in the future.

The small states also contained many men interested in western lands. For example, in New Jersey speculators held title to lands in the West based on Indian deeds. After the Virginia cession of the Northwest these men, usually organized in companies, sought to defend their interests. Control of the national government, or a strong voice in it, would surely come easier if representation remained equal among the states. Land speculators were also influential in Connecticut which had long claimed the Wyoming Valley in Pennsylvania for itself. A special federal writ had turned this grab aside, but the state's government, undaunted, managed to extract the Connecticut Reserve, a very large area, to feed to insatiable speculators.[9]

Virtually all of the small states wanted western lands. Western lands under national control might be sold to pay off public debts. To ensure this happy event, equality in Congress seemed necessary. A strong national government under the control of large states aroused fears that it might cut off small states from western revenues, and their veterans from a landed stake. And what, lacking state equality, was to prevent the large from growing larger at the expense of the small by drawing off their farmers with promises of low taxes in the West?

Large and small states shared reasons for supporting the creation of a powerful central government. Both wanted commerce regulated; both feared upheavals like Shays's Rebellion, which a national government might forestall or speedily suppress; both had a stake in solid public finance and the protection of creditors; both saw that a national government might stimulate the economy; and both saw the need for

9. Brant, *James Madison: Father*, 62, 65; Richard P. McCormick, *Experiment in Independence: New Jersey in the Critical Period, 1781–1789* (New Brunswick, N.J., 1950), chap. 9, *passim*.

protection of the republic in a rapacious world of monarchy. And both were composed of citizens who had fought together in the glorious cause.

To describe the states as if they were human beings with minds and hearts is necessary, even helpful, up to a point, but sometimes probably distorts the truth. It suggests the absence of disagreement in Maryland or New Jersey to say that each had such designs on western lands. Land companies in each had such designs, and because of their power succeeded in making their desires into something approaching state policy. But there were also men in each who did not care or who despised the land companies. There is still another danger in referring to the states as if they were people: no state sat in the Convention; delegates did. Saying that in the Convention Virginia defended landed interests is a convenient shorthand and in most respects is not distorting. But the delegates in Philadelphia made hundreds of decisions while they both represented complicated interests at home and spoke for themselves. The relation between what was commonly felt to be a state interest and a delegate's decision on some matter of government, say whether the President should serve for four or six years or whether Congress or electors should choose him, is seldom clear. In most decisions about the frame of government and its powers all we can perceive are the dispositions of delegates and how their dispositions expressed the interests of dominant social and economic groups in their states. We should not assume, however, that a delegate's vote was predetermined; and we should not discount the power of the deliberations to change men's minds. The Convention met for almost four months. During that time it generated its own forces, chiefly through discussion and argument. In all these deliberations, reason and intellect made their impress, just as did irrationality and passion, chance and accident.

II

In the first four days after the Convention opened, it elected George Washington as its chairman, and William Jackson, who had served as an assistant to the secretary at war, its secretary. It also adopted rules which had been prepared by a committee of George Wythe, Alexander Hamilton, and Charles Pinckney. At this time, the Convention decided to keep its proceedings a secret, a wise decision making candor and flexibility possible, both essential to the accommodation of differences. Some promise of differences appeared in the credentials of the delegations which the Convention read in the opening sessions. Delaware's, for example, instructed its delegates not to agree to any system depriving the states of the customary equality of suffrage in the Congress.[10]

On May 29, Edmund Randolph turned the Convention to its work by offering the Virginia Plan. Randolph sang his song—music and lyrics by James Madison—in a tempo appropriate to a dirge. The present situation of America, the Convention was given to understand, was not good. In fact, Randolph said, there existed such a crisis as to promise the fulfillment of the prophecies of an American downfall. To prevent a downfall and to forestall anarchy—his speech suggested that the two were indistinguishable—a change in government was necessary, a conclusion that could hardly have surprised that assemblage.

The "change" proposed in the Virginia Plan implied that the Articles of Confederation should be discarded even though the first resolution offered by Randolph simply declared that they were to be "corrected and enlarged." This resolution was followed by fourteen more which laid out the framework for a powerful central government. The major branch of this government was to be a "national legislature" composed of two houses, the first popularly elected and the second chosen by the first from nominations of the state legislatures. This national legislature would choose the executive and the judiciary. Its legislative authority would include all the powers of the Confederation Congress and in addition a general grant "to legislate in all cases to which the separate states are incompetent, or in which the harmony of the United States may be interrupted by the exercise of individual legislation." Besides this general grant, it was empowered "to negative all laws passed by the several states, contravening in the opinion of the national legislature the articles of Union." The national legislature in effect would decide when the new constitution had been violated by state laws, and it would veto them. The national legislature would be a powerful body but not an unrestrained one: the Virginia Plan called for a check on it through the operation of a Council of Revision, composed of the executive and a "convenient number" of judges, who might veto statutes. The national legislature possessed the authority to play the final hand in the game, however, for it might re-enact legislation over the Council's veto.[11]

The tenth resolve of the Plan provided for the admission of new states, and the eleventh guaranteed a republican government to old and new states. The fourteenth resolve required state officials to take an oath to support the new constitution, and the final one provided for ratification in state conventions convened for the purpose.

10. Farrand, I, 2–13.
11. *Ibid.*, 18–23; *ibid.*, III, 593–94.

The day following the introduction of the Virginia Plan, May 30, the Convention resolved itself into a committee of the whole, in order to permit discussion and action unencumbered by the fairly rigid rules agreed upon earlier. During the next two weeks the delegates learned at first hand just how important careful preparation is in deliberative bodies. For the preparation of the Virginians and the thoughtfully conceived plan of government they offered their colleagues gave them the initiative. They had framed the terms of the discussion, and now in these two weeks they and their supporters in the large states forced the pace of deliberations and, for the most part, controlled the Convention. Their opponents from the small states found themselves on the defensive, forced always to deal with the questions raised by the large, and compelled to answer and refute rather than to propose.

Not that the large states had everything their own way in these early days of the meeting or even that they agreed upon everything among themselves. As soon as the committee of the whole began its review of the Virginia Plan, Gouverneur Morris suggested that the first resolve— that the Convention should correct and enlarge the Articles—ought to be "postponed." Morris and everyone else recognized that Randolph had proposed much more than correction and enlargement, and Randolph now had to admit it. Instead of the first, he now offered three propositions which made clear that national sovereignty would replace state sovereignty if the Virginia Plan were accepted. The committee eased its way over these shoals by agreeing that a national government ought to be established consisting of a "supreme" legislature, executive, and judiciary. It then entered the really dangerous waters of representation in the legislature. The Virginia Plan proposed that representation should be allocated according to population. The actual formula used had been derived by Madison in 1783, reckoning five slaves as three freemen for purposes of establishing state financial contributions to the Congress. The committee had hardly begun to discuss representation when Delaware's George Read reminded everyone that his state's commission forbade its delegates to agree to any departure from state equality. If the Convention discarded equality, Read reminded, he and his colleagues might have to go home, a threat which doubtless irritated men who wanted to discuss the problem. But Read's ploy worked, and the Convention decided that representation was a matter that could wait for a few days.[12]

12. *Ibid.*, I, 33–38.

Virtually every other resolution Randolph offered made its way into the discussions of the next two weeks. How the first branch—the lower house—should be elected was taken up on May 31 and decided in favor of the people. Disagreement occurred immediately afterwards over the election of the upper house. The committee turned to the executive during the next two days with little luck. Should the executive be one or many? A single executive smacked of monarchy to Randolph, who pointed out that "the permanent temper of the people was adverse to the very semblance of monarchy." Two days later James Wilson punctured Randolph's arguments for a plural executive by pointing out that they dealt more with what people would say about a single executive than genuine objections to it. "All know," Wilson remarked, "that a single magistrate is not a king." Wilson's most telling rebuttal was his reminder that all the states had decided on a single executive for themselves in their recently drafted constitutions. The vote that followed Wilson's speech confirmed his judgment, seven to three in favor of a single executive.[13]

The provision for a judicial branch raised difficult questions, especially of the method of appointment, which the committee found easier to postpone than to answer. It agreed rather easily that a fair method of admitting new states should be included in the new constitution and then began discussion of ratification of whatever new arrangements the Convention might produce. Over the next few days the committee fleshed out agreement achieved in the previous week, decided on a transition from government under the old Articles to the new, resolved to guarantee a republican form of government to the states and to require state officials to support the new constitution. It also approved the ratification by special conventions, the method proposed under the Virginia Plan. By June 13 the committee had finished its work and reported the results to the Convention. The results were substantially the Virginia Plan without the Council of Revision, which most delegates recognized as a clumsy contrivance sure to make mischief. Madison's near-mad scheme to give the Congress a veto over state legislation remained in the Plan. The principle of equality of representation in the Congress did not survive these deliberations as the committee recommended allocation of representatives in both houses according to population with a slave counting as three-fifths of a man.[14]

13. For discussions of the Virginia Plan, *ibid.*, 45–239 (quotations are on 88, 96).
14. *Ibid.*, 235–37.

Representation and the means of selecting representatives provided subjects which might have deadlocked the committee of the whole. The large states had their way as the small scrambled about trying to pull themselves together. The small did succeed in substituting election of the second house by state legislatures for the means recommended in the Virginia Plan—election by the lower house.[15]

Although nothing appears in the notes of the debates, representation in Congress and election of its members must have been connected in the delegates' minds. If both houses were popularly elected, as James Wilson desired, the argument for apportioning representatives by population would be almost irresistible. Hence the debate over the selection of the lower house carried an extraordinary, though unspoken, meaning.

Roger Sherman of Connecticut almost made this meaning explicit in his opposition to popular election in the following sentence: "If it were in view to abolish the State Governments the elections ought to be by the people." In other words if the state governments were to be preserved they must elect the officers of the national government. Early in the Convention, Sherman also professed a strong animus against the people saying that they "should have as little to do as may be about the Government. They want information and are constantly liable to be misled." Later when the protection of state rights was not at stake, Sherman proved more sympathetic to popular control than these first statements suggest.[16]

Sherman's ally in opposing elections by the people, Elbridge Gerry of Massachusetts, does not seem to have opposed such elections for Sherman's reasons. Gerry, who decried a leveling spirit, insisted simply that "The evils we experience flow from the excess of democracy."[17]

The day after the committee of the whole reported its revision of the Virginia Plan, William Paterson of New Jersey stood up and asked for an adjournment of a day to allow several delegations time to offer a "purely federal" plan to the Convention. The Convention adjourned and the next day, June 15, when Paterson presented the New Jersey Plan, the meaning of "purely federal" became clear. Paterson's plan— the production of delegates from Delaware, New York, Connecticut, Maryland, as well as New Jersey—included several provisions clearly borrowed from Virginia's proposals, but retained the essential structure

15. *Ibid.*, 156, 235.
16. For Sherman's comments, *ibid.*, 133, 48.
17. *Ibid.*, 48.

of the old Confederation—a Congress of one house in which the states were equally represented. The Congress would appoint a plural executive, and the executive would appoint a supreme court of rather limited jurisdiction. State equality remained the primary concern of New Jersey's delegation and of those from the other states that helped in composing the alternative to the Virginia Plan. These states did not object to a powerful central government—the New Jersey Plan required that congressional statutes "and all Treaties made and ratified under the authority of the United States shall be the supreme law of the respective states so far forth as those acts or treaties shall relate to the said states or their citizens." Should a state refuse to observe a statute or a treaty, the executive was empowered to compel its adherence. And the Congress would enjoy new powers, most notably to tax and to regulate commerce.[18]

The New Jersey Plan's first resolution described those that followed as measures which "revised, corrected and enlarged" the Articles of Confederation, a nice—and wicked—touch, lifted from Randolph's unamended plan. As an enlargement of the Articles, it would of course have to win the approval of the Congress and the state legislatures. There was nothing in the New Jersey Plan calculated to rouse democratic sympathies.

Paterson described his proposal in measured terms. It involved, he said, no violation of the people's trust; it "accorded with the powers of the Convention" and the "sentiments of the people." What Paterson meant in this part of his speech was that the Convention was approaching revolutionary action in approving the Virginia Plan with its fresh structure and its requirement that the new constitution receive popular ratification. His plan in contrast brought no threat to constitutionalism or public confidence.[19]

The committee of the whole listened and understood. In the next three days James Wilson compared the two plans and suggested that a legislature composed of only one house invited a "legislative despotism." "If the legislative authority be not restrained," Wilson said, "there can be neither liberty nor stability; and it can only be restrained by dividing it within itself, into distinct and independent branches. In a single House there is no check, but the inadequate one, of the virtue and good sense of those who compose it." Wilson also took up Paterson's contention that the Virginia Plan exceeded the authority of the Convention by

18. *Ibid.*, 242–45; *ibid.*, III, 611–16.
19. *Ibid.*, I, 250.

stating that the Convention could "conclude nothing" but was "at liberty to propose anything."[20]

Those arguments found sympathetic listeners in the large states. But it remained for Charles Pinckney and James Madison to isolate the underlying difference between the two parties of adherents. The "whole," according to Pinckney, came to this: "give New Jersey an equal vote, and she will dismiss her scruples, and concur in the National system." Madison, who spoke on June 18, the day after Hamilton gave a long, irrelevant discourse praising elective monarchy, pointed out that New Jersey and the other like-minded states might someday rue their advocacy of the equality of states. The prospect of many new states formed out of the West should make New Jersey pause; these states would undoubtedly enter the Union "when they contained but few inhabitants. If they should be entitled to vote according to their proportions of inhabitants, all would be right and safe." But let them "have an equal vote, and a more objectionable minority than ever might give law to the whole."[21]

The debate stopped when Madison finished, and the vote showed the weakness of the small states. Only New Jersey and New York voted for Paterson's plan, and the committee reported out the Virginia proposals. The small states wanted to control the government and agreed that state equality offered the means. But at this time they could not agree on much more.[22]

Small-state delegates attempted to collect themselves in the next couple of days as the Convention took up the report of the committee of the whole, the revised Virginia Plan. The large states first raised defeated spirits in the small by agreeing that the first resolution should read that the "Government of the United States ought to consist of a supreme Legislative, Executive, and Judiciary" rather than the "national" government. The word "national" excited small-state suspicions of the intentions of the large, and the change in wording went at least part way toward reassuring them. But the reassurance they most craved was equality in the national legislature. Three of them—New Jersey, Delaware, and New York—immediately opposed the resolution calling for a Congress of two houses. They had no hope of making their opposition stick; rather they intended to extract a concession to equality of the states. Roger Sherman offered a compromise almost at once, saying that "if

20. For Wilson's speech, *ibid.*, 252–55 (quotations on 253, 254).
21. *Ibid.*, 255, 314–22 (for Madison's speech).
22. *Ibid.*, 322.

the difficulty on the subject of representation cannot be otherwise got over, he would agree to have two branches, and a proportional representation in one of them, provided each State had an equal voice in the other." The large states refused the bait and landed their own fish, approval of a two-house legislature, with ease.[23]

Aristocratic bias, or planters' interest, next made itself felt in a motion, offered by General Charles Cotesworth Pinckney of South Carolina, that the lower house should be elected as the state legislatures directed rather than by the people. The play here for planter control with the protection of slavery in mind escaped no one. Of the southern states, however, only South Carolina joined by Connecticut, New Jersey, and Delaware, supported this motion. The Virginia Plan's provision that the people should choose the first branch then won approval with only New Jersey opposing.[24]

The problem of the second branch remained unsolved, and, though the Convention spent part of the last days of June discussing such matters as who should pay representatives and what qualifications they should have, it persisted in popping up. On June 27 the Convention began still another effort at dealing with it. These efforts unfortunately served not only to clarify premises but to harden them. That result, though not unanticipated perhaps, stands as another instance in history of good intentions leading to unintended results.[25]

The question of why the delegates debated the issue of representation so forcefully is not as simple as it seems. They might have abandoned what was by this time their usual practice and simply voted, much after all had been said about representation. But the delegates were, for all their practicality, much too imaginative to allow an opportunity to pass without examining once again the major division among them. They were men of pride; some may have believed that they might change the minds of the opposition. In any case almost all dreaded failure— and they were staring at failure. They had no choice but to argue out their differences. Since the large states were urging the acceptance of a constitutional system which could only reduce small-state power, they saw the debates as providing a chance to reassure the small. Over the next few days both Madison and Wilson denied the existence of a "combination" of the large against the others in the Union. Madison reviewed

23. *Ibid.*, 335–44 (Sherman quotation on 343).
24. *Ibid.*, 358–60.
25. *Ibid.*, 383–443.

the interests of Massachusetts, Pennsylvania, and Virginia and found nothing that threatened a "combination."[26]

Size certainly did not draw them together, he concluded. "Experience rather taught a contrary lesson." Among individuals, the rich and eminent more commonly fought one another than combined against the weak. Among nations, an analogous situation existed—for example, "Carthage and Rome tore one another to pieces instead of uniting their forces to devour the weaker nations of the Earth." Among the ancient and modern confederacies the contentions, not the coalitions, of Sparta, Athens, and Thebes proved fatal to the smaller members of the Amphictyonic Confederacy. And if large states *"singly"* should prove threatening would not the safety of the small be secured best if the Union provided a "perfect incorporation" of the thirteen states, a Union which would have the strength to protect all its citizens from any part?[27]

There is no reason not to accept as genuine the small states' fears of the large. They had heard a great deal about majoritarian tyranny in recent months and were to listen to a good deal more. Where, they asked, was the majority but in the large? Madison, Randolph, and Wilson had reproached the small states for their refusal to comply with congressional requisitions and had expressed the impatience of the large states with the small. The small after all were being asked to change a system in which their weight had been evident. No one could anticipate clearly what the new would do to their power, and they, like the large states, wanted to exercise as much control as possible in the Union.[28]

Ellsworth, Sherman, and Johnson, all from Connecticut, made the heart of the case for equality of representation with minor, though long-winded, aid from Luther Martin. The essential weakness in the argument for proportional representation, they insisted, was that it rested on a misunderstanding of the Confederacy. The states in reality were joined together by an agreement much like a treaty; they were free and sovereign. Now they were asked to give up their equal voices in the Union, in effect to be consolidated out of existence, for as Bedford of Delaware explained, "there was no middle way between a perfect consolidation and a mere confederacy of the states." Bedford's rhetoric may have embarrassed his colleagues from the small states; they sought not a continuation of the old system but rather a compromise that would give the states an equal voice in the upper house. Still, Bedford's extravagance

26. *Ibid.*, 446–49.
27. *Ibid.*, 448, for the quotations. See also, *ibid.*, 463–65 (Madison), 467 (Gerry).
28. See, e.g., *ibid.*, 450 (Sherman), 468–69 (Ellsworth).

had its uses; most notably it made the compromisers look more reasonable and moderate than they really were. Ellsworth himself, a sober and careful advocate, argued that "No instance of a Confederacy has existed in which an equality of voices has not been exercised by the members of it," an inaccurate assessment of history he was soon to choke back down. In any case there was no need for so drastic a change as popular representation in both houses, Ellsworth contended. "We are running from one extreme to another. We are razing the foundations of the building. When we need only repair the roof. No salutary measure has been lost for want of a majority of the states, to favor it," an argument—if true—that made the existence of the Convention a little hard to understand.[29]

There were also principles at stake; both sides agreed on that. The small states saw their version of the government as representing the ideals of the Revolution. Their principles were the rights of man. They professed not to understand why anyone would wish to depart from a constitution that defended their rights. Martin's remark "that the language of the States being sovereign and independent, was once familiar and understood," but now seemed "strange and obscure," carried genuine bewilderment.[30]

What Luther Martin described as the language of the states did not impress Madison and Wilson as the language of the Revolution. Both rejected the small-state contention that a treaty bound the Confederation together. Far from a union of equals, the Confederation possessed some—but not enough—authority over the states. The examples Madison cited, though not the stuff of the ordinary operations of government, made his point: "In the cases of captures, of piracies, and of offenses in a federal army, the property and persons of individuals depend on the laws of Congress." What was proposed would lengthen this list and would grant "the highest prerogative of supremacy" to the "National Government." In this government of considerable power, simple justice required that the majority rule. Wilson agreed and rejected the Connecticut proposal of a compromise—the lower house to be apportioned according to population, the upper according to state equality—and cited statistics which purported to show that such an arrangement would permit the minority to control the majority. Seven states, Wilson noted, might control six; seven with one-third of the country's population would control six with two-thirds of the population. "Can we forget," he asked, "for

29. *Ibid.*, 490–92, 500–502 (Bedford), 484–85 (Ellsworth).
30. *Ibid.*, 468.

whom we are forming a Government? Is it for men, or for the imaginary beings called States? . . . The rule of suffrage ought on every principle to be the same in the second as in the first branch."[31]

Madison phrased the argument even more passionately than Wilson. He denied flatly that the states were sovereign—"in fact they are only political societies. There is a gradation of power in all societies, from the lowest corporation to the highest sovereign. The states never possessed the essential rights of sovereignty. These were always vested in Congress." The states, Madison argued, "are only great corporations, having the power of making by-laws, and these are effectual only if they are not contradictory to the general confederation. The states ought to be placed under the control of the general government—at least as much so as they formerly were under the King and British Parliament." And from these propositions about the character of the states—devoid of sovereignty, mere corporations, properly under the thumb of the national government—it followed that since America was a republic, representation must be based on the people.[32]

The knowledge of history in Madison's arguments is impressive, his logic is impeccable, and his failure to convince small-state delegates completely understandable. The large states were simply asking too much in expecting the small to accept a status as "corporations," analogous to "counties," in a great unitary—the word used more often was "consolidated"—government. Madison's language was so stark, his conception of federal-state relations so clear-cut that the implications of the Virginia Plan could not escape anyone. What the small states required was assurance that individual rights would be protected under a new constitution and that state lines would not be obliterated. The second concern may indeed have been uppermost in their minds. Logic, history, reason were weak weapons in a struggle against local feeling, especially when that feeling had a long history of its own.[33]

Feelings found expression on the last day of June. The discussions had eaten deeply of energies, apparently to no good purpose. The small had proposed what they considered to be a compromise; the large under the prod of Madison and Wilson had refused it. With deadlock apparent and failure of the Convention possible, an obviously frustrated and angered Bedford accused the large-state delegations of speaking to the

31. *Ibid.*, 447, 482–84.
32. *Ibid.*, 471–72.
33. For Madison's later comments on his language in this speech, see Brant, *James Madison: Father*, 85–87.

small with a "dictatorial air" and warned that if the large dissolved the meeting the small would begin the search for foreign allies. These words set off a small explosion in King of Massachusetts, who responded with reproaches of his own. Bedford—not he—had spoken with "dictatorial language"; Bedford—not he—had been vehement; Bedford—not he—had declared himself willing to abandon "our common Country." This exchange occurred on Saturday. Two days later, on Monday, July 2, the Convention divided five states to five, with Georgia split, on the motion to provide equality of representation in the second branch. Roger Sherman described the Convention then as "at a full stop." A few minutes of discussion revealed that no one wished to remain at a stop; nor did anyone want the Convention to dissolve. With only New Jersey and Delaware voting "no," the Convention then decided to submit the matter to a grand committee which was instructed to work out a compromise.[34]

The grand committee included neither Madison nor Wilson. One delegate sat from each state, Franklin from Pennsylvania and Mason from Virginia. The Convention chose the committee by ballot, and its composition promised that some accommodation would be forthcoming. The Convention thus stated its intentions of continuing and of writing a constitution.[35]

The report delivered by the committee has been usually referred to as the Great Compromise. In fact it conceded the small-state formula as Ellsworth and the Connecticut delegation had devised it—one representative for every 40,000 inhabitants, the count to reckon five slaves as three freemen; the lower house to have the sole right to originate money bills; equality of representation in the upper house.

For the most part reactions followed the usual lines. Gerry, although not altogether pleased with the report, presented it to the Convention and in the next two weeks defended it. He, like several members from large states, may have felt compelled to give his support because of his part in drafting the report. Not all shared this feeling, but any defectors from the older alignment were important. They included Franklin, George Mason, and a man largely unknown to most delegates, William R. Davie of North Carolina.[36]

Madison opposed and said so with great force. There was something new in his tone, a threatening edge as he spoke of the possibility of

34. Farrand, I, 490–93 (Bedford and King), 510, 511–16.
35. *Ibid.*, 516.
36. *Ibid.*, 524–26.

"the principal states comprehending a majority of the people" agreeing on a "just and judicious plan" which all other states might "by degrees" accede to, phrasing that implied an attempt to form a union outside the Convention. Gouverneur Morris objected in wild terms—"This Country must be united. If Persuasion does not unite it, the sword will." And "the Gallows and Halter will finish the work of the sword." Bedford and others reproached him for this talk, and the work of trying to find agreement continued.[37]

As was becoming the custom of the Convention, further committees were resorted to as each of the main clauses of the original report were taken up. Whether intended or not, this tactic served to tie more delegates to the report or to some version closely resembling it. Everyone knew that the clause allowing each state a vote in the upper house was, as Gerry said on July 7, "the central question." Gerry declared himself willing to agree to it rather than have no accommodation at all. Still, the other clauses received close scrutiny and were the subjects of intense discussions.[38]

The discussions differed from earlier ones. They were spare, almost dry, lacking in references to ancient and modern confederacies and to the ideas of political theory. Principles were stated flatly in a few words. The delegates cut away the context and eschewed indirection in favor of direct assertions about the interests of their individual states. Thus they spent many hours on the number of representatives each state would have in the lower house. They speculated on population growth, trying to anticipate the changes that would have to be accommodated. With growth in mind, Gerry and King argued for a motion which would have forever restricted representatives from new states in the West to a number no greater than "the representatives from such of the thirteen United States as shall accede to this Confederation." On this point a sense of fairness obtruded itself and coupled to the interests of states with large backcountries produced a majority against the motion.[39]

A desire to avoid a deadlock produced agreement on one of the sorest points in the Convention: the proposal, originally by Gouverneur Morris (who later regretted it), to make representation in the lower house proportionate to direct taxation. Direct taxation was to be levied on the basis of five slaves counting as three freemen. This equation turned stomachs but seemed necessary if South Carolina and Georgia were to be persuaded to stay within the Union.

37. *Ibid.*, 527–29 (Madison), 529–31 (Morris), 531–32 (Bedford).
38. *Ibid.*, 550.
39. *Ibid.*, 548–606, *passim; ibid.*, II, 203 (on Gerry and King's motion).

The entire proposal won approval on July 16, including the crucial recommendation of equality in the upper house. The vote proved to be as close as possible: Massachusetts divided, with Gerry and Caleb Strong in favor and King and Gorham in opposition; the small-state coalition held together and with North Carolina's support carried the motion; Pennsylvania, Virginia, South Carolina, and Georgia opposed. New York, which surely would have approved, could not vote—Lansing and Yates had gone home.[40]

III

The Convention thus solved the problem of power. The national government would be one of strength, and the small states believed that they would have an important hand in its exercise. From this point on, the persistent nationalism of the delegates found expression. With the "compromise" the old alignments collapsed, and divisions thereafter, such as they were, followed sectional and property lines. Not that sectional and property interests fully defined the issues. The Convention after all was in the process of framing a constitution. With the question of power pretty well disposed of, political theory and experience, favorite references of many, could be consulted more directly than when the primary issue lay between large and small states.

The nationalism of the small states appeared immediately as the Convention resumed its business after deciding on equality in the upper house. The sixth resolution of the Virginia Plan was under examination, a resolution dealing with the powers of the national legislature. Roger Sherman moved that the powers should be enumerated, a motion that lost badly—in part because Sherman had not included direct taxation on his list. Bedford immediately proposed that the national legislature be empowered "to legislate in all cases for the general interests of the Union, and also in those to which the States are separately incompetent." Randolph responded with a short assessment which held that Bedford's idea involved the violation of all the laws and constitutions of the states, a "formidable" idea he said. Bedford insisted that his version of the grant of power was no more formidable than the one Randolph had given the Convention. With that, discussion ended, and Bedford's motion passed. The vote revealed that the old coalitions had been shattered: Connecticut opposed and was joined by Virginia, South Carolina, and Georgia. The six states in favor included Massachusetts, Pennsylvania, and the remainder of the small states.[41]

40. *Ibid.*, II, 15–16.
41. *Ibid.*, 25–27.

What powers the national legislature should exercise involved tangled issues which would come up again, and no delegate imagined that Bedford's motion settled them. The executive branch exposed complexities almost as tortuous, and the Convention failed to master them in the next two weeks. It tried, however, in long sessions which heard Madison and Wilson argue for bringing the people into the heart of the process of electing the executive. Gouverneur Morris, although never a champion of democracy, joined them. His reasons owed more to his fear of intrigue in the national legislature than to his faith in the people. Wilson and Madison noted that the people would be uninvolved in the intimate processes of government, which would also be free of the faction and intrigue normally accompanying those processes. Only leaders of quality would likely produce an outstanding executive. This reasoning may have struck others as rather strained; in any event on July 17 the Convention decided on election of the executive by the national legislature. This decision seemed unsatisfactory to many, but it stood for the time being while the delegates thrashed about over the term of the executive, whether he should be eligible for re-election, be subject to impeachment, and be given a veto over legislation.[42]

The debates that followed were confused. The delegates may not have felt fatigue after reaching compromise on equality in the second branch, but they showed impatience. They also realized that much remained to be accomplished, and when agreement seemed impossible they pushed ahead to fresh resolutions. Before they adjourned on July 26, for ten days, in order to give a committee of detail—surely an ill-chosen name—time to pull together a constitution in the rough, they managed to make several important decisions. To James Madison's dismay, they tossed out his cherished notion of a congressional veto of state laws. They also decided that the judiciary should be appointed by the upper house, another decision unsatisfactory to Madison; and they agreed that provisions should be made for amendment of the constitution. Ellsworth and Paterson, in a revival of their earlier partnership, argued that the state legislatures should ratify whatever constitution the Convention drafted. Madison argued for popular ratification and carried the Convention with him.

Throughout the last days of July, when these matters came up, the Convention returned over and over again to the definition of the executive. No clear alignments persisted throughout the convoluted discussions

42. *Ibid.*, 29–32, 33–128, *passim.*

and votes of these days. There were consistent lines of argument, however: Madison and Wilson strongly urged election by the people, or at least election by some body of electors chosen by the people. Madison also argued strongly for giving the authority to revise laws to the executive and a part of the judiciary. His and Wilson's reasons hinged on their conviction that the national legislature would likely encroach on all other authority and would be an "overmatch for them" even if they did cooperate. As Madison saw things: "Experience in all the States had evinced a powerful tendency in the Legislature to absorb all power into its vortex. This was the real source of danger to the American Constitutions; and suggested the necessity of giving every defensive authority to the other departments that was consistent with republican principles." Ellsworth, who did not agree with Madison on the method of election, agreed with him on executive and judicial cooperation.[43]

There were by previous standards other curious alignments until finally on July 26, the Convention put the results of its agreements and disagreements into the hands of the committee of detail. This group was charged to draft a constitution which conformed to the decisions already taken in the Convention. It had also to reckon with the "decisions" the Convention had been unable to make, including several about the executive. Charles Cotesworth Pinckney also delivered his own charge, a warning that if the committee failed to find a way of preventing the emancipation of slaves and the taxation of slaves, his state would withhold its support. The Convention listened politely and then carefully selected a committee which included Pinckney's colleague John Rutledge, who served as chairman of the group. The other members were Randolph, Gorham, Ellsworth, and James Wilson.[44]

The committee of detail reported on August 6 as scheduled. It apparently had worked together without major disagreements. Randolph and Wilson seem to have written most of the report, a document which in rough became the Constitution after further revision. The committee of detail had heeded C. C. Pinckney's warning not to tamper with slavery. The seventh article of the report contained a flat injunction against prohibiting the importation of persons. As far as the rest of the report was concerned, the committee had drawn on the Virginia Plan and earlier decisions of the Convention, and it had incorporated the powers of Congress set forth in the Articles of Confederation. It had also added a number of ideas of its own and ignored one of the most important

43. *Ibid.*, 74 (quotation).
44. *Ibid.*, 85, 95–96, 97.

of the Convention's: the general grant of power to Congress which Bedford had moved. Still, the Congress as envisioned by the committee would not lack authority—it could tax just about as it wished except that direct taxes must be in proportion to a census, a requirement also intended to protect slavery. Congress was also authorized "to make all laws that shall be necessary and proper for carrying into execution" the powers it and the government were vested with.[45]

Although the Convention modified portions of the report, it responded generally with favor. It left intact the structure of government recommended by the committee, and it accepted the enumeration of powers, though it would do much more about legislative power in following weeks. What the Convention refused to do may have been almost as important as any of its responses to the report. The committee of detail had recommended that the electors of the lower house be the same as those choosing the more numerous branch of the states' legislatures. Gouverneur Morris feared or professed to fear that this provision invited tyranny. "The time is not distant," Morris argued, "when this Country will abound with mechanics and manufacturers who will receive their bread from their employers." Morris doubted that these workers could resist the opportunity of selling their votes to the rich who would set themselves up as an aristocracy. To forestall this development Morris urged that the suffrage be confined to freeholders, men of property—"the best guardians of liberty," as John Dickinson, who agreed, called them.[46]

The association of liberty with property had long found approval in England and America, and it proved hard at first for the Convention to resist Morris's amendment. Wilson and Ellsworth disputed Morris's claims at once, joined soon by Mason and Rutledge. Madison seemed for a time unable to make up his mind but he did state that on "its merits alone, the freeholders of the country would be the safest depositories of republican liberty." What prevented Madison from voting for Morris's proposal may have been a feeling that the ordinary people of the nation would be repelled by it and would then reject the constitution. Benjamin Franklin helped reinforce this notion in an effective answer to Morris. Franklin reminded the Convention of the people's "virtue and public spirit" which, he said, had contributed so much to the winning of the war. Debate stopped soon after Franklin spoke, and Morris's motion was rejected.[47]

45. The report is in *ibid.*, 177–89.
46. *Ibid.*, 202–3 (Morris), 202 (Dickinson).
47. *Ibid.*, 203–4 (Madison), 204–5 (Franklin).

This decision on the suffrage did not consume much time. Yet it involved a revealing set of motives and premises. It drew on republican theory; it elicited short analyses of the American people and predictions of what they might become; it also forced the delegates to consider how politics actually worked. Was there anything else below the surface? A regard for property and a class bias surely were; they indeed inhered in republican theory.

All of these dispositions, motives, and concerns figured in the review of the rest of the report. By this time the delegates understood one another well, and for the most part they found explaining their assumptions unnecessary. They pushed through a variety of recommendations, accepting some, changing many, and postponing a try at cracking apparently uncrackable nuts. In the final week of August they put together another compromise, one that left them feeling uneasy and perhaps guilty.

The committee of detail had proposed that Congress be prohibited from taxing importations of slaves. As had become the practice of the Convention, the committee had not used the word "slave" but everyone understood which "persons" the committee had in mind in recommending the prohibition. The committee had also included a clause providing that no navigation act should be passed without the assent of two-thirds of the members present in each house.[48]

The barrier against taxing the slave trade was intended to ease the not-so-tender sensibilities of South Carolinian and Georgian planters. One of the Carolinians warned the Convention in the discussion that neither the Carolinas nor Georgia would approve the constitution if the slave trade were not protected. No doubt C. C. Pinckney and perhaps others as well were issuing similar threats. Whether such predictions were really necessary to obtain protection of the trade is doubtful. The Convention knew that it was near the end of its work, and its spirit was by this time very much in accord with compromise. Still there were members who felt revulsion at any concessions to slavery. Most who did seem to have said so. Rufus King, by this time thoroughly disenchanted with catering to planters' interests, contained his anger and remarked only of the injustice of protecting one sort of property. John Dickinson was considerably blunter. George Mason reckoned the costs of indulging the slave interests in providential terms, saying that slave masters were petty tyrants. "They bring the judgment of heaven

48. Article VII [VI], Sect. 4, 6, in *ibid.*, 183.

on a Country. As Nations cannot be rewarded or punished in the next world they must be in this. By an inevitable chain of causes and effects providence punishes national sins, by national calamities." These words undoubtedly came from Mason's conscience—he himself owned slaves and lived off their labor. But Mason was a Virginian, and his state, which currently had a surplus of slaves, would profit by selling them southward should the importation be stopped. The Carolinians were convinced, as C. C. Pinckney said a few weeks later, that deprived of slaves, South Carolina would soon be a "desert waste." Pinckney questioned whether Mason and the Virginians opposed the trade from principle—or from purse.[49]

Concern for purse was not confined to the deep southern states. Northern business would have been affected by the requirement of two-thirds approval for navigation acts, and so might southern planters with staples to sell. The southerners feared that a Congress controlled by the North might bar foreign ships from carrying American trade and that without such competition American shippers would plunder the southerners. Northern delegates naturally considered the proposed two-thirds provision to be unfair—it gave a veto to a minority in the southern states.

Given the mood of the Convention a compromise was almost inevitable, and in this last week of August it was concluded. A provision against any prohibition of the slave trade before 1808 was agreed to, and, a few days later, the delegates from South Carolina and Georgia supported a change to a simple majority for passage of navigation acts. At the time of the concession to the advocates of the slave trade, Madison remarked laconically: "Twenty years will produce all the mischief that can be apprehended from the liberty to import slaves." Gouverneur Morris's comment had more bite: he was for making the clause read that "importation of slaves into North Carolina, South Carolina, and Georgia shall not be prohibited." Luther Martin laid bare the savage irony of the situation—a people opposing Great Britain's attempts to enslave them now take measures to assure themselves a supply of slaves, all the while claiming freedom on the grounds of the natural rights of mankind. But Madison's final judgment a few months later that "Great as the evil is, a dismemberment of the union would be worse"—was more persuasive to most white Americans.[50]

On August 31, two days after beating back an attempt to untie this arrangement, the Convention selected a committee on unfinished parts

49. *Ibid.*, 370 (Mason), 372–73 (Dickinson), 373 (King); *ibid.*, III, 254 (Pinckney).
50. *Ibid.*, II, 415 (Madison and Morris); *ibid.*, III, 211–12 (Martin), 325 (Madison).

to bring in a report on still unresolved questions. Included among these questions was a recommendation of the committee of detail that Congress receive power

> to provide, as may become necessary, from time to time, for the well managing and securing the common property and general interests and welfare of the United States in such manner as shall not interfere with the Governments of individual States in matters which respect only their internal Police, or for which their individual authorities may be competent.[51]

This grant was immense. It summed up earlier proposals by Madison and Sherman, and the already approved resolution by Bedford. The committee on unfinished parts had to decide whether to include this clause in the general enumeration of Congressional powers or to set a more modest limit. It had also to consider how taxing authority should be defined, for what purposes, who should originate money bills, the powers of the Senate, and the method of selecting the President.

This last problem had already vexed the convention for weeks—both Madison and Wilson agreed that it had caused more heartburn than anything else—and it continued to undergo discussion. The committee made its recommendations on it and the other questions in the early days of September. The President, it said, should be elected by the people through an electoral college, serve for four years, and be eligible for re-election. Should no candidate receive a majority, the Senate should choose from the five receiving the most votes. The committee cut the Senate down to size by proposing that it not make treaties and choose Supreme Court judges and ambassadors, responsibilities the Convention had seemed determined to vest it with. Nor would the Senate be permitted to originate money bills although it might amend them. The massive grant of power to do virtually all things in the name of the general welfare was quietly discarded, replaced by a narrower but still powerful authorization. This grant pertained to the authority of Congress to spend and lend: "The legislature shall have power to lay and collect taxes, duties, imposts, and excises, to pay the debts and provide for the common defence and general welfare of the United States."[52]

This wording made its way into the Constitution as did the other solutions proposed by the committee. The one important revision of

51. *Ibid.*, II, 367.
52. *Ibid.*, 497.

the committee's work concerned the method of electing the President. By this time the electoral college had won acceptance, but disagreement persisted over who should act if it was unable to reach a majority. The committee on unfinished parts had recommended that the Senate choose, a recommendation acceptable to most of the small-state delegates. After further discussion and much unsuccessful maneuvering the convention apparently was swayed by Mason and Wilson who argued that giving the Senate this power would create "an aristocracy worse than absolute monarchy." Roger Sherman suggested a way out of this tangle: election by the House of Representatives, each state delegation casting one vote.[53]

The most important work of the Convention was completed by September 8, when one more committee was chosen—a committee of style and arrangement—charged to revise the mass of articles into the coherent form of a constitution. Madison and Alexander Hamilton both sat on this committee, but the real work was done by Gouverneur Morris, who had the pen of a gifted editor. Morris slashed the accumulation of excess words, reorganized those remaining, and rewrote the Preamble. When he and the committee were done, they discovered that they had satisfied the Convention, a body not easily satisfied.[54]

On September 17, the delegates signed. George Mason, still unhappy over the decision to drop the two-thirds requirement for the passage of navigation acts, refused as did Edmund Randolph and Elbridge Gerry. Randolph explained that without promise of another convention which would consider amendments he would have to withhold his signature, although he had not decided on whether to oppose or support ratification. Gerry's reasons do not seem entirely clear; a sympathetic account of his refusal lays it to his belief that the Constitution was not appropriate to a republican people.[55]

The others did not agree and signed, apparently sharing a hope that ratification might follow without difficulty. Ratification was given in the next nine months, but not without difficulty and a certain amount of strain. Perhaps the difficulty was inevitable. On the whole it was minor, given what the Americans had already overcome.

53. *Ibid.*, 515, 527.
54. *Ibid.*, 547, 553.
55. *Ibid.*, 644–45 (Randolph); George Athan Billias, *Elbridge Gerry: Founding Father and Republican Statesman* (New York, 1975), 200–205, is a fine account of this matter and others.

26

Ratification:
An End and a Beginning

What had happened in the Constitutional Convention? A fairly common opinion in 1787 had it that there had been a withdrawal of the original commitment to the principles of the American Revolution. Those of this persuasion pointed out that the Constitution virtually destroyed the old Confederation of sovereign states and replaced it with what they called "consolidated" government. In this government, power and sovereignty lay at the center—not in the individual states. In the year following the close of the federal Convention there were to be many variations on the meaning of consolidation.

Since 1787 many historians have expanded these opinions, and describe the Constitution as the expression of a conservative movement. Not many any longer see it as the product of a conspiracy by holders of public securities, all bent on lining their own pockets and those of their class. Perhaps more argue that in the Constitution an elite established a frame of government which, for a short time at least, successfully curbed a growing democracy. The Constitution in this interpretation was a conservative response to a profound move toward democracy stimulated by the Revolution. In 1776, we are told, the democracy captured the Revolution and proclaimed its great principles. In the process, democratic political arrangements were fashioned, in particular the state constitutions and the Articles of Confederation. These institutions and the ideals they embodied presumably all revolved around the premise that sovereignty lay in the people. The historians who detect a democracy surging into public life in 1776 insist that the years from 1776 to 1781 saw the Revolution defined, and they judge all that took place afterwards against those years, against what they presume to be the true standard of revolutionary action.

This argument is parochial and in some ways ahistorical, presuming as it does to lay down a norm against which later history is rendered invalid. For the Revolution was a complex set of events taking place over almost thirty years, events which in fact went through a number of phases. To assume that one phase is more "revolutionary," or more "conservative," than another inhibits understanding of them all.

Once independence was won and peace made, revolutionary issues changed. The period before 1783 had one set of problems, all connected to establishing independence. The period following concerned many of the same problems, especially of how free men should govern themselves. Yet these periods differ too—a war dominated the years between 1775 and 1783, a war with its own imperatives and objectives. Everyone recognized that some of the methods of governance resorted to in war were not suitable for peace. Thus, though the problems after the war look similar to those of the earlier years, concerning as they did governance, they were in fact different because they occurred in a context of peace. It is true that in the 1780s Americans had to face problems inherited from the war, but independence and peace put these problems in a new setting.

When the war ended, men of affairs—merchants, lawyers, large farmers, and planters—were running the Congress, the state legislatures, and the army. They were men of vision and not without passion, but the concern for a virtuous republic probably was not as prominent in their minds as it had been earlier, or as it had been in the minds of the likes of Samuel Adams. Rather, efficiency in commerce and energy in government seemed almost as important as virtue—and essential to it. Their vision, perhaps their dreams, now focused on large organizations, including the nation, and the power that these organizations could muster. Their preoccupations were natural given the problems that remained from the war and given their own experience in government, especially in the Congress and the army.

Such men wrote the Constitution. They did so in a mood marked by disenchantment. For the delegates shared the widespread suspicion that virtue might be in flight from a deteriorating America. But they were not devoid of hope based on the American achievements of the previous thirty years. These achievements remained so dazzling that few if any among the delegates were disposed to give up an equally powerful conviction that the American experiment in republicanism would yield a great example to the world.

These complex attitudes give evidence of the persistence of Protestant and Whiggish values which had saturated American atmospheres in the 1760s and up to at least 1779. They testify as well to the strength of the old morality and its power to shape perceptions of politics. For public life in the 1780s, as before the war, was understood to derive its health from the morality of the people. A virtuous people, most Americans agreed, were a people who valued frugality, despised luxury, hated corruption, and preferred moderation and balance to extremes of any sort, especially in the orders of society. Above all else they were a people who retained a sense of responsibility to public interests even when those interests clashed with private purposes.

The slackening in these old standards and the lust for private gain that seemed to follow the war convinced the delegates to the Convention that a reordering of American government was necessary. Their disillusionment with the people's behavior forced them to admit to themselves the truth of a previously inadmissible proposition: the people themselves might be the source of tyranny. This recognition marked the appearance of a new realism in American constitutionalism which, like the radical Whig ideology at its center, had been prone, at least early in the Revolution, to idolize the people. This older version of Whig thought had conceived of the problem of politics as the opposition of the ruler to the ruled. How, this politics asked, was the ruler to be controlled, for if he were not controlled he would become a tyrant. Now in the 1780s, and most clearly in the Constitutional Convention, a new source of tyranny was identified—the people themselves.

Along with the new realism about politics went a new realism about society. The older Whig theory had assumed that because the people were one, all their interests were the same. From this assumption came all the facile talk about the public good, as if the people had only one thing on their minds. During the war political thought began to accommodate itself to the existence of interest groups, factions in eighteenth-century parlance, and thereby gained an unusual accuracy. At the Convention, James Madison spelled out the sources of faction and argued that in a large and complicated nation factionalism could be made to protect private rights. Madison's brilliant insight anticipated the course of two hundred years of American political life. He attained this prophetic accuracy at least in part because he saw deeply into the nature of the society that had emerged from the Revolutionary War.

American society had not been transformed by the war, but the basis for change had been laid. War had trained up a body of men accustomed to think in national terms and to work in large organizations. The war indeed had brought something approaching the beginnings of an organizational revolution to America. The nation was the greatest example of this change and the inspiration for all the lesser organizations. It had not replaced the states of course, but it provided a very different arena for the economy and for public policy. During the war, men in and out of the army had sought to serve their nation, and themselves, in raising military forces and in providing food, weapons, ammunition, and the other supplies required to maintain an institution of many men on a demanding mission. Although the army virtually disbanded in 1783, the experience of the previous eight years could not be dispensed with. Nor did anyone wish to turn the clock back—acquisitive appetites remained powerful in America and grew with the means of satisfying them. The war had reinforced them and, unconfined but disciplined and managed by men with a new sense of the fruitfulness of large-scale operations, they would make America a thriving nation. In the Constitution the delegates had created a framework through which the economy could find itself. The Constitution after all stopped state regulation of interstate commerce, it stopped wild schemes in public finance, and it virtually guaranteed an environment congenial to business. American business needed freedom and it needed order. The Constitution promised to provide both.

That freedom and order were tied to virtue had long appeared obvious to Americans. That virtue could not survive amidst anarchy was equally plain. The Constitution, its makers believed, would protect virtue. On the face of things, including the debates in the Convention, the idea that the Constitution expressed a moral view seems absurd. There were no genuine evangelicals in the Convention, and there were no heated declarations of Christian piety. Yet the Constitution managed to capture some of the morality long common in American life and clearly present in the first days of the Revolution.

For the Constitution confined power, power which had long been understood as threatening virtue as well as liberty. It aimed to thwart majoritarian tyranny, but it did not deny that sovereignty resided in the people. Government should serve the people, and in the Constitution the delegates sought to create a framework which would make such service effective, though not at the cost of the oppression of the minority. Hence the moderation of the Constitution, with its three balanced branches and its careful enumeration of powers. These restraints seemed promising to the founders for several reasons, not the least of which was that they would operate against corruption as well as majoritarian excess. Corruption sprang from an unbridled prerogative, irresponsible power which had in the colonial past sent hordes of placemen who sucked up American substance. In the Revolution the Americans drove out such creatures, and in the Constitution they sought through new means to achieve an old purpose, a virtuous public life. And that life could survive, Americans agreed, only if corruption in the broadest sense, as a general decay of society and morality, could be avoided. The restraints built into the Constitution might be depended upon to prevent corruption in the technical, or Whiggish, sense, the undue influence of the executive in the legislature and perhaps even in the newer form so graphically described by Madison, as majoritarian tyranny. But underlying any successful constitutionalism there had to be a virtuous people. The founders, especially Franklin, Madison, and Wilson, believed that the Convention must risk all, indeed risk the Revolution, by trusting the virtue of the American people.

Madison thought that the risk might be less in America than elsewhere because of the size of the country and the variety of its people. Spread over an enormous land, divided by state lines and by different interests, factions determined to dominate others would have difficulty concerting their actions. The history of the Revolution, which saw the people barely able to pull themselves together in the face of British oppression, verified this analysis. With peace they had in many states, however, formed irresponsible, even tyrannical majorities. But what could be done in a state might be impossible to duplicate in a nation composed of many varieties of factions and spread from the Atlantic to the Mississippi.

Thus the delegates placed their trust in the people because they had no choice: a republic had to found itself on the people. Their suspicions of popular power led to a preoccupation with restraints and curbs on the undue exercise of power by heedless majorities. At the same time the delegates' belief in majority rule, as an indispensable part of republican government, remained strong. Confining the majority—the source of power and therefore potentially of tyranny—had to be done. The limits protected the rights of the minority and of property, rights which had helped set the revolutionary process in motion in the 1760s.

But it was also necessary that the majority possess the freedom to exercise constitutional powers. The founders therefore concentrated on making the national legislature representative of the people. The great compromise removed the Senate from direct popular control, an arrangement Madison and Wilson had favored, but even so the Congress would be more democratic than it had been under the Articles of Confederation.

The House of Representatives after all would be popularly elected. Thus the people would be both free and confined—the people whatever their rank, station, or number. Free, because a republic required a virtuous people; confined, because the people of all sorts had human frailties.

The delegates phrased these assumptions in the language of republicanism. Though they did not resort to religion, they did indirectly invoke the old moral certainties familiar to the children of the twice-born. They did most clearly in the discussions in Philadelphia which considered the people's selfishness, their passions, and their propensity to do evil. And the Constitution itself, by establishing a government which seemed capable of restraining some of the worst impulses of man, especially his instinct to dominate others, spoke to a persistent concern in Protestant culture.[1]

II

The concern over power appeared immediately in the discussions which greeted the publication of the Constitution. It soon became apparent that not everyone agreed that power had been sufficiently curbed, especially power exercised from afar. Some of those who raised questions about the Constitution in the early autumn of 1787 did so in a language that suggested that they thought they faced a revival of tyranny in America. Thus they spoke of a "despotic aristocracy" behind the Constitution, and sometimes of a "masked aristocracy," masked presumably out of a desire to conceal authoritarian purposes. They also played on the words of the Constitution itself. The official who would head the executive branch was rendered as the "president-general" and sometimes as "our new king."[2]

In his letter of September 17 transmitting the Constitution to Congress, George Washington, as president of the Convention, may have given critics an opening by referring to the "consolidation of our Union" as one of the purposes of the Convention. Whatever the source, "consolidation" became almost immediately one of the most highly charged words of the process of ratification. The critics argued that the Constitu-

1. This interpretation is based on my reading of a variety of sources and studies. Perhaps the most influential interpretation of the drafting of the Constitution—and the most harmful to understanding—is Charles Beard's *An Economic Interpretation of the Constitution of the United States* (New York, 1913).
2. Cecelia M. Kenyon, ed., *The Antifederalists* (Indianapolis, Ind., 1966), 8, 17 (Letters of "Centinel"), 43 (Pennsylvania Minority), 86 (Philadelphiensis). (I have reduced the capitals in several of these words to the lower case.)

tion would establish a "consolidated government" in which the national government would exercise all powers at the expense of the states.[3]

The critics failed, however, to appropriate the one word to describe themselves which might have strengthened their arguments. The word was "Federalist." It was the supporters of the Constitution who began calling themselves Federalists as soon as the Convention closed, leaving their opponents to be almost inevitably branded as the Antifederalists, a much less useful name to a group which wished to identify state loyalties with themselves. The most important fact about Antifederalist thought was its opposition to the transfer of authority from the states to the national government. Perhaps most Antifederalists had approved the idea of amending the Articles of Confederation, at least to the extent of adding the authority to tax and to regulate commerce to Congress's powers. But the Constitution surprised and dismayed them by the extent of the changes it made and by the complexity it introduced into the structure of government. They had believed that the Convention would propose amendments to the Articles of Confederation that would go into effect only after ratification by all thirteen states. Now in September 1787 they faced a proposal for an entirely new constitution which would establish an entirely new government. And the new constitution was to become effective when only nine of the thirteen states approved.

The opposition to the Constitution should not have surprised anyone. The Revolution after all had been fought over questions of governance and rights. A generation of Americans had come to maturity amidst discussions of the nature of representation, of legislative and executive authority, of constitutionalism itself, and the need to protect individual rights. Another generation had grown old in the defense of independence and the right to self-government. Confronted by a major change in governing arrangements, the revolutionaries would have betrayed themselves and their recent achievements had they not asked questions about the change.

Those who found unsatisfactory the answers given to their questions opposed the Constitution. They voted for delegates who promised to vote against ratification; they published articles and tracts advocating rejection; they agitated and talked; they formed committees; and some served as delegates in the state conventions.

They did not arm themselves and secede from the Union. They did not make another revolution despite all their talk about the tyranny

3. Charles C. Tansill, ed., *Documents Illustrative of the Formation of the Union of the American States* (Washington, D.C., 1927), 1003–4.

hovering in the wings. Nor did anyone imprison them. The ratification process, in short, remained peaceful, despite the wild rhetoric it generated. And when it was completed, there was no fresh exodus from the United States such as the loyalists had made.

In tone and substance, nothing marked ratification so much as the controversy between Federalists and Antifederalists in Pennsylvania. One of the two political parties in the state, the "Constitutionalists," a name derived from their advocacy of the Pennsylvania constitution of 1776, included within its number a strong contingent of democrats who detected a conspiracy against the people in the Constitutional Convention. For example, Samuel Bryan, the son of George Bryan, a draftsman of the constitution of 1776, published a series of newspaper essays which described the division over the federal Constitution as dividing the people from the "wealthy and ambitious, who in every community think they have a right to lord it over their fellow creatures."[4] Thereafter, until ratification was completed in America, an undercurrent of class antagonism ran through much of the debate. In Pennsylvania, this antagonism represented considerable popular feeling. Elsewhere the call to the people to beware of the rich and the well-born may have been little more than a political tactic.[5]

As an explanation of behavior, conspiracy gains in persuasiveness as it is personified. In Pennsylvania the conspirators at hand were well known to everyone. The rich and well-born were the Republicans who had opposed the Pennsylvania constitution and who now supported the federal; they included Robert Morris, who had attended the Convention. In "The Chronicle of Early Times," Morris appeared as "Robert the Cofferer," interested only in the fortunes of "the mill," the Bank of North America. The Constitution erected a wall around the mill to protect it from the multitude: "And he reported to them faithfully all that had been done, and how the enemies of the mill had been put to flight." Assisting Robert the Cofferer were James Wilson, tagged here as "James the Caledonian," and Gouverneur Morris, who appeared as "Gouvero the cunning man." These three, and their cohorts, plotted to make the mill their own, to keep it free of popular control, and to share among themselves the corn, i.e., the money, it produced.[6]

---

4. Merrill Jensen et al., eds., *Documentary History of the Ratification of the Constitution* (3 vols. to date, Madison, Wis., 1976–   ), II, 159. (This essay is also reprinted in Kenyon, ed., *The Antifederalists*.)
5. See especially Jensen et al., eds., *Doc. Hist. of Ratification*, II, 128–640.
6. *Ibid.*, 182–85.

The Antifederalists in Pennsylvania also made charges of substance against the Constitution which echoed through the arguments in every state. Two issues seemed important almost everywhere. The first concerned a lack of a bill of rights: protections of speech, religion, trial by jury, all the traditional rights free Englishmen had long enjoyed. To the claim that the Constitution failed to afford such protection there was no answer, though the Federalists in Pennsylvania gave one. Under the Constitution, James Wilson said in a widely reported speech, the national government would exercise only those powers given it; all others were reserved to the states. Since no powers were given Congress to "shackle or destroy" the free press, or—by implication—other traditional rights, no bill of rights was necessary ("it would have been superfluous and absurd to have stipulated with a federal body of our own creation, that we should enjoy those privileges, of which we are not divested either by the intention or the act, that has brought that body into existence").[7]

The second question raised by the Antifederalists, in Pennsylvania, widely repeated elsewhere, concerned the nature of representation in a republic. Everyone agreed that the great authority on republics was Montesquieu. The Antifederalists claimed in his name that a republic could not survive in a nation which covered a large territory and must in time yield to despotism. "Centinel" may have been the first in Pennsylvania to point to the problem a national government would face in attending "to various local concerns and wants." Size alone would render satisfaction of local desires difficult. The number of representatives allotted to the new government simply increased the difficulty. Fifty-five men in the House of Representatives must attend to the interests of a country which extended over hundreds of thousands of square miles. This number invited "corruption and undue influence"; presumably only a very large number could stave off attempts at bribery. And if the representatives managed to avoid being corrupted, they would lose their sense of "accountability" through their long tenure in office—a term was two years, twice as long as the usual state term. Indeed the probability was that no number, however large, could adequately represent the people of a large nation. Adequate representation in Antifederalist minds implied the existence of representatives who shared fully their constituents' interests, passions, and opinions. The representative in an ideal situation would relay the desires of local interests. He would not reason or act

7. *Ibid.*, 168.

independently; his commission simply called for him to register the judgment of the people.[8]

James Madison had anticipated these charges in the Convention. Far from being unsuited to the republican form, Madison argued, a large nation offered ideal circumstances for its successful application. For the weakness of a republic lay in its tendency toward instability and tyranny, a tendency which would be effectively controlled in a large nation containing a variety of interests. Madison's reasoning rested on several suppositions. First, he assumed that instability inhered in a republic because by definition a republic contained within its assemblies a democratic element. And democracy lent itself to flux through its direct expression of the passions of the people. Democracy was the people governing themselves without the benefit of confining, or limiting, institutions.[9]

Madison's assumption about democracy was based on still another about human beings: man, by nature, preferred to follow his passions rather than his reason; he invariably chose short-term over long-term interests. Creatures of passion, of selfishness, and sometimes of wickedness, men in political society would always have difficulty in accepting responsibility for the public interest and they would succumb rather easily to opportunities to deprive others of their rights, if by doing so, they seemed to serve themselves.[10]

Thus, in a republic covering a large nation, bringing together men of various interests—factions in Madison's parlance—forming a majority capable of repressing a minority would always be difficult. Their large number and their variety would in effect lead them to block one another out. Madison's mature statement of his theory of factions appeared in the *Federalist* No. 10:

> The smaller the society, the fewer probably will be the distinct parties and interests composing it; the fewer the distinct parties and interests, the more frequently will a majority be found of the same party; and the smaller the number of individuals composing a majority, and the smaller the compass within which they are placed, the more easily

8. *Ibid.*, 164, 165. See also Cecelia M. Kenyon, "Men of Little Faith: The Anti-Federalists on the Nature of Representative Government," *WMQ*, 3d Ser., 12 (1955), 3–46.

9. *Federalist*, No. 10.

10. See, e.g., Nos. 37 and 57 of the *Federalist*. And see also the fine discussions of the theory of human nature expounded in the *Federalist*: B. F. Wright, "The Federalist on the Nature of Political Man," *Ethics*, 59 (1949), 1–31; and James P. Scanlon, "The Federalist and Human Nature," *Review of Politics*, 21 (1959), 657–77.

will they concert and execute their plans of oppression. Extend the sphere and you take in a greater variety of parties and interests; you make it less probable that a majority of the whole will have a common motive to invade the rights of other citizens; or if such a common motive exists, it will be more difficult for all who feel it to discover their own strength and to act in unison with each other.[11]

Wilson's restatement of Madison's theory was less powerful but clear enough to be picked up in the debates that followed those in Pennsylvania. Once, of course, the *Federalist* began appearing in late October 1787, the Federalists came into possession of the most powerful body of political thought ever produced in America. These essays, by Alexander Hamilton, John Jay, and James Madison, offered much more than a theory of representation. They dissected the circumstances under which power was exercised in America in the 1780s; they provided a critique of the Articles of Confederation; and they explained how the new government under the Constitution would work. Most important, they reassured Americans concerned about reconciling power and liberty.[12]

We cannot know exactly how discussions of constitutional issues affected delegates to the state ratifying conventions. But they must have moved some of the delegates; several of the arguments in print were repeated, with variations, in these conventions, and very little of substance appeared outside that did not receive a hearing within. On the other hand, the process of ratification, state by state, may have served to diminish the power of political ideas to persuade. And it may have increased the importance of strictly local interests. Ratification was a series of state actions, and each state convention had almost of necessity to consider the Constitution in the light of its state's interests. That these interests included a perception that political freedom was essential to all aspects of a state's well-being was tacitly acknowledged by all. Still, we do not know how in a delegate's mind a definition of his state's well-being incorporated a particular notion of representation, or a theory of the structure of government, or a particular sense of individual rights. What is clear is that state interests were discussed in ratifying conven-

11. On *Federalist* No. 10, see Douglass Adair, "The Tenth Federalist Revisited," and " 'That Politics May Be Reduced to a Science': David Hume, James Madison, and the Tenth Federalist," in Trevor Colbourn, ed., *Fame and the Founding Fathers: Essays by Douglass Adair* (New York, 1974), 75–106.

12. Readers interested in the *Federalist* papers may read them in several excellent modern editions, including those edited by Jacob E. Cooke, Clinton Rossiter, and Benjamin F. Wright.

tions as well as principles of governance. It is also clear that there was a "logic" to ratification, with individual states responding to the actions of others. To say that there was "momentum" in ratification oversimplifies a complex process. But states were influenced by their neighbors, and the rapid approval by three states in December, followed by two others in January, helped get ratification off to a good start.

III

Article VII of the Constitution provided that the "Ratification of the Conventions of nine States" would put it into effect. By implication the four states remaining outside could go their separate ways when nine others approved—or, join the Union. This procedure of getting the new government under way ignored the Articles of Confederation which had required that amendments receive unanimous approval. It also ignored the state legislatures except for one particular—by common understanding they would have to call for elections of the ratifying conventions. In transmitting the Constitution to the Congress, Washington expressed this understanding as "the Opinion of this Convention."[13]

The Constitution, with Washington's letter, reached the Congress on September 20. The Congress included among its number critics of the Constitution. One of them, Richard Henry Lee of Virginia, suggested that Congress should first amend the Constitution and then send it to the states. The states, Lee's argument ran, would then have a choice: either to ratify the original or to amend it and to send the revised version to a second constitutional convention. The Congress included more friends to the Constitution than enemies—eighteen members who had served as delegates returned to Congress in late September—but they did not want to wound the critics. Therefore, though they refused Lee's proposal, they refrained from forcing through an endorsement. Instead the Congress contented itself, after gentle prodding by the majority, with simply sending the Constitution to the states without a recommendation.[14]

When the message from Congress reached the state legislatures, they began to act. Delaware's had met even before the Convention dissolved in order to listen to a report from Richard Bassett, a member who had sat as a delegate. Now, with the Constitution in hand, it called a special election. The ratifying convention, which met soon afterwards,

13. Tansill, ed., *Documents*, 1005.
14. Jensen et al., eds., *Doc. Hist. of Ratification*, I, 345–46.

wasted no time and on December 7, 1787, gave the state's approval unanimously.[15]

The reasons for Delaware's eagerness are clear. Its people, most of whom were small farmers, felt vulnerable. Their economic dependence upon their larger neighbors may have been responsible for a part of this feeling—their profitable milling businesses imported wheat from Pennsylvania—but Delaware's size and history probably were more important. Delaware was a dwarf beside Pennsylvania's immense size and population, and even Maryland overshadowed it. Its history also worked to make its people think of union—until 1776, for example, it had always shared a governor with Pennsylvania.

In 1787 the state enjoyed a thriving economy. The millers grinding imported wheat flourished; trade had picked up after the war; and public indebtedness was light. The possibility of life alone, however, was difficult to conceive of. The ratifying convention brought together farmers who had the intelligence to see where political realism lay. The result was a rapid meeting and a vote of thirty in favor, none opposed.

Pennsylvania moved almost as swiftly. By some rough handling of reluctant legislators, the Federalists forced through a vote in the legislature authorizing the meeting of a ratifying convention. A few hours later the legislature dissolved in preparation for the election of a successor to itself; the action in favor of convening a body to consider ratification had been a near thing.

The arguments over the Constitution were amplified in Pennsylvania for several weeks before the election. Organization may have been even more important, and here the Federalists gained the advantage. The key to the election of the convention lay in Philadelphia and the surrounding countryside. Both the city and the farms around it fell to the Federalists—with artisans, shopkeepers, and farmers voting in favor of delegates

15. To reconstruct the history of ratification in the states, I have drawn heavily from two books by Forrest McDonald, *We The People: The Economic Origins of the Constitution* (Chicago, 1958) and *E Pluribus Unum: The Formation of the Federal Republic, 1776–1790* (Boston, 1965). Among state studies, the following are especially valuable: Philip A. Crowl, *Maryland During and After the Revolution* (Baltimore, 1943); Richard P. McCormick, *Experiment in Independence: New Jersey in the Critical Period, 1781–1789* (New Brunswick, N.J., 1950); Irwin H. Polishook, *Rhode Island and the Union, 1774–1795* (Evanston, Ill., 1969). I have also drawn from Jonathan Elliot, ed., *The Debates of the Several State Conventions on the Adoption of the Federal Constitution* (5 vols., Philadelphia, 1836–45). The quotation below from P. Henry's second long speech is in *ibid.*, III, 47.

pledged to ratification. If the Antifederalists had a chance in Pennsylvania, they had to capture the western sector and to play on suspicions of concentrated power. Federalist organization carried the struggle. Shortly after it was elected, Pennsylvania's ratifying convention voted on December 12 two to one in favor of the Constitution.

Six days later New Jersey's convention voted unanimously in favor of ratification, and on January 2, 1788, the twenty-six members of Georgia's convention did the same. In a general way both states acted, as Delaware had before them, to escape the weakness of isolation. New Jersey could not survive alone, and the Constitution promised advantages to every major group in the state. Georgia's weakness was more apparent than New Jersey's. The Creek Indians threatened survival of the state, and a strong national government seemed to promise security. Local attachments, which persisted almost everywhere else in America, were weak in Georgia, which was populated by recent immigrants who had not yet rooted themselves deeply.

Connecticut had a different set of reasons for ratifying, but it too could not survive outside a union. It wanted to rid itself of economic bondage to New York, and the Constitution, by placing the regulation of foreign commerce with the new government, offered the means. A week after Georgia acted, Connecticut voted by better than three to one in favor of the Constitution.

Thus within a period of just over a month, five states had ratified the Constitution. One of them, Pennsylvania, would be essential to any union of the states. The other four, though small and relatively weak, had helped give force to the process of ratification, a process which would reach a completion of sorts with the adherence of four more states.

The first of the four, Massachusetts, approved early in February by a vote of 187 to 168. Opposition to the Constitution had formed in several parts of the state with the western area especially hostile. The bitterness of rebellion still lingered there. Small farmers, the victims of eastern power, were understandably suspicious of an even more remote authority. The Federalists, recognizing that the contest would be close, took pains to woo John Hancock and Samuel Adams. Both were popular men; both distrusted the transactions at Philadelphia. The road to Hancock's sympathies lay in his vanity, which the Federalists carefully cultivated, even going so far as to suggest apparently that he might expect to become Vice President in the new government. Hancock took the bait like a hungry fish. Samuel Adams was vain in his own way. He could not bear to be separated from "the people," and when Paul Revere and a group of artisans let him know that they fancied the Constitution, he joined the Federalists. Along with approval, the Massachusetts convention recommended amendments to the Constitution, proposals that guarantees of civil liberties be added.

Maryland, which ratified next, in April, considered amendments, but adopted none. Ratification was voted easily a week after the convention opened. The decision in South Carolina, a month after Maryland's, came in a closer vote, 149 to 73, but probably was never in doubt. South Carolina had not yet recovered from the terrible damages of the war and had everything to gain in the Union. Its public debt was heavy, and assumption of it by the national government would be welcome. Union with other states also offered security, and in South Carolina public concern about defense remained strong.

With South Carolina's vote, eight states were in the Union. Two powerful states remained uncommitted—Virginia and New York. North Carolina and Rhode Island had already expressed their distaste for the Constitution, and New Hampshire's convention, which met first in February, refused to act. This refusal arose from an opposition which, though strong, was not prepared to burn all bridges. By June, public opinion had swung behind the Constitution, in part because of the ratification by other states—especially next-door Massachusetts. Still the vote was almost evenly divided, 57 to 47 in favor of ratification.

Would Virginia and New York come in? Delegates in both states twisted and turned before voting. The condition of Virginia's economy may have persuaded some planters to look with favor on the Constitution. There was little money in the state, but much indebtedness. A strong stable government, some planters said, would make borrowing from abroad possible.

Patrick Henry led the Antifederalists in the convention. Much of his attack had a certain eloquence, but more was simply shapeless. Much of what Henry said was a play on this sentence (from his second long speech): "My great objection is, that it does not leave us the means of defending our rights, or of waging war against tyrants." Edmund Pendleton, among others, cut through Henry's oratory like a sharp knife. Whether Federalist arguments moved men or not, the Federalists gained an edge in the convention. Edmund Randolph's decision to support the Constitution undoubtedly helped just as the immense prestige of George Washington must have. In any case the final vote, though not heavily on the side of the Constitution, was favorable.

Virginia ratified in late June. A month later New York gave its approval in a tough fight which saw Hamilton lead the way. News from Virginia undoubtedly swayed delegates, and the threat of New York City to secede from the state if the Constitution were not approved forced some delegates to back the Constitution.

With New York in, only North Carolina and Rhode Island remained out. North Carolina delayed joining the Union until November 1789; Rhode Island held back until May of the following year. By the time it gave approval, the administration of President Washington had been in office for over a year.

Epilogue
The Enduring Truths

Before the American Revolution many Americans lived by standards implicit in such words as grace, calling, frugality, thrift, and virtue. During the Revolution they came also to speak of honor, glory, and sacrifice. The Americans were not a perfect people before the Revolution; nor did they approach perfection during the war. But despite their lapses and their failures, they left these words unsoiled, as good as they had been before the Revolution.

Between 1776 and 1789 the Americans had to reconsider the meaning of these old words and some others as well—independence, the nation, liberty, and equality. War and crisis had brought them to this reconsideration and had stimulated their imaginations. The revolutionaries indeed had managed to think in two extraordinarily different ways: they had learned to see things as they are and to imagine how they might be. The old truths had endured while new standards were raised. The test the Americans now faced lay in getting the best out of themselves in the service of old and new.

Abbreviated Titles

AHR	*American Historical Review*
Andrews, *Colonial Period*	Charles M. Andrews, *The Colonial Period of American History* (4 vols., New Haven, Conn., 1934–38)
Bailyn, *Ordeal of Hutchinson*	Bernard Bailyn, *The Ordeal of Thomas Hutchinson* (Cambridge, Mass., 1974)
BF Papers	Leonard W. Labaree et al., eds., *The Papers of Benjamin Franklin* (21 vols. to date, New Haven, Conn., 1959–)
BG	*Boston Gazette*
BRC, *Reports*	Boston Records Commission, *Reports of the Boston Records Commissioners* (31 vols., Boston, 1876–1904)
Bridenbaugh, *Cities in Revolt*	Carl Bridenbaugh, *Cities in Revolt: Urban Life in America, 1743–1776* (New York, 1955)
Burnett, *Continental Congress*	Edmund Cody Burnett, *The Continental Congress* (New York, 1941)
Butterfield et al., eds., *Diary of John Adams*	Lyman H. Butterfield et al., eds., *Diary and Autobiography of John Adams* (4 vols., Cambridge, Mass., 1961)
Channing and Coolidge, eds., *Barrington-Bernard Correspondence*	Edward Channing and Archibald Cary Coolidge, eds., *The Barrington-Bernard Correspondence, 1760–1770* (Cambridge, Mass., 1912)
Copeland, ed., *Correspondence of Edmund Burke*	Thomas W. Copeland, ed., *The Correspondence of Edmund Burke* (10 vols., Chicago, 1958–78)
CSM, *Pubs.*	Colonial Society of Massachusetts, *Publications*
"Diary of John Rowe"	"Diary of John Rowe," Massachusetts Historical Society, *Proceedings*, 2d Ser., 10 (Boston, 1896), 60–108
EHD	Merrill Jensen, ed., *English Historical Documents*, vol. IX: *American Colonial Documents to 1776* (New York, 1955)
EHR	*English Historical Review*
Farrand	Max Farrand, ed., *The Records of the Federal Convention of 1787* (rev. ed., 4 vols., New Haven, Conn., 1966)

Fortescue, ed., *Correspondence of George the Third* Sir John Fortescue, ed., *The Correspondence of King George the Third from 1760 to December 1783* (6 vols., London, 1927–28)

Freeman, *GW* Douglas Southall Freeman, *George Washington: A Biography*, completed by J. A. Carroll and Mary W. Ashworth (7 vols., New York, 1948–57)

Gipson, *American Loyalist* Lawrence Henry Gipson, *American Loyalist: Jared Ingersoll* (1920; reprint ed., New Haven, Conn., 1971)

Gipson, *British Empire* Lawrence Henry Gipson, *The British Empire Before the American Revolution* (15 vols., Caldwell, Idaho, and New York, 1936–70)

GW Papers George Washington Papers, Library of Congress, Washington, D.C., microfilm, 124 reels

GW Writings John C. Fitzpatrick, ed., *The Writings of George Washington from the Original Manuscript Sources, 1745–1799* (39 vols., Washington, D.C., 1931–44)

HL Henry E. Huntington Library, San Marino, California

HLQ *Huntington Library Quarterly*

JCC Worthington C. Ford et al., eds., *Journals of the Continental Congress, 1774–1789* (34 vols., Washington, D.C., 1904–37)

Jensen, *Founding* Merrill Jensen, *The Founding of a Nation: A History of the American Revolution, 1763–1776* (New York, 1968)

JIH *Journal of Interdisciplinary History*

JM Papers W. T. Hutchinson, William M. E. Rachal, and Robert Rutland eds., *The Papers of James Madison* (12 vols. to date, Chicago and Charlottesville, Va., 1962–   )

McIlwaine and Kennedy, eds., *Jour. Va. Burgesses* H. R. McIlwaine and John Pendleton Kennedy, eds., *Journals of the House of Burgesses of Virginia (1619–1776)* (13 vols., Richmond, Va., 1905–15)

LMCC Edmund C. Burnett, ed., *Letters of Members of the Continental Congress* (8 vols., Washington, D.C., 1921–36)

Lovejoy, *Rhode Island Politics* David S. Lovejoy, *Rhode Island Politics and the American Revolution, 1760–1775* (Providence, R.I., 1958)

MdHM *Maryland Historical Magazine*

MHS, *Colls.* Massachusetts Historical Society, *Collections*

MHS, *Procs.* Massachusetts Historical Society, *Proceedings*

Morgan, ed., *Prologue* Edmund S. Morgan, ed., *Prologue to Revolution: Sources and Documents on the Stamp Act Crisis, 1764–1766* (Chapel Hill, N.C., 1959)

Morgan and Morgan, *Stamp Act Crisis* — Edmund S. Morgan and Helen M. Morgan, *The Stamp Act Crisis: Prologue to Revolution* (Chapel Hill, N.C., 1953)

NCHR — *North Carolina Historical Review*

NEQ — *New England Quarterly*

PAH — *Perspectives in American History*

Peckham, *Toll* — Howard H. Peckham, ed., *The Toll of Independence: Engagements and Battle Casualties of the American Revolution* (Chicago, 1974)

PMHB — *Pennsylvania Magazine of History and Biography*

Rakove, *Beginnings of National Politics* — Jack N. Rakove, *The Beginnings of National Politics: An Interpretive History of the Continental Congress* (New York, 1979)

SCHM — *South Carolina Historical Magazine*

Sheer and Rankin, *Rebels and Redcoats* — George F. Sheer and Hugh F. Rankin, *Rebels and Redcoats* (New York, 1957)

Stedman, *History of the American War* — Charles Stedman, *The History of the Origin, Progress, and Termination of the American War* (2 vols., Dublin, 1794)

Stevens, ed., *Clinton-Cornwallis Controversy* — Benjamin Franklin Stevens, ed., *The Campaign in Virginia 1781. An Exact Reprint of Six Rare Pamphlets on the Clinton-Cornwallis Controversy with . . . Letters . . .* (2 vols., London, 1888)

Syrett and Cooke, eds., *Papers of Hamilton* — Harold C. Syrett and Jacob E. Cooke, eds., *The Papers of Alexander Hamilton* (26 vols., New York, 1961–79)

TJ Papers — Julian P. Boyd et al., eds., *The Papers of Thomas Jefferson* (19 vols. to date, Princeton, N.J., 1950–)

VG — *Virginia Gazette* (Williamsburg)

VMHB — *Virginia Magazine of History and Biography*

Ward — Christopher Ward, *The War of the Revolution*, ed. John Richard Alden (2 vols., New York, 1952)

Wickwires, *Cornwallis* — Franklin B. and Mary Wickwire, *Cornwallis: The American Adventure* (New York, 1970)

Willcox, *Portrait of a General* — William B. Willcox, *Portrait of a General: Sir Henry Clinton in the War of Independence* (New York, 1964)

Willcox, ed., *Clinton's Narrative* — William B. Willcox, ed., *The American Rebellion: Sir Henry Clinton's Narrative of His Campaigns, 1775–1782, With an Appendix of Original Documents* (New Haven, Conn., 1954)

WMQ — *William and Mary Quarterly*

Bibliographical Note

More than any work that I have written, this one draws on the studies of other historians. I have used with great profit books and essays by Bernard Bailyn, Julian P. Boyd, Irving Brant, E. James Ferguson, Douglas Southall Freeman, Lawrence Henry Gipson, Ira D. Gruber, Merrill Jensen, Forrest McDonald, Piers Mackesy, Edmund S. and Helen M. Morgan, Lewis Namier, J. H. Plumb, John Shy, Christopher Ward, Franklin B. and Mary Wickwire, and William B. Willcox, and a great many others. In mentioning these scholars, I do not mean to imply that I agree with all that they have written; nor would they agree with everything in this book.

On most of the important problems discussed in this book, I have read some of the eighteenth-century sources. I cite them in the footnotes but not in this bibliographical note. I have, of course, read only a small sample.

In the note that follows, I have not repeated all the citations appearing in the footnotes nor have I listed all the studies that I have consulted. Rather I have indicated some of the major studies that I believe will be helpful to anyone wishing to pursue further investigation of the Revolution. There is no full or satisfactory bibliography of the American Revolution; and there probably cannot be. Most of the studies cited in the footnotes and this note contain bibliographies on their subjects. The literature on the Revolution is enormous, of course, and it is growing.

W. A. Speck, *Stability and Strife: England, 1714–1760* (Cambridge, Mass., 1977) is a fine starting point for study of the English background. Besides the works cited in my footnotes, see also H. J. Habakkuk, "England," in A. Goodwin, ed., *The European Nobility in the Eighteenth*

Century (London, 1967), and J. D. Chambers, *Population, Economy and Society in Pre-industrial England* (Oxford, 1972). English crowds are studied most helpfully in E. P. Thompson, "The Moral Economy of the English Crowd in the Eighteenth Century," *Past and Present,* 50 (1971). For the Anglican church, see Norman Sykes, *Church and State in England in the Eighteenth Century* (Cambridge, 1934). On financial change, P. G. M. Dickson, *The Financial Revolution* (Oxford, 1967) is outstanding; R. Davis, *A Commercial Revolution: English Overseas Trade in the Seventeenth and Eighteenth Centuries* (London, 1967) is short, but helpful. See also J. D. Chambers and G. E. Mingay, *The Agricultural Revolution, 1750–1780* (London, 1966) and Phyllis Deane, *The First Industrial Revolution* (Cambridge, 1965).

Biographies which sketch in the "times" of the subjects are often informative. J. H. Plumb, *Sir Robert Walpole: The Making of a Statesman* and *Sir Robert Walpole: The King's Minister* (Boston, 1956, 1961) are superb. See also Reed Browning, *The Duke of Newcastle* (New Haven, Conn., 1975) and Ross J. S. Hoffman, *The Marquis: A Study of Lord Rockingham, 1730–1782* (New York, 1973). The biographies cited in my footnotes are particularly helpful, especially those by Basil Williams (Pitt) and John Brooke (George III).

Edmund S. Morgan and Helen M. Morgan, *The Stamp Act Crisis: Prologue to Revolution* (Chapel Hill, N.C., 1953), and three books by Bernard Bailyn, *The Ideological Origins of the American Revolution* (Cambridge, Mass., 1967), *The Origins of American Politics* (New York, 1968), and *The Ordeal of Thomas Hutchinson* (Cambridge, Mass., 1974) offer penetrating analyses of the ideological basis of American resistance to British measures before independence.

The political cast of that resistance is thoroughly reconstructed in Merrill Jensen, *The Founding of a Nation: A History of the American Revolution 1763–1776* (New York, 1968), and in such studies of states as Robert J. Taylor, *Western Massachusetts in the Revolution* (Providence, R.I., 1954), Charles A. Barker, *The Background of the Revolution in Maryland* (New Haven, Conn., 1940), Jere R. Daniell, *Experiment in Republicanism: New Hampshire Politics and the American Revolution, 1741–1794* (Cambridge, Mass., 1970), Kenneth Coleman, *The American Revolution in Georgia, 1763–1789* (Athens, Ga., 1958), W. W. Abbot, *The Royal Governors of Georgia, 1754–1775* (Chapel Hill, N.C., 1959), David S. Lovejoy, *Rhode Island Politics and the American Revolution, 1760–1776* (Providence, R.I., 1958), Ronald Hoffman, *A Spirit of Dissension: Economics, Politics, and the Revolution in Maryland* (Baltimore,

1973), Oscar Zeichner, *Connecticut's Years of Controversy, 1750–1776* (Chapel Hill, N.C., 1949), Bernard Mason, *The Road to Independence: The Revolutionary Movement in New York, 1773–1777* (Lexington, Ky., 1966), Larry R. Gerlach, *Prologue to Independence: New Jersey in the Coming of the American Revolution* (New Brunswick, N.J., 1976), Richard M. Jellison, ed., *Society, Freedom, and Conscience: The Coming of the Revolution in Virginia, Massachusetts, and New York* (New York, 1976).

A brilliant essay by Perry Miller, "From the Covenant to the Revival," in *Nature's Nation* (Cambridge, Mass., 1967), provides a valuable starting point for studying the relationship of religion to the Revolution. Alan Heimert, *Religion and the American Mind* (Cambridge, Mass., 1966) is suggestive, as are Edmund S. Morgan, *The Gentle Puritan: A Life of Ezra Stiles, 1727–1795* (New Haven, Conn., 1962), Henry F. May, *The Enlightenment in America* (New York, 1976), Ernest Lee Tuveson, *Redeemer Nation: The Idea of America's Millennial Role* (Chicago, 1968), James West Davidson, *The Logic of Millennial Thought: Eighteenth-Century New England* (New Haven, Conn., 1977), Frederick V. Mills, Sr., *Bishops by Ballot: An Eighteenth-Century Ecclesiastical Revolution* (New York, 1978), Carl Bridenbaugh, *Mitre and Sceptre: Transatlantic Faiths, Ideas, Personalities, and Politics, 1689–1775* (New York, 1962), and Philip Greven, *The Protestant Temperament* (New York, 1977).

Other studies which aid in understanding the coming of the Revolution are Carl Bridenbaugh, *Cities in Revolt: Urban Life in America, 1743–1776* (New York, 1955), Gary B. Nash, *The Urban Crucible: Social Change, Political Consciousness, and the Origins of the American Revolution* (Cambridge, Mass., 1979), Jack Greene, *The Quest for Power: The Lower Houses of Assembly in the Southern Royal Colonies, 1689–1776* (Chapel Hill, N.C., 1963), Charles S. Olton, *Artisans for Independence: Philadelphia Mechanics and the American Revolution* (Syracuse, N.Y., 1975), Alison Gilbert Olson, *Anglo-American Politics: The Relationship between Parties in England and Colonial America* (Oxford, 1973), Roger J. Champagne, *Alexander McDougall and the American Revolution in New York* (Schenectady, N.Y., 1975), Aubrey C. Land, *The Dulanys of Maryland* (Baltimore, 1955), Pauline Maier, *From Resistance to Revolution: Colonial Radicals and the Development of American Opposition to Britain, 1765–1776* (New York, 1972), J. R. Pole, *Representation in England and the Origins of the American Republic* (London, 1966), Michael Kammen, *A Rope of Sand: The Colonial Agents, British Politics, and the American Revolution* (Ithaca, N.Y., 1968), David Ammerman,

In the Common Cause: American Response to the Coercive Acts of 1774 (Charlottesville, Va., 1974), Richard D. Brown, *Revolutionary Politics in Massachusetts: The Boston Committee of Correspondence and the Towns, 1772–1774* (Cambridge, Mass., 1970).

The grand studies by Douglas Southall Freeman, Christopher Ward, Piers Mackesy, John Richard Alden, William B. Willcox, Franklin B. and Mary Wickwire, Ira D. Gruber, and John Shy are essential reading for an understanding of the war between Britain and America. Page Smith, *A New Age Now Begins: A People's History of the American Revolution* (2 vols., New York, 1976) provides an excellent account of military operations. Mark M. Boatner III, *Encyclopedia of the American Revolution* (Bicentennial ed., New York, 1976) is one of the most helpful works ever written about the war. Charles Royster, *A Revolutionary People at War: The Continental Army and American Character, 1775–1783* (Chapel Hill, N.C., 1979) supplies thoughtful assessments of the officers and men of the army. See also Jonathan G. Rossie, *The Politics of Command in the American Revolution* (Syracuse, N.Y., 1975), Jonathan R. Dull, *The French Navy and American Independence: A Study of Arms and Diplomacy, 1774–1787* (Princeton, N.J., 1975), Don Higginbotham, *The War of American Independence: Military Attitudes, Policies, and Practice, 1763–1789* (New York, 1971), Eric Robson, *The American Revolution in Its Political and Military Aspects* (London, 1955), Theodore G. Thayer, *Nathanael Greene, Strategist of the American Revolution* (New York, 1960), and M. F. Treacy, *Prelude to Yorktown, the Southern Campaigns of Nathanael Greene* (Chapel Hill, N.C., 1963).

There is much about British military forces and British strategy in the books cited above. Two books on supply and logistics are especially important: R. Arthur Bowler, *Logistics and the Failure of the British Army in America, 1775–1783* (Princeton, N.J., 1975) and Norman Baker, *Government and Contractors: The British Treasury and War Supplies, 1775–1783* (London, 1971). On other aspects of the British effort in America see George A. Billias, ed., *George Washington's Opponents* (New York, 1969), J. E. D. Binney, *British Public Finance and Administration, 1774–1792* (Oxford, 1959), David Syrett, *Shipping and the American War, 1775–1783* (London, 1970), and Paul H. Smith, *Loyalists and Redcoats: A Study in British Revolutionary Policy* (Chapel Hill, N.C., 1964), an especially valuable book.

The key books on the diplomacy of the Revolution are Samuel Flagg Bemis, *The Diplomacy of the American Revolution* (Washington, D.C., 1935, and Bloomington, Ind., 1957), Richard B. Morris's brilliant *The*

Peacemakers: The Great Powers and American Independence (New York, 1965), Felix Gilbert, *To the Farewell Address: Ideas of Early American Foreign Policy* (Princeton, N.J., 1961), and essays by James H. Hutson and William C. Stinchcombe in Lawrence S. Kaplan, ed., *The American Revolution and "A Candid World"* ([Kent, Ohio], 1977).

Society, the American economy, and politics during and immediately after the war are tangled subjects. Several books by Merrill Jensen offer suggestive starting places, though they must be read with care (and skepticism): *The Articles of Confederation* (Madison, Wis., 1940; paperback ed., 1959), *The New Nation: A History of the United States during the Confederation, 1781–1789* (New York, 1950), *The American Revolution within America* (New York, 1974). Readers of Jensen's work on the "critical period," a phrase John Fiske applied to the 1780s, will also find Edmund S. Morgan's "Conflict and Consensus," chapter 6, in *The Challenge of the American Revolution* (New York, 1976), suggestive. Jackson Turner Main has also contributed several valuable books on the internal revolution—*The Antifederalists: Critics of the Constitution, 1781–1788* (Chapel Hill, N.C., 1961), *The Social Structure of Revolutionary America* (Princeton, N.J., 1965), and *Political Parties before the Constitution* (Chapel Hill, N.C., 1973). Jack N. Rakove, *The Beginnings of National Politics: An Interpretive History of the Continental Congress* (New York, 1979) is also valuable.

For thoughtful appraisals of women in the Revolution, see Mary Beth Norton, *Liberty's Daughters: The Revolutionary Experience of American Women, 1750–1800* (Boston and Toronto, 1980) and Linda K. Kerber, *Women of the Republic: Intellect & Ideology in Revolutionary America* (Chapel Hill, N.C., 1980); for Indians, Barbara Graymont, *The Iroquois in the American Revolution* (Syracuse, N.Y., 1972) and James H. O'Donnell III, *Southern Indians in the American Revolution* (Knoxville, Tenn., 1973); for blacks, Winthrop D. Jordan, *White Over Black: American Attitudes Toward the Negro, 1550–1812* (Chapel Hill, N.C., 1968), Edmund S. Morgan, *American Slavery, American Freedom: The Ordeal of Colonial Virginia* (New York, 1975), Benjamin Quarles, *The Negro in the American Revolution* (Chapel Hill, N.C., 1961), William M. Wiecek, *The Sources of Antislavery Constitutionalism in America, 1760–1848* (Ithaca, N.Y., 1977), and Duncan J. Macleod, *Slavery, Race and the American Revolution* (Cambridge and New York, 1974).

Questions concerning law entered almost every aspect of revolutionary development. James H. Kettner's *The Development of American Citizenship, 1608–1870* (Chapel Hill, N.C., 1978) is a superb study. See also

Morton J. Horwitz, *The Transformation of American Law, 1780–1860* (Cambridge, Mass., 1977), John Phillip Reid's *In a Defiant Stance* (University Park, Pa., 1977) and his *In Defiance of the Law* (Chapel Hill, N.C., 1981).

On matters relating to constitutionalism in the 1780s, Forrest McDonald, *We The People: The Economic Origins of the Constitution* (Chicago, 1958) is essential. Although they provide different perspectives, so are the following: E. James Ferguson, *The Power of the Purse: A History of American Public Finance, 1776–1790* (Chapel Hill, N.C., 1961), Gordon S. Wood, *The Creation of the American Republic, 1776–1787* (Chapel Hill, N.C., 1969). There is no substitute for reading *The Federalist,* but in undertaking that enjoyable task, the essays of Douglass Adair, in Trevor Colbourn, ed., *Fame and the Founding Fathers* (New York, 1974), are helpful, and Garry Wills, *Explaining America: The Federalist* (New York, 1981) is stimulating and perceptive.

Index

Connecticut, 23, 37, 42, 43, 124, 131, 175, 277, 507, 514, 626, 632, 635, 641; Association in, 260; British raids in, 536; and Continental Army, 304, 344, 348, 349, 413, 524; emancipation in, 558; Gage on, 286; governor of, 104; Great Awakening in, 103; legislature, 103, 104, 124, 161, 234; militia, 280; and Navy Board, 527; nonimportation in, 182; politics in, 102–4, 141–42; and ratification, 662; speculators in, 627; Stamp Act in, 76, 105–7; and western lands, 104

Connecticut Gazette (Hartford), 105

Connecticut River, 377

Connecticut River valley, 29

Conscription, 511

Considerations on the Nature and Extent of the Legislative Authority of the Parliament. See Wilson, James

Conspiracy: and American liberties, 126–28, 130–35, 656; and Bute, 137; Otis-Adams faction on, 170; and Quartering Act, 151; and Revenue Act, 150–51; and Rhode Island charter, 100; and Stamp Act, 126–28

Constitution (Brit.): Americans on, 6, 120–22; in colonies, 49; Continental Congress on, 244; and fundamental law, 121–22; George III on, 18; and liberty, 6; Thomas Paine on, 318–19

Constitution (U.S.), 647, 660; and class antagonism, 656; as conservative movement, 649–64; criticism of, 654–55 (*see* Antifederalists); and separation of powers, 652

Constitutional Convention (1787), 600, 621, 622–48, 649, 651, 653; aristocratic bias in, 635; and class antagonism, 656; compromise in, 626, 639; and congressional powers, 646–48; and executive, 642; and judiciary, 642; and large states, 626–27, 636, 641; and New Jersey plan, 633; and slave trade, 643–46; and small states, 626, 627; and state interests, 626–37; and Virginia plan, 630, 635; and western lands, 627

Constitutionalists, 620, 656

Constitutions, state, 603–21. *See also names of individual states*

Continental Congress, First, 234–52; and the Association, 248, 257; and British trade, 242, 243; colonial response to, 250–52; and colonial rights, 243–44; Dartmouth on, 260; and Declaration of Rights, 247; delegates to, 234, 239–42, 251–53; Galloway's Plan of Union, 245–46; and nonconsumption, 247–48; and nonexportation, 246–48; and nonimportation, 246–48; voting rules of, 243

Continental Congress, Second, 278–81, 327–32, 443, 451, 466, 493, 494, 528, 593–98; and army officers, 340, 347, 453–54, 580; army supplies in, 465, 516; and Canada invasion,

280, 304; and commissary department, 415, 512–19; and commissioners in France, 403–4; composition of, 278; demobilizes military, 582–84; and foreign powers, 320–22, 398–405; and French treaties, 405; and independence, 312–14, 316, 327–32, 400–401; and Loyalist property, 574; and medical service, 520; and militia, 467; and "model treaty," 401; moderates in, 313, 321–22, 324; naval policy of, 527; and peace commission, 571; and quartermaster department, 512–19; raises Continental Army, 313, 510; and Revolutionary War, 279–80, 333, 334, 453, 511–19; and sectional divisions, 588; southern army in, 463; and the states, 316–17, 324, 585; and troop recruitment, 350, 364–65; and the West, 585, 588–90

Conway, Gen. Henry, 108, 112, 146–52 *passim;* and Declaratory bill, 114; on stamp tax, 76, 117

Cooper, Samuel, 208, 209, 219

Cooper River (S.C.), 441, 448

Copp's Hill (Boston), 284, 287

Cork, Ireland, 512

Cornwallis, Lord Charles, 422, 452–59, 461, 470, 475–87, 491, 496, 499, 502, 519, 535, 559, 564, 575; at Camden, 454–57; in the Carolinas, 469; and Clinton, 447–48, 560–63, 577–78; and Fort Lee, 349, 354; and Long Island, 341, 343, 344; and Loyalists, 479, 495; at Monmouth Court House, 427–28; and New Jersey retreat, 354–55; in North Carolina, 479–88; and Parliament, 437; and Princeton, 362; in South Carolina, 451; southern campaign, 476–87; strategy of, 488; as tactician, 576; Washington on, 566; and Yorktown, 561, 562, 566, 569–70

Coryell's Ferry, Pa., 421

Countess of Scarborough, 532–34

Cowan's Ford, N.C., 477

Cowpens, S.C., battle of, 470–76, 481, 505

Coxe, Tench, 443

Coxe, William, 95

Coxe's Mill, N.C., 453

Crammond, Maj., 542

Cranbury, N.J., 421, 423

Creek Indians, 234, 662

Cromwell, Oliver, 29

Crook, Robert, 101–2

Cross Creek, N.C., 487

Crosswicks, N.J., 421

Crown, the, 23, 25, 40, 132, 227, 338; American attitudes toward, 5, 235. *See also* Monarchy

Crown Point, N.Y., 277, 373

Cruger, Col. John, 462, 491, 493

Currency Act, 62, 208

Cushing, Thomas, 161, 211; as congressional delegate, 239, 244; and convention of towns,